An Essay on the Development of Christian Doctrine

Editor's books on Newman

Newman Today (ed.), 1990

Newman: *Anglican Difficulties* (ed.), 1994

Newman: *Conscience and Papacy* [Letter to the Duke of Norfolk] (ed.), 2002

Newman: *The Mother of God* [A Letter to Pusey on Occasion of his *Eirenicon*] (ed.), 2003

Newman's Challenge, 1999

Newman to Converts: An Existential Ecclesiology, 2001

Edtitor's books on the Church

Les tendances nouvelles de l'ecclésiologie, 1957[1] 1963[2]

And on This Rock: The Witness of One Land and Two Covenants, 1978[1] 1987[2] 1997[3]

The Keys of the Kingdom: A Tool's Witness to Truth, 1986[1] 2001[2]

Catholic Essays, 1990

The Gist of Catholicism and Other Essays, 2001

Why Believe in the Church?, 2002

For the full list of books by the editor, see p. [434]

John Henry Newman

An Essay on the Development of Christian Doctrine

[1845]

with an Introductory Essay and Notes by
Stanley L. Jaki

Real View Books

2003

Real View Books
4237 Kinfolk Court
Pinckney, Michigan 48169

www.realviewbooks.com

Newman, J. H. (1801-1890)

Jaki, Stanley L. (1924-)

J. H. Newman: An Essay on the Development Christian Doctrine

1. Facts and ideas of development 2. Identity of the Church of Rome
with the Church of the Apostles 3. History of dogma

ISBN 1-892548-32-1

Newman's two portraits on the cover represent him at 40 and 80 respectively. See also the fourth motto on p. [x].

Manufactured in the United States of America

Contents

CHAPTER I.

ON THE DEVELOPMENT OF IDEAS.

CHAPTER II.

ON THE DEVELOPMENT OF CHRISTIAN IDEAS, ANTECEDENTLY CONSIDERED.

CHAPTER III.

ON THE NATURE OF THE ARGUMENT IN BEHALF OF THE EXISTING DEVELOPMENTS OF CHRISTIANITY.

CHAPTER IV.

ILLUSTRATIONS OF THE ARGUMENT IN BEHALF OF THE EXISTING DEVELOPMENTS OF CHRISTIANITY.

CHAPTER V.

ILLUSTRATIONS CONTINUED.

CHAPTER VI.

ILLUSTRATIONS CONTINUED.

CHAPTER VII.

APPLICATION OF THE FOURTH TEST OF FIDELITY IN DEVELOPMENT.

CHAPTER VIII.

ILLUSTRATIONS CONCLUDED.

"Catholicity and Christianity
had in my mind become identical,
so that to give up the one was to give up the other."

An Essay on the Development of Christian Doctrine

"I give tests of a true development, founded on the nature of the case. These tests secure the substantial immutability of Christian doctrine—and I think my comparison is, that modern R. Catholicism looks different from primitive Catholicism in no other sense, than a friend, whom we see after a lapse of years, seems at first strange to us, till after a few minutes the old features revive in spite of the changes."

Newman to John Cowley Fisher, October 14, 1861

"To me the words 'development of dogma' are substantially nothing but the process by which, under the magisterium of the Church, implicit faith becomes explicit."

Newman to Lord Acton, June 23, 1862

"The very reason I became a Catholic was because the present Roman Catholic Church is the *only Church*, which is like, and it is very like, the primitive Church, the Church of St Athanasius. I have said this in print [*Development*, pp. {97-98}]. It is almost like the photograph of the primitive Church, or at least it does not differ from the primitive near so much as the photograph of a man of 40 differs from his photograph when he was 20. *You know that it is the same man.*"

Newman to Mrs. Helbert, August 30, 1869

Foreword

The present work is a wholly reset but otherwise exact text of Newman's *Essay on the Development of Christian Doctrine* as it left the press in late November 1845, or less than two months after he had joined, on October 8, the Catholic Church as the One True Fold. By then part of the book had been typeset and within three more weeks Newman was able to give the full set of proofs to Bishop Wiseman. Without reading it, the future Cardinal advised Newman that the book should be published in the form it had by October 6 when Newman dated the book's Advertisement in which he listed his former erroneous views on Rome in order to disavow them once more.

A second edition by the same publisher, James Toovey in Piccadilly, followed in February 1846 and was identical with the first apart from some typographical corrections. Thirty-two years later Newman, as he was preparing all his books for a definitive edition, produced a third edition of the *Development*, which wholly superseded the first two, copies of which are rare. The Penguin Books edition, in which the first edition reappeared in 1972, has surely not done justice to the scholarly seriousness of Newman's grappling in the *Development* with important historical matters, which he carefully documented in numerous notes. In that reissue practically all the many notes of the original have been omitted.

The differences between the first edition and the definitive edition are considerable. Not a few pages of Newman's copy of the first edition, into which he wrote in ink the changes, look rather black. In making the changes Newman showed himself to be a meticulous stylist as he replaced many words with their synonyms and rephrased many statements, without adding anything really new. In the definitive edition Newman left out two sets of consecutive pages, amounting to almost forty pages in all. One of those sets contains a most interesting analysis of the development of Methodism. He also rearranged the material in at least one notable instance. In the definitive edition Newman moved to almost the beginning of the book the section which deals with the need for the development of an organ whose function is to decide infallibly between genuine and non-genuine developments. He was obviously intent on making an emphatically Catholic book even more decidedly Catholic.

Mr. Gerard Tracey, the late and much regretted Archivist of the Birmingham Oratory, told me during our last conversation in November 2002 that two Canadian scholars have for years been preparing an edition of the *Development* that would contain all the passages that Newman moved, changed, or left out from the first edition, or added to it as he prepared the definitive edition. Mr. Tracey also thought that such an edition would be so large, complex, and expensive as to foreclose its being ever widely used.

Therefore an exact presentation of the text of the first edition should seem justified for more than one reason. Whereas Newman's references to patristic works are clear even in their succinctness to anyone familiar with that literature, different is the case with his manner of quoting modern authors, often very much dated nowadays. Additions to Newman's references are given in editorial < > parentheses. No effort was made to emulate the monumental complicatedness of the critical apparatus attached to the German translation of 1969, which is very uncritical in some crucial respects.

This new edition, which follows the original even in its sometimes outmoded typographical style and gives its page-numbering between { }, is preceded by an Introductory Essay in which special attention is paid to Newman's own views on his book. He put on paper, mostly in his letters, all those views prior to the publication of the definitive edition. Many of those views of his have been signally ignored in the Introductions prefixed to various re-editions of the definitive edition as well as in the large literature which that edition has prompted, especially in recent decades. It should therefore be very eye-opening to find that Newman well in advance protested those who took his book for a pretext to promote what he called "extravagating" in matters doctrinal or to foment ecumenical syncretism.

The book has a pathos and exudes a resolve which are responsible in part for phrases that are among the most incisive, the most telling, and stylistically the most beautiful Newman had ever penned. They deserve to be savored in exactly the form in which Newman originally gave them. This is a special duty of those who share Newman's visceral conviction that man has the sacred obligation to find fully what God revealed to man for his own eternal salvation. Newman did not write this book or any of his books to entertain mere academics, including theologians. At one point he referred to some of these as "sciolists," that is, those who make a pretentious and superficial display of their learning. Whether such or not, they still have to discover and appreciate the spiritual drama that runs through this immortal book. It is not a doctoral dissertation or a Habilitationschrift with a thesis whose truth or fallacy makes no real difference for the ultimate destiny of a human mind created in the image of God.

Newman wrote this book first to convince himself once and for all that groundless are most of the objections raised against the basic Roman Catholic claim that the Church of Rome is the direct and only legitimate continuation of the Church of the Apostles. He knew, and said so in the *Development,* that a lifetime is not enough to unravel all real and conceivable objections to that claim. Further, he wrote the book for those who had, as he once did, Anglo-Catholic convictions. They held the view that if they followed Rome's liturgical and devotional practices they had fully Roman convictions and their staying within the Church of England did not amount to fomenting the hideous sin of schism.

This was precisely the view which Newman wanted to undermine by showing in the *Development* that objections to Rome's claims are logically fallacious and spiritually destructive. To one prominent Anglo-Catholic, who tried to hold out but eventually converted, Newman wrote that he could understand that there is One Church or that there is no Church, but the idea that there are several Churches made no sense to him.

Newman's spiritual and intellectual struggle to gain hold of the One True Fold is the gist of the *Development*. Everything else there is of secondary importance, however precious.

The Feast of Pentecost 2003   S. L. J.

Introductory Essay

Newman an evolutionist?

Apart from the *Apologia pro vita sua*, which stands in a class by itself among Newman's books, no other book of his has made a greater impact than the *Essay on the Development of Christian Doctrine*, a work whose publication followed closely on Newman's conversion in early October 1845. But unlike the *Apologia,* whose impact was huge and immediate, the *Development* made its mark slowly, as if to conform to its author's view of true developments. Again, whereas the *Apologia* was rarely the target of patent misconstructions, it became eventually fashionable to cast the *Development* into frameworks alien to it.

At times the very timing of this clashed with what Newman tried to achieve with the *Development.* On the hundredth anniversary of Newman's death Clifford Langley, religion reporter of *The Times* (London), quoted without qualification the view of "the novelist A. N. Wilson" that Newman "was the only Victorian intellectual of the first rank who had not been disabused of Christian faith by the theories of Charles Darwin: and Newman himself said he was happy 'to go the whole hog' with Darwin's hypothesis of natural selection."[1] In using that idiom Newman certainly showed his bent for putting a point strongly, but he also spoke dismissively about Darwinian evolution. While one would not expect from Mr. Wilson's type of writers to do serious research, Newmanists, who cast Newman into the role of an evolutionist, have little excuse for not having done their homework.[2]

Newman spoke of the development of single entities— whether the state, the church, or an idea—as all being subject to that law of life which is to grow. Newman called corruption any growth which led to a loss of identity. Darwin, however, was interested in such growth of any species which issued in a species whose members no longer could interbreed with members of the parent species. Further, in the *Origin of Species* Darwin drew the picture of an endless proliferation into innumerable species, all ready to feed upon one another. If Newman had really anticipated Darwin, he should have called his book not an *Essay on the Development of Christian Doctrine,* but an essay on the issuance of ever new sets of doctrines among Christians forming ever more numerous mutually hostile groups. Had Newman been a forerunner of Darwin, he would then have contended that all such doctrines, each being an intellectual "species," are equally justified. In that case Newman would never have converted, but would have pleaded that all should be free to convert into anything else or at least to imagine that one remains the same, though cast on the waves of endless changes. But in the *Development* Newman portrayed the growth of one single Church. In a little noted phrase in that book, Newman held high Saint Augustine for never referring to the Donatists as a Church.[3] Patristic ecumenists, especially when they parade in Newman's cloak, better take note both of this and of the nature of schism as Newman viewed it.

Had Newman worked along Darwinian lines, he would have served as an instance of what Disraeli lampooned in his *Tancred; or, a New Crusade.* There Lady Constance urges Tancred, a young aristocrat, to read "The Revelations of Chaos," because "it explains everything, and is written in a very agreeable style. . . . It is impossible to contradict anything in it." This had to be the case, if it were true, as she claimed, that "all is development." The principle is correct, she went on, because "all is explained by geology and astronomy." The latter explains how "a cluster of vapour, the cream of the milky way, a sort of celestial cheese, churned into light." Geology in turn explains that "we are a link in the chain, as inferior animals were that preceded us: we in turn shall be inferior; all that will remain of us will be some relics in a new red sandstone. This is development. We had fins, we may have wings."[4]

This was, of course, incidental in *Tancred*, whose author wanted to prove the superiority of Jews and their faith over Christians and their creeds. In conjuring up "The Revelations of Chaos," a fictitious bestseller, Disraeli aimed at Robert Chambers' *Vestiges of the Natural History of Creation*, published in 1844, which had for its indirect target the Mosaic account of creation in six days, the chief perspective of the fixity of species as well. But by 1844 the idea of evolution and development had been for some time gaining acceptance under the guise of progress, the great slogan which found itself glorified through the opening of the Grand Exhibition in the Crystal Palace in 1851.[5] And Newman himself insisted on doctrinal development in public and in print at least two years before he wrote the *Development* during the months preceding his conversion.

Doctrinal development posed a challenge hardly more for a Roman Catholic than for an Anglican, who felt to be a Catholic. Such were all Anglicans who with Newman looked upon themselves as Anglo-Catholics and whose number the Anglican Newman wanted to increase as much as possible. It was to them that Newman preached on Purification Day in 1843 on "The Theory of Developments in Religious Doctrines." There he spoke of the history of one's opinions as instancing "no abrupt revolution, or reaction . . . but the birth of an idea, the development, in explicit form, of what was already latent within it." By then he had warned his hearers that he was not concerned with "the question who is the legitimate framer and judge of these dogmatic inferences under the Gospel, or if there be any. Whether the Church is infallible, or the individual, or the first ages, or none of these, is not the point here, but the theory of developments itself."[6]

No sooner had these words appeared in print than attention was drawn to Newman's fondness for the word "development."

But to see the history of doctrines in terms of development Newman did not have to fall back on De Maistre and Möhler, as implied by William Palmer (1803-1885), whom Newman called in the *Apologia* the only thoroughly learned man among the early Tractarians. Palmer, of whom more later, had for some time distanced himself from Newman when he brought out in 1843 his *Narrative of Events connected with the Publication of the Tracts for the Times*. There Palmer deplored the Romanizing tendencies of some Tractarians and in particular their fondness for the word "development," with Newman being Palmer's chief target.[7]

Newman did not have to borrow from De Maistre and Möhler the notion that everything developed. Nor did Newman have to rely on those two for the idea that, contrary to the instinct of taking an entity, such as a river, to be clearer at its source, the entity becomes more discernible in its developed form. Had Newman referred to the fact that the "British oak" is far more discernible as a stately tree than a mere seedling, Palmer, very much an advocate of the Church of England, could have hardly objected. If anyone then Palmer had to realize that the first decades of the Church of England showed no pristine clarity, whether doctrinally or organizationally.

By focusing on development, äewman merely unfolded the obvious fact that insofar as anything lived, it had to develop and that this meant change upon change, even if identity has not suffered in the process. This is is what he meant when he noted, in one of the most often quoted passages of the *Development*, that "here below to live is to change, and to be perfect is to have changed often."[8] Yet nothing would have been farther from Newman's thinking than the notion that the conceptual "mechanism" of theological development as set forth in the *Development* was an engine to promote endless innovations. Newman would be greatly distressed on seeing Catholic efforts, at times on very high level, to fuel developments most consciously. It would not escape his attention that such efforts are eagerly picked up by journalistic antennas and dished out to vast audiences. A case in point is what appeared from the pen of W. McGurn, chief editorial writer for the *Wall Street Journal*. What he wrote there on March 28, 2003, led to further communications by him where he recalled an interview that John Allen had with Archbishop Renato Martino, the Vatican's representative to the United Nations. To Allen's question about whether the Archbishop no longer held the idea of just wars, the reply was "absolutely." The reason for this, according to the Archbishop, was that the Church's teaching "about just war was evolving along the same lines as the Church's doctrine about death penalty." One indeed gains the impression that the doctrine is being pushed to evolve. Promoters of such deliberate "developments," even in much smaller ecclesial matters, such as liturgical changes, would draw upon their heads the displeasure of a Newman most respectful of liturgical rules and traditions.

For whatever the "mechanism" which unfolds what is already latent in any early phase of genuine ecclesial development, Newman also stated something most basic underlying that mechanism: "Bold outlines, which cannot be disregarded, rise out of the records of the past, when we look to see what it will give up to us: they may be dim, they may be incomplete but they are definite."[9] If pressed for an answer about the entity whose outlines he saw boldly emerging, Newman, so fond of biblical images would, most likely, have referred to the mountains which surround Jerusalem as symbols of God's guarding his own plan of salvation (Ps 124: 1-2). The outlines then would stand for a vast mountain range which a special act of God placed athwart human history, beginning with the promise to the first Eve that her and Adam's fall would turn into a unparalleled benefit for all their descendants through the cooperation of the Second Eve, who would become the Mother of the Savior.

Newman is fully aware that it is not his theory of development which makes the Church, but the Church, the living body of Christ, that makes developments within it not only possible but also necessary. Even the slightest oversight of the order of this sequence bodes ill for a proper grasp of what Newman's theory of development can deliver and what it cannot and was never meant to deliver. Newman phrased this in a negative way when he added to his dictum about bold outlines: "Whatever be historical Christianity, it is not Protestantism. If ever there were a safe truth, it is this."[10] Are these the words of someone who ought be read "ecumenically," with an eye on a hypothetical Third and Fourth Vatican Council so that the Church might be turned into an entity which is a chain of ever fleeting moments? For Newman those bold outlines stand in witness to something permanent, whereas Protestantism is the permanence of fragmentation which erodes all distinct contours.

The gist of the Development

Had Newman dwelt somewhat on those bold outlines, he would have made even clearer the gist of the *Development*. It was not so much about the analysis of conceptual changes, it was not even about some mystical force operating through the allegorical meaning of many a biblical phrase, but about a huge fact. After all, for Newman those bold outlines were not ideas but the combined effect of a vast array of facts which he marshalled from Church history and from the writings of Church Fathers.

For only the vision of such facts as aggregating into bold outlines can provide on behalf of Newman's theory of development a substratum, or a skeleton, without which it will, as indeed this happened in more recent decades, become the prey of interpretations that are much more germane to psychology than to dogma and history. Much earlier, disregard of the ecclesial reality visible in bold outlines could seem to justify the charge that Newman's arguments were at times circular. He supposed, so that charge went, what he meant to prove. But for him the reality of the Church as having kept its identity from Apostolic times to the present was not a supposition. He sees that entity, even though, for the sake of argument, he writes at times as if it were a mere idea. For he argues not so much on his own behalf as on behalf of those whom he had taught to be Anglo-Catholic. There is indeed some truth in a remark of Thomas Mozley, who in 1843 was close to becoming a Roman Catholic, but did not because Newman told him to wait until the moment when he would feel an overwhelming push from Heaven. Newman was then playing for time as he was writing the *Development,* because he expected "further light from his Heavenly Guide."[11]

This is not contradicted entirely by Newman's repeated assertions that he would not have become a Catholic without having written the *Development.* About Newman's own assertions concerning this or that, it remains true what he told much later concerning development: no one can have all the relevant considerations present in one's mind at a given moment. But there was one overwhelming consideration present in Newman's mind as he was writing the *Development.* It was the huge fact of the One Church, the one vast range of God's mountains and of their outlines piercing the sky, the vault of Heaven writ large.

Newman himself recalled and specified the very origin of this perception of his about the Church of Rome as the sole vestibule to Heaven. It is unlikely that Newman would have seen for the first time Augustine's words, "securus judicat orbis terrarum . . . ," when he saw them in an essay which Nicholas Wiseman, the future Cardinal Archbishop of Westminster, published about a four-volume collection of the *Tracts for the Times* that appeared between 1834 and 1838. Wiseman showed, mainly through lengthy quotations from Augustine's writings against the Donatists, that the various claims of the Tractarians about the Church of England not being in schism were a mere echo of what the Donatists had brought up long ago against the arguments of Catholics about the One True Fold.[12]

On reading that essay, Isaac Williams, Newman's former curate at Saint Mary's, saw immediately the portent of those words, which at first made no impression on Newman. But before long they began ringing in his ears like the sounds of a church bell. Within a little over a year, the impact of those words made Newman write his Tract 90, in which he not only claimed that a Roman Catholic interpretation of the Thirty-nine Articles was possible, but also that Anglo-Catholics had the right to worship as Roman Catholics within the Church of England. Of course, Newman was rebuffed by the Establishment, which, however, could not help rebuffing itself. It soon agreed to an intercommunion with the Lutheran State Church, giving thereby one more proof of its radically Protestant nature.

In two more years Newman retracted his previous anti-Rome statements, which proved that a profound change had taken place in his perception of Rome. Of course, he always knew that the Church of Rome was far greater than the Church of England and had been great long before there was an Anglican Church. But Newman now began to see that greatness in a wholly new light. With his bent on psychological analysis, Newman could have anticipated those moderns who in our times made so popular the mental process called paradigm shift, had Wiseman's article contained a most precious anti-Donatist dictum of Augustine. In a little known piece against the Donatists, Augustine refers to Isaiah's words about the House of God which is also God's mountain (Is 2:2) and challenges the Donatists to see the mountain which is the Catholic Church. Newman, so keen to man's proneness to sin, would not have taken offense at Augustine's comment that the Donatists had sinfully blinded themselves to that gigantic reality.[13] Newman might have experienced right then what the blind man did after Jesus touched his eyes and scales fell from them.

This would have almost certainly happened to the still Anglican Newman had his attention been called to a Sermon which Augustine preached in memory of Saint Fructuosus, bishop of Toledo, who died for his faith during the persecution of Decius. Augustine especially cherished in the Acta of the bishop the answer he had given to his deacon who begged for his prayers once in the presence of God. The bishop almost refused the request: "I am bound to pray for the whole Catholic Church spread over the world, spread from the East to the West," went the bishop's reply as he ascended the stake, a reply which Augustine interpreted as follows: "If you wish that I should pray for you, do not leave her [the Church] for whom I pray."[14]

The words "securus judicat . . ." were slowly performing a transformation in Newman's mind, so that it became fully Roman Catholic by the time he began to write the *Development*. He knew that after putting on paper all his considerations about the Church of Rome as remaining the same through all her changes, he had to act and convert, even if he had not gained any further insight. By early 1844 the Church of Rome had emerged before his eyes not so much as geographically monumental, but rather as spanning across all Christian history. That history was much more than what a political historian could see. The core of it was spiritual, though clearly translatable into facts. Seeing this allowed Newman to draw three powerful parallels between the Church of Rome of his day and the Church of pre-Nicene, Nicene, and post-Nicene times.

The first of those parallels deals with the hostility shown by pagans and Jews during the first three centuries and the reaction of the Church to it. The hostility was a relentless defamation and recurrent bloody persecution to which the Church reacted with a humble but also steely endurance. The Church responded in the same way also to Gnostics, Marcionites and other early heretics. Newman drew the second parallel after he had surveyed at length the insidiousness of Arius, the Arians, and the semi-Arians, and the heroic stance of Athanasius and others on behalf of orthodoxy as held up by Rome. This parallel stretched into what the Church had to suffer for the purity of faith during the fifth century in the hands of the Nestorians. But the most telling is the third parallel, in which the sixth century Church is shown as being flooded over everywhere by heretics and schismatics, while the Catholic Church, though caught in that murky flood of "ecclesial diversification," was still clearly recognized and in no small measure on account of its being tied to the See of Rome.

In very modern parlance, the Catholic Church, and only that Christian Church, is alone the target of unremitting enmity by a secularist world, of insidious opposition by all "Christian" denominations, and an entity that much more than in Newman's day is today similar to an archipelago. In the vast stretches of ecclesial waters Catholic dioceses are so many islands, surrounded by a large variety of Christian churches that can agree, for all their efforts to unite, only in their protests against Rome. And these protesters do everything to be present everywhere in formerly Catholic lands. While modern democracy helps Catholic missionary efforts in non-Catholic lands, it also exposes the Catholic realms to a relentless proselytizing by non-Catholics. Newman foresaw all this as he kept speaking of an age of infidelity to be around the corner in which only the Church of Rome would remain a faithful witness.

Those three parallels are part of the longest section of the *Development* that deals with the first characteristic, the preservation of type, of genuine development. Much shorter is Newman's treatment of the other factors, or the principle of continuity, the power of assimilation, early anticipation, logical sequence, preservative additions, and chronic continuance. None of these suggests the random events of "evolution." All those factors imply much more than intangible psychological processes, which Newman, now and then, brings into play. Most importantly, Newman's listing and explanation of these factors is preceded by an Introduction in which he presents the problems which the *Development* is meant to answer. Among these problems the chief is the fearful alternative on which Newman allows no tergiversation whatsoever. Either the present Roman Catholic Church is the organic and sole continuation of the Church established by Christ, or He, Christ, cannot be imagined to have established a Church. In the *Apologia* Newman would present that alternative as the impossibility of finding a middle road between Rome and atheism.[15] Such an alternative meant the difference between spiritual life and spiritual death.

Did this mean that the Church of England was a corpse? Without using such a strong word, Newman implied this when he first spoke about the consideration that drove his writing of the *Development*. The occasion was the letter Newman received from Samuel Charles Wilks, editor of the *Christian Observer,* who saw in Newman's conversion the proof that he was right when years earlier he expressed his misgivings about the devotees of "Anglican principles" as being on the road to Rome. "I do not think," Newman wrote to Wilks on November 8, 1845, "at all more than I did, that the Anglican principles I advocated at the date [1838] you mention, lead to the Church of Rome." According to Newman the essence of those principles was the taking of "*antiquity* not the *existing Church*, as the oracle of truth; and holding that the *Apostolical Succession* is a sufficient guarantee of Sacramental Grace, without *union with the Christian Church throughout the world*. I think them [those principles] still the firmest, strongest bulwark against Rome—that is *if they can be held*. They have been held by many, and are far more difficult to refute than those of any other religious body."

Sacramental grace meant the supernatural life conveyed by the sacraments. Could this flow of grace be had in terms "Anglican principles"? According to those principles one was supposed to hold what Antiquity had always held and one was not supposed to hold anything else, as Roman Catholics allegedly did. Bishop Bull's *Defensio fidei nicenae* (1685) was the best exposition of the claim that the tenets of the Nicene Creed could directly be read out from the New Testament and from the ante-Nicene patristic literature. And since that Creed contained no subsequent Romish tenets and devotions, the position of the Church of England could appear far more genuinely Apostolic than that of Rome. "I have felt all along," Newman wrote to Wilks, "that Bishop Bull's theology was the only theology on which the English Church could stand—I have felt that opposition to the Church of Rome was *part* of that theology; and that he who could not protest against the Church of Rome was no true divine in the English Church." Newman did not soften much this statement by distinguishing between protest and hostility: "I have never said, nor attempted to say, that any one in office in the Church of England, whether Bishop or incumbent, could be otherwise than in hostility to the Church of Rome." But it was incumbent on all of them that they should protest.

Yet, it is not the hostile or unhostile attitude shown by this or that Anglican bishop toward Rome, which is the crucial point Newman wanted to make. That point is tied to the word "protest," a word evoking Protestantism and its willful break with Rome. The Church of England could perhaps claim that its break with Rome was not heresy but a mere schism. This was, however, a sufficient crime to stifle the flow of sacramental grace in a schismatic body. That lifeblood the Church of England could not have because, being a consciously schismatic body, it had severed itself from the trunk of the tree of life.

Later, especially in speaking to prospective converts from Anglo-Catholicism, Newman took pains to elaborate on that point, so shocking to anyone who had led a most devout life as an Anglican and made frequent recourse to its communion service. Newman assured them of the validity of their baptism, which, anyhow depended on the intention of the minister to do what the Church of Christ always did. But when it came to the Anglican Eucharist, Newman the Catholic never failed to insist that such a Eucharist was useful only in the measure of personal piety. And since the Church of England was ambivalent about the sacraments of ordination and confirmation, and even more so on confession and extreme unction, and spoke of marriage merely as an "honorable state," Newman drew the inference: Anglicans could be in the state of grace, but they were not so in virtue of their being of the Church of England, which was a mere wreck, as Newman put it bluntly in his *Anglican Difficulties*, a series of lectures he delivered in London in the late Spring of 1850.

But it was not possible to hold fast to the bold outlines as embodied in the Church of Rome and not to see at the same time that the Church of Rome of the mid-nineteenth century was different from the Rome of early patristic times. The difference had to be accounted for, and this is what Newman tried to explain by insisting that any genuinely living entity had to develop, and this meant change, though within limits. Thus, to recall a favorite simile of Newman, on some reflection one could recognize that the same man was shown by two photographs taken decades apart.

Still Newman did not write the *Development* to prove that Rome showed a sameness across many centuries. Rather, he wrote it on the assumption, indeed in the firm belief, that the Rome of the day was the Church established by Christ. Therefore, and this what he said later, the *Development* was meant by him merely to remove some objections to seeing Rome in that light. The *Development* was not to be taken for a theological treatise, and not even for a piece of systematic apologetics, but for a set of arguments *ad hominem*, the man being a typical Anglo-Catholic, the only type of Anglican of interest to Newman. He did not write it for Protestants, let alone for future modernists, willful or well-meaning, the latter coming from among the protagonists of the "new" theology and its many hapless victims.

The *Development* exudes from start to end the conviction of a Catholic, and also of a Catholic who has an unusually vast command of facts at his disposal. In writing that book, Newman did not want to "demonstrate" Rome's case, but merely to show that changes of Rome posed no serious objection to it. Most importantly, Newman wanted to show this not so much by theorizing about change, but by marshalling facts upon facts that lost their meaning unless they represented genuine development.

The role which Newman attributed to facts as he worked out his theory of development is part and parcel of the *Development* and transpires in a so far unnoticed or ignored aspect of it: the strikingly frequent occurrence there of the word "fact." In the very first page of the Introduction to the *Development* Newman refers to facts and in particular to the Christian religion as a fact seven times. In that Introduction the Christian religion is held high as something that cannot be treated as a "matter of private opinion." Then Newman distances himself from "a hypothesis which has no claim on our time and attention till facts are adduced on which it is built, for which it accounts." In Chapter 2 the words "fact" and "facts" occur over twenty times, including one passage in which Newman excoriates a German Church historian (Gieseler) for shifting his facts. Newmanists, who left no page unexamined in Newman's Anglican's writings to find the word "development," still have to see the importance which Newman the Anglican attributed to the facts of ecclesiastical history as he found them mostly in Fleury's vast work, of which he had translated into English a section dealing with the Nicene Church's belief in ecclesiastical miracles.[16]

Newman who already in the first page of the *Development* attributed "objective existence" to the Christian religion, uses heavily in that Chapter 2 the words "object" and "objective." Subjectivists, who would take comfort in Newman's statements that the "mind cannot take in an object fully" and that "whole objects do not create in the mind whole ideas," would do well to recall that Newman declares the Christian religion, like the Jewish, to be an "objective religion." He states that "revealed religion comes to us as a whole objectively" and that if it is not a series of facts, then "objective religion has not been given." He also states that "the doctrine of infallibility secures for religion its objects," that it "impresses objectiveness on religion," and that the principle of development must imply the "principle of objectiveness." Nowhere does Newman suggest that the subjective mental states of the knower are the condition for objects to exist, though such states may color one's grasp of objects. In the *Development* Newman refers time and again to Truth writ large. Then there is in the *Development* a full chapter on the role of Rome as the guardian of revealed truth: Just as the apostles were the guardians of truth, "apostles are harbingers of Popes." Once more Newman piles facts upon facts to make his point.

All this brings us to the question of the actual pulling together of all those facts, that is, to the actual writing of the *Development*. Newman began to fill notebooks on a systematic presentation of the topic of development shortly after he moved to Littlemore in 1842. After discarding several schemes, he did not start writing the *Development* until January 1845. A mere look at the many references in the *Development* can but make one think that "writing [it] in the space of nine months was an extraordinary achievement." This remark of the learned Oratorian editors of *The Correspondence of John Henry Newman with John Keble and Others . . . 1839-1845*,[17] is not entirely correct even if one considers the fact that Newman wrote out the actual text of the *Development* in less than seven months as he had to discard everything he had put on paper during January and February.

He surely did not discard some books from which many pages entered the *Development* in the form of quotations that were at times several pages long. He heavily used his own *Prophetical Office* and *University Sermons* to illustrate good and faulty uses of the notion of development. As Anglican he was increasingly aware of the fact that the Church of England had to show development if it was a genuine Church. Newman also kept at close range the works of such non-Catholic historians as Gibbons, Guizot, and Gieseler, and monographs by Anglican divines on pagan and Jewish attitudes to the early Church. Last but no least he readily referred to the ideas of his favorite author, Bishop Butler. Almost a third of the *Development* consists of quotations from a dozen authors, while it still remains a most original work. And as in other cases, once Newman gained the leading idea of what he was going to present, he did not refuse to use material wherever he found it. Nor did he spare himself from chaining himself, so to speak, to his writing desk, where some visitors found him standing pale and exhausted.

In his long letter of June 10, 1845, to Mrs. William Froude, Newman complained that he had much more material on hand than he could use, his difficulty being how "to bring them into shape." He admitted that he had no hope of finishing the work before the autumn, if at all: "I have not written a sentence, I suppose, which will stand or hardly so. Perhaps one gets over-sensitive even about style, as one gets on in life." Thirty-three years later when he brought out the definitive edition of the *Development*, he surely showed himself a stickler for style by introducing great many changes, many of them purely stylistic. At any rate, Newman told Mrs. Froude that he felt tired and hoped "to lay aside the actual writing for three weeks or so." If he did, then it becomes an even greater miracle that an "unfinished" work was ready for the printer about three months later in such a "finished" form.

Yet, if one looks at the closing sections of the book, especially on the pages that deal with devotion to Mary, one cannot help being touched there by a tone which is spiritually enthusiastic, perhaps mystical, revealing a distinct ease on Newman's part. A detail, which is hardly ever noted by Newmanists, but stood out very much in Newman's memory, may give the clue to that tone and ease, as if indicating that the writing of the *Development* was for him a downhill course from late August on. The clue to this is in a very brief note Newman sent on August 22, 1867, to Pusey, to congratulate him on his birthday. Newman ended the note with the remark: "August 22 was also the day on which in 1845 I saw my way clear to put a miraculous medal round my neck." A dozen or so years after it had first been minted in Paris, at the urging of Catherine Labouré, the miraculous medal found its way to a cow barn in Littlemore to perform one of the greatest marvels of theological history. The pages on Mary are so many jewels. Twenty years later, when Newman felt he had to rise to the defense of her Lady against the strange cogitations of Pusey, he found in those pages a mine of information for making it clear that Pusey's and other High-Church Anglicans' reluctance to be enthusiastic about Mary, the Mother of God, had nothing to do with the Fathers.[18]

For all that final help from Heaven, the "finished" form of the *Development* is surely imperfect and Newman repeatedly noted this during the ensuing decades. It had a built-in imperfection concerning its chief explanatory device, namely, the difference between the individual mind's growth in perceiving a topic, and the "communal" mind of the Church, which is a mind only in an analogous sense. Newman never confronted this problem in its width and depth. It is a major problem even if one presents a dogmatic or theological treatise on development, let alone if the treatise, as is the case with the *Development*, is largely, though not entirely, a piece of apologetic, or, rather, a vast canvass about the early centuries of the Church in a very special perspective. But even if Newman had repeated the words "bold outlines" throughout the *Development*, Anglican critics of it would have hardly written differently. Not for them some plain truths and facts, either then or now.

Anglican critics

That so many Anglicans rushed to review the *Development* tells much about the threat it posed to them. The bishops tried to ignore Newman's secession, let alone its documentary justification, the *Development*. Newman himself recalled in the *Apologia* that more than a full year before he "seceded" to Rome, an Anglican bishop foretold it and also slighted its significance well in advance. The bishop, Newman wrote, "thought it worthwhile to give out to the world that 'the adherents of Mr. Newman are few in number. A short time will now probably suffice to prove this fact. It is well known that he is preparing for secession; and, when this event takes place, it will be seen how few will go with him'."[19] Whatever the number of those who immediately followed Newman, the number of Anglican reviews of the *Development* betrayed a deep apprehension.

There was, in addition, the speed with which some of the reviews were printed. George Moberly, Head-Master of Winchester School and future bishop of Salisbury, used the printing of the second edition of his book, *The Sayings of the Great Forty Days between the Resurrection and Ascension regarded as the Outlines of the Kingdom of God, in Five Discourses*, to deal with the *Development*. He did so by adding to the seven-page long Preface of the first edition another Preface of fifty-five pages, signed on December 29, 1845, a little over a month after the *Development* came off the press. Had Moberly pondered the gist of Newman's argument, he would have thought twice before charging Newman and those who followed him to Rome with having "incurred the guilt of schism."[20] Had not Newman set great store by the Fathers' viewing the sin of schism so gravely and had not Anglican divines taken so lightly the possibility of being guilty of that sin? Was the Church of England, eager to pose in the garb of the Fathers, so innocent of that sin? For whatever the question of Rome's alleged innovations, and regardless of Newman's "theory," the weight of Christendom lay with Rome in Antiquity, no less then in Moberly's time.

Newman's theory could be analyzed to the point where it bore no likeness to what he said. Newman rested his theory on putting facts first, a vast series of facts, and especially the "bold outlines" they formed together. Severed from those facts and from some most crucial factual considerations, without which, as Newman said, the theory was of little use, it surely could be turned and twisted to no end. Of all concepts only those of numbers are at safe remove from their being abused by the human intellect, prone to yield to its resentment of truth. All other concepts are so many slippery fish, of which those used in theology are so many notorious examples. And if one were convinced as Moberly was that in the forty days between His resurrection and ascension Christ specifically imparted to the Apostles all the tenets of the Nicene Creed, one merely constructed a conundrum especially cumbersome for Anglicans. While Matthew's Gospel contained the Trinitarian formula dear to Anglicans, like Moberly, they preferred to take lightly the words the risen Christ spoke when he committed to Peter the care of his entire flock, and did so in a triple rhythm expressive of utmost emphasis. Was such a commission to cease with Peter's death, whereas the role of the Apostles would continue in the office of bishops?

At any rate, was it so certain that the Church of England of Moberly's time, or of any time, was identical with the Church of the Apostles? Were the problems which Newman outlined in the Introduction mere illusions? What to make of the formation of the scriptural Canon? Would matters have not turned out differently, had Christ told the Eleven to preach only after the New Testament had been fully written up? Did the New Testament support the patently Protestant components of Anglicanism? Could Anglicans be so assured that their barbs aimed at Rome had not hit Canterbury prior to their reaching their intended target? There is not a trace of these questions in Moberly's long Preface. It was a lame escape from the clutches of Newman's idea of development to claim, as Moberly did, that in the New Testament we have all that Christ taught, whether in those forty days or prior to them.

Among the Tractarians proper, William Palmer became the chief critic of the *Development*, and to the surprise of nobody. Palmer had first made a name for himself with his *Origines liturgicae* (1832), a historical study of the sources of the rituals of the Church of England. This book brought him in contact with John Keble, Hurrel Froude, and Hugh James Ross, then editor of the *British Critic*. They formed an "Association of Friends of the Church" to help the latter recover its spiritual roots. Soon Newman appeared on the scene and used the Association to promote the printing of Tracts. Newman also wanted to modify the principles of the Association in a distinctly Catholic direction, which Palmer resisted from the first. His *Narrative,* already mentioned, was a broadside against the Catholic interpretation of the Thirty-nine Articles and similar Romanizing tendencies. By then Palmer had published his two-volume *Treatise on the*

Church of Christ (1838). The book's aim was to confirm Anglican students of theology in the belief that the Church of England was a legitimate branch, together with Rome and Greece, of the Church Catholic. Two years later Palmer came out with *A Compendious Ecclesiastical History from the Earliest Period to the Present Time*, to further the same aim. Still another year later Palmer criticized Wiseman's critique of Newman's interpretation of the Thirty-nine Articles. Clearly, Palmer wanted not a whiff of Romanism, to which he invariably reacted with considerable animus.

All this must be kept in mind in taking a look at Palmer's *The Doctrine of Development and Conscience, considered in Relation to the Evidences of Christianity and of the Catholic System*. In that book Palmer tried to answer not only Newman's *Development* but also a book very different from it, namely, Ward's *The Ideal of the Christian Church* (1843), which was a reply to Palmer's *Narrative*. The choice of two different targets could make rather problematic for Palmer a consistent approach. Further, he did not really want to approach either book. He treated both piecemeal, without facing up to what Newman in particular presented as his aim and strategy. Palmer skirted around Newman's starting point, the inadequacy of Vincent of Lerins' rule as brought out by glaring lacunae and contradictions in the patristic record, which as such told heavily against Bull. The structure of Palmer's book of 340 pages would not have allowed its readers to reconstruct, in its essentials, of what Newman said in the *Development*.

Palmer began with bemoaning the current infatuation with the idea of progress, which surely was not applicable to Newman, a visceral conservative. Further, the four-page-long table of contents shows that Palmer cared not for Newman's concern about the sin of schism. And since Newman did not depend on De Maistre and Möhler, it was not appropriate for Palmer to end his book with a long summary of the theories of those two. Fortunately, for the sake of clarity, Palmer did not make good on his promise that he would follow up his first volume with a second. At any rate, Palmer's claim that the *Development*'s argument was rationalist could sound believable only for those who cast their lot with a recourse to faith and conscience, both taken by Palmer in a transparently Protestant sense. As to his handling of patristic evidence, Palmer provided an instance of those whom Newman later lampooned as Patristico-Protestants. Concerning Palmer's defense of conscience, it reappeared in a revealing document, the anonymous pamphlet with which Palmer came to the aid of Gladstone when the latter challenged, in 1875, Newman on conscience, papal infallibility, and civic loyalty.[21]

It was not a Catholic but an Anglican, the Tractarian Richard W. Church, that offered a most incisive remark on Palmer's book. In the newly established daily, *The Guardian*, where he was in charge of book reviews, Church praised Palmer's mastery of facts and his customary ability not to let the main points escape his attention, but he also felt that in the latter respect Palmer had now failed: "He hits blots better than he deals with them, . . . he fails . . . in grappling satisfactorily with keen and subtle arguments and in mastering the perplexed and difficult state of things to which the theories he examines are applied."[22] But then what of those who did not consider the theory at all and ignored the facts? Church's remark was indeed an unintended exposure of the entire range of Anglican rejoinders to the *Development* and surely of the one to be reviewed next.

Frederick D. Maurice (1805-1872), another Anglican to come out in book form with a critique of the *Development*, was the kind of Anglican who threw himself into any theological dispute, without having a proper theological training and even some clear convictions. Coming from a Quaker background, he had received baptism in the Church of England in 1831, when he was already twenty-six, and taken holy orders three years later, without any systematic schooling in theology. For the rest of his life he remained an eclectic, leaning toward latitudinarianism. Never in personal touch with the principal figures of the Tracta-

rian movement, Maurice approved of the Jerusalem bishopric as
a sign of the catholicity of the Church, for which he was sharply
rebuked by Palmer. Maurice had no sympathy for the Catholicism
of the Tractarians' "Church principles," let alone for Newman's
advocacy of them.

Given the doctrinal heterogeneity of the Church of England
bishops, Maurice could easily endear himself now to this prelate,
now to another. His appointment, in 1840, as professor of
English literature at King's College in London was an evidence
of this tactic of his and so was also his appointment, in 1845, by
the Archbishop of Canterbury to the Warburton lectureship,
which he gave in 1846. To the printed form of those three
lectures on the Epistle to the Hebrews, covering 96 pages,
Maurice added a Preface of 128 pages that dealt with Newman's
Development. He took great pains to make it appear that the long
Preface integrally related to the lectures themselves. He firmly
believed that Newman had been sincere all the time and motivated by the deepest spiritual concerns. But if one took one's stand
as Maurice did in his three lectures on the subjective intensity of
faith and not on what one specifically had to believe, then no
sacraments, no apostolical succession counted by comparison. He
failed to consider why the author of the Epistle to the Hebrews
said not a word on that Christian rite, the Eucharistic supper,
although it had by then been central for decades, as shown by
Paul's Second Letter to the Corinthians. Maurice rather asked:
"Will a mere belief in the Fathers, or in [Apostolic] Succession,
avail to answer the question, 'Is GOD really among us or no?'"
Then, with a veiled reference to what he saw to be rationalism as
the underlying force of Newman's query, Maurice concluded:
"We shall satisfy, not stifle the questions of others; our own
ground will be what it has ever been, but we shall *know* that we
are standing on the Rock of Ages."[23] Protestants loved to make
the "Rock of Ages" synonymous with faith, and of faith the
author of the Letter to the Hebrews spoke eloquently, but he also
enjoined obedience to those set above the faithful with an eternal

responsibility for them. Such obvious considerations were beyond Maurice's purview.

By far the longest of early Anglican discussions of Newman's book came from the pen of James Bowling Mozley (1803-1878), whose brother, Thomas, had married Newman's oldest sister Harriet. Neither of the brothers was a prominent student in Oxford. James Mozley owed his eventual appointment in 1871 as Regius Professor of Divinity in Oxford to his much earlier support of Gladstone's first election to Parliament. Following Newman's conversion, Mozley stated that "at that moment he could no more leave the Church of England than fly." His High-Church convictions that endeared him to Newman, Keble, and Pusey turned out to be skin deep. Though first a critic of the Gorham Judgment, five years of subsequent reflections, as he put it, convinced him of its correctness. This revealed that he was an evangelical Protestant in High-Church clothing.

Tractarians could not therefore gain much by the fact that Mozley took over the editorship of *Christian Remembrancer* following the demise of the *British Critic* as an organ of High-Church views. As editor Mozley could easily publish in the *Christian Remembrancer* a hundred-fifty-five-page-long review[24] of Newman's *Development*, which Newman considered interesting on particulars. Thirty-three years later, when Newman brought out the definitive edition of the *Development*, he expressed his wish, through Anne Mozley, sister-in-law of Newman's sister Jemima, that James Mozley would write again at length on the *Development*. As a result Mozley brought out in book form his original review, without alterations, of the *Development*'s first edition.

Though using so many pages to present and criticize Newman's work, Mozley stated at the start that all that space was not enough for the task. Therefore he claimed the liberty to deal only with the historical parts of Newman's book. In other words, he chose to pick holes in various details without considering Newman's basic line of argument and his insistence on "bold outlines." No wonder that at the end Mozley's could command the semblance of being on firm ground when he wrote: "So then we ask Mr Newman what is his theory? For we confess we are unable to make it out."[25] No wonder, one may add. For contrary to the claim Mozley made in the same breath, Newman did not derive his argument from a mere idea of the Church, but from the reality of the Church, generating an idea of it, which in turn was reflected in a vast array of facts, all forming a "bold outline." That array Mozley damned with faint praise as he registered Newman's command of patristic history and left it at that.

In the many pages of Mozley's review one would look in vain for a concise summary of Newman's argument. One could not even find out from that review Newman's starting point, or the threat posed by the rule of Vincent of Lerins to Anglican theology. Mozley's review glosses over the three major parallels Newman drew about the Church of old and the present Church of Rome. Mozley did not confront Newman's references to patristic views on the grievousness of consciously living in the sin of schism. The review was a vast illustration of what a review ought not to be, unless, of course, its writer feels at liberty to present primarily his own views. Though well written, Mozley's review was not to the point, a very doctrinal point. This was precisely to be expected from one, who, in Newman's words, "never held it [Anglicanism] simply as a doctrine, as a truth—but as an *ethos*."[26] The apparently strongest part of Mozley's review was his recourse to Orestes Brownson, a recent American convert, who had just begun to publish against the *Development* a series of heated articles, from the first of which Mozley quoted long passages with obvious delight.

In December 1845, William Archer Butler (1814-1848), professor of moral philosophy at the University of Dublin, began to publish in the *Irish Ecclesiastical Gazette* a series of articles on Newman's work, which were brought out together five years later as a book, *Letters on the Development of Christian Doctrine, in Reply to Mr Newman's Essay,* through the editorial care of the Rev. Thomas Woodward. This hefty book of four hundred pages, preceded by an extremely detailed table of contents running to forty pages[27] is worth recalling only because of Butler's astonishment over the vast number of quotations in Newman's book. Butler hoped that their reliability would one day be the object of a close scrutiny. Well, no subsequent critic of Newman's book found his quotations wanting in accuracy.

Years later Newman briefly referred in a letter to Henry Wilberforce to Butler's work and also to those of Moberly, Maurice, and Mozley, but he did not mention William J. Irons, author of *The Theory of Development Examined with Reference Especially to Mr. Newman's Essay and to the Rule of St. Vincent of Lerins.*[28] Vicar of Brompton, Middlesex, in 1846, Irons later tried to dislodge the Oratorians from their present location on the pretext that the Oratory was not at least 300 yards away from the nearest Protestant Church. Irons, who is best remembered for his hymn translation, "Day of wrath! O day of mourning," of the "Dies irae," zealously defended the Established Church in many publications, among them a spirited pamphlet-reply, *Apologia pro vita ecclesiae Anglicanae,* to Newman's *Apologia.*[29] In his *Theory* Irons began with a general view of the topic, followed by a discussion of Newman's theory of it. According to Irons "the theory has no ideal unity whatsoever, if regarded apart from its subject matter, which is the Roman Church. It is rather a number of theories, more or less analogous, kept together by an ingenious writer for a definite purpose, but having no internal oneness—and therefore not being capable of being submitted to any test."[30]

The illusory character of this conclusion escaped Irons because no less than others he failed to appreciate Newman's starting point: the overwhelming reality of a "Catholic" ecclesial reality, *the* Church indeed. Oversight of this could then make many a particular argument in the *Development* appear circular. For Newman did not try to derive the Church from the idea of development, but wanted to show that the Church, if it was living, had to develop. Failing to see this logic, Irons brought to a close the next section, that dealt with the Rule of Vincent of Lerins, with the remark that Newman said nothing more than that Christianity developed into the Pope and that the Popes develop ad infinitum. The next section on "Popedom" ended with a question about the problem of schism: "Did Newman ever meet with anyone who maintained that the apostolic succession is everything?" But this question merely proved that Irons had little use for Laud, Andrewes, Bull and other notable figures of Anglican theology, who had been very much concerned with doctrinal continuity, besides that "everything" or apostolic continuity. The last section was about the finality of the revealed truth, which Irons thought to reside in the sacraments and the creeds, though hinting that Truth was invisible because of the miserable divisions of Christians. Once more a heretic's or a schismatic's attack on the very visible Rome led to the "invisible" Church of the Reformers.

Somewhat shorter was the pamphlet, *Romanism as Represented by the Rev. John Henry Newman, Briefly Considered with Some Illustrations of its Necessary Tendency*,[31] by A. Irvine, vicar of St. Margaret's in Leicester. After reviewing Newman's earlier anti-Roman argumentations, Irvine concluded that "the sole change is in Mr. Newman himself."[32] There was surely a change, and a very great change in Newman himself, but its real reason Irvine either could not, or was not willing to see. He ignored Newman's reference to the bold outlines, to the seriousness of the sin of living in the state of schism, and to the fact that Newman finally saw what had been obvious beforehand, namely, a monumental reality very much visible.

While Irvine was not a scholar by any measure, historical scholarship marked Henry Hart Milman's career. His first major work *The History of the Jews* (1830) treated the chosen people as an ordinary semitic tribe, which greatly displeased Newman, who was to report about this in the *Apologia*. For, surely, even on purely historical grounds there was something out of the ordinary in that history, and it had to appear monumental precisely because of the puniness of that tribe in comparison with the great cultures surrounding it. But just as Milman could not see this feature there, he failed to see it in Christianity itself, in spite of the fact that he spent much time on producing an edition of Gibbon's *Rise and Fall of the Roman Empire* that was full of critical correctives of Gibbon's treatment of the Church.

Milman, who began his academic career as professor of poetry in Oxford, had already been dean of Saint Paul's for five years when he came out with his magnum opus, *The History of Latin Christianity down to the Death of Pope Nicholas V*, first published in 1855. There he celebrated "the Latin Church" without paying attention to what gave a special mark to Roman Christianity, in distinction from its Eastern forms. Milman did not see what Newman called "the bold outlines" of Church history and of the history of doctrine when he wrote a review of the *Development* for the March 1846 issue of *Quarterly Review*,[33] the leading British periodical of the nineteenth century, until the *Contemporary Review* took its place.

Long enough was the space, a full sixty pages, for Milman to do what is required by objectivity. But from first to last he harped on matters subjective, and in a condescending style. He unctuously wished Newman well: "May his restless spirit at length have repose!" Milman kept on with this kind of well-wishing for the rest of a long paragraph, in which he contrasted Newman's opting for "cloistral practices" with the bravery of those who face the challenges of living Christianity "either in the high places or in the domestic sanctuaries of life." Milman, on his way to the safe comforts (pecuniary and social) of the Deanship of St. Paul's Cathedral, had no eyes for the hardships of those "cloistral practices."

No wonder. Already in the next paragraph of his review Milman conjured up with a reference to Coleridge the merits of a psychological approach to Newman's personal problems, which sowed "the bitter seeds of religious dissension in many families." Not for Milman the idea that Christ came to bring divisions.

There could be no room for such plain Gospel truths in a review which came to a close with an encomium of a spiritual bravery that has no need for trusting in the presumed infallibility of some humans (popes). As one might expect, Milman failed to specify what that bravery stood for in matters of belief and morals. It was the old story of claiming to oneself the Gospel without specific Gospel truths, the very attitude which Newman bemoaned as the enduring feature of Anglicanism.

Milman was not one of those who were driven by a zeal to revive religiosity in the English Church along decidedly non-Romanist lines. These could but look with contempt at the *Development*, and at times even at its author. This was certainly true of their leader, Samuel Wilberforce, Bishop of Oxford from 1844, and subsequently bishop of Exeter. Zealous though hardly an intellectual, he was the only one of the four Wilberforce brothers not to convert. On December 6, 1845, he wrote to Gladstone, asking him whether he had seen Newman's book, which he described as being "acute, perhaps beyond anything he has written." The bishop, who earned himself the nickname "Soapy Sam" and went down in history as T. H. Huxley's hapless opponent on Darwin's theory, thought that Newman's book was not such as to "overthrow the faith of many." But the bishop also thundered at an ordination ceremony in Christ Church Cathedral that Newman had been "borne upon the wings of an unbridled passion into the bosom of an unfathomable superstition."[34]

The bishop's reason for slighting Newman's book was precisely the one which Newman's more perceptive Anglican readers felt to have been undermined by Newman, even when they did not agree with him that Rome was the successor of the Church of the Apostles. The reason given by the bishop was a rather simplistic restatement of Bull's position that the written Word was given to the Church as a source from which "to draw out and define with logical accuracy" the truth whenever a heresy created the necessity. Therefore the bishop had to conclude that Newman's book "has no force whatever."

Gladstone's reply, written on December 10, was a subtle rebuttal of that position and in more than one sense. First, Gladstone stated that Newman's "secession (an event so unexampled) was an epoch in the history of the Church of England." His book deserved to be answered "by one or more of our very best heads." Then Gladstone's took up the question of development: "I am not able to convince myself that 'to draw out with logical accuracy' what is actually in Scripture, constitutes the whole expository gift of the Church. It is long since I read Vincentius [of Lerins]; but I have always taken it for granted that there is necessarily in the Church some power of 'development'." If such was the case, Gladstone had to admit that it was "extremely difficult to draw with precision against Newman the limits of this power." Gladstone felt that if alive Bishop Butler might be up to the task. A poor way of trying to dispose of a book which, according to Gladstone, called for an answer "constructive as well as destructive."[35] Precisely this was the kind of answer which a Church of England caught in its Protestant veneration of the Bible could never give. It could not do even something much less. Four decades later Gladstone still bemoaned the fact that Anglicans had not yet sized up for themselves the calamitous importance of Newman's secession.[36] More than a century later Anglicans can do no better than to claim that Newman is still one of them, to illustrate the extent to which English pragmatism can befog one's vision.

A very mean attack on the argument of the *Development* came, characteristically enough, from a Broad Church cleric, Julius Hare, Archdeacon of Lewes from 1840 on, whose most popular book carried the title *The Guessing at Truth*.[37] The only distinctive character of truth Hare allowed was the kind of fideism he imbibed while in Germany, where he had spent part of his younger years. In his last book, *The Vindication of Luther against his Recent English Assailants* (1855), Hare rose to the defense of the Lutheran ingredients of the English Reformation. His first major publication, *The Victory of Faith*, the text of sermons he delivered in Cambridge in 1839, stood for the Lutheran principle of justification by faith alone. And just as Luther could dismiss imperiously any counterargument, so did Hare handle Newman's *Development*: "Take a sentence or two here and there from this Father, and a couple of expressions from another, add half a canon of this Council, a couple of incidents out of some ecclesiastical historian, an anecdote for a chronicler, two conjectures of some critic, and half a dozen drachms of a schoolman, mix them up in rhetoric *quant. suff.*, and shake them well together—and thus we get at a theological development."[38] In all this Hare's chief aim was to keep as many Christians as possible within the Established Church, whatever the great variety into which they "developed" their faith.

Newman, ready to throw himself into any dispute about worthy causes, refrained from answering any of the foregoing reactions to the *Development* and many others written by his former co-religionists.[39] In a sense he silently made his face like flint to those vilifying him for obeying his conscience, although they distanced themselves from Rome in the name of their own individual conscience. But on occasion he also wondered whether it had been fully right for him to publish the *Development*. Years later, when the question arose of whether recent converts should publish, Newman answered, on October 27, 1867, in the negative and with an eye on himself: "My experience goes to persuade me that Anglicans think that such an act in a recent convert is especially out of place, and (however erroneously) pretentious. They think that one who is learning has no business to teach; and that he can say nothing but [what] he is primed with by others." To Newman's excuse, he was not, when he wrote the *Development*, primed by recent Catholic writings on the topic, certainly not by those of Moehler and De Maistre, and not even by Wiseman's dicta on developments in the Church. Yet the *Development* is a work that teaches Catholics a great deal, though many of them want to learn from it notions which Newman did not teach either there or in any other of his works.

Catholic reactions

Immediate Catholic reactions to the *Development* were few. On December 20 and 27, 1845, and on January 10, 1846, *The Tablet* carried fairly long and favorable reports about the *Development*, but their writer, a certain "H" (possibly Husenbeth, a Catholic historian), nowhere touched on the problem which eventually became the chief preoccupation of Catholic theologians trying to cope with a development that was not a matter of syllogisms. Strangely, only in the last of those reports did the writer take up the general plan of Newman's argumentation. The first instalment dealt with what "H" felt might give the greatest delight to the readers of *The Tablet,* namely, the blows the book delivered against Anglicans and especially Anglo-Catholics.

The unsigned review in the December 1845 issue of the *Dublin Review* treated Newman's book together with the books other former Tractarians, Frederick Oakeley and T. W. Marshall, both converts. They were hailed as proofs of a reorientation of Anglicans toward Rome. Three-fourths of the review[40] dealt with Newman's book, which, so the reviewer insisted, "contains not a theological treatise, but an essay" and was written before its author joined the Catholic Church. Although the reviewer gave a systematic account of the book, he failed to notice the importance of Newman's reference to "bold outlines" and to the sin of schism. The reviewer said of the development of doctrine only that it was, according to Vincent of Lerins' old observation, similar to the growth of a seed into a plant. Quite enthusiastic was the reviewer about the profoundly religious tone of Newman's statements on the growth of the doctrinal and devotional aspects of the Catholic attitude toward Mary.

In January 1846, Bishop James Gillis (1862-1864), already coadjutor bishop of the Eastern District in Scotland and from 1852 on Vicar Apostolic there, wrote to Newman that he had given a series of lectures on the *Development* in Edinburgh that created great interest there, adding that he hoped to publish them for the benefit of those who could not attend. As one educated in

Saint Sulpice in Paris and ready to print many of his pastoral charges,[41] Bishop Gillis may have produced lectures of great interest on the *Development*, but apparently they were not printed.[42] In that respect similar was the fate of the reaction, very negative though, of Alexander Grant, Vice-Rector of the Scottish College in Rome and consultant for English affairs for *Annali delle scienze religiose*, the Vatican's unofficial voice. In its spring 1846 issue Grant stated that he would review there Newman's work, but apparently failed to do. But he did not fail to charge Newman, in conversations at least, of "material heresy" and spoke of the *Development* as "Newman's hobby."[43]

The charge of material heresy was made openly and forcefully by Orestes Augustus Brownson, one of the greatest as well as most forgotten American minds of the nineteenth century. The storm Brownson wanted to create blew itself out rather quickly, in spite of the fact that he at first found on his side some bishops in America. Brownson's main objections to the *Development* lay in its author's insistence that there was a development of doctrine and that this development arose in terms of an "implicit feeling under secret supernatural guidance." As to this second point, Brownson saw it as an indirect endorsement of fideism. As to the first point, he felt it flew in the face of the Church's teaching that she had always taught the same thing.[44] Brownson failed to see that Newman not only spoke of Christianity as an idea but also, and primarily, as a fact. It was therefore easy for Brownson to submit to unsparing conceptual analysis Newman's dicta about ideas.

To Brownson's chagrin, the *Dublin Review* refused to engage in a theological debate about something which in its editor's opinion was not a theological work at all but a mere essay on thoughts that led to Newman's conversion.[45] Brownson kept coming up with further attacks on Newman's book, saying among other things that "it deserves to be excluded from every Catholic library for its unorthodox forms of expression, as scandalous even if not as heretical, erroneous or rash."[46] Wisely enough, the *Dublin Review* did not rise to the bait and merely restated its view that Newman's work was "not a theological treatise. As such it could not be the subject of theological criticism, and therefore it would be presumptuous to come to its defence!"[47] But just as Brownson failed to see what was really important in the *Development*, the *Dublin Review*, too, was mistaken in thinking that theological questions, apart from other questions, were not to be raised about that book.[48]

The attitude of the *Dublin Review* clearly reflected the views of Bishop Wiseman, who first wanted Newman to bring out the *Development* with "Catholic" corrections. Wiseman formed this intention of his after consulting also with Dr. Russell in May-nouth, of whom Newman was to speak warmly in the *Apologia* as a most tactful and thoughtful person. Newman himself was ready to throw the proofs of the *Development* into the fire, as he put it in a letter to Dr. Baggs, Vicar Apostolic of the London District, if the book really contained false doctrines. However, on learning from Newman that some Anglicans would deeply resent it if the book were to come out in a "revised" form, Wiseman, without opening the packet that contained the proofs, told Newman to proceed with the publication.[49]

As far as the notion of development was concerned, Wiseman could hardly be in disagreement. He must have remembered the sermon he preached at the opening of the new church of St. Mary at Derby in early October 1839 on the parable of the mustard seed. Newman most likely was unaware of this, but he would have certainly found mirrored in it the very judgment he began to form on Anglicanism from that year on. The Reformers, said Wiseman, "imagined that . . . whatever development in outward or inward life it [Christianity] had exhibited was an addition to what God had revealed. If they could not find in His written word the practices observed, to their full extent, and the very terms applied to them, as they admitted no power of development, they rejected all these its results, and generally with them the principles from which they gradually evolved."[50]

Still to be published in full is the letter which F. C. Husenbeth, a Catholic priest and historian, wrote to Newman on December 5, 1845, partly to thank Newman for a complimentary copy of the *Development*. While Husenbeth took the view that the book could do much good for Anglicans, he held it to be the work of one who still had to reach the level of manhood in perceiving Catholicism.[51] After reading the *Development* four times, Edward Caswall, perhaps the greatest religious poet next to Keble of Victorian times, converted to Catholicism on January 18, 1847, and eventually became an Oratorian. But James Hope and Manning were not moved until they saw that the Anglican hierarchy failed to make a stand, in 1850, against the Privy Council, which directed the Bishop of Exeter, a High-Church man, to install the Rev. Gorham, although the latter denied the sacramental value of baptism.[52]

Newman on the Development: phase one

No sufficient attention has yet been paid to Newman's own view on the *Development*. On November 9, 1845, a day after Newman wrote to Wilks, he wrote to Mrs. Bowden, informing her that his readiness to make changes was declined by Bishop Wiseman and that if ever changes were to be made, they would all be made public. Newman insisted that he had no notion of having said "anything against true doctrine." At any rate, he preferred "nothing said about it [the book] at present."

Far more important is the letter which Newman wrote on December 18 to Elizabeth Anstice, widow of Joseph Anstice, professor of classical literature at King's College, and a good friend of Gladstone. Mrs. Anstice, who became a Catholic in September 1845, a month before Newman did, wrote to Newman, because her brother-in-law, James Spencer Northcote, hesitated about converting on account of a question about the Fourth Lateran Council in 1215.

While Newman held Northcote's question important, he expressed his puzzlement over the fact that Northcote had found the *Development* difficult to understand. "It is a shame," Newman wrote, "he should say so. He really must get into the argument, which is not difficult—In so very large a question as the Roman, he really cannot expect to see his way ever through every difficulty. My book attempts to show that *so much* may be said for the *consistency* of the Roman system, which is the outward token and test of its *infallibility*, that it is safest and best to submit to it. But as to particular questions such as Mr. Northcote is perplexing himself with, they are endless—life is not long enough for them." This echoed the *Development's* concluding words about the shortness of this life and the immeasurable length of eternity.

Then there followed a warning, most timely then as now, about the futility of getting lost in details: "I am far from denying that a strong case of apparent exception to the infallibility is not sufficient to make a person pause—but to *begin* with particular cases is to begin at the wrong end. If he will overcome his dread of my obscurities, he will see, that my very argument is to show that we were intended to begin with antecedent probabilities and general presumptions, and to take large and broad views of the subject, instead of entangling ourselves with particular questions. When we have lost our way, we mount up to some eminence to look about us, but he [Northcote] plunges into the nearest thicket to find out his bearings." Clearly, Newman had in mind the importance of focusing on "bold outlines" and seemed to disavow in advance lengthy essays and books that deal with subtle conceptual processes, intuitions, and psychological preconditions as being the key to the *Development*.

It was with such concerns in mind that Newman asked Mrs. Anstice to focus on two principles if the reading of the *Development* was not become a futile enterprise. First, difficulties and insoluble problems would forever remain in this earthly condition of ours and in this respect the Scriptures themselves were no exception. Second, in this life one could not work out a perfect consistency about any historical fact, including the long series of facts of salvation history and its implementation in and by the Church. Those who, like Mr. Northcote, tried to achieve this merely made their own minds "the measure, the arbiter, of perfect consistency." Then, Newman asked, would not all stand on their own ground "according to their respective success in making all things consistent? or rather must there not be *some general* ground which all may stand upon?" The latter, Newman added, "is furnished by the quantum of evidence, which all enquirers may have for the consistency of the Catholic system and history."

It would be most tempting to savor for a while that priceless phrase, "quantum of evidence," so modern in flavor but also so crucial for grasping what came first for Newman. Not ideas, not even antecedent probabilities, however telling, but evidence. The phrase reflected the emphasis which Newman put on facts as the ground on which his hypothesis of development had to rest. In an act which showed Newman's confidence in the evidence he had provided, he urged Mrs. Anstice to ask her brother-in-law to take another look at the *Development*: "I really do think you should make him read my book; it may have no effect on him; but till he does so, he is standing, I do think, in a very unreal position, without being aware that it is thought so by others, or why it is thought so." And with the zeal he had for the eternal salvation of souls, Newman continued: "Pray write me at once what you have to say to these remarks—and I shall be able to answer you when I send the answer to Mr. Northcote." It was to rest on a parallel which Newman drew between himself and others: The *Development* was for Newman a monumental witness on behalf of his concern for his own eternal salvation, which could be had only within the One True Fold as long as one was convinced that Jesus had come to set up such a Fold. For others, too, the *Development*, so Newman thought, was to serve as a means for facilitating that very end, and not a means for specious hairsplitting about development, writ in low case or in upper case.

Newman's next major statement about the thrust of the *Development* was the letter he wrote to Northcote on February 8,

1846. By then Northcote had joined, in January 1846, the Catholic Church where he had been preceded by his wife, Susannah Spencer Ruscombe Poole, one of three sisters who had become Catholic in November 1845. Following the death of his wife in 1853, Northcote studied for the priesthood under Newman in Birmingham and ended his priestly career as Provost of the Cathedral Chapter there. So much for the background of Newman's letter to Northcote about the *Development* and in reference to a correspondent of Northcote himself.

The correspondent was a future convert, William Henry Buckle (1793-1871), related to George Buckle of Oriel College, and to Mrs. Hawkins, wife of the Provost there. Since Buckle had no time to read the whole of the *Development*, Northcote asked Newman to set forth "a few of the leading popular arguments in the matter." Newman, always ready to turn the table, began: "It is unreasonable in any one to object that the grounds a person gives for his conversion cannot be expressed in a formula, but require some little time and consideration to master; which seems to be your correspondent's complaint of my Volume." Not that Newman would shrink from the pastoral task of helping, but he felt doubtful about the possibility of finding such a formula and of its usefulness: "If I could express them [the arguments in the *Development*] in a formula, they could not really be more intelligible or comprehensible—indeed to show this as a general principle is the main object of the Essay. Catholicism is a deep matter; you cannot take it up in a teacup." Or in thick volumes, whose authors skirt the very basics of what Newman said.

Newman distanced himself from two pitfalls in reference to the task of summing up the *Development*. One was to give its thrust in a sentence: "Any dogmatic or sententious proposition would too surely be misunderstood. If I said, for instance, 'I have become a Catholic because I must be either a Catholic or an infidel' men would cry out 'So he has flung himself into the Catholic Church to escape infidelity,' whereas I should only mean that Catholicity and Christianity had in my mind become identical, so that to give up the one was to give up the other." If there was ever a phrase penned by Newman whereby he concisely presented his thinking, it was this phrase, which surely renders the marrow of the *Development*, and aptly serves as its motto for this re-edition of it.

Newman also felt that were he to do justice to his reasons for becoming a Catholic in a few words, let alone doing this in print, he would betray himself as well as the cause: I would "wantonly expose myself and my cause to the hasty and prejudiced criticisms of opponents. This I will not do. People shall not say, 'We have now got his reasons, and know their worth.' No, you shall not get them, you cannot get them, except at the cost of some portion of the trouble I have been at myself. You cannot buy them for a crown piece—You cannot take them in your hand at your will, and toss them about."

This meant that instead of an easy barter, one had to offer one's very mind and will. What Newman said in the *Apologia* about a total reform of one's thinking and intentions,[53] was anticipated as Newman continued his letter to Northcote: "You must consent to *think*—and you must exercise such resignation to the Divine Hand which leads you, as to follow it any whither. I am not assuming that my reasons are sufficient or unanswerable, when I say this—but describing the way in which alone our intellect can be successfully exercised on the great subject in question, if the intellect is to be the instrument of conversion. Moral proofs are grown into, not learnt by heart."

Newman, always very practical, did not fail to hint at some concrete aid. He asked Northcote to recommend to Mr. Buckle to read p. 138 of the *Development*. There, "I state my conviction that were St Athanasius and St Ambrose now to come to Oxford, they would go to Mass in St Clement's." The latter was a simple Catholic mission church there, so different from the splendid Gothic churches and chapels in Oxford, all bathed in the rays of sun filtered through stained glass windows and caressed by the soft melodies of evensong, with exquisite organ music thrown in for good measure for the delight of well-heeled people. Athanasius and Ambrose would not be misled. They were saints with the unerring instinct of saints about holiness and mindful of the rule that the Gospel would be preached to the poor.

Newman also recommended that Northcote suggest to Mr. Buckle to read Chapters iv and v of the *Development* and specified them as pp. 204-317. Those pages, Newman wrote, "your correspondent might read without troubling himself with the rest of the Essay. The argument of those Chapters is this: that the general type of Christendom, and the relation of part with part, in early times and in the present is one and the same—that the Catholic Church and sects and heresies then, correspond to the Roman, Protestant, and other communions now—and in particular that the Anglican Church corresponds to the Semi-Arian body, or the Nestorian, or the Monophysite."

Here was a signal evidence about Newman's own estimate of what really was important in the *Development*. Its pages were about facts put together to form a vast threefold painting, a sort of triptych on which Newman drew, as if it were an altar piece, three parallels. On each there was the present Church of Rome, juxtaposed, first to the pre-Nicene Church, then to the Nicene Church, and finally to the Church of the fifth and sixth centuries. In all the three parallels the Church of Rome of Newman's day corresponded to three phases of the early history of Church, the correspondence all the more convincing because in each case it appeared in different hues. Newman did not think that his own cogitations about the life of ideas, let alone about their psychological underpinnings, were the real strength of the *Development*. They alone would have turned that book into a Romantic period piece with a Hegelian touch.

Newman's reference to the Monophysites should seem especially important in these very days when a prominent American academic made a wholesale assault, with the help of a prestigious American University Press, on Newman's character both as an Anglican and as a Catholic. In both phases of his life,

Newman, according to that book, was a disingenuous self-server, ready to invent things. It is claimed in that book that in writing the *Apologia* in 1864 Newman invented the notion that already in 1839 he saw the Church of England as mirroring what the Monophysites did a thousand and a half years earlier.[54] Could Newman expect either Northcote, a close friend of his from Tractarian days, or Buckle, who had close connections with Oriel, to believe him in early 1846, if on a most important point a recollection of his about his state of mind in 1839 was a mere fiction? Had this been the case, Buckle would not have converted in December 1848, nor would his wife have followed him after New Year's day.[55] Northcote, Buckle, and others had to read the *Development* with eyes which were Newman's when he was writing it, if they were to profit by it. Those eyes were fixed on total obedience to the supernatural, no matter where it led, and to the gigantic reality of the Catholic Church as the supernatural's unique framework.

Such a view about Newman's frame of mind had to be transmitted to Pius IX, who otherwise would not have shown to him a signal benevolence. On March 20, 1846, Newman informed Miss Giberne, who converted before Newman did, that His Holiness had sent him a silver crucifix and a particle of the Cross, with indulgences attached to it. Newman, fond of registering coincidences, found most propitious for the eventual success of the *Development* both the day, February 27, on which the granting of the relic was registered in Rome, and the fact that he received word of this on March 15. The former day was the anniversary of the publication, five years earlier, of Tract 90. On the other day, again five years earlier, the Heads of Oxford Colleges denounced Tract 90. Newman wrote: "The process of condemnation was just as long as the time it has taken to do me honor. What makes this especially acceptable is this—that it is an indirect approval of my book—at least a negative approval—for, if the book had any thing in it very dangerous or unsound, I suppose the honor would not have been paid me."

Newman judged matters most accurately, yet he did not wish to occupy himself, at least for the time being, with the *Development*. Still he could not ignore the *Development* as he tried to help prospective converts. One of them was Henry Wilberforce, who still tried to shore up his Anglican position with objections to the difference between the development of practice and doctrine. Without entering into a systematic discussion of this question, Newman referred to the fact that the practice of infant baptism had long preceded its doctrinal justification.

No passage or paragraph in those letters of Newman to Henry Wilberforce is similar to the tone of the letter which Newman, shortly before his departure to Rome, wrote to Lord Adare on August 31, 1846.[56] He began with lines full of indirect allusions to what his writing of the *Development* served as a prelude for: "In going abroad I follow my own deliberate judgment—and I trust it will not be for long—but at my time of life and with my stationary habits it is a very great trial—I know it is ungrateful and unbelieving in me, however, to be downcast—for as yet never have I been called to any thing, but strength has been given me in doing it and a reward after it was done—And I do not at all doubt that I shall look back with pleasure on what is at the time so painful."

Newman was not in a mood for further controversy such as vibrating through all the pages of the *Development:* "You may fancy I am not in cue for controversy—and really I have in a measure, at least for the time, forgotten controversy—for controversy is a means to an end—and when one has raised a building, why keep up the scaffolding? and when one enjoys the shore, why count the billows which preceded the landing? I do not say this to defend selfishness, but to account for what, for a time at least, is an incapacity. Would that all others had what I have—and many in time, I trust, will have it—though of some I despair, if it is right to say or feel such a thing." The *Development* was a means to an end, and not a means for endless "developing." It had to be viewed as something serving an end, which was on hand because the arguments set forth in that book meant to put an end to futile footdragging about joining the One True Fold.

Lord Adare brought up a book which T. Allies, who was to become Newman's intellectually most prominent convert, had just written on the patriarchal system of the Church as a justification for a separate Church in England which was not schismatic. Newman felt that Allies' book did not touch the argument of the *Development*. "It is not a greater difficulty to suppose the patriarchal theory developed into, or (if you will) [was] superseded . . . , than to admit that the Apostles' Creed has been developed into the Athanasian. The Athanasian is at first sight as different from the Apostles' [Creed] as the Papal Church from the primitive. If the primitive Church can be proved to be anti-papal, it can as easily (I should say as sophistically) be proved to be Arian." Newman's remark that Allies' book did not touch on the argument of the *Development* could just as well be said of all Anglican criticisms of it.

What Newman said to Lord Adare echoed the tone of the *Development* at its best, and the same was true of what Newman added: "Next I have said that in all fair reasoning, when no great existing objections or suspicions are in the way, we should take the later state of the Church as the *interpretation* of the words and deeds of the earlier. Thus the fulfillment of a prophecy interprets the wording in which it is conveyed—the event is made the legitimate comment upon the text. As then we take the decision of Nicea as the true measure of the words of the Ante-Nicene Fathers, so we ought to take other decisions on the question of the Papacy as the rule and standard of the variable acts and words (if so) which preceded them." This advice is the reverse of what has become so popular lately to give: start with a hypothetical reconstruction of the Church of the Fathers and then insist that the Church of today should conform to it.

Then there followed something most central to Newman's ecclesiology. In the *Development*, Newman wrote, I have made the Papacy a *doctrine*, which may fairly be taken on faith without a bit of evidence in its favor, on the *Church's warrant*, supposing there be no great antecedent objection to it, and no facts clearly irreconcilable with it—or, which is rather the state of the case, supposing there is much for it, and some things apparently against it—whereas Allies, I believe, takes it as a primary and elementary point, to be proved simply by historical evidence in order to the determination *which* is the Church. This is just the reverse to my mode of reasoning in my book."

Finally, Newman admitted some defects in the *Development* at least in the sense that certain points there were not stated as clearly and as fully as they should have been. Still Newman felt that he was justified in saying in the *Development,* to which he kept referring as "the Essay," that "the early Fathers are often, not in expression only, but in thought, mistaken, i.e. individually, or some of them, nay sometimes many of them at once." He gave the reason as follows: "People do not know what they hold and what they do not, till a subject is sifted. When a question suddenly comes on them, they are startled, and perhaps give an answer contrary to what they mean. I have seen this—e.g. when the Tracts first began, an Evangelical Bishop, who wished to be candid towards them, began reading one—'Well,' he said, 'I suppose I admit this—and I admit that etc.' In the event, I believe, he turned round—and was true to the legitimate development of his opinions—but when the matter came suddenly upon him, he spoke in an unreal way, as not grasping the points in dispute." Such was an incisive warning about how not to engage with the train of thought in the *Development*. It was meant to be taken in as a whole and not as a piecemeal offering, as if served up on a smorgasbord.

Newman then brought up another point as not set forth with sufficient clarity in the *Development*. The point related to the difference between a sudden reaction to something new and a calm consideration of it. There was further the difference between "partial and false developments, unauthorized private developments, or developments of a particular prevalent tone of thought. We must distinguish between the obiter dicta and the decisions of divines, between what they do under excitement and in matters personally interesting to themselves, and what they pronounce coolly. Moreover persons often do not know the effect of what they say—hence in examinations or cross-examinations counsel and interested parties are always on the watch to make the examinee explain himself."

Two months after Newman wrote that letter he arrived in Rome on November 1846, with his fame preceding him there, and he soon had opportunity to exchange views on "doctrinal development" with Fr. Perrone, the leading Roman theologian at that time. As a Jesuit, Perrone could not be unappreciative of the labors of the famed seventeenth-century Jesuit Denis Petavius to establish the continuity of Christian doctrine on a historical basis, that became known as positive theology. Nor could Perrone be unaware of the fact that Bishop Bull had strongly attacked Petavius for holding that only the Magisterium could make clear what was not clear in Tradition. Bull argued in his famed *Defensio fidei Nicenae* that during the centuries preceding the Council of Nicea the Trinitarian dogma, together with other basic Christian tenets, was fully present not only in the New Testament, but also in the pre-Nicene literature.

Rather similar, in a sense, to Bull's method was that of Perrone, who at that time prepared a book to show that the still to be defined dogma of the Immaculate Conception of Mary was explicitly contained in the New Testament, or at least it could be derived by straightforward syllogisms from scriptural verses. In his encounters with Perrone Newman held his ground about the necessity of a development that implied more than syllogisms. His objections were left unanswered by Perrone. Newman also found that his book began to be spoken of by some theologians in Rome as being erroneous.

The evidence for all this is in the long letters Newman wrote on November 15, 1846, from Rome to Fr. Dalgairns, who was in

Paris at that time and had informed Newman about the forthcoming translation of the book into French. Needless to say, Newman was apprehensive whether the translation would be accurate. A week later Newman wrote again to Dalgairns. This time his letter contained a paragraph that dealt specifically with points pertaining to his theory. Newman recalled that he had insistently asked Fr. Perrone whether the Roman tradition alone was decisive concerning the formation of the scriptural Canon. Perrone failed to give him a definite answer, which, of course, could come only if one admitted some form of development.

A few months later Newman submitted to Perrone a summary in Latin of what he meant by "doctrinal development," a document which lay in manuscript until 1935 and therefore will be taken up later. Upon returning from Rome, Newman became too heavily involved in a number of practical matters to have time for theological theorizing. He set up the Oratory in Birming-ham, gave the lectures on Anglican Difficulties in the Spring of 1850, and still another series of lectures a year later on the actual position of Catholics in England. He also defended himself in the Achilli trial and for over six years spent much time and energy on setting up a Catholic University in Dublin—to mention only a few major encumbrances of his. His brief editorship of the *Rambler* ended in controversies which prompted him to prefer even more his retirement in the Oratory.

Newman on the Development: phase two
Newman was far from forgetting the *Development* in the midst of all that. He was reminded of it by those Anglo-Catholics who turned to him for advice as they groped their way to Rome, often under the impact of their having read that book. In general, he told them that the *Development*'s aim was essentially negative, namely, to remove difficulties, and that if it had a positive aim, it was to show the apostolicity of the Church of Rome. Nowhere in those letters does Newman as much as hint at the view, very popular a century later, that the *Development* was an engine

whereby one could generate ever new developments as if these were good just because they implied novelties.[57]

The latter view was of a piece with modern preconceptions, whereas Newman vehemently reacted to the claim that the *Development* aimed at reconciling Christianity with modern thought. This happened when it was reported to him that according to the Spring 1861 issue of the *Quarterly Review* Thomas De Quincey, famed for his *Confessions of an English Opium Eater*, had held that "there was a good deal in Newman's theory of development, not as tending to Romanism, but as helping to harmonise Scripture with modern thought."[58] To John Cowley Fisher, a Catholic and author of *Liturgical Purity, Our Rightful Inheritance*, who had made the report, Newman wrote on October 14, 1861: "I wonder if he [De Quincey] saw even the outside of my book on doctrinal development. If he ever saw it, he would have known that the object of it, and the matter of it, was solely and entirely to answer the very objection which he makes <implies>."

Had De Quincey glanced at the cover, he would have seen there the motto, "Oculi mei defecerunt in salutare tuum" (my eyes were exhausted in viewing your salvation—verse 82 from Psalm 118, Vulgate), which surely did not support modern naturalism and rationalism. The motto rather evoked salvation history, a history of the supernatural. This is to be kept in mind if one is to grasp the weight of the fact that Newman used in the next breath the word "religiously," as he jotted down one of his most telling reflections on what he meant by true development: "I lay down, that no one can religiously speak of development, without giving the *rules* which keep it from extravagating endlessly. And I give seven tests of a true development, founded on the nature of the case. These tests secure the substantial immutability of Christian doctrine—and I think my comparison is, that modern R. Catholicism looks different from primitive Catholicism in no other sense, than a friend, whom we see after a lapse of years, seems at first sight strange to us, till after a few minutes the old features revive in spite of the changes."

"To speak religiously" of the development of Christian doctrine are words that should serve as warning posts against taking Newman's ideas on doctrinal development for the vehicle of an intellectual game. For him the working out of those ideas, and especially during the ten months preceding his conversion, was not only a "religious" task, but a task so existentially religious that it could only be measured by the alternative between being forever either in God's presence, or in its opposite for which the word "hell" remains the only unequivocal label.

That place may also be properly described with a recourse to Newman's phrase, "extravagating endlessly," which is the process that prevents one from reaching a satisfactory conclusion about anything and from reaching one's God-given target, which is God himself. To remain at a safe remove from that condition one may take Newman's advice to read the *Development* "religiously" and to think religiously when speaking of development, an advice hardly ever heeded by most of those who, as will be seen, have written profusely in recent decades on the *Development*. Compared with that advice quite secondary should seem Newman's view about his book's future: "I feel confident that when the day comes when men shall read it, instead of conjecturing its contents, they will feel that it is worthy [of] their attention." In the same letter Newman also stated that he had not read the *Development* since he had published it in 1845. On the same day, October 14, 1861, Newman wrote to another correspondent that "any number of copies of my Essay on Development of Doctrine may be had at Toovey's Piccadilly, tho' the booksellers say that it is out of print."

Newman's next utterance on the *Development* came in reaction to a communication from Lord Acton, who, on June 23, 1862, asked him to comment on a paper which J. B. Morris had sent him on doctrinal development for publication in *Home and Foreign Review*. Morris—a Tractarian, a convert, for a short time an Oratorian, and later a priest—was well known to Newman, who found Morris' paper to reflect a personal character bent on extremism. Lest his own ideas on development be confused with those of Morris, Newman wrote to Acton on July 8 that unlike Morris, who did not specify what he meant by doctrinal development, he held it to be no more "than a more intimate apprehension, and a more lucid enunciation of the original dogma." In an obvious reference to the *Development*, Newman added: "If I said more than this, I think I had not worked out my meaning, and was confused." Next, Newman stated that "if a St Polycarp had been asked whether our Lady was immaculately conceived, he would, after some reflection and clarification of the terms, have answered in the affirmative."

This statement remains possibly Newman's most illuminating utterance about his own view of doctrinal development. It is noteworthy that Newman singled out Saint Polycarp, who still conversed with the Apostle John and was therefore the last direct link to the Apostles' kerygma. Had Newman singled out Saint Irenaeus, who as a young man was in contact with Saint Polycarp, he would not have been able to say that in his best judgment the immediately post-Apostolic generation needed only "some reflection and clarification" to recognize in Rome's teaching at any time, the teaching of the Apostles. The phrase was a powerful vote on Newman's part of the view of doctrinal development which is a going from the implicit to the explicit rather than a mystical reflection on the Church's communal mind.

Newman reconfirmed this view as he slighted, in concluding his letter to Acton, the importance of a meticulous investigation of minute facts: "Whether the minute facts of history will bear me out in this view, I leave to others to determine." This could hardly please Acton, a historian intent on setting forth all such facts. He was to become a spirited opponent of the definition of papal infallibility as one not in agreement with all facts. Acton clearly did not grasp the significance of what Newman added: "Accordingly, to me the words 'development of dogma' are substantially nothing but the process by which, under the magisterium of the Church, implicit faith becomes explicit."

This illustrated that Newman's position was much closer to that of those who then, or before, or later, put the emphasis on what connects the implicit with the explicit. As to Newman's slighting of "the minute facts of history" it made sense only if one insisted, as Newman did in the *Development* (but omitted to do in this letter), that unless one fell back again and again on the "bold outlines" that stand out clearly, anyone discoursing about his ideas of doctrinal development would find himself caught in a thicket of obscurities, posed by facts about which not enough information is available.

Equally revealing about Newman's own thinking in reference to the *Development* is the reply he wrote on October 15, 1862, to Daniel Radford of Liverpool, who had sent him a paper on the question of whether "St Peter's Successor and the Bishop of Rome are necessarily one and the same." In his letter Radford asked: "How do spiritual gifts come through mere electors to a see? How and when did the electors in this particular case get their authority to confer these gifts. . .?" Newman began his reply that he himself had considered that argument against Rome around 1836 as he was writing his *Prophetical Office*, but did not include it in that book because he thought he had not properly argued the point.

Radford's letter found Newman in Deal (Kent), which he was to leave the next day, and therefore he excused himself for not being able to consult books in order to discuss Radford point in detail. Newman, however, noted that he had already dealt with Radford's question in the *Development* and in one of the last lectures of *Anglican Difficulties*. He also recalled that once he had come to understand better the Catholic system, "the objection vanished as a mist before the sun—and I thought I had deluded myself with an ingenious puzzle." Newman admitted that to say this was "no answer to a grave argument." To his excuse Newman recalled that because of his circumstances he could not formulate that answer. Further, he was tired of controversy and had no wish to deal with what appeared to him mere objections.

For, Newman continued, objections have no value when confronted with total certainty. And such was his certainty, he wrote, that
the present Roman communion was identical with the Church of
Saint Cyprian and the Church of the Apostles: "I say to myself, if
a mind can come to a solid immovable conclusion, mine has
done so—I have a clear anticipation that there is no possible
argument which has a chance of interfering with my conviction
that what is called the "Roman communion" is a continuation of
that ecclesiastical body to which St Cyprian belonged, and which
the Apostles founded." This kind of argumentation implied a
readiness to perceive "bold outlines" and to surrender to them,
partly because they stand out so boldly. As such they call for
bold steps and for unflinching courage in perseverance.

In a phrase, which should but irritate the present academic
mentality for which irrational is any certainty on any point
whatsoever, Newman added: "This does not seem to me irrational. I say the same, and I suppose you would do so also, as to
the question of the Being of a God. Surely these are points on
which we have a right to be certain. This being the case with me,
I feel it almost impossible at my age to engage in what presents
itself to me in the light of a *skiamachia* [fighting with shadows]."
In the draft of his letter Newman made the point even stronger,
but possibly because he felt it would unnecessarily irritate
Radford, the copy he sent to Radford did not contain the
following: "Now I hope I am saying nothing rash, but according
to my own personal apprehension I think there are fewer
objections to the divine origin of the Roman communion than
there are to the being of a God. 'There is God. He has a Son who
is one God with Him—the Son came on earth—He founded a
communion to perpetuate His presence here—the Roman
communion is the communion which He founded,' these
propositions are all certain to me. I have no doubt or fear about
any of them—and since really there can be no degrees in that
certainty which is without doubt or fear, I suppose I am right in
saying I am as sure that the Roman communion is from God as

there is a God at all." Those propositions are the quintessence of Newman's theology. Any presentation of that theology, or of any part of it, which does not reflect those propositions is a farce.

In leaving out that magnificent but very strong statement, Newman may have thought of Saint Paul who was careful to give just milk to infants in faith and spare them solid food. It is another matter whether leading Newmanists would be ready to take themselves as well as their readers for mere infants and offer this as an excuse for not quoting that statement of Newman on the flimsy ground that Newman did not communicate it. But they feel uneasy even about statements of Newman which he included in that letter, and did so second thought and in the form of lengthy notes to his reply so that it cover some particulars in Radford's letter. Newman's dismantling of Radford's claim that the Anglican communion was on a par with the Roman Church would not be particularly important had it not included Newman's reflections, with an eye on the *Development,* on what had really motivated him to become a Catholic. It was the great fact of the "sacramentum unitatis" of the Church of the Fathers, and the fact that the Roman communion of the day forcefully showed that unity over the whole world, and that it alone did so.

Newman himself put a sharp light on all this, when two years later, following the publication of the *Apologia*, he received a letter from Henry Cleveland, rector in Darlington, who wanted to know, with other "sincere and anxious inquirers after Truth," how "the maxim of St. Augustine (securus judicat orbis terrarum) is *per se* calculated to produce that extraordinary influence upon the mind which you attribute to it in your Apologia." To this communication of June 25, 1864, Newman replied as concisely as possible. He stated that his study of the history of fifth century showed him first not that Rome was right, but that the argument "which I had used for Anglicans—was wrong." It was on this negative insight that the words of Saint Augustine suddenly threw a positive light: Those "words came as a key, or rather an expression or aphorism, of the state of the case."[59]

But back to the letter to Radford which contains what was truly the working of that key once it fell in Newman's hands or rather lodged in his mind. All of a sudden it provided a concrete historical expression to a general and most fearsome alternative and did so with a direct reference to the argument of the *Development.* Nothing is right in reference to Christianity, unless the Church Christ founded is identical with the Church of Rome: "I certainly did not become a Catholic, as others have, on the ground 'Ubi Petrus, ibi Ecclesia,' but because, whereas the Church is to last to the end of the world, unless that large Communion which happens to be Roman be the Church, the Church has failed. This I think will be found to be the argument of my Essay—and I have insisted on this point strongly in my last lecture on Anglican Difficulties." It is enough to read this statement with half open eyes in order to purge oneself of the illusion that Newman can be read "ecumenically."

In the lengthy notes Newman added to his letter to Radford there is another passage which shows the light in which Newman saw the *Development.* The context was his illustration of a point there, that devotion to Mary in particular could readily precede doctrinal specifications about her and that excesses in that devotion were always kept in check by other parts of the Catholic doctrinal systems, such as the doctrine about the real presence of Christ in the Eucharist. Newman, always ready to speak concretely, recalled to Bradford the dying hours of a dear Catholic friend of his, a lady convert, who had been visited at her deathbed by a Protestant acquaintance. The latter, on seeing her recite the rosary, urged her not to let anything, however holy, come between her soul and her Savior, because that might make her forget Him. "Forget Him?" she replied. "Why, he was with me just now in this room—". She had just received communion, remarked Newman, who added: "There was nothing in her devotion to our Lady to obscure the incommunicable claim of her Maker upon her love and loyalty. And, in the doctrine of development, as I have held and hold it, the teaching of the later

Church does not supersede, but does fortify that of the ancient." Then he asked gravely: "What is it that enables us to say of Gregory, or Hildebrand, or Pius: this man is the head, and except through him there is no communion with Christ or heaven?"

Newman's next reference to the *Development* came in a letter which he wrote on February 15, 1868, to Stanislas Flanagan, a former Oratorian and still a good friend of Newman and of his former confrères there. Flanagan, since 1864 a parish priest in Ireland, began to be agitated about Newman's idea on development when he read a reply of Ignatius Ryder, a Birmingham Oratorian, to the claim of W. G. Ward that all doctrinal statements of a pope were infallible. The reply reflected Newman's own thinking on the depositum as something that had not been clearly and fully given to the Apostles by Jesus himself. Flanagan wrote to Ryder that he found this most troubling and this is why Newman hastened to explain himself in a long letter, which first saw print in 1958 in an article published in the *Gregorianum*,[60] and quickly became a document, taken, rather wrongly, for the most precise formulation by Newman of what he meant by doctrinal development.

It was largely overlooked that the precision could not be had in severance from facts, from the "bold outlines." For one had to be seized first by the overwhelming fact of the Catholic Church as always centered on Rome in order to speak confidently of the mind of the Church which was developing under the infallible guidance of a magisterium. Severed from that fact there remained an intrinsic vagueness of a communal mind, of many minds taken *per modum unius*, to recall Newman's expression. Newman fully granted the mysterious workings of such a communal mind, while he also insisted that it unfolded not by logical steps what is contained in the original depositum. The notion of the Church at any given time was a "vision" of what the Apostles had in mind, and "not logical" propositions, "and therefore consistent with errors of reasoning and of fact in the enunciation after the manner of an intuition or an instinct."[61] To those who would say then that in that case everything goes, and that this was a far cry from his view of the development as a step from the implicit to the explicit, Newman could have only one answer: to fall back on paraphrasing his expression of "bold outlines." He could have only said that such a range could be seen even if all its slopes and crevices had not yet been mapped out fully. As to those Anglicans who dwelt on such difficulties, he would have merely reminded them of the saying that those who live in glass houses should not throw stones.

Newman on the Development: phase three

In 1862 Newman could, with some semblance of truth, say to Radford: "I have not read my book since I published it in 1845." Newman had no right whatsoever to say the same eight years later when his attention was drawn to the *Development* by John Thomas Seccombe (1835-1895). An odd figure Seccombe certainly was. After earning his degree in medicine, he turned an Anglican clergyman and, for good measure, had himself consecrated by an orthodox bishop in 1867, which his second wife did not find out until after his death. Aware of Newman's opposition to the definition of papal infallibility, Seccombe wrote to Newman on December 5, 1869, telling him that though he firmly believed in the true Church, he could not decide between Rome and Eastern Orthodoxy. One reason for Seccombe's reluctance to choose Rome was that although the Orthodox Church completely answers to every requirement of an infallible guide, she alone of all denominations of Christians does not appear to demand the submission of Englishmen." A priceless remark. Seccombe seemed to forget that the Church of England demanded no submission even from her Englishmen. Even in earlier times that Church merely suppressed dissenters and especially Roman Catholics, but tolerated within its fold anyone with the strangest views, provided he did not rock the boat too wildly.

Newman replied on the 14th, apologizing that his reply to Seccombe was the twentieth he had to write on that day. While stating that he did not come into the Church on the basis of the pope's infallibility, which is held as a doctrine by the large majority of Catholics, Newman quickly turned the table on Seccombe: "The Greek Church seems to me out of Court by the very fact you mention, its not claiming infallibility. Did our Lord intend Councils to cease with the Seventh? Why has not the Greek Church held a council these last 1000 years? In the Latin, there is the continuation of all the functions which went on the early Church—there is no suspended animation." Then Newman offered Seccombe a copy of the *Development*. Surely, if there was a book in which the ancient Church's will to rule was set up in magnificent parallels with the will of the Church of Rome to rule, it was that very book, which most recent Newmanists still have to read in its own light and not in the fluorescence of their infatuation with modernity.

Seccombe replied, thanking Newman for the copy, and referred to the Synods held by the Orthodox. Newman's reply, written on January 2, 1870, was terse: "I was referring, not to ordinary Synods, but to Ecumenical Councils, when I was referring to the Greek Church. In their Confession answering to the Creed of Pope Pius, they acknowledge 'the Seven Councils, the Seven Sacraments,' etc. Of course, they condemn modern heresies as the Kirk condemns the 'Papists' and the Socinians and the Church of England [condemns] the Pelagians of old times. My main reason for becoming a Catholic was that the present Latin communion was the only one which answered to the early Church in all substantial matters. My Essay is to answer the Objection 'The Roman Church has added to the faith.' The Greek Church answers in very many things—but it has no political life, such as an ecclesiastical body ought to–and it takes no account of the Pope—not so much as their old Saints took of him."

As one would expect from one who in 1877 became one of the founders of F. G. Lee's "Order for Corporate Reunion," Seccombe resented Newman's remark in the *Development* that "the Church must possess a political life and, if this be so, there is no choice between the Church of Rome, which possesses such a kind of life and no Church at all . . ." But at least Seccombe noted that crucial phrase, which so many "learned" students of Newman's idea of development still have to discover. Add to this that Newman deplored the foregoing "Order" and similar movements to promote corporate reunion, because, in his view, they all undermined the individual's sense of duty to look for and find the true Church, the sole Ark of Salvation.[62]

In telling Seccombe that he had not read the *Development* since its publication, Newman seemed to forget what he had said five years earlier to Manning, who congratulated him on his *Letter to Pusey* as an outstanding defense of Catholic devotion to Mary. Newman must have re-read at least parts of the *Development*, if it was true that, as he wrote to Manning, he had "cogged out" much of that *Letter* from the *Development*.[63] Another letter that prompted Newman to take up the *Development* came to him only a few days prior to the moment when the new Italy's troops were about putting an end to the Papal States, an event which Newman took for a divine answer to the definition of papal infallibility a few months earlier. Since it was no secret at all that Newman was greatly perplexed, it was natural for John Pym Yeatman, a lawyer and legal historian, who had recently converted, to turn to Newman with his queries on papal infallibility. As in other cases when Newman did not really know the state of mind of the inquirer, he was reluctant to recommend any book of his. Still he called Yeatman's attention to his book on Miracles, to appear again in a few weeks, and added: "I have also written on the Development of Catholic doctrine and have, I almost think, said that the definition of the Pope's infallibility was to be expected. So people say, but I have not read the book, since I wrote it, and don't know where to look for the passage."[64]

Newman's other hyperbole, that the *Development* was a book that nobody read, clashed with what Bishop Moriarty wrote to him on February 20, 1870, from the Vatican Council: "Strange to say, if ever this definition comes, you will have contributed much towards it. Your treatise on development has given the key. A Cardinal said the other day—'We must give up the first ten centuries, but the infallibility is an obvious development of the supremacy.' Of course development was ever at work in the Church, but you brought it out and placed it on a pedestal."

What Newman said in reply was full of lopsided phrases: "As to development I am quite aware of what you say. It has been my fate to have my book attacked by various persons, praised by none—till at last it is used against me. However, I cannot be sorry for it, for without it I never should have become a Catholic." As has been shown, the *Development* was attacked by not a few, but it was surely not true that it had received no praise. What about the review in the *Tablet*? Also, praise was implied in the fact that the *Development* came out in a second edition in early 1846, and in the same year in a German transla-tion, and by 1848 in two different French translations of which more later. Patently exaggerated and unjustified was it on New-man's part to write to Moriarty that his eminent friend "seems to think *anything* is development." Then to make matters worse, Newman brought up extravagant details, such as the reasoning that if a Pope reigned longer than Saint Peter this would show by "development" that such a pope ceased to be a pope.

There followed further such exaggerations on Newman's part when he began, in 1874, to prepare a definitive edition of his works. The turn of the *Development* did not come until the summer of 1877. On June 26 and again on August 23 he wrote in his diary that he had started work on it. The corrected text was not sent to the printer until November 1, 1877. The span of two to three months should alone suggest that the changes would be many and at times very significant. It must not have been easy for the typesetter to work from that over-corrected copy. The amount of corrections put Newman on the defensive when he wrote on December 23, 1877, to Mrs. Froude that he "had made no substantial alterations" to the book. This was true enough, depending on what one meant by substantial. But it was also true that Newman, to quote him "nearly turned it [the *Development*] inside out as far as arrangement goes." Four months later, on April 23, 1878, when that final edition had already appeared, Newman himself gave a telltale sample of the extent of that rearrangement as he wrote to the Free Kirk theologian David Brown that a reference to the Free Kirk on pp. 76 and 77 in the first edition, could be found on pp. 18 and 19 of the new.

Newman did not leave untouched any paragraph of the original edition. Countless were the purely stylistic changes, and many of the notable changes, partly additions, partly omissions. Whereas the original consisted in eight chapters, the definitive edition contained twelve. The seven tests of development, treated in the first edition in four chapters, were now given each a separate chapter. Whereas in the first edition the idea of development, both in its true and wrong forms were treated in one unit, they were now distributed in two. The antecedent arguments and the historical arguments also appeared separately in the definitive edition. The longest section which Newman omitted from the first edition are pages {182} to {202} in which Newman listed instances to show that deductive reasoning had its role in history, ethics, and religion. He also left out most of the pages of "Specimens of Theological Science," as well as some four pages in the Introduction that dealt with Wesley and his movement.[65]

Nothing of this was noted at that time. The one who might have noted these difference and make much of them would have been Mozley. On July 6, when Newman wrote to Anne Mozley, whom twelve years earlier he had chosen to be editor of his correspondence from his Anglican years, he suggested to her that her brother's long critique of the first edition of the *Development* be reissued.[66] Mr. Mozley, a man of so acute a mind, would, Newman thought, find many faults with the new edition just as he did with the first, but about the substance of the book Newman felt confident. In fact he began his letter by saying: "I have myself the fullest confidence in my argument—I have never doubted it—my faith in it has been rekindled by my recent perusal of it." For only with such confidence could Newman also say that he looked forward to counterarguments, though not to what today is called psychohistory, or the replacing of arguments of substance with imputations of personal motives. Newman called this tactic, so dear to some latter-day "intellectual" historians, the "poisoning of the well."

Newman could stir the same well in the sense that he loved to be rhapsodic, and biting, too, if necessary. He readily exaggerated in order to make a point. Writing books was a travail to him, and he likened it, again and again, to a woman's birth pangs. One can hardly think that the poet Aubrey De Vere took Newman literally on reading in his letter of January 20, 1878, that he "didn't mean to open the book again." Newman hoped to be done with book writing once his revision of his translation of Saint Athanasius was finished, and looked forward to his remaining years free of "composition." But Newman could rightly worry that the rearrangement of the material of the first edition might imply "serious mistakes in logic, references, etc."

Possibly the most telling of Newman's own reflections on the *Development* was his view that he had at least brought a crucial question to the fore. The question derived from the patently problematic aspects of early patristic literature as reflecting the faith of the early Church. In reference to Moberly's marshaling patristic texts telling against papal supremacy, Newman had, already on June 6, 1846, called the attention of Henry Wilberforce to the fact that Moberly would call him a reckless disputant were he to remind Moberly of passages against the Eternal Son's Immensity. Newman also reminded Wilberforce that it was simply improper to remain in a "half and half position" in which one quoted the Fathers only insofar as they agreed with one, without quoting their contrary statements.

Twenty five years later Newman returned to those early critics of the *Development* as he wrote, on February 5, 1871, to Fr. Coleridge, who had urged him to answer Fr. Harper's criticism of the *Grammar*. Newman declined: "I think I never answered any critique of any writing of mine in my life. My Essay on Development was assailed by Dr. Brownson, on one side, and Mr. Archer Butler on the other, at great length. Brownson, I believe, thought me a Pantheist, and sent my work to Rome, by some American Bishop. Mr Butler has been lauded by his people as having smashed me." One could only admire Newman's trust that time would vindicate truth and him as well. Once more he quoted his favorite line in George Crabbe's *Tales of the Hall* about Time being the Father of Truth. But surely no passing of time would abolish a major fact about the historical record of the early Church. The record was far from being complete and Newman held it to be his achievement of having brought this to the attention of Catholics: "Let those who think I ought to be answered, those Catholics, first master the great difficulty, the great problem, and then, if they don't like my way of meeting it, find another. Syllogising won't meet it."

This was true in several, though not in all respects. By then Newman himself used the form of syllogism, which is to go from the implicit to the explicit, as he defended in 1865 Mary's Immaculate Conception in his reply to Pusey's *Eirenicon*.[67] Still Newman was fully justified in saying to Fr. Coleridge that while the *Development* "may be full of defects, and certainly characterised by incompleteness and crudeness, . . . it is something to have started a problem, and mapped in part a country, if I have done nothing more." The *Development* is indeed a great start and also a tremendous assurance. The *Development* made, in the long run, Catholics think in a new way about their remote past, while it also gave them a priceless assurance that, because the past fully belonged to them, so did the present and the future as well. But in order to gain that assurance they have to read the *Development* with the eyes of its author. He started with a notion of the Church steeped in sacramental life and ready to oppose fallen nature as it raises its bewitching head against the supernatural. If they do not see this in the present Church of Rome, they shall take their uncertain ideas for the Church of the Fathers. Conversely, a genuine focusing on the Church of Ambrose and Athanasius, both great and heroic saints, will make Rome beckon in the distance. This happened to Newman and the *Development* is the unparalleled presentation of the final phase of his mind's growing into the One True Fold.

Catholics on the Development: phase one

The new and definitive edition of the *Development,* in which Newman tried to remedy some of those defects, made no immediate impact, just as the first two editions failed to influence a debate which had been going on from the 1820s and reached its apogee in the declaration of Vatican I on doctrinal development. This in spite of the fact that Newman, as already noted, was very much spoken of by some Council Fathers as the one whose ideas on development would make possible the definition of papal infallibility. Newman himself paid scant attention to the keen reaction of Rome to pre-modernistic ideas on doctrinal development as maintained in particular by Lamennais and Hermes. In that story, as set forth in M. G. McGrawth's doctoral thesis, *The Vatican Council's Teaching on the Evolution of Dogma,* published on the eve of the opening of Vatican II,[68] Newman's *Development* is rightly disregarded. Catholic theologians did not seem to show willingness to profit when Newman explained, in his reply to Gladstone in 1875, in terms of development the gradual rise of ecclesiastical awareness of papal authority.[69] It was one thing to appreciate Newman's dissecting Gladstone's reasoning and another to appreciate the train of thought whereby Newman vindicated the Catholic position in all its historical framework. Much the same happened ten years earlier following Newman's defense of Marian dogmas and devotions in his reply to Pusey's *Eirenicon.*[70]

No Catholic theologian observed that when Newman brought out in 1878 a new and definitive edition of the *Development,* he made a Catholic book even more Catholic. This he did by moving forward the section on the guiding role which the papacy plays in guiding doctrinal development. No hint about this came when Henry Nutcombe Oxenham, a convert with no small eccentricity, brought out in 1881 the third edition of his *The Catholic Doctrine of the Atonement: An Historical Review*, which carried the subtitle, *With an Introduction on the Principle of Theological Developments*.[71] Oxenham referred to Newman's *Development* only once, as he recalled Gladstone's strictures of Samuel Wilberforce's unjust criticism of the *Development*.[72]

Many years had to pass before there appeared in print a most interesting comment from Mark Pattison, a friend of Newman's from Tractarian times, to whom Newman sent a copy of the new edition. In thanking Newman, on April 5, 1878, Pattison marveled that Newman "should have first started the idea—and the word—Development, as the key to the history of church and [that] since then it has gradually become the dominant idea of all history, biology, physics, and in short has metamorphosed our view of every science, and of all knowledge." Pattison ignored that Newman had disapproved of metamorphoses that played havoc with the original form. The fact that Newman a few years later visited Pattison during his last sickness showed that Newman remained driven by the same major concern: to bring people into the One True Fold and thereby promote their eternal salvation. He could but be pleased with another passage in Pattison's letter: "Thirty-two years! I cannot trust myself to speak of the many threads which connect heart and mind with that distant time. Another and yet the same! I often wonder if other men have gone through such a mental change without losing their personal identity." A perfect, though unwitting comment on what Newman tried to safeguard in anyone's thinking about the Church as its endless changes and transformations were considered. That in recent years Pattison's phrase has been seized upon as an indication that Newman's work anticipated Darwin, proves many a mind's ability to metamorphose, that is, to extravagate endlessly. Worse, this becomes quite respectable if done with profuse invocations of Newman.

Newman had already been dead when his *Development* began to be subjected, in various measures, to that metamorphosis. This outcome surely contrasted with the procedure of the first translators of Newman's book. J. A. M. Brühl, a Catholic priest and author of reports about new and favorable developments of Catholicism in France and England, presented in 1846 his German translation without adding an introduction to it. He omitted the line, which in the original indicated, right under Newman's name, that he was the author of "Lectures on the Prophetical Office of the Church." Brühl replaced that line with "A Justification of his [Newman's] conversion to the Catholic Church." Thus was the book's gist presented right away to the typical German reader.[73]

About that time two French translations appeared in quick succession. The first was the work of Mme Louise Boyeldieu d'Auvigny, who used the second edition of the original. With a sure grasp of what Newman's work was about, she added a subtitle, "Preuves de la vérité catholique," which spoke louder than a special introduction might have.[74] The second translation was produced by Jules Gondon a year later.[75] When this translation was reissued a year later in Belgium in a reset format, it carried the subtitle, "ou motifs de retour à l'Eglise catholique," which echoed the subtitle of the translation by Mme Boyeldieu d'Auvigny.[76] While Dalgairns, Newman's fellow Oratorian, felt that Gondon's translation was more accurate,[77] Fr. Dupuy's modern scrutiny, of which more later, vindicated the merits of Mme Boyeldieu d'Auvigny's translation.[78]

These two French translations had been largely forgotten by the end of the century, although the history and development of dogma had for some time commanded considerable attention. This happened partly because H. Taine applied Darwin's evolutionary ideas to literary and ideological development. There was also the impact of A. Harnack's rationalist approach to the history of dogma. The extent to which a French theologian could discuss all this, and with a total disregard of Newman's *Develop-*

ment, is well illustrated in the series of lectures which Andrew de la Barre, a Jesuit, gave at the Institut Catholique in Paris in 1897 and published under the title, *La vie du dogme catholique. Autorité—Evolution.*[79] He kept referring to De Maistre and Möhler as he battled the positivists and the rationalists, but had room for Newman's book only in the concluding bibliography. Again, about the same time Newman was hardly visible in two long articles which the Jesuit L. de Grandmaison published in the August 5 and 20, 1898, issues of the *Etudes* that were reprinted in book form thirty years later under the title, *Le dogme chrétien. Sa nature—ses formules—son développement.*[80]

All this slighting of Newman suddenly changed when in 1905 Henri Bremond brought out an improved version of Gondon's translation of the *Development*.[81] A fourth or "nou-velle édition" followed in 1908 with the title *Newman* (par Henri Bremond) with *Développement du dogme chrétien* being only a subtitle. In a long preface Bremond defended himself for not giving the full text of Newman's work (Bremond also left out the notes), and also for the fact that his Introduction was too suggestive. In fact, as will be seen, by 1908 there arose in France quite a debate about Newman, with the involvement of such whom Lebreton called "Newmaniaques" or Newmaniacs.[82]

No small part in stirring that debate was played by Bremond as he engaged the support of Mgr Mignot, Archbishop of Albi, who contributed a "Lettre-Preface," long on rhetoric but short on substance. Bremond himself added two publications by Newman from his Anglican period concerning "development" to justify his own presentation of Newman. Yet while those earlier pieces by Newman did not convey the sense of necessity of converting to Rome, the *Development* certainly did, and did so with a keen sense that one's eternal salvation was at stake and that issue was anything but academic.

Somehow that keen sense was the very point which Bre-mond, the future historian of the religious sentiments in France during the 16th and 17th centuries, tried to play down. From

Bremond's monograph, *Le mystère de Newman* (1905), which quickly appeared in English translation,[83] one could hardly gain the impression that Newman had converted essentially for an objective reason. Bremond saw mysteries in Newman where there were none, and ignored the mystery, or the supernatural reality, which counted most for Newman. All was psychology with Bremond, whose writings then or later had much to do with the portrayal of religious sentiment, surely a psychological topic. To what extent did Bremond see the pitfalls of the psychological approach to dogma is another matter. But about that time, Charles Sarolea, most of whose writings dealt with geopolitical questions, applied the psychological method to Newman and reached the conclusion that Newman's development into Catholicism was a necessary outcome of his personal make-up.[84] Then it followed that the *Development*, too, was a piece of cogitation which implied a foregone conclusion. It was also about that time that William James, a founder of experimental psychology, and one with wide information about thinking in that field, let it be known that most psychologists did not believe in free will. He should have therefore spelled out clearly that his memorable studies of the varieties of religious experience could only prove that such experiences were the inevitable sublimation of latent urges. And here Catholic modernists of the early twentieth century could not disagree with James, who luckily ignored Newman's works. This is to be kept in mind in respect to their interpretation of Newman's *Development*.

Bremond's undeniable mastery of style was most effective in spreading wrong notions about Newman's *Development*. It did not help Newman's reputation that Bremond asked George Tyrell, soon to be excommunicated as a chief modernist, to write an Introduction running over ten pages to the French translation of Newman's *Development*. A champion of "catholicism" as distinct from "Catholicism," Tyrell here, too, did his best to take the sharp and clear edges out of Newman's intellectual and spiritual profile and from what the *Development* was about. By then

Newman's name began to be tied ever more frequently, especially in France, to modernist presentations of doctrinal development.

It was therefore inevitable that the appearance of the Encyclical *Pascendi* (1907) would be taken by some for an indirect disavowal of Newman's ideas on development. The chief opponent of such an interpretation of the Encyclical was E. T. O'Dwyer, bishop of Limerick. His *Cardinal Newman and the Encyclical Pascendi Dominici Gregis: An Essay*[85] was originally intended for the *Dublin Review*, but failed to appear there after the Bishop refused to accede to the view of Wilfrid Ward, the editor, that certain passages in the Encyclical were not sufficiently clear and as such cast undue suspicion on too many. After giving details about his skirmish with Ward, who had already been busy for over ten years writing Newman's biography, Bishop O'Dwyer listed the main propositions of modernism as condemned by the Encyclical: Man cannot recognize by the use of his reason the existence of God; there can be no such a thing as a revelation of a supernatural order; moral conscience is purely subjective. It was easy for the Bishop to quote passage after passage, mainly from Newman's *Idea of a University* and from the *Grammar of Assent,* to show that on all those crucial points Newman held the very opposite of those modernist errors.

Finally, the Bishop came to Newman's theory of development in general and to his idea of the development of Christian doctrine in particular. The bishop raised two questions: "(a) is his [Newman's] theory admissible according to the principles of Catholic Theology, and (b) is it covered, or touched in any wise, by the condemnations of the recent Encyclical?" To the first question the bishop gave, with all submission, his "personal opinion, little as it is worth, that in its broad outlines it [Newman's theory] is thoroughly sound and orthodox, and most serviceable for the interpretation of the facts of the history of the dogma." As to the second, the bishop stated that nothing short of an "explicit statement by the Supreme authority of the Holy See would convince" him to the contrary. The bishop could not see how anyone could find anything in common between Newman's views on development and the views of modernists. About these the Bishop acidly remarked that "the word development is the only thing they hold in common."[86]

Bishop O'Dwyer summed up the gist of the *Development* as follows: Its "whole scope and purpose . . . was to show that in the Church this original revelation has been preserved, that whatever definitions have been pronounced in the course of ages, they but declare authoritatively, what it has contained from the beginning, and, consequently, that the faith of every Catholic of the present time is identical with that of the Church of Apostolic times." As a confirmation of this the Bishop quoted from the *Development*'s Introduction, the paragraph which comes to an end with the words: "This may be called the Theory of the Development of Doctrine."[87]

The Bishop had not only the modernists for his target, but also those Catholics who rejected Newman's theory of development, while they "harp upon the phrase [of Newman] that religion is vital." One could only wish that the bishop had noted what was the unwitting chink in Newman's theory. According to the bishop "Newman speaks of the influence of the living thoughts and feelings of men who are the recipients of Christ's revelation." This was true enough. Time and again Newman personified, indeed reified ideas as if they could do thinking on their own. Had Newman kept speaking of the thoughts and feelings of living men, instead of the living thoughts and feelings of men, and done so invariably, he would have taken the wind out of the sail of many of Newman's misguided admirers. They were, as will be seen, most intent on discoursing on the life of ideas and on living developments, and, for good measure, on whatever they could find psychological in Newman's dicta.

The bishop soon had the satisfaction of receiving a letter from the highest authority in which his defence of Newman was fully vindicated. In that letter, dated March 10, 1908, Pius X began: "We wish to assure you that your pamphlet, in which you show that the writings of Cardinal Newman, far from differing from our Encyclical Letter *Pascendi*, are in reality in closest accord with it, has our heartiest approval." Later, the Pope referred to his predecessor Leo XIII as one who had created Newman a cardinal, and made a most pertinent observation: "Would that they [the Modernists] had really followed the authority of Newman, not that they might search his volumes in the light of their preconceived ideas, in order to draw from them, with deliberate dishonesty, what they claim supports their opinions, but rather that they might adopt as their own the sincerity and integrity of Newman principles, acquire his spirit, and follow his example."[88]

Had this letter been in print by late winter 1908, when the noted Jesuit L. Grandmaison sent to press an article on the evolution of dogma, he might not have written that Newman's book "raises more questions than answers, opens more avenues than explores. He is a brilliant innovator rather than a safe teacher."[89] Eleven years later this phrase was used by the Flemish Dominican M. M. Tuyaerts both as a shield for himself and as a sword against Newman in a "theological study on the development of dogma," which began with a survey of various expositions of that development. The authors surveyed there were Harnack, Sabatier, Günther, Loisy, Tyrell, Blondel, and Newman. The first five were plain rationalists or modernists. As to Blondel, he was an enigma and still is. Placed in such a company New-man could hardly appear in his true light.[90] Tuyaerts did not as much as hint that since none of the others showed any interest in Newman's ideas, it was hardly justified to put him in their company.

After the pope's letter appeared in print, Thomists disagreeing with Newman could either be silent on him, or to praise him, without saying much about his ideas. Already before the Encyclical the silent treatment was the case in J. V. Bainvel's *De magisterio vivo et de traditione* (1905),[91] and, after the Encyclical, in A. Gardeil's *Le donné révélé et la théologie* (1910).[92] R.

Schultes' *Introductio in historiam dogmatum* (1922), the text of lectures given at the Angelicum, contained a page-long appraisal of Newman's work, but hardly such as to make students of theology develop an interest in him.[93]

In none of these books was it pointed out that Newman had to be ignored by rationalist cultivators of the history of dogma, because with doctrine, Newman always writes with a profoundly existential commitment to the concretely supernatural. He always writes as one who wants to save souls, his own and the soul of others who for him mostly came from the ranks of Anglo-Catholics. He showed signal interest in only one agnostic, in the husband of Mrs. Froude, one of Newman's great converts. Newman had him largely in mind as he wrote over twenty years the *Grammar of Assent*, which precisely because of this "pastoral" concern of its author, hardly made a ripple in philosophical circles. One has to be a Catholic, animated with a zeal for the supernatural, to appreciate Newman the controversialist (fearless defender of the faith) as he viewed himself.

Yet if a Catholic writer's interest is mainly in abstract propositions his sincere praises of Newman will be brief. Such is the case in the Dominican Francisco Marin-Sola's *La evolucion homogenea del dogma católico* (1922), which first appeared in a series of articles in *La ciencia tomista* from 1911 on. Although it subsequently appeared twice, in 1952 and 1963, in the series "Biblioteca de autores cristianos," it made its broader impact in the French version, *L'évolution homogène du dogme catholique*, first published in 1922 and again in 1924.[94] Marin-Sola considered Newman's work to be within the confines of orthodoxy, but he clearly did not wish to take up Newman's insistence that syllogisms were not enough to cope with the development of dogma. The very word "homogeneous" in the title of Marin-Sola's work indicated that his theory meant an unfolding of the explicit from the implicit. He failed to note that Newman spoke of development in that vein and therefore the "Thomist" view was not as foreign to his thinking as some imagined and still do.

Although Pierre Batiffol made use of Marin-Sola's work during the Malines Conversations in the 1920s, neither he, nor other Catholic participants there insisted on a point on which Newman had insisted very much, namely, that Anglican objections to Rome as a fomenter of novelties hit Rome via Canterbury.[95] Anglo-Catholics, to say nothing of mere Anglicans, were at that Conference (or today for that matter) no longer interested in the fact that Bull's position could not be justified on historical grounds. As to the earlier, or Caroline Anglican divines, their writings showed less coherence than those of Bull.

Catholics on the Development: phase two

The fact of the vulnerability of Canterbury was overlooked in the long article on doctrinal development which R. Draguet contributed to *Apologétique*, published in 1945,[96] and which was symptomatic of a new Catholic approach to the *Development*. Draguet not only began his article with a reference to Newman, but he also presented him as the first who had offered a "theological" solution to the question posed by dogmatic developments. But then a problem arose for the apologists who had to work with purely rational means. Could the infallibility of the Church be brought in as a "rational" starting point? Draguet's positive answer would have been convincing had he emphasized Newman's phrase about "bold outlines," and emphasized it in a way in which Newman did not, although only when this is done can a theory of doctrinal development take on a rational solidity.

In Draguet's handling of the problem one could see various facets of a "new" approach to Newman and to his thought. The intuitive and aesthetic elements in Newman's thought began to be stressed at a disregard of Newman's fondness for facts, of his repeated endorsements of the principle of objective truth, and of the obviousness, in Newman's eyes, of the four great Notes of the Church. The "novelty" of this new approach can easily be seen if one studies side by side two major anthologies of Newman's thought, separated by about fifty years. One is

Characteristics of John Henry Newman, published in 1874 and already in its fifth edition by 1880. Most importantly, the book's compiler, William Samuel Lilly, a prominent barrister, had Newman's approval for his labors.[97] The other book, similar in size, grew out of small volumes in which Erich Przywara, Jesuit editor of the *Stimmen der Zeit,* presented in the early 1920s excerpts from Newman's works. These small volumes made their real impact when they were published together in English as *Newman Synthesis.*[98] Przywara, an ardent promoter of the idea of a new, more complete Catholicism, in which existentialism, phenomenology, and aestheticism were to be fully integrated, surely saw to it that the "synthesis" should not include any of Newman's "old fashioned" ideas. Thus "integration" once more functioned as "elimination."

The reader of *Newman Synthesis* hardly learns from the texts there how important for Newman was the visible, the juridical Church, which imposes "imperially" its belief. No trace in that "Synthesis" of that gist of Newman's thought which he spelled out with almost painful sharpness when he prepared his *Via Media* for the definitive edition of his works. Since Newman wanted to dispel any future oversight of his thorough disapproval of the idea that there could be a Church between Rome and Protestantism (which Anglicanism in his mind really was), he wrote for that edition of the *Via Media* a hundred-page-long introduction, which contains this statement: "Christianity, then, is at once a philosophy, and a religious rite; as a religion, it is Holy; as a philosophy, it is Apostolic; as a political power, it is imperial, that is, One and Catholic. As a religion its special centre of action is pastor and flock; as a philosophy, the Schools; as a rule, the Papacy and its Curia."[99] Yes the Curia, the *bête noire* for the stalwarts of the "new" theology, although they love to take cover by profusely invoking Newman's name, though covering up what he really wrote and stood for.

Max Scheler was also a main figure in that strange re-orientation or rather disorientation toward a "more complete"

Catholicism, and remained an inspiration for it even after he turned from a convert into a renegade ("sit venia verbo"). The new completeness had only a veneer of real fullness. It took its strength from big phrases which showed a studied avoidance of the "negative aspects" of Catholic thought, aspects very essential to Newman's conception of Catholicism. No place in that "new" Catholicism for the dogma of original sin, of eternal damnation, let alone of election—all so dear to Newman.

It is an old story that French and German intellectuals love to accuse one another of implementing mad ideas invented by the other side. Already Heine had made that accusation from the German side. He did so with an eye on Napoleon, who surely did his best to implement the new world order as madly dreamed up by Saint Simon and other French social engineers. The coming of Hitler then gave plenty of cover for the French to see themselves as the blameless knights in a modern culture wallowing in madness and, logically enough, freeing itself of its Christian moorings with a frenzy.

Yet, on the level of a "new" presentation of Newman's thought, the French surely did not wish to be left behind by the Germans. When largely forgotten were the efforts of some who cozied up, with profuse invocations of Newman, to rank modernists in the opening years of the century, there came, in 1933, Jean Guitton with his *La philosophie de Newman*, tellingly enough with the subtitle: *Essai sur l'idée de développement*.[100] Guitton gave summaries of Newman's thought under four headings: Religion and dogma, religion and tradition, religion and progress, and the bearing of the idea of development. In the first, Guitton presented Newman's writings on Arianism, in the second his *Via Media*, in the third his *Development*, in the fourth Guitton promoted himself: he first presented Hegel's ideas on unfolding, then Spencer's idea on evolution, and then Newman's idea on development. Guitton's reader could not learn that Newman worked with no concern for those two, but rather had a notion of development which for its health had to be anchored in the concrete supernatural reality of the Church. Guitton concluded with the extravagant claim that Newman's insistence on life implied that there was an ambiguity in such notions as potency, duration, growth, and time. All this would have appeared to Newman as sheer "extravagating."

Guitton's book came to a close with two appendices. One dealt with Newman and the ante-Nicene Fathers, the other with Newman's relation to modernism and Anglo-Catholicism. Guitton's combination of these two supported a very thwarted vision on his part, which appeared also in the fact that he dedicated his book to Lord Halifax. Guitton preferred not to know of the strange machinations by which Lord Halifax had hoodwinked Cardinal Mercier into hosting the ill-begotten Malines conversations between 1921 and 1925.[101] Nor did Guitton see noteworthy Newman's merciless critique of Anglo-Catholicism in a series of lectures given in London in 1850.

In his Introduction Guitton presented "the reconciliation of the Church with the modern world" as Newman's chief aim. Well, Newman had a very negative view of the modern world and foresaw a large-scale apostasy to come, indeed the coming of the Antichrist in the guise of modernity. At any rate, Newman had already scorned that aim as read by De Quincey into the *Development*. The last section of that Introduction dealt with "the metaphysics of development" as "the move of the absolute through history." The carriers of that move, according to Guitton, were Newman, Saint Augustine, and Hegel. Strange eyes were needed to see anything really common between Hegel and the other two.

Obviously it was not with an eye on Guitton's presentation of Newman's thought that Pius XII told him in a private audience in 1956 that he should not be surprised if Newman would eventually be declared a doctor of the Church.[102] Not that in that case some Newmanists would reconsider their own ideas about Newman, instead of foisting them on Newman's writings, by reading these very selectively. In doing so, they fail to realize how much they owe to the impact of World War II, which in addition to great political, social, and economic dislocations, produced enormous changes in thinking as well, and all too often not for the better. Worse, dreams about a prosperous and progressive future were taken for sober considerations. Newman's writings (very selectively read) quickly became a preferred vehicle to promote what he would have called a new wave of extravagating.

Newman for one would have been greatly agitated by some aspects of an ecumenical reorientation which thrives on a studied replacement of the categories of truth versus error, right versus wrong, with the categories of narrow-minded versus inclusive, of progressive versus conservative, the latter being all too often taken for retrogressive, or possibly dinosauric. A small but telling example of this new approach with respect to the reconsideration of the *Development* is an essay by Maurice Nédoncelle (1905-1976), a chief French Newmanist of the mid-twentieth century. Nédoncelle presented James Mozley as a remarkable critic of Newman and did so in an ecumenical context,[103] without telling bluntly that a "remarkable" critic could still be dead wrong and that Newman was always most alive to the difference between what was true and what was erroneous.

This was in 1975 or thirty years after the publication of *Oeuvres philosophiques de Newman.*"[104] This book, produced on wartime paper of the poorest quality, was remarkable not so much by its running to over 600 pages, but by the fact that one third of it was taken up by an introduction written by Nédoncelle. Still another third of the *Oeuvres* came from the *Development*, the remaining third from Newman's *Essay on Aristotle's Poetics*, from the *Apologia*, and from the *Grammar of Assent*.

To cast the *Développement* in the mold of philosophy was to present it in its weakest aspect. This signaled unmistakable tendentiousness which was glaring in Nédoncelle's introduction. The latter consisted in a series of sections that dealt in turn with Newman's life, with the question of whether he was a philosopher, with his solitary connection with God, with his moral personalism, with moral conscience as evidence of God, with the problem of belief, with economy and development, and with Newman's humanism. All these were legitimate topics. But was it right, for instance, to make no reference to what Newman held to be most important while recalling his having had, at the age of fifteen, the realization that he was alone with God? For just about the same time, Newman also had two other major experiences. One was his discovery, from reading Joseph Milner's *History of the Church of Jesus Christ,* that a genuinely spiritual Church had existed for fifteen hundred years prior to the coming of Luther. The other was his reading about the same time Thomas Newton's *Dissertations on Prophecies that Have Remarkably Been Fulfilled*, with the last of the prophecies dealing with the Church of Rome as an embodiment of the Antichrist.

These two books would not have made such an impression on young Newman had his notion of God not been from the start about a God who was the God of biblical salvation history. Tellingly it was about that time that Newman was seized with the notion that he was one of the elect, hardly an experience within a purely natural or philosophical religion. Those two books would not have made such an impression on Newman had his thinking not been riveted, however confusedly at that time, on the reality of the Church as the organic continuation of biblical salvation history. All that Newman offered in the way of philosophy was meant to be a mere underpinning to that great ecclesial reality. Newman never tried to derive the reality of the Church and its development from philosophy or from "spiritual experience." He offered philosophy in the *Development* only to explain why Christian doctrines did grow and had to grow as time went on.

This fact could not emerge in Nédoncelle's vast Introduction and much less in its section on Newman's *Development* which began with the strange argument that although Newman did not speak of German idealists, nor of Hegel in particular, he might very well have learned about things German through conversations with Pusey and Blanco White, both of Oriel.[105] It is within such a dubiously argued perspective that Nédoncelle viewed Newman's idea on the development of doctrine. Tellingly, Nédoncelle's selections from the *Development* do not contain the all-important Introduction, with its emphatic reference to "bold outlines," nor the three great factual parallels Newman drew about the Church of the Fathers and the Church of Rome. Nor did Nédoncelle recall all this in his Introduction and in his *La philosophie religieuse de John Henry Newman*. To make matters worse, Nédoncelle, already "docteur ès lettres" and "Maitre de conférences" at the Faculty of Catholic theology of the University of Strasbourg, presented that latter work as a doctoral dissertation in theology.[106]

Nédoncelle was led by a personalist philosophy which issued in such works of his whose titles speak for themselves. He authored a monograph on Baron von Hügel,[107] books on personalist philosophy, on intersubjectivity and ontology, on love and the person, on the phenomenology of prayer, on the human person and nature, as well as on the history of religious thought in England from 1850 to the present. Last but not least, he conducted a symposium on Henri Bremond. It would be most wrong to think that such an orientation of thought should raise even the slightest doubt on the personal orthodoxy of Nédoncelle, who finished his career as Honorary Dean of the Faculty of Theology of the University of Strasbourg. In a "Colloque" held in his memory at the same University in 1979, he was quoted as being deeply disturbed by some post-Conciliar developments: "I was never willing to cover up, by some stupid readiness to compromise, harmful to everybody, the nature of the Church which is ours." But he, who as professor of theology taught mainly ecclesiology, was also quoted there as one who did not consider the Church of England as a purely natural construct but as a "transnatural" entity channelling the grace of God.[108]

Nédoncelle does not seem to have noticed, or wanted to notice, that Newman most emphatically considered the Church of England a purely natural political product and that he, as a Catholic, never spoke of *our* Church but always of *the* Church. And such is the gist also of the *Development*.

Twenty years after there appeared those selections in French from the *Development*, there followed its text in full. The translator, the Oratorian Marcel Lacroix, relied on Gondon's translation and was helped in the work of updating the notes by A. Pompen and Louis Bouyer, a well known convert from Calvinism and also an Oratorian. The brief introduction written by Bouyer deserves mention because it ends with a warm endorsement of the works of Walgrave and Nédoncelle as outlining what the notion of development ought to be in a Catholic sense, which is also fully Newmanian. Unfortunately, Bouyer noted, this was not yet widely accepted within Catholic theological circles. As a result, Bouyer continued, Chadwick, "the best historian of the Catholic notion of doctrinal development, failed to understand that a notion of it which is not strictly deductive need not be a fluid notion on the basis of which one can justify anything."[109] Bouyer, who failed to explain why Newman's theory, though not strictly deductive, was anything but "fluid," was once more carried away by his bent on poetizing.

In the same year, 1964, there appeared still another French translation, produced by Luce Gerard, and introduced by J. H. Walgrave,[110] who had already published a lengthy study on Newman's ideas on the development of dogma.[111] A curious study for more than one reason. As a Dominican, Walgrave was obviously aware of the importance of the work of his confrère Marin-Sola, who stood solidly in the Thomist tradition of doing theology. As was already noted, Marin-Sola did not consider Newman's approach to the question, except for some brief laudatory remarks on it. Walgrave in turn did not consider the factor really germane in Newman's thought to Thomism. The factor was visible in Newman's scattered but instinctively emphatic assertions of a realist epistemology, which, however, he never articulated in detail. These scattered remarks were very visible in the *Development* for anyone with an eye on Newman's frequent use there of such words as fact, object, objective, and truth. There he wrote the last word again and again as Truth.

Walgrave personalized and psychologized, so to speak, Newman's ideas on development. The second and by far the longest part of Walgrave's book had for its title, "La croissance de la foi et du dogme. Le problème du développement," but the titles of the three chapters within that part showed that Walgrave's interest lay with psychology. In the first of those chapters Walgrave discussed Newman and psychology, in the second the general psychology of development, and in the third the "differential" psychology of development. It was in such an incongruous framework that Walgrave dealt with distinctly epistemological questions in Newman's discourse on development, without noting the vigorously realist remarks there.

Walgrave saw Newman as being caught between a Scylla and a Charybdis, but actually his own approach to Newman was in that predicament. His article, "Development, Doctrine of," in the *New Catholic Encyclopedia*[112] showed all too well the inner logic of that psychologist approach to something which, in Newman's case, was not psychological at all, in spite of all his attention to the personal. Walgrave made much of Newman's letter of February 15, 1868, to Fr. Flanagan on doctrinal development, a letter in which Newman insisted that the historical process of the development of doctrine does not become logical "just because theologians afterwards can reduce them to their relations to other doctrines." According to Walgrave's summary Newman's position was as follows: "Together with the historical continuity of the message, divine grace 'fosters in the bosom of intuition' (*Fifteen Sermons* . . .) 'an intimate sense' (Newman-Perrone paper), 'a real apprehension' (*A Grammar of Assent*) of the divine mystery. Development, then, is a historical process; all that makes the history of the Church conditions the process of development."[113] Newman was not that all-inclusive. As a logician he would have frowned on theories which, because of their amplitude, are unable to make the mind converge on the point at dispute.

In spite of Walgrave's focusing on the psychological, he listed much of the vast literature concerning the *Development*, and did this also in his introduction to the French translation mentioned above. Aiming at completeness in marshaling the bibliography did not amount, in Walgrave's case either, to seeing what is essential. In that failure Walgrave was surpassed by a German priest, J. Artz, who provided most of a plethora of notes to the modern German translation of the *Development*.[114] For all his good intentions, Artz showed time and again a preoccupation in which the categories of right and wrong are replaced with the categories of positive and negative, or progressive and traditional. According to Artz, Newman's appraisal of Luther was "negative" as if anything really "positive" could be found in the Lutheran Luther's dicta which he had not owed to his Catholic past. Artz also found merit in studies in which Newman was correlated with Hegel.[115] No evidence of serious and independent studies of the *Development* and its background can be found in the introductions written to modern translations in Italian[116] and in Spanish,[117] but those introductions attest a bent for trendy phrases and prolificity.

From Bossuet to Newman, from Newman to Congar

In such an atmosphere prevailing in Catholic circles, one could not expect a firm and clear reaction to major Anglican efforts to reclaim Newman to themselves. One was connected with the fact that Longman's warehouse was bombed out in the London Blitz in 1940. To make at least some of the volumes of the definitive edition of Newman's works available, Longmans assigned the task of editing to Charles Frederick Harrold, who between 1925 and 1943 taught English literature at Ohio State University.[118] The re-edition of the *Development* appeared in 1948, with

Harrold's brief preface and a much longer introduction by him.[119] Both contain more than one inexact detail, such as Harrold's quoting Grandmaison's statement that from its first edition on the *Development* influenced all Catholic thinking on the subject. It should be noted that the influence during the latter part of the nineteenth century was minimal. During the twentieth century the influence did not become robust until its midpoint and after. This Introductory Essay is aimed in part at bringing out the nature of that influence so that facts may be distinguished from clichés.

Harrold himself rightly criticized the cliché about a similarity between Newman and Darwin, but he also claimed that unlike the notion of evolution in Darwin's work, that of development in Newman's work was not clear. One wonders whether Harrold read Darwin with any care. And he surely was careless in failing to refer to Newman's insistence on "bold outlines," on facts, on truth, and on the basic perspective stressed by Newman. Newman did not mean to write a book that would be "basic" for Catholics and an intellectual experience for others. He meant to offer truth valid for everybody, especially for Anglo-Catholics. The best part of that re-edition remains the Appendix by O. I. Schreiber. For the first time there appeared in print a meticulous account of the many differences between the first and the definitive editions of the *Development*.[120]

While the volumes edited by Harrold saw wide circulation, the introductions he provided hardly reflected Newman's firmest convictions. These were skirted in a different way in Owen Chadwick's *From Bossuet to Newman: The Idea of Doctrinal Development*, the text of his Birkbeck Lectures, given in 1955-57.[121] Chadwick, who subsequently made a name for himself as an intellectual historian, did not produce a book without merit, although it was less original than it appeared to be. Chadwick was not original even in showing that Newman's cursory reference to De Maistre and Möhler meant no real familiarity on his part with those two notable writers.[122] But why, one may ask, did Chadwick, who quoted Newman's devastating passage on history and Protestantism, choose not to quote Newman's words on "bold outlines"? The reason may be that Chadwick tried to make it appear that in spite of Newman's book, Rome and Canterbury were much in the same position. This is what one had to expect from a future member of the Archbishop of Canterbury's commission on Church and State.

Chadwick thought to convey that presumed parity by presenting, time and again, only one side of the picture. Not for him Newman's observation that Anglican missiles aimed at Rome reach their target by first hitting Canterbury, insofar as the latter wants to appear "Catholic." Newman was of interest to Chadwick only inasmuch as Newman's work seemed to hit Rome and not Canterbury. Chadwick's book came to a close with a reference to the *Lamentabili* (1907), a Decree in which Pius X imposed on Catholic theologians the duty to hold that Revelation ended with the death of the last Apostle. Chadwick's reference supported his question of whether the *Lamentabili* could be defended in terms of the *Development*. He failed to distinguish there some cogitation from a visceral vision.

Once more offense was used as the best defense. Was the Anglican position, insofar as it was "Catholic," Clearly, Chadwick did not want to consider the question of whether Canterbury's position was any more defensible than Rome's. Chadwick gave away his tactic by beginning his book with a little story about Sir Henry Wotton, who on visiting a friendly priest's church in Rome, found, as the Vespers were sung, a choirboy sent to him with a piece of paper on which the officiating priest wrote: "Where was your religion to be found before Luther?" Sir Henry sent the choirboy back to the priest after having written on the same piece of paper: "My religion was to be found then, where yours is not be found now, in the written Word of God." Such was indeed the essence of all answers to Newman's *Development* by Anglicans, whether they fancied themselves to be Catholic or professed themselves what they were and are, plain Protestant. For as Newman was fond to note, the Bible was all the religion of Anglicans.

Like all Protestants, Anglicans still have to find an answer to the slow development of the list of the canonical books of the New Testament, which they hold in common with Catholics. But whereas Catholics can fall back on an infallible Church for assurance, Protestants cannot do so even when they put on Catholic liturgical paraphernalia. The use of such paraphernalia makes it even more difficult for them to place themselves in the perspective, very much Newman's, which shows the Church of England to be far more lamentable than whatever there can be lamented in the Church of Rome. Not by the farthest stretch of imagination may it appear that it is easier to defend the Lambeth Conference of 1930, which condoned contraception, or to defend the present Archbishop of Canterbury, who "theologically" approves stable homosexual unions and favors women bishops, than to reconcile the *Development* with the *Lamentabili.*

Part of the impact of Chadwick's book can be seen in a flurry of dissertations on the *Development.* The most ambitious of these was *A Critical Examination of the Aims and Method of Argument of Newman's Essay on the Development of Christian Doctrine*, which Nicholas Lash presented at Cambridge Universi-ty in 1971. Its substance and thrust appeared four years later in Lash's *Newman on Development: The Search for an Explanation in History.*[123] This book makes one wonder whether one should not take in a reverse sense a reflection which Fr. George Ryder, of the Birmingham Oratory, made about a hundred years ago on the erstwhile reaction of Roman theologians to the *Development.* According to Fr. Ryder, whom Chadwick quotes with visible delight, the Roman theologians saw Newman to be a "formidable engine of war on their side, but they were distinctly aware that they did not thoroughly understand the machinery. And so they came to think, some of them, that it might perhaps one day go off itself or in the wrong direction."[124] As handled by Lash, the *Development* looks as if proving the case when one shoots himself in the leg, and with the full honors of an Imprimatur obtained by the publisher Sheed and Ward. To promote its increasingly progressive agenda, that publishing house had by then made much of the ultraliberal leanings of a diocesan authority in the Northeastern United States. Within ten years after the conclusion of Vatican II, signs of disarray (extravagating, Newman would say) were everywhere visible within the Catholic Church, including the theological sector. In that process Newman's writings were heavily used or rather abused, a fact which still needs a full airing.

In 1974 A. Mead, an episcopalian clergyman from Connecticut, presented at Oxford a dissertation under the title: "A Critical Investigation of the Controversy between Newman and the Tractarians over the Development of Doctrine," which fortunately remains unpublished. It would be a great misfortune for Newman's reputation to have in print Mead's claim that the *Development* had laid the groundwork for a reconciliation between the Anglican and the Roman positions. No such hapless contention can be found in the dissertation which Lawrence J. Henry presented at the University of Texas in 1973. The dissertation, "The Genesis of John Henry Newman's Theory of Development and the Reception of his 'Essay on the Development of Christian Doctrine'," would have deserved to be published for at least Henry's meticulous effort to track down as many elusive documents as possible.[125]

Quite the opposite is true of William C. Hunt's dissertation, *Intuition: The Key to John Henry Newman's Theory of Doctrinal Development*, presented at the Catholic University of America in 1967.[126] The entire second part of that dissertation is on the *Grammar of Assent*, in which Newman uses the word "intuition," but neither in the first nor in the definitive edition of the *Development*. There, however, he emphatically spoke, as he did also in the *Grammar*, about man's knowing directly and immediately the external world, a mental feat surely different from intuition. That Newman did not mean something mysterious by intuiting is transpiring also from the fact that Butler and Samuel Johnson used that word in such a very plain sense. These are the only two significant authors Hunt quotes as ones who used the word intuition, prior to Newman, whereas all his other examples postdate the *Development*. There is indeed a danger that an indiscriminate reliance on the word "intuition" may generate fog instead of illumination.

Something special is to be said of the Foreword which Fr. G. Weigel wrote to what became the most widely used modern edition of the *Development*, namely, its Image Book issue. Not so much because of Fr. Weigel's ambivalent reaction there to Chadwick's book, whose gist he should have seen as being thoroughly anti-Catholic, regardless of its suavely Anglican packaging. That Foreword's dubious character relates to Weigel's presentation there of Newman's epistemology as underlying his theory of development and pointing toward present Catholic grappling with epistemological questions. There is much more than meets the eye in Weigel's dictum that "Newman evolved his own epistemological meditations with an Olympian unconcern for either of those two thinkers [i. e. Kant and Hegel]."[127] Was not this a roundabout endorsement of Maréchal's contention, much applauded by his confrères, that Kant should be grafted on Aquinas to save Thomism for modern times? Weigel should have rather recalled that Newman left his own copy of the first English translation of Kant's *Critique* half uncut, with the remark, that there is no point wasting time on a philosopher who does not conclude to anything.[128]

An equally telling aspect of Weigel's meditations on epistemology relates to his claim that Newman's epistemology was existential.[129] By 1960 the word "existential" had been around long enough to take on widely different meanings. Therefore a specification of the sense in which Newman's meditations could be seen as existential should have been given. But in that case, a vague ground would have been pulled from under Weigel's further assertion that a new methodology in epistemology was foreshadowed in Newman's writings, of which Weigel singled out the *Grammar*. But the *Grammar*, as well as the *Development*, is larded with brief though forceful declarations that state the primacy of a direct and immediate registering of reality as the first step in mental activity. Once this primacy is ignored everything goes in epistemology and consequently in theology. This is an inevitable development, though the kind which Newman would have branded as plain corruption. What happened in Catholic philosophical and theological circles since 1960 or so speaks louder than words. Worse, this kind of "development" is taken for a great step toward an epistemological high ground about which Weigel admits that we still have no name for it. Wittgenstein's advice, that what one cannot express, one has to be silent thereof, should come to mind.

The last four decades have produced a plethora of articles on Newman's *Development*. Some of them may pass for prime specimens of obscurantism, which always is on hand when one attempts, so to speak, to build an edifice with tools fit for interior decoration alone.[130] And from most of those articles one fails to understand why Newman converted to the Catholic Church at all. Again and again it is suggested, at least between the lines, that what Newman did was good for him, but not necessarily for others. Those authors are unaware that Pusey offered that interpretation of Newman's conversion shortly after it had come about, and that Dean Church offered it again in the wake of Newman's death. About Pusey it was Newman's most considered view that it was impossible to ascertain what Pusey believed in. As to Dean Church, he himself stated in the same context that he did not really believe in supernatural dogmas. It may have been therefore natural for him to serve as Dean of Saint Paul's Cathedral.

There is much reason to exclaim: "Let the true Newman stand up," that is, let his true countenance reappear from the thick veneer applied on him by the "new" theology. The latter is responsible for the popularity of that fuzzy syncretism which, in various degrees, pervaded the papers presented at a conference held in Oriel College March 29 - April 1, 1966, and published as *The Rediscovery of Newman: An Oxford Symposium.*[131] Telling-ly, the Symposium was half Anglican and half Roman Catholic, with Archbishop Ramsey leading the roster of speakers. His Grace unabashedly supported the view that Newman should be fully acceptable to both sides, a claim with no saving grace to it.

The only essays with intrinsic merit in that "rediscovery" of Newman dealt with the history of the growth of attention paid to Newman in Germany, France, and England. Of those surveys the one by Fr. Dupuy dealing with the French scene contained hints that now and then something was wrong with "development."[132] The paper by Walgrave, that dealt with the Low Countries, was blatantly void of critical observations. No wonder. This is not the place to review the blossoming of strange studies on Newman in that country. Suffice it to say that it was there that a future Cardinal Archbishop of Utrecht came out in 1940 with a study of Newman and Hegel, as if the thoughts of the two had anything in common, or anything but a superficial similarity.[133] As to the paper that dealt with England, it had for its author H. Francis Davis, who twenty years earlier had come out with an article on "Newman and the Psychology of the Development of Doc-trine."[134] He made no effort to hint that one could have a development of doctrine in terms of psychology and also in terms of doctrine which is independent of one's psychological state. He would have done well had he recalled that in Catholic publica-tions occasioned by the centenary of Newman's conversion little had been said about Newman's concern for converts.[135] It may have been unnerving to point a finger at a failure of the nerve.

In that Oxford Conference the Abbot of Downside (Dom Butler) provided the concluding essay, "Newman and the Second Vatican Council," a perfect echo of his paper "On the Signifi-cance of Newman Today: The Theory of Development,"[136] published just after John XXIII announced his intention to convoke Vatican II. Abbot Butler praised Newman's anticipation

of Darwin's emphasis on change, without referring to Newman's
emphatic reference to the obviousness of bold outlines that
showed permanence. With such a myopic perspective one could
ignore the glaring difference between what Newman put in
writing again and again and what the Documents of Vatican II
did not contain. They are as cursory as possible on original sin, a
most central concern for Newman, and there are only five lines
there on the never ending hostility between the Church and the
World, by which Newman set so great a store.[137] Only when such
facts are kept in mind will one see the shallowness of a remark
which Cardinal Gracias of Bombay made three years after the
Council. According to him, Newman was a major influence in
the Second Vatican Council.[138] Newman, who could be very
distrustful of General Councils, would know what to say and
would certainly protest the fact that the remark became a
hallowed shibboleth in Newmanian circles and beyond.

That Newman was not of such influence at Vatican II can
easily be gathered by anyone, who can distinguish that Council
from sanguine ideas about it. As to the Council, heavy volumes
that deal with its preparation and its procedures, are practically
silent about Newman.[139] It is safe to say, that Newman, and
certainly the true Newman, was almost as absent in spirit from
Vatican II as he was physically absent from Vatican I. But even if
one considers the specific influence of Newman's *Development*
on the modern Catholic theological literature on the development
of doctrine, one may be in for a rude jolt as long as facts count
more than trendy phrases.

That true Newman was not really to the liking of the most
resolute critics of the narrowness of the Scholastic, or Thomistic,
treatment of doctrinal development could already transpire from
a hitherto unnoticed feature of a momentous article which Henry
de Lubac published in 1948 in *Recherches de science religieuse*
on "Le problème du développement du dogme."[140] He analyzed
the position of such Dominican authors as Tuyaerts, Gardeil,
Marin-Sola and others, and of such Jesuit authors as Boyer and

Dhanis, sparing none of them. But Newman's name did not appear even sparingly in that long article. Perhaps the author of that article sensed that what he had just said in his *Le Surnaturel* would not square with Newman's very traditional statements on the supernatural. Newman would certainly be taken aback by the intentional lopsidedness of De Lubac's *Catholicism* on the social aspects of the dogma. For Newman would once more insist that whatever the social embedment of the individual faithful in the Church as the body of Christ, he or she would not differ from what Newman sensed most concretely. For whether one is seized, as Newman was, at the age of fifteen with the overwhelming realization that one was created for God alone, or whether this dawned on one when the call of the angel of death sounded from around the corner, the outcome was exactly the same. May no one around that soul be then in the predicament of the author of *A Grief Observed* (who, tellingly, did not like Newman) and to discover to one's own chagrin that not even a most beloved wife fails to belong to God alone.

On a less dramatic but still momentous level, a keen reader of De Lubac's essay may note his curious insistence that a new language is needed to overcome what may appear to many a conceptual Thomistic straitjacket. Indeed soon a plethora of new words, some of which might have done credit to Heidegger's verbal contortionism, appeared in the pages of a new theological literature. That Walgrave was the author, twenty years later, of an article on "Development and language," only accentuates the significance of this development. This enrichment of theological vocabulary, be it from psychology, has not promoted appreciation of long hallowed theological terms that alone can convey anything similar to the elemental simplicity of Chesterton's dictum: "There *is* an Is!" If God deigned to give his own name as He who Is, one should be rather careful about making plain reality appear overcomplicated. This also holds about exegesis and especially if the exegete takes his inspiration from Newman. But then the exegete should realize that Newman was very traditional in matters biblical. This fact hardly transpires from the pages of a book, *Bible et tradition chez Newman*, whose author presented it as a guide to "the sources of the theory of development," as Newman conceived matters.[141]

But the document which most glaringly, as well as most unintentionally, shows the absence of Newman in the mainstream of publications on doctrinal development during the twentieth century, is Aidan Nichols' *From Newman to Congar*, published in 1996.[142] It offers many interesting details, though also some "surprises" such as that Suarez was a Jesuit Cardinal and that the Collège Stanislas in Paris was directed by Jesuits.[143] The introduction of the book leaves no doubt about Nichols' conviction that in the wake of Vatican II Catholic theology achieved a splendid synthesis of doctrinal development and a full resolution of its thorny issues.

Well, if such a conviction is taken for something founded in facts, one can only wonder why the book's very first chapter on Newman contains no reference to his insistence on facts, on bold outlines, and on his dictum that history is not the forte of Protestantism. Nichols does not show any surprise over the fact that none of the big names, who are treated by him chapter by chapter, had written anything significant on Newman and development, although they wrote profusely on development. Obviously this was a blessing in disguise in the case of Tyrell, whom Nichols lets depart from this life as being separated from the Church "only sacramentally." In Blondel's case Nichols found nothing disturbing in relation to epistemology.

All is beautifully developing in Nichols' work after he gets beyond his Dominican confrères, Tuyaerts, Gardeil, and Marin-Sola as well their Jesuit allies, such as Boyer and Dhanis. Nichols presents the thought of de Lubac, Rousselot, Rahner, Schillebeeckx, and Congar as an ascending movement toward the peak of theological perfection. Only Newman is missing as a figure who would have been studied by these illustrious writers. Newman is, of course, at the start of all that, but only, and this

Nichols does not state, inasmuch as Newman himself stated, and did so proudly, that he put a problem into focus. His handling of it was very different from what all those illustrious names have offered.

The fact that Newman's name occurs, outside the chapter on him, about twenty times in Nichols' book can unduly impress anyone who does not care to look up those pages. The references are invariably incidental. In other words, on that basis alone one should be wary of thinking that there is an organic development on doctrinal development from Newman to Congar. There is none and there remain huge problems. Nichols should still realize the astonishment Newman would feel on reading Congar's encomiums on Luther as a theologian greater than Aquinas and Augustine, and greater even than Saint Paul himself.[144] Had Nichols studied Newman for Newman's sake, instead of using him as a prop on behalf of a hazily novel perspective, he would have thought twice about telling a group of Anglo-Catholics that they should be credited for cultivating the theological riches of the Caroline Anglican divines, about who he was still at the beginning of the learning curve. Newman would reiterate what he had said about them in his *Anglican Difficulties.* Even more importantly, he would repeat that according to him efforts aimed at a corporate reunion between Rome and Canterbury can only result among Anglo-Catholics in a decrease of their sense of personal moral obligation to be inside the One True Fold.[145]

The Development's Newman

Even if one assumes that Newman was wrong, it remains most un-Newmanian to make it appear that he did not say, and say emphatically, certain things, just because his dicta do not chime with the shibboleths of the "new" theology. But since truth prevails, in the long run at least, the true Newman will ultimately emerge from under the thick layers of the cosmetic make-ups that have been pasted on his mental and spiritual physiognomy so as to make him the great prophet of an "inclusive" ecclesial outlook.

Those responsible for that face-lifting, which began with Bremond, clamor, with copious invocations of Newman's name, for ever new developments so that they may distract from monumentally perennial ecclesiological truths which Newman had not ceased emphasizing from the *Development* on. They studiously ignore his words about "bold outlines" so that in the guise of minute investigations they may promote the cause of ultimate fuzziness. They are no better than those who would insist on the lack of a superhighway, or perhaps of an air-conditioned ski-lift, up to Mount Everest, so that they may distract from the massive contours of the Himalayas piercing the sky. The hard-hitting mottos used in this book may not wake them from their theologizing slumber.

For those who read Newman for his own sake, the true Newman will keep standing out boldly, because already in the *Development* he was utterly true to himself. Though not yet formally Catholic, he was wholly Catholic as he wrote it, because he did so with a total respect for the supernatural realities embedded in the visible Catholic Church and nowhere else. This is why he produced a book which exudes the ethos of the supernatural so strongly in some of its pages as to make one think that one reads not a book of controversy, but a most inspired book on spirituality, guided by Truth, writ large.

The true Newman will withstand clever efforts to draw his portrait at variance with what he emphatically stated following his conversion in his books and especially in his letters to converts. The true Newman will have a perennial comeback in the teeth of endless distortions of what he said and stood for. There is prophecy in the words of a dear professor of his at the Gregorianum, Fr. Mazio, words which Newman himself recalled from a distance of twenty-five years to Fr. Coleridge: "Fr Mazio said of my Development, 'I do not know how it is, but so it is that all these startling things Mr Newman brings them round at the end to a good conclusion'."[146] Newman could quote this confidently because he never tried to hide that not everything was perfect in the *Development*, yet he knew that he had subtly brought it a conclusion, which is very reliable.

Insofar as it contained a theory, which is a conceptual construct, the *Development* was not unitary. Newman himself stated there that he employed a number of various approaches according to the cases he had to consider. This will surprise only those who forget that Thomas Aquinas readily borrowed from Plato whenever this or that Platonic notion appeared to him more suited to cast light on this or that aspect of Catholic teaching. He did not thereby become a Platonist, nor a syncretist. He knew what is demanded by the priority of facts, the bold and massive facts of Revelation, over theorizing about them. There is no hidden anti-Romanism in Newman's *Development* just because he had a predilection for the Alexandrian Fathers' Platonism as different from the Aristotelianism of Catholic dogma.[147] Newman also showed great fondness for Aristotle's *Poetics*.

Conceptually, Plato and Aristotle are perfectly reconcilable. The difference between the two consists in the fact that they explained differently the origin of ideas in the human mind. Aristotle fully perceived that Plato did not explain anything by claiming that eternal ideas somehow implanted themselves in the mind, taken for a particle from the universal Mind. While Aristotle also viewed the human mind to be such a particle, he stated that the mind could gain ideas only by perceiving them in the material, the sensory. This, too, was no explanation in the sense of being a reduction of matter to mind or vice versa, but an assertion of the obvious and natural way in which the human mind operates in surrendering to facts and objects. In the *Development* Newman himself kept asserting the priority of facts over ideas. This is why he could indulge in emotions about those facts and, on occasion, in poetizing about them. Therefore a reading of the *Development* for its own sake will fly in the face of those who put the premium, that is, the primacy on the emotive, and forget that while man can form concepts about the emotive, concepts themselves are not emotions.

In the *Development* Newman made it abundantly clear that the judgment of the infallible organ on this or that development will forever have to remain conceptual. That organ, the papacy in particular, is guided by that negative assistance which is its infallibility. The latter is not a gift to fill the incompleteness of the patristic record, nor can it conceptualize what by its nature escapes conceptualization, such as the mystical sense. That organ has no special eyes to follow the slow growth of awareness in the individual minds of the faithful about a particular doctrine. Nor can it trace the phases of the "collective mind" of the Church about the same.

Most importantly, the Newman of the *Development* emphatically stated that even when that infallible organ does not speak infallibly, though still emphatically, it "has in all cases a claim on our obedience."[148] This statement of his is interesting not so much because it precedes his quoting Bellarmine to the same effect, but because it reoccurs again and again in his subsequent writings, public and private, and in particular in his great rebuttal, the *Letter to the Duke of Norfolk*, of Gladstone's claim that belief in papal infallibility voids a Catholic's civil loyalty. For that phrase he did not have to search through the *Development*, which he was not particularly eager to re-read at that time. The phrase simply welled up from the funds of his deepest convictions, all of which, including his profound devotion to Mary, are obviously present in the *Development*.

Between those two books Newman published the *Apologia*, or a defense of his having held sincerely a variety of religious opinions as they kept developing in him during his pre-Catholic years. But when in the last chapter of the *Apologia* Newman speaks of his religious opinions during his first twenty Catholic years, he roundly states that he has no "development" to recount. And why should he, who characterized the moment of his conversion as one that made him see, in the words of Simeon's "Nunc dimittis," the salvation delivered by the Lord himself. Since that moment he could grow in tasting and understanding

that salvation, but not handle it as something developing in the
sense of evolving.

In the *Development* there is no trace whatever of an
evolution of dogma along the lines made famous by Darwin. The
thinking, all too often very muddled, of Darwin was a far cry
from Newman's. He most likely never read all the *Origin of
Species,* nor Chambers' *Vestiges of the Natural History of
Creation*, although it was the rage of the day just when he
converted. One could only wish that Newman had taken a
serious look at the *Origin*. In that case his sensitivity to the many
meanings of basic words bandied around by Darwin would have
greatly helped him to disentangle the scientific wheat there from
the philosophical chaff. Then Newman might have pointed out
that the development of dogma shares in the perplexity posed by
the evolution of species on the purely natural level before
supernatural considerations come into play. One can safely posit
the fact of biological evolution, partly because otherwise the vast
succession of living forms would be deprived of rational
explanation. Yet the recognition of the fact of evolution does not
provide the mechanism whereby such a succession becomes a
reality. Natural selection does not become an explanation just
because it is achieving the status of a shibboleth. Or to quote the
now almost half-a-century-old remark of Professor James Gray
of Cambridge: "No amount of argument, or clever epigram, can
disguise the inherent improbability of orthodox [evolutionary]
theory; but most biologists feel it is better to think in terms of
improbable events than not to think at all."[149]

What remains true of Darwin's *Origin of Species*, or of the
theory set forth therein, remains true of Newman's *Development*.
Newman's analysis of conceptual changes and his listing of their
psychological underpinnings can go only so far. And whatever
the anticipatory character of true doctrine, it is not strictly
predictive, just as one cannot predict the forms of future species
on the basis of Darwinian mechanism. In close parallel with the
theory of biological evolution, the theory of doctrinal develop-

ment is essentially retrospective and not prospective. Newman could say that papal infallibility would eventually be defined as a tenet of faith, but he could have hardly predicted its eventual wording, nor the time, and much less the fact that Döllinger's mean-spirited attacks on Pio Nono and Vatican I would make many Council Fathers join forces with the resolute infallibilists.

Still, there is a huge difference between biological and theological evolution. The former must, in order to remain scientific, eschew the idea of a break in the natural process, let alone the idea of a divine intervention to bridge the apparent gaps in it. Evolutionary biologists must therefore look favorably on the idea that life could naturally evolve from non-living matter. But the theological evolution must rest on an unparalleled divine intervention into human affairs, which is the utterly supernatural fact of the Incarnation. Already in reference to the fact of Revelation Newman stated that there were considerable limitations to the guiding idea of Butler, his favorite philosopher. Only up to a point could one argue, as Butler did, that for all its imperfections the natural remained a firm pointer to the existence of God, and therefore the great imperfections in the biblical story did not discredit the notion of a Revelation. But Newman went beyond Butler, when he emphatically claimed in the *Development* that there is no parallel whatsoever in the natural order to the fact of the Incarnation.

Yet even the special character of biblical Revelation was enough to irritate Matthew Arnold, although he claimed to be an admirer of Newman from his Oxford Days. Arnold, who in a lecture given in Birmingham on October 16, 1871, suggested that Christianity was a derivation from other religions, asked Newman to specify the pages in Butler on the special status of biblical religion. In his reply of December 3, 1871, Newman dealt with other questions in Arnold's letter,[150] and only in the end did he make a passing reference to Butler. Newman might have reminded Arnold, who for all his good intentions could not grasp the supernatural, that even more strongly than in the *Apologia* did he, in the *Development*, put an emphasis on the underivable character of the Incarnation. Teilhardians, who talk blissfully of their idol's presentation of Christ as an Omega point, should think twice before they pose as Newman's spiritual heirs.

The role of the supernatural in an ultimately supernatural doctrinal development also relates to the mystical or allegorical sense of the Bible to which Newman assigned a very strong role. He did so with the proviso that the sense in question, which cannot by itself guarantee its conceptualization, would be especially protected by the action of an infallible organ within the Church. It is also well to recall that Newman himself reached back, spontaneously in his letters, as well as thematically in his reply to Pusey's *Eirenicon*, to the conceptual connection between the implicit and the explicit in order to explain development as a continuity, and especially in Mariology. This is why efforts, of which the work of Marin-Sola is the towering example, will forever remain indispensable to cope with the development of doctrine.

Yet, while those efforts and that of Newman may, in some parts, be conceptually irreducible to one another, they all must rest on the same common foundation: the fact of a huge entity, the Church, living through history, morally as well as doctrinally, and living in its members. The true greatness of the *Development* is not in the hypothesis it contains, but in Newman's greatness as a Catholic, in his dramatically persuasive presentation of facts as illustrative of a Fact, the fact of the Church remaining the same in the welter of change. As such, those facts are not like those listed in an ordinary stock-taking of dry goods that can be neatly arranged on shelves.

Almost every page of the *Development* reverberates with emotions because Newman searched for a truth that alone can liberate man—liberate him from that error which is sin and which clashes with God's plan of salvation. About the existence of that very plan Newman never had a moment of doubt. It stood out for him all the time in bold outlines or contours, though it took him many painful years to recognize the crucial point. In order to conceptualize one's perception of those outlines or rather their gradual emergence from the dim past, the words must be written not in some contortionist script but in a "timelessly" Roman typefont which alone makes clear the fountain from which Truth bubbles forth all the time.

As a Catholic, Newman was not for a moment ashamed of what it takes to be the kind of Catholic for whom Christ is the same yesterday, today, and forever, and so is the Church Christ left behind to protect His being taken for the Road, the Truth, and the Life. Syllogizing is not enough to grasp all that, but even less enough for the purpose is to psychologize about it, let alone to take cover under a pleasing but hollow rhetoric coated in phenomenological theologese. For the latter, time is always long enough, unlike for the *Development*'s Newman, for whom time was short but eternity was immeasurably long, and yet to be decided within the span of a very fleeting life on earth.

---

[1] C. Langley, "Lead Kindly Light, amidst the Encircling Gloom," *The Times*, Feb. 7, 1989, p. 12.

[2] Anyone who cares to peruse the evidence I presented in my essay, "Newman and Evolution" (*Downside Review*, Feb. 1991, pp. 16-34, reprinted as ch. 12 in my *Newman's Challenge* [Grand Rapids, Mich.: Wm. B. Eerdmans, 2000]), will know what to think of the statement in M. J. Cameron's Introduction to his re-edition as a Penguin book of the first edition of the *Development*, where he speaks of "Newman's early conversion to Darwin's theory" (p. 43 note).

[3] See text p. {269}.

[4] Originally published in 1847. See reprint of the 1905 edition (London: John Lane), pp. 148-49.

[5] See on this my *The Purpose of It All* (Edinburgh: Scottish Academic Press, 1990), ch. 1, "Progress for Scant Purpose."

[6] *University Sermons*, pp. 320-21.

[7] See reprint of 1883 (London: Rivingtons), pp. 146, 150-51.

[8] See below, p. {39}. The passage runs the same in the definitive edition.

[9] See below, p. {5}. In the definitive edition Newman made this sentence even more forceful by adding "bold masses of colour" after "bold outlines."

[10] See below, p. {5}.

[11] T. Mozley, *Reminiscences, chiefly of Oriel College and the Oxford Movement* (London: Longmans, Green and Co., 1882), vol. 2, p. 398.

[12] *The Dublin Review*, Vol. VII, August & November 1839, pp. 139-180. For Wiseman's quoting the passage, see p. 154. Contrary to Wiseman, who refers to Contra Epist. Parm. Lib. III, cap. 3, the passage is in cap. 4. See Migne PL 43:101.

[13] *In Joannis epistolam ad Parthos*, Tract. I, PL 35:1987.

[14] Sermo 273, PL 38:1249. It is also quoted in Butler's *Lives of the Saints*, ed. H. Thurston and D. Attwater (New York: P. J. Kenedy & Sons, 1962), vol. 1, pp. 137-38.

[15] See *Apologia* (Image Book Edition, New York: Doubleday, 1956), pp. 286, 290, 321 and 322.

[16] On Newman's part in that translation see note 22 to ch. III.

[17] London: Longmans, Green and Co., 1937, p. 366.

[18] See the Introduction to my re-edition of Newman's *Letter to Pusey*, under the new title, *The Mother of God* (Pinckney, Mich.: Real View Books, 2002).

[19] *Apologia*, Image Book Edition, p. 313.

[20] London: F. and J. Rivington, 1846, p. viii.

[21] Originally published as *Letter to the Duke of Norfolk* (1875). See the Introduction of my re-edition, with notes, as *Conscience and Papacy* (Pinckney, Mich.: Real View Books, 2002).

[22] Quoted in L. J. Henry, *The Genesis of John Henry Newman's Theory of Development and The Reception of his "Essay on the Development of Christian Doctrine"* (Dissertation, University of Texas, 1973), pp. 173-74 (available through UMI Dissertation Service).

[23] *The Epistle to the Hebrews . . . With a Preface containing a Review of Mr. Newman's Theory of Development* (London: John W. Parker, 1846), p. cxxviii.

[24] J. Mozley, "Newman on Development," *Christian Remembrancer* 13 (1847), pp. 111-265.

[25] J. Mozley, *The Theory of Development: A Criticism of Dr Newman's Essay on the Development of Christian Doctrine* (London: Rivington's, 1878; New York: E. P. Dutton, 1879). See p. 222 in the American edition.

[26] *Letters and Diaries of John Henry Newman* (Oxford: Oxford University Press, 1965—), vol. 11, p. 348. Unless otherwise noted, letters of Newman are quoted from this work and referenced only by their dates.

[27] Published again four years later.

[28] London: F. and J. Rivington, 1846.

[29] This is not included among Irons' eighteen publications listed in the entry on him in the *Dictionary of National Biography* (vol. 10, p. 482), where he is also described as a Bampton Lecturer and a protégé of Gladstone.

[30] Ibid., p. 44.

[31] London: F. and J. Rivington, 1846, 66pp.

[32] Ibid., p. 26.

[33] "Newman on the Development of Christian Doctrine," *Quarterly Review* 77 (1846), pp. 404-65.

[34] Quoted in L. J. Henry's dissertation, *Newman and Development* (see note 20 above), p. 146, a work discussed here on p. xcv.

[35] For these two letters, see A. R. Ashwell, *Life of the Right Reverend Samuel Wilberforce . . . with Selections from his Diaries and Correspondence* (London: John Murray, 1880), vol. 1, pp. 328-29.

[36] See G. B. Smith, *The Life of the Right Honourable William Ewart Gladstone* (New York: G. P. Putnam, 1880), p. 499.

[37] See *Guessing at Truth: The Life of Julius Charles Hare* (Shepherdstown: Patmos Press, 1979), by N. M. Distad, who is very sympathetic to Hare's "inclusive" Christianity.

[38] Quoted in Edwin Abbott, *The Anglican Career of Cardinal Newman* (London: Macmillan, 1892), vol. 2, p. 380.

[39] Such as W. B. Barter (late-Fellow of Oriel), *Postscript to the English Church not in Schism, Containing a Few Words on Mr. Newman's Theory of Development* (London: F. and J. Rivington, 1846), G. S. Faber, *Letters on Tractarian Secessions to Popery, with Remarks on Mr. Newman's Principle of Development* (London: W. R. Dalton, 1846), and R. Maguire, *The "Oxford Movement;" Strictures on the "Personal Reminiscences," and Revelations of Dr. Newman, Mr. Oakeley, and Others* (2nd ed.; London: Seeley, Jackson and Halliday, 1855.) The last work of 24 pages contains invectives but no argumentation as one may expect from one who is identified on the title page as the "Clerical Secretary to the Islington Protestant Institute." There were, in addition, several reviews in the *English Churchman*, and in other ecclesiastical periodicals, of which a number is listed in *John Henry Newman: A Bibliography of Secondary Studies* (Front Royal: Christendom College Press, 1980) by John R. Griffin, who, unfortunately, all too often lists (and does incorrectly) books and articles taken from secondary sources.

[40] Vol. XIX (September and December, 1845), pp. 522-538.

[41] The Scottish National Library in Edinburgh lists 31 of them. Even more are in the Scottish Catholic Archives there.

[42] Contrary to its being listed by Griffin as a publication, it cannot be found in either of the two places in Edinburgh.

[43] Quoted in O. Chadwick, *From Bossuet to Newman: The Idea of Doctrinal Development* (Cambridge: University Press, 1957), p. 179.

[44] References are to *The Works of Orestes A. Brownson*, collected and arranged by Henry F. Brownson (Detroit: Thorndike Nourse, 1884), where volume XIV begins with five articles of Brownson on Newman's *Development* and on the idea of doctrinal development. For quotation, see p. 12.

[45] See p. 325 in the June 1847, issue of the *Dublin Review*, where Art. III is a review of Brownson's article.

[46] "Newman's Theory of Christian Doctrine," in *Brownson's Quarterly Review*, New Series, Vol. I, Nr. 1, January 1847, p. 84. In *The Works*, vol. XIV, p. 73. The article begins with Brownson's statement that he reviewed a copy of the "American reprint" of Newman's work. It was published by D. Appleton in New York (n. d.) in a wholly reset format of 206 densely printed pages.

[47] See the issue of December 1847, p. 376, with a pointed reference there to the earlier statement.

[48] Of the numerous studies on Brownson's criticism of the *Development*, the most detailed is the unpublished Laval University dissertation by D. Walsh, *Brownson's Rejection of Newman's Theory of Development* (1966). See also D. Barnes, "Brownson and Newman: The Controversy Re-Examined," *Emerson Society Quarterly* 50 (1967), pp. 9-20.

[49] Details about all this are in Newman's letter of November 7, 1845, to Wiseman, and in the editorial notes attached to it. Seventeen years later Newman most emphatically referred to that letter of his to Bishop Baggs, and he did so also in letters to Bishop Ullathorne and to Ward, written on the same day, December 30, 1862.

[50] Quoted in W. Ward, *The Life and Times of Cardinal Wiseman* (London: Longmans, Green & Co., 1897), vol. 1, p. 319. The excerpt from that sermon cover six pages (pp. 314-19) and contain such statements that "the Hierarchy was not planted by our Saviour, nor by the apostles themselves, in a systematic form; but the episcopal body, if I may so speak, evolved from itself, in the season, the priestly order" (p. 316). Surely, this was as daring as anything Newman could say.

[51] Quoted in Chadwick, *From Bossuet to Newman*, p. 236.

[52] About the implications of the Gorham Judgment for Anglo-Catholics, see the Introduction to my re-edition of Newman's *Anglican Difficulties* (Fraser, Mich.: Real View Books, 1994), pp. vi-vii.

[53] *Apologia* (Image Book Edition), p. 325.

[54] Frank M. Turner, of course, author of *John Henry Newman: The Challenge to Evangelical Christianity* (New Haven: Yale University Press, 2002). See my review, "Newman: an Apostate?" in *New Oxford Review* May 2003, pp. 37-46.

[55] Contrary to a statement in W. Ward, *John Henry Newman* (London: Longmans, 1911), vol. I, p. 121. See also Northcote to Newman on Feb 1, 1846.

[56] Lord Adare (Edwin Richard Windham until 1850, when on his father's death he became 3rd Earl of Dunraven) first met Newman in Oxford in 1839. By then he had been for two years Conservative M.P. for Glamorsganshire. A friend of Montalambert, Lord Adare became Catholic in 1852. As such he met Newman in Birmingham in 1855, four years after he had left Parliament. He was also the brother-in-law of William Monsell, another friend of Newman.

[57] All those epistolary statements of Newman are discussed in my *Newman to Converts: An Existential Ecclesiology* (Pinckney, Mich.: Real View Books, 2001).

[58] Neither Fisher, nor the editors of Newman's *Letters and Diaries* reported correctly either the issue of the *Quarterly Review* (January-April, vol. 110) or the context, a review there of *Selections, Grave and Gay, from writings published and unpublished by Thomas De Quincey* (Edinburgh: 1854-60, in 14 vols.), where the statement occurs on p. 17. In that long review (pp. 1-35) one also learns that De Quincey was most strongly against Catholic Emancipation

as it would lead "to the recognition of Irish Romanism as the Irish Church, a clear deviation from the idea of the Catholic Church. And this is precisely the view of the most orthodox, learned, and enlightened Anglicans" (p. 33). No wonder that De Quincey did not learn about the doctrine of baptismal regeneration until it was brought to the light by the case of "the now half forgotten Mr. Gorham." A perfect illustration of the ability of Anglicans to forget, within a mere ten years, even some most embarrassing facts.

[59] *Letters and Diaries*, vol. 21, p. 135.

[60] H. M. de Achával, "An Unpublished Paper by Cardinal Newman on the Development of Doctrine," *Gregorianum* 39 (1958), pp. 585-596.

[61] Ibid., p. 596.

[62] See on this my *Newman to Converts*, pp. 388-90.

[63] See my re-edition of Newman's *Letter to Pusey*, under the main title: *The Mother of God* (see note 18 above), p. li.

[64] This letter was written on Sept. 17, 1870.

[65] Many more such details are given in an essay which is cited in note 120 below.

[66] See note 24 above.

[67] See my Introduction to *The Mother of God* (note 18 above), p. lxxii.

[68] Rome: Pontificium Athenaeum Internationale "Angelicum" 1960. The thesis was defended in January 1953.

[69] See note 21 above, pp. xxxix-xl.

[70] See my re-edition of Newman's *Letter to Pusey*, under the main title: *The Mother of God* (see note 18 above).

[71] London: W. Allen, 1881, pp. 1-82. The work was dedicated to Döllinger.

[72] Ibid., pp. 36-37 (note).

[73] *Ueber die Entwickelung der christlichen Lehre* (Schaffhausen: Hurter'sche Buchhandlung 1846), xvi + 445pp. An interesting list of Brühl's publications is in *Gestamtverzeichnis der deutschprachigen Schrifttums, 1700-1910* (München: G. K. Saur, 1979-1987), vol. 21. p. 37.

[74] *Développement de la doctrine chrétienne, preuves de la vérité catholique* (Paris: Lagny Frères, 1846), XIV + 416pp. Unfortunately, she is not listed in standard biographical dictionaries, although some of her works relating to Christian social action are still in print.

[75] *Histoire du développement de la doctrine chrétienne* (Paris: Sagnier et Bray, 1848), XVI + 459pp. Gondon (1812-1873?) was a journalist associated with the French Catholic weekly, *L'Univers*. He also translated Newman's *Discourses to Mixed Congregations* and published a *Notice biographique sur le R. P. Newman* (Paris: Sagnier et Bray, 1853) a work of 137 pp., which ended with a report on the Achilli trial. In that *Notice* Gondon merely touched on his translation of Newman's *Development*, while he quoted at length autobiographical passages from Newman's *Difficulties of Anglicans*. Newman's impact on French Catholics would have been different had Gondon translated this latter work, which is still to appear in French.

[76] *Histoire de la doctrine chrétienne, ou motifs de retour à l'Eglise catholique* tr. also Jules Gondon (Liège: J. G. Lardinois 1849), XIX + 475pp.

[77] See *Letters and Diaries*, vol. 11, p. 289.

[78] In his article, "Newman's Influence in France," in J. Coulson and A. M. Allchin, *The Rediscovery of Newman: An Oxford Symposium* (London: Sheed and Ward, 1967), the French Dominican B. D. Dupuy speaks (p. 166) favorably of Mme D'Auvigny's translation (p. 166), but a contrary view is given by Chadwick (see note 43 above, p. 175), who does not seem to have seen it because he speaks of her as "a M. d'Avrigny" and calls her he.

[79] Paris: Lethielleux, 1898.

[80] Paris: Beauchesne, 332pp.

[81] *Le développement du dogme chrétien* (Paris: Bloud, 1905), 280pp. In the series "La Pensée Chrétienne. Textes et études."

[82] I may have originated the English form, which I have used in several of my earlier publications on Newman. The French form I did not see until I found it, in March 2002, in perusing Dupuy's article, "Newman's Influence in France" (see note 78 above, p. 166).

[83] London: Williams and Norgate, 1907, 358pp. The translator was H. Corrance.

[84] C. Sarolea, *Cardinal Newman and His Influence on Religious Thought and Life* (Edinburgh: T. & T. Clark, 1908).

[85] London: Longmans, Green and Co., 1908, 44pp.

[86] Ibid., p. 38.

[87] Ibid., p. 39. In this edition the passage occurs on p. {24}.

[88] In its original Latin the pope's letter is found in *Acta Sanctae Sedis* 41 (1908), pp. 200-202. I am quoting from the translation of E. D. Benard, *Preface to Newman's Theology* (St. Louis: B. Herder, 1945), pp. 155-56.

[89] L. Grandmaison, "Le développement du dogme chrétien," *Revue pratique d'apologétique*, April 1, 1908, p. 33. In this article, of which the first part dealt with Harnack and Sabatier, and the second with Newman, the latter's theory was described as "eclectic." Grandmaison failed to note Newman's reference to "bold outlines" and all that was implied in that expression.

[90] *L'Evolution du dogme. Etude théologique* (Louvain: Nova et Vetera, 1919), 254pp. Newman is discussed there on pp. 27-32.

[91] Paris: Beauchesne, 159pp.

[92] Paris: Gabalda; see especially, pp. 151-68.

[93] Paris: Lethielleux, 1922, 355pp; see pp. 290-91.

[94] Fribourg: Oeuvres de St. Paul, 536 and 368pp.

[95] See my essay, "The Malines Conversations and What was Malign there," *New Oxford Review*, May 2003, pp. 37-46.

[96] Paris: Bloud & Gay, 1948. The article runs from p. 1097 to p. 1122. The book was the work of thirty-eight collaborators, gathered from among leading French and Flemish theologians, under the direction of M. Brillant, M. Nédoncelle, and Canon Coppens.

[97] The book had for subtitle: *Being Selections Personal, Historical, and Religious from His Various Works* (5th ed.; London: C. Kegan Paul, 1880), carried on its title page the phrase, "with the author's [Newman's] approval." A volume of xvi + 447 pages, it had an extensive subject index, which can show at a glance what Lilly held to be essential in Newman's thinking.

[98] London: Sheed and Ward, 1930, 379pp.

[99] Longmans ed., p. xl.

[100] Paris: Boivin et Cie, 1933.

[101] See my article quoted in note 95.

[102] See my *Newman to Converts: An Existential Ecclesiology*, p. 508.

[103] M. Nédoncelle, "Le Développement de la doctrine chrétienne: J. B. Mozley, critique anglicane de Newman," in *Oecumenica: Jahrbuch für ökumensiche Forschung, 1971-72* (Minneapolis: Augsburg Publishing House, 1972), pp. 156-74. Nédoncelle ignores that according to Newman Mozley wanted the ethos of Anglicanism without dogmas.

[104] Paris: Aubier, 1945. 669pp. Collection bibliothèque philosophique. S. Jankélévitch was the translator.

[105] Ibid., p. 137-38.

[106] Strasbourg: Sostralib, 1946, 324pp. A dozen or so years later Nédoncelle appraised in the same incomplete perspective recent works on Newman *Development*, such as the ones by Walgrave, Chadwick, Dr. Zeno, and others in his "Chronique de théologie fondamentale: Newman et le développement dogmatique," *Revue des sciences religieuses* 32 (1958), pp. 197-213.

[107] It appeared in English translation in 1937.

[108] *La pensée philosophique et religieuse de Maurice Nédoncelle* (Paris: Tequi, 1981), pp. 44-45.

[109] *Essai sur le développement de la doctrine chrétienne*, tr. M. Lacroix, L. Bouyer, A. Pompen (Paris: Desclée de Brouwer, 1964), pp. 14-15. This volume is part of the series *Textes newmaniens*.

[110] *Essai sur le développement de la doctrine chrétienne* (Paris: Editions du Centurion, 1964), 435pp, in Collection L'Eglise en son temps.

[111] J. H. Walgrave, *Newman: Le Développement du dogme* (Tournai: Casterman, 1957), 398pp.

[112] See pp. 940-44, and especially p. 943.

[113] "Doctrine, Development of," *The New Catholic Encyclopedia*, vol. 4. p. 943. In the updated form of that article, also by Walgrave, in the second edition of the same *Encyclopedia* (2002), the most recent entry in the bibliography is from 1973.

[114] *Uber die Entwicklung der Glaubenslehre* (Mainz: Matthias Grünewald Verlag, 1969), liv + 662pp, vol. 8 of *Ausgewählte Werke* (1951-1975). Actually it was a revised form of a translation originally prepared by Theodor Häcker.

[115] About Arzt's strange preconceptions very revealing are his dicta about Newman and Hegel, Newman and Kant, and Newman and Luther. See pp. ibid., pp. XXVII-XXVIII, 549-50, and 553.

[116] *Lo sviluppo della dottrina cristiana* (Bologna: Società editrice il Mulino, 1967) with an introduction (pp. v-lx) by Alfonso Prandi. This translation reappeared in 2003 (Milano: Jaca Book), "a cura di Luca Obertello e Postfazione di Gaetano Lettieri." The text of this translation is not the same as the one which appeared as *Lo sviluppo del domma cristiano.* in 1908 under the name of Romolo Murri, a promoter of modernism.

[117] *Ensayo sobre el desarrollo de la doctrina cristiana* with a rather "trendy" presentation (pp. 11-16) by Fernando Rodriguez Garrapucho. In the series Biblioteca Oecumenica Salmanticensis, vol. 24 (Salamanca, 1997), 496pp. (with or without Newman's notes**?.

[118] An Anglican, Harrold (1897-1948) taught English literature at Ohio State University from 1935 until 1943. He wrote his thesis at Yale University on "The Method and Sources of Carlyle's *French Revolution*" (1924). Ten years later he published his *Carlyle and German Thought*. In 1945 Longmans in London published his *John Henry Newman: An Expository and Critical Study of his Mind, Thought, and Art*, xv + 472pp. Two years earlier the same publisher brought out his *A Newman Treasury. Selections from the Prose Works of John Henry Newman*, which hardly conveys to its reader that the One True Fold was a paramount consideration for Newman. Most of the Newman volumes edited by Harrold came out in 1947, a year before his tragic death by suicide.

[119] New York, London, Toronto: Longmans, Green and Co., xxxvii + 440pp., with an Appendix by Ottis I. Schreiber.

[120] Schreiber also gave a parallel listing of the major shifts of pages from the first to the final edition.

[121] *From Newman to Bossuet: The Idea of Doctrinal Development* (see note 43 above).

[122] Suffice it to recall A. Minon's long study "L'attitude de Jean-Adam Moehler (1796-1838) dans la question du développement du dogme," *Ephemerides Theologicae Lovanienses* 16 (1939), pp. 328-384.

[123] London: Sheed and Ward, 1975.

[124] See Chadwick, *From Bossuet to Newman*, pp. 169-170.

[125] A xerographic copy of it is available via www.il.proquest.com.

[126] This dissertation of viii + 320 pages was directed by Eugene M. Burke.

[127] Image Books edition, p. 19.

[128] For this and other relevant statements of Newman on German idealists, see my *Newman's Challenge*, p. 223.

[129] Image Book edition, p. 19.

[130] The most widely discussed of such articles had for its author Anthony A. Stephenson, "Cardinal Newman and the Development of Doctrine," *Journal of Ecumenical Studies* 3 (1966), pp. 463-85. His style and phraseology could but throw off even such proponents as De Lubac of a new language to be used in theology. In his reply to various criticisms Stephenson claimed "that in 1845 the Catholic-Protestant conflict could have have been relatively easily resolved." *ibid.*, 5 (1968), p. 374. The history of that conflict prior to 1854 and up to 1950

gives that evaluation of the conflict. Stephenson is unable to see the difference between the essential and the accidental, because he operates with the categories of weak and strong propositions, an elastic distinction made popular by writings on the philosophy of science. Also very telling is his rejection of the claim of a critic of his, according to whom Vatican II was consciously guided everywhere by Newman's ideas about the need for reformulations. It is still to be shown that Newman's thought actually served as such a guide.

[131] London: Sheed and Ward, 1967, under the joint editorship of J. Coulson and A. M. Allchin.

[132] See Dupuy's essay quoted in note 78 above.

[133] J. Willebrands, "De ontwickeling der idee volgens Newman vergeleken met Hegel," *Bijdragen* 7 (1946), pp. 60-79. The paper was first presented at a congress of Thomistic scholars in Witten. Willebrands had by then published articles, also in Dutch, in *Studia Catholica* (1941) on personalism in Newman and on his Christian Platonism.

[134] *The Dublin Review,* April 1945 (Nr 433), pp. 97-107.

[135] For an Australian Catholic's observation that in 1945 no interest in converts could be found in England, see my *Newman to Converts*, p. 476.

[136] *The Dublin Review*, 233 (1959), pp. 337-46.

[137] It should be enough to contrast what Newman kept saying of the coming of the Antichrist as couched in material amenities, with what is on hand in the studiedly brief reference to the undying conflict between the world and the Church in par. 37 of the Pastoral Constitution on the Church in the Modern World. The point that such a conflict derives from Original Sin can hardly be gathered from the Documents of Vatican II which makes only one generic reference to that Sin.

[138] In an article written for the Friends of Cardinal Newman and published in *The Examiner*, May 21, 1977. For a discussion of Cardinal Gracias' most lopsided views on the pre- and post-Vatican II Church in reference to Newman, see my *Newman to Converts: An Existential Ecclesiology*, pp. 480-84.

[139] See, for instance, S. Garofalo and T. Federici (eds.), *Dizionario del Concilio Ecumenico Vaticano Secondo* (Rome: Unedi - Unione Editoriale, 1969) and J. Grootaers, *Actes et acteurs à Vatican II* (Leuven: University Press, 1998) where Newman is merely mentioned (pp. 342-43). The thirty years separating these two great volumes obviously did not produce any evidence to the contrary.

[140] Volume 35, pp. 130-160.

[141] This book, written by Jean Stern, was published by Aubier in Paris in 1967 as a title in the series "Théologie," directed by professors of theology at Lyon-Fourvière.

[142] With the subtitle, *The Idea of Doctrinal Development from the Victorians to the Second Vatican Council* (Edinburgh: T & T Clark, 1990).

[143] See ibid., pp. 136 and 179.

[144] In setting up Congar as the summit of development in thinking about the development of doctrine, Nichols would have done well to think what Newman

would have thought about Congar's statement: "Cet homme [Luther] est un des plus grands génies religieux de toute l'histoire. Je le mets à cet égard sur le même plan que saint Augustin, saint Thomas d'Aquin ou Pascal. D'une certaine manière, il est encore plus grand. Il a repensé tout le christianisme. Il en a donné une nouvelle synthèse, une nouvelle interprétation. . . . Luther fut un homme d'Eglise." Quoted in *Une vie pour la vérité. Jean Puyo interroge le Père Congar* ([Paris]: Le Centurion, [1975]), p. 59. For Newman found nothing so detrimental for the prospects of Catholicism within the Church of England than Lutheranism's early penetration into it. As to how Luther, whose philosophy was Ockhamism, could "rethink the entire Christianity" is a question to which there must be a pointed reply in Aquinas, who well in advance could destroy transcendental Thomism by his statement that the mind learns from sensory experience even about the categories of the mind. Congar's encomium of Luther makes sense only if one ignores the monumental researches which the Dominican Denifle and the Jesuit Grisar produced on Luther less than a century ago. Does the road to "true reform in the Church" consist in ignoring anything that preceded the rise of the "new theology"? Is not the road to false reform in view when one has endless interfaith conferences and the practical end of summons to convert to the One True Fold?

[145]   See chapter 23 "Sober Ecumenist," in my *Newman to Converts.* Newman's letter of March 3, 1866, to Ambrose Phillipps de Lisle, a convert and advocate of corporate reunion, should be read in extenso.

[146]   February 5, 1871.

[147]   As done by Allen Brent, "Newman and Perrone: Unreconcilable Theses on Development," *Downside Review* 102 (October 1984), pp. 276-89.

[148]   See pp. {124-25}.

[149]   See my Gifford Lectures, *The Road of Science and the Ways to God* (Chicago: University of Chicago Press, 1978), p. 289.

[150]   These related to the need for an orientation of the Church toward democratic political trends. While Newman endorsed that need, he distanced himself from those who could not be patient, and referred to the rise of Communism as a reason for caution on the part of the Vatican!

AN ESSAY

ON THE

DEVELOPMENT

OF

CHRISTIAN DOCTRINE.

BY

JOHN HENRY NEWMAN,

AUTHOR OF LECTURES ON THE PROPHETICAL OFFICE OF THE CHURCH.

OCULI MEI DEFECERUNT IN SALUTARE TUUM,

ET IN ELOQUIUM JUSTITIÆ TUÆ.

LONDON:

JAMES TOOVEY, 192, PICCADILLY.

M.DCCC.XLV.

ADVERTISEMENT

It is now above eleven years since the writer of the following pages, in one of the early Numbers of the Tracts for the Times, expressed himself thus:—

"Considering the high gifts, and the strong claims of the Church of Rome and its dependencies on our admiration, reverence, love and gratitude, how could we withstand it, as we do; how could we refrain from being melted into tenderness, and rushing into communion with it, but for the words of Truth itself, which bid us prefer it to the whole world? 'He that loveth father or mother more than Me, is not worthy of Me.' How could we learn to be severe, and execute judgment, but for the warning of Moses against even a divinely-gifted teacher who should preach new gods, and the anathema of St. Paul even against Angels and Apostles who should bring in a new doctrine?"[1]

He little thought, when he so wrote, that the time would ever come, when he should feel the obstacle, which he spoke of as lying in the way of communion with the Church of Rome, to be destitute of solid foundation.

The following Work is directed towards its removal.

Having in former Publications directed attention to the supposed difficulty, he considers himself bound to avow his present belief that it is imaginary.

I

He has neither the ability to put out of hand a finished composition, nor the wish to make a powerful and moving representation, on the great subject of which he treats. His aim will be answered, if he succeeds in suggesting thoughts, which in God's good time may quietly bear fruit, in the minds of those to whom that subject is new; and which may carry forward inquirers, who have already put themselves on course.

If at times his tone appears positive or peremptory, he hopes this will be imputed to the scientific character of the Work, which requires a distinct statement of principles, and of the arguments which recommend them.

He hopes too he shall be excused for his frequent quotations from himself; which are necessary in order to show how he stands at present in relation to various of his former Publications.

His more important changes of opinion will be seen of course by referring to his Lectures on the Prophetical Office of the Church, published in the beginning of 1837. In these Lectures there are various statements which he could wish unsaid; but he thinks it right to draw the reader's especial attention to the following passage, which he retracts with the others:—

"We must take and deal with things as they are, not as they pretend to be. If we are induced to believe the professions of Rome, and make advances towards her as if a sister or a mother Church, which in theory she is, we shall find too late that we are in the arms of a pitiless and unnatural relative, who will but triumph in the arts which have inveigled us within her reach. No; dismissing the dreams which the romance of early Church history, and the high doctrines of Catholicism, will raise in the inexperienced mind, let us be sure that she is our enemy, and will do us a mischief when she can. In speaking and acting on this conviction, we need not depart from Christian charity towards her. We must deal with her as we would towards a friend who is visited by derangements; in great affliction, with all affectionate tender thoughts, with tearful regrets and a broken heart, but still with a steady eye and a firm hand. For in truth she is a Church beside herself; abounding in noble gifts and rightful titles, but unable to use them religiously; crafty, obstinate, wilful, malicious, cruel, unnatural, as madmen are. Or rather, she may be said to resemble a demoniac, possessed with principles, thoughts and tendencies not his own; in outward form and in natural powers what God has made her, but ruled within by an inexorable spirit, who is sovereign in his management over her, and most subtle and most successful in the use of her gifts. Thus she is her real self only in name; and till God vouchsafe to restore her, we must treat her as if she were that evil one which governs her. And, in saying this, I must not be supposed to deny that there is any real excellence in Romanism even as it is, or that any really excellent men are its adherents. Satan ever acts on a system; various, manifold, and intricate, with parts and instruments of different qualities, some almost purely evil, others so unexceptionable that, in themselves and detached from the end to which all is subservient, they are really "Angels of Light," and may be found so to be at the Last Day. In Romanism there are some things absolutely good, some things only just tainted and sullied, some things corrupted, and some things in themselves sinful; but the system itself so called must be viewed as a whole, and all parts of it as belonging to the whole, and in connexion with their practical working and the end which they subserve."[2]

He will add that there is one statement in these Lectures, about which he has never seen any reason at all for changing his opinion. It is this:—

"In England the Church co-operates with the State in exacting
subscription to the Thirty-nine Articles as a test, and that not only of the
Clergy, but also of the governing body in our Universities, *a test against
Romanism.*"

Such a statement is quite consistent with a wish, on
which he has before now acted, to correct popular misap-
prehensions both of the Roman Catholic doctrines, and of
the meaning of the Thirty-nine Articles.

Some years since a retractation of his appeared in the
public prints, which he is desirous of formally acknowledging here, and of preserving. It is as follows:—

"It is true that I have at various times, in writing against the Roman
system, used not merely arguments, about which I am not here speaking,
but what reads like declamation.

"1. For instance, in 1833, in the *Lyra Apostolica*, I called it a 'lost
Church.'

"2. Also, in 1833, I spoke of 'the Papal Apostasy' in a work upon the
Arians.

"3. In the same year, in No. 15 of the series called the 'Tracts for the
Times,' in which Tract the words are often mine, though I cannot claim it
as a whole, I say—

'True, Rome is heretical now—nay, she has thereby forfeited her orders; yet,
at least, she was not heretical in the primitive ages. If she has apostatized, it was at
the time of the Council of Trent. Then, indeed, it is to be feared the whole Roman
Communion bound itself, by a perpetual bond and covenant, to the cause of
Antichrist.'

"Of this and other Tracts a friend, with whom I was on very familiar
terms, observed, in a letter some time afterwards, though not of this

particular part of it—'It is very encouraging about the Tracts—but I wish I could prevail on you, when the second edition comes out, to cancel or materially alter several.' The other day accidentally put in my way the Tract on the Apostolical Succession in the English Church; and it really does seem so very unfair, that I wonder if you could, even in the extremity of οἰκονομια and φενακισμός have consented to be a party to it.

"On the passage above quoted, I observe myself, in a pamphlet published in 1838—

"I confess I wish this passage were not cast in so declamatory a form; but the substance of it expressed just what I mean."

"Also, in 1833, I said—

"Their communion is infected with heresy; we are bound to flee it as a pestilence. They have established a lie in the place of God's truth, and, by their claim of immutability to doctrine, cannot undo the sin they have committed." Tract 20.

"5. In 1835, I said, in a magazine—

'The spirit of old Rome has risen again in its former place, and has evidenced its identity by its works. It has possessed the Church there planted, as an evil spirit might seize the demoniacs of primitive times, and makes her speak words which are not her own. In the corrupt Papal system we have the very cruelty, the craft, and the ambition of the Republic; its cruelty in its unsparing sacrifice of the happiness and virtue of individuals to a phantom of public expediency, in its forced celibacy within, and its persecutions without; its craft in its falsehoods, its deceitful deeds and lying wonders; and its grasping ambition in the very structure of its polity, in its assumption of universal dominion: old Rome is still alive; no where have its eagles lighted, but it still claims the sovereignty under another pretence. The Roman Church I will not blame, but pity—she is, as I have said, spell-bound, as if by an evil spirit; she is in thraldom.'

"I say, in the same paper—

'In the book of Revelation, the sorceress upon the seven hills is not the Church of Rome, as is often taken for granted, but Rome itself, that bad spirit which, in its former shape, was the animating principle of the fourth monarchy. In St. Paul's prophecy, it is not the Temple or Church of God, but the man of sin in the Temple, the old man or evil principle of the flesh which exalteth itself against God. Certainly it *is* a mystery of iniquity, and one which may well excite our dismay and horror, that in the very heart of the Church, in her highest dignity, in the seat of St. Peter, the evil principle has throned itself, and rules. It seems as if that spirit has gained subtlety by years; Popish Rome has succeded to Rome Pagan: and would that we had no reason to expect still more crafty developments of Antichrist amid the wreck of institutions and establishments which will attend the fall of the Papacy!.....I deny that the distinction is unmeaning. Is it nothing to be able to look on our mother, to whom we owe the blessing of Christianity, with affection instead of hatred, with pity indeed, nay and fear, but not with horror? Is it nothing to rescue her from the hard names which interpreters of prophecy have put on her, as an idolatress and an enemy of God, when she is deceived rather than a deceiver?"

"I also say—

'She virtually substitutes an external ritual for moral obedience; penance for penitence, confession for sorrow, profession for faith, the lips for the heart: such at least is her system as understood by many.'

"Also I say, in the same paper—

'Rome has robbed us of high principles which she has retained herself, though in a corrupt state. When we left her, she suffered us not to go in the beauty of holiness; we left our garments and fled.'

"Against these and other passages of this paper the same friend, before it was published, made the following protest:—'I only except from this general approbation your second and most superfluous hit at the poor Romanists. You have first set them down as demoniacally possessed by the evil genius of Pagan Rome, but notwithstanding are able to find something to admire in their spirit, particularly because they apply ornament to its proper purposes: and then you talk of their churches: and all that is very well, and one hopes one has heard the end of name-calling, when all at once you relapse into your Protestantism, and deal in what I take leave to call slang.'

"Then, after a remark which is not to the purpose of these extracts, he adds—'I do not believe that any Roman Catholic of education would tell you that he identified penitence and penances. In fact I know that they often preach against this very error as well as you could do.'

"6. In 1834 I also used, of certain doctrine of the Church of Rome, the epithets 'unscriptural,' 'profane,' 'impious,' 'bold,' 'unwarranted,' 'blasphemous,' 'gross,' 'monstrous,' 'cruel,' 'administering deceitful comfort,' and 'unauthorised,' in Tract 38. I do not mean to say that I had not a definite meaning in every one of these epithets, or that I did not weigh them before I used them.

"With reference to this passsage the same monitor had said— 'I must enter another protest against your cursing and swearing at the end of the first *Via Media* as you do. (Tract 38.) What good can it do? I call it uncharitable to an excess. How mistaken we may ourselves be on many points that are only gradually opening to us!'

"I withdrew the whole passage several years ago.

"7. I said in 1837 of the Church of Rome—

'In truth she is a Church beside herself,' &c. [see above.]

"8. In 1837, I also said in a review—

'The Second and Third Gregories appealed to the people against the Emperor for a most unjustifiable object, and in, apparently, a most unjustifiable way. They became rebels to establish image-worship. However, even in this transaction, we trace the original principle of Church power, though miserably defaced and perverted, whose form
> 'Had yet not lost
All her original brightness, or appeared
Less than Archangel ruined and the excess
Of glory obscured.'

Upon the same basis, as is notorious, was built the Ecclesiastical Monarchy. It was not the breath of princes, or the smiles of a court, which fostered the stern and lofty spirit of Hildebrand and Innocent. It was the neglect of self, the renunciation of worldly pomp and ease, the appeal to the people.'

"I must observe, however, upon this passsage, that no reference is made in it (the idea is shocking) to the subject of Milton's lines who ill answers to the idea of purity and virtue defaced, of which they speak. An application is made of them to a subject which I considered, when I so wrote, to befit them better, viz. the Roman Church as viewed in a certain exercise of her power in the person of the two Popes.

"Perhaps I have made other statements in a similar tone, and that, again, when the statements themselves were unexceptionable and true. If you ask me how an individual could venture, not simply to hold, but to publish such views of a communion so ancient, so wide-spreading, so fruitful in Saints, I answer that I said to myself, 'I am not speaking my own words, I am but following almost a *consensus* of the divines of my Church. They have ever used the strongest language against Rome, even the most able and learned of them. I wish to throw myself into their system. While I say what they say, I am safe. Such views, too, are necessary for our position.' Yet I have reason to fear still, that such language is to be ascribed, in no small measure, to an impetuous temper, a hope of approving myself to persons I respect, and a wish to repel the charge of Romanism.

"An admission of this kind involves no retractation of what I have written in defence of Anglican doctrine. And as I make it for personal reasons, I make it without consulting others. I am as fully convinced as ever, indeed I doubt not Roman Catholics themselves would confess, that the Anglican doctrine is the strongest, nay the only possible antagonist of their system. If Rome is to be withstood, it can be done in no other way."

Of course he now withdraws the arguments alluded to, as far as they reflect upon the Church of Rome, as well as the language in which they were conveyed.

LITTLEMORE,
  Oct. 6, 1845.

POSTSCRIPT

Since the above was written, the Author has joined the Catholic Church. It was his intention and wish to have carried his Volume through the Press before deciding finally on this step. But when he got some way in the printing, he recognised in himself a conviction of the truth of the conclusion to which the discussion leads, so clear as to supersede further deliberation. Shortly afterwards circumstances gave him the opportunity of acting upon it, and he felt that he had no warrant for refusing to do so.

His first acOhis Work for revision to the proper authorities; but the offer was declined on the ground that it was written and partly printed before he was a Catholic, and that it would come before the reader in a more persuasive form, if he read it as the author wrote it.

It is scarcely necessary to add that he now submits every part of the book to the judgment of the Church, with whose doctrine, on the subjects of which it treats, he wishes all his thoughts to be coincident.

[1] Records of the Church, xxiv. p. 7.
[2] Proph. Off. pp. 103, 4.

INTRODUCTION

CHRISTIANITY has been long enough in the world to justify us in dealing with it as a fact in the world's history. Its genius and character, its doctrines, precepts, and objects cannot be treated as matters of private opinion or deduction, unless we may reasonably so regard the Spartan institutions or the religion of Mahomet. It may indeed legitimately be made the subject-matter of theories; what is its moral and political excellence, what its due location in the range of ideas or of facts which we possess, whether it be divine or human, whether original or eclectic, or both at once, how far favorable to civilization or to literature, whether a religion for all ages or for a particular state of society, these are questions upon the fact, or professed solutions of the fact, and belong to the province of opinion; but to a fact do they relate, on an admitted fact do they turn, which must be ascertained as other facts, and surely has on the whole been so ascertained, unless the testimony of so many centuries is to go for nothing. Christianity is no dream of the study or the cloister. It has long since passed beyond the letter of documents and the reasonings of individual minds, and has become public property. Its "sound has gone out into all lands," and its "words unto the ends of the world." It has from the first had an objective existence, and has thrown itself upon the great concourse of men.

1

Its home is in the world; and to know what {2} it is, we must seek it in the world, and hear the world's witness of it.

The hypothesis, indeed, has met with wide reception in these latter ages, that Christianity does not fall within the province of history,—that it is to each man what each man thinks it to be, and nothing else; and thus in fact is a mere name for a number of different religions all together, at variance one with another, and claiming the same appellation, not because they can assign any one and the same doctrine as the common foundation of all, but because certain points of agreement may be found here and there of some sort or other, by which each in its turn is connected with one or another of its neighbours. Or again, it has been maintained, or implied, that all existing denominations of Christianity are wrong, none representing it as taught by Christ and His Apostles; that it died out of the world at its birth, and was forthwith succeeded by a counterfeit or counterfeits which assumed its name, though they inherited but a portion of its teaching; that it has existed indeed among men ever since, and exists at this day, but as a secret and hidden doctrine, which does but revive here and there under a supernatural influence in the hearts of individuals, and is manifested to the world only by glimpses or in gleams, according to the number or the station of the illuminated, and their connexion with the history of their times.

This is what, with more or less distinctness, is said or thought; and it is sufficient to observe upon it simply that it *is* an hypothesis, which has no claim on our time and attention till facts are adduced on which it is built, or for which it accounts. Till it is shown why we should view the matter differently, it is natural, or rather necessary, it is agreeable to our modes of proceeding in parallel cases, to consider that the society of Christians {3} which the Apostles left on earth were of that religion to which the Apostles had converted them; that the external continuity of name, profession, and communion is a *primâ facie* argument for a real continuity of doctrine; that, as Christianity began by manifesting itself to all mankind, therefore it went on to manifest itself; and that the more, considering that prophecy had already determined that it was to be a power visible in the world and sovereign over it, characters which are accurately fulfilled in that historical Christianity to which we commonly give the name. It is not a great assumption, then, but rather mere abstinence from the wanton admission of a principle which would necessarily lead to the most vexatious and preposterous scepticism,[1] to take it for granted that the Christianity of the second, fourth, seventh, twelfth, and sixteenth, and intermediate centuries is in its substance the very religion which Christ and his Apostles taught in the first, whatever may be the modifications for good or evil which lapse of years, or the vicissitudes of human affairs have impressed upon it.

I am not denying the abstract possibility of extreme changes. The substitution is certainly, in idea, supposable of a counterfeit Christianity for the original, by means of the adroit innovations of seasons, places, and persons, till, according to the familiar illustration, the "blade" and the "handle" are successively renewed, and identity is lost without the loss of continuity. It is possible; but it must not be assumed. The *onus probandi* is with those who assert what is unnatural to expect; to be just able to doubt is no warrant for disbelieving.

Accordingly, some writers have gone on to give reasons from history for their refusing to appeal to it. They say that, when they come to look into {4} the history of Christianity, they find its doctrines so variously represented, and so inconsistently maintained by its professors, that, however natural it be *a priori*, it is useless, in fact, to seek in history the matter of that Revelation which has been vouchsafed to mankind; that they cannot be historical Christians if they would. They say, in the words of

Chillingworth, "There are popes against popes, councils against councils, some fathers against others, the same fathers against themselves, a consent of fathers of one age against a consent of fathers of another age, the Church of one age against the Church of another age." And it must be allowed to such persons that, while reason antecedently suggests an historical inquiry, as the means of arriving at a knowledge of Christianity, it makes no promise that difficulties will not embarrass its course, or even preclude its satisfactory completion. The remoteness or nearness of the times, the scantiness or the abundance of materials, the multitude of details, the depth and intricacy of the system, the subtle intermixture of received teaching and personal opinion, and the disorder which is inevitable in any mass of historical facts,—the problem of finding a point of view from which minds born under the gracious shelter of Revelation may approximate to an external and general survey of it,—these are considerations which lead to misgivings, that, even though history be the true mode of determining the character of Christianity, still it cannot be satisfactorily used for the purpose.

Now it cannot be denied that this anticipation is in a measure, though only in a measure, fulfilled. It is not fulfilled in such sense that an inquirer, coming to history, would not obtain a certain definite impression what Christianity was, and certain general views of its doctrines, principles, and characteristics. The nature and temper of the religion, as a matter of fact, no one can mistake, whether he {5} accept it or stumble at it. No one, for instance, will say that Christianity has not always taught benevolence and mercy; that it has sanctioned injustice, or made light of impurity; that its spirit has been sceptical; that is has discountenanced what is called the sacramental principle, or the principle of mystery. Bold outlines, which cannot be disregarded, rise out of the records of the past, when we look to see what it will give up to us: they may be dim, they may be incomplete, but they are definite;—there is that which they are not, which they cannot be. Whatever be historical Christianity, it is not Protestantism. If ever there were a safe truth, it is this.

And Protestantism has ever felt it. I do not mean that every Protestant writer has felt it; for it was the fashion at first, at least as a rhetorical argument against Rome, to appeal to past ages, or to some of them; but Protestantism, as a whole, feels it, and has felt it. This is shown in the determination already referred to, of dispensing with historical Christianity altogether, and of forming a Christianity from the Bible alone: men never would have put it aside, unless they had despaired of it. It is shown by the long neglect of ecclesiastical history in England, which prevails even in the English Church. Our popular religion scarcely recognises the fact of the twelve long ages which lie between the Councils of Nicaea and Trent, except as affording one or two passages to illustrate its wild interpretations of certain prophesies of St. Paul and St. John. It is melancholy to say it, but the chief, perhaps the only English writer who has any claim to be considered an ecclesiastical historian, is the infidel Gibbon. German Protestantism, on the other hand, has been of a bolder character; it has calmly faced and carefully surveyed the Christianity of eighteen hundred years, and it frankly avows that it is a mere religion of man and the {6} accident of a period. It considers it a syncretism of various opinions springing up in time and place, and forming such combinations one with another as their respective characters admitted; it considers it as the religion of the childhood of the human mind, and curious to the philosopher as a phenomenon.

And the utter incongruity between Protestantism and historical Christianity is true whether the latter be regarded in its earlier or in its later centuries. Protestants can as little bear its Ante-nicene as its Post-tridentine period. I have elsewhere observed on this circumstance: "So much must the Protestant grant that, if such a system of doctrine as he would now intro-

duce ever existed in early times, it has been clean swept away as
if by a deluge, suddenly, silently, and without memorial; by a
deluge coming in a night, and utterly soaking, rotting, heaving
up, and hurrying off every vestige of what it found in the
Church, before cock-crowing: so that "when they rose in the
morning_ her true seed 'were all dead corpses"—nay dead and
buried—and without grave-stone. "'The waters went over them;
there was not one of them left; they sunk like lead in the mighty
waters." Strange antitype, indeed, to the early fortunes of
Israel!—then the enemy was drowned, and "Israel saw them dead
upon the seashore." But now, it would seem, water proceeded as
a flood "out of the serpent's mouth," and covered all the witnesses, so that not even their dead bodies "lay in the streets of the
great city." Let him take which of his doctrines he will, his
peculiar view of self-righteousness, of formality, of superstition;
his notion of faith, or of spirituality in religious worship; his
denial of the virtue of the sacraments, or of the ministerial
commission, or of the visible Church; or his doctrine of the
divine efficacy of the Scriptures as the one appointed instrument
of religious teaching; and let him consider how far antiquity, as it
has come down to us, will {7} countenance him in it. No, he
must allow that the alleged deluge has done its work; yes, and
has in turn disappeared itself, it has been swallowed up in the
earth mercilessly as itself was merciless."[2]

That Protestantism, then, is not the Christianity of history, it
is easy to determine; but there is a determination which is
difficult. It is difficult to complete, to finish from history that
picture of the divine religion which, even in its outlines, is
sufficient to condemn Protestantism, though not sufficient to
imprint upon our minds the living image of Christianity. Confused, inaccurate knowledge is no knowledge. It is the very fault
we find with youths under education that they use words without
meaning, that they are wanting in precision and distinctness, that

they are ignorant of what they know and what they do not know. We account this a great defect of mind, which must be overcome. Now our difficulty lies in getting beyond this half-knowledge of Christianity, if we make history our teacher; in obtaining from it views serviceable, ready, for belief and practice, whole views, definite answers to definite questions, critical decisions between truth and error, explanations of its own variations, measures of its meaning. History is not a creed or a catechism; it gibes lessons rather than rules; it does not bring out clearly upon the canvass the details which were familiar to the ten thousand minds of whose combined movements and fortunes it treats. Such is it from its very nature; nor can the defect ever be fully remedied. This must be admitted; at the same time, Principles may be laid down with considerable succss as keys to its various notices, enabling us to arrange and reconcile them.

Such a key, as regards the teaching of Christianity, it has been imagined was contained in the celebrated dictum of Vincentius,—a method of accounting for whatever variations we may find in the {8} historical testimonies concerning it, of separating authoritative doctrine from opinion, of rejecting what is faulty, and combining and forming a theology. That "Christianity is what has been held always, everywhere and by all," certainly promises a solution of the perplexities, an interpretation of the meaning of history. What can be more natural than that divines and bodies of men should speak sometimes from themselves, sometimes from tradition? what more natural than that individually they should say many things on impulse, or under excitement, or as conjectures, or in ignorance? what more certain than that they must have been all instructed and catechised in the Creed of the Apostles? what more evident than that what was their own would in its degree be peculiar, and differ from what was similarly private and personal in their brethren? what more conclusive than that the doctrine that was common to all at once was not really their own, but public property in which they had a joint interest, and proved by the concurrence of so many witnesses to have come from an apostolical source? Here, then, we have a short and easy method for reconciling the various informations of ecclesiastical history with that antecedent probability in its favour, which nothing but its actual variations would lead us to neglect.

Such is the rule of historical interpretation which has been professed in the English school of divines; and it contains a majestic truth, and offers an intelligible principle, and wears a reasonable air. It is congenial, or, as it may be said, native to the Anglican mind, which takes up a middle position, neither discarding the Fathers nor acknowledging the Pope. It lays down a simple rule by which to measure the value of every historical fact as it comes, and thereby provides a bulwark against Rome while it opens an assault upon Protestantism. Such is its promise; but its difficulty lies in applying it in {9} particular cases. The rule is most serviceable in determining what is not, than what is Christianity; it is irresistible against Protestantism, and in one sense indeed it is irresistible against Rome also, but in the same sense it is irresistible against England. It admits of being interpreted in one of two ways: if it be narrowed for the purpose of disproving the catholicity of the Creed of Pope Pius, it becomes also an objection to the Athanasian; and if it be relaxed to admit the doctrines retained by the English Church, it no longer excludes certain doctrines of Rome which that Church denies. It cannot at once condemn St. Thomas and St. Bernard, and defend St. Athanasius and St. Gregory Nazianzen.

This general defect in its serviceableness has been heretofore felt by those who appealed to it. It has been said: "The Rule of Vincent is not of a mathematical or demonstrative character, but moral, and requires practical judgment and good sense to apply it. For instance, what is meant by being "taught *always*?" does it mean in every century, or every year, or every month? Does *"everywhere"* mean in every country, or in every diocese? and does "'the *Consent of Fathers*'_ require us to produce the direct testimony of every one of them? How many Fathers, how many places, how many instances constitute a fulfilment of the test propsed? It is, then, from the nature of the case, a condition which never can be satisfied as fully as it might have been. It admits of various and unequal application in various instances; and what degree of application is enough must be decided by the same principles which guide us in the conduct of life, which determine us in politics, or trade, or war, which lead us to accept Revelation at all, for which we have but probability to show at most, nay, to believe in the existence of an intelligent Creator."[3]

{10} So much was allowed by the writer; but then he added:—

"This character, indeed of Vincent's Canon, will but recommend it to the disciples of the school of Butler, from its agreement with the analogy of nature; but it affords a ready loophole for such as do not wish to be persuaded, of which both Protestants and Romanists are not slow to avail themselves."

This is the language of disputants who are more intent on assailing others than defending themselves; as if similar loopholes were not necessary for Anglican theology.

He elsewhere says: "What there is not the shadow of a reason for saying that the Fathers held, what has not the faintest pretensions of being a Catholic truth, is this, that St. Peter or his successors were and are universal Bishops, that they have the whole of Christendom for their one diocese in a way which other Apostles and Bishops had and have not."[4] Most true, if, in order that a doctrine be considered Catholic, it must be formally stated by the Fathers generally from the very first; but, on the same understanding the doctrine also of the apostolic succession in the episcopal order "has not the faintest pretensions of being a Catholic truth."

Nor was this writer without a feeling of the difficulty of his school; and he attempted to meet it by denying it. He wished to maintain that the sacred doctrines admitted by the Church of England into the Articles were taught in primitive times with a distinctness which could not be fancied to attach to the characteristics of Rome.

"We confidently affirm," he said in another publication, "that there is not an article in the Athanasian Creed concerning the Incarnation which is not anticipated in the controversy with the Gnostics. There is no question which the Apollinarian {11} or the Nestorian heresy raised which may not be decided in the words of Irenaeus and Tertullian."[5]

This may be considered as true. It may be true also, or shall here be assumed, for there will be an opportunity of recurring to the subject, that there is also a *consensus* in the Anti-nicene Church for the doctrines of Our Lord's Consubstantiality and Coeternity with the Almighty Father. Let us allow that the whole circle of doctrines, of which our Lord is the subject, was consistently and uniformly confessed by the Primitive Church, though not ratified formally in Council. But it surely is otherwise with the Catholic doctrine of the Trinity. I do not see in what sense it can be said that there is a *consensus* of primitive divines in its favour, which will not avail also for certain doctrines of the Roman Church which will presently come into mention. And this is a point which the writer of the above passages ought to have more distinctly brought before his mind and more carefully weighed; but he seems to have fancied that Bishop Bull proved the primitiveness of the Catholic doctrine concerning the Holy Trinity as well as concerning our Lord.

Now it should be clearly understood what it is which must be shown by those who would prove it. Of course the doctrine of our Lord's divinity itself partly implies and partly recommends the doctrine of the Trinity; but implication and suggestion belong to another kind of proof which has not yet come into consideration. Moreover the statements of a particular father may certainly be of a most important character; but one divine is not equal to a Catena. We must have a whole doctrine stated by a whole Church. The Catholic Truth in question is made up of a number of separate propositions, each of which, if maintained without the rest, is a heresy. In order then to prove that all the Ante-nicene writers taught it, it is not enough to prove that each has gone far enough to be a heretic—not {12} enough to prove that one has held that the Son is God, (for so did the Sabellian, so did the Macedonian,) and another that the Father is not the Son, (for so did the Arian,) and another that the Son is equal to the Father, (for so did the Tritheist,) and another that there is but One God, (for so did the Unitarian,) not enough that many attached in some sense a Threefold Power to the idea of the Almighty (for so did almost all the heresies that ever existed, and could not but do so, if they accepted the New Testament at all;) but we must show that all these statements at once, and others too, are laid down by as many separate testimonies as may fairly be taken to constitute a "*consensus* of doctors." It is true indeed that the subsequent profession of the doctrine in the Universal Church creates a presumption that it was held even before it was professed; and it is fair to interpret the early Fathers by the later. This is true, and admits of application to certain other doctrines besides that of the Blessed Trinity in Unity; but there is as little room for antecedent probabilities as for the argument from intimations in the *Quod semper, quod ubique, quod ab omnibus*, as it is commonly understood by English divines. What we need is a sufficient number of Anti-nicene statements, each distinctly anticipating the Athanasian Creed.

Now let us look at the leading facts of the case, in appealing to which I must not be supposed to be ascribing any heresy to the holy men whose words have not always been sufficiently full or exact to preclude the imputation. First, the Creeds of that early day make no mention in their letter of the Catholic doctrine at all. They make no mention indeed of a Three; but that there is any mystery in the doctrine, that the Three are One, that They are coequal, coeternal, all increate, all omnipotent, all incomprehensible, is not stated, and never could {13} be gathered from them. Of course we believe that they imply it, or rather intend it. God forbid we should do otherwise! But nothing in the mere letter of those documents leads to that belief. To give a deeper meaning to their letter, we must interpret them by the times which came after.

Again, there is one and one only great doctrinal Council in Ante-nicene times. It was held at Antioch, in the middle of the third century, on occasion of the incipient innovations of the Syrian heretical school. Now the Fathers there assembled, for whatever reason, condemned, or at least withdrew, when it came into the dispute, the word "Homoüsion," which was received at Nicaea as the special symbol of Catholicism against Arius.[6]

Again, the six great Bishops and Saints of the Ante-nicene Church were St. Irenaeus, St. Hippolytus, St. Cyprian, St. Gregory Thaumaturgus, St. Dionysius of Alexandria, and St. Methodius. Of these, St. Dionysius is accused by St. Basil of having sown the first seeds of Arianism;[7] and St. Gregory is allowed by the same learned Father to have used language concerning our Lord, which he only defends on the plea of an economical object in the writer.[8] St. Hippolytus speaks as if he were ignorant of our Lord's Eternal Sonship;[9] St. Methodius speaks incorrectly at least upon the Incarnation;[10] {14} and St. Cyprian does not treat of theology at all. Such is the incompleteness of the extant teaching of these true saints, and, in their day, faithful witnesses of the Eternal Son.

Again, Athenagoras, St. Clement, Tertullian, and the two SS. Dionysii would appear to be the only writers whose language is at any time exact and systematic enough to remind us of the Athanasian Creed. If we limit our views of the teaching of the Fathers by what they expressly state, St. Ignatius may be considered as a Patripassian, St. Justin arianizes, and St. Hippolytus is a Photinian.

Again, there are three great doctrinal writers of the Antenicene centuries, Tertullian, Origen, and, we may add, Eusebius, though he lived some way into the fourth. Tertullian is heterodox on the doctrine of our Lord's divinity,[11] and indeed ultimately fell altogether into heresy and schism; Origen is, at the very least, suspected, and must be defended and explained rather than cited as a witness of orthodoxy; and Eusebius was an Arian.

Moreover it may be questioned whether any Antenicene father distinctly affirms either the numerical Unity or the Coequality of the Three Persons; except perhaps the heterodox Tertullian, and that chiefly in a work written after he had become a Montanist:[12] yet to satisfy the Anti-roman use of *Quod Semper* &c., surely we ought not to be left for these great articles of doctrine to the testimony of a later age.

{15} Further, Bishop Bull allows that "nearly all ancient Catholics who preceded Arius have the appearance of being ignorant of the invisible and incomprehensible (*immensam*) nature of the Son of God;"[13] an article expressly contained in the Athanasian Creed under the sanction of its anathema.

It must be asked, moreover, how much direct and literal testimony the Ante-nicene Fathers give, one by one, to the divinity of the Holy Spirit. This alone shall be observed, that St. Basil, in the fourth century, finding that if he distinctly called the Third Person in the Blessed Trinity by the name of God, he should be put out of the Church by the Arians, pointedly refrained from doing so on occasion on which his enemies were on the watch; and that, when some Catholics found fault with him, St. Athanasius took his part.[14] Could this possibly have been the conduct of any true Christian, not to say Saint, of a later age? that is, whatever be the true account of it, does it not suggest to us that the testimony of those early times lies very unfavourably for the application of the rule of Vincentius?

Let it not be for a moment supposed that I impugn the orthodoxy of the early divines, or the cogency of their testimony among fair inquirers; but I am trying them by that *unfair* interpretation of Vincentius, which is necessary in order to make him available against the Church of Rome. And now, as to the positive evidence which the Fathers offer in behalf of the Catholic doctrine of the Trinity, it has been drawn out by Dr. Burton, and seems to fall under two heads. One is the general *ascription of glory* the the Three Persons together, both by fathers and churches, and that on continuous tradition and from the earliest times. Under the second fall certain *distinct statements* of *particular* Fathers; thus we find the word "Trinity" used by {16} St. Theophilus, St. Clement, St. Hippolytus, Tertullian, St. Cyprian, Origen, St. Methodius; and the Divine *Circumincessio*, the most distinctive portion of the Catholic doctrine, and the unity of power, or again, of substance, are declared with more or less distinctness by Athenagoras, St. Irenaeus, St. Clement, Tertullian, St. Hippolytus, Origen, and the two SS. Dionysii. This is pretty much the whole of the evidence.

Perhaps it will be said we ought to take the Ante-nicene Fathers as a whole, and interpret one of them by another. This is to assume that they are all of one school, which is a point to be proved; but it is even doubtful whether, on the whole, such a procedure would strengthen the argument. For instance, as to the second head of the two, Tertullian is the most formal and elaborate of these Fathers in his statements of the Catholic doctrine. "It would hardly be possible" says Dr. Burton, after quoting a passage, "for Athanasius himself, or the compiler of the Athanasian Creed, to have delivered the doctrine of the Trinity in stronger terms than these."[15] Yet Tertullian must be considered heterodox on the doctrine of our Lord's eternal existence.[16] If then we are to argue from his instance to that of the other Fathers, we shall be driven to the conclusion that even the most exact statements are worth nothing more than their letter, are a warrant for nothing beyond themselves, and are consistent with heterodoxy where they do not expressly protest against it.

And again, as to the argument derivable from the Doxologies, it must not be forgotten that one of {17} the passages in St. Justin Martyr includes the worship of the Angels. "We worship and adore," he says, "Him and the Son who came from Him and taught us these things, and the host of those other good Angels, who follow and are like Him, and the Prophetic Spirit."[17] A Unitarian[18] might argue from this passage that the glory and worship which the early Church ascribed to our Lord was not more definite than that which St. Justin was ready to concede to creatures.

Thus much on the doctrine of the Holy Trinity. Let us proceed to another example. There are two doctrines which are generally associated with the name of a Father of the fourth and fifth centuries, and which can allege little definite testimony in their behalf before his time,—Purgatory and Original Sin. The dictum of Vincent admits both or excludes both, according as it is or is not rigidly taken; but if used as the "Lesbian Rule," then of course it can be made to admit Original Sin and exclude Purgatory.

On the one hand, the notion of suffering, or trial, or punishment after this life, in the case of the faithful departed, or rather vague forms of the doctrine of Purgatory, has almost a *concensus* in its favour of the four first ages of the Church, though some Fathers state with far greater openness and decision than others. It is, as far as words go, the Confession of St. Clement of Alexandria, Tertullian, St. Perpetua, St. Cyprian,

Origen, Lactantius, St. Hilary, St. Cyril of Jerusalem, St. Ambrose, St. Basil, St. Gregory of Nazianzus, and of Nyssa, St. Chrysostom, St. Jerome, St. Paulinus, and St. Augustine. And, on the other hand, there is an agreement {18} of Fathers from the first that mankind has derived some disadvantage from the sin of Adam.

Next, when we consider the two doctrines more distinctly,—the doctrine that between death and judgment there is a time or state of punishment; and the doctrine that all men, naturally propagated from fallen Adam, are in consequence born destitute of original righteousness,—we find, on the one hand, several, such as Tertullian, St. Perpetua, St. Cyril, St. Hilary, St. Jerome, St. Gregory Nyssen, as far as their words go, definitely declaring a doctrine of Purgatory: whereas no one will say that there is a testimony of the Fathers, equally strong, for the doctrine of Original Sin, though it is difficult to make any definite statement about their teaching without going into a discussion of the subject.

On the subject of Purgatory there were, to speak generally, two schools of opinion; the Greek, which contemplated a trial of fire at the last day through which all were to pass; and the African, resembling more nearly the present doctrine of the Roman Church. And so there were two principal views of Original Sin, the Greek and the African or Latin. Of the Greek, the judgment of Hooker is well known, though it must not be taken in the letter: "The heresy of freewill was a millstone about the Pelagians' neck; shall we therefore give sentence of death inevitable against all those Fathers in the Greek Church which, being mispersuaded, died in the error of freewill?"[19] Bishop Taylor, arguing for an opposite doctrine, bears a like testimony: "Original Sin," he says, as it is at the day commonly explicated, was not the doctrine of the primitive Church; but when Pelagius had puddled the stream, St. Austin was so angry that he stamped

and disturbed it more. And truly, I do not think that the gentlemen that urged against me St. Austin's opinion do well consider
that I profess to {19} follow those Fathers who were before him;
and whom St. Austin did forsake, as I do him, in the question."[20] The same is asserted or allowed by Jansenius, Petavius,
and Walch,[21] men of such different schools that we may surely
take their agreement as proof of the fact. A late writer, after
going through the testimonies of the Fathers one by one, comes
to the conclusion, first, that "the Greek Church in no point
favoured Augustine, except in teaching that from Adam's sin
came death, and (after the time of Methodius,) an extraordinary
and unnatural sensuality also;" next that "the Latin Church
affirmed, in addition, that a corrupt and contaminated soul, and
that, by generation, was carried on to his posterity,"[22] a doctrine
denied by St. Augustine and the Church since; and, lastly, that
neither Greeks nor Latins held the doctrine of imputation. It may
be observed, in addition, that the doctrine of Original Sin appears
neither in the Apostles' nor the Nicene Creed.

One additional specimen shall be given as a sample of many
others:—I betake myself to one of our altars to receive the
Blessed Eucharist; I have no doubt whatever on my mind about
the Gift which that Sacrament contains; I confess to myself my
belief, and I go through the steps on which it is assured to me.
"The Presence of Christ is here, for It follows upon the Consecration; and Consecration is the prerogative of Priests; and Priests
are made by Ordination; and Ordination comes in direct line {20}
from the Apostles. Whatever be our other misfortunes, every link
in our chain is safe; we have the Apostolic Succession, we have a
right form of consecration: therefore we are blessed with the
great Gift." Here the question rises in me, "Who told you about
that Gift?" I answer, "I have learned it from the Fathers: I believe
the Real Presence because they bear witness to it. St. Ignatius
calls it 'the medicine of immortality;' St Irenaeus says that 'our

flesh becomes incorrupt, and partakes of life, and has the hope of the resurrection,' as 'being nourished from the Lord's Body and Blood;' that the Eucharist 'is made up of two things, an earthly and a heavenly;'[23] perhaps Origen and perhaps Magnes, after him, say that it is not a type of our Lord's Body, but His Body; and St. Cyprian uses language as awful as can be spoken, of those who profane it. I cast my lot with them, I believe as they." Thus I reply and then the thought comes upon me a second time, "And do not the same ancient Fathers bear witness to another doctrine, which you disown? Are you not as a hypocrite, listening to them when you will, and deaf when you will not? How are you casting your lot with the Saints, when you go but half-way with them? For of whether of the two do they speak the more frequently of the Real Presence in the Eucharist, or of the Pope's Supremacy? You accept the lesser evidence, you reject the greater."

In truth, scanty as the Anti-nicene notices may be of the Papal Supremacy, they are both more numerous and more definite than the adducible testimonies in favour of the Real Presence. The testimonies to the latter are confined to a few passages such as those just quoted. On the other hand, of a passage in St. Justin, Bishop Kaye remarks, "Le Nourry infers that Justin maintained the doctrine of Transubstantiation; it might in my opinion be more plausibly urged in favour of {21} Consubstantiation, since Justin calls the consecrated elements Bread and Wine, though not common bread and wine[24]. . . We may therefore conclude that, when he calls them the Body and Blood of Christ, he speaks figuratively." "Clement," observes the same author, "says that the Scripture calls wine a mystic *symbol* of the holy blood. . . . Clement gives various interpretations of Christ's expressions in John vi. respecting His flesh and blood; but in no instance does he interpret them literally. . . His notion seems to have been that, by partaking of the bread and wine in the

Eucharist, the soul of the believer is united to the Spirit, and that by this union the principle of immortality is imparted to the flesh."[25] "It has been suggested by some," says Waterland, "that Tertullian understood John vi. merely of faith, or doctrine, or spiritual actions; and it is strenuously denied by others." After quoting the passage, he adds, "All that one can justly gather from this confused passage is that Tertullian interpreted the bread of life in John vi. of the Word, which he sometimes makes to be vocal, and sometimes substantial, blending the ideas in a very perplexed manner; so that he is no clear authority for construing John vi. of doctrines, &c. All that is certain is that he supposes the Word made flesh, the Word incarnate to be the heavenly bread spoken of in that chapter."[26] Origen's general observation relating to that chapter is, that it must not be literally, but figuratively understood."[27] Again, "It is plain enough that Eusebius followed Origen in this matter, and that both of them favoured the same mystical or allegorical construction; whether constantly and uniformly I need not say."[28] I will but add the incidental testimony afforded on a late occasion:—how far the Anglican doctrine of the Eucharist depends on the times before the Nicene {22} Council, how far on the times after it, may be gathered from the circumstance that, when a memorable Sermon was published on the subject, out of about one hundred and forty passages from the Fathers appended in the notes, not in formal proof, but in general illustration, only fifteen were taken from Ante-nicene writers.

With such evidence, the Ante-Nicene testimonies which may be cited in behalf of the authority of the Holy See, need not fear a comparison. Faint they may be one by one, but at least they are various, and are drawn from many times and countries, and thereby serve to illustrate each other, and form a body of proof. Thus St. Clement, in the name of the Church of Rome, writes a letter to the Corinthians, when they were without a bishop; St. Ignatius of Antioch addresses the Roman Church, and it only out of the Churches to which he writes, as "the Church which has the first seat in the place of the country of the Romans;" St. Polycarp of Smyrna betakes himself to the Bishop of Rome on the question of Easter; the heretic Marcion, excommunicated in Pontus, betakes himself to Rome; Soter, Bishop of Rome, sends alms, according to the custom of his Church, to the Churches throughout the empire, and, in the words of Eusebius, "affectionately exhorted those who came to Rome, as a father his children;" the Montanists from Phrygia come to Rome to gain the countenance of its Bishop; Praxeas, from Africa, attempts the like, and for a while is successful; St. Victor, Bishop of Rome, threatens to excommunicate the Asian Churches; St. Irenaeus speaks of Rome as "the greatest Church, the most ancient, the most conspicuous, and founded and established by Peter and Paul," appeals to its tradition, not in contrast indeed, but in preference to that of other Churches, and declares that "in this Church, every Church, that is, the faithful from every side must meet" or "agree {23} together, *propter potiorem principalitatem.*" "O Church, happy in its position," says Tertullian, "into which the Apostles poured out, together with their blood, their whole doctrine." The presbyters of St. Dionysius, Bishop of Alexandria, complain of his doctrine to St. Dionysius of Rome; the latter expostulates with him, and he explains. The Emperor Aurelian leaves "to the Bishops of Italy and of Rome" the decision whether or not Paul of Samosata shall be dispossessed of the see-house at Antioch; St. Cyprian speaks of Rome as "the See of Peter and the principal Church, whence the unity of the priesthood took its rise, . . . whose faith has been commended by the Apostles, to whom faithlessness can have no access;" St. Stephen refuses to receive St. Cyprian's deputation, and separates himself from various Churches of the East; Fortunatus and Felix, deposed by St. Cyprian, have recourse to Rome; Basilides, deposed in Spain, betakes himself to Rome and gains the ear of St. Stephen.

Whatever objections may be made to this or that particular fact, and I do not think any valid ones can be raised, still, on the whole, I consider that a cumulative argument rises from them in favour of the active and the doctrinal authority of Rome, much stronger than any argument which can be drawn from the same era for the doctrine of the Real Presence.

If it be said that the Real Presence appears by the Liturgies of the fourth or fifth century to have been the doctrine of the earlier, since those very forms probably existed from the first in Divine worship, this is doubtless an important truth; but then it is true also that the writers of the fourth and fifth centuries fearlessly assert, or frankly allow, that the prerogatives of Rome were derived from apostolic times, and that because it was the See of St. Peter.

Moreover, if the resistance of St. Cyprian and {24} Firmilian to the Church of Rome, in the question of baptism by heretics, be urged as an argument against her primitive authority, or the earlier resistance of Polycrates of Ephesus, let it be considered, first, whether all authority does not necessarily lead to resistance; next, whether St. Cyprian's own doctrine is not more weighty than his act; thirdly, whether he was not already in error in the main question under discussion, and Firmilian also; and, lastly, which is the chief point, whether, in like manner, we may not object against the Real Presence the words of Tertullian, who explains, "This is my Body," by "a figure of my Body," and of Origen, who speaks of "our drinking Christ's Blood not only in the rite of the Sacraments, but also when we receive his discourses,"[29] and says that "that Bread which God the Word acknowledges as His Body is the Word that nourishes souls,"[30]—passages which admit of a Catholic interpretation when the Catholic doctrine is once proved, but which *primâ facie* run counter to that doctrine.

It does not seem possible, then, to avoid the conclusion that, whatever the proper key for harmonizing the records and documents of the early and later Church, and true as the dictum of Vincentius must be considered in the abstract, and possible as its application might be in his own age, when he might almost ask the primitive centuries for their testimony, it is hardly available now or effective of any satisfactory result. The solution it offers is as difficult as the original problem.

A second hypothesis, far more widely adopted, not less plausible, and in a certain measure reconcilable with the former, is that of an early corruption of Christianity from external sources, Oriental, Platonic, and Polytheistic; an hypothesis which is certainly sufficient in the abstract to account both for variations which may exist in doctrine and {25} practice, and for the growth of opinion on particular points. Some light may be thrown on this hypothesis as we proceed; meanwhile, however freely it may be assumed and largely applied, it has no claims on our attention till it is drawn out scientifically;—till we are distinctly informed what the real Christian doctrine or evangelical message is, or if there be any; from what sources it is drawn; how those sources are ascertained to us; and what is a corruption.

A third hypothesis, which has been put forward by divines of the Church of Rome, is what has been called the *Disciplina Arcani*. It is maintained that doctrines which are associated with the later ages of the Church were really in the Church from the first, but not publicly taught, and that for various reasons: as, for the sake of reverence, that sacred subjects might not be profaned by the heathen; and for the sake of catechumens, that they might not be oppressed or carried away by a sudden communication of the whole circle of revealed truth. And indeed the fact of concealment can hardly be denied, in whatever degree it took the shape of a definite rule, which might vary with persons and places. That it existed even as a rule, as regards the Sacraments, seems to be confessed on all hands. That it existed in other respects, as a practice, is plain from the nature of the case, and from the writings of the Apologists. Minucius Felix and Arnobius, in controversy with Pagans, imply a denial that then the Christians used altars; yet Tertullian speaks expressly of the *Ara Dei* in the Church. What can we say, but that the Apologists deny altars *in the sense* in which they ridicule them; or, that they deny that altars *such as* in the Pagan altars were tolerated by Christians? And, in like manner, Minucius allows that there were no temples among Christians; yet they are distinctly recognised in the edicts of the Dioclesian era, and are known to have {26} existed at a still earlier date. It is the tendency of every dominant system, such as the Paganism of the Ante-nicene centuries, to force its opponents into the most hostile and jealous attitude, from the apprehension which they naturally feel, lest, in these points in which they approximate towards it, they should be misinterpreted and overborne by its authority. The very fault now found with clergymen of the English Church, who wish to conform their practices to her rubrics, and their doctrines to her divines of the seventeenth century, is, that whether they mean it or no, whether legitimately or no, still in matter of fact, they will be sanctioning and encouraging the religion of Rome, in which there are similar doctrines and practices, more definite and more influential; so that, at any rate, it is inexpedient to attempt what is sure to be mistaken. That is, they are required to exercise a *disciplina Arcani*; and a similar reserve was inevitable on the part of the Catholic Church, at a time when priests and altars and rites all around it were devoted to malignant and incurable superstitions. It was wrong indeed to deny, but it was a duty to withold, the ceremonial of Christianity; and Apologists might be sometimes tempted to deny absolutely what at furthest could only be denied under conditions. An idolatrous Paganism tended to repress the externals of Christianity, as at this day, the presence of Protestantism is said to repress, though for another reason, the exhibition of the Roman Catholic religion.

On various grounds, then, it is certain that portions of the Church system were held back in primitive times, and of course this fact goes some way to account for that apparent variation and growth of doctrine which embarrasses us when we would consult history for the true idea of Christianity; yet it is no key to the whole difficulty, as we find it, for an obvious reason;—the variations continue {27} beyond the time when it is conceivable that the discipline was in force.

The following Essay is directed towards a solution of the difficulty which has been stated,—the difficulty which lies in the way of using the testimony of our most natural informant concerning the doctrine and worship of Christianity, viz. the history of eighteen hundred years. The view on which it is written has at all times, perhaps, been implicitly adopted by theologians, and, I believe, has recently been illustrated by several distinguished writers of the continent, such as De Maistre and Möhler: viz. that the increase and expansion of the Christian Creed and Ritual, and the variations which have attended the process in the case of individual writers and Churches, are the necessary attendants on any philosophy or polity which takes possession of the intellect and heart and has had any wide or extended dominion; that, from the nature of the human mind, time is necessary for the full comprehension and perfection of great ideas; and that the highest and most wonderful truth, though communicated to the world once for all by inspired teachers, could not be comprehended all at once by the recipients, but, as received and transmitted by minds not inspired and through media which were human, have required only the longer time and deeper thought for their full elucidation. This may be called the *Theory of Developments*; and, before proceeding to treat it, two remarks may be in place.

First, it is undoubtedly an hypothesis to account for a difficulty; and such too are the various explanations given by astronomers from Ptolemy to Newton of the apparent motions of the heavenly bodies. But it is as unphilosophical on that account to object to the one as to object to the other. Nay, more so; for an hypothesis, such as the present, rests {28} upon facts as well as accounts for them, and independent of the need of it, is urged upon us by the nature of the case. Nor is it more reasonable to express surprise, that at this time of day a theory is necessary, granting for argument's sake that the theory is novel, than to have directed a similar wonder in disparagement of the theory of gravitation, or the Plutonian theory in geology. Doubtless, the theory of the Secret and the theory of Developments are expedients, and so is the dictum of Vincentius; so is the art of grammar or the use of the quadrant; it is an expedient to enable us to solve what has now become a necessary and an anxious problem. For three hundred years the documents and the facts of Christianity have been exposed to a jealous scrutiny; works have been judged spurious which once were received without a question; facts have been discarded or modified which were once first principles in argument; new facts and new principles have been brought to light; philosophical views and polemical discussions of various tendencies have been maintained with more or less sucess. Not only have the relative situation of controversies and theologies altered, but infidelity itself is in a different,—I am obliged to say in a more hopeful position,—as regards Christianity. The facts of revealed religion, though in their substance unaltered, present a less compact and orderly front to the attacks of its enemies, and allow of the introduction of new conjectures and theories concerning its sources and its rise. The state of things is not as it was, when an appeal lay to the supposed works of the Areopagite, or the primitive Decretals, or to St. Dionysius's answers to Paul, or to the Coena Domini of St. Cyprian. The assailants of dogmatic truth have got the start of its adherents of whatever Creed; philosophy is completing what criticism has begun; and apprehensions are not unreasonably excited lest we should have a new world to conquer {29} before we have weapons for the warfare. Already infidelity has its views and ideas, on which it arranges the facts of ecclesiastical history; and it is sure to consider the absence of any antagonist theory as an evidence of the reality of its own. That the hypothesis, here to be adopted, accounts not only for the Athenasian Creed, but for the Creed of Pope Pius, is no fault of those who adopt it. No one has power over the issues of his principles; we cannot manage our argument, and have as much of it as we please and no more. An argument is needed, unless Christianity is to abandon the province of argument; and those who find fault with the explanation here offered of its historical phenomena will find it their duty to provide one of their own.

And as no aim at Roman Catholic doctrine need be supposed to have given a direction to the inquiry, so neither can a reception of that doctrine be immediately based on its results. It would be the work of a life to apply the Theory of Developments so carefully to the writings of the Fathers, and the history of controversies and councils, as thereby to vindicate the reasonableness of every decision of Rome; much less can such an undertaking be imagined by one who, in the middle of his days, is beginning life again. So much, however, might be gained even from an Essay like the present,—a solution of such a number of the reputed corruptions of Rome, as might form a fair ground for trusting her, where the investigation had not been pursued.

---

[1] On "The Difficulties of Latitudinarianism," vide Tracts for the Times, No. 85, Lecture 2. <Tract 85, "Lectures on the Scripture Proofs of the Doctrine of the Church," Lecture II, "The Difficulties of Latitudinarianism," pp. 15-26. In

citing from the Tracts, Newman refers to their edition in six volumes (Oxford, 1840-42). It was reissued in facsimile by AMS Press, New York, 1969.>

2 Church of the Fathers, p. 327.

3 Proph. Office, pp. 68, 69, ed. 2.

4 Ibid, p. 221.

5 British Critic, July 1836, p. 193. <"The Brothers' Controversy, being a genuine corespondence between a Clergyman of the Church of England and a Layman of Unitarian Opinions.">

6 This of course has been disputed, as is the case with almost all facts which bear upon the decision of the controversy. I shall not think it necessary to notice the possibility of the fact of objections on questions upon which the world may now be said to be agreed; e.g. the arianizing tone of Eusebius.

7 σχεδὸν ταυτησὶ τῆς νῦν περιθρυλλουμένης ἀσεβείας, τῆς κατὰ τὸ Ἀνόμοιον λέγω, οὗτος ἐστὶν, ὅσα γε ἡμεῖς ἴσμεν, ὁ πρῶτος ἀνθρώποις τὰ σπέρματα παρασχών. Ep. ix. 2.

8 Bull, Defens. F. N. ii 12, § 6. <George Bull (1634-1710), Defensio fidei nicenae (1685), in The Works, ed. E. Burton (Oxford, 1827). vol. V.>

9 "The authors who make the generation temporary, and speak not expressly of any other, are these following: Justin, Athenagoras, Theophilus, Tatian, Tertullian, and Hippolytus."—Waterland, vol. i. part 2, p. 104. <Daniel Waterland (1683-1740) was a Cambridge theologian and chaplain ordinary to the King. Newman refers to Waterland's Critical History of the Athanasian Creed (1723) in The Works of the Rev. Daniel Waterland (Oxford, 1843).>

10 "Levia sunt," says Maran in his defence, "Quae in Sanctissimam Trinitatem hic liber peccare dicitur, paulo graviora quae in mysterium Incarnationis." Div. Jes. Christ, p. 527. Shortly after, p. 530, "In tertiâ oratione nonnulla legimus Incarnationem Domini spectantia, quae subabsurdè dicta fateor, nego impiè cogitata." <Prudent Maran (1683-1762), Maurist Benedictine, Divinitas Domini Nostri Jesu Christi manifesta in Scripturis et Traditione . . . (1746).>

11 Bishop Bull, who is tender towards him, allows, "Ut quod res est dicam, cum Valentinianis hic et reliquo gnosticorum grege aliquatenus locutus est Tertullianus; in re ipsâ tamen cum Catholicis omninò sensit."–Defens. F. N. iii. 10, § 15. <see note 8 above.>

12 Adv. Prax.

13 Defens. F. N. iv. 3, § 1. <See note 8 above.>

14 Basil. ed. Ben. vol. 3, p. xcvj.

15 Ante-nicene Test. to the Trinity, p. 69. <Edward Burton (1794-1836), Testimonies of the Ante-Nicene Fathers to the Trinity (1831).>

16 "Quia et Pater Deus est, et judex Deus est, non tamen ideo Pater et judex semper, qui Deus semper. Nam nec Pater potuit esse ante Filium, nec judex ante delictum. Fuit autem tempus, cum et delictum et Filius non fuit, quod

judicem, et qui Patrem Dominum faceret."—*Contr. Herm.* 3.

[17] Vid. infra, towards the end of the Essay, where more will be said on the passage.

[18] There seems no reason why we should not allow the title Unitarian as we allow that of Presbyterian. Error is generally partial truth.

[19] Of Justification, 26. <Richard Hooker (1653-1600), *A Learned Discourse on Justification, Works, and how the Foundation of Faith is overthrown* (1590) in *The Works*, ed. W. S. Dobson (London: G. Cowie, 1825), II, pp. 498-547.>

[20] Works, vol. ix. p. 396. <Jeremy Taylor, *An Answer to a Letter Written by the R. R. the L^d B^p of Rochester, concerning the Chapter of Original Sin in the 'Unum Neccessarium'* (1656), in *The Works*, ed., R. Heber (London: C. J. Rivington, 1826), vol. ix, pp. 361-401).>

[21] Quamvis igitur quam maximè fallantur Pelagiani, quum asserant, peccatum originale ex Augustini profluxisse ingenio, antiquam vero ecclesiam illud plane nescivisse; diffiteri tamen nemo potest, apud Graecos patres imprimis inveniri loca, quae Pelagianismo favere videntur. Hinc et C. Jansenius, 'Graeci,' inquit, 'nisi caute legantur et intelligantur, praebere possunt occasionem errori Pelagiano;' et D. Petavius dicit, 'Graeci originalis fere criminis raram, nec disertam mentionem scriptis suis attigerunt.'—*Walch. Miscell. Sacr.* p. 607. <Johann Georg Walch (1693-1775), *Miscellanea sacra, sive Commentationum ad historiam ecclesiasticam sanctioresque disciplinas pertinentium collectio* (Amsterdam, 1744).>

[22] Horn, Comment. de Pecc. Orig. 1801, p. 98. <Iohannis Horn Verdensis, *Commentatio de sententiis eorum patrum quorum auctoritas ante Augustinum plurimum valuit de peccato originali* (Göttingen: H. Dietirich, 1801).>

[23] Haer. iv. 18, § 5.

[24] Justin Martyr, ch. 4.

[25] Clem. Alex. ch. 11.

[26] Works, vol. vii. p. 118-120. <See note 9 above.>

[27] Ibid. p. 121.

[28] Ibid. p. 127.

[29] Numer. Hom. xvi. 9 <PG 12:701>

[30] Interp. Com. in Matt. 85 <PG 13:1754-55>

CHAPTER I.

ON THE DEVELOPMENT OF IDEAS.

SECTION I.

ON THE PROCESS OF DEVELOPMENT IN IDEAS.

IT is a characteristic of our minds to be ever engaged in passing judgments on the things which come before them. No sooner do we learn, but we judge; we allow nothing to stand by itself: we compare, contrast, abstract, generalize, adjust, classify; and we view all our knowledge in the associations with which these processes have invested it.

Of the judgments thus exercised, some are mere opinions, which come and go, or remain with us only till an accident displaces them, whatever influence they may exert meanwhile. Others are firmly fixed in our minds and have a hold over us, whether they are principles of conduct, or are views of life and the world, or fall under the general head of belief. These habitual judgments often go by the name of ideas, and shall be called so here.

Of these ideas,—religious, political, or otherwise relating to human affairs,—some are real, that is, represent facts existing; and others are mere imaginations, and stand for nothing external to themselves. Thus the heathen mythology, or the Cartesian system of vortices, supplied a variety {31} of ideas, which were but fanciful and unreal; whereas the idea of a saint, or a hero, or a tyrant, or what are called the laws of motion, are the representatives of things.

Ideas thus described, being of the nature of judgments, must, properly speaking, be considered as true by those who hold them. The absence, however of this condition of course does not change their nature: thus poets are familiar with fable; orators and pleaders make a case or embellish a character; and philosophers lay down some great principle, not necessarily as representing a fact, but as a generalization of phenomena, convenient, fact or not, for the purpose of science.

The number of persons holding an idea is no warrant for its objective character, else the many never could be wrong; for uniformity of education, or the sympathy kindled by enthusiasm, may carry many minds into one state, in which belief in certain ideas, and the mistake of formulae or usages for external truths, will be natural and necessary. Such are popular superstitions; or the law of honour, as pressed by men of the world; or the heated notions created by mob oratory; all of which are baseless and untrue as they are influential. Again, a whole train of investigation or inference may depend on the original admission of some one proposition which is false; and the consequent unanimity with which separate minds regard and treat the same matters may be unfairly taken as a concurrent evidence of the truth of the conclusions at which they arrive.

But when one and the same idea is held by persons who are independent of each other, and are variously circumstanced, and have possessed themselves of it by different ways, and when it presents itself to them under very different aspects, without losing its substantial unity and its identity, and when it is thus variously presented, yet {32} recommended to persons similarly circumstanced; and when it is presented to persons variously circumstanced, under aspects, discordant indeed at first sight, but reconcilable after such explanations as their respective states of mind require; then it seems to have a claim to be considered the representative of an objective truth.

For instance, there is a general sentiment obtaining at very different times and places, and variously expressed, concerning the danger of unmixed prosperity, or security, or high spirits; as signified in the proverbs, "Pride will have a fall," and "Many a slip," or the Scotch saying about persons who are "fie," or the Greek φθονερὸν ὁ δαίμων, and the like; which is proved by that manifold testimony to be well founded, or to be a real law in human affairs.

"Great is Diana of the Ephesians," is an instance, on the other hand, of a popular cry long sustained, to which numbers and energy contribute no credibility.

An idea ever presents itself under different aspects to different minds, and in proportion to that variety will be the proof of its reality and its distinctness. On the other hand, meager and monotonous statements, and those simply reiterated, as in the case of the Ephesian clamour, betoken ideas which are unreal, or which are not properly understood by the speakers. Or such characteristics denote mystery, that is, dim information taken on faith; as we see in the theological enunciations of Scripture.

Ideas are not ordinarily brought home to the mind, except through the medium of a variety of aspects; like bodily substances, which are not seen except under the clothing of their properties and influences, and can be walked round and surveyed on opposite sides and in different perspectives and in contrary lights. And as views of a material object may be taken from points so remote or so {33} distinct that they seem at first sight incompatible, and especially as their shadows will be disproportionate or even monstrous, and yet all these will be harmonized together by taking account of the point of vision or the surface of projection, so also the representations of an idea, even all the misrepresentations, are capable of a mutual reconciliation and adjustment, and of a resolution into the subject to which they belong, and their contrariety, when explained, is an argument for

its substantiveness and integrity, and their variety for its originality and power.

For instance, persons who have not cultivated the science of
music are often slow to believe that harmonies of its masters are
more than a display of skill, or than literally a composition,
which falls in with the fancy of particular persons, and is taken
up by others as a fashion; as though its laws were conventional,
and proficiency in it a mere successful application of general
talent to a medium of exhibition accidentally chosen, and as if
the satisfaction it affords were felt not spontaneously but upon
rule, the mere approbation of those who were witnessing
instances of conformity to principles which they had themselves
arbitrarily propounded: that is, they do not believe in the
existence of truths or laws about the beauty of sounds in the
nature of things, external to particular minds, affecting various
persons variously, and mastered by them in various degrees, as
the case may be. An instance in point may be mentioned of a
person under this impression, who was greatly astonished to be
told by another who had some knowledge of the art, and a
sensibility to musical creations, that, in spite of this, he was not
able to compose; for he took it for granted that any one of fair
abilities who knew the rules could put them into practice, and
impart to himself a pleasure which was of his own making. But
ideas which are conversant {34} with realities are not ours at will, but
then only and as far as is given us; and they present themselves very
variously, and in various measures to individual minds.

Since an idea, as has already been said, cannot be viewed
except under particular aspects, the formal statements under
which it is conveyed are practically identical with itself. They
introduce us to that idea from which they are derived, and, so far
as they seem to oppose, they correct each other, and serve to
impress a fuller and more exact representation of their original
upon the mind.

And hence, if the illustration on which we are proceeding be correct, there is no one aspect such, as to go the depth of a real idea, no one term or proposition which can duly and fully represent it; though of course one representation of it will be more just and appropriate than another, and though when an idea is very complex, it is allowable to consider its distinct aspects as if separate ideas, for the sake of convenience. Thus with all our intimate knowledge of animal life, and the structure of particular animals, we cannot give a true definition of any one of them, but are forced to enumerate properties and accidents by way of description. Nor can we enclose in a formula that intellectual fact, or system of thought, which we call the Platonic philosophy, or that historical phenomenon of doctrine and conduct which we call the heresy of Montanus or of Manes. Again, of Protestantism and Lutheranism in its doctrine of justification, this would be an approximation to the truth; but it is plain that to argue or act as if these were adequate definitions would be a serious mistake. Sometimes an attempt has been made to ascertain the "leading idea," as it has ben called, of Christianity; a remarkable essay as directed towards a divine religion, when, even in the instance of the {35} works of man, the task is beyond us. Thus, the one idea of the Gospel has been decided by some to be the restoration of our fallen race, by others philanthropy, by others the spirituality of true religious service, by others the salvation of the elect, by others the union of the soul with God. All these representations are truths, as being aspects of Christianity, but none of them is the whole truth. For Christianity has many aspects: it has its imaginative side, its philosophical, its ethical, its political; it is solemn, and it is cheerful; it is indulgent, and it is strict; it is light, and it is dark; it is love, and it is fear.

When an idea, whether real or not, is of a nature to interest and possess the mind, it is said to have life, that is, to live in the mind which is the recipient of it. Thus, mathematical ideas, real as they are, cannot be called living, for they have no influence and lead to nothing. But when some great enunciation, whether true or false, about human nature, or present good, or government, or duty, or religion, is carried forward into the public throng and draws attention, then it is not only passively admitted in this or that form into the minds of men, but it becomes a living principle within them, leading them to an ever-new contemplation of itself, an acting upon it and a propagation of it. Such is the doctrine of the natural bondage of the will, or of individual responsibility, or of the immortality of the soul, or of the rights of man, or of the divine rights of kings, or of the hypocrisy and tyranny of priestcraft, or of the lawfulness of self-indulgence,—doctrines which are of a nature to arrest, attract, or persuade, and have so far the *primâ facie* appearance of reality that they may be looked at on many sides and strike various minds very variously. Let one such idea get possession of the popular mind, or the mind of any set of persons, and it is not difficult to {36} understand the effects which will ensue. There will be a general agitation of thought, and an action of mind both upon itself and upon other minds. New lights will be brought to bear upon the original idea, aspects will multiply, and judgments will accumulate. There will be a time of confusion, when conceptions and misconceptions are in conflict; and it is uncertain whether anything is to come of the idea at all, or which view of it is to get the start of the others. After a while some definite form of doctrine emerges; and, as time proceeds, one view of it will be modified or expanded by another, and then, combined with a third, till the idea in which they centre will be to each mind separately what at first it was only to all together. It will be surveyed, too, in its relation to other doctrines or facts, to other natural laws or established rules, to the varying circumstances of times and places, to other religions, polities, philosophies, as the case may be. How it stands affected towards other systems, how

it affects them, how far it coalesces with them, how far it
tolerates, when it interferes with them, will be gradually wrought
out. It will be questioned and criticized by enemies, and explained by well-wishers. The multitude of opinions formed
concerning it, in these respects and many others, will be collected, compared, sorted, sifted, selected, or rejected, and gradually
attached to it, or separated from it, in the minds of individuals
and of the community. It will, in proportion to its native vigour
and subtlety, introduce itself into the framework and details of
social life, changing public opinion and supporting or undermin-
ing the foundations of established order. Thus in time it has
grown into an ethical code, or into a system of government, or
into a theology, or into a ritual, according to its capabilities; and
this system, or body of thought, theoretical and practical, thus
laboriously gained, will after all be only the adequate representation of the original idea, being {37} nothing else than what that
very idea *meant* from the first,—its exact image as seen in a
combination of the most diversified aspects, with the suggestions and
corrections of many minds, and the illustration of many trials.

This process is called the development of an idea, being the
germination, growth, and perfection of some living, that is,
influential truth, or apparent truth, in the minds of men during a
sufficient period. And it has this necessary characteristic,—that,
since its province is the busy scene of human life, it cannot
develop at all, except either by destroying, or modifying and
incorporating with itself, existing modes of thinking and acting.
Its development then is not like a mathematical theorem worked
out on paper, in which each successive advance is a pure
evolution from a foregoing, but it is carried on through individuals and bodies of men; it employs their minds as instruments, and
depends upon them while it uses them. And so as regards their
existing opinions, principles, measures, and institutions, it
develops in establishing relations between them and itself, in

giving them a meaning, in creating what may be called a jurisdiction over them, in throwing off from itself what is utterly heterogeneous in them. It grows when it incorporates; and its purity consists, not in isolation, but in its continuity and sovereignty. This it is which imparts to the history both of states and of religions its especially turbulent or polemical character. Such is the explanation of the wranglings whether of Schools or of Parliaments. It is the warfare of ideas, striving for mastery, each of them enterprising, engrossing, imperious, more or less incompatible with the rest, and rallying followers or rousing foes according as it acts upon the faith, the prejudices, or the interests of individuals.

Moreover, an idea not only modifies, but, as has been implied, is modified or at least influenced by {38} the state of things in which it is carried out, and depends in various ways on the circumstances around it. Its development proceeds quickly or slowly; the order of succession in its separate stages is irregular; it will show differently in a small sphere of action and in an extended; it may be interrupted, retarded, mutilated, distorted, by external violence; it may be enfeebled by the effort of ridding itself of domestic foes; it may be impeded and swayed or even absorbed by counter energetic ideas; it may be coloured by the received tone of thought into which it comes, or depraved by the intrusion of foreign principles, or at length shattered by the development of some original fault within it.

But, whatever be the risk of corruption from intercourse with the world around it, such a risk must be undergone, if it is duly to be understood, and much more if it is to be full exhibited. It is elicited by trial, and struggles into perfection. Nor does it escape the collision of opinion even in its earlier years; nor does it remain truer to itself, and more one and the same, though protected from vicissitude and change. It is indeed sometimes said that the stream is clearest near the spring. Whatever use may fairly be made of this image, it does not apply to the history of a philosophy or sect, which, on the contrary, is more equable, and purer, and stronger, when its bed has become deep, and broad, and full. It necessarily rises out of an existing state of things, and for a time, savours of the soil. Its vital element needs disengaging from what is foreign and temporary, and is employed in efforts after freedom, more vigorous and hopeful as its years increase. Its beginnings are no measure of its capabilities, nor of its scope. At first, no one knows what it is, or what it is worth. It remains perhaps for a time quiescent: it tries, as it were, its limbs, and proves the ground under it, and feels its way. From time to time, it makes essays {39} which fail, and are in consequence abandoned. It seems in suspense which way to go; it wavers, and at length strikes out in one definite direction. In time it enters upon strange territory; points of controversy alter their bearing; parties rise and fall about it; dangers and hopes appear in new relations, and old principles reappear under new forms; it changes with them in order to remain the same. In a higher world it is otherwise; but here below to live is to change, and to be perfect is to have changed often.

I conclude with an example: No one but will allow that Wesleyanism represents an idea, a doctrine, system, and polity; no one but will connect it with the well-known divine and preacher whose name it bears. Yet, when we look back upon its course during the hundred years since it commenced, how many are the changes and vicissitudes through which the man is connected with his work! so much so that it is a most difficult task, and one which perhaps must be reserved for a later age, duly to review its history,—to say what really belongs and what is foreign to it, to find a key for the whole and a clue for the succession of its parts. The event alone still future, which will bring its completion, will also bring its interpretation.

When Mr. Wesley began his religious movement at Oxford,[1] first, he visited the sick and prisoners, communicated weekly, fasted on Wednesday and Friday, employed himself in meditation and prayer, and apparently meditated a single life, being, as he afterward considered, in a state of great spiritual ignorance. Moreover, he travelled on foot that he might save money for the poor, doubted the lawfulness of secular studies, and, though in orders, {40} resolved for his soul's sake, never to undertake parochial duty. We read, too, of his letting his hair flow on his shoulders when it was the universal fashion to wear it dressed.

Next he goes as a Missionary to Georgia to convert the Indians; and on his voyage, progressing in his asceticism, he wholly leaves off flesh and wine, sleeps on the floor, and rises at four in the morning. Then, he is zealous for the Rubric, withholding Baptism from children except by immersion, repelling one Dissenter from the communion, unless he were re-baptized, and refusing to bury another. Then, he forms an attachment to a lady who came to him for religious advice, disappoints her in obedience to his Moravian directors, denies her the communion on the ground of duplicity towards himself, is prosecuted for defamation, and escapes for England while the trial is pending.

On his return, he falls under the influence of Boehler, and experiences what he considers conversion and assurance. He preaches the new-birth, and the phenomenon of convulsions follows among his hearers; pulpits are closed against him, and he preaches in the fields. Converts lead to religious companies; companies to meeting-houses; meeting-houses to a lay-ministry, to which he reluctantly consents. The class system and itinerancy follow.

Four years had hardly passed since his return from America, and all this was done. Methodism had come into existence as a society and as a doctrine; and its first extravagances had given way to order, though to miracles it still laid claim. Charges of favouring Pope and Pretender are preferred; and the new

Societies have to avow in emphatic terms their attachment to the house of Hanover and the Church of England. Other calumnies, however, succeed: mobs rise and ill-treat the new religionists in various places.

The theology of the sect becomes of a definite {41} character; it consists in the doctrines of the sensible new-birth, the suddenness of conversion, assurance, the gift of perfection, and, what these tenets imply, the inefficacy of forms under the gospel, whether rites, polity, or even creeds.

When he is towards fifty, Mr. Wesley marries: his wife is a jealous, violent-tempered woman, who, at the end of twenty years, leaves him for good, running off with his papers.

Soon after his return from America, he had commenced the Annual Conference of Preachers, regulated, if the word be not a misnomer here, on this principle, that in matters of practice each should be ruled, as far as his conscience would allow, by the majority; but in matters of opinion by himself alone. He establishes this body with the avowal that his followers will either leaven the whole Church or be thrust out; after a time, he begins to doubt whether presbyters may not ordain; next, he obtains orders for some of his lay-assistants from a so-styled Bishop of Arcadia; at length, when he is past eighty, he himself consecrates one of his followers as Bishop for the ordination of clergy in his American congregations.

Even in his own day, and much more since his death, his variations of opinion become successive excuses for fresh sects. What he had received from tradition, or learned from contemporaries, or crudely imagined, or thrown out hastily, became matter for development in others. Thus, whereas he had separated from Whitfield from hatred of Calvinism and had been not unwilling to praise, not only St. Ignatius Loyola, but Pelagius and Servetus, Relly, re-acting from Whitfield, extended the principle of comprehension, and gave birth to the Universalists in the United States, who now number at least five hundred and fifty Churches. Again, when Bell professed the gifts of miracles and prophecy, Maxfield supported him, and seceded with {42} a number of brethren, professing that man might be absolutely perfect, infallible, and beyond temptation.

Immediately on Wesley's death arose an agitation in favour of conferring on preachers the administration of the Sacraments; an innovation which he had on the whole steadily withstood. Kilham, who wrote a book in behalf of the measure, with the significant title of "Progress of Liberty," was expelled by the Conference, and, at the end of six years after Wesley's death, had founded the Methodist New Connexion. The principle which led to this secession from the body worked its way within it, and had its slow development in the course of twenty years. In 1816 the Conference admitted it; and then a secession took place, in the opposite direction, on the principle of respecting, as Wesley had enjoined, the prerogatives of the Established Church. The new body called themselves "Church Methodists," while they named the parent-society which they had left "Dissenting Methodists," and professed to be "members of the Church of England" like Mr. Wesley, having "no design to interfere with the Church or with dissenting societies."

Others have wished to perpetuate the bodily extravagances which attended Wesley's first preaching; and hence the Primitive Methods, or Ranters, who even admit of female preachers, and form the largest body of the Wesleyan family in Great Britain which has separated from the Conference. Another secession is that of the Bryanites; another of the Independent Methodists, who reject a "hired ministry," as they call it, and admit nothing but lay teachers. And another is that of the Protestant Methodists, who objected, or at least objected in 1828, to ministerial education, the growth of a sacerdotal spirit, and the ornaments of worship, as displayed in the Conference Connexion. Later still is Dr. Warren's secession, which has issued in the {43} Wesleyan Association, founded on the general principle of the New Connexion.

Though these various seceding bodies amount in this country to above a third of the mother-persuasion, they are most of them comparatively small, and would never be confounded with it. The Conference Connexion remains the representative of the Wesleyan ideas; in its gradual independence and growing substantiveness, in its conservative spirit in politics, in its doctrines of the new-birth, justification, and assurance, it is following or developing the principles of its founder. In its rivalry of the Establishment, it has acted against his feelings and advice; in the growth of the hierarchical element, it has abandoned his principle for his example; in its violence against the Church of Rome, it has forgotten the first years of his religious life; in its care for ministerial education, and its relinquishment of field-preaching, it shows that the point is reached in its course when order takes the place of enthusiasm.

Varieties in a teacher, and schisms among his followers, are an evidence of life; though life is no criterion of truth, for unreal but plausible, or isolated ideas may powerfully affect multitudes. On the other hand, they do not argue the absence of one real idea in the movement in which they are found, but only that this man or that is not infallible.

SECTION II.

ON THE KINDS OF DEVELOPMENT IN IDEAS.

To attempt an accurate analysis or complete enumeration of the processes of thought, whether purely speculative or practical, which come under the notion of development, exceeds the pretensions of an Essay like the present; but, without some general {44} view of the various mental exercises which go by the name, we shall have no security against confusion in our reasoning and exposure to criticism.

1. First, then it must be borne in mind that the word is commonly used, and is used here, in three senses indiscriminately, from defect of our language; on the one hand for the process of development, on the other for the result; and again either generally, for a development true or not true, (that is faithful or unfaithful to the ideas from which it started,) or exclusively for a development deserving the name. A false or unfaithful development is called a corruption.

2. Next, it is plain that *mathematical* developments, that is, the system of truths drawn out from mathematical definitions or equations, do not fall under our present subject, though altogether analogous to it. There can be no corruption in such development, because they are conducted on strict demonstration; and the conclusions in which they terminate, being necessary, cannot be declensions from the original idea.

3. Nor, of course, do *physical* developments, as the growth of an animal or vegetable nature, come into consideration; excepting that, as mathematical, they may be taken as illustrations of those developments to which we have to direct our attention.

4. Nor have we to consider *material* developments, which, though effected by human contrivance, are still physical; as the development, as it is called, of the national resources. We speak, for instance, of Ireland, the United States, or the valley of the Indus, as admitting of a great development; by which we mean that those countries have fertile tracts, or abundant products, or broad and deep rivers, or central positions for commerce, or capacious and commodious harbours, the materials and instruments of wealth, and these turned to insufficient account. Development in this case will {45} proceed by establishing marts, cutting canals, laying down railroads, erecting factories, forming

docks, and similar works, by which the natural riches of the country may be made to yield the largest return and to exert the greatest influence. In this sense, art is the development of nature, that is, its adaptation to the purposes of utility and beauty, the human intellect being the developing power.

5. When such developments as have last been mentioned are connected with some continuous intellectual process on which they depend, they are developments of an idea, and may be called *political*; as we see them in the growth of States or the changes of a Constitution. Barbarians descend into southern regions from cupidity, and their warrant is the sword: this is no intellectual process, nor is it the mode of envelopment exhibited in civilized communities. Where civilization exists, reason, in some shape or other, is the incentive or the pretence of development. When an empire enlarges, it is on the call of its allies, or for the balance of power, or from the necessity of a demonstration of strength, or from a fear for its frontiers. It lies uneasily in its territory, it is ill-shaped, it has unreal boundary lines, deficient communication between its principal points, or defenceless or turbulent neighbours. Thus, of old time, Euboea was necessary for Athens, and Cythera for Sparta; and Augustus left his advice, as a legacy, to confine the Empire between the Atlantic, the Rhine and Danube, the Euphrates, and the Arabian and African deserts. In this day, we hear of the Rhine being the natural boundary of France, and the Indus of our Eastern empire; and we predict that, in the event of a war, Prussia will change her outlines in the map of Europe. The development is material; but an idea gives unity and force to its movement.

And so in national politics, a late writer remarks {46} of the Parliament of 1628-29, in its contest with Charles, that, so far from encroaching on the just powers of a limited monarch, it never hinted at the securities which were necessary for its measures. However, "twelve years more of repeated aggressions," he adds, "taught the Long Parliament what a few sagacious men might perhaps have already suspected; that they must recover more of their ancient constitution from oblivion; that they must sustain "its partial weakness by new securities; that, in order to render the existence of monarchy compatible with that of freedom, they must not only strip it of all it had usurped, but of something that was its own."[2] Whatever be the worth of this author's theory, his facts or representations are an illustration of a political development.

Again, at the present day, that Ireland should have a population of one creed, and a Church of another, is felt to be a political arrangement so unsatisfactory, that all parties seem to agree that either the population will develop in power or the Establishment in influence.

Developments in polities, though really the growth of ideas, are often capricious and intricate from the nature of their subject-matter. They are influenced by the character of sovereigns, the rise and fall of statesmen, the fate of battles, and the numberless casualties of the world. "Perhaps the Greeks would be still involved in the heresy of the Monophysites," says Gibbon, "if the Emperor's horse had not fortunately stumbled. Theodosius expired, his orthodox sister succeeded to the throne."[3]

Again, it often happens, or generally, that various distinct and incompatible elements are found in the origin or infancy of polities, or indeed of philosophies, some of which must be ejected before any satisfactory developments can take place, if any. And they are commonly ejected by the gradual {47} growth of the stronger. The reign of Charles the First, just referred to, supplies an instance in point.

Sometimes discordant ideas are for a time connected and concealed by a common profession or name. Such is the case of coalitions in politics and comprehensions in religion, of which commonly no good is to be expected. Such is an ordinary function of committees and boards, and the sole aim of conciliations and concessions, to make contraries look the same, and to secure an outward agreement where there is no other unity.

Again, developments, reactions, reforms, revolutions, and changes of various kinds are mixed together in the actual history of states, as of philosophical sects, so as to make it very difficult to exhibit them in any scientific analysis.

Often the intellectual process is detached from the practical, and posterior to it. Thus it was after Elizabeth had established the Reformation that Hooker laid down his theory of Church and State as one and the same, differing only in idea; and after the Revolution and its political consequences, that Warburton wrote his "Alliance." A new theory is now again needed for the constitutional lawyer, to reconcile the existing state of things with the just claims of religion. And so, again, in Parliamentary conflicts, men come to their conclusions by the external pressure of events or the force of principles, they do not know how; they have to speak, and they look about for arguments: and a pamphlet is published on the subject in debate, or an article appears in a Review, to furnish common places for the many.

Other developments, though political, are strictly subjected and consequent to the ideas of which they are the exhibitions. Thus Locke's philosophy was a real guide, not a mere defence of the Revolution era, operating forcibly upon Church and government in and after his day. Such too were the theories {48} which preceded the overthrow of the old regime in France and other countries at the end of the last century.

Again, perhaps there are polities founded on no ideas at all, but on mere custom, as among the Asiatics.

6. In other developments the intellectual character is so prominent that they may even be called *logical*, as in the Anglican theory of the Royal Supremacy, which has been created in the courts of law, not in the cabinet or on the field. Hence it is carried out with a consistency and minute application which the history of constitutions cannot exhibit. It does not merely exist in statutes, or in articles, or in oaths, it is realized in details: as in the *congé d'èlire* and letter-

missive on appointment of a Bishop;—in the forms observed in Privy Council on the issuing of State Prayers;—in certain arrangements observed in the Prayer-book, where the universal or abstract Church precedes the King, but the national or really existing body follows him; in printing his name in large capitals, while the Holiest are in ordinary type, and in fixing his arms in churches instead of the Crucifix; moreover, perhaps, in placing "sedition, privy conspiracy, and rebellion," before "false doctrine, heresy, and schism."

Again, when some new philosophy or its portions are introduced into the measures of the Legislature, or into the concessions made to a political party, or into commercial or agricultural policy, it is often said, "We have not seen the end of this;" "It is an instalment of future concessions;" "Our children will see." We feel that it has unknown bearings and issues.

The admission of Jews to municipal offices has lately been defended[4] on the ground that it is the introduction of no new principle, but a development of one already received; that is great premisses have been decided long since and that the present age has but to draw {49} the conclusion; that it is not open to us to inquire what ought to be done in the abstract, since there is no ideal model for the infallible guidance of nations; that change is only a question of time, and that there is a time for all things; that the application of principles ought not to go beyond the actual case, neither preceding nor coming after an imperative demand; that in point of fact Jews have lately been chosen to offices, and that in point of principle the law cannot refuse to legitimate that election.

In theology, the adoption of the word θεοτόκος at Ephesus as a test of orthodoxy is an instance of a logical development.

7. Another class of developments may be called *historical*; I mean when a fact, which at first is very imperfectly apprehended except by a few, at length grows into its due shape and complete proportions, and spreads through a community, and attains general reception by the accumulation, agitation, and concurrence of testimo-

ny. Thus some reports die away; others gain a footing, and are ultimately received as truths. Courts of law, Parliaments, newspapers, letters and other posthumous documents, historians and biographers, and the lapse of years which dissipates parties and prejudices, are in this day the instruments of the development. Accordingly the Poet makes Truth the daughter of Time.[5] Thus at length approximations are made to a right appreciation of facts and characters. History cannot be written except in an after-age. Thus by development the Canon of the New Testament has been formed. Thus public men are content to leave their reputation to posterity; great re-actions take place in opinion; nay, sometimes men outlive opposition and obloquy. Thus Saints are canonized in the Church, long after they have entered into their rest.

{50} 8. *Moral* developments are not properly matter for controversy, but are natural and personal, substituting what is congruous, desirable, pious, decorous, generous, for strictly logical inference. Bishop Butler supplies us with a remarkable instance in the beginning of the Second Part of his "Analogy." As principles imply applications, and general propositions include particulars, so, he tells us, do certain relations imply correlative duties, and certain objects demand certain acts and feelings. He observes that, even though we were not enjoined to pay divine honours to the Second and Third Persons of the Holy Trinity, what is predicated of Them in Scripture would be an abundant warrant, an indirect command, nay, a logical reason, to do so. "Does not," he asks, "the duty of religious regards to both these Divine Persons as immediately arise, to the view of reason, out of the very nature of these offices and relations, as the inward good-will and kind intention which we owe to our fellow-creatures arises out of the common relations between us and them?" He proceeds to say that he is speaking of the inward religious regards of reverence, honour, love, trust, gratitude, fear, hope. "In what external manner this inward worship is to be expressed, is a matter of pure revealed command; . . . but the worship, the internal worship itself, to the Son and the

Holy Ghost, is no further matter of pure revealed command than as the relations they stand in to us are matter of pure revelation; for, the relations being known, the obligations, to such internal worship are obligations of reason, arising out of those relations them selves." Here is a development of doctrine into worship: in like manner the doctrine of the beatification of the Saints has been developed into their *Cultus*; of the θεοτόκος, or Mother of God, into *hyperdulia* and of the Real Presence into Adoration of the Host.

A development converse to that which Butler speaks of, must next be mentioned. As objects {51} demand feelings, so do feelings imply acts and objects. Thus conscience, the existence of which we cannot deny, is as proof of the doctrine of a Moral Governor, which alone gives it a meaning and a scope; that is, the doctrine of a Judgment to come is a development of the phenomenon of conscience. Again, it is plain that passions and affections are in action in our minds before the presence of their proper objects; and their activity would of course be an antecedent argument of extreme cogency in behalf of the real existence of those objects, supposing them un-known. And so again, the social principle, which is innate in us, gives a divine sanction to society and government. And the doctrine of post-baptismal sin and the usage of prayers for the faithful departed have developed into the doctrine of Purgatory. And rites and ceremonies are natural means through which the mind relieves itself of devotional and penitential emotions. And sometimes the cultivation of awe and love towards what is great, high, and unseen, has led a man to the abandon-ment of his sect for some more Catholic form of Christianity.

Aristotle furnishes us with an instance of this kind of develop-ment in his account of the happy man. After showing that his definition of happiness includes in itself the pleasurable, which is the most obvious and popular idea of happiness, he goes on to say that still external goods are necessary to it, about which the definition said nothing; that is, a certain prosperity is by moral fitness, not by logical necessity, attached to the happy man. "For it is impossible," he observes, "or not easy, to practise high virtue without abundant means. Many deeds are done by the instrumentality of friends, wealthy and political power; and of some things the absence is a cloud upon happiness, as of noble birth, of hopeful children, and of personal appearance: for a person utterly deformed, or low-born, or bereaved and childless, cannot quite be {52} happy: and still less if he have very worthless children or friends, or they were good and died."[6]

This process of development has been well delineated by a living French writer, in his Lectures on European Civilization, who shall be quoted at some length. "If we reduce religion," he says, "to a purely religious sentiment . . . it appears evident that it must and ought to remain as purely personal concern. But I am either strangely mistaken, or this religious sentiment is not the complete expression of the religious nature of man. Religion is, I believe, very different from this, and much more extended. There are problems in human nature, in human destinies, which cannot be solved in this life, which depend on an order of things unconnected with the visible world, but which unceasingly agitate the human mind with a desire to comprehend them. The solution of these problems is the origin of all religion; her primary object is to discover the creeds and doctrines which contain, or are supposed to contain it.

"Another cause also impels mankind to embrace religion. From whence do morals originate? whither do they lead? is this self-existing obligation to do good, an isolated fact, without an author, without an end? does it not conceal, or rather does it not reveal to man, an origin, a destiny, beyond this world? The science of morals, by these spontaneous and inevitable questions, conducts man to the threshold of religion, and displays to him a sphere from whence he has not derived it. Thus the certain and never-failing sources of religion are, on the one hand, the problems of our nature; on the other, the necessity of seeking for morals a sanction, an origin, and an aim. It, therefore, assumes many other forms beside that of a pure sentiment; it appears a union of doctrines, of precepts, of promises.

This is what truly constitutes religion; {53} this is its fundamental character; it is not merely a form of sensibility, an impulse of the imagination, a variety of poetry.

"When thus brought back to its true elements, to its essential nature, religion appears no longer a purely personal concern, but a powerful and fruitful principle of association. It is considered in the light of a system of belief, a system of dogmas. Truth is not the heritage of any individual, it is absolute and universal; mankind ought to seek and profess it in common. Is it considered with reference to the precepts that are associated with its doctrines? A law which is obligatory on a simple individual, is so on all; it ought to be promulgated, and it is our duty to endeavour to bring all mankind under its dominion. It is the same with respect to the promises that religion makes, in the name of its creeds and precepts; they ought to be diffused; all men should be incited to partake of their benefits. A religious society, therefore, naturally results from the essential elements of religion, and is such a necessary consequence of it that the term which expresses the most energetic social sentiment, the most intense desire to propagate ideas and extend society, is the word *proselytism*, a term which is especially applied to religious belief, and in fact consecrated to it.

"When a religious society has ever been formed, when a certain number of men are united by a common religious creed, are governed by the same religious precepts, and enjoy the same religious hopes, some form of government is necessary. No society can endure a week, nay, more, no society can endure a single hour, without a government. The moment, indeed, a society is formed, by the very fact of its formation, it calls forth a government,—a government which shall proclaim the common truth which is the bond of the society, and promulgate and maintain the precepts that {54} this truth ought to produce. The necessity of a superior power, of a form of government, is involved in the fact of the existence of a religious, as it is in that of any other society.

"And not only is a government necessary, but it naturally forms itself . . . When events are suffered to follow their natural laws, when force does not interfere, power falls into the hands of the most able, the most worthy, those who are most capable of carrying out the principles on which the society was founded. Is a warlike expedition in agitation? The bravest take command. Is the object of the association learned research, or a scientific undertaking? The best informed will be the leader . . . . The inequality of faculties and influence, which is the foundation of power in civil life, has the same effect in a religious society . . . . Religion has no sooner arisen in the human mind than a religious society appears; and immediately a religious society is formed, it produces its government."[7]

9. It remains to allude to what, unless the word were often so vaguely and carelessly used, I should be led to call *metaphysical* developments; I mean such as are a mere analysis of the idea contemplated, and terminate in its exact and complete delineation. Thus Aristotle draws the character of a magnanimous or of a munificent man; thus Shakespeare might conceive and bring out his Hamlet or Ariel; and thus, in the sacred province of theology, the mind may be employed in developing the solemn ideas which it has hitherto held implicitly, and without subjecting them to its reflecting and reasoning powers.

I have already treated of this subject at length in a former work, from which it will be sufficient here to quote some sentences in explanation:—

"The mind which is habituated to the thought of God, of Christ, of the Holy Spirit, naturally turns {55} with a devout curiosity to the contemplation of the object of its adoration, and begins to form statements concerning it, before it knows whither, or how far, it will be carried. One proposition necessarily leads to another, and a second to a third; then some limitation is required; and the combination of these opposites occasions some fresh evolutions from the original idea, which indeed can never be said to be entirely exhausted. This process is its development, and results in a series, or rather body, of dogmatic statements, till what was an impression on the Imagination has become a system or creed in the Reason.

"Now such impressions are obviously individual and complete above other theological ideas, because they are the impressions of Objects. Ideas and their developments are commonly not identical, the development being but the carrying out of the idea into its consequences. Thus the doctrine of Penance may be called a development of the doctrine of Baptism, yet still is a distinct doctrine; whereas the developments in the doctrines of the Holy Trinity and the Incarnation are mere portions of the original impression, and modes or representing it. As God is one, so the impression which He gives us of Himself is one, so the impression which He give us of Himself is one; it is not a thing of parts; it is not a system; nor is it anything imperfect and needing a counterpart. It is the vision of an object. When we pray, we pray, not to an assemblage of notions or to a creed, but to One Individual Being; and when we speak of Him, we speak of a Person, not of a Law or Manifestation. This being the case, all our attempts to delineate our impression of Him go to bring out one idea, not two, or three, or four; not a philosophy, but an individual idea in its separate aspects.

"This may be fitly compared to the impressions made on us by the senses. Material objects are real, whole, and individual; and the impressions which they make on the mind, by means of the {56} senses, are of a corresponding nature, complex and manifold in their relations and bearings, but, considered in themselves, integral and one. And, in like manner, the ideas which we are granted of Divine Objects under the Gospel, from the nature of the case and because they are ideas, answer to the originals so far as this, that they are whole, indivisible, substantial and may be called real, as being images of what is real. Objects which are conveyed to us through the senses stand out in our minds, as I may say, with dimensions and aspects and influences various, and all of these consistent with one another, and many of them beyond our memory or even knowledge, while we contemplate the objects themselves; thus forcing on us as persuasion of their reality from the spontaneous congruity and coincidence of these accompaniments, as if they could not be creations of our minds, but were the images of external and independent beings. This of course will take place in the case of the sacred ideas which are the objects of our faith. Religious men, according to their measure, have an idea or vision of the Blessed Trinity in Unity, of the Son Incarnate, and of His Presence, not as a number of qualities, attributes, and actions, not as the subject of a number of propositions, but as one and individual, and independent of words, like an impression conveyed through the senses.

"Particular propositions, then, which are used to express portions of the great idea vouchsafed to us, can never really be confused with the idea itself, which all such propositions taken together can but reach and cannot exceed. As definitions are not intended to go beyond their subject, but to be adequate to it, so the dogmatic statements of the Divine Nature used in our confessions, however multiplied, cannot say more than is implied in the original idea, considered in its completeness, without the risk of heresy. Creeds and dogmas live in the one idea which they are designed to express, and {57} which alone is substantive; and are necessary only because the human mind cannot reflect upon it, except piecemeal, cannot use it in its oneness and entireness, or without resolving it into a series of aspects and relations. And, in matter of fact, these expressions are never equivalent to it. We are able, indeed, to define the creations of our minds, for they are what we make them and nothing else; but it were as easy to create what is real as to define it. And thus the Catholic dogmas are, after all, but symbols of a divine fact, which, far from being compassed by those very propositions, would not be exhausted, not fathomed, by a thousand."[8]

SECTION III.

ON THE CORRUPTION OF AN IDEA.

§ 1.

Distinctive Tests between Development and Corruption.

Since the developments of an idea are nothing else than its adequate representation and its fulfillment, in its various aspects, relations, and consequences, and since the causes which stimulate may {58} also distort its growth, as is seen in the corruptions of truth with which the world abounds, rules are required to distinguish legitimate developments from those which are not.

Here the most ready test is suggested by the analogy of physical growth, which is such that the parts and proportions of the developed form correspond to those which belong to its rudiments. The adult animal has the same make as it had on its birth; young birds do not grow into fishes; nor does the child degenerate into the brute, wild or domestic, of which is by inheritance lord. "Imitetur," says Vincentius, "animarum religio rationem corporum, quae licet annorum processu numeros suos evolvant et explicent, eadem tamen quae erant remanent."[9] Unity in type is certainly the most obvious characteristic of a faithful development.

Yet this illustration must not be pressed to the extent of denying all variation, nay, considerable alteration of proportion and relation, in the development of the parts or aspects of an idea. Such changes in outward appearance and internal harmony occur in the instance of the animal creation itself. The fledged bird differs from its rudimental form in the egg. The butterfly is the development, but not in any sense the image, of the grub. The whale claims a place among mammalia, though we might fancy that, as in the child's game of catscradle, some strange introsusception had been permitted, to make it so like, yet so contrary to the animals with which it is itself classed. And, in like manner, if beasts of prey were once in paradise, and fed upon grass, they must have presented bodily phenomena very different from the structure of muscles, claws, teeth, and viscera which now fit them for a carnivorous existence. Eutychius, Patriarch of Constantinople, on his death-bed, grasped his own hand {59} and said, "I confess that in this flesh we shall all rise again;" yet flesh and blood cannot inherit the kingdom of God, and a glorified body has attributes incompatible with its present condition on earth.

More subtle still are the variations which are consistent or inconsistent with identity in political and religious developments. The Catholic doctrine of the Holy Trinity has ever been accused by heretics of interfering with that of the Divine Unity out of which it grew, and even believers will at first sight consider that it tends to obscure it. But Petavius says, "I will affirm, what perhaps will surprise the reader, that that distinction of Persons which, in regard to *proprietates* is in reality most great, is so far from disparaging the Unity and Simplicity of God that this very real distinction especially avails to the doctrine that God is One and most Simple."[10]

Again, Arius asserted that the Second Person of the Blessed Trinity was not able to comprehend the First, whereas Eunomius's characteristic tenet was that all men could comprehend God as fully as the Son comprehended Him Himself; yet no one can doubt that Eunomianism was a true development, not a corruption of Arianism.

The same individual may run through systems of philosophy or belief, which are in themselves irreconcilable, without inconsistency, since in him they may be nothing more than accidental instruments or expressions of what he is inwardly from first to last. The political doctrines of the modern Tory resemble those of the primitive Whig; yet few will deny that the Whig and Tory characters have each a discriminating type. Calvinism has changed into Unitarianism; yet this is no corruption, even if it be not, strictly speaking a development; for Harding, in controversy with Jewell, surmised the coming change three centuries since, and it has occurred not in one country, but in many.

{60} The history of national character supplies an analogy, rather than an instance strictly in point; yet there is so close a connexion between the development of minds and of ideas that it is allowable to refer to it here. Thus we find England of old the most loyal supporter, and England of late the most jealous enemy, of the Holy See. As great a change is exhibited in France, once the eldest born of the Church and the flower of her Knighthood, now democratic and lately infidel. Yet, in both nations, these great changes cannot be well called corruptions.

Or again, let us reflect on the ethical vicissitudes of the chosen people. How different is their groveling and cowardly temper on leaving Egypt from the chivalrous spirit, as it may be called, of the age of David, or, again, from the bloody fanaticism which braved Titus and Hadrian! How different that impotence of mind which yielded even at the sight of a pagan idol, from the stern iconoclasm and bigoted nationality of later Judaism! How startling the apparent absence of what would be called talent in this people during their supernatural Dispensation, compared with the gifts of mind which various witnesses assign to them now!

And, in like manner, ideas may remain, when the expression of them is indefinitely varied; and we cannot determine whether a professed development is truly such or not, without some further knowledge than the mere fact of this variation. Nor will our feelings serve as a criterion. It must have been an extreme shock to St. Peter to be told he must slay and eat beasts, unclean as well as clean, though such a command was implied already in that faith which he held and taught; a shock, which a single effort, or a short period, or the force of reason would not suffice to overcome. Nay, it may happen that a representation which varies from its original may be felt as more true and faithful than one which has more pretensions to be exact. So {61} it is with many a portrait which is not striking: at first look, of course, it disappoints us; but when we are familiar with it, we see in it what we could not see at first, and prefer it, not to a perfect likeness, but to many a sketch which is so precise as to be a caricature.

And, in like manner, real perversions and corruptions are often not so unlike externally to the doctrine to which they belong, as are changes which are consistent with it and true developments. When Rome changed from a Republic to an Empire, it was a real alteration of polity or a corruption; yet in appearance the change was small. The old offices or functions of government remained: it was only that the Imperator, or Commander in Chief, concentrated them in his own person. Augustus was Consul and Tribune, Supreme Pontiff and Censor, and the Imperial rule was, in the words of Gibbon, "an absolute monarchy disguised by the forms of a commonwealth." On the other hand, when the dissimulation of Augustus was exchanged for the ostentation of Dioclesian, the real alteration of constitution was trivial, but the appearance of change was great. Instead of plain Consul, Censor, and Tribune, Dioclesian became Dominus or King, assumed the diadem, and threw around him the forms of a court.

Nay, one cause of corruption in religion is the refusal to follow the course of doctrine as it moves on, and an obstinacy in the notions of the past. Certainly: as we see conspicuously in the history of the chosen race. The Samaritans who refused to add the Prophets to the Law, and the Sadducees who denied what lay in the Book of Exodus, were in appearance but faithful adherents to the primitive doctrine. Our Lord found His people precisians in their obedience to the letter; He condemned them for not being led on to its spirit, that is, to its developments. The Gospel is the development of the Law; yet what difference {62} seems wider than that which separates the unbending rule of Moses from the "grace and truth" which "came by Jesus Christ?" Samuel had of old time fancied that the tall Eliab was the Lord's anointed; and Jesse had thought David only fit for the sheepcote; and when the Great King came, He was "as a root out of a dry ground:" but strength came out of weakness, and out of the strong sweetness.

So it is in the case of our friends; the most obsequious are not always the truest, and seeming cruelty is often the most faithful. We know the conduct of the three daughters in the fable towards the old King. She who had found her love "more richer than her tongue," and could not "heave her heart into her mouth," was in the event alone true to her father.

Natural then as it is at first sight to suppose that an idea will always be the exact image of itself in all stages of its history, experience does not bear out the anticipation. To discover the tests of as true development, as distinguished from a corruption, we must consider the subject more attentively.

Perhaps it will help us in the difficulty to consider the literal meaning of the word corruption, as used by material substances. Corruption is a breaking up of the subject in which it takes place, or its resolution into its component parts, which involves eventually a loss unity. Again, it is only applied to organized matter; a stone may be crushed to powder, but cannot be corrupted. Moreover, since organization involves, corruption must in consequence destroy, both life and growth; for which reason it is opposed by philosophers to generation. If this analogy is to be followed, the corruption of philosophical and political ideas is a process ending in dissolution of the body of thought and usage which was bound up, as it were, into one {63} system; in the destruction of the norm or type, whatever it may be considered, which made it one; in its disorganization; in its loss of the principle of life and growth; in its resolution into other distinct lives, that is, into other ideas which take the place of it.

Moreover, corruption, as seen in the physical world, not only immediately precedes dissolution, but immediately follows upon development. It is the turning-point or transition-state in that continuous process by which the birth of as living thing is mysteriously connected with its death. In this it differs from as re-action, innovation, or reform, that it is a state to which a development tends from the first, at which sooner or later it arrives, and which is its reversal, while it is its continuation. Animated natures live on till they die; they grow in order to decrease; and every hour which brings them nearer to perfection, brings them nearer to their end. Here the resemblance and the difference between a development and corruption are brought into close juxtaposition. The corruption of an idea is that state of a development which undoes its previous advances.

If the process is suspended and the state chronic, then it is called decay; but it is called corruption when it hastens to a crisis, as a fever, or the disturbance of system consequent on poisoning, in which the bodily functions are under preternatural influence, whereas in decay there is a loss of activity and vigor.

Thus, without considering the analogy as strict, or sufficient to rest an argument upon, we may use it to introduce several rules for drawing the line between a development and a corruption. That development, then, is to be considered a corruption which *obscures or prejudices its essential idea*, or which *disturbs the laws of development* which constitute its organization, or which *reverses its course* {64} *of development;* that is *not* a corruption which is *both a chronic and an active state* or which is *capable of holding together* the component parts of a system. From this analysis seven tests of a development may be drawn of varying cogency and independence.

§ 2.

First Test of a true Development; Preservation of Idea.

That the essential idea or type which a philosophical or political system represents must continue under all its developments, and that its loss is tantamount to the corruption of the system, will scarcely be denied. When, for instance, we pronounce a monastic institution to have been in a state of corruption, we mean that it had departed from the view or professions in which it was founded. Judges are corrupt, when they are guided in their decisions, not by justice and truth, but by the love of lucre or respect of persons. Severity in living may be carried to excess as well as indulgence; but we predicate corruption, not of the extreme, which preserves, but of that which destroys, the type of self-restraint.

This is in substance acknowledged in a variety of other cases. An empire or a religion may have many changes: but when we speak of its developing, we consider it to be fulfilling, not to be belying its destiny; so much so that we even take its actual fortunes as a comment on its early history, and call its policy a mission. The Popes present a very different appearance to the historian of the world, when in apostolical poverty or in more than imperial power; but, while they protect the poor, reconcile rival sovereigns, convert barbarians, and promote civilization, he recognizes their function {65} in spite of the change, and is contented to praise them.

It has been argued by a late writer, whether fairly or not does not interfere with the illustration, that the miraculous vision and dream of the Labarum could not have really taken place, as reported by Eusebius, because it is counter to the original type of Christianity. "For the first time," he says, on occasion of Constantine's introduction of the standard into his armies, "the meek and peaceful Jesus became a God of battle, and the Cross, the holy sign of Christian Redemption, a banner of bloody strife... This was the first advance to the military Christianity of the middle ages, a modification of the pure religion of the Gospel, if directly opposed to its genuine principles, still apparently indispensable to the social progress of men."[11]

Again, a popular leader may go through a variety of professions, he may court parties and break with them, he may contradict himself in words, and undo his own measures, yet there may be a steady fulfillment of certain objects, of adherence to certain plain doctrines, which impress upon beholders, not his scrupulousness, but his sincerity and consistency. On the other hand, a statesman loses his position, and hurts his influence, in proportion as he is neglectful of the special charges or duties which he began by undertaking.

One of the obvious arts in debate and diplomacy is to anticipate the possible developments of a measure as to be able to hit upon amendments, or modifications, which are contrary to them, and which in consequence, if carried, necessarily nullify the measure itself, without professing to do so; all developments being parts of an original idea, and what is inconsistent with it being no development.

This test, however, is too obvious and too close upon demonstration to be easy of application in {66} particular cases. It implies an insight into the essential idea in which a system of thought is set up, which often cannot be possessed, and, if attempted, will lead to mere theorizing. As to Christianity,

considering the unsystematic character of its inspired documents
and the all but silence of contemporary history, if we attempt to
determine its one original profession, undertaking, or announcement, we shall be reduced to those eclectic and arbitrary
decisions which have in all ages been so common, and have been
censured in a former place. Thus, of old time, the Author of the
Clementines gives this rule for separating what he considers the
spurious from the genuine portion of Scripture: "Every thing is
false which contradicts the divine perfections."[12] On the other
hand, in a work just published, we are told, "Seize the general
tendency of the pure Gospel into one concentrated thought, and
you will be persuaded that Jesus's words, "The body profiteth
nothing," are as a master-key to the whole of His revelation. But
how totally inconsistent with this leading principle is the account
of Jesus's conception!"[13] Nothing can be easier, and nothing
more trifling, than private determinations about "the essentials,
the peculiar doctrines, the vital doctrine, the great truths, simple
views, or leading idea of the Gospel."[14]

The first test, then, of a faithful or legitimate or development is
its *preservation of the essential idea* of the doctrine or polity
which it represents.

§ 3.

Second Test; Continuity of Principles.

As in mathematical creations figures are formed on distinct
formulae, which are the laws under which they are developed, so
it is in ethical and political {67} subjects. Doctrines expand
variously according to the mind, individual or social, into which
they are received; and the peculiarities of the recipient are the
regulating power, the law, the organization, or, as it may be

called, the form of the development. The life of doctrines may be said to consist in the law or principle which they embody.

The science of grammar affords another instance of the existence of special laws in the formation of systems. Some languages have more elasticity than others, and greater capabilities; and the difficulty of explaining the fact does not lead us to doubt it. There are languages, for instance, which have a capacity for compound words, which, we cannot tell why, is in matter of fact denied to others. We feel the presence of a certain character or genius in each, which determines its path and its range; and to discover and enter into it is one part of refined scholarship. And when particular writers, in consequence perhaps of some theory, tax a language beyond its powers, the failure is conspicuous. Very subtle, too, and difficult to draw out, are the principles on which depends the formation of proper names in a particular people, In works of fiction, names or titles, significant or ludicrous, must be invented for the characters introduced; and some authors excel in their fabrication, while others are equally unfortunate. Foreign novels, perhaps, attempt to frame English surnames, and signally fail; yet what every one feels to be the case, no one can analyse: that is, our surnames are constructed on a law which is only exhibited in particular instances, and which rules their formation on certain, though subtle, determinations.

And so in philosophy, the systems of physics or morals, which go by celebrated names, proceed upon the assumption of certain {68} conditions which are necessary for every stage of their development. The Newtonian theory of gravitation is based on certain axioms; for instance, that the fewest causes assignable for phenomena are the true ones: and the application of science to practical purposes depends upon the hypothesis that what happens to-day will happen to-morrow.

And so in military matters, the discovery of gunpowder developed the science of attack and defence in a new instrumentality. Again, it is said that when Napoleon began his career of victories, the enemy's generals pronounced that his battles were fought against rule, and that he ought not to conquer.

So states have their respective policies, on which they move forward, and which are the conditions of their well-being. Thus it is sometimes said that the true policy of the American Union, or the law of its prosperity, is not the enlargement of its territory, but the cultivation of its internal resources. Thus Russia is said to be weak in attack, strong in defence, and to grow, not by the sword, but by diplomacy. Thus Islamism is said to be the form or life of the Ottoman, and Protestantism of the British Empire; and the admission of European ideas into the one, or of Catholic ideas into the other, to be the destruction of the respective conditions of their power. Thus Augustus and Tiberius governed by dissimulation; thus Pericles in his "funeral Oration" draws out the principles of the Athenian commonwealth, viz., that it is carried on, not by formal and severe enactments, but by the ethical character and spontaneous energy of the people.

The political principles of Christianity, if it be right to use such words of a divine polity, are laid down for us in the Sermon on the Mount. Contrariwise to other empires, Christians conquer by yielding; they gain influence by hating it; they possess the earth by renouncing it. Gibbon speaks of the "vices of the clergy" as being "to a philosophic eye far less dangerous than their virtues."[15]

{69} Again, as to Judaism, it may be asked on what law it developed; that is, whether Mahometanism may not be considered as a sort of Judaism, as formed by the presence of a different class of influences. In this contrast between them, perhaps it may be said that the expectation of a Messiah was the principle or law which expanded the elements, almost common to Judaism with Mahometanism, into their characteristic shape.

One of the points of discipline to which Wesley attached most importance was that of preaching early in the morning. This was his principle. In Georgia, he began preaching at five o'clock every day, winter and summer. "Early preaching," he said, "is the glory of the Methodists; whenever this is dropt, they will dwindle away into nothing, they have lost their first love, they are a fallen people."

Now these instances show, as has been incidentally observed of some of them, that the destruction of the special laws or principles of a development is its corruption. Thus, as to nations, when we talk of the spirit of a people being lost, we do not mean that this or that act has been committed, or measure carried, but that certain lines of thought or conduct by which it has grown great are abandoned. Thus the Roman Poets consider their State in course of ruin because its *prisci mores* and *pietas* were failing. And so we speak of countries or persons as being in a false position, when they take up a course of policy, or assume a profession, inconsistent with their natural interests or real character. Judaism, again, was rejected when it rejected the Messiah.

Thus the *continuity or alteration of the principles* on which an idea has developed is a second mark of discrimination between a true development and a corruption.

{70}   § 4.

Further Remarks on the Second Test.

A comparison of the principles of a philosophy or religion with its doctrines may tend to throw further light on the nature of a development; though it is difficult to go into the subject as fully as is necessary, without incurring the charge of subtlety, and becoming intricate and obscures.

Principles are abstract and general, doctrines relate to facts; doctrines develop, and principles do not; doctrines grow and are enlarged, principles are illustrated; doctrines are intellectual, and principles are more immediately ethical and practical. Systems live in principles and represent doctrines. Personal responsibility is a principle, the Being of God is a doctrine; from that doctrine all theology has come in due course, whereas the principle is not clearer under the Gospel than in paradise, and depends, not on belief in an Almighty Governor, but on conscience.

Yet the difference between the two sometimes merely exists in our mode of viewing them; and what is a doctrine in one philosophy is a principle in another. Personal responsibility may be made a doctrinal basis, and develop into Arminianism or Pelagianism. Again, it may be discussed whether infallibility is a principle or a doctrine of the Church of Rome, and dogmatism a principle or doctrine of Christianity. Again, consideration for the poor is a doctrine of the Church considered as a religious body, and a principle when she is viewed as a political power.

Doctrines stand to principles, as the definitions to the axioms and postulates of mathematics. Thus the 15th and 17th propositions of Euclid I. are developments, not of the three first axioms, which are required in the proof, but of the definition of a right {71} angle. Perhaps the perplexity, which arises in the mind of a beginner, on learning the early propositions of the second book, arises from these being more prominently exemplifications of axioms than developments of definitions. He looks for developments from the definition of the rectangle, and finds but various particular cases of the general truth, that "the whole is equal to its parts."

Doctrines stand to principles, if it may be said without fancifulness, as the principle of fecundity to generation, though this analogy must not be strained. Doctrines are developed by the operation of principles, and develop differently according to those principles. Thus a belief in the transitiveness of worldly goods leads the Epicurean to enjoyment, and the ascetic to mortification; and, from their common doctrine of the sinfulness of matter, the Alexandrian Gnostics became sensualists, and the Syrian devotees. The same philosophical elements, received into a certain sensibility or insensibility to sin and its consequences, leads one mind to the Church of Rome; another to what, for want of a better word, may be called Germanism.

Again, religious investigation sometimes is conducted on the principle that it is a duty "to follow and speak the truth," which really means that it is no duty to fear error, or to consider what is safest, or to shrink from scattering doubts, or to regard the responsibility of misleading; and thus it terminates in heresy or infidelity, without any blame to religious investigation in itself.

Again, to take a different subject, what constitutes a chief interest of dramatic compositions and tales, is to use external circumstances, which may be considered their law of development, as a means of bringing out into different shapes, and showing under new aspects, the peculiarities of personal character, according as either those circumstances or those peculiarities vary in the personages introduced.

{72} Principles are popularly said to develop when they are but exemplified; thus the various sects of Protestantism, unconnected as they are with each other, are called developments of the principle of Private Judgment, of which really they are but applications and results.

A development, to be faithful, must retain both the doctrine and the principle with which it started. Doctrine without its correspondent principle remains barren, if not lifeless, of which the Greek Church seems an instance; or it forms those hollow professions which are familiarly called "shams," as a zeal for an established Church and its creed, on merely conservative or temporal motives. Such, too, was the Roman Constitution between the reigns of Augustus and Dioclesian.

On the other hand, principle without its corresponding doctrine may be considered as the state of religious minds in the heathen world, viewed relatively to Revelation; that is, of the "children of God who are scattered abroad."

Pagans may have, heretics cannot have, the same principles as Catholics; if the latter have the same, they are not real heretics, but in ignorance. Principle is a better test of heresy than doctrine. Heretics are true to their principles, but change to and fro, backwards and forwards, in opinion; for very opposite doctrines may be exemplifications of the same principle. Thus the Antiochenes and other heretics sometimes were Arians, sometimes Sabellians, sometimes Nestorians, sometimes Monophysites, as if at random, from fidelity to their common principle, that there is no mystery in theology. Thus Calvinists become Unitarians from the principle of private judgment. The doctrines of heresy are accidents and soon run to an end; its principles are everlasting.

This, too, is often the solution of the paradox "Extremes meet," and of the startling re-actions {73} which take place in individuals; viz., the presence of some one principle or condition, which is dominant in their minds from first to last. If one of two contradictory alternatives be necessarily true on a certain hypothesis, then the denial of the one leads, by mere logical consistency and without direct reasons, to a reception of the other. Thus the question between the Church of Rome and Protestantism falls in some minds into the proposition, "Rome is either the pillar and ground of the Truth or she is Antichrist;" in proportion, then, as they revolt from considering her the latter are they compelled to receive her as the former. Hence, too, men may pass from infidelity to Rome, and from Rome to infidelity, from a conviction in both courses that there is no tangible intellectual position between the two.

Protestantism, viewed in its more Catholic aspects, is doctrine without principle; viewed in its heretical, it is principle without doctrine. Many of its speakers, for instance, use eloquent language about the Church and its characteristics: some of them do not realize what they say, but use high words and general statements about "the faith," and "primitive truth," and "schism," and "heresy," to which they attach no definite meaning; while others speak of "unity," "universality," and "Catholicity," and use the words in their own sense and for their own ideas. The same remark applies to that Anglo-Germanism which has for some time been coming into fashion; its doctrine of the Sacraments is either a "sham" or a "myth."

§ 5.

The Third Test; Power of Assimilation.

In the physical world whatever has life is characterized by growth, so that in no respect to grow is to cease to live. It grows by taking into its own substance external materials; and this absorption {74} or assimilation is completed when the materials appropriated come to belong to it or enter into its unity. Two things cannot become one, except there be a power of assimilation in one or the other. Sometimes assimilation is effected only with an effort; it is possible to die or repletion, and there are animals who lie torpid for a time under the contest between the foreign substance and the assimilating power. And different food is proper for different recipients.

This analogy may be taken to illustrate certain peculiarities in the growth or development in ideas, which were noticed in the opening Section. It is otherwise with mathematical and other abstract creations, which, like the soul itself, are solitary and self-dependent; but doctrine and views which related to man are not placed in a void, but in the crowded world, and make way for themselves by interpenetration, and develop by absorption. Facts and opinions, which have hitherto been regarded in other relations and grouped round other centres, henceforth are gradually attracted to a new influence and subjected to a new sovereign. They are modified, laid afresh, thrust aside, as the case may be. A new element of order and composition has come among them; and its life is proved by this capacity of expansion, without disarrangement or dissolution. An eclectic, conservative, assimilating, healing, moulding process, *a unitive power* is of the essence, and a third test, of a faithful development.

Thus a power of development is a proof of life, not only in its essay, but in its success; for a mere formula either does not expand or is shattered in expanding. A living idea becomes many, yet remains one.

The attempt at development shows the presence of a principle, and its success the presence of an idea. Principles stimulate thought, and an idea keeps it together.

{75} The idea never was that throve and lasted, yet, like mathematical truth, incorporated nothing from external sources. So far from the fact of such incorporation implying corruption, as is sometimes supposed, development implies incorporation. Mahometanism may be in external developments scarcely more than a compound of other theologies, yet no one would deny that there has been a living idea somewhere in that religion, which has been so strong, so wide, so lasting a bond of union in the history of the world. Why it has not continued to develop after its first preaching, if this be the case, as it seems to be, cannot be determined without a greater knowledge of that religion, and how far it is merely political, how far theological, than we commonly possess.

In Christianity, opinion, while a raw material, is called philosophy or scholasticism; when a rejected refuse, it is called heresy.

Ideas are more open to an external bias in their commencement than afterwards; hence the great majority of writers who consider the Medieval Church corrupt, trace its corruption to the first four centuries, not to what are called the dark ages.

That an idea more readily coalesces with certain ideas than with others does not show that it has been unduly influenced, that is, corrupted by them, but that it has an antecedent affinity to them. At least it shall be assumed here that, when the Gospels speak of virtue going out of our Lord, and of His healing with the clay which He had moistened, they afford instances, not of a perversion of Christianity, but of affinity to notions which were external to it; and that St Paul is not biased by Orientalism, though he said that it was "excellent not to touch a woman."

Thus in politics, too, ideas are sometimes proposed, discussed, rejected, or adopted, as it may happen. Sometimes they are shown to be unmeaning {76} and impossible; sometimes they are true, but partially so, or in subordination to other ideas, with which, in consequence they are as wholes or in part incorporated, as far as these have affinities to them. Mr. Bentham's system was an attempt to make the circle of legal and moral truths developments of certain principles of his own;—those principles of his may, if it so happen, prove unequal to the weight of truths which are eternal, and the system founded on them may break into pieces; or again, a State may absorb certain of them, for which it has affinity, that is, it may develop in Benthamism, yet remain in substance what it was before. In the history of the French Revolution we read of many middle parties, who attempted to form theories of constitutions short of those which they would call extreme, and successfully failed from the want of power or reality in their characteristic ideas. The Semiarians attempted a middle way between orthodoxy and heresy, but could not stand their ground; at length part fell into Macedonianism, and part joined the Church.

The stronger and more living is an idea, that is, the more powerful hold it exercises on the minds of men, the more able is it to dispense with safeguards, and trust to itself against the danger of corruption. As strong frames exult in their agility, and healthy constitutions throw off ailments, so parties or schools that live can afford to be rash, and will sometimes be betrayed into extravagances, yet are brought right by their inherent vigour. On the other hand, unreal systems are commonly decent externally. Forms, subscriptions, or Articles of religion are indispensable when the principle of life is weakly. Thus Presbyterianism has maintained its original theology in Scotland where legal subscriptions are enforced, while it has run into Arianism or Unitarianism where that protection is away. We have yet to see whether the Free Kirk can keep its present {77} theological ground. The Church of Rome can consult expedience more freely than other bodies, as trusting to her living tradition, and is sometimes thought to disregard principle and scruple when she is but dispensing with forms. Thus Saints are often characterized by acts which are no patterns for others; and the most gifted men are, by reason of their very gifts, sometimes led into fatal inadvertences. Hence vows are the wise defence of unstable virtue, and general rules the refuge of feeble authority.

And so much may suffice on the *unitive power* of faithful developments, which constitutes their third characteristic.

§ 6.

The Fourth Test; Early Anticipation.

Since when an idea is living, that is, influential and operative in the minds of recipients, it is sure to develop according to the principles on which they are formed; instances of such a process, though vague and isolated, may occur from the very first, though a lapse of time be necessary to bring it to perfection. And since developments are in great measure only aspects of the idea from which they come, and all of them are natural consequences of it, it is often a matter of accident in what order they are carried out in individual minds; and it is in no wise strange that here and there definite specimens should very early occur, which, in the historical course are not found till a late day. The fact, then, of such early or recurring intimations of tendencies, which afterwards are fully realized, is a sort of evidence that those later and more systematic fulfillments are but in accordance with the original idea.

Nothing is more common, for instance, than accounts or legends of the anticipations, which great {78} men have given in boyhood of the bent of their minds, as afterwards displayed in their history; so much so that the popular expectation has sometimes led to the invention of them. The child Cyrus mimics a despot's power, and St. Athanasius is elected Bishop by his playfellows. In the Book of Job, we find a special doctrine of the Gospel anticipated at so early a date that Warburton even considers it a difficulty in his particular theory, and is led in consequence to make Ezra the writer.

To turn to profane history. It is observable that in the eleventh century, when the Russians were but Pirates upon the Black Sea, Constantinople was their aim; and that a prophecy was in circulation in that city that they should one day gain possession of it.

In the reign of James the First, we have a curious anticipation of the system of influence in the management of political parties, which was developed by Sir R. Walpole a century afterwards. This attempt is traced by a living writer to the ingenuity of Lord Bacon. "He submitted to the King that there were expedients for more judiciously managing a House of Commons; . . . that much might be done by forethought towards filling the House with well-affected persons, winning or blinding the lawyers . . . and drawing the chief constituent bodies of the assembly, the country gentlemen, the merchants, the courtiers, to act for the King's advantage; that it would be expedient to tender voluntarily certain graces and modifications of the King's prerogative," &c.[16] The writer adds, "This circumstance, like several others in the present reign, is curious, as it shows the rise of a systematic parliamentary influence, which was one day to become the mainspring of government."

Arcesilas and Carneades, the founders of the later Academy, are known to have innovated on the {79} Platonic doctrine by inculcating a universal scepticism; and they did this, as if on the authority of Socrates, who had adopted the method of *ironia* against the Sophists, on their professing to know everything. This, of course, was an insufficient plea. However, could it be shown that Socrates did on one or two occasions evidence deliberate doubts on the great principles of theism or morals, would any one deny that the innovation in question had grounds for being considered a true development, not a corruption?

It is certain that, in the idea of Monachism, prevalent in ancient times, manual labour had a more prominent place than study; so much so that De Rancé, the celebrated Abbot of La Trappe, in controversy with Mabillon, maintained his ground with great plausibility against the latter's apology for the literary occupations for which the Benedictines of France are so famous. Nor can it be denied that the labours of such as Mabillon and Montfaucon are at least a development upon the simplicity of the primitive institution. And yet it is remarkable that St. Pachomius, the first author of a monastic rule, enjoined a library in each of his houses, and appointed conferences and disputations three times a week on religious subjects, interpretation of Scripture, or points of theology. St. Basil, the founder of Monachism in Pontus, one of the most learned of the Greek Fathers, wrote his theological treatises in the intervals of agricultural labour. St. Jerome, the author of the Latin version of Scripture, lived as a poor monk in a cell at Bethlehem. These, indeed, were but exceptions in the character of early Monachism; but they suggest its capabilities and anticipate its history. Literature is certainly not inconsistent with its idea.

In the controversies with the Gnostics, in the second century, striking anticipations occasionally occur, in the works of their opponents, of the formal dogmatic teaching developed in the Church in the {80} course of the Nestorian and Monophysite controversies in the fifth. Paul of Samosata, one of the first disciples of the Syrian school of theology, taught a heresy sufficiently like Nestorianism, in which that school terminated, to be mistaken for it in later times; yet for a long while after him the characteristic of the school was Arianism, an opposite heresy.

Lutheranism, as is well known, has by this time become almost simple heresy or infidelity; it has terminated, if it has even yet reached its limit, in a denial both of the Canon and the Creed, nay, of many principles of morals. Accordingly the question arises, whether these conclusions are in fairness to be connected with its original teaching or are a corruption. And it is no little aid towards its resolution to find that Luther himself at one time rejected the Apocalypse, called the Epistle of St. James, "straminea," condemned the word "Trinity," fell into a kind of Eutychianism as holding the omnipresence of our Lord's Manhood, and in a particular case, sanctioned bigamy. Calvinism, again, in various distinct countries, has become Socinianism, and Calvin seems to have denied our Lord's Eternal Sonship and ridiculed the Nicene Creed.

Another evidence, then, of the faithfulness of an ultimate development is its *definitive anticipation* at an early period in the history of the idea to which it belongs.

§ 7.

The Fifth Test; Logical Sequence.

Though it is a matter of accident in what order or degree developments of a common idea will show themselves in this or that place, particular minds or communities taking different courses, yet on a large field they will on the whole be gradual and orderly, nay, in *logical sequence.* It may be asked whether a development is itself a logical process; and if by {81} this is meant a conscious reasoning from premisses to conclusion, of course the answer must be in the negative. An idea grows in the mind by remaining there; it becomes familiar and distinct, and is viewed in its relations; it suggests other ideas, and these again others, subtle, recondite, original, according to the character, intellectual and moral, of the recipient; and thus a body of thought is gradually formed without his recognising what is going on within him. And all this while, or at least from time to time, external circumstances elicit into formal statement the thoughts which are coming into being in the depths of his mind; and soon he has to begin to defend them; and then again a further process must take place, of analysing his statements and ascertaining their dependence one on another. And thus he is led to regard as consequences, and to trace to principles, what hitherto he has discerned by a moral perception, and adopted on sympathy; and logic is brought in to arrange and inculcate what no science was employed in gaining.

And so in the same way, such intellectual processes, are carried on silently and spontaneously in the mind of a party or school, of necessity come to light at a later date, and then present themselves not without an intelligible order. Then logic has its function, not of discovery, but of propagation; analogy, the nature of the case, antecedent probability, application of principles, congruity, expedience, are some of the methods of proof on which the development is continued from mind to mind and established in the faith of the community.

Yet even then the analysis is not made on a principle, or with any view to its whole course and finished results. Each argument is brought for an immediate purpose; minds develop step by step, without looking behind them or anticipating their goal, and without either intention or promise of {82} forming a system. Afterwards, however, this logical character which the whole wears becomes a test that the process has been a true development, not a perversion or corruption, from its evident naturalness; and in some cases from the gravity, distinctness, precision, and majesty of its advance, and the harmony of its proportions, like the tall growth, and graceful branching, and rich foliage, of some vegetable production.

The process of development, thus capable of a logical expression, has sometimes been invidiously spoken of as rationalism and contrasted with faith. But though a particular doctrine or opinion which is subjected to development may happen to be rationalistic, and, as is the original, such are its results; and though we may develop erroneously, that is, reason incorrectly, yet the developing itself as little deserves that imputation in any case, as an inquiry into an historical fact, which we do not thereby make but ascertain,—for instance, whether or not St. Mark wrote his Gospel with St. Matthew before him, or Solomon brought his merchandize from Tartessus or some Indian port. Rationalism is the preference of reason to faith; but one does not see how it can be faith to adopt the premisses, and unbelief to accept the conclusion.

For instance, let us take a definition which some years since was given of rationalism. To rationalize is "to ask improperly how we are to *account for* certain things, to be unwilling to believe them unless they can be accounted for, that is, referred to something else as a cause, to some existing system, as harmonizing with them or taking them up into itself. . . . Rationalism is characterized by two peculiarities, its love of systematising, and its basing its system upon personal experience or the evidence of sense."[17] If this be rationalism, it is totally distinct from development; to develop is to {83} receive conclusions from received truth, to rationalize is to receive *nothing* but conclusions from received truths; to develop is positive, to rationalize is negative; the essence of development is to extend belief, of rationalism to contract it.

At the same time it may be granted that the spontaneous process which goes on within the mind itself is higher and choicer than that which is logical; for the latter, being scientific, is common property, and can be taken and made use of by minds who are strangers, in any true sense, both to the ideas in question and to their development.

Thus, the holy Apostles would know without words all the truths concerning the high doctrines of theology, which controversialists after them have piously and charitably reduced to formulae, and developed through argument. Thus St. Justin or St. Irenaeus might be without any digested ideas of Purgatory or Original Sin, yet have an intense feeling, which they had not defined or located, both of the fault of our first nature and the liabilities of our nature regenerate. Thus St. Antony said to the philosophers who came to mock him, "He whose mind is in health does not need letters;" and St. Ignatius Loyola, while yet an unlearned neophyte, was favoured with transcendent perceptions of the Holy Trinity during his penance at Manresa. Thus St. Athanasius himself is more powerful in statement and exposition than in proof; while in Bellarmine we find the whole series of doctrines carefully drawn out, duly adjusted with one another, and exactly analyzed one by one.

The history of empires and of public men supplies so many instances of political logic, that it is needless to do more than allude to them. It is illustrated by the words of Jeroboam, "Now shall this kingdom return to the house of David, if this people go up to do sacrifice in the house of the Lord at Jerusalem. . . . Wherefore the king took {84} counsel and made two calves of gold, and said unto them, Behold thy gods, O Israel."

A specimen of logical development, most interesting, though most painfully so, is afforded us in the history of Lutheranism as it has of late years been drawn out by various English writers. Luther started on a double basis, his dogmatic principle being contradicted by his right of private judgment, and his sacramental by his theory of justification. The sacramental element never showed signs of life; but on his death, that which he represented in his own person as a teacher, the dogmatic, gained the ascendancy; and "every expression of his upon controvert points became a norm for the party, which, at all times the largest, was at last coextensive with the Church itself. This almost idolatrous veneration was perhaps increased by the selection of declarations of faith, of which the substance on the whole was his, for the symbolical books of his Church."[18] Next a reaction took place; private judgment was restored to the supremacy. Calixtus put reason, and Spener the so-called religion of the heart, in the place of dogmatic correctness. Pietism for the present died away; but rationalism developed in Wolf, who professed to prove all the orthodox doctrines, by a process of reasoning, from premises level with the reason. It was soon found that the instrument which Wolf had used for orthodoxy, could as plausibly be used against it;—in his hands it had proved the Creed; in the hands of Semler, Ernesti, and others, it disproved the authority of Scripture. What was religion to be made to consist in now? A sort of philosophical Pietism followed; or rather Spener's pietism and the original theory of justification were analyzed more thoroughly, and issued in various theories of Pantheism, which from the first was at the bottom of Luther's doctrine and personal character.

And this appears to be the state {85} of Lutheranism at present, whether we view it in the philosophy of Kant, in the open infidelity of Strauss, or in the religious professions of the new Evangelical Church of Prussia. Applying this instance to the subject which it has been brought to illustrate, I should say that the equable and orderly march and natural succession of views, by which the creed of Luther has been changed into the infidel or heretical philosophy of his present representatives, is a proof that that change is no perversion or corruption, but a faithful development of the original idea.

This is but one out of many instances with which the history of the Church supplies us. The fortunes of a theological school are made the measure of the teaching of its founder. The great Origen died after his many labours in peace; his immediate pupils were saints and rulers in the Church; he has the praise of St. Athanasius, St. Basil, and St. Gregory Nazianzen, and furnishes materials to St. Ambrose and St. Hilary; yet, as time proceeded, a definite heterodoxy was the growing result of his theology, and at length, three hundred years after his death, he was condemned, and, as has generally been considered, in an Ecumenical Council.[19] "Diodorus of Tarsus," says Tillemont, "died at an advanced age, in the peace of the Church, honoured by the praises of the greatest saints, and crowned with a glory, which, having ever attended him through life, followed him after his death;"[20] yet St. Cyril of Alexandria considers him and Theodore of Mopsuestia the true authors of Nestorianism, and he was placed in the event by the Nestorians among their saints. Theodore himself was condemned {86} after his death by the same Council which is said to have condemned Origen, and is justly considered the chief rationalizing doctor of antiquity; yet he was in the highest repute in his day, and the eastern synod complains, as quoted by Facundus, that "Blessed Theodore, who died so happily, who was so eminent a teacher for five and forty years, and overthrew every heresy, and in his lifetime experienced no imputation from the orthodox, now after his death so long ago, after his many conflicts, after his ten thousand books composed in refutation of errors, after his approval in the sight of priests, emperors, and people, runs the risk of receiving the reward of heretics, and of being called their chief."[21] There is a certain continuous advance and determinate path which belong to the history of a doctrine, policy, or institution, and which impress upon the common sense of mankind, that what it ultimately becomes is the issue of what it was at first. This sentiment is expressed in the proverb, not limited to Latin, *Exitus acta probat*; and is sanctioned by Divine Wisdom, when, warning us against false prophets, It says, "Ye shall know them by their fruits."

Logical sequence, then, is a fifth characteristic of developments, which are faithfully drawn from the ideas to which they profess to belong.

§ 8.

The Sixth Test; Preservative Additions.

As developments which are preceeded by definite indications have a fair presumption in their favour, so those which do but contradict and reverse the course of doctrine which has been developed before them, and out of which they spring, are certainly corrupt; for a corruption is a development in that very stage in which it ceases to illustrate, and begins to prejudice, the acquisitions gained in its previous history.

{87} It is the rule of creation, or rather of the phenomena which it presents, that life passes on to its termination by a gradual, imperceptible course of change. There is ever a maximum in earthly excellence, and the operation of the same causes which made things great makes them small again. Weakness is but the resulting product of power. Events move in cycles; all things come round, "the sun ariseth and goeth down, and hasteth to his place where he arose." Flowers first bloom, and then fade; fruit ripens and decays. The fermenting process, unless stopped at the due point, corrupts the liquor which it has created. The grace of spring, the richness of autumn are but for a moment, and worldly moralists bid us *Carpe diem*, for we shall have no second opportunity. Virtue seems to lie in a mean, between vice and vice; and, as it grew out of imperfection, so to grow in enormity. There is a limit to human knowledge, and both sacred and profane writers witness that overwisdom is folly. And in the political world states rise and fall, the instruments of their aggrandizement becoming the weapons of their destruction. And hence tHe frequent ethical maxims, such as, *"Ne quid nimis,"* *"Medio tutissimus,"* "Vaulting ambition," which seem to imply that too much of what is good is evil.

So great a paradox of course cannot be maintained as that truth literally leads to falsehood, or that there can be an excess of virtue; but the appearance of things and the popular language about them will at least serve us in obtaining a test for the discrimination of a development of an idea from its corruption.

A true development, then, may be described as one which is conservative of the course of development which went before it, which is that development and something besides: it is an addition which illustrates, not obscures, corroborates, not corrects, {88} the body of thought from which it proceeds; and this is its characteristic as contrasted with a corruption.

For instance, a gradual conversion from a false to a true religion, plainly, has much of the character of a continuous process, or a development, in the mind itself, even when the two religions, which are the limits of its course, are antagonist. Now let it be observed, that such a change consists in addition and increase chiefly, not in destruction. "True religion is the summit and perfection of false religions; it combines in one whatever there is of good and true separately remaining in each. And in like manner the Catholic Creed is for the most part the combination of separate truths, which heretics have divided among themselves, and err in dividing. So that, in matter of fact, if as religious mind were educated in, and sincerely attached to some form of heathenism or heresy, and then were brought under the light of truth, it would be drawn off from error into the truth, not by losing what it had, but by gaining what it had not, not by being unclothed, but by being 'clothed upon,' 'that mortality may be swallowed up of life.' That same principle of faith which attaches it to its original wrong doctrine would attach it to the truth; and that portion of its original doctrine, which was to be cast off as absolutely false, would not be directly rejected, but indirectly, *in* the reception of the truth which is its opposite. True conversion is ever of a positive, not a negative character."[22]

Such too is the theory of the Fathers as regards the doctrines fixed by Councils, as is instanced in the language of St. Leo. "To be seeking for what has been disclosed, to reconsider what has been {89} finished, to tear up what has been laid down, what is this but to be thankful for what is gained?"[23] Vincentius of Lerins, in like manner, speaks of the development of Christian doctrine, as *Profectus fidei non permutatio.*[24] And so as regards the Jewish Law, our Lord said that He came "not to destroy, but to fulfil."

Mahomet is accused of contradicting his earlier revelations by his later, "which is a thing so well known to those of his sect that they all acknowledge it; and therefore when the contradictions are such as they cannot solve them, then they will have one of the contradictory places to be revoked. And they reckon in the whole Alcoran about a hundred and fifty verses which are thus revoked."[25]

Schelling, says Mr. Dewar, considers "that the time has arrived when an esoteric speculative Christianity ought to take

the place of the exoteric empiricism which has hitherto prevailed." This German philosopher "acknowledges that such a
project is opposed to the evident design of the Church, and of her
earliest teachers."[26]

When Roman Catholics are accused of substituting another
Gospel for the primitive Creed, they answer that they hold, and
can show that they hold, the doctrines of the Incarnation and
Atonement, as firmly as any Protestant can state them. To this it
is replied that they do certainly profess them, but that they
obscure and virtually annul them by their additions; that the
cultus of St. Mary and the Saints is no development of the truth,
but a corruption, because it draws away the mind and heart from
Christ. They answer that, so far from this, it subserves, illustrates
-trates, protects the doctrine of our Lord's condescension and
mediation. Thus the parties in controversy join issue on the
common ground, that a developed doctrine which reverses {90} the
course of development which has preceded it, is no true development but a corruption. This subject, however, will come before
us by and bye.

Blackstone supplies us with an instance in another subject
matter, when he observes that "when society is once formed,
government results of course, as necessary to preserve and to
keep that society in order."[27]

When the Long Parliament proceeded to usurp the
executive, they impaired the popular liberties which they seemed
to be advancing; for the security of those liberties depends on the
separation of the executive and legislative powers, or on the
enactors being subjects, not executors of the law.

And in the history of ancient Rome, from the time that the
privileges gained by the tribunes in behalf of the people became
an object of ambition to themselves, the development had
changed into a corruption. Thus, too, the Greek demagogue
became the tyrant.

And thus a sixth test of a true development is its being *an addition which is conservative* of what has gone before it.

§ 9.

The Seventh Test; Chronic Continuance

Since the corruption of an idea, as far as the appearance goes, is a sort of accident or affection of its development, being the end of a course, and a transition-state leading to a crisis, it is, as has been observed, a brief and rapid process. While ideas live in men's minds, they are ever enlarging into fuller development; they will not be stationary in their corruption any more than before it; and dissolution is that further state to which corruption tends. Corruption cannot, therefore, be of {91} long standing; and thus *duration* is another test of a faithful development.

Si gravis, brevis; si longus, levis; is the Stoical topic of consolation under pain; and of a number of disorders it can even be said, The worse, the shorter.

Sober men are indisposed to change in civil matters, and fear reforms and innovations, lest, if they go a little too far, they should at once run to some great calamities before a remedy can be applied. The chance of a slow corruption does not strike them. Revolutions are generally violent and swift; now, in fact, they are the course of a corruption.

The course of heresies is always short: it is an intermediate state between life and death, or what is like death; or, if it does not result in death, it is resolved into some new, perhaps opposite, course of error, which lays no claim to be connected with it. And in this way indeed an heretical principle will continue in life many years, first running one way, then another.

The abounding of iniquity is the token of the end approaching; the faithful in consequence cry out, How long? as if delay opposed reason as well as patience. Three years and a half are to complete the reign of Antichrist.

Nor is it any real objection that the world is ever corrupt, and yet, in spite of this, evil does not fill up its measure and overflow; for this arises from the external counteractions of truth and virtue, which bear it back; let the Church be removed, and the world will soon come to its end.

And so again, if the chosen people age after age became worse and worse, till there was no recovery, still their course of evil was continually broken by reformations, and was thrown back upon a less advanced stage of declension.

It is true that decay, which is one form of corruption, is slow; but decay is a state in which there {92} is no violent or vigorous action at all, whether of a conservative or a destructive character, the hostile influence being powerful enough to enfeeble the functions of life, but not to quicken its own process. And thus we see opinions, usages, and systems, which are of venerable and imposing aspect, but which have no soundness within them, and keep together from a habit of consistence, or from dependence on political institutions; or they become almost peculiarities of a country, or the habits of a race, or the fashions of society. And then, at length, perhaps they go off suddenly and die out under the first rough influence from without. Such are the superstitions which pervade a population, like some ingrained die or inveterate odour, and which at length come to an end, because nothing lasts forever, but which run no course, and have no history; such was the established paganism of classical times, which was the fit subject of persecution, for its first breath made it crumble and disappear. Such apparently is the state of the Nestorian and Monophysite communions; such might have been the condition of Christianity had it been absorbed by the feudalism of the middle ages; such too is that Protestantism or (as it sometimes calls itself) attachment to the Establishment, which is not unfrequently the boast of the respectable and wealthy among ourselves.

Whether Mahometanism external to Christendom, and the Greek Church within it, fall under this description is yet to be seen. Circumstances can be imagined which would even now rouse the fanaticism of the Moslem; and the Russian despotism does not venture upon the usages, though it may domineer over the priesthood, of the national religion.

Thus, while a corruption is distinguished from decay by its energetic action, it is distinguished from a development by its *transitory character*. {93} And thus we have a seventh and final test of a development.

This is all that need here be said on the criteriae between a development and a corruption. We shall have occasion for them hereafter. Meanwhile it is plain that they are only of a practical character, and not determined on any logical principle of division; and the instances which have been arranged under one head might in some cases have been referred to another.

[1] This sketch is for the most part taken from Southey, but in no case from any authority later than 1837. <Robert Southey (1774-1843>, author of *Life of Wesley; and the Rise and Progress of Methodism*, 1820).>

[2] Hallam's Constit. Hist. ch. vii. p. 572. <Henry Hallam (1777-1859), *Constitutional History of England from the Accession of Henry VIII to the Death of George II*, first published in 1827.>

[3] Ch. xlvii.

[4] Times Newspaper of March 1845.

[5] Crabbe's Tales. <George Crabbe (1754-1832), *Tales of the Hall* (1819), IX, 200.

[6] Eth. Nic. i. 8.

[7] Guizot Europ. Civil. Lect. v. Beckwith's Translation. <F. P. G. Guizot, *Lectures on European Civilization*, Oxford, 1837.>

[8] University Sermons, pp. 330-333.

[9] Commonit. 29.

[10] De Deo. ii. 4, § 8.

[11] Milman, Hist. of Christ. iii. 1 <Henry Hart Milman (1791-1868), Dean of St. Paul's), *The History of Christianity from the Birth of Christ to the Abolition of Paganism* (London, 1840), in 3 vols.>

[12] Hom. ii. 38.

[13] Bl. White's Autobiography, vol. ii. p. 110. <*The Life of the Rev. Joseph Blanco White, written by himself with Portions of his Correspondence*, edited by John Hamilton Thom (London: J. Chapman, 1845). Blanco White (1775-1841) was a Spanish priest, son of an Irishman who settled in Seville, and a Spanish mother. After becoming an Anglican clergyman, Blanco White was member, from 1826 on, of the Oriel Common Room, where he had friendly ties with Newman. Eventually he turned Unitarian and died a pantheist.>

[14] Tracts for the Times, No. 85, p. 15. <See note 1 to Introduction>

[15] Ch. xlix.

[16] Hallam's Const. Hist. ch. vi. p. 461. <See note 2 above.>

[17] Tracts for the Times, No. 73, § 1, init. <"On the Introduction of Rationalistic Principles into Religion," § 1, "The Rationalistic and the Catholic Spirit Compared," p. 2.>

[18] Pusey on German Rationalism, p. 21, note. <E. B. Pusey, *An Historical Inquiry into the Probable Causes of the Rationalist Character Lately Predominant in the Theology of Germany* (London: C. J. Rivington, 1828).>

[19] Halloix <Jean Halloix (1571-1656), *Origines defensus . . .* (Paris, 1648>, Valesius <Henricus Valesius (1603-76), whose editions, with translations into French, of the Church historians Eusebius, Socrates and Sozomen entered in Migne PG>, Lequien, <Michel Lequien (1661-1733), *Oriens Christianus, in quatuor patriarchatus digestus . . . opus postumum* (Paris, 1740)>, Gieseler <Johann K. L. Gieseler (1792-1854), *Lehrbuch der Kirchengeschichte* (1823); English translation *Textbook of Ecclesiastical History*, 1836>, Döllinger <Ignaz von Döllinger (1799-1890), Patristic scholar and Church historian>, &c. say that he was condemned, not in the fifth Council, but in the Council under Mennas.

[20] Mem. Eccl. tom. viii. p. 562.

[21] Def. Tr. Cap. viii. init. <*Sacrosanctum Concilium Tridentinum . . . cum citationibus . . .* (Bassani, 1842), suis typis Remondini edidit.>

[22] Tracts for the Times, No. 85, p. 73. A remark follows about Roman Catholics and the primitive faith, which may be better applied to the Roman faith and those who oppose it. <see note 14 above, Lecture VI, "External Difficulties of the Canon and the Catholic Creed, Compared.">

[23] Ep. 162.

[24] Ib. p. 309.

[25] Prideaux, Life of Mahomet, p. 90.<Humphrey Prideaux (1648-1724) Dean of Norwich, was an orientalist and author of *The History of the Life of the Great Impostor Mahomet* (1696) and other works relating to Mahomet.>

[26] German Protestantism, p. 176. <Duncan Dewar, *German Protestantism and the Right of Private Judgment in the Interpretation of Holy Scriptures. A Brief History of German Theology, from the Reformation to the Present Time. In a Series of Letters to a Layman* (Oxford: J. H. Parker, 1834)>

[27] Vol. i. p. 118. <W. Blackstone, *Commentaries on the Laws of England* (London, 1765-69).>

CHAPTER II.

ON THE DEVELOPMENT OF CHRISTIAN IDEAS ANTECEDENTLY CONSIDERED.

SECTION I

ON THE PROBABILITY OF DEVELOPMENTS IN CHRISTIANITY.

1. If Christianity is a fact, and can be made subject-matter of exercises of the reason, and impressed an idea on our minds, that idea will in course of time develop in a series of ideas connected and harmonious with one another, and unchangeable and complete, as is the external fact itself which is thus represented. It is the peculiarity of the human mind, that it cannot take an object in, which is submitted to it, simply and integrally. It conceives by means of definition or description; whole objects do not create in the intellect whole ideas, but are, to use a mathematical phrase, thrown into series, into a number of statements, strengthening, interpreting, correcting each other, and with more or less exactness approximating, as they accumulate, to a perfect image. There is no other way of learning or of teaching. We cannot teach except by aspects of views, which are not identical with the thing itself which we are teaching. Two persons will convey the same truth to another, yet by methods and representations altogether different. The same person will treat the same

89

argument differently in an essay or {95} speech, according to the accident of the day of writing, or of the audience, yet it will be the same.

And the more claim an idea has to be considered living, the more various will be its aspects; and the more social and political is its nature, the more complicated and subtle will be its developments, and the longer and more eventful will be its course. Such is Christianity; and whatever has been said in the last Chapter about the development of ideas generally, becomes of course an antecedent argument for its progressive development.

It may be objected that inspired documents, such as the Holy Scriptures, at once determine its doctrine without further trouble. But they were intended to create an idea, and that idea is not the sacred text, but in the mind of the reader; and the question is, whether that idea is communicated to him, in its completeness and minute accuracy, on its first apprehension, or expands in his heart and intellect, and comes to perfection in the course of time. Nor could it be maintained without extravagance that the letter of the New Testament, or of any assignable number of books, comprises a delineation of all possible forms which a divine message will assume when submitted to a multitude of minds.

Nor is the case altered by supposing that inspiration did for the first recipients of the Revelation what the Divine Fiat did for herbs and plants in the beginning, which were created in maturity. Still, the time at length came, when its recipients ceased to be inspired; and on these recipients the revealed truths would fall, as in other cases, at first vaguely, and generally, and would afterwards be completed by developments.

Nor can it fairly be made a difficulty that thus to treat of Christianity is to level it in some sort of sects and doctrines of the world, and to impute to it the imperfections which characterize the productions {96} of man. Certainly it is a degradation of a divine work to consider it under an earthly form; but it is no irreverence, since the Lord Himself, its Author and Owner, bore one also. Christianity differs from other religions and philosophies, in what it has in addition to them; not in kind, but in origin; not in its nature, but in its personal characteristics; being informed and quickened by what is more than intellect, by a Divine Spirit. It is externally what the Apostle calls an "earthen vessel," being the religion of men. And, considered as such, it grows "in wisdom and stature;" but the powers which it yields, and the words which proceed out of its mouth, attest its miraculous nativity.

Unless then some special ground of exception can be assigned, it is as evident that Christianity, as a doctrine and worship, will develop in the minds of recipients, as that it conforms in other respects, in its external propagation or its political framework, to the general methods by which the course of things is carried forward.

2. Again, if Christianity be an universal religion, suited not to one locality or period, but to all times and places, it cannot but vary in its relations and dealings towards the world around it, that is, it will develop. Principles require a very various application according to persons and circumstances, and must be thrown into new shapes according to the form of society which they are to influence. Hence all bodies of Christians develop the doctrines of Scripture. Few but will grant that Luther's view of justification had never been stated in words before his time; that his phraseology and his positions were novel, whether called for by circumstances or not. It is equally certain that the doctrine of justification defined at Trent was, in some sense, new also. The refutation and remedy of errors cannot precede their rise; and thus the fact of false developments or corruptions involves the {97} correspondent manifestation of true ones. Moreover, all parties appeal to Scripture, that is, argue from Scripture; but argument implies deduction, that is, development. Here there is no difference

between early times and late, between a Pope *ex cathedrâ* and an individual Protestant, except that their authority is not on a par. On either side the claim of authority is the same, and the process of development.[1]

Accordingly, the common complaint of Protestants against the Church of Rome is, not simply that she has added to the primitive or the Scriptural doctrine, but that she contradicts it, and moreover imposes her additions as fundamental truths under sanction of an anathema. For themselves they deduce by quite as subtle a method, and act upon doctrines as implicit and on reasons as little analyzed in time past, as Catholic schoolmen. What small prominence has the Royal Supremacy in the New Testament, or the lawfulness of bearing arms, or the duty of public worship, or the substitution of the first day of the week for the seventh, or infant baptism, to say nothing of the fundamental principle that the Bible and the Bible only is the religion of Protestants! These doctrines and usages, true or not, which is not the question here, are surely gained, not by a mere exercise of argument upon words and sentences placed before the eyes, but by the unconscious growth of ideas habitual to the mind.

3. And, indeed, when we turn to the consideration of particular doctrines on which the Scripture lays the greatest stress, we shall see that it is absolutely impossible for them to remain in the mere letter of Scripture, if they are to be more than mere words, or to convey a definite idea to the recipient. When it is declared that "the Word became flesh," three {98} wide questions open upon us on the very announcement. What is meant by "the Word," what by "flesh," what by "became?" The answers to these involve a process of investigation, and are developments. Moreover, when they have been made, they will suggest a series of secondary questions; and thus at length a multitude of propositions is the result, which gather round the inspired sentence of which they come, giving it externally the form of a doctrine, and creating or deepening the idea of it in the mind.

It is true that, so far as such statements of Scripture are mysteries, they are relatively to us but words, and cannot be developed. But as a mystery implies in part what is incomprehensible, so does it in part imply what is not so; it implies a partial manifestation, or a representation by economy. Because then it is in a measure understood, it can so far be developed, though each result in the process will partake of the dimness and confusion of the original impression.

4. This moreover should be considered, that great questions exist in the subject-matter of which Scripture treats, which Scripture does not solve; questions too so real, so practical, that they must be answered, and answered, unless we suppose a new revelation from the revelation which we have, that is, by development. Such is the question of the Canon of Scripture and its inspiration: whether Christianity depends upon a written document as Judaism, if so, on what writings and how many;— whether that document is self-interpreting, or requires a comment, and whether any authoritative comment or commentator is provided;—whether the revelation and the document are commensurate, or the one outruns the other, that is, whether or not the revelation is partly documentary and partly traditional, and whether or not the document is but partially the revelation, the revelation in an {99} uninspired organ, or the revelation with additions;—all these questions surely find no solution on the surface of Scripture, nor indeed under the surface in the case of most men, however long and diligent might be their study of it. Nor were these difficulties settled by authority, as far as we know, at the commencement of the religion; yet surely it is quite conceivable that an Apostle might have dissipated them all in a few words, had Divine Wisdom thought fit. But in matter of fact the decision has been left to time, to the slow process of thought, the influence of mind upon mind, the issues of controversy, and the growth of opinion.

To take another instance:—if there was a point on which a rule was desirable from the first, it was concerning the course which Christian parents were bound to pursue towards their children. It would be natural indeed in any Christian father, in the absence of express direction, to bring his children for baptism; such in this instance would be the practical development of his faith in Christ and love for his offspring; still a development it is,—necessarily required, yet, as far as we know, not provided for his need by the Revelation as originally given.

Another very large field of thought, full of practical considerations, yet, as far as our knowledge goes, but partially occupied by any apostolical judgment, is that which the question of the effects of Baptism opens upon us. That they who came in repentance and faith to that Holy Sacrament received remission of sins, is undoubtedly the doctrine of the Apostles; but is there any means of a second remission for sins committed after it? St. Paul's Epistles, where we might expect an answer to our inquiry, contain no explicit statement on the subject; what they do plainly say does not diminish the difficulty;—viz., first that Baptism is intended for the pardon of sins before it, not in prospect; {100} next, that those who have received the gift of Baptism live in a state of holiness, not of sin. How does doctrine like this meet the actual state of the Church as we see it at this day?

Considering that it was expressly predicted that the Kingdom of Heaven, like the fisher's net, should gather every kind, and that the tares should grow with the wheat until the harvest, a graver and more practical question cannot be imagined than that which it has pleased the Divine Author of the Revelation to leave undecided, unless indeed there be means in that Revelation for its own growth or development. As far as the letter goes of the inspired message, "there is not one of us but has exceeded by transgression its revealed provisions, and finds himself in consequence thrown upon those infinite resources of Divine Love which are stored in Christ, but have not been drawn out into form in its appointments."[2] Since then Scripture needs completion, the question is brought to this issue, whether defect or or inchoateness in its doctrines be or be not an antecedent probability in favour of a development of them.

There is another subject, though not so immediately practical, on which Scripture does not, strictly speaking, keep silence, for then there would be no basis for development, but says so little as to require, and so much as to suggest, information beyond its letter,—the intermediate state between death and the Resurrection. Considering the length of time which separates Christ's first and second coming, the millions of faithful souls who are exhausting it, and the intimate concern which every Christian has in the determination of its character, it might have been expected that Scripture would have spoken explicitly concerning it, whereas in fact its notices are but brief and obscure. We might indeed have argued that this silence was intentional, {101} with a view of discouraging speculations upon the subject, except for the circumstance that, as in the question of our post-baptismal state, its teaching seems to proceed upon an hypothesis inapplicable to the state of the Church since the time it was delivered. As Scripture contemplates Christians, not as backsliders, but as saints, so does it apparently represent the Day of Judgment as immediate, and the interval of expectation as evanescent. It leaves on our minds the general impression that Christ was returning on earth at once, "the time short," worldly engagements superseded by "the present distress," persecutors urgent, Christians sinless and expectant, without home, without plan for the future, looking up to heaven. But outward circumstances have changed, and with the change, of necessity, a different application of the revealed word became necessary, that is, a development. When the nations were converted and offences abounded, then the Church came out to view, on the one hand as an establishment, on the other as a remedial system, and passages of Scripture aided and directed the development which before were of inferior account. Hence the doctrine of Penance as the complement of Baptism, and of Purgatory as the explanation of the Intermediate State. So reasonable is this development of the original creed, that, when Baptism was lately expounded without the doctrine of Penance, it was accused by English Churchmen of Novatianism, while heterodox thinkers have before now urged the doctrine of the sleep of the soul as the only successful preventive of belief in Purgatory.

Thus developments of Christianity are proved to have been in the contemplation of its Divine Author, by an argument parallel to that by which we infer intelligence in the system of the physical world. In whatever sense the need and its supply are a proof of design in the visible creation, in the same do the {102} gaps, if the word may be used, which occur in the structure of the original creed of the Church, make it probable that those developments, which grow out of the truths which lie around them, were intended to complete it.

Nor can it be fairly objected that in thus arguing we are contradicting the great philosopher, who tells us that "upon supposition of God affording us light and instruction by revelation, additional to what He has afforded us by reason and experience, we are in no sort judges by what methods, and in what proportion, it were to be expected that this supernatural light and instruction would be afforded us,"[3] because he is speaking of our judging *before* a revelation is given. He observes that "we have no principles of reason upon which to judge beforehand, how it were to be expected Revelation should have been left, or what was most suitable to the divine plan of government," in various respects; but the case is altogether altered when a Revelation is vouchsafed, for then a new precedent, or what he calls "principle of reason," is introduced, and from what is actually put into our hands we can form a judgment whether more is to be expected. Butler, indeed, as a well-known passage of his work shows, is far from denying the principle of progressive development.

5. The method of revelation observed in Scripture abundantly confirms this anticipation. For instance, Prophecy, if it had so happened, need not have afforded a specimen of development; separate predictions might have been made to accumulate as time went on, prospects might have opened, definite knowledge might have been given, by communications independent of each other, as St. John's Gospel or the Epistles of St. Paul are unconnected with the first three Gospels, though the doctrine of each Apostle is a development of their matter. But the Revelation is, in matter of fact, not of this nature, but a process of development: the earlier prophecies are pregnant {103} texts out of which the succeeding announcements grow; they are types. It is not that first one truth is told, then another; but the whole truth or large portions of it are told at once, yet only in their rudiments, or in miniature, and they are expanded and finished in their parts, as the course of revelation proceeds. The Seed of the woman was to bruise the serpent's head; the scepter was not to depart from Judah till Shiloh came, to whom was the gathering of the people. He was to be Wonderful, Counsellor, the Prince of Peace. The question of the Ethiopian rises in the reader's mind, "Of whom speaketh the Prophet this?" Every word requires a comment. Accordingly, it is no uncommon theory with unbelievers, that the Messianic idea, as they call it, was gradually developed in the minds of the Jews by a continuous and traditional habit of contemplating it, and grew into its full proportions by a mere human process; and so far seems certain, without trenching on the doctrine of inspiration, that the books of Wisdom and Ecclesiasticus are developments of the writings of the Prophets, expressed under or elicited by current ideas in the Greek

philosophy, and ultimately adopted and ratified by the Apostle in his Epistle to the Hebrews.

But the whole Bible, not its prophetical portions only, is written on the principle of development. As the Revelation proceeds, it is ever new, yet ever old. St. John, who completes it, declares that he writes no "new commandment unto his brethren," but an old commandment which they "had from the beginning." And then he adds, "A new commandment I write unto you." The same test of development is suggested in our Lord's words on the Mount, as has already been noticed, "Think not that I am come to destroy the Law and the Prophets; I am not come to destroy, but to fulfil." He does not reverse, but perfect, what has gone before. Thus with respect to the evangelical view of the rite of {104} sacrifice, first the rite is enjoined by Moses; next Samuel says, "to obey is better than sacrifice;" then Hosea, "I will have mercy and not sacrifice;" Isaiah, "Incense is an abomination unto me;" then Malachi, describing the times of the Gospel, speaks of the "pure offering" of wheatflour; and our Lord completes the development, when He speaks of worshipping "in spirit and in truth." If there is anything yet to explain, it will be found in the usage of the Christian Church immediately afterwards, which shows that sacrifice was not removed, but truth and spirit added.

Nay, the *effata* of our Lord and His Apostles are of a typical structure, parallel to the prophetic announcements above mentioned, and predictions as well as injunctions of doctrine. If then the prophetic sentences have had that development which has really been given them, first by succeeding revelations, and then by the event, it is probable antecedently that those doctrinal, political, ritual, and ethical sentences, which have the same structure, should admit the same expansion. Such are, "This is My Body," or "Thou art Peter, and upon this Rock I will build My Church," or "Suffer little children to come unto Me," or "The pure in heart shall see God."

On this character of our Lord's teaching, the following passage may suitably be quoted. "His recorded words and works when on earth . . . come as the declarations of a Lawgiver. In the Old Covenant, Almighty God first of all spoke the Ten Commandments from Mount Sinai, and afterwards wrote them. So our Lord first spoke his own Gospel, both of promise and of precept, on the Mount, and His Evangelists have recorded it. Further, when He delivered it, He spoke by way of parallel to the Ten Commandments. And His style, moreover, corresponds to the authority which He assumes. It is of that solemn, measured, and severe character {105} which bears on the face of it tokens of its belonging to One who spake as none other man could speak. The Beatitudes, with which His Sermon opens, are an instance of this incommunicable, style, which befitted, as far as human words could befit, God Incarnate.

"Nor is this style peculiar to the Sermon on the Mount. All through the Gospels it is discernible, distinct from any other part of Scripture, showing itself in solemn declarations, canons, sentences, or sayings, such as legislators propound, and scribes and lawyers comment on. Surely everything our Saviour did and said is characterized by mingled simplicity and mystery. His emblematical actions, His typical miracles, His parables, His replies, His censures, all are evidences of a legislature in germ, afterwards to be developed, a code of divine truth which was ever to be before men's eyes, to be the subject of investigation and interpretation, and the guide in controversy. 'Verily, verily, I say unto you,'—'But, I say unto you,'—are the tokens of a supreme Teacher and Prophet.

"And thus the Fathers speak of His teaching. 'His sayings,' observes St. Justin, 'were short and concise; for He was no rhetorician, but His word was the power of God.' And St. Basil, in like manner, 'Every deed and every word of our Saviour Jesus Christ is a crown of piety and virtue. When then thou hearest word or deed of His, do not hear it as by the way, or after a simple and carnal manner, but enter into the depth of His contemplations, become a communicant in truths mystically delivered to thee.'

"As instances in point, I would refer, first, to His discourse with Nicodemus. We can hardly conceive but He must have spoken during His visit much more than is told us in St. John's Gospel; but so much is preserved as bears that peculiar character which became a Divine Lawgiver, and was {106} intended for perpetual use in the Church. It consists of concise and pregnant enunciations, on which volumes of instructive comment might be written. Every verse is a canon of Divine Truth.

"His discourse to the Jews, in the fifth chapter of St. John's Gospel, is perhaps a still more striking instance.

"Again, observe how the Evangelists heap His words together, though unconnected with each other, as if under a divine intimation, and with the consciousness that they were providing a code of doctrine and precept for the Church. St. Luke, for instance, at the end of his ninth chapter,&c . . . Here are six solemn declarations made one after another, with little or no connexion.

"The twenty-second chapter of St. Matthew would supply a similar series of sacred maxims; or, again the eighteenth, in which the separate verses, though succeeding one the other with somewhat more of connexion, are yet complete each in itself and very momentous.

"No one can doubt, indeed, that as the narratives of His miracles are brought together in one as divine signs, so His sayings are accumulated as lessons.

"Or take, again, the very commencement of His prophetical ministrations, and observe how His words run. He opens His mouth with accents of grace, and still they fall into expressive sentences. The first: 'How is it that ye sought Me? wist ye not that I must be about My Father's business?' The second: 'Suffer it to be so now, for thus it becometh us to fulfil all righteousness.' The third: 'Woman, what am I to thee? Mine hour is not yet come.' The fourth: 'Take these things hence; make not My Father's house a house of merchandize.' The fifth: 'Repent ye, for the Kingdom of Heaven is at hand.'

"The same peculiarity shows itself in His conflict with Satan. He strikes and overthrows him, as {107} David slew Goliath, with a sling and with a stone, with three words selected out of the Old Testament: 'Man shall not live by bread alone, but by every word which proceedeth out of the mouth of God.' Thou shalt not tempt the Lord thy God.' 'Thou shalt worship the Lord thy God, and Him only shalt thou serve.'

"In like manner, what He uttered from time to time at His crucifixion even goes by the name of His seven last words.

"Again: His parables and often His actions, as His washing His disciples' feet and paying the tribute, are instances of a similar peculiarity."[4]

Moreover, while it is certain that developments of Revelation proceeded all through the Old Dispensation down to the very end of our Lord's ministry, on the other hand, if we turn our attention to the beginnings of apostolical teaching after His ascension, we shall find ourselves unable to fix an historical point at which the growth of doctrine ceased, and the rule of faith was once for all settled. Not on the day of Pentecost, for St. Peter had still to learn at Joppa about the baptism of Cornelius; not at Joppa and Caesarea, for St. Paul had to write his Epistles; not on the death of the last Apostle, for St. Ignatius had to establish the doctrine of Episcopacy; not then, nor for many years after, for the Canon of the New Testament was still undetermined. Not in the Creed, which is no collection of definitions, but a summary of certain *credenda*, an incomplete summary, and, like the Lord's Prayer or the Decalogue, a mere sample of divine truths, especially of the more elementary. No one doctrine can be named which starts *omnibus numeris* at first, and gains nothing from the investigations of faith and the attacks of heresy. The Church went forth from the world in haste, as the Israelites from Egypt "with their dough before it was leavened, {108} their kneading troughs being bound up in their clothes upon their shoulders."

Moreover, the political developments contained in the historical parts of Scripture are as striking as the prophetical and the doctrinal. Can any history wear a more human appearance than that of the rise and growth of the chosen people to which I have just alluded? What had been determined in the counsels of the Lord of heaven and earth from the beginning, what was immutable, what was announced to Moses in the burning bush, is afterwards represented as the growth of an idea under successive emergences. The Divine Voice in the bush announced the Exodus of the children of Israel from Egypt and their entrance into Canaan; and added, as a token of the certainty of His purpose, "When thou hast brought forth the people out of Egypt, ye shall serve God upon this mountain." Now this sacrifice or festival, which was but incidental and secondary in the great deliverance, is for a while the ultimate scope of the demands which Moses makes upon Pharaoh. "Thou shalt come, thou and the elders of Israel, unto the King of Egypt, and you shall say unto him, The Lord God of the Hebrews hath met with us, and now let us go, we beseech thee, three days' journey into the wilderness, that we may sacrifice to the Lord our God." It was added that Pharaoh would first refuse their request, but that after miracles he would let them go altogether, nay, with "jewels of silver and gold, and raiment." Accordingly the first request of Moses was, "Let us go, we pray thee, three days' journey into the desert and sacrifice unto the Lord our God." Before the plague of frogs the warning is repeated, "Let My people go that they may serve Me;" and after it Pharaoh says, "I will let the people go, that they may do sacrifice unto the Lord." It occurs again before the plague of flies; and after it Pharaoh offers to let the {109} Israelites sacrifice in Egypt which Moses refuses on the ground that they will have to "sacrifice the abomination of the Egyptians before their eyes." "We will go three days' journey into the wilderness," he proceeds, "and sacrifice to the Lord our God;" and Pharaoh then concedes their sacrificing in the wilderness, "only," he says, "You shall not go very far away." The demand is repeated separately before the plagues of murrain, hail, and locusts, no mention being yet made of anything beyond a service or sacrifice in the wilderness. On the last of these interviews, Pharaoh asks an explanation, and Moses extends his claim: "We will go with our young and with our old, with our sons and with our daughters, with our flocks and with our herds will we go, for we must hold a feast unto the Lord." That it was an extension seems plain from Pharaoh's reply: "Go now ye that are men and serve the Lord, for that ye did desire." Upon the plague of darkness Pharaoh concedes the extended demand, excepting the flocks and herds; but Moses reminds him that they were implied, though not expressed in the original wording: "Thou must give us also sacrifices and burnt offerings, that we may sacrifice unto the Lord our God." Even to the last, there is no intimation of their leaving Egypt for good; the issue was left to be wrought out by the Egyptians. "All these thy servants," says Moses, "shall come down unto me, and bow themselves unto me, saying, Get thee out, and all the people that follow thee, and after that I will go out;" and accordingly, after the judgment on the first-born, they were thrust out at midnight, with their flocks and herds, their kneading troughs and their dough, laden, too, with the spoils of Egypt, as had been fore-ordained, yet apparently by a combination of circumstances, or the complication of a crisis. Yet Moses knew that their departure from Egypt was final, for he took the bones of Joseph with him; and that {110} conviction broke on Pharaoh soon, when he and his asked themselves, "Why have we done this, that we have let Israel go from serving us?" But this progress of events, vague and uncertain as it seemed to be, notwithstanding the miracles which attended it, had been directed by Him who works out gradually what He has determined absolutely; and it ended in the parting of the Red Sea, and the destruction of Pharaoh's host, on his pursuing them.

Moreover, from what occurred forty years afterwards, when they were advancing upon the promised land, it would seem that the original grant of territory did not include the country east of Jordan, held in the event by Reuben, Gad, and half the tribe of Manasseh; at least they undertook at first to leave Sihon in undisturbed possession of his country, if he would let them pass through it, and only on his refusing his permission did they invade and appropriate it.

6. It is in point to notice also the structure and style of Scripture, a structure so unsystematic and various, and a style so figurative and indirect, that no one would presume at first sight to say what is in it and what is not. It cannot, as it were, be mapped, or its contents catalogued; but after all our diligence, to the end of our lives and to the end of the Church, it must be an unexplored and unsubdued land, with heights and valleys, forests and streams, on the right and left of our path and close about us, full of concealed wonders and choice treasures. Of no doctrine whatever, which does not actually contradict what has been delivered, can it be peremptorily asserted that it is not in Scripture; of no reader, whatever be his study of it, can it be said that he has mastered every doctrine which it contains. Butler's remarks on this subject were just now alluded to. "The more distinct and particular knowledge," he says, "of those {111} things, the study of which the Apostle calls 'going on unto perfection,'" that is, of the more recondite doctrines of the gospel, "and of the prophetic parts of revelation, like many parts of natural and even

civil knowledge, may require very exact thought and careful consideration. The hindrances too of natural and of supernatural light and knowledge have been of the same kind. And as it is owned the whole scheme of Scripture is not yet understood, so, if it ever comes to be understood, before the "restitution of all things," and without miraculous interpositions, it must be in the same way as natural knowledge is come at, by the continuance and progress of learning and of liberty, and by particular persons, attending to, comparing, and pursuing intimations scattered up and down it, which are overlooked and disregarded by the generality of the world. For this is the way in which all improvements are made, by thoughtful men tracing on obscure hints, as it were, dropped us by nature accidentally, or which seem to come into our minds by chance. Nor is it at all incredible that a book, which has been so long in the possession of mankind, should contain many truths as yet undiscovered. For all the same phenomena, and the same faculties of investigation, from which such great discoveries in natural knowledge have been made in the present and last age, were equally in the possession of mankind several thousand years before. And possibly it might be intended that events, as they come to pass, should open and ascertain the meaning of several parts of Scripture."[5] Butler of course was not contemplating the case of new articles of faith, or developments imperative on our acceptance, but he surely bears witness to the probability of developments in Christian doctrine considered in themselves, which is the point at present in question.

{112} It may be added that, in matter of fact, all the definitions or received judgments of the early and medieval Church rest upon definite, even though sometimes obscure sentences of Scripture. Thus Purgatory may appeal to the "saving by fire," and "entering through much tribulation into the kingdom of God;" the communication of the merits of the Saints to our "receiving a prophet's reward" for "receiving a prophet in the name of a

prophet," and "a righteous man's reward" for "receiving a righteous man in the name of a righteous man;" the Real Presence to
"This is My Body;" Absolution to "Whatsoever sins ye remit, they
are remitted;" Extreme Unction to "Anointing him with oil in the
Name of the Lord;" Voluntary poverty to "Sell all that thou hast;"
obedience to "He was in subjection to His parents;" the honour paid
to creatures, animate or inanimate, to *Laudate Dominum in sanctis
Ejus*, and *Adorate scabellum pedum Ejus*; and so of the rest.

7. Lastly, while Scripture no where recognises itself or
asserts the inspiration of those passages which are most essential,
it distinctly anticipates the development of Christianity, both as a
polity and as a doctrine. In one of our Lord's parables "the
Kingdom of Heaven" is even compared to "a grain of mustard-
seed, which a man took and hid in his field; which indeed is the
least of all seeds, but when it is grown it is the greatest among
herbs, and becometh a tree," and, as St. Mark words it, "shooteth
out great branches, so that the birds of the air come and lodge in
the branches thereof." And again, in the same chapter of St.
Mark, "So is the kingdom of God, as if a man should cast seed
into the ground, and should sleep, and rise night and day, and the
seed should spring and grow up, he knoweth not how; for the
earth bringeth forth fruit of herself." Here an internal element of
life, whether principle or doctrine, is spoken of rather {113} than
any mere external manifestation; and it is observable that the
spontaneous, as well as the gradual, character of the growth is
intimated. This description of the process corresponds to what has
been above observed respecting development, viz., that it is not
an effect of wishing and resolving, or of forced enthusiasm, or of
any mechanism of reasoning, or of any mere subtlety of intellect;
but comes of its own innate power of expansion within the mind
in its season, though with the use of reflection and argument and
original thought, more or less as it may happen, with a dependence on the ethical growth of the mind itself, and with a reflex

influence upon it. Again, the Parable of the Leaven describes the development of doctrine in another respect, in its active, engrossing and assimilating power.

From the necessity, then, of the case, from the history of all sects and parties in religion, and from the analogy and example of Scripture, we may fairly conclude that Christian doctrine admit of formal, legitimate, and true developments, or of developments contemplated by its Divine Author.

The general analogy of the world, physical and moral, confirms this conclusion, as we are reminded by the great authority who has already been quoted in the course of this Section. "The whole natural world and government of it," says Butler, "is a scheme or system; not a fixed, but a progressive one; a scheme in which the operation of various means takes up a great length of time before the ends they tend to can be attained. The change of seasons, the ripening of the fruits of the earth, the very history of a flower is an instance of this; and so is human life. Thus vegetable bodies, and those of animals, though possibly formed at once, yet grow up by degrees to a mature state. And thus rational agents, who animate these latter bodies, are naturally directed to form each his own manners and character {114} by the gradual gaining of knowledge and experience, and by a long course of action. Our existence is not only successive, as it must be of necessity, but one state of our life and being is appointed by God to be a preparation for another; and that to be the means of attaining to another succeeding one; infancy to childhood, childhood to youth, youth to mature age. Men are impatient, and for precipitating things; but the Author of Nature appears deliberate throughout His operations, accomplishing His natural ends by slow successive steps. And there is a plan of things beforehand laid out, which, from the nature of it, requires various systems of means, as well as length of time, in order to the carrying on its several parts into execution. Thus, in the daily course of natural providence, God operates in the very same manner as in the dispensation of Christianity, making one thing subservient to another; this, to somewhat farther; and so on, through a progressive series of means, which extend, both backward and forward, beyond our utmost view. Of this manner of operation, everything we see in the course of nature is as much an instance as any part of the Christian dispensation."[6]

SECTION II.

ON THE PROBABILITY OF A DEVELOPING AUTHORITY IN CHRISTIANITY.

It has now been made probable that developments of Christianity were but natural, as time went on, and were to be expected; and that these natural and true developments, as being natural and true, were of course contemplated and taken into account by its Author, who in designing the work designed its legitimate results. These may be called absolutely {115} "the developments" of Christianity. That there are such is surely a great step gained in the inquiry; it is a momentous fact. The next question is, *What* are they? and to a theologian, who could take a general view, and also possessed an intimate and minute knowledge of its history, they would doubtless on the whole be easily distinguishable by their own characters, and require no foreign aid to point them out, no external authority to ratify them. But it is difficult to say who is exactly in this position. Considering that Christians, from the nature of the case, live under the bias of the doctrines, and in the very midst of the facts, and during the process of the controversies, which are to be the subject of criticism, since they are exposed to the prejudices of birth, education, locality, personal attachment, and party, it can hardly be maintained that in matter of fact a true development carries with it always its own certainty even to the learned, or that history, past or present, is secure from the possibility of a variety of interpretations.

I have already spoken on this subject in a very different connexion:—

"Prophets or Doctors are the interpreters of the revelation; they unfold and define its mysteries, they illuminate its documents, they harmonize its contents, they apply its promises. Their teaching is a vast system, not to be comprised in a few sentences, not to be embodied in one code or treatise, but consisting of a certain body of Truth, pervading the Church like an atmosphere, irregular in its shape from its very profusion and exuberance; at times separable only in idea from Episcopal Tradition, yet at times melting away into legend and fable; partly written, partly unwritten, partly the interpretation, partly the supplement of Scripture, partly preserved in intellectual expressions, partly latent in the spirit and temper of Christians; poured to and fro in closets and upon the housetops, in {116} liturgies, in controversial works, in obscure fragments, in sermons, in popular prejudices, in local customs. This I call Prophetical Tradition, existing primarily in the bosom of the Church itself, and recorded in such measure as Providence has determined in the writings of eminent men. Keep that which is committed to thy charge, is St. Paul's injunction to Timothy; and for this reason, because from its vastness and indefiniteness it is especially exposed to corruption, if the Church fails in vigilance. This is that body of teaching which is offered to all Christians even at the present day, though in various forms and measures of truth, in different parts of Christendom, partly being a comment, partly an addition upon the articles of the Creed."[7]

If this be true, certainly some rule is necessary for arranging and authenticating these various expressions and results of

Christian doctrine. No one will maintain that all points of belief are of equal importance. "There are what may be called minor points, which we may hold to be true without imposing them as necessary;" "there are greater truths and lesser truths, points which it is necessary, and points which it is pious to believe."[8] The simple question is, How are we to discriminate the greater from the less, the true from the false.

This need of an authoritative sanction is increased by considering after M. Guizot's suggestion, that Christianity, though represented in prophecy as a kingdom, came into the world as an idea rather than an institution, and has had to wrap itself in clothing and fit itself with armour of its own providing, and to form the instruments and methods of its prosperity and warfare. If the developments, which have above been called *moral*, are to take place to any great extent, and without them it is difficult to see how Christianity can exist at all, if {117} only its relations towards civil government have to be ascertained, or the qualifications for the profession of it have to be defined, surely an authority is necessary to impart decision to what is vague and confidence to what is empirical, to ratify the successive steps of so elaborate a process, and to secure the validity of inferences which are to be made the premisses of more remote investigations.

Tests, it is true, for ascertaining the correctness of developments in general have been drawn out in a former Chapter, and shall presently be used; but they are insufficient for the guidance of individuals in the case of so large and complicated a problem as Christianity, though they aid our inquiries and support our conclusions in particular points. They are of a scientific and controversial, not of a practical character, and are instruments rather than warrants of right decisions. While, then, on the one hand, it is probable that some means will be granted for ascertaining the legitimate and true developments of Revelation, it appears, on the other, that these means must of necessity be external to the developments themselves.

Reasons shall be given in the present Section for asserting that, in proportion to the probability of true developments of doctrine and practice in the Divine Scheme, is the probability also of the appointment in that scheme of an external authority to decide upon them, thereby separating them from the mass of mere human speculation, extravagance, corruption, and error, in and out of which they grow. This is the doctrine of the infallibility of the Church; for by infallibility I suppose is meant the power of deciding whether this, that, and a third, and any number of theological or ethical statements are true.

1. Let the state of the case be carefully considered. If the Christian doctrine, as originally taught, admits of true and important developments, {118} as was argued in the foregoing Section, this is a strong antecedent argument in favour of a provision in the Dispensation for putting a seal of authority upon those developments. The probability of their being known to be true varies with their truth. The two ideas are certainly quite distinct of revealing and guaranteeing a truth, and they are often distinct in fact. There are various revelations all over the earth which do not carry with them the evidence of their divinity. Such are the inward suggestions and secret illuminations granted to so many individuals; such are the traditionary doctrines which are found among the heathen, that "vague and unconnected family of religious truths, originally from God, but sojourning, without the sanction of miracle or a definite home, as pilgrims up and down the world, and discernible and separable from the corrupt legends with which they are mixed, by the spiritual mind alone."[9] There is nothing impossible in the notion of a revelation occurring without evidences that it is a revelation; just as human sciences are a divine gift, yet are reached by our ordinary powers and have no claim on our faith. But Christianity is not of this nature:

it is a revelation which comes to us as a revelation, as a whole, objectively, and with a profession of infallibility; and the only question to be determined relates to the matter of the revelation. If then there are certain great truths, or proprieties, or observances, naturally and legitimately resulting from the doctrines originally professed, it is but reasonable to include these true results in the idea of the revelation, to consider them parts of it, and if the revelation be not only true, but guaranteed as true, to anticipate that they will be guaranteed inclusively. Christianity, unlike other revelations of God's will, except the Jewish, of which it is a continuation, is an objective religion, or a revelation {119} with credentials; it is natural then to view it wholly as such, and not partly *sui generis*, partly like others. Such as it begins, such let it be considered to continue: if certain large developments of it are true, they must surely be accredited as true.

2. An objection, however, is often made to the doctrine of infallibility *in limine*, which is too important not to be taken into consideration. It is urged that, as all religious knowledge rests on moral evidence, not on demonstration, our relief in the Church's infallibility must be of this character; but what can be more absurd than a probable infallibility, or a certainty resting on doubt?—I believe, because I am sure; and I am sure, because I think. Granting then that the gift of infallibility be adapted, when believed, to unite all intellects in one common confession, it is as difficult of proof as the developments which it is to prove, and nugatory therefore, and in consequence improbable in a Divine Scheme. "The advocates of Rome," it has been urged as an *argumentum ad hominem*, yet it will serve to express the objection as used for its own sake, "insist on the necessity of an infallible guide in religious matters, as an argument that such a guide has really been accorded. Now it is obvious to inquire how individuals are to know with certainty that Rome *is* infallible . . . how any ground can be such as to bring home to the mind

infallibly that she is infallible; what conceivable proof amounts to more than a probability of the fact; and what advantage is an infallible guide, if those who are guided have, after all, no more than an opinion, as the Romanists call it, that she is infallible?"[10]

This argument, however, except when used, as is intended in this passage, against such persons as would remove all doubt from religion, is certainly a {120} fallacious one. For since, as all allow, the Apostles were infallible, it tells against their infallibility, or the infallibility of Scripture, as truly as against the infallibility of the Church; for no one will say that the Apostles were made infallible for nothing, yet we are only morally certain that they were infallible. Further, if we have but probable grounds for the Church's infallibility, we have but the like for the impossibility of certain things, the necessity of others, the truth, the certainty of others; and therefore the words *infallibility, necessity, truth,* and *certainty* ought all of them to be banished from the language. But why is it more inconsistent to speak of an uncertain infallibility than of a doubtful truth or a contingent necessity, phrases which present ideas clear and undeniable? In truth we are playing with words when we use arguments of this sort. When we say a person is infallible, we mean no more than that what he says is always true, always to be believed, always to be done. The term is resolvable into these phrases as its equivalents; either then the phrases are inadmissible, or the idea of infallibility must be allowed. A probable infallibility is a probable gift of never erring; a reception of the doctrine of a probable infallibility is faith and obedience towards a person founded on the probability of his never erring in his declarations or commands. What is inconsistent in this idea? Whatever then be the particular means of determining infallibility, the abstract objection may be put aside.

3. Again, it is sometimes argued that such a dispensation would destroy our probation, as dissipating doubt, precluding the exercise of faith, and obliging us to obey whether we wish it or

no; and it is urged that a Divine Voice spoke in the first age, and difficulty and darkness rest upon all subsequent ones; as if infallibility and personal judgment were incompatible; but this is to confuse the subject. We {121} must distinguish between a revelation and the reception of it, not between its earlier and later stages. A revelation, in itself divine, and guaranteed as such, may be received, doubted, argued against, perverted, rejected, by individuals according to the state of mind of each. Ignorance, misapprehension, unbelief, and other causes, do not at once cease to operate because the revelation is in itself true and in its proofs irrefragable. We have then no warrant at all for saying that an accredited revelation will exclude doubts and difficulties, or dispense with anxious diligence on our part, though it may in its own nature tend to do so. Infallibility does not interfere with moral probation; the two notions are perfectly distinct. It is no objection then to the idea of an arbitrary authority, such as I am imposing, that it lessens the task of personal inquiry, unless it be an objection to the authority of Revelation altogether. A Church, or a Council, or a Pope, or a Consent of Doctors, or a Consent of Christendom, limits the inquiries of the individual in no other way than Scripture limits them: it does limit them; but while it limits their range, it preserves intact their probationary character; we are tried as really, though not on so large a field. To suppose that the doctrine of a permanent authority in matters of faith interferes with our freewill and responsibility is, as before, to forget that there were infallible teachers in the first age, and heretics and schismatics in the ages subsequent. There may have been a supreme authority from first to last, and a moral judgment from first to last. Moreover, those who maintain that Christian truth must be gained solely by personal efforts are bound to show that methods, ethical and intellectual, are granted to individuals sufficient for gaining it; else the mode of probation they advocate is less, not more, perfect than that which proceeds upon external authority. On the whole, then, no argument against continuing the principle {122} of objectiveness into the developments of Revelation is deducible from the conditions of our moral responsibility.

4. Perhaps it will be urged that the Analogy of Nature is against our anticipating the continuance of an external authority which has once been given; because, in the words of the profound thinker who has already been cited, "We are wholly ignorant what degree of new knowledge it were to be expected God would give mankind by revelation, upon supposition of His affording one; or how far, and in what way, He would interpose miraculously to qualify them to whom He should originally make the revelation for communicating the knowledge given by it, and to secure their doing it to the age in which they should live, and to secure its being transmitted to posterity;" and because "we are not in any sort able to judge whether it were to be expected that the revelation should have been committed to writing, or left to be handed down, and consequently corrupted, by verbal tradition, and at length sunk under it."[11] But this reasoning does not here apply, as has already been observed; it contemplates only the abstract hypothesis of a revelation, not the fact of an existing revelation of a particular kind, which may of course in various ways modify our state of knowledge, by settling some of those very points on which, before it was given, we had no means of deciding. Nor can it, as I think, be fairly denied that the argument from Analogy in one point of view tells against anticipating a revelation at all, for an innovation upon the physical order of the world is by the very force of the terms inconsistent with its ordinary course. We cannot then regulate our antecedent view of the character of a revelation by a test which, applied simply, overthrows the very notion of a revelation altogether. Anyhow, Analogy is in some sort violated by the fact of a {123} revelation, and the question before us only relates to the extent of that violation.

I will hazard a distinction here between the facts of revelation and its principles;—the argument from Analogy is more concerned with its principles than with its facts. The revealed facts are special and singular, from the nature of the case: but it is otherwise with the revealed principles; they are common to all the works of God: and if the Author of Nature be the Author of Grace, it may be expected that, while the two systems of facts are distinct and independent, the principles displayed in them will be the same, and form a connecting link between them. In this identity of principle lies the Analogy of Natural and Revealed Religion, in Butler's sense of the word. The doctrine of the Incarnation is a fact, and cannot be paralleled by anything in nature;[12] the doctrine of Mediation is a principle, and is abundantly exemplified in its provisions. Miracles are facts; inspiration is a fact; divine teaching once for all, and a continual teaching, are each a fact; probation by means of intellectual difficulties is as principle both in nature and in grace, and may be carried on in the system of grace either by a standing ordinance of teaching or by one definite act of teaching, and that with an analogy as perfect in either case to the order of nature; nor can we succeed in arguing from the analogy of that order against a standing guardianship of revelation without arguing also against its original bestowal. Supposing the order of nature once broken by the introduction of a revelation, the continuance of that revelation is but a question of degree; and the circumstance that a work has begun makes it more probable than not that it will proceed. We have no reason to suppose that there is so great a distinction of dispensation between ourselves and the first generation of Christians, as that they had a living infallible guidance, and we have not.

{124} The case then stands thus:—that Revelation has introduced a new law of divine governance over and above those laws which appear in the natural course of the world; and henceforth our argument for a standing authority in matters of faith proceeds on the analogy of Nature, and from the fact of Christianity. Preservation is involved in the idea of creation. As the Creator rested on the seventh day from the work which He had made, yet He "worketh hitherto;" so He gave the Creed once for all in the beginning, yet blesses its growth still, and dispenses its increase. His word "shall not return unto Him void, but accomplish" His pleasure. As creation argues continual governance, so are Apostles harbingers of Popes,

5. Moreover, it must be borne in mind that, as the essence of all religion is authority and obedience, so the distinction between natural religion and revealed lies in this, that the one has a subjective authority, and the other an objective. Revelation consists in the manifestation of the Invisible Divine Power, or in the substitution of the voice of a Lawgiver for the voice of conscience. The supremacy of conscience is the essence of natural religion; the supremacy of Apostle, or Pope, or Church, or Bishop, is the essence of the revealed; and when such external authority is taken away, the mind falls back again upon that inward guide[13] which it possessed even before Revelation was vouchsafed. Thus, what conscience is in the system of nature, such is the voice of Scripture, or of the Church, or of the Holy See, as we may determine it, in the system of Revelation. It may be objected, indeed, that conscience is not infallible; it is true, but still it is ever to be obeyed. And this is just the prerogative which controversialists assign to the See of St. Peter; it is not in all cases infallible, it may err beyond its special province, but it has even in all {125} cases a claim on our obedience. "All Catholics and heretics," says Bellarmine, "agree in two things: first that it is possible for the Pope, even as Pope, and with his own assembly of councillors, or with General Council, to err in particular controversies of fact, which chiefly depend on human information and testimony; secondly, that it is possible for him

to err as a private Doctor, even in universal questions of right, whether of faith or of morals, and that from ignorance, as sometimes happens to other doctors. Next, all Catholics agree in other two points, not, however, with heretics, but solely with each other: first, that the Pope with General Council cannot err, either in framing decrees of faith or general precepts of morality; secondly, that the Pope, when determining anything in a doubtful matter, whether by himself or with his own particular Council, *whether it is possible for him to err or not, is to be obeyed* by all the faithful."[14] And as obedience to conscience, even supposing conscience ill-informed, tends to the improvement of our moral nature, and ultimately of our knowledge, so obedience to our ecclesiastical superior may subserve our growth in illumination and sanctity, even though he should command what is extreme or inexpedient, or teach what is external to his legitimate province.

6. The common sense of mankind does but support a conclusion thus forced upon us by analogical considerations. It feels that the very idea of revelation implies a present informant and guide, and that an infallible one; not a mere abstract declaration of truths not known before to man, or a record of history, or the result of an antiquarian research, but a message and a lesson speaking to this man and that. This is shown by the popular notion which has prevailed among us since the Reformation, that the Bible itself is such a guide; {126} and which succeeded in overthrowing the supremacy of Church and Pope, for the very reason that it was a rival authority, not resisting merely, but sup-planting it. In proportion, then, as we find, in matter of fact, that the inspired Volume is not calculated or intended to subserve that purpose, are we forced to revert to that living and present guide, which, at the era of her rejection, had been so long recognized as the dispenser of Scripture according to times and circumstances, and the arbiter of all true doctrine and holy practice to her children: We feel a need, and she alone

of all things under heaven supplies it. We are told that God has spoken. Where? In a book? We have tried it, and it disappoints; it disappoints, that most holy and blessed gift, not from fault of its own, but because it is used for a purpose for which it was not given. The Ethiopian's reply, when St. Philip asked him if he understood what he was reading, is the voice of nature: "How can I, unless some man shall guide me?" The Church undertakes that office; she does what none else can do, and this is the secret of her power. "The human mind," it has been said, "wishes to be rid of doubt in religion; and a teacher who claims infallibility is readily believed on his simple word. We see this constantly exemplified in the case of individual pretenders among ourselves. In Romanism the Church pretends to it; she rids herself of competitors by forestalling them. And probably, in the eyes of her children, this is not the least persuasive argument for her infallibility, that she alone of all Churches dares claim it, as if a secret instinct and involuntary misgivings restrained those rival communions which go so far towards affecting it."[15] These sentences, whatever be the errors of their wording, surely express a great truth. The most obvious answer, then, to the question, why we yield {127} to the authority of the Church in the questions and developments of faith, is, that some authority there must be if there is a revelation, and other authority there is none but she. In the words of St. Peter to her Divine Master and Lord, "To whom shall we go?" Nor must it be forgotten in confirmation, that Scripture expressly calls the Church "the pillar and ground of the Truth," and promises her as by covenant that "the Spirit of the Lord that is upon her, and His words which He has put in her mouth shall not depart out of her mouth, nor out of the mouth of her seed, nor out of the mouth of her seed's seed, from henceforth and for ever."[16]

7. And if the very claim to infallible arbitration in religious disputes is of so weighty importance and interest in all ages of

the world, much more is it welcome at a time like the present, when the human intellect is so busy, and thought so fertile, and opinion so definitely divided. The absolute need of a spiritual supremacy is at present the strongest of arguments in favour of its supply. Surely, either an objective revelation has not been given, or it has been provided with means for impressing its objectiveness on the world. If Christianity be a social religion, as it certainly is, and if it be based on certain ideas acknowledged as divine, or a creed, which shall here be assumed, and if these ideas have various aspects, and make distinct impressions on different minds, and issue in consequence in a multiplicity of developments, true, or false, or mixed, as has been shown, what influence will suffice to meet and to do justice to these conflicting conditions, but a supreme authority ruling and reconciling individual judgments by a divine right and a recognized wisdom? In barbarous times the will is reached through the senses; but in an age in which reason, as it is called, is the standard of truth and right, it is abundantly evident to any one, {128} who mixes ever so little with the world, that, if things are left to themselves, every individual will have his own view of things, and take his own course; that two or three agree together to-day to part tomorrow; that Scripture will be read in contrary ways and history will be analyzed into subtle but practical differences; that philosophy, taste, prejudice, passion, party, caprice, will find no common measure, unless there be some supreme power to control the mind and to compel agreement. There can be no combination on the basis of truth without an organ of truth. As cultivation brings out the colours of flowers, and domestication the hues of animals, so does education of necessity develop differences of opinion; and while it is impossible to lay down first principles in which all will unite, it is utterly unreasonable to expect that this man should yield to that, or all to one. I do not say there are no eternal truths, such as the poet speaks of,[17] which all acknowledge in private, to be the basis of public union and action. The only general persuasive in matters of conduct is authority; that is, when truth is in question, a judgment which we consider superior to our own. If Christianity is both social and dogmatic, and intended for all ages, it must, humanly speaking, have an infallible expounder. Else you will secure unity of form at the loss of unity of doctrine, or unity of doctrine at the loss of unity of form; you will have to choose between a comprehension of opinions and a resolution into parties, between latitudinarian and sectarian error; you may be tolerant or intolerant of contrarieties of thought, but contrarieties you will have. By the Church of England a hollow uniformity is preferred to an infallible chair; and by the sects of England, an interminable division. Germany and Geneva began with persecution, and {129} have ended in scepticism. The doctrine of infallibility is a less violent hypothesis than this sacrifice either of faith or of charity. It secures the objects, without, to say the least, violating the letter of the revelation.

8. I have called the doctrine of Infallibility an hypothesis: let it be so considered for the sake of argument, that is, let it be considered to be a mere position, supported by no direct evidence, but required by the facts of the case, and reconciling them with each other. That hypothesis is indeed, in matter of fact, maintained and acted on in the largest portion of Christendom, and from time immemorial; but let this coincidence be accounted for by the need. Moreover, it is not a naked or isolated fact, but the animating principle of a large scheme of doctrine which the need itself could not simply create; but let this system be merely called its development. Yet even as an hypothesis, which has been held by one out of various communions, it may not be lightly put aside. Some hypothesis all parties, all controversialists, all historians must adopt, if they would treat of Christianity at all. Gieseler's "Text Book" bears the profession of being a dry analysis of Christian history; yet on inspection it will be found to

be written on a positive and definite theory, and to bend facts to meet it. An unbeliever, as Gibbon, assumes one hypothesis, and an Ultra-montane, as Baronius, adopts another. The school of Hurd and Newton consider that Christianity slept for centuries upon centuries, except among those whom historians call heretics. Others speak as if the oath of Supremacy or the *congé d'élire* could be made the measure of St. Ambrose, and they fit the Thirty-nine Articles on the fervid Tertullian. The question is, which of all these theories is the simplest, most natural, the most persuasive. Certainly the notion of development {130} under infallible authority is not a less grave, a less winning hypothesis, than the chance and coincidence of events, or the Oriental Philosophy, or the working of Antichrist, to account for the rise of Christianity and the formation of its theology.

---

[1] Vid. Proph. Office, vii. where this parallel is insisted on, though with a different object.

[2] Justification, lect. xiii.

[3] Butler's Anal. ii. 3. <Joseph Butler (1692-1753), *The Analogy of Religion, Natural and Revealed, to the Constitution and Course of Nature* (1736).

[4] Proph. Office, pp. 356-361.

[5] <Butler's Anal.>, ii. 3; vide also ii. 4, fin.

[6] Analogy, ii. 4, ad fin.

[7] Proph. Office, pp. 305, 306.

[8] Ibid. pp. 301, 310

[9] Arians, ch. v. sect. 3, p. 89.

[10] Proph. Office, p. 148.

[11] Anal. ii. 3.

[12] Univ. Serm. pp. 33, 34.

[13] Univ. Serm. pp. 34, 35.

[14] De Rom. Pont. iv. 2. <*De Romano Pontici*, or Disputatio III, in *Disputationes de controversiis christianae fidei adversus hujus temporis haereticos* (1586).>

[15] Proph. Office, p. 141.

[16] Tim. iii. 16; Isaiah lix. 21.

[17] Οὐ γάρ τι νῦν γε κἀχθές, κ.τ.λ. <"not today, nor yesterday," etc., Sophocles, *Antigone*, 456.>

CHAPTER III.

ON THE NATURE OF THE ARGUMENT
IN BEHALF OF
EXISTING DEVELOPMENTS IN CHRISTIANITY.

SECTION I.

PRESUMPTIVE CHARACTER OF THE PROOF.

In proceeding to the consideration of the character of the argument adducible in behalf of the truth of the existing developments of Christianity, we must first direct our attention to the preponderating force of antecedent probability in all practical matters, where it exists. If this probability is great, it almost supersedes evidence altogether. This is instanced in every day's experience: whether the particular conclusion, in this or that case, be true or not is not here the question; the correctness of the process itself is shown by its general adoption. "Trifles light as air," the poet tells us, "are to the jealous, confirmations strong, as proofs of Holy Writ." Did a stranger tell us in a crowd to mind our purses, we should believe him, though in the sequel he turned out to be the thief, and gave us warning in order to gain them. A single text is sufficient to prove a doctrine to the well-disposed or prejudiced. "Not forsaking the assembling of ourselves together" is sufficient to lead the Christian mind to observe the

123

duty of social worship and "Forbidding to marry" is sufficient proof that Rome is Antichrist to those who {132} have been educated in that doctrine. Again, to take an instance in different matter, when we are fully convinced that an important step which another proposes is in itself right, we insist but generally on self-examination, waiting, and other preparation in his particular case; but in proportion as we are doubtful of its religiousness and happiness do we make much of these, lengthening his probation and putting obstacles in the way of his moving. Again, it is plain that a person's after course for good or bad brings out the passing words or obscure actions of previous years. Then we make the event a presumptive interpretation of the past, of those past indications of his character which were too few and doubtful to bear insisting on at the time, and would have seemed ridiculous had we attempted to do so. And the antecedent probability is found to triumph over contrary evidence, as well as to sustain what agrees with it. Every one may know of cases in which a plausible charge against an individual was borne down at once by weight of character, though that character was incommensurate of course with the circumstances which gave rise to suspicion, and had no direct neutralizing force to destroy it. On the other hand, it is sometimes said, and even if not literally true will serve in illustration, that not a few of the culprits in our criminal courts are not legally guilty of that particular crime on which a verdict is found against them, being convicted not so much upon the particular evidence, as on the presumption arising from their want of character and the memory of former offences. But this presumptive character of belief and conviction, and especially of faith, I have pointed out in other publications.

"Faith is reasoning of a religious mind, or of what Scripture calls a right or renewed heart, which acts upon presumptions rather than evidence, which speculates and ventures on the future when {133} it cannot make sure of it. Thus, to take the instance of

St. Paul preaching at Athens: he told his hearers that he came as a messenger from that God whom they worshipped already, though ignorantly, and of whom their poets spoke. He appealed to the conviction that was lodged within them of the spiritual nature and the unity of God; and he exhorted them to turn to Him who had appointed One to judge the whole world hereafter. This was an appeal to the antecedent probability of a Revelation, which would be estimated variously, according to the desire of it existing in each breast. Now what was the evidence he gave in order to concentrate those various antecedent presumptions, to which he referred in behalf of the message which he brought? Very slight, yet something; not a miracle, but his own word that God had raised Christ from the dead; very like the evidence to the mass of men now, or rather not so much. No one will say it was strong evidence; yet, aided by the novelty, and what may be called originality, of the claim, its strangeness and improbability considered as a mere invention, and the personal bearing of the Apostle, and supported by the full force of the antecedent probabilities which existed and which he stirred within them, it was enough."[1]

Again: "The proofs commonly brought, whether for the truth of Christianity, or for certain doctrines from texts of Scripture, are commonly strong or light, not in themselves, but according to the circumstances under which the doctrine professes to come to us, which they are brought to prove; and they will have a great or small effect upon our minds, according as we admit those circumstances or not. Now the admission of those circumstances involves a variety of antecedent views, presumptions, admitted analogies, and the like, many of which it is very difficult to detect and analyze. {134} One person, for instance, is convinced by Paley's argument from the Miracles, another is not; and why? Because the former admits that there is a God, that He governs the world, that He wishes the salvation of man, that the light of nature is not sufficient for man, that there is no other way of introducing a Revelation but miracles, and that men, who were neither enthusiasts nor impostors, could not have acted as the Apostles did, unless they had seen the miracles which they attested; the other denies some one, or more of these statements, or does not feel the force of some other principle more recondite and latent still than any of these, which is nevertheless necessary to the validity of the argument."[2]

The same principle applies in the argument in behalf of the ecclesiastical miracles: "The main point to which attention must be paid is the proof of their antecedent probability. If that is established, the task is nearly accomplished. If the miracles alleged are in harmony with the course of Divine Providence in the world, and with the analogy of faith as contained in Scripture, if it is possible to account for them, if they are referrible to a known cause or system, and especially if it can be shown that they are recognised, promised, or predicted in Scripture, very little positive evidence is necessary to induce us to listen to them, or even accept them, if not individually, yet viewed as a collective body. In that case, they are but the natural effects of supernatural agency."[3]

And in like manner, in proportion as there is reason for presuming the correctness of the existing developments of Christianity, shall we dispense with a formal historical argument in their favour, and content ourselves with such accidental corroborating evidences as the stream of time has washed upon our shores; and it has been shown above, that {135} there is very fair or strong reason for presuming them correct, if it be reasonable to expect developments of Christianity at all. This then is the next point to insist upon.

I observe then, that, when we are convinced that the idea of Christianity, as originally revealed, cannot but develop, and know, on the other hand, that large developments do exist in matter of fact, profession to be true and legitimate, our first impression naturally must be that these developments are what they pretend to be. Moreover, the very scale on which they have been made, their high antiquity yet present promise, their gradual formation yet precision, their harmonious order, dispose the imagination most forcibly towards the belief that a teaching so young and so old, not obsolete after so many centuries, but vigorous and progressive, is the very development contemplated in the Divine Scheme. And then we have to consider that from first to last other developments there are none, except those which have possession of Christendom; none, that is, of prominence and permanence sufficient to deserve the name. In early times the heretical doctrines were confessedly barren and short-lived, and could not stand their ground against Catholicism. As to the medieval period I am not aware that the Greeks present more than a negative opposition to the Latins. And now in like manner the Tridentine Creed is met by no rival developments; there is no antagonist system. Criticisms there are in plenty, but little of positive teaching anywhere; seldom an attempt on the part of any opposing school to master its own doctrines, to investigate their sense and bearing, to determine their relation to the decrees of Trent and their distance from them. And when at any time this attempt is by chance in any measure made, then an incurable contrariety does but come to view between portions of the theology thus developed, and {136} a war of principles; an impossibility moreover of reconciling that theology with the general drift of the formularies in which its elements occur, and a consequent appearance of unfairness and sophistry in adventurous persons who aim at forcing them into consistency; and, further, a prevalent understanding of the truth of this presentation, authorities keeping silence, eschewing a hopeless enterprise and discouraging it in others, and the people plainly intimating that they think both doctrine and usage, antiquity and development, of very little matter at all; and, lastly, the evident despair of even the better sort of men who, in consequence, when they set great schemes on foot, as for the conversion of the heathen world, are afraid to agitate the question of doctrines to which it is to be converted, lest through the opened door they should lose what they have, instead of gaining what they have not. To the weight of recommendation which this contrast throws upon the developments commonly called Catholic, must be added the argument which arises from the coincidence of their consistency and permanence, with their claim of an infallible sanction—a claim, the existence of which, in some quarter or other of the Divine Dispensation, is, as we have already seen, antecedently probable. All these things being considered, I think few persons will deny the very strong presumption which exists, that, if there are developments in Christianity, the doctrines propounded by successive Popes and Councils, through so many ages, are they.

A further presumption in behalf of these doctrines arises from the general opinion of the world about them. Christianity being one, all its doctrines are necessarily developments of one, and, if so, are of necessity consistent with each other, or form a whole. Now the world fully enters into this view of those well-known developments which claim the name of Catholic. It allows them that {137} title, it considers them to belong to one family, and refers them to one theological system. It is scarcely necessary to set about proving what is urged by their opponents even more strenuously than by their champions. Their opponents avow that they protest, not against this doctrine or that, but against one and all; and they seem struck with wonder and perplexity, not to say with awe, at a consistency which they feel to be superhuman, though they will not allow it to be divine. The system is confessed on all hands to bear a character of integrity and indivisibility upon it, both at first view and on inspection. Hence such sayings as the "Tota jacet Babylon" of the distich. Luther did but a part of the work, Calvin another portion, Socinus finished it. To take up with Luther, and to reject Calvin and Socinus, would be, according to that epigram, like living in a house without a roof to it. This, I say, is no private judgment of this man or that, but the common opinion and experience of all countries. The two great divisions of religion feel it, Roman Catholic and Protestant, between whom the controversy lies; sceptics and liberals, who are spectators of the conflict, feel it; philosophers feel it. A school of divines indeed there is, dear to memory, who have not felt it; and their exception will have its weight,—till we reflect that the particular theology which they advocate has not the prescription of success, never has been realized in fact, or, if realized for a moment, had no stay; moreover, that, when it has been enacted by human authority, it has scarcely travelled beyond the paper on which it was printed, or out of the legal forms in which it was embodied. But, putting the weight of these revered names at the highest, they do not constitute more than an exception to the general rule, such as is found in every subject that comes into discussion.

And this general testimony to the oneness of {138} Catholicism extends to its past teaching relatively to its present, as well as to the portions of its present teaching one with another. No one doubts, with such exception as has just been allowed, that the Roman Catholic communion of this days is the successor and representative of the Medieval Church, or that the Medieval Church is the legitimate heir of the Nicene; even allowing that it is a question whether a line cannot be drawn between the Nicene Church and the Church which preceded it. On the whole, all parties will agree that, of all existing systems, the present communion of Rome is the nearest approximation in fact to the Church of the Fathers, possible though some may think it to be nearer still to that Church on paper. Did St. Athanasius or St. Ambrose come suddenly to life, it cannot be doubted what communion they would mistake for their own. All differences of opinion, whatever protests, if we will, would find themselves more at home with such men as St. Bernard or St. Ignatius Loyola, or with the lonely priest in his lodging, or the holy sisterhood of mercy, or the unlettered crowd before the altar, than with the rulers or members of any other religious community. And may we not add, that were the two Saints, who once sojourned in exile or on embassage, at Treves, to come more northward still, and to travel until they reached another fair city, seated among groves, green meadows, and calm streams, the holy brothers would turn from many a high aisle and solemn cloister which they found there, and ask the way to some small chapel where mass was said in the populous alley or forlorn suburb? And on the other hand, can any one who has but heard his name, and cursorily read his history, doubt for one instant how, in turn, the people of England, "we, our princes, our priests, and our prophets," Lords and Commons, Universities, {139} Ecclesiastical Courts, marts of commerce, great towns, country parishes, would deal with Athanasius,—Athanasius who spent his long years in fighting against kings for a theological term?

SECTION II.

CHARACTER OF THE EVIDENCE.

There is a well-known remark of Aristotle's that "it is much the same to admit the probabilities of a mathematician and to ask demonstration from an orator." Some things admit of much closer and more careful handling than others; and we must look for proof in every case according to the nature of the subject-matter which is in debate, and not beyond it. Evidence may have an air of nature even in its deficiencies; and it recommends itself to us, when it carries with it its explanation why it is such as it is, not fuller or more exact.

Sometimes, indeed, we cannot discover the law of silence of deficiency, which is then simply unaccountable. Thus Lucian, for whatever reason, hardly notices Roman authors or affairs.[4] Maximus Tyrius, who wrote several of his works at Rome, nevertheless makes no reference to Roman history. Paterculus, the historian, is mentioned by no ancient writer except Priscian. What is more to our present purpose, Seneca, Pliny the elder, and Plutarch are altogether silent about Christianity; and perhaps Epictetus also, and the Emperor Marcus. The Jewish Mishna, too, compiled about A.D. 180, is silent about Christianity; and the Jerusalem and Babylonish Talmuds almost {140} so, though the one was compiled A.D. 300, and the other A.D. 500.[5] Eusebius, again, is very uncertain in his notice of facts; he does not speak of St, Methodius, nor of St. Anthony, nor of the martyrdom of St. Perpetua, nor of the miraculous power of St. Gregory Thaumaturgus; and he mentions Constantine's cross, not in his Ecclesiastical History, where it would naturally find a place, but in his Life of the Emperor. Moreover, those who receive that wonderful occurrence, which is, as one who rejects it allows,[6] "so inexplicable to the historical inquirer," have to explain the difficulty of the universal silence on the subject of all the Fathers of the fourth and fifth centuries, excepting Eusebius.

In like manner, Scripture has its unexplained omissions. No religious school finds its own tenets and usages on the surface of it. The remark applies also to the very context of Scripture, as in the obscurity which hangs over Nathaniel or the Magdalen. It is a remarkable circumstance that there is no direct intimation all through Scripture that the Serpent mentioned in the temptation of Eve was the evil spirit, till we come to the vision of the woman and child, and their adversary, the Dragon, in the twelfth chapter of the Revelations.

Omissions, thus absolute and singular, when they occur in the evidence of facts or doctrines, are of course difficulties; on the other hand, very frequently they admit of explanation. Silence may arise from the very notoriety of the facts in question, as in the case of the seasons, the weather, or other natural phenomena; or from their sacredness, as the Athenians did not mention the mythological Furies; or from external constraint, as the omission of statues of Brutus and Cassius in the procession. Or it may proceed from fear or disgust, {141} as on the arrival of unwelcome news; or from indignation, or hatred, or contempt, or perplexity, as Josephus is silent about Christianity, and Eusebius passes over the deaths of Crispus in his life of Constantine; or from other strong feeling, as implied in the poet's sentiment, "Give sorrow words;" or from policy or other prudential motive, or propriety, as Queen's Speeches do not mention individuals, however influential in the political world, and newspapers after a time were silent about the cholera. Or, again, from the natural and gradual course which the fact took, as in the instance of inventions and discoveries, the history of which is on this account often obscure; or from loss of documents or other direct testimonies, as we should not look for theological information in a treatise on geology.

Again, it frequently happens that omissions proceed on some law, as the varying influence of an external cause; and then, so far from being a perplexity, they may even confirm such evidence as occurs, by becoming, as it were, its correlative. For instance, an obstacle may be assignable, fact, or principle, or law, which ought, if it really exists, reduce or distort the indications of its presence to that very point, or in that very direction, and with the variations, and in the order and succession, which occur in its actual history. At first sight it might be a suspicious circumstance that but one or two manuscripts of some celebrated document were forthcoming; but if it were known that the sovereign power had exerted itself to suppress and destroy it at the time of its publication, and that the extant manuscripts were found just in those places where history witnessed to the failure of the attempt, the coincidence would be highly corroborative of that evidence which alone remained.

This is a principle familiar in mixed sciences, as often as an abstract truth to be extracted from {142} physical facts, as they present themselves to the experimentalists. Thus a writer on Mechanics, after treating of the laws of motion, observes, "These laws are the simplest principles to which motion can be reduced and upon them the whole theory depends. They are not indeed self-evident, nor do they admit of accurate proof of experiment, on account of the great nicety required in adjusting the instruments and making the experiments; and on account of the effects of friction, and the air's resistance, which cannot entirely be removed. They are, however, constantly, and invariably, suggested to our senses, and they agree with experiment as far as experiment can go; and the more accurately the experiments are made, and the greater care we take to remove all those impediments which tend to render the conclusions erroneous, the more nearly do the experiments coincide with these laws."[7] And thus a converging evidence for facts or doctrines through a certain period may, under circumstances, be as cogent a proof of their presence throughout that period, as the *Quod semper, quod ubique, quod ab omnibus.*

And so with respect both to the Canon and the Creed: "We depend upon the fourth and fifth centuries thus:—As to Scripture, former centuries do not speak distinctly, frequently, or unanimously, except of some chief books, as the Gospels; but we see in them, as we believe, an ever-growing tendency and approximation to that full agreement which we find in the fifth. The testimony given at the latter date is the limit to which all that has been before said converges. For instance, it is commonly said, *Exceptio probat regulam*; when we have reason to think that a writer or an age *would* have witnessed so and so, *but* for this or that, and that this or that were mere incidents of his position, then he or it may be said to *tend towards* such {143} testimony. In this way the first centuries tend towards the fifth. Viewing the matter as one of moral evidence, we seem to see in the testimony of the fifth the very testimony which every preceding century gave, accidents excepted, such as the present loss of documents once extant, or the then existing misconceptions which want of intercourse between the Churches occasioned. The Fifth century acts as a comment on the obscure text of the centuries before it, and brings out a meaning, which with the help of the comment any candid person sees really to be theirs. And in the same way as regards the Catholic creed, though there is not so much to explain and account for. Not so much; for one, I suppose, will deny that in the Fathers of the fourth century it is as fully developed, and as unanimously adopted, as it can be in the fifth. And, again, there had been no considerable doubts about the Epistle to the Hebrews or the Apocalypse; or, if any, they were started by individuals, as Origen's about eternal punishment, not by Churches, or at once condemned by the general Church, as in the case of heresies, or not about any primary doctrine, such as the Incarnation or Atonement: and all this in spite of that want of free intercourse which occasioned doubts about portions of the Canon. Yet in both cases, we have at first an *inequality* in the evidence, for what was afterwards universally received as divine;—the doctrines of the Holy Trinity and of Episcopacy, and, again, the four Gospels, being generally witnessed from the first; but certain other doctrines, being at first rather practised and assumed than insisted on, as the necessity of infant baptism; and certain books, as the Epistle to the Hebrews and the Apocalypse, doubted or not admitted in particular countries. And as the unanimity of the fifth century as regards the Canon clears up and {144} overcomes all previous differences, so the abundance of the fourth as to the Creed interprets, develops, and combines all that is recondite or partial in previous centuries as to doctrine, acting similarly as a comment, not indeed, as in the case of the Canon, upon a perplexed and disordered, but upon a concise text. In both cases, the after centuries contain but the termination of the testimony of the foregoing."[8]

And if this be true in a case in which development of doctrine is not supposed, much more will it hold when the doctrine itself in question is growing, and an increase in the evidence does but faithfully represent the condition of the original on which it depends.

Thus it is possible to have too much evidence; that is, evidence so full or exact as to throw suspicion over the case for which it is adduced. The genuine Epistles of St. Ignatius contain none of those ecclesiastical terms, such as "Priest" or "See," which are so frequent afterwards; and they quote Scripture sparingly. The interpolated Epistles quote it largely; that is, they are too Scriptural to be Apostolic. Few persons, again, who are acquainted with the primitive theology, but will be sceptical at first reading of the authenticity of such works as the longer Creed of St. Gregory Thaumaturgus, or St. Hippolytus contra Beronem, from the precision of the theological language.

The influence of circumstances upon the expression of opinion or testimony supplies another form of the same law of omission. "I am ready to admit," says Paley, "that the ancient Christian advocates did not insist upon the miracles in argument so frequently as I should have done. It was their lot to contend with notions of magical agency, against which the mere production of the facts was not sufficient for the convincing of their adversaries; I do {145} not know whether they themselves thought it quite decisive of the controversy. But since it is proved, I conceive with certainty, that the sparingness with which they appealed to miracles was owing neither to their ignorance nor their doubt of the facts, it is at any rate an objection, not to the truth of the history, but to the judgment of its defenders."⁹ And in like manner, Christians were not likely to entertain the question of the abstract allowableness of images in the Catholic ritual, with the actual superstitions and immoralities of paganism before their eyes. Nor were they likely to determine the place of St. Mary in our reverence, before they had duly secured, in the affections of the faithful, the supreme glory and worship of God Incarnate, her Eternal Lord and Son. Nor would they recognise Purgatory as a part of the Dispensation, till the world had flowed into the Church, and a habit of corruption had been superinduced. Nor could ecclesiastical liberty be asserted, till it had been assailed. Nor would a Pope arise, but in proportion as the Church was consolidated. Nor would monachism be needed, while martyrdoms were in progress. Nor could St. Clement give judgment on the doctrine of Berengarius, nor St. Dionysius refuse the Ubiquists, nor St. Irenaeus denounce the Protestant view of Justification, nor St. Cyprian draw up a theory of persecution. There is "a time for every purpose under the heaven;" "a time to keep silence and a time to speak."¹⁰

Sometimes when the want of evidence about a series of facts or doctrines is unaccountable, in the course of time an unexpected explanation or addition is found as regards a portion of them, which suggests a ground of patience as regards the historical obscurity of the rest. Two instances are obvious to mention, of an accidental silence of clear primitive testimony as to important doctrine, and {146} its removal. In the number of the articles of Catholic belief which the Reformation especially resisted, were the Mass and the sacramental virtue of Ecclesiastical Unity. Since the date of that movement, the shorter Epistles of St. Ignatius have been discovered, and the early Liturgies verified; and this with most men has put an end to the controversy about those doctrines. What has happened to them may happen to others; and though it does not happen to others, yet that it has happened to them, is to those others a sort of compensation for the obscurity in which their early history continues to be involved.

SECTION III.

METHOD OF CONDUCTING THE INQUIRY.

It seems, then, that we have to deal with a case something like the following: Certain doctrines come to us, professing to be Apostolic, and possessed of such high antiquity that, though we are able to assign the date of their formal establishment to the fourth, or fifth, or eighth, or thirteenth century, as it may happen, yet their substance may, for what appears, be coeval with the Apostles, and be expressed or implied in texts of Scripture. Further, these existing doctrines are universally considered, without any question, to be the representatives in each age of the doctrines of the times preceding them, and thus are thrown back to a date indefinitely early, even though their ultimate junction with the Apostolic Creed be denied. Moreover, they are confessed to form on body one with another, so that to reject one is to disparage the rest, and they include in their own unity even those primary articles of faith, such as that of the Incarnation, which many an impugner of the system of {147} doctrine, as a system, professes to accept, and which, do what he will, he cannot intelligibly separate, whether in point of evidence or of internal character from others which he disavows. Further, those doctrines occupy the whole field of theology, and leave nothing to be supplied, except in detail, by any other system; while, in matter of fact, no rival system is forthcoming, so that we have to choose between this theology and none at all. Moreover, this theology alone makes provision for that direction of opinion and conduct, which seems externally to be the special aim of Revelation; and fulfills the promises of Scripture, by adapting itself to the various problems of thought and practice which meet us in life. And, further, it is the nearest approach, to say the least, to the religion of the early Church, nay, to that of the Apostles and Prophets; for all will agree so far as this, that Elijah, Jeremiah, the Baptist, and St. Paul are in their history and mode of life (I do not speak of measures of grace, no, nor of doctrine and conduct, for these are points in dispute, but) in what is external and meets the eye (and this is no slight resemblance when things are viewed as a whole and from a distance),—these saintly and heroic persons, I say, are more like a Dominican preacher, or a Jesuit missionary, or a Carmelite friar, more like St. Toribio, or St. Vincent Ferrer, or St. Francis Xavier, or St. Alphonso Liguori, than to any individuals, or to any classes of men that can be found in other communions. And then, in addition, is the high antecedent probability that Providence would watch over His own work, and would direct and ratify those developments of doctrine which were inevitable.

Last of all, it has appeared, that in practical questions we are intended to guide our course chiefly by presumptions, such as the foregoing, and only secondarily by inquiries into evidence and by direct proof; and that in the case of developments, {148} a growth, a scantiness, a variation, an interruption of evidence, nay even silence, are to be expected, and are sometimes even necessary, and that exactness and fulness of evidence may even prejudice the doctrine for which it is adduced, because they are improbable.

If this is, on the whole, a true view of the general shape under which the existing body of developments commonly called Catholic present themselves before us, antecedently to our looking into the particular evidence on which they stand, I think we shall be at no loss to determine what both logical truth and duty prescribe to us as to our reception of them. It is very little to say that we should treat them as we are accustomed to treat other alleged facts and truths, and the evidence for them which bring with them a fair presumption of evidence in their favour. Such are of every day's occurrence; and what is our behavior towards them? We meet them, not with suspicion and criticism, but with a frank confidence. We do not in the first instance exercise our reason upon opinions which are received, but our faith. We do not begin with doubting; we take them on trust, and we put them on trial, and that, not of set purpose, but spontane- ously. We prove them by using them, by applying them to the subject-matter, or the evidence, or the body of circumstances, to which they belong, as if they gave it its interpretation or its colour, as a matter of course; and only when they fail, in the event, in illustrating phenomena or harmonizing facts, do we discover that we must reject the doctrines or the statements which we had in the first instances taken for granted. Again, we take the evidence for them, whatever it be, as a whole, as forming a combined proof; and we interpret what is obscure in it by such portions as are clear. Moreover, we bear with them in proportion to the strength of the antecedent probability in their favour, we are patient with difficulties in their {149} application, with apparent objections to them drawn from matters of fact, deficien- cy in their comprehensiveness, or want of neatness in their working, if their claims on our attention are considerable.

Thus the whole school of physical philosophers take Newton's theory of gravitation for granted, because it is generally received, and use it without rigidly testing it first, each for himself, by phenomena; and if phenomena are found which it does not satisfactorily solve, this does not trouble them, for they are sure that a way must exist of explaining them, consistently with that theory, though it does not occur to themselves.

Again, if we found a concise or obscure passage in one of Cicero's letters to Atticus, we should not scruple to admit as its true explanation a more implicit statement in his *Ad Familiares*. Aeschylus is illustrated by Sophocles in point of language, and Thucydides by Aristophanes in point of history. Horace, Persius, Suetonius, Tacitus, and Juvenal may be made to throw light on each other. Even Plato may gain a commentator in Plotinus, and St. Anselm is interpreted by St. Thomas. Two writers, indeed, may be known to differ, and then we do not join them together as fellow-witnesses to common truths; Luther has taken on himself to explain St. Augustine, and Voltaire, Pascal, without persuading the world that they have a claim to do so; but in no case do we begin with doubting that a comment disagrees with its text, when there is a *primâ facie* congruity between them. We elucidate the one by the other, though, or rather because, the former is fuller and clearer than the latter.

Thus too we deal with Scripture, when we have to interpret the prophetical text and the types of the Old Testament. The event which is the development is also the interpretation of the prediction; it provides a fulfilment by imposing a meaning. And we accept certain events as the fulfilment of {150} prophecy from the broad correspondence of the one with the other, in spite of many incidental difficulties. The difficulty, for instance, in accounting for the fact that the dispersion of the Jews followed upon their keeping, not their departing from their Law, does not hinder us from insisting on their present state as an argument against the infidel. Again, we readily submit our reason on competent authority, and accept certain events as an accomplishment of predictions, which seem very far removed from them; as the passage, "Out of Egypt have I called My Son." Nor do we find a difficulty, when St. Paul appeals to a text of the Old Testament which stands otherwise in our Hebrew copies; as the words, "A body hast Thou prepared Me." We receive such difficulties on faith, and leave them to take care of themselves. Much less do we consider mere fulness in the interpretation, or definiteness, or again strangeness, as a sufficient reason for depriving the text, or the action to which it is applied, of the advantage of it. We make no objection that the words themselves come short of it, or that a previous fulfilment satisfies it. A reader who came to the inspired text by himself, beyond the influence of that traditional acceptation which happily encompasses it, would be surprised to be told that the Prophet's words, "A Virgin shall conceive," &c., and "Let all the Angels of God worship Him," refer to our Lord; but assuming the intimate connexion between Judaism and Christianity, and the inspiration of the New Testament, we do not scruple to believe it. We rightly feel that it is no prejudice to our receiving the prophecy of Balaam in its Christian meaning, that it is adequately fulfilled in David; or the history of Jonah, that it has a moral in itself; or the meeting of Abraham and Melchizedek, that it is too brief and simple to mean any great thing.

{151} Butler corroborates these remarks, when speaking of the particular evidence of Christianity. "The obscurity or unintelligibleness," he says, "of one part of a prophecy does not in any degree invalidate the proof of foresight arising from the appearing completion of those other parts which are understood. For the case is evidently the same as if those parts which are not understood, were lost, or not written at all, or written in an unknown tongue. Whether this observation be commonly attended to or not, it is so evident that one can scarce bring one's self to set down an instance in common matters to exemplify it."[11] He continues, "Though a man should be incapable, for want of learning, or opportunities of inquiry, or from not having turned his studies this way, even so much as to judge whether particular prophecies have been throughout completely fulfilled; yet he may see, in general, that they have been fulfilled to such a degree, as, upon very good ground, to be convinced of foresight more than human in such prophesies, and of such events being intended by them. For the same reason also, though, by means of the deficiencies in civil history, and the different accounts of historians, the most learned should not be able to make out to satisfaction that such parts of the prophetic history have been minutely and throughout fulfilled; yet a very strong proof of foresight may arise from that general completion of them which is made out; as much proof of foresight, perhaps, as the Giver of prophesy intended should ever be afforded by such parts of prophecy."

He illustrates this by the parallel instance of fable and concealed satire. "A man might be assured that he understood what an author intended by a fable or parable, related without any application or moral, merely from seeing it to be easily (152) capable of such application, and that such a moral might naturally be deduced from it. And he might be fully assured that such persons and events were intended in a satirical writing, merely from its being applicable to them. And, agreeably to the last observation, he might be in a good measure satisfied of it, though he were not informed in affairs, or in the story of such persons, to understand half the satire. For his satisfaction, that he understood the meaning, of these writings, would be greater or less in proportion as he saw the general turn of them to be capable of such application, and in proportion to the number of particular things capable of it." And he infers hence, that if a known course of events, or the history of a person as our Lord, is found to answer on the whole to the prophetical text, it becomes at once the right interpretation of that text, in spite of difficulties in detail. And this rule of interpretation may obviously be applied to the parallel case of doctrinal passages, when a certain creed, which professes to have been derived from Revelation, comes recommended to us on strong antecedent grounds, and presents no striking opposition to the sacred text.

The same author observes that the first fulfilment of a prophecy is no valid objection to a second, when what seems like a second has once taken place; and, in like manner, an interpretation of doctrinal texts may be literal, exact, and sufficient, yet in spite of all this may not embrace the full scope of their meaning; and that fuller scope, if it so happen, may be less satisfactory and precise, as an interpretation, than their primary and narrow sense. In such cases the justification of the larger interpretation lies in some antecedent probability, such as Catholic consent; and the ground of the narrow is the context, and the rules of grammar; and, whereas the argument of the critical {153} commentator is that the sacred text *need not* mean more than the letter, those who adopt a deeper view of it maintain, as Butler in the case of prophecy, that we have no warrant for putting a limit to the sense of words which are not human but divine.

Now it is but a parallel exercise of reasoning to interpret the previous steps of a development by the later; and the same grudging and jealous temper, which refuses to enlarge the sacred text for teaching and prophecy, will occupy itself in carping at the Ante-nicene testimonies for Nicene or Medieval doctrines and usages. When "I and My Father are One" is urged in proof of our Lord's unity with the Father, heretical disputants do not see why the words must be taken to denote more than a unity of will. When "This is My Body" is alleged as a warrant for the change of the Bread into the Body of Christ, they explain away the words into a figure, because such is their most obvious interpretation. And, in like manner, when Roman Catholics urge St. Gregory's invocations, they are told that these are but rhetorical; or St. Clement's allusion to Purgatory, that perhaps it was Platonism; or Origen's language about Praying to Angels and the merits of Martyrs, that it is but an instance of his heterodoxy; or St. Cyprian's exaltation of the *Cathedra Petri*, that he need not be contemplating more than a figurative or abstract see; or the general testimony to the spiritual authority of Rome in primitive times, that it arose from its temporal greatness; or Tertullian's language about Tradition and the Church, that he took a lawyer's view of those subjects; whereas the early condition, and the evidence, of each doctrine respectively, ought consistently to be interpreted by means of the doctrine itself which was ultimately attained.

Those who will not view the beginning in the light of the result, are equally unwilling to let {154} the whole elucidate the parts. The Catholic doctrines, as I have already had occasion to observe, are members of one family, and suggestive, or correlative, or confirmatory, or illustrative of each other. In other words, one furnishes *evidence* to another, and all to each of them; if this is proved, that becomes probable; if this and that are both probable, but for different reasons, each adds to the other its own probability. The Incarnation is the antecedent of the doctrine of Mediation, and the archetype both of the Sacramental principle and of the merits of Saints. From the doctrine of Mediation follow the Atonement, the Mass, the merits of Martyrs and Saints, their invocation and *cultus*. From the Sacramental principle come the Sacraments properly so called; the unity of the Church, and the Holy See as its type and centre; the authority of Councils; the sanctity of rites; the veneration of holy places, shrines, images, vessels, furniture, and vestments. Of the Sacraments, Baptism is developed into Confirmation on the one hand; into Penance, Purgatory, and Indulgences on the other; and the "Eucharist into the Real Presence, adoration of the Host, Resurrection of the body, and the virtue of relics. Again, the doctrine of the Sacraments leads to the doctrine of Justification; Justification to that of Original Sin; Original Sin to the merit of Celibacy. Nor do these separate developments stand independent of each other, but by cross relations they are connected, and grow together while they grown from one. The Mass and the Real Presence are parts of one; the veneration of Saints and their relics are parts of one; their intercessory power, and the Purgatorial

State, and again the Mass and that State are correlative; Celibacy is the characteristic mark of Monachism and the Priesthood. You must accept the whole or reject the whole; reduction does but enfeeble, and amputation mutilate. It is trifling to receive all but something which is as integral as any {155} other portion; and, on the other hand, it is a solemn thing to receive any part, for, before you know where you are, you may be carried on by a stern logical necessity to accept the whole.

Moreover, since the doctrines all together make up one integral religion, it follows that the several evidences which respectively support those doctrines belong to a whole, and must be thrown into a common stock, and all are available in the defence of any. A collection of weak evidences makes up a strong evidence; again, one strong argument imparts cogency to collateral arguments which are in themselves weak. For instance, as to the miracles, whether of Scripture or the Church, "the number of those which carry with them their own proof now, and are believed for their own sake, is small, and they furnish the grounds on which we receive the rest."[12] Again, no one would fancy it necessary, before receiving St. Matthew's Gospel, to find primitive testimony in behalf of every chapter and verse: when only part is proved to have been in existence in ancient times, the whole is proved, because that part is but part of a whole; and when the whole is proved, it shelters such parts as for some incidental reason have no evidence of their antiquity. Again, it would be enough to show that St. Augustine knew the Italic version of the Scriptures, if he quoted it once or twice. And, in like manner, it will be generally admitted that the proof of the Being of the Second Person in the Godhead lightens indefinitely the burden of proof necessary for belief in a Third Person; and that, the Atonement being in sort a correlative of eternal punishment, the evidence for the former doctrine virtually increases the evidence for the latter. And so, Protestants would feel that it told little, except as an omen of victory, to reduce an opponent to a denial of Transubstantiation, if he still adhered firmly to the Invocation of Saints, Purgatory, the Seven Sacraments, and {156} the doctrine of merit; and little too for one of their own party to condemn the adoration of the Host, the supremacy of Rome, the acceptableness of celibacy, auricular confession, communion under one kind and tradition, if he was zealous for the doctrine of the Immaculate Conception.

The principle on which these remarks are made has the sanction of some of the deepest of English Divines. Bishop Butler, for instance, who has so often been quoted, thus argues in behalf of Christianity itself, though confessing at the same time the disadvantage which in consequence the revealed system lies under. "Probable proofs," he observes, "by being added, not only increase the evidence, but multiply it. Nor should I dissuade any one from setting down what he thought made for the contrary. . . . The truth of our religion, like the truth of common matters, is to be judged by all the evidence taken together. And unless the whole series of things which may be alleged in this argument, and every particular thing in it, can reasonably be supposed to have been by accident (for here the stress of the argument for Christianity lies), then is the truth of it proved; in like manner, as if, in any common case, numerous events acknowledged were to be alleged in proof of any other event disputed, the truth of the disputed event would be proved, not only if any one of the acknowledged ones did of itself clearly imply it, but though no one of them, singly, did so, if the whole of the acknowledged events, taken together, could not in reason be supposed to have happened, unless the disputed one were true.

"It is obvious how much advantage the nature of this evidence gives to those persons who attack Christianity, especially in conversation. For it is easy to show, in a short and lively manner, that such and such things are liable to objection, that this and another thing is of little weight in itself; {157} but impossible to show, in like manner, the united force of the whole argument in one view."[13]

In like manner, Mr. Davison condemns that "vicious manner of reasoning," which represents "any insufficiency of the proof, in its several branches, as so much objection;" which manages "the inquiry so as to make it appear that, if the divided arguments be inconclusive one by one, we have a series of exceptions to the truths of religion instead of a train of favourable presumptions, growing stronger at every step. The disciple of Scepticism is taught that he cannot fully rely on this or that motive of belief, that each of them is insecure, and the conclusion is put upon him that they ought to be discarded one after another, instead of being connected and combined."[14] No work perhaps affords more specimens in a short compass of the breach of the principle of reasoning inculcated in these passages, than Barrow's Treatise on the Pope's Supremacy.

The remarks of these two writers relate to the duty of combining doctrines which belong to one body, and evidences which relate to one subject; and few persons would dispute it in the abstract. The application which has been here made of the principle is this,—that where a doctrine comes recommended to us by strong presumptions of its truth, we are bound to received it unsuspiciously, and use it as a key to the evidences to which it appeals, or the facts which it professes to systematize, whatever may be our ultimate judgment about it. Nor is it enough to answer, that the voice of one particular Church, denying this so-called Catholicism, is an antecedent probability which outweighs all others and claims our prior obedience, loyally and without reasoning, to its own interpretation. This may excuse individuals certainly, in beginning with doubt and distrust of the Catholic developments, but it only shifts the blame.

{158}

SECTION IV.

INSTANCES IN ILLUSTRATION.

The rule of interpretation which has been above insisted on must now be applied in illustration, to several of the developments which go by the name of Catholic. Properly speaking, the consideration of particular cases belongs to the later chapters of this Essay; but sufficient will remain for the subject-matter of those chapters, though these instances are turned to our present purpose.

1. In the question raised by various learned men in the seventeenth and following century, concerning the view of the early Fathers on the subject of our Lord's Divinity, the one party estimate their theology by the literal force of their separate expressions or phrases, or by the philosophical opinions of the day; the other, by the doctrine of the Catholic Church, as afterwards authoritatively declared. The one party argues that those Fathers *need not* have meant more than what was afterwards considered heresy; the other answers that there is *nothing to prevent* their meaning more. Thus the position which Bull maintains seems to be nothing beyond this, that the Nicene Creed is a *natural key* for interpreting the body of Ante-nicene theology. His very aim is to explain difficulties; now the notion of difficulties and their explanation implies a rule to which they are apparent exceptions, and in accordance with which they are to be explained. Nay, the title of the work, which is a "Defence of the Creed of Nicaea," shows that he is not seeking a conclusion but imposing a view. And he proceeds both to defend the Creed by means of the Fathers against Sandius, and to defend the Fathers by means of the Creed against Petavius. {159} He defends Creed and Fathers by reconciling one with the other. He allows their language is not such as they would have used after the Creed had

been imposed; but he says in effect that, if we will but take it in our hands and apply it to their writings, we shall bring out and harmonize their teaching, clear their ambiguities, and discover their anomalous statements to be few and insignificant. In other words, he begins with a presumption, and shows how naturally facts close round it and fall in with it, if we will but let them. He does this triumphantly, yet he has an arduous work; out of about thirty writers whom he reviews, he has, for one cause or other, to explain nearly twenty.

2. The Canonicity, that is, the divine authority, of the books of the New Testament, is a subject to which allusion has been already made, and which furnishes a second illustration of the logic by which the facts and doctrines of Christianity are established. There are particular books, to which the Test of Vincentius, *Quod semper, &c.*, cannot be applied. The state of the argument is thus presented to us by Less: "All the Scriptures of our New Testament, it is confessed, have not been received with universal consent as genuine works of the Evangelists and Apostles. But that man must have predetermined to oppose the most palpable truths, and must reject all history, who will not confess that the greater part of the New Testament has been universally received as authentic, and that the remaining books have been acknowledged as such by the majority of the ancients."[15]

For instance, as to the Epistle of St. James. It is true, it is contained in the old Syriac version in the second century; but Origen, in the third century, is the first writer who distinctly mentions it among the Greeks; and it is not quoted by name by any Latin in the fourth. St. Jerome speaks of {160} its gaining credit "by degrees, in process of time." Eusebius says no more than that it had been, up to his time, acknowledged by the majority; and he classes it with the Shepherd of St. Hermas and the Epistle of St. Barnabas.[16]

Again: "The Epistle to the Hebrews, though received in the East, was not received in the Latin Churches till St. Jerome's time. St. Irenaeus either does not affirm, or denies that it is St. Paul's. Tertullian ascribes it to St. Barnabas. Caius excludes it from his list. St. Hippolytus does not receive it. St. Cyprian is silent about it. It is doubtful whether St. Optatus received it."[17]

Again, St. Jerome tells us, that in his day, towards A.D. 400, the Greek Church rejected the Apocalypse, but the Latin received it.

Again: "The New Testament consists of twenty-seven books in all, though of varying importance. Of these, fourteen are not mentioned at all till from eighty to one hundred years after St. John's death, in which number are the Acts, the Second to the Corinthians, the Galatians, the Colossians, the Two to the Thessalonians, and St. James. Of the other thirteen, five, viz. St. John's Gospel, the Philippians, the First of Timothy, the Hebrews, and the First of St. John are quoted but by one writer during the same period."[18]

On what ground, then, do we receive the Canon as it comes to us, but on the authority of the Church of the fourth and fifth centuries? The Church at that era decided,—not merely bore testimony, but passed a judgment on former testimony,—decided that certain books were of authority. We receive that decision as true; that is, we virtually apply to a particular case the doctrine of her infallibility. And in proportion as the cases multiply in which we are obliged to trust her decision, do {161} we approach, in fact, to the belief that she is infallible.

3. In the beginning of the fifteenth century, the Council of Constance decreed, that, "though in the primitive Church the Sacrament" of the Eucharist "was received by the faithful under each kind, and by the laity only under the kind of Bread; since it is most firmly to be believed, and in no wise doubted, that the whole Body and Blood of Christ is truly contained as well under the kind of Bread as under the kind of Wine."

Now the question is, whether the doctrine here laid down, and carried into effect in the usage here sanctioned, was entertained by the early Church, and may be considered a just development of its principles and practices. I answer that, starting with the presumption that the Council is right, which is the point here to be assumed, we shall find quite enough for its defence, and shall be satisfied to decide in the affirmative; we shall readily come to the conclusion that the Communion under either kind is lawful, each kind conveying the full gift of the Sacrament.

For instance, Scripture affords us two instances of what may reasonably be considered the administration of the Bread without the Wine; viz. our Lord's own example towards the two disciples at Emmaus, and St. Paul's conduct at sea during the tempest. Moreover, St. Luke speaks of the first Christians as continuing in the Apostles' doctrine and fellowship, and "in *breaking of bread*, and in prayer," not mentioning the Cup.

Again, St. Paul says that "whosoever shall eat this Bread or drink this Cup of the Lord unworthily, shall be guilty of the Body and Blood of the Lord." And while he does but say "the Cup of blessing which {162} we *bless*," without speaking of the communication, he says of the Bread, "which we *break*;" and proceeds, "We, being many, are one *bread* and one body for we are all partakers of that one Bread," without mentioning the Cup. And our Lord, in like manner, says absolutely, "he that *eateth* Me, even he shall live by Me."

Many of the types of the Holy Eucharist, as far as they go, tend to the same conclusion; such as the Paschal Lamb, the Manna, the Shewbread, the sacrifices from which the blood was poured out, and the miracle of the loaves, which are figures of the bread alone; while the water from the rock, and the Blood from our Lord' side correspond to the Wine without the Bread. Others are representations of both kinds; as Melchizedek's feast, and Elijah's miracle of the meal and oil.

And further, it certainly was the custom in the early Church, under circumstances, to communicate in one kind, as we learn from St. Cyprian, St. Dionysius, St. Basil, St. Jerome, and others. For instance, St. Cyprian speaks of the communion of an infant under Wine, and of a woman under Bread; and St. Ambrose speaks of his brother in shipwreck folding the Bread in a handkerchief, and placing it round his neck; and the monks and hermits in the desert can hardly be supposed to have been ordinarily in possession of consecrated Wine as well as Bread. From the following letter of St. Basil, it appears that, not only the monks, but the whole laity of Egypt ordinarily communicated in Bread only. He seems to have been asked by his correspondent, whether in time of persecution it was lawful, in the absence of priest or deacon, to take the communion "in our own *hand*," that is, of course, the Bread; he answers that it may be justified by the following parallel cases, in mentioning which he is altogether silent about the Cup. "It is plainly no fault," he says, "for long custom affords instances which {163} sanction it. For all the monks in the desert, where there is no priest, keep the communion at home, and receive (partake) it from themselves (*aph heauton*). In Alexandria too, and in Egypt, each of the laity, for the most part, has the Communion in his house, and when he will, he receives it from himself. For when once the priest has celebrated the Sacrifice and given it, he who has taken it [away] as a whole together, and then partakes of it daily, reasonably ought to think that he partakes and receives from him who [once] gave it."[19] It should be added, that in the beginning of the Letter he had been led to speak of the communion in both kinds, and says that it is "good and profitable."

Here we have the usage of Pontus, Egypt, Africa, and Milan. Spain may be added, if a late author is right in his view of the meaning of a Spanish Canon;[20] and Syria, as well as Egypt, at least at a later date, since Nicephorus[21] tells us that the Acephali, having no Bishops, kept the Bread which their last priests had consecrated, and dispensed crumbs of it every year at Easter for the purposes of Communion.

But it may be said, that "after all it is so very {164} hazardous and fearful a measure actually to withdraw from Christians one-half of the Sacrament, that, in spite of these precedents, some direct warrant is needed to reconcile the mind to it. There might have been circumstances which led St. Cyprian, or St. Basil, or the Apostolical Christians before them to curtail it, about which we know nothing. It is not therefore safe in us, because it was safe in them." Certainly a warrant is necessary; and just such a warrant is the infallibility of the Church. If we can trust her implicitly, there is nothing in the state of the evidence to form an objection to her decision in this instance, and in proportion as we find we can trust her does our difficulty lessen. Moreover, children, not to say infants, were at one time admitted to the Eucharist, at least to the Cup; on what authority are they now excluded from Cup and Bread also? St. Augustine considered the usage to be of Apostolical origin; and it continued in the West down to the twelfth century; it continues in the East among Greeks, Russo-Greeks, and the various Monophysite Churches to this day, and that on the ground of its almost universality in the primitive Church.[22] Is it a less innovation to suspend the Cup, than to cut off children from Communion altogether? Yet we acquiesce in the latter deprivation without a scruple. It is safer to acquiesce with, than without, an authority; safer with the belief that the Church is infallible, than with the belief that she may err.

4. The chief tokens extant of the existence of the Papal authority, in the first three centuries, were cursorily mentioned in the Introductory Chapter. Here, as in other cases, the plan of the work has obliged us to lay down what afterwards we have to take up, and to break into parts what ought to be viewed as a whole.

With a view, then, of furnishing another illustration {165} of the peculiar logical method on which I have been insisting, let us proceed to consider the disposition, or *lie* of the evidence which is adducible in the first five centuries in behalf of the supremacy of the Holy See; not, indeed, minutely going through it, and establishing it, but saying enough to point out how the Ante-nicene centuries may be viewed in the light of the Post-nicene, whereas Protestants resolve the latter into the dimness and indistinctness of the former.

The question is this, whether there was not from the first a certain element at work or in existence, which, for some reason or other, did not at once show itself upon the surface of ecclesiastical affairs, and of which events in the fourth century are the development; and whether the evidence of its existence and operation, which does occur in the earlier centuries, be it much or little, is not just as ought to occur upon such an hypothesis.

For instance, it is true, St. Ignatius is silent in his Epistles on the subject of the Pope's authority; but if that authority was not, and could not be in active operation then, such silence is not so difficult to account for as the silence of Seneca or Plutarch about Christianity itself, or of Lucian about the Roman people. St. Ignatius directed his doctrine according to the need. While Apostles were on earth, there was the display neither of Bishop nor Pope; their power had no prominence, as being exercised by Apostles. In course of time, first the power of the Bishop displayed itself, and then the power of the Pope. When the Apostles were taken away, Christianity did not at once break into portions; yet separate localities might begin to be the scene of internal dissensions, and a local arbiter in consequence would be wanted. Christians at home did not yet quarrel with Christians abroad; they quarrelled at home among themselves. St. Ignatius applied the fitting remedy. The {166} *Sacramentum Unitatis* was acknowledged on all hands; the mode of fulfilling and the means of securing it would vary with the occasion; and the determination of its essence, its seat, and its laws would be a gradual consequence of a gradual necessity.

This is but natural, and is parallel to instances which happen daily. It is a common occurrence for a quarrel and a lawsuit to bring out the state of the law, and the most unexpected results often follow. St. Peter's prerogative would remain a mere letter, till the complication of ecclesiastical matters became the cause of ascertaining it. While Christians were "of one heart and one soul," it would be suspended; love dispenses with laws. Christians knew that they must live in unity, and they were in unity; in what that unity consisted, how far they could proceed, as it were, in bending it, and what at length was the point at which it broke, was an irrelevant as well as unwelcome inquiry. Relations often live together in happy ignorance of their respective rights and properties, till a father or a husband dies; and then they find themselves against their will in separate interests, and on divergent courses, and dare not move without legal advisers. Again, the case is conceivable of a corporation or an Academical body, going on for centuries in the performance of the routine business which came in its way, and preserving a good understanding between its members, with statutes almost a dead letter and no precedents to explain them, and the rights of its various classes and functions undefined,—then, suddenly thrown back by the force of circumstances upon the question of its formal character as a body politic, and in consequence developing in the relation of governors and governed. The *regalia Petri* might sleep, as the power of a Chancellor has slept; not as an obsolete, for they never had been carried into effect, but as a mysterious privilege, which was not understood; as an unfulfilled prophecy. For St. Ignatius to speak of Popes, when it was a matter of Bishops, would have been {167} like sending an army to arrest a housebreaker. The Bishop's power indeed was from God, and the

Pope's could be no more; he was our Lord's representative, and had a sacramental office: but I am speaking, not of its intrinsic sanctity, but of its duties.

When the Church, then, was thrown upon her own resources, first local disturbances gave exercise to Bishops, and next ecumenical disturbances gave exercise to Popes; and whether communion with the Pope was necessary for Catholicity would not and could not be debated till a suspension of that communion had actually occurred. It is not a greater difficulty that St. Ignatius does not write to the Asian Greeks about Popes, than that St. Paul does not write to the Corinthians about Bishops. And it is a less difficulty that the Papal supremacy was not formally acknowledged in the second century, than that there was no formal acknowledgment of the doctrine of the Holy Trinity till the fourth. No doctrine is defined till it is violated.

And in like manner, it was natural for Christians to direct their course in matters of doctrine by the guidance of mere floating, and as it were, endemic tradition, while it was fresh and strong; but in proportion as it languished, or was broken in particular places, did it become necessary to fall back upon its special homes, first the Apostolic Sees, and then the See of St. Peter.

Moreover, an international bond and a common authority could not be consolidated, were it ever so certainly provided, while persecutions lasted. If the Imperial Power checked the development of Councils, it availed also for keeping back the power of the Papacy. The Creed, the Canon, in like manner, both remained undefined. The Creed, the Canon, the Papacy, Ecumenical Councils, all began to form, as soon as the Empire relaxed its tyrannous oppression of the Church. And as it was natural that her monarchical power should display itself when the Empire became Christian, so was it natural also that {168} further developments of that power should take place when that Empire fell.

Moreover, when the power of the Holy See began to exert itself, disturbance and collision would be the necessary consequence. Of the Temple of Solomon, it was said that "neither hammer, nor axe, nor any tool of iron was heard in the house, while it was in building." This is a type of the Church above; it was otherwise with the Church below, whether in the instance of Popes or Apostles. In either case, a new power had to be defined; as St. Paul had to plead, nay, to strive for his Apostolic authority, and enjoined St. Timothy, as Bishop of Ephesus, to let no man despise him: so Popes too have not therefore been ambitious because they did not establish their authority without a struggle. It was natural that Polycrates should oppose St. Victor; and natural too that St. Cyprian should both extol the See of St. Peter, yet resist it when he thought it went beyond its province. And at a later day it was natural that Emperors should rise in indignation against it; and natural on the other hand, that it should take higher ground with a younger power than it had taken with an elder and time-honoured.

We may follow Barrow here without reluctance, except in his imputation of motives.

"In the first times," he says, "while the Emperors were pagans, their [the Popes'] pretences were suited to their condition, and could not soar high; they were not then so mad as to pretend to any temporal power, and a pittance of spiritual eminency did content them."

Again: "The state of the most primitive Church did not well admit such an universal sovereignty. For that did consist of small bodies incoherently situated, and scattered about in very distant places, and consequently unfit to be modelled into one political society, or to be governed by one head especially considering their condition under persecution and poverty. What convenient resort for {169} direction on justice could a few distressed Christians in Egypt, Ethiopia, Parthia, India, Mesopotamia, Syria, Armenia, Cappadocia, and other parts have to Rome!"

Again, "Whereas no point avowed by Christians could be so apt to raise offence and jealousy in pagans against our religion as this, which setteth up a power of so vast extent and huge influence; whereas no novelty could be more surprising or startling than the creation of an universal empire over the consciences and religious practices of men; whereas also this doctrine could not be but very conspicuous and glaring in ordinary practice, it is prodigious that all pagans should not loudly exclaim against it," that is if it had then been in operation.

And again: "It is most prodigious that, in the disputes managed by the Fathers against heretics, the Gnostics, Valentinians, &c., they should not, even in the first place, allege and urge the sentence of the universal pastor and judge, as most evidently conclusive argument, as the most efficacious and compendious method of convincing and silencing them."

Once more: "Even Popes themselves have shifted their pretences, and varied in style, according to the different circumstances of time, and their variety of humours, designs, interests. In time of prosperity, and upon advantage, when they might safely do it, the Pope almost would talk high and assume much to himself; but when they were low, or stood in fear of powerful contradiction, even the boldest Popes would speak submissively or moderately."[23]

On the whole, supposing the power to be divinely bestowed, yet in the first instance more or less dormant, a history could not be traced out more probable, more suitable to that hypothesis, than the actual course of the controversy which took place age after age upon the Papal Supremacy.

{170} It will be said that all this is a theory. Certainly it is: it is a theory to account for facts as they lie in the history, to account for so much being told us about the Papal authority in early times, and not more; a theory to reconcile which is, and what is not recorded about it; and, which is the principal point, a theory to connect the words and acts of the Ante-nicene Church with that antecedent probability of a monarchical principle in the Divine Scheme, and that actual exemplification of it in the fourth century, which forms their presumptive interpretation. All depends on the strength of that presumption. Supposing there be otherwise good reason for saying that the Papal Supremacy is part of Christianity, there is nothing in the early history of the Church to contradict it.

It follows to inquire in what this presumption consists? It has, as I have said, two parts, the antecedent probability of the Popedom, and the actual state of the Post-nicene Church. The former of these reasons has unavoidably been touched upon in what has preceded. It is the absolute need of a monarchical power in the Church which is our ground for anticipating it. Blackstone has expressed the principle in a sentence, quoted in an earlier page, as it relates to kingly power. A political body cannot exist without government, and the larger is the body the more concentrated must the government be. If the whole of Christendom is to form one Kingdom, one head is essential; at least this is the experience of eighteen hundred years. As the Church grew into form, so did the power of the Pope develop; and wherever the Pope has been renounced, decay and division have been the consequence. We know of no other way of preserving the *Sacramentum Unitatis*, but a centre of unity. The Nestorians have had their "Catholicus;" the Lutherans of Prussia have their general superintendant; even the Independents, I believe, have {171} had an overseer in their Missions. The English Church affords an observable illustration of this doctrine. As her prospects have opened, and her communion extended, the See of Canterbury has become the natural centre of her operations. It has at present the jurisdiction in the Mediterranean, at Jerusalem in Hindostan, in North America, at the Antipodes. It has been the organ of communication, when a Prime Minister would force the

Church to a redistribution of her property, or a Protestant Sovereign would bring her into friendly relations with his own communion. Eyes have been lifted up thither in times of perplexity; thither have addresses been directed and deputations sent. Thence issue the legal decisions, or the declarations of Parliament, or the letters, or the private interpositions, which shape the fortunes of the Church, and are the moving influence within her separate dioceses. It must be so; no Church can do without its Pope. We see before our eyes the centralising process by which the See of St. Peter became the Sovereign Head of Christendom.

If such be the nature of the case, it is impossible, if we may so speak reverently, that an Infinite Wisdom, which sees the end from the beginning, in decreeing the rise of an universal Empire, should not have decreed the development of a ruler.

To this must be added the general probability, which has been shown in the foregoing Chapter, that all true developments of doctrine and usage which have been permitted, and this in the number, have been divinely approved; and, again, the probability in particular in favour of the existence, in some quarter, of an infallible authority in matters of faith.

And on the other hand, as the counterpart of these anticipations, we are met by certain announcements in Scripture, more or less obscure and needing a comment, and claimed by the Papal See as having {172} their fulfilment in itself. Such are the words, "Thou art Peter, and upon this rock I will build My Church; and the gates of hell shall not prevail against it, and I will give unto Thee the Keys of the Kingdom of Heaven." Again: "Feed my lambs, feed my sheep." And "Satan hath desired to have you; I have prayed for thee, and when thou art converted, strengthen thy brethren." Such, too, are various other indications of the Divine purpose as regards St. Peter, too weak in themselves to be insisted on separately, but not without a confirmatory power; such as his new name, his walking on the sea, his miraculous draught of fishes on two occasions, our Lord's preaching out of his boat, and His appearing first to him after His resurrection.

It should be observed, moreover, that a similar promise was made by the patriarch Jacob to Judah: "Thou art he whom thy brethren shall praise: the sceptre shall not depart from Judah till Shiloh come;" yet it was not fulfilled for perhaps eight hundred years, during which long period we hear little or nothing of the tribe descended from him. In like manner, "On this rock, I will build My Church," "I give unto thee the Keys," "Feed my sheep," are, not precepts merely, but prophecies and promises, promises to be accomplished by Him who made them, prophecies to be interpreted by the event,—by the history, that is, of the fourth and fifth centuries, though they had a partial fulfilment even in the preceding period, and a still more noble development in the middle ages.

For instance, we have seen in an earlier Chapter that St. Cyprian allows to the Roman See the name of the *Cathedra Petri*; and even Firmilian is a witness that the See of Rome claimed it. Now in the fourth and fifth centuries this title and its logical results became prominent. Thus, St. Julius, who was Pope during the persecution of St. Athanasius (A.D. 342), remonstrated by letter with the Eusebian {173} party for "proceeding on their own authority as they pleased," and then, as he says, "desiring to obtain our concurrence in their decisions, though we never condemned him. Not so have the constitutions of Paul, not so have the traditions of the Fathers directed; this is another form of procedure, a novel practice. . . For what we have received from the blessed Apostle Peter, that I signify to you; and I should not have written this, as deeming that these things are manifest unto all men, had not these proceedings so disturbed us."[24] St. Athanasius, by preserving this protest, has given it his sanction. Moreover, it is alluded to by Socrates; and his account of it has the more force, because he happens to be incorrect in the details, and therefore did not borrow it from St. Athanasius:—"Julius wrote back," he says, "that they acted against the Canons, because they had not called him to a Council, the Ecclesiastical Canon commanding that the Churches ought not to make Canons beside the will of the Bishop of Rome."[25] And Sozomen: "It was a sacerdotal law, to declare invalid whatever was transacted beside the will of the Bishop of the Romans."[26] On the other hand, the heretics themselves, whom St. Julius withstands, are obliged to acknowledge that Rome was "the School of the Apostles and the Metropolis of orthodoxy from the beginning;" and two of their leaders (Western Bishops,) some years afterwards recanted their heresy before the Pope in terms of humble confession.

Another Pope, St. Damasus, in his letter addressed to the Eastern Bishops against Apollinaris (A.D. 382), calls those Bishops his sons. "In that your charity pays the due reverence to the Apostolical See, ye profit the most yourselves, most honoured sons. For if, placed as we are in that Holy Church, in which the Holy Apostle sat and taught, how it becometh us to direct the helm to which we have {174} succeeded, we nevertheless confess ourselves unequal to that honour; yet do we therefore study as we may, if so be we may be able to attain to the glory of his blessedness."[27] "I speak," says St. Jerome to the same St. Damasus, "with the successor of the fisherman and the disciple of the Cross. I, following no one as my chief but Christ, am associated in communion with thy blessedness, that is, with the See of Peter. I know that on that rock the Church is built. Whosoever shall eat the Lamb outside this House is profane; if a man be not in the Ark of Noe, he shall perish when the flood comes in its power."[28] St. Basil entreats St. Damasus to send persons to arbitrate between the Churches of Asia Minor, or at least to make a report on the authors of their troubles, and the party with which the Pope should hold communion. "We are in no wise asking anything new," he proceeds, "but what was customary with blessed and religious men of former times, and especially with yourself. For we know, by tradition of our fathers of whom we have inquired, and from the information of writings still preserved among us, that Dionysius, that most blessed Bishop, while he was eminent among you for orthodoxy and other virtues, sent letters of visitation to our Church of Caesarea, and of consolation to our fathers, with ransomers of our brethren from captivity." In like manner, Ambrosiaster, a Pelagian in his doctrine, which is not to the purpose, speaks of the "Church being God's house, whose ruler at this time is Damasus."[29]

"We bear," says St. Siricius, another Pope, (A.D. 385,) "the burden of all who are laden; yea, rather the blessed Apostle Peter beareth them in us, who, as we trust, in all things protects and defends us the heirs of his government."[30] And he in turn ins confirmed by St. Optatus. "You cannot deny your {175} knowledge," says the latter to Parmenian, the Donatist, "that, in the city Rome, on Peter first hath an Episcopal See been conferred, in which Peter sat, the head of all the Apostles, . . . in which one See unity might be preserved by all, lest the other Apostles should support their respective Sees; in order that he might be at once a schismatic and a sinner, who against that one See (*singularem*) placed a second. Therefore that one See (*unicam*), which is the first of the Church's prerogatives, Peter filled first; to whom succeeded Linus; to Linus, Clement; to Clement, &c., &c. . . to Damasus, Siricius, who at this day is associated with us, (*socius,*) together with whom the whole world is in accordance with us, in the one bond of communion, by the intercourse of letters of peace."[31]

Another Pope: "Diligently and congruously do ye consult the *arcana* of the Apostolical dignity," says St. Innocent to the Council of Milevis (A.D. 417), "the dignity of him on whom, beside those things which are without, falls the care of all the

Churches; following the form of the ancient rule, which you know, as well as I, has been preserved always by the whole world."[32] Here the Pope appeals, as it were, to the Rule of Vincentius; while St. Augustine bears witness that he did not outstep his prerogative, for, giving an account of this and another letter, he says, "He [the Pope] answered us as to all these matters as it was religious and becoming in the Bishop of the Apostolic See."[33]

Another Pope: "We have especial anxiety about all persons," says St. Celestine (A.D. 425), to the Illyrian Bishops, "on whom, in the holy Apostle Peter, Christ conferred the necessity of making all persons our concern, when He gave him the Keys of opening and shutting." St. Prosper, his contemporary, confirms him, when he calls Rome "the seat of Peter, which, being made to the world the head {176} of pastoral honour, possesses by religion what it does not possess by arms;" and Vincent of Lerins, when he calls the Pope "the head of the whole world."[34]

Another Pope: "Blessed Peter," says St. Leo, (A.D. 440, &c.), "hath not deserted the helm of the Church which he had assumed . . . His power lives and his authority is pre-eminent in his See."[35] "That immoveableness, which, from the Rock of Christ, he, when made a rock, received, has been communicated also to his heirs."[36] And as St. Athasius and the Eusebians, by their contemporary testimonies, confirm St. Julius; and St. Jerome, St. Basil, and Ambrosiaster, St. Damasus; and St. Optatus, St. Siricius; and St. Augustine, St. Innocent; and St. Prosper and Vincent, St. Celestine; so do St. Peter Chrysologus, and the Council of Chalcedon confirm St. Leo. "Blessed Peter," says Chrysologus, "who lives and presides in his own see, supplies truth of faith to those who seek sit."[37] And the Ecumenical Council of Chalcedon, addressing St. Leo respecting Dioscorus, Bishop of Alexandria: "He extends his madness even against him to whom the custody of the vineyard has been committed by the

Saviour, that is, against thy Apostolical holiness."[38] But the instance of St. Leo will occur again in a later Chapter.

The acts of the fourth century speak as strongly as its words. We may content ourselves here with Barrow's admissions:—

"The Pope's power," he says, "was much amplified by the importunity of persons condemned or extruded from their places, whether upon just accounts, or wrongfully, and by faction; for they, finding no other more hopeful place of refuge and redress, did often apply to him: for what will not men do, whither will not they go in straits? Thus did Marcion go to Rome, and sue {177} for admission to communion there. So Fortunatus and Felicissimus in St. Cyprian, being condemned in Afric, did fly to Rome for shelter; of which absurdity St. Cyprian doth so complain. So likewise Martianus and Basilides in St. Cyprian, being outed of their Sees for having lapsed from the Christian profession, did fly to Stephen for succour, to be restored. So Maximus, the Cynic, went to Rome, to get a confirmation of his election at Constantinople. So Marcellus, being rejected for heterodoxy, went thither to get attestation to his orthodoxy, of which St. Basil complaineth. So Apiarius, being condemned in Africa for his crimes, did appeal to Rome. And, on the other side, Athanasius being with great partiality condemned by the Synod of Tyre; Paulus and other bishops being extruded from their sees for orthodoxy; St. Chrysostom being condemned and expelled by Theophilus and his complices; Flavianus being deposed by Dioscorus and the Ephesine synod; Theodoret being condemned by the same, did cry out for help to Rome. Chelidonius, Bishop of Besançon, being deposed by Hilarius of Arles for crimes, did fly to Pope Leo."

Again: "Our adversaries do oppose some instances of popes meddling in the constitution of bishops; as Pope Leo I. saith, that Anatolius did 'by the favour of his assent obtain the bishopric of Constantinople.' The same pope is alleged as having confirmed

Maximus of Antioch. The same doth write to the Bishop of Thessalonica, his vicar, that he should 'confirm the elections of bishops by his authority.' He also confirmed Donatus, an African bishop:—'We will that Donatus preside over the Lord's flock, upon condition that he remember to send us an account of his faith.'. . Pope Damasus did confirm the ordination of Peter Alexandrinus."

And again: "The Popes indeed in the fourth {178} century began to practise a fine trick, very serviceable to the enlargement of their power; which was to confer on certain bishops, as occasion served, or for continuance, the title of their vicar or lieutenant, thereby pretending to impart authority to them: whereby they were enabled for performance of divers things, which otherwise by their own episcopal or metropolitical power they could not perform. By which device they did engage such bishops to such a dependence on them, whereby they did promote the papal authority in provinces, to the oppression of the ancient rights and liberties of bishops and synods, doing what they pleased under pretence of this vast power communicated to them; and for fear of being displaced, or out of affection to their favourer, doing what might serve to advance the papacy. Thus did Pope Celestine constitute Cyril in his room. Pope Leo appointed Anatolius of Constantinople. . . . Pope Simplicius to Zeno, Bishop of Seville: 'We thought it convenient that you should be held up by the vicariat authority of our see.' So did Siricius and his successors constitute the bishops of Thessalonica to be their vicars in the dioceses of Illyricum, wherein being then a member of the western empire they had caught a special jurisdiction; to which Pope Leo did refer in those words, which sometimes are impertinently alleged with reference to all bishops, but concern only Anastasius, Bishop of Thessalonica: "We have entrusted thy charity to be in our stead; so that thou art called into part of the solicitude, not into plenitude of the authority." So did Pope Zosimus bestow a like pretence of vicarious power upon the Bishop of Arles, which city was the seat of the temporal exarch in Gaul."[39]

More ample testimony for the Papal Supremacy is scarcely necessary than what is contained in {179} these passages: the simple question is, whether the clear light of the fourth and fifth centuries may be fairly taken to illuminate the dim notices of the preceding.

SECTION V.

PARALLEL INSTANCES.

Bacon is celebrated for destroying the credit of a method of reasoning much resembling that which it has been the object of this Chapter to recommend. "He who is not practised is doubting," he says, "but forward in asserting and laying down such principles as he takes to be approved, granted, and manifest, and, according to the established truth thereof, receives or rejects everything, as squaring with or proving contrary to them, is only fitted to mix and confound things with words, reason and madness, and the world with fable and fiction, but not to interpret the works of nature."[40] But he was aiming at the application of these modes of reasoning to what should be strict investigation, and that in the province of physics; and this he might well censure, without attempting what is impossible, to banish them from history, ethics, and religion. Physical facts are present; they are submitted to the senses, and the senses may be satisfactorily tested, corrected, and verified. To trust to anything but sense in a matter of sense is irrational; why are the senses given us but to supersede less certain, less immediate informants? We have recourse to reason or authority to determine facts, when the senses fail us; but with the senses we begin. We deduce, we form inductions, we abstract, we theorize from facts; we do not begin with surmise and conjecture, much less do we look to the tradition of past ages, or the {180} decree of foreign teachers, to determine matters which are in our hands and under our eyes.

But it is otherwise with history, the facts of which are not present; it is otherwise with ethics, in which phenomena are more subtle, closer, and more personal to individuals than other facts, and not referrible to any common standard by which all men can decide upon them. In such sciences, we cannot rest upon mere facts, if we would, because we have not got them. We must do our best with what is given us, and look about for aid from any quarter; and in such circumstances the opinions of others, the traditions of ages, the prescriptions of authority, antecedent auguries, analogies, parallel cases, these and the like, not indeed taken at random, but, like the evidence from the senses, sifted and scrutinized, obviously become of great importance.

And further, if we proceed on the hypothesis that a merciful Providence has supplied us with means of gaining such truth as concerns us, in different subject-matters, though with different instruments, then the simple question is, what those instruments are which are proper to a particular case. If they are of the appointment of a Divine Protector, we may be sure that they will lead to the truth, whatever they are. The less exact methods of reasoning may do His work as well as the more perfect, if He blesses them. He may bless antecedent probabilities in ethical inquiries, who blesses experiment and induction in the art of medicine.

And if it is reasonable to consider medicine, or architecture, or engineering, in a certain sense, divine arts, as being divinely ordained means of our receiving divine benefits, much more may ethics be called divine; while as to religion, it directly professes to be the method of recommending ourselves to Him and learning

His will. If then it be His gracious purpose that we should learn it, the means He gives for learning it, be they promising or not {181} to human eyes, are sufficient because they are His. And what they are at this particular time, or to this person, depends on His disposition. He may have imposed simple prayer and obedience on some men as the instrument of their attaining to the mysteries and precepts of Christianity. He may lead others through the written word, at least for some stages of their course; and if the formal basis on which He has rested His revelations be, as it is, of an historical and philosophical character, then antecedent probabilities, subsequently corroborated by facts, will be sufficient, as in the parallel case of other history, to bring us safely to the matter, or at least to the organ, of those revelations.

Moreover, in subjects which belong to moral proof, such, I mean, as history, antiquities, political science, ethics, metaphysics, and theology, which are pre-eminently such, and especially in theology and ethics, antecedent probability may have a real weight and cogency which it cannot have in experimental science; and a mature politician or divine may have a power of reaching matters of fact in consequence of his peculiar habits of mind, which is never given in the same degree to physical inquirers, who, for the purposes of this particular pursuit, are very much on a level. And this last remark at least is confirmed by Lord Bacon, who confesses "Our method of discovering the sciences does not much depend upon subtlety and strength of genius, but lies level to almost every capacity and understanding;"[41] though surely sciences there are, in which genius is everything, and rules all but nothing.

It will be a great mistake then to suppose that, because this eminent philosopher condemned presumption and prescription in inquiries into facts which are external to us all, therefore authority, tradition, verisimilitude, analogy, and the like, are mere "idols of {182} the den," or "of the theatre" in history or ethics.

Here we may oppose to him an author in his own line as great as he is: "Experience," says Bacon, "is by far the best demonstration, provided it dwell in experiment; for the transferring of it to other things judged alike is very fallacious, unless done with great exactness and regularity."[42] But Niebuhr takes the contrary side: "Instances are not arguments," he grants, when investigating an obscure question of Roman history,—"instances are not arguments, but in history are scarcely of less force; above all, where the parallel they exhibit is in the progressive development of institutions."[43] Here this sagacious writer recognises the true principle of historical logic, while he exemplifies it.

1. Nor is this all; it is remarkable that not even in physics can real genius submit to the trammels of that *Novum Organum* of investigation, which, as Bacon truly says, is so important, so necessary, in the case of the many. "Sir Isaac Newton," says Bacon's editor, "appears to have had a very extraordinary method of making discoveries; but as that great philosopher did not think proper to reveal it, philosophers of an inferior rank can only guess at it, and admire what they do not fully understand. Where the business of investigation depended upon experiments, as particularly in his excellent inquiries about light, he seems first *to have imagined in his mind how things were*, and afterwards contrived his experiments on purpose to show *whether those things were as he had preconceived* them or not; and according to the information thus obtained, whether from his own experiments and observations, or those of others, he altered and improved his notions. . . . At other times this great philosopher observed the stricter laws of induction. . . . So that he seems to have used all sorts of methods by turns."[44]

{183} 2. Nay, it is remarkable too that the very professors of profane learning, who often show so great a contempt for the use of antecedent processes of reasoning in religious inquiries, do not scruple to apply their own conclusions in science or history as a presumptive interpretation of the matter of revelation. The inspired histories, and the doctrines of the Church, are often analyzed on principles, and subjected to systems, totally alien from Scripture and theology. Some theory of politics, antiquities, language, or geology is forcibly imposed upon the facts of religion, whether those facts are disposed to admit it or not. Thus M. Dupuis turned Christianity into a form of Mithraism. Thus Heeren speaks of Samuel's "scheme of making the office of Judge hereditary in his own family," and "his crafty policy in the election which he could not impede," and describes Solomon's reign as "the brilliant government of a despot from the interior of his seraglio;" by a process similar to that by which men of narrow minds impute their own motives to another, to account for his actions.

This, however, is but the abuse of a legitimate method, which must not be condemned merely because, like other instruments, its success or failure depends upon the hand which applies it. It is of universal use in scientific and literary research, and, whether it ends in a true or false conclusion, the process is ever the same. And this is the point on which I am here insisting, that it is no peculiarity of Catholic and orthodox reasoning, but is equally found in infidel and heretical [noun?] and in history or ethics, as well as in theology.

3. For instance: if it be an assumption to interpret every passage of a primitive author which bears upon doctrine or ritual by the theology of a later age, it surely is an assumption also to argue, if his statement is incomplete, that he held no more than he happened to say, or if it is the most ancient {184} testimony now extant, that no one held the same before him. The former is the assumption of those who hold that the developments of Christian doctrine are faithful; the latter of those who consider that the existing creed is the accidental result of various natural causes and human elements. Such is the assumption which runs through Gieseler's most able and useful Text-book of Ecclesiastical

History, and which gives to his analysis a reckless and arbitrary tone such as cannot be surpassed by the most dogmatic Schoolman.

To take the first specimen which occurs:—he mentions the author of the Pastor as an Apostolical Father,[45] adding in the note that the work itself claims to be written by Hermas, the disciple of St. Paul, that it is quoted by St. Irenaeus as "Scripture," and that it is often cited by St. Clement and others; moreover, that though others have given it to Hermas, brother of Pope Pius, "this is only conjecture." Thus he begins: however, some pages later it is assumed to be a "spurious writing" of the second century;[46] one of those which taught Chiliasm, as did all the other spurious writings of the period. Next, on those spurious writings he grounds the assertion "that no one can hesitate to consider Chiliasm universal" in that age; and he corroborates this conclusion by the hypothesis that "such notions as it offered were not unnecessary to animate men to suffer for Christianity." He then traces the doctrine to the Apocalypse, and alludes to several Greek Fathers, St. Justin, and St. Irenaeus, who held it. Then, with this doctrine, which he represents as universal, he connects the belief that till the millennium "the souls of the dead were to be kept in the world below," referring in the note (that is, in proof of what he considers a Catholic doctrine of the second century) to passages written by Tertullian when a Montanist in the beginning of the third. Lastly, he observes that "the fancied enjoyments of" this Catholic {185} Millennium, which were to animate the martyrs, "were in a high degree sensual and earthly."

In like manner he implies that a certain Unitarian doctrine was not considered heresy at Rome and in Asia Minor in the beginning of the third century, because Praxeas was not at once condemned or detected by the Pope, nor the school to which Noetus belonged by the Asian bishops,[47] and he suggests in a note that the Victorinus, who is said in an anonymous work to have supported Praxeas, is really Pope Victor.

Again, in the instance of Pope Julius in the fourth century, he maintains without hesitation the genuineness of a letter ascribed to him by the Council of Ephesus, (which he certainly would have rejected, had he acted in the critical or rather sceptical temper usual in his school,) merely, I will say, because that letter is of an Apollinarian character, and, if genuine, in its present form, might be considered to compromise the infallibility of a Pope.[48]

Again, speaking of Christianity at large in the same century, he tells us that "the populace were disposed to consider *every* obscure grave as the grave of a martyr," solely referring to Sulpicius's life of St. Martin, where we do but read that the barbarous peasants of Gaul had falsely fancied that a certain spot in a monastery, where former Bishops were said to have erected an altar, was a martyr's grave.

Such is the looseness of reasoning, and the negligence of facts, which all writers more or less exhibit, who consider that they are in possession of a sure hypothesis on which to interpret evidence and employ argument.

4. The fault of Gieseler, as it seems to me, is his distorting facts to serve a theory; if Catholic controversialists have at any time done the like, they have done what their hypothesis did not require. If the Catholic hypothesis is true, it neither needs nor is benefited by unfairness. Adverse facts should {186} be acknowledged; explained if but apparent; accounted for if real; or let alone and borne patiently as being fewer and lighter than the difficulties of other hypotheses. In illustration I proceed to make use of the following passage from a work already quoted, though I condemn its tone and drift, and think its statements exaggerated. However, *mutatis mutandis*, I acquiesce in it. After mentioning the Greek doctrine of the judgment-fire and its difference from the Roman doctrine of Purgatory, in time, place, and subjects, the writer observes that certain passages from the Fathers which

contain it are enumerated by Bellarmine, first as testimonies in his inductive proof in favour of Purgatory, and then as exceptions to the doctrine thereby established. Then he proceeds:—

"Now, do I mean to accuse so serious and good a man as Bellarmine of wilful unfairness in this procedure? No. Yet it is difficult to enter into the state of mind under which he was led into it. However we explain it, so much is clear, that the Fathers are only so far of us in the eyes of Romanists as they prove the Roman doctrines, and in no sense are allowed to interfere with the conclusions which their Church has adopted; that they are of authority when they seem to agree with Rome, of none if they differ. But if I may venture to account in Bellarmine's own person for what is in controversy confessedly unfair, I would observe as follows, though what I say may seem to border on refinement.

"A Romanist, then, cannot really argue in defence of the Roman doctrines; he has too firm a confidence in their truth, if he is sincere in his profession, to enable him critically to adjust the due weight to be given to this or that evidence. He assumes his Church's conclusion as true; and the facts or witnesses he adduces are rather brought to receive an interpretation than to furnish a proof. His highest aim is to show the mere consistency of his theory, {187} its possible adjustment with the records of Antiquity. I am not here inquiring how much of high but misdirected moral feeling is implied in this state of mind; certainly as we advance in perception of the Truth, we all become less fitted to be controversialists.

"I consider, then, that when he first adduces the above-mentioned Fathers in proof of Purgatory, he was really but interpreting them; he was teaching what they ought to mean,—what in charity they must be supposed to mean,—what they might mean, as far as the very words went,—probably meant, considering the Church so meant,—and might be taken to mean, even if their authors did not so mean, from the notion that they spoke vaguely, and, as children, that they really meant something else than what they formally said, and that, after all, they were but the spokesmen of the then existing Church, which, though in silence, certainly held, as being the Church, that same doctrine which Rome has since defined and published. So much as to its first use of them; but afterwards, in noticing what he considers erroneous opinions on the subjects, he treats them, not as organs of the Church Infallible, but as individuals, and interprets their language by its literal sense, or by the context, and in consequence condemns it. The Fathers in question, he seems to say, really held as modern Rome holds; for if they did not, they must have dissented from the Church of their own day; for the Church then held as modern Rome holds. And the Church then held as Rome holds now because Rome is the Church, and the Church ever holds the same. How hopeless then is it to contend with Romanists, as if they practically agreed with us as to the foundation of faith, however much they pretend to it! Ours is Antiquity; theirs the existing Church. Its infallibility is their principle; belief in it is a deep {188} prejudice quite beyond the reach of anything external. It is quite clear that the combined testimonies of all the Fathers, supposing such a case, would not have a feather's weight against a decision of the Pope in Council, nor would it matter at all, except for the Father's sake who had by anticipation opposed it. They consider that the Fathers ought to mean what Rome has since decreed, and that Rome knows their meaning better than they did themselves.

"Let us then understand the position of the Romanists towards us; they do not really argue from the Fathers, though they seem to do so. They may affect to do so in our behalf, happy if by an innocent stratagem they are able to convert us; but all the while in their own feelings they are taking a far higher position. They are teaching, not disputing or proving. They are interpreting what is obscure in Antiquity, purifying what is alloyed, correcting what is amiss, perfecting what is incomplete, harmonizing what is various. They claim and use all its documents as ministers and organs of that one infallible Church, which once forsooth kept silence, but since has spoken; which by a divine gift must ever be consistent with herself, and which bears with her her own evidence of Divinity."[49]

5. A partial illustration is afforded us of the point in question in the views taken by various schools of the sense of the formularies of the English Church; partial, because these views are never proofs of the truth of doctrine, but are mere methods for interpretation and comment. Opposite parties come with their own creeds, and use them as keys to Prayer-book, Articles, and other authoritative documents. Now the test of an admissible hypothesis will be its incorporating without force the whole circle of statements of which it takes cognizance. Some of these may be *primâ facie* {189} adverse, and the difficulty may be reasonably solved; some may be at least accounted for, and their objective force suspended; others, it may be, cannot be explained, and must not be explained away. But when the mind is under the influence of some particular theory, (as, for instance, that the views of the original writers, or that the present understanding of the nation, is their legitimate interpretation,) it will be strongly tempted to evade and distort them, erring, not in arranging them on a general principle, but in forgetting that, though statements often are ambiguous, yet they often are not so, and in that case must be suffered to speak for themselves.

In the following passage a writer frankly confesses a difficulty in the way of his theory, and, instead of treating it with violence, leaves it.

"The Fathers," says Mr. Scott, writing on the doctrine of regeneration, "soon began to speak on this subject in unscriptural language; and our pious reformers, from an undue regard to them and to the circumstances of the times, have retained a few expressions in the liturgy, which not only are inconsistent with their other doctrine, but also tend to perplex men's minds, and mislead their judgment on this important subject. It is obvious, however, from the words above cited and many other passages, that they never supposed the mere outward administration of baptism to be *regeneration*, in the strict sense of the word; nor can any man, without the most palpable absurdity, overlook the difference between the baptism that is "outward in the flesh," and "that of the heart, by the Spirit, whose praise is not of men but of God."[50]

6. It is not intended here to question the substantial accuracy of Gibbon's account of the Paulicians, (A.D. 660,) which has received the approval of later writers; but still it will afford an instance of the necessity, under which historians lie, of framing {190} hypothetical views, if they would present to the reader a distinct and consistent narrative. Photius and Petrus Siculus call the Paulicians a brand of the Manichees, and go through a detail of their doctrine in accordance with this imputation; and in this testimony Gibbon acquiesces, as Neander and others since. There is this difficulty, however, in admitting it:—that (besides the utter absence, I believe, of any testimony to the existence of Manicheeism in their neighbourhood, up to the time of their rise,) these religionists actually disowned the name of Manichee, anathematized Manes, and abjured both his theology and even that of the Gnostic Valentinus. But if we are not to trust Peter and Photius for the origin, how shall we trust them for the doctrine of the Paulicians? especially as a notion about their origin may have biassed those writers in their account of the doctrine.

Gibbon solves this difficulty by the following hypothesis. He finds that, in the fourth century, Gnostics were congregated in the villages and mountains about the Euphrates, and that a trace of the Marcionites is found, though at some distance from the river, in Theodoret's personal history in the fifth. He knows nothing of them later; but he sees that the Paulicians rose at Samosata, near the Euphrates. It suggests itself, therefore, to him, that, though they did not profess themselves Manichees, perhaps they were some remnant of Gnostics popularly called Manichees, in spite of their disowning Valentinus. For the Gnostics rejected the Old Testament, and held the doctrine of two Principles, which Photius and Petrus Siculus impute to the Paulicians; and are very likely to have had the other Paulician peculiarities, such as contempt of images and relics, neglect of St. Mary, and disbelief in the Eucharistic change, because they separated off from the Church before these {191} points were formally settled. So far, well; but it appears that the people, out of whom the Paulicians arose, were not well acquainted with the Gospels, which would seem to show they were Catholic laymen; but then he reflects that it is not impossible but the Gnostic laity were forbidden the use of the Scriptures too. This completes his theory; and enables him forthwith to set forward in the vigorous and flowing passage that follows, his apologies and explanations skilfully falling into their places as he proceeds:—

"The Gnostics, who had distracted the infancy, were oppressed by the greatness and authority of the Church. Instead of emulating or surpassing the wealth, learning, and numbers of the Catholics, their obscure remnant was driven from the capitals of the east and west, and confined to the villages and mountains along the borders of the Euphrates. Some vestige of the Marcionites may be detected in the fifth century; but the numerous sects were finally lost in the odious name of the Manicheeans; and these heretics, who presumed to reconcile the doctrines of Zoroaster and Christ, were pursued by the two religions with equal and unrelenting hatred. Under the grandson of Heraclius, in the neighbourhood of Samosata, more famous for the birth of Lucian than for the title of a Syrian kingdom, a reformer arose, esteemed by the Paulicians as the chosen messenger of truth. In his humble dwelling of Mananalis, Constantine entertained a deacon, who returned from Syrian captivity, and received the inestimable gift of the New Testament, which was already concealed from the vulgar by the prudence of the Greek, and perhaps of the Gnostic, clergy. These books became the measure of his studies, and the rule of his faith; and the Catholics, who dispute his interpretation, acknowledged that his text was genuine and sincere. . . . In the gospel, and the epistles of St. Paul, his {192} faithful follower investigated the creed of primitive Christianity; and, whatever might be the success, a Protestant reader will applaud the spirit of the inquiry.

"But if the Scriptures of the Paulicians were pure, they were not perfect. Their founders rejected the two epistles of St. Peter, the apostle of the circumcision, whose dispute with their favourite for the observance of the law could not easily be forgiven. They agreed with their Gnostic brethren in the universal contempt for the Old Testament, the books of Moses and the prophets, which have been consecrated by the decrees of the Catholic Church. With equal boldness, and doubtless with more reason, Constantine, the new Sylvanus, disclaimed the visions, which, in so many bulky and splendid volumes, had been published by the oriental sects; the fabulous productions of the Hebrew patriarchs and the sages of the East; the spurious gospels, epistles, and acts, which in the first age had overwhelmed the orthodox code; the theology of Manes, and the authors of the kindred heresies; and the thirty generations, or eons, which had been created by the fruitful fancy of Valentine. The Paulicians sincerely condemned the memory and opinions of the Manicheean sect, and complained of the injustice which impressed that invidious name on the simple votaries of St. Paul and of Christ.

"Of the ecclesiastical chain, many links had been broken by the Paulician reformers; and their liberty was enlarged as they reduced the number of masters, at whose voice profane reason must bow to mystery and miracle. The early separation of the Gnostics had preceded the establishment of the Catholic worship; and against the gradual innovations of discipline and doctrine, they were as strongly guarded by habit and aversion as by the silence of St. Paul and the Evangelists. The objects, which had been transformed by the magic of {193} superstition, appeared to the eyes of the Paulicians in their genuine and naked colours. An image made without hands was the common workmanship of a mortal artist, &c. The miraculous relics were an heap of bones and ashes, &c.; the true and vivifying cross was, &c.; the Body and Blood of Christ, a loaf of bread, and a cup of wine, the gifts of nature and the symbols of grace; the Mother of God was degraded, &c., and the Saints and Angels were no longer solicited, &c. . . . In the practice, or at least in the theory of the Sacraments, the Paulicians were inclined to abolish all visible objects of worship; and the words of the gospel were, in their judgment, the baptism and communion of the faithful.

"A creed thus simple and spiritual was not adapted to the genius of the times; and the rational Christian, who might have been contented with the light yoke and easy burden of Jesus and His Apostles, was justly offended that the Paulicians should dare to violate the Unity of God, the first article of natural and revealed religion. . . . They likewise held the eternity of matter, a stubborn and rebellious substance, the origin of a second principle, &c. . . . The apostolic labours of Constantine-Sylvanus soon multiplied the number of his disciples; the secret recompense of spiritual ambition. The remnant of the Gnostic sects, and especially the Manicheeans of Armenia, were united under his standard; many Catholics were converted or seduced by his arguments; and he preached with success in the region of Pontus and Cappadocia, which had long since imbibed the religion of Zoroaster.". . &c.

Now I conceive there is nothing in this sketch, though it seems so precarious on an analysis, which is fairly open to objection, except that the author has not mentioned its hypothetical character.

7. Another writer of history may be mentioned, who uses hypothesis as well as fact, and presumption {194} as well as evidence, but is properly careful to discriminate between them. Disquisition cannot be conducted in a more logical tone than it assumes in the present Bishop of St. David's History of Greece; yet it would not be logical, if, when engaged upon the early portions of it, where evidence is wanting, it did not proceed by means of general truths, and appeal to common places larger than the particular points on which he has to decide. Thus, when discussing the origin of the Grecian mythology, he introduces one or two passages from Herodotus and Homer which bear upon the subject; and then interprets or modifies them by a view of his own, founded on presumptions. He refers to Agamemnon's oath in the Iliad, addressed not only to Jupiter, but to the omniscient sun, rivers, and earth, and to the gods of vengeance in the realms below; he refers also to Herodotus's testimony or opinion, or rather that of the priests of Dodona, that "the Pelasgians," that is, the early possessors of the country, "once sacrificed only to nameless deities;" and to the statement of the same author, that the religion underwent two changes, one from the introduction of Egyptian rites, the other from the poems of Homer and Hesiod, who gave names and histories to the gods.

These are his four facts; and he submits them to the action of the following antecedent probabilities. He observes that "the Greek was formed to sympathize strongly with the outward world; in all the objects around him he found life, or readily imparted it to them out of the fulness of his own imagination. This was not a poetical view, the privilege of extraordinary minds, but the popular mode of thinking and feeling, cherished

undoubtedly by the bold forms and abrupt contrasts, and all the
natural wonders of a mountainous and sea-broken land. A people
so disposed and situated {195} is not immediately impelled to
seek a single universal source of being. The teeming earth, the
quickening sun, the restless sea, the rushing stream, the irresistible storm, every display of superhuman which it beholds, rouses
a distinct sentiment of religious awe. Everywhere it finds deities,
which however may not for a long time be distinguished by name
from the objects in which their presence is manifested."[51] This is
the first stage of the author's development of Greek religion,
viz., the worship of nature; and he at once appropriates to it
Agamemnon's invocation, which he seems to consider but a
specimen of "all the traces of the primitive religion to be found
in the later Greek mythology." He also identifies it with Herodotus's Pelagic period, and interprets his "nameless deities" by
"invisible powers." This interpretation, he says, "is highly
probable in itself;" and he confirms it "by the example of the
ancient Persians."

Then he proceeds, after the example, but not on the theory
of Herodotus, "to trace the steps by which this simple creed was
transformed into the complicated system of Greek mythology."
Herodotus, as we have seen, had referred to the Egyptian religion
and to the poets. Dr. Thirlwall rejects the notion of any direct
influence of Egypt in the process: first, on the fair antecedent
ground that the information came from the priests of that country,
who were neither acquainted with Grecian mythology, nor
unbiassed witnesses in a question so nearly touching their
national pride; and next, from what certainly is of the nature of
evidence, that there is very little of a foreign character in the
mythology. Yet, though he considers it of native growth, he will
not grant to Herodotus that the poets were its authors, or that its
matter and its ritual are allegorical, or philosophy its origin and its
{196} latent interpretation. This opinion he considers to be "repugnant

to all analogy as well as to all internal evidence." Accordingly, he conjectures that the mythology arose from the gradual development of popular ideas and feelings, brought into shape, as regards the persons, provinces, functions, and mutual relations of the deities, by many generations of sacred bards, and especially in the course of the heroic age. And thus the Hellenic period, in which the heroic is included, is contrasted with the Pelasgic.

Shortly afterwards he debates the question, whether human sacrifices entered into the religion of the Greeks, which has been disputed on account of the silence of Homer on the subject; and he reasonably concludes that such mere silence "would not in the slightest degree shake the authority of the numerous legends" which record them; that in the Iliad itself twelve Trojans are immolated by Achilles to the shade or memory of Patroclus; moreover, that the notion of propitiating an offended deity, or that foreign example, might lead to that cruel superstition, and that the bloodless dedication of living persons, which was very ancient, might, not inconsistently with the manners of the heroic age, be changed into a dedication of blood.

Who will deny the fairness of these conclusions? yet how singularly are they independent of definite facts! And if such are allowable where speculation is harmless, why may they not be a duty when action is imperative?

Heeren, who has already been noticed, after an elaborate review of the state, monuments, and commerce of Meroe, ends by observing "that the first seats of commerce were also the first seats of civilization."[52] When we examine the proofs of this "great conclusion which," he says, "becomes in a manner forced upon us," it seems to consist merely in this, that the cities of which he has treated {197} were both centres of civilization and marts of commerce. There is no fact adduced to decide for us, by what Lord Bacon would call an *experimentum crucis*, whether the commerce led to the civilization or the civilization to the commerce. He adopts however, as I have said, the former of these two propositions; and he supports it by a purely antecedent argument. "Exchange of merchandize," he observes, "led to the exchange of ideas, and by mutual friction was first kindled the sacred flame of humanity."

Whether this antecedent reasoning be correct need not here be determined. So much may plausibly be advanced in its favour, that, of the needs respectively supplied by commerce and civilization, those supplied by commerce are far the most urgent, and are likely to have engaged the earlier attention; food has a prior claim on us to books. Yet it is remarkable that Heeren, instead of troubling himself with any closer proof than is contained in the words which have been quoted from him, had already suggested to us a previous hypothesis, which supersedes the question of this alternative altogether, viz., that religion led *both* to commerce and civilization. He insists, as one of the three great facts which he has proved, that the chief marts were also "establishments of a priest caste, who as a dominant race had their principal seat at Meroe,"[53] whence they sent out colonies, which in their turn became builders of cities and temples, and likewise the founders of states; "a caste whose civilization was bound to their religion,"[54] the fame of whose piety and justice spread even to the Greeks,[55] "whose progress in architecture, and in a certain degree in the pictorial arts, is still one of the greatest problems, though one of the greatest certainties;" and, on the other hand, "who, by sending out colonies, guided the course of trade."

And here, again, to prove the dependence of commerce on religion, ingenious and satisfactory as he {198} is, he is equally antecedent in his arguments, as when he would prove the dependence of civilization on commerce. His proof mainly consists of certain powerful presumptions, that trade in the East must extend under the shadow of religion, confirmed by instances, not of ancient, but modern times. Those countries,[56] he says, are desert wilds, inhabited by nomadic tribes; there is no security for the merchant but in sacred places. Besides, religion is a festive principle, and requires the goods of this world for its due exercise; fairs are naturally both devotional and commercial assemblages. Caravans of pilgrims are trading caravans. Mecca is still the seat of religion and commerce. "The rapidity with which a place rises in the East, when once it has obtained a sanctuary that becomes the object of a pilgrimage, and by means becomes a place of trade, almost surpasses belief,"[57] as Tenta, a city of the Delta, has risen in our own day. Burkhardt[58] found a priestly establishment at Damer, in the isle of Meroe, of five hundred houses, which was also a trading state. These sacred characters are much reverenced by their wild neighbours, and two of them accompanied his caravan as guards. "It would require an armed force," he adds, "to pass here without the aid of some of these religious men." Antecedent or collateral considerations such as these, he thinks he brings home with sufficient cogency to the immediate proposition to which he has committed himself, if he can produce just one or two distinct facts in evidence, such as the probable fact that the celebrated Temple of Ammon was also the halt of a caravan. And, doubtless, he proceeds in this method of reasoning, on the latent but very reasonable principle, that it is impertinent to ask for what it is hopeless to obtain.

9. One more instance of the same method shall be supplied from Mosheim. He prefaces his Dissertation, "*De turbatâ per recentiores Platonicos* {199} *Ecclesiâ*," by a caution that he is giving but a sketch of the alleged corruption, and of the grounds on which it is proved; yet as much as a sketch he certainly means to give. Now what he has undertaken to show is a fact, the fact of an extensive effect wrought on the Church by the Neo-platonic philosophy;—whether he shows it by means of direct evidence, instances or testimony, or of existing causes which involve it, or

of results which presuppose it, or of circumstances which presume and betoken it. We want actual proof, if it be possible, of a definite process; of certain wrong principles, first, in Neo-platonism, and then, in matter of fact, passing from Neo-platonism into the Church, and corrupting it. Now let us see how far he answers our reasonable demand.

On the face of the history, we find that Eclecticism existed in the Church before the Eclectic sect was heard of. Athenagoras's extant works, as Mosheim refers to them, show that he was an Eclectic, that is, chose out the best opinions from all philosophies, when he was a Christian. St. Clement, again, expressly gives the name of philosophy *par excellence*, "not to the Stoic, Platonic, Epicurean, or Aristotelic," but "to whatever is good in each collected together," or "to an Eclectic system," using the very word; and whereas some Christians spoke against philosophy, he, on the contrary, considered it as a preparation for Christianity. Moreover, Ammonius, the founder of the Neo-platonic, or Eclectic sect, who was a contemporary of St. Clement, was a Christian, and had been educated at the Catechetical School of Alexandria. And, indeed, from the nature of the case, the principle of Eclecticism must have been exercised by the Church from the first, and except upon that principle no Christian could be a philosopher at all; for Christianity, treating of the same subject-matter as heathen philosophy had undertaken, could not avoid {200} giving judgment on the attempts of its several sects and pronouncing how far each was right and where wrong.

This is a *primâ facie* view of the case, which Mosheim has to meet; and he attempts to do so by maintaining that one Potamo, and Eclectic philosopher, who lived at the end of the second century, was really of the date of Augustus, and preceded Christianity,—a supposition which Brucker and others disprove. He observes, too, that Athenagoras, as we have seen, was an

Eclectic after he joined the Church, apparently with a view of suggesting that he was an Eclectic before it; and that St. Clement pronounced that true philosophy was Eclectic, as if this avowal implied the presence of a heathen Eclectic school; and that Pantaenus, being called by one author a Stoic, and by another a Pythagorean, before he was a Christian, probably was neither, but professed the Eclectic principle; and that since Christian philosophers were in the practice of following the Stoics in ethics, Aristotle in dialectics, Plato in theology, therefore they were corrupted by heathen Eclecticism; moreover, that St. Augustine certainly confesses that philosophers joined the Church without giving up their paganism, because he speaks of Platonists, who, with only the change of a few words and sentiments, had become Christians; lastly, that Origen's Platonic opinions are well known, and that his pupils were raised to the highest dignities in the Eastern Church.

What we have a right to demand is some antecedent probability, or specimen of evidence, to show that any one doctrine or principle was in the Neo-platonic sect before it was in the Catholic Church, and that it passed from the former into the latter; yet even assuming that there were certain anticipations which is far from proved, no proof does {201} Mosheim bring of such a communication or corruption as is in question.

He proceeds to speak in detail of the external and internal evils which Neo-platonism inflicted on the Church; with the external we are not concerned.

Under the latter head, he mentions the history of Synesius, in the *fifth* century, who, being a Platonic philosopher, was consecrated a Bishop without renouncing his opinions; and next he refers to the *heretical* author of the Clementines, to show "what mischief to Christian interests had been caused by that wisdom of the Alexandrians."

Then he compares the frauds and falsehoods of heathens and heretics; the doctrine of pious frauds countenanced by the Judaic writer last mentioned, by the ancient priests of Egypt, and by Pythagoras and Plato; moreover, the numerous spurious writings of the first ages, and false accounts of miracles, with the principle of economy sanctioned by Origen, St. Chrysostom, and Synesius, down to the time of St. Augustine; by way of proving that the principle of the economy came from the philosophical extravagances.

Lastly, he proceeds to assert that Platonism has introduced into the Church wrong opinions about human liberty, the state of the dead, the human soul, the Holy Trinity and kindred doctrines, religious contemplation, and the interpretation of Scripture; and wrong practices in rites and usages, as fasting, abstinence, and continence; but he still does not offer any proof of these assertions.

It is plain that, in the whole of this elaborate Essay, there are but two of his statements which are at all of the nature of an argument in behalf of the matter of fact which he proposes to prove: the one, that Origen is said to have introduced Platonic doctrine into his writings; the other, that Synesius is charged with not renouncing his Platonism on {202} becoming a Bishop. Of these, the instance of Synesius is an isolated one; while Origen was never countenanced by the Church even in his day, and has no distinct connexion with the Neo-platonists.

If it be asked how a clear and sensible mind, such as the writings of Mosheim evince, could reason so loosely, the answer is ready. He took it for granted that the Catholic doctrines and usages were wrong; and in that case, since there is a resemblance between the philosophical and the Catholic, there is certainly a very strong presumption that the Catholic were actually derived from the philosophical. Accordingly, throughout his dissertation, he is but arranging and interpreting the facts of history by his thesis, and not proving his thesis by the facts.

These instances may suffice in illustration of a method of reasoning, ordinary and necessary when facts are scarce; often easy to handle aright, but very frequently difficult and dangerous; open to great abuse, and depending for its success or failure far more on the individual exercising it than on rules which can be laid down; a method which, if delicate and doubtful when used in proof of the Catholic Creed, is far less certain and far less satisfactory in the many instances in which it is applied to scientific and historical investigations.

[1] Univ. Serm. pp. 195, 196.

[2] Univ. Serm. pp. 269, 270.

[3] Essay on Miracles, p. lxxvi.

[4] Lardner's Heath. Test. p. 22. <Nathaniel Lardner (1684-1768), *A Large Collection of Ancient Jewish and Heathen Testimonies to the Truth of Christian Religion with Notes and Observations* (1764-67), in 4 vols.>

[5] Paley's Evid. p. i. prop. 1, 7. <William Paley, *A View of the Evidences of Christianity,* 1793>

[6] Milman, Christ. vol. ii, p. 352. <see note 11 to ch. 1>

[7] Wood's Mechan. p. 31. <James Wood, *The Principles of Mechanics*, vol. 3. pt. 1 in his *The Principles of Natural Philosophy* (Cambridge, 1790-99), in 4 vols.

[8] Tracts for the Times, vol. v. pp. 102-104. <Tract 85, "Lectures on the Scripture Proofs of the Doctrine of the Church," Lecture VIII, "Difficulties of Jewish and Christian Faith Compared," pp. 102-115. <see note 1 to the Introduction>

[9] Evidences, iii. 5.

[10] Evidences, iii. 5.

[11] Anal. ii. 7.

[12] Essay on Miracles, p. ci.

[13] Anal. ii. 7.

[14] On Prophecy, i. p. 28. <J. Davison (1777-1834), *Discourses on Prophecy, in which are considered its structure, use, and inspiration, being the substance of twelve sermons preached in the Chapel of Lincoln's Inn, in the lecture founded by the Right Reverend William Warburton* (London: John Murray, 1824).>

[15] Authent. N. T. p. 237. <Gottfried Less (1736-1797), *The Authenticity, Incorrupted Preservation, and Credibility of the New Testament,* tr. from the German by R. Kingdon (London: F. C. and J. Rivington, 1804).>

¹⁶ According to Less.

¹⁷ Tracts for the Times, No. 85, p. 78. <see note 8 above; Lecture VI, "External Difficulties of the Canon and the Catholic Creed," pp. 70-85.>

¹⁸ Ibid. p. 80.

¹⁹ Ep. 93.

²⁰ Vid. Concil. Bracar. ap. Aguirr. Conc. Hisp. t. ii. p. 676. <José Sáenz de Aguirre (1630-1699), *Collectio maxima Conciliorum omnium Hispaniae et novi orbis* (Salamanca, 1686).> "That the cup was not administered at the same time is not so clear; but from the tenor of this first Canon in the Acts of the Third Council of Braga, which condemns the notion that the Host should be steeped in the chalice, we have no doubt that the wine was withheld from the laity. Whether certain points of doctrine are or are not found in the Scriptures is no concern of the historian; all that he has to do is religiously to follow his guides, to suppress or distrust nothing through partiality." *Dunham, Hist. of Spain and Port* vol i. p. 204. <S. Astley Dunham, *The History of Spain and Portugal*, 1830, a volume in the *Cabinet Encyclopedia*.> If *pro complemento communionis* in the Canon merely means "for the Cup," at least the Cup is spoken of as a complement; the same view is contained in the "confirmation of the Eucharist," as spoken of in St. German's Life. Vid. Lives of Saints, No. 9, p. 28.

²¹ Niceph. Hist. xviii. 45. Renaudot, however, tells us of two Bishops at the time when the schism was at length healed. Patr. Al. Jac. p. 248. However, these had been consecrated by priests, p. 145. <Eusebius Renaudot (1646-1720), *Historia patriarcharum Alexandrinorum Jacobitarum* (1713).>

²² Vid. Bingh. Ant. xv. § 7 <J. Bingham, *The Antiquities of the Christian Church* (1708-1722), 10 vols.>; and Fleury, Hist. xxvi. 50, note *g*. <Claude Fleury (1640-1723), *Histoire ecclésiastique* (1691-1765). Newman refers to his own translation, with notes, *The Ecclesiastical History of M. L'abbé Fleury from A.D. 400 to A. D. 429* (Oxford: J. H. Parker, 1843).>

²³ Pope's Suprem. ed. 1836, pp. 26, 27, 157, 171, 222. <Isaac Barrow (1630-77). Master of Trinity College, Cambridge, *A Treatise of the Pope's Supremacy, to which is added a Discourse on the Unity of the Church*, first ed. by Archbp. Tillotson, London 1680.>

²⁴ Athan. Hist. Tract. Oxf. tr. p. 56.

²⁵ Hist. ii. 17.

²⁶ Hist. iii. 10.

²⁷ Theod. Hist. v. 10.

²⁸ Constant, Epp. Pont. p. 546. <Pierre Coustant (1654-1721), *Epistolae romanorum pontificum et quae ad eos scripta sunt a S. Clemente I usque ad Innocentium III* . . . (Paris, apud L. D. Delatour, A. U. Coustelier, 1721-), vols.>

²⁹ In 1 Tim. iii. 14, 15.

[30] Constant, p. 624. <see note 28 above.>

[31] ii. 3.

[32] Constant, pp. 896, 1064.

[33] Ep. 186, 2.

[34] De. Ingrat. 2. Common. 41.

[35] Serm. De Natal. iii. 3.

[36] Ibid. v. 4.

[37] Ep. ad Eutych. fin.

[38] Concil. Hard. t. ii. p. 656.

[39] Barrow on the Supremacy, ed. 1836, pp. 263, 331, 384. <see note 23 above>.

[40] Aphor. 5, vol. iv. p. xi. ed. 1815.

[41] Nov. Org. i. 2, § 26, vol. iv. p. 29.

[42] Nov. Org. § 70, p. 44.

[43] Hist. of Rome, vol. i. p. 345, ed. 1828. <Barthold Georg Niebuhr (1776-1831), *Römische Geschichte*. 1828-32>, *The History of Rome*, tr. J. C. Hare <Cambridge: J. Taylor, 1828-42), in 3 vols.>

[44] Vol. v. p. 219.

[45] Engl. tr. vol. 1, pp. 67, 68. <See note 19 to Introduction.>.

[46] pp. 99, 100.

[47] p. 127

[48] p. 228.

[49] Proph. Off. pp. 84-87.

[50] Essays, ch. xii. p. 201. <Thomas Scott (1747-1821), *Essays on the most Important Subjects on Religion*, 1793. Newman said of Scott in the *Apologia*, that he owed him his very soul.>

[51] Vol. i. p. 184. <Connop Thirlwall (1779-1875), bishop of St. David's, was best known for his *History of Greece* (London: Longmans, 1835), in 8 vols.>

[52] Hist. Res. vol. 4, p. 475. Oxf. tr. <Arnold H. Ludwig Heeren (1760-1842), *Historical Researches into the Politics, Intercourse and Trade of the Principal Nations of Antiquity* (Oxford: D. A. Talboys, 1833-34), in 6 vols.).>

[53] p. 471.

[54] p. 475.

[55] p. 477.

[56] p. 448.

[57] p. 449.

[58] p. 425.

CHAPTER IV.

ILLUSTRATIONS OF THE ARGUMENT IN BEHALF OF EXISTING DEVELOPMENTS OF CHRISTIANITY.

No one will be disposed to deny that the body of doctrine which at this day goes by the name of Catholic is at once the historical and the logical continuation of the body of doctrine so-called in the eighteenth, in the seventeenth, in the sixteenth, and so back in every preceding century successively till we come to the first. Whether it be a corrupt development or a legitimate, conducted on sound logic or fallacious, the present so-called Catholic religion is the successor, the representative, and the heir of the religion of the so-called Catholic Church of primitive times.

Neither can any one, I think, deny, after following the line of thought which has just been brought to a conclusion, that the doctrines of which the present Catholic religion consists are *primâ facie* the correct, true, faithful, legitimate developments of the doctrines which preceded them, and not their corruptions; that a very strong case ought to be made out against that religion, to prove that it is materially corrupt, and not in its substance Apostolic.

We have now to proceed a step further,—to apply these so-called Catholic doctrines, thus favourably recommended to our notice, the tests which have already been framed to distinguish between development and corruption; that is, in the fair and reasonable temper which is demanded {204} of us by this *primâ facie* likelihood of their fidelity to their originals. I ought rather to say,—to suggest how those tests may be applied, for this is all that can be expected in an undertaking like the present.

SECTION I.

APPLICATION OF THE FIRST TEST OF FIDELITY IN DEVELOPMENT.

THE CHURCH OF THE FIRST CENTURIES.

It was said, then, that true development retains the *essential idea* of the subject from which it has proceeded, and a corruption loses it. What then is the true idea of Christianity? and is it preserved in the developments commonly called Catholic, and in the Church which embodies and teaches them?

Here, it must be observed, according to a foregoing remark, that the forms and types of divine creations are not, strictly speaking, ascertainable; they are facts. No one can define an oak, or an eagle, or a lion, or any other of the objects which arrest us, and which we gaze upon externally. We can but describe them. We multiply properties or qualities which attach to them, and thereby impress upon the mind analytically an image of that which we cannot philosophically express. Let us now pursue the same way with the Church. Let us take it as the world now views it in its age; and let us take it as the world once viewed it in its youth; and let us see whether there be any great difference between the early and the later description of it. The following statement will show my meaning:—

There is a religious communion claiming a divine commission, and calling all other religious bodies {205} around it heretical or infidel; it is a well-organized, well-disciplined body; it is a sort of secret society, binding together its members by influences and by engagements which it is difficult for strangers to ascertain. It is spread over the known world; it may be weak or insignificant locally, but it is strong on the whole from its continuity; it may be smaller than other religious bodies together, but larger than each separately. It is a natural enemy to governments external to itself; it is intolerant and engrossing, and tends to a new modelling of society; it breaks laws, it divides families. It is a gross superstition; it is charged with the foulest crimes; it is despised by the intellect of the day; it is frightful to the imagination of the many. And there is but one communion such.

Place this description before Pliny or Julian; place it before Frederick the Second or Guizot. "Apparent dirae facies." Each knows at once, without asking a question, who is meant by it. One object, and only one, absorbs each item of the detail of the delineation.

The *primâ facie* view of early Christianity, in the eyes of witnesses external to it, is presented to us in the brief but vivid descriptions given by Tacitus, Suetonius, and Pliny, the only heathen writers who distinctly mention it for the first hundred and fifty years.

Tacitus is led to speak of the religion, on occasion of the conflagration of Rome, which was popularly imputed to Nero. "To put an end to the report," he says, "he laid the guilt on others, and visited them with the most exquisite punishment those, namely, who, held in abhorrence for their crimes, (*per flagitia invisos,*) were popularly called Christians. The author of that profession (*nominis* was Christ, who in the reign of Tiberius, was capitally punished by the Procurator, Pontius Pilate. The deadly superstition (*exitiabilis superstitio*), though {206} checked for a while, broke out afresh; and that, not only through Judaea, the original seat of the evil, but through the City also, whither all things atrocious or shocking (*atrocia aut pudenda*) flow together from every quarter and thrive. At first certain were seized who avowed it; then, on their report, a vast multitude were convicted, not so much of firing the city, as of hatred of mankind (*odio humani generis.*)" After describing their tortures, he continues, "In consequence, though they were guilty and deserved most signal punishment, they began to be pitied, as if destroyed not for any public object, but from the barbarity of one man."

Suetonius relates the same transactions thus:—

"Capital punishments were inflicted on the Christians, a class of men of a new and magical superstition (*superstitionis novae et maleficae*)." What gives additional character to this statement is its context; for it occurs as one out of various police or sumptuary or domestic regulations which Nero made; such as "controlling private expenses, forbidding taverns to serve meat, repressing the contests of theatrical parties, and securing the integrity of wills."

When Pliny was Governor of Pontus, he wrote his celebrated letter to the Emperor Trajan, to ask advice how he was to deal with the Christians, whom he found there in great numbers. One of his points of hesitation was whether the very profession of Christianity was not by itself sufficient to justify punishment: "whether the name itself should be visited, though clear of flagitious acts (*flagitia*), or only when connected with them." He says, he had ordered for execution such as persevered in their profession, after repeated warnings, "as not doubting, whatever it was they professed, at any rate contumacy and inflexible obstinacy ought to be punished." He required them to invoke the gods, to sacrifice wine and frankincense to the {207} images of the Emperor, and to blaspheme Christ; "to which," he adds, "it is said no real Christian can be compelled." Renegades informed him that "the sum total of their offence or fault was meeting before light on an appointed day, and saying with one another a form of words (*carmen*) to Christ, as if to a god, and binding themselves by oath, not to the commission of any wickedness, but against the commission of theft, robbery, adultery, breach of trust, denial of deposits; that, after this, they were accustomed to separate, and then to meet again for a meal, but eaten together and harmless; however, that they had even left this off after his edicts enforcing the Imperial prohibition of *Hetaeriae* or Associations." He proceeded to put two women to the torture, but "discovered nothing beyond a bad and excessive superstition" (*superstitionem pravam et immodicam*), "the contagion" of which," he continues, "had spread through villages and country, till the temples were emptied of worshippers."

In these testimonies, which will form a natural and convenient text for what is to follow, we have various characteristics brought before us of the religion to which they related. It was a superstition, as all three writers agree; a bad and excessive superstition, according to Pliny; a magical superstition according to Suetonius; a deadly superstition, according to Tacitus. Next, it was embodied in a society, and moreover a secret and unlawful society or *hetaeria*; and it was a proselytizing society; and its very name was connected with "flagitious," "atrocious," and "shocking" acts.

Now these few points, which are not all which might be set down, contain in themselves a distinct and significant description of Christianity; but they have far greater meaning when illustrated by the history of the times, the testimony of later writers, and the acts of the Roman government towards its {208} professors. It is impossible to mistake the judgment passed on the religion by these three writers, and still more clearly by other writers and Imperial functionaries. They evidently associated Christianity with the oriental superstitions, whether propagated by individuals or embodied in a rite, which were in that day traversing the Empire, and which in the event acted so remarkable a part in breaking up the national forms of worship, and so in preparing the way for Christianity. This, then, is the broad view which the educated heathen took of Christianity; and, if it had been very unlike those rites and curious arts in external appearance, they would not have confused it with them.

Changes in society are, by a providential appointment, commonly preceded and facilitated by the setting in of a certain current in men's thoughts and feelings in that direction towards which a change is to be made. And, as lighter substances whirl about before the tempest and presage it, so words and deeds, ominous but not effective of the coming revolution, are circulated beforehand through the multitude, or pass across the field of events. This was specially the case with Christianity, as became its high dignity; it came heralded and attended by a crowd of shadows, shadows of itself, impotent and monstrous as shadows are, but not at first sight distinguishable from it by common spectators. Before the mission of the Apostles, a movement, of which there had been earlier parallels, had begun in Egypt, Syria, and the neighbouring countries, tending to the propagation of new and peculiar forms of worship throughout the Empire. Prophecies were afloat that some new order of things was coming in from the East, which increased the existing unsettlement of the popular mind; pretenders made attempts to satisfy its wants, and old traditions of the Truth, embodied for ages in local or in national religions, gave to these attempts a {209} doctrinal and ritual shape, which became an additional point of resemblance to that Truth which was soon visibly to appear.

The distinctive character of the rites in question lay in their appealing to the gloomy rather than to the cheerful and hopeful feelings, and in their influencing the mind through fear. The notions of guilt and expiation, of evil and good to come, and of dealings with the invisible world, were in some shape or other pre-eminent in them, and formed a striking contrast to the classical polytheism, which was gay and graceful, as was natural in a civilized age. The new rites, on the other hand, were secret; their doctrine was mysterious; their profession was a discipline, beginning in a formal initiation, manifested in an association, and exercised in privation and pain. They were from the nature of the case proselytizing societies, for they were rising into power; nor were they local, but vagrant, restless, intrusive, and encroaching. Their pretensions to supernatural knowledge brought them into easy connexion with magic and astrology, which are as attractive to the wealthy and luxurious as the more vulgar superstitions to the populace.

Such were the rites of Cybele, Isis, and Mithras; such the Chaldeans, as they were commonly called, and the Magi; they came from one part of the world and during the first and second century spread with busy perseverance to the northern and western extremities of the empire.[1] Traces of the mysteries of Cybele, a Syrian deity, if the famous temple of Hierapolis was hers, have been found in Spain, in Gaul, and in Britain, as high up as the wall of Severus. The worship of Isis was the most widely spread of all the pagan deities; it was received in Ethiopia and in Germany, and even the name of Paris has {210} been fancifully traced to it. Both worships, as well as the Science of Magic, had their colleges of priests and devotees, which were governed by a president, and in some places were supported by farms. Their processions passed from town to town, begging as they went and attracting proselytes. Apuleius describes one of them as seizing a whip, accusing himself of some offence, and scourging himself in public. These strollers, *circulatores* or *agyrtae* in classical language, told fortunes, and distributed prophetical tickets to the ignorant people who consulted them. Also, they were learned in the doctrine of omens, of lucky and unlucky days, of the rites of expiation and of sacrifices. Such an *agyrtes* or itinerant was the notorious Alexander of Abonotichus, till he managed to establish himself in Pontus, where he carried on so successful an imposition that his fame reached Rome, and men in office and station intrusted him with their dearest political secrets. Such a wanderer, with as far more religious bearing and a high reputation for virtue, was Apollonius of Tyana, who professed the Pythagorean philosophy, claimed the gift of miracles, and roamed about preaching, teaching, healing, and prophesying from India and Alexandria to Athens and Rome. Another solitary proselytizer, though of an earlier time and an avowed profligacy, had been the Sacrificulus, viewed with such horror by the Roman Senate, as introducing the infamous Bacchic rites into Rome. Such, again, were those degenerate children of a divine religion, who, in the words of their Creator and Judge, "compassed sea and land to make one proselyte," and made him "twofold more the child of hell than themselves."

These vagrant religionists for the most part professed a severe rule of life, and sometimes one of fanatical mortification. In the mysteries of Mithras, the initiation[2] was preceded by fasting and abstinence, {211} and a variety of painful trials; it was made by means of a baptism as a spiritual washing; and it included an offering of bread, and some emblem of a resurrection. In the Samothracian rites it had been a custom to initiate children; confession too of greater crimes seems to have been required, and would naturally be involved elsewhere in the inquisition prosecuted into the past lives of the candidates for initiation. The garments of the converts were white; their calling was considered as a warfare (*militia*), and was undertaken with a *sacramentum*, or military oath. The priests shaved their heads and wore linen, and when they were dead were buried in a sacerdotal garment. It is scarcely necessary to allude to the mutilation inflicted on the priests of Cybele; one instance of their scourgings has already been mentioned; and Tertullian speaks of their high priest cutting his arms for the life of the Emperor

Marcus.[3] The priests of Isis, in lamentation for Osiris, tore their breasts with pine cones. This lamentation was a ritual of observance, founded on some religious mystery: Isis lost Osiris, and the initiated wept in memory of her sorrow; the Syrian goddess had wept over dead Thammuz, and her mystics commemorated it by a ceremonial woe; in the rites of Bacchus, an image was laid on a bier at midnight,[4], which was bewailed in metrical hymns; the god was supposed to die, and then to revive. Nor was this the only worship which was continued through the night; while some of the rites were performed in caves.

Only a heavenly light can give purity to nocturnal and subterraneous worship. Caves were at that time appropriated to the worship of the infernal gods. It was but natural that these wild religions should be connected with magic and its kindred {212} arts; magic has at all times led to cruelty, and licentiousness would be the inevitable reaction from a temporary strictness. An extraordinary profession, when men are in a state of nature, makes hypocrites or madmen, and will in no long time be discarded except by the few. The world of that day associated together in one company, Isiac, Phrygian, Mithriac, Chaldean, wizard, astrologer, fortune-teller, itinerant, and, as was not unnatural, Jew. Magic was professed by the profligate Alexander, and was imputed to the grave Apollonius. The rites of Mithras came from the Magi of Persia; and it is obviously difficult to distinguish in principle the ceremonies of the Syrian Taurobolium from those of the Necyomantia in the Odyssey, or of Canidia in Horace. The Theodosian Code calls magic generally a "superstiOtion;" and magic, orgies, mysteries, and "sabbathizings," were referred to the same "barbarous" origin. "Magical superstitions," the "rites of the Magi," the "promises of the Chaldeans," and the "Mathematici," are familiar to the readers of Tacitus. The Emperor Otho, an avowed patron of oriental fashions, took part in the rites of Isis, and consulted the Mathematici. Vespasian, who also consulted them, is heard of in Egypt as performing miracles at the suggestion of Serapis. Tiberius, in an edict, classes together "Egyptian and Jewish rites;" and Tacitus and Suetonius, in recording it, speak of the two religions together as *"ea superstitio."*[5] Augustus had already associated them together as superstitions, and as unlawful, and that in contrast to others of a like foreign origin. "As to foreign rite (*peregrinae ceremoniae*)" says Suetonius, "as he paid more reverence to those which were old and enjoined, so did he hold the rest in contempt.[6] He goes on to say that, even on the judgment-seat, he had recognised the Eleusinian priests, into whose mysteries he had been {213} initiated at Athens; "whereas, when travelling in Egypt, he had refused to see Apis, and had approved of his grandson Caligula's passing by Judaea without sacrificing at Jerusalem." Plutarch speaks of magic as connected with the mournful mysteries of Orpheus and Zoroaster, with the Egyptian and the Phrygian; and, in his Treatise on Superstition, he puts together in one clause, as specimens of that disease of mind, "mud, filth, sabbathizings, fallings of the face, unseemly postures, foreign adorations."[7] Ovid mentions in consecutive verses the rites of "Adonis lamented by Venus," "The Sabbath of the Syrian Jew," and the "Memphitic Temple of Io in her linen dress."[8] Juvenal speaks of the rites, as well as the language and the music, of the Syrian Orontes having flooded Rome; and in his description of the superstition of the Roman women, he places the low Jewish fortune-teller between the pompous priests of Cybele and Isis, and the bloody witchcraft of the Armenian haruspex and the astrology of the Chaldeans.[9]

The Christian, being at first accounted a kind of Jew, was even on this score included in whatever odium, and whatever bad associations, attended on the Jewish name. But in a little time his independence of the rejected people was clearly understood, as even the persecutions show; and he stood upon his own ground.

Still his character did not change in the eyes of the world; for favour or for reproach, he was still associated with the votaries of secret and magical rites. The Emperor Hadrian, noted as he is for his inquisitive temper, and a partaker in so many mysteries,[10] still believed that the Christians of Egypt allowed themselves in the worship of Serapis. They are brought into connexion with the magic of Egypt in the history of what is commonly called the Thundering Legion, so far as this, {214} that the providential rain which relieved the Emperor's army, and which the Church ascribed to the prayers of the Christian soldiers, is by Dio Cassius attributed to an Egyptian magician who obtained it by invoking Mercury and other spirits. This war had been the occasion of one of the first recognitions which the state had conceded to the Oriental rites, though statesmen and emperors, as private men, had long taken part in them. The Emperor Marcus had been urged by his fears of the Marcomanni to resort to these foreign introductions, and is said to have employed Magi and Chaldeans in averting an unsuccessful issue of the war. It is observable that, in the growing countenance which was extended to these rites in the third century, Christianity came in for a share. The chapel of Alexander Severus contained statues of Abraham, Orpheus, Apollonius, Pythagoras, and our Lord. Here indeed, as in the case of Zenobia's Judaism, an eclectic philosophy aided the comprehension of religions. But, immediately before Alexander, Heliogabalus, who was no philosopher, while he formally seated his Syrian idol in the Palatine, while he observed the mysteries of Cybele and Adonis, and celebrated his magic rites with human victims, intended also, according to Lampridius, to unite with his horrible superstition "the Jewish and Samaritan religions and the Christian rite, that so the priesthood of Heliogabalus might comprise the mystery of every worship."[11] Hence, more or less, the stories which occur in ecclesiastical history of the conversion or good-will of the emperors to the Christian faith, of Hadrian, Mammaea, and others, besides Heliogabalus and Alexander. Such stories might often mean little more than that they favoured it among other forms of Oriental superstition.

What has been said is sufficient to bring before the mind an historical fact, which indeed does not {215} need evidence. Upon the established religions of Europe the East had renewed her encroachments, and was pouring forth a family of rites which in various ways attracted the attention of the luxurious, the political, the ignorant, the restless, and the remorseful. Armenian, Chaldee, Egyptian, Jew, Syrian, Phrygian, as the case might be, was the designation of the new hierophant; and magic, superstition, barbarism, jugglery, were the names given to his rite by the world. In this company appeared Christianity. When then three well-informed writers call Christianity a superstition and a magical superstition, they were not using words at random, or the language of abuse, but they were describing it in distinct and recognised terms as cognate to those gloomy, secret, odious, disreputable religions which were making so much disturbance up and down the empire.

The impression made on the world by the circumstances of the rise of Christianity receives a sort of confirmation after their time, in the appearance of the Gnostic and kindred heresies, which issued from the Church during the second and third centuries. Their resemblance in ritual and constitution to the Oriental rites, sometimes their historical relationship, is undeniable; and certainly it is a singular coincidence, that Christianity should be first called a magical superstition by Suetonius, and then should be found in the intimate company, and seemingly the parent, of a multitude of magical superstitions, if there was nothing in the religion itself to give rise to such a charge.

The Gnostic family[12] suitably traces its origin to a mixed race, which had commenced its history by associating Orientalism with Revelation. After the captivity of the ten tribes, Samaria was colonized by "men from Babylon and Cushan, and from Ava, and from Hamath, and from Sepharvaim," who were {216} instructed at their own instance in "the manner of the God of the land," by one of the priests of the Church of Jeroboam. The consequence was, that "they feared the Lord and served their own gods." Of this country was Simon, the reputed patriarch of the Gnostics; and he is introduced in the Acts of the Apostles as professing those magical powers which were so principal a characteristic of the Oriental mysteries. His heresy, though broken into a multitude of sects, was poured over the world with a Catholicity not inferior to that of Christianity. St. Peter, who fell in with him originally in Samaria, seems to have encountered him again at Rome. At Rome, St. Polycarp met Marcion of Pontus, whose followers spread through Italy, Egypt, Syria, Arabia, and Persia, Valentinus preached his doctrines in Alexandria, Rome and Cyprus; and we read of his disciples in Crete, Caesarea, Antioch, and other parts of the East. Bardesanes and his followers were found in Mesopotamia. The Carpocratians are spoken of at Alexandria, at Rome, and in Cephallenia; the Basilidians spread through the greater part of Egypt; the Ophites were apparently in Bithynia and Galatia; the Cainites or Caians in Africa, and the Marcosians in Gaul. To these must be added several sects, which, though not strictly of the Gnostic stock, are associated with them in date, character, and origin;—the Ebionites of Palestine, the Cerinthians, who rose in some part of Asia Minor, the Encratites and kindred sects, who spread from Mesopotamia to Syria, Cilicia, and other provinces of Asia Minor, and thence to Rome, Gaul, Aquitaine, and Spain; and the Montanists, who, with a town in Phrygia for their metropolis, reached at length from Constantinople to Carthage.

"When [the reader of Christian history] comes to the second century," says Dr. Burton, "he finds that Gnosticism, under some form or other, was professed {217} in every part of the then civilized world. He finds it divided into schools, as numerously and as zealously attended as any which Greece or Asia could boast in their happiest days. He meets with names totally unknown to him before, which excited as much sensation as those of Aristotle or Plato. He hears of volumes having been written in support of this new philosophy, not one of which has survived to our own day."[13] Many of the founders of these sects had been Christians; others were of Jewish parentage; others were more or less connected in fact with the Pagan rites to which their own bore so great a resemblance. Montanus seems even to have been a mutilated priest of Cybele; the followers of Prodicus professed to possess the secret books of Zoroaster; and the doctrine of dualism, which so many of the sects held, is to be traced to the same source. Basilides seems to have recognised Mithras as the Supreme Being, or the Prince of Angels, or the Sun, if Mithras is equivalent to Abraxas, which was inscribed upon his amulets: on the other hand, he is said to have been taught by an immediate disciple of St. Paul. Marcion was the son of a Bishop of Pontus; Tatian, a disciple of St. Justin Martyr.

Whatever might be the history of these sects, and though it may be a question whether they can be properly called "superstitions," and though many of them numbered educated men among their teachers and followers, at least in ritual and profession they closely resembled the vagrant Pagan mysteries which have been above described. Their very name of "Gnostic" implied the possession of a secret, which was to be communicated to their disciples. Ceremonial observances were the preparation, and symbolical rites the instrument of initiation. Tatian and Montanus, the representatives of very distinct {218} schools, agreed in making asceticism a rule of life. The followers of each of these sectaries abstained from wine; the Tatianites and Marcionites from flesh; the Montanists kept three Lents in the year. All the

Gnostic sects seem to have condemned marriage on one or other reason.[14] The Marcionites had three baptisms or more; the Marcosians had two rites of what they called redemption; the latter of these was celebrated as a marriage, and the room adorned as a marriage-chamber. A consecration to a priesthood then followed with anointing. An extreme unction was another of their rites, and prayers for the dead one of their observances. Bardesanes and Harmonius were famous for the beauty of their chants. The prophecies of Montanus were delivered, like the oracles of the heathen, in a state of enthusiasm or ecstasy. To Epiphanes, the son of Carpocrates, who died at the age of seventeen, a temple was erected in the island of Cephallenia, his mother's birthplace, where he was celebrated with hymns and sacrifices. A similar honour was paid by the Carpocratians to Homer, Pythagoras, Plato, Aristotle, as well as to the Apostles; crowns were placed upon their images, and incense burned before them. In one of the inscriptions found at Cyrene, about twenty years since, Zoroaster, Pythagoras, Epicurus, and others are put together with our Lord, as guides of conduct. These inscriptions also contain the Carpocratian tenet of a community of women. I am unwilling to allude to the Agapae and Communions of certain of these sects, which were not surpassed in profligacy by the Pagan rites of which they were an imitation. The very name of Gnostic became an expression for the worst impurities, and no one dared eat bread with them, or use their culinary instruments or plates.

These profligate excesses are found in connection {219} with the exercise of magic and astrology.[15] The amulets of the Basilidians are still extant in great numbers, inscribed with symbols, some Christian, some with figures of Isis, Serapis, and Anubis, represented according to the gross indecencies of the Egyptian mythology.[16] St. Irenaeus had already connected together the two crimes in speaking of the Simonians: "Their mystical priests," he says, "live in lewdness, and practise magic, according to the ability of each. They use exorcisms and incantations; love-potions too, and seductive spells; the virtue of spirits, and dreams, and all other curious arts, they diligently observe."[17] The Marcosians were especially devoted to these curious practices, which are also ascribed to Carpocrates and Apelles. Marcion and others are reported to have used astrology. Tertullian speaks generally of the sects of his day: "Infamous are the dealings of the heretics with sorcerers very many, with mountebanks, with astrologers, with philosophers, to wit, such as are given to curious questions. They everywhere remember, 'Seek and ye shall find.'"[18]

Such were the Gnostics; and to external and prejudiced spectators, whether philosophers, as Celsus and Porphyry, or the multitude, they wore an appearance sufficiently like the Church to be mistaken for her in the latter part of the Ante-nicene period, as she was confused with the Pagan mysteries in the earlier.

Of course it may happen that the common estimate concerning a person or a body is purely accidental and unfounded; but in such cases it is not lasting. Such were the calumnies of child-eating and impurity in the Christian meetings, which were almost extinct by the time of Origen, and which might arise from the world's confusing {220} them with the pagan and heretical rites. But when it continues from age to age, it is certainly an index of a fact, and corresponds to definite qualities in the object to which it relates. In that case, even mistakes carry information; for they are cognate to the truth, and we can allow for them. Often what seems like a mistake is merely the mode in which the informant conveys his testimony, or the impression which a fact makes on him. Censure is the natural tone of one man, in a case where praise is the natural tone of another; the very same character or action inspires one mind with enthusiasm, and another with contempt. What to one man is magnanimity, to another is romance, and pride to a third, and pretence to a fourth, while to a fifth it is simply unintelligible; and yet there is a certain analogy in their separate testimonies, which conveys to us what the thing is like and what it is not like. When a man's acknowledged note is superstition, we may be pretty sure we shall not find him an Academic or an Epicurean; and even words which are ambiguous, as "atheist" or "reformer," admit of a sure interpretation when we are informed of the speaker. In like manner, there is a certain general correspondence between magic and miracle, obstinacy and faith, insubordination and zeal for religion, sophistry and argumentative talent, craft and meekness, as is obvious. Let us proceed then in contemplating this reflexion, as it may be called, of primitive Christianity in the mirror of the world.

All three writers, Tacitus, Suetonius, and Pliny, call it a "superstition;" this is no accidental imputation, but is repeated by a variety of subsequent writers and speakers. The charge of Thyestean banquets scarcely lasts a hundred years; but, while pagan witnesses are to be found, the Church is accused of superstition. The heathen disputant in Minucius calls Christianity, "*Vana et demens* {221} *superstitio*." The lawyer Modestinus speaks, with an apparent allusion to Christianity, of "weak minds being terrified *superstitione numinis*." The heathen magistrate asks St. Marcellus whether he and others have put away "vain superstitions," and worship the gods whom the emperors worship. The Pagans in Arnobius speak of Christianity as "an execrable and unlucky religion, full of impiety and sacrilege, contaminating the rites instituted from of old with the superstition of novelty." The anonymous opponent of Lactantius calls it, "*Impia et anilis superstitio*." Dioclesian's inscription at Clunia was, as it declared, an occasion of "the total extinction of the superstition of the Christians, and the extension of the worship of the gods." Maximin, in his Letter upon Constantine's Edict, still calls it a superstition.[19]

Now what is meant by the word thus attached by a *consensus* of heathen authorities to Christianity? At least, it cannot mean a religion in which a man might think what he pleased, and was set free from all yokes, whether of ignorance, fear, authority, or priestcraft. When heathen writers call the Oriental rites superstitions, they evidently use the word in its modern sense; it cannot surely be doubted that they apply it in the same sense to Christianity. But Plutarch explains for us the word at length, in his Treatise which bears the name: "Of all kinds of fear," he says, "superstition is the most fatal to action and resource. He does not fear the sea who does not sail, nor war who does not serve, nor robbers who keeps at home, nor the sycophant who is poor, nor envy who is a private man, nor an earthquake who lives in Gaul, nor thunder who lives in Ethiopia; but he who fears the gods fears everything, earth, seas, air, sky, darkness, light, noises, silence, sleep. Slaves sleep and forget their masters; of the fettered doth sleep lighten the chain; inflamed wounds, ulcers cruel and agonizing, are suspended {222} to the sleeping. Superstition alone has come to no terms with sleep; but in the deep sleep of her victims, as though they were in the realms of the impious, she raises horrible spectres, and monstrous phantoms, and various pains, and whirls the miserable soul about, and persecutes it. They rise, and, instead of making light of what is unreal, they fall into the hands of quacks and conjurers, who say, "Call the crone to expiate, bathe in the sea, and sit all day on the ground." He goes on to speak of the introduction of "uncouth names and barbarous terms" into "the divine and national authority of religion;" observes that whereas slaves, when they despair of freedom, may demand to be sold to another master, superstition admits of no change of gods, since "the god cannot be found whom he will not fear, who fears the gods of his family and his birth, who shudders at the Saving and the Benignant, who has a trembling and dread at those from whom we ask riches and wealth, concord, peace, success of all good words and deeds." He says, moreover, that, while death is to all men an end of life, it is not so to the superstitious; for them "there are deep gates of hell to yawn, and headlong streams of at once fire and gloom are opened, and darkness with its many phantoms encompasses, ghosts presenting horrid visages and wretched voices, and judges and executioners, and chasms and dens full of innumerable miseries."

Presently, he says that in misfortune or sickness the superstitious man refuses to see physician or philosopher, and cries, "Suffer me, O man, to undergo punishment, the impious, the cursed, the hated of gods and spirits. The Atheist," with whom all along he is disadvantageously contrasting the superstitious, "wipes his tears, trims his hair, doffs his mourning; but how can you address, how help the superstitious? He sits apart in sackcloth or filthy rags; and often he strips himself and rolls in the mud, and tells out his sins and offences, as having {223} eaten and drunken something, or walked some way which the divinity did not allow. . . . And in his best mood, and under the influence of a good-humoured superstition, he sits at home, with sacrifice and slaughter all round him, while the old crones hang on him as on a peg, as Bion says, any charm they fall in with." He continues, "What men like best are festivals, banquets at the temples, initiations, orgies, votive prayers, and adorations. But the superstitious wishes indeed, but is unable to rejoice. He is crowned and turns pale; he sacrifices and is in fear; he prays with a quivering voice, and burns incense with trembling hands, and altogether belies the saying of Pythagoras, that we are then in best case when we go to the gods; for superstitious men fare most wretchedly and evilly, approaching the houses or shrines of the gods as if they were the dens of bears, or the holes of snakes, or the caves of whales."

Here we have a vivid picture of Plutarch's idea of the essence of Superstition; it was the imagination of the existence of an unseen ever-present Master; the bondage of a rule of life, of a continual responsibility; obligation to attend to little things, the impossibility to escape from duty, the inability to choose or change one's religion, interference with the enjoyment of life, a melancholy view of the world, sense of sin, horror at guilt, apprehension of punishment, dread, self-abasement, depression, anxiety and endeavor to be at peace with heaven, and error and absurdity in the methods chosen for the purpose. Such too had been the idea of the Epicurean Velleius, when he shrank with horror from the "*sempiternus dominus*" and "*curiosus Deus*" of the Stoics.[20] Such, surely, was the meaning {224} of Tacitus, Suetonius, and Pliny. And hence of course the frequent reproach cast on Christians as credulous, weak-minded, and poor-spirited. The heathen objectors in Minucius and Lactantius speak of their "old-woman's tales."[21] Celsus accuses them of "assenting at random and without reason," saying "do not inquire, but believe." They lay it down," he says elsewhere, "Let no educated man approach, no man of wisdom, no man of sense, but if a man be unlearned, weak in intellect, an infant, let him come with confidence. Confessing that these are worthy of God, they evidently desire, as they are able, to convert none but fools, and vulgar, and stupid, and slavish, women and boys." They "take in the simple, and lead him where they will." They address themselves to "youths, house-servants, and the weak in intellect." They "hurry away from the educated, as not fit subjects of their imposition, and inveigle the rustic."[22] "Thou," says the heathen magistrate to the Martyr Fructuosus, "who as a teacher dost disseminate a new fable, that fickle girls may desert the groves and abandon Jupiter; condemn, if thou art wise, the anile creed."[23]

Hence the epithets of itinerant, mountebank, conjurer, cheat, sophist, sorcerer, heaped upon the teachers of Christianity; sometimes to account for the report or appearance of their miracles, sometimes to explain their success. Our Lord was said to have learned His miraculous power in Egypt; "wizard, mediciner, cheat, rogue, conjurer," were the epithets applied to him by the opponents of Eusebius;[24] they "worship that crucified sophist," says Lucian;[25] "Paul, who surpasses all the conjurers and imposters who ever lived," is Julian's account of the Apostle. "You have sent through the whole world," says St. Justin to Trypho, "to preach that {225} a certain atheistic and lawless sect has spring from one Jesus, a Galilean cheat."[26] "We know," says Lucian, speaking of Chaldeans and Magicians, "the Syrian from Palestine, who is the sophist in these matters, how many lunatics, with eyes distorted and mouth in foam, he raises and sends away restored, ridding them from the evil at a great price."[27] "If any conjurer came to them, a man of skill and knowing how to manage matters," says the same writer, "he made money in no time, with a broad grin at the simple fellows."[28] The officer who had custody of St. Perpetua feared her escape from prison "by magical incantations."[29] When St. Tiburtius had walked barefoot on hot coals, his judge cried out that Christ had taught him magic. St. Anastasia was thrown into prison as a mediciner; the populace called out against St. Agnes, "Away with the witch," *Tolle magam, tolle maleficam*. When St. Bonosus and St. Maximilian bore the burning pitch without shrinking, Jews and Gentiles cried out, *Isti magi et malefici*. "What new delusion," says the heathen magistrate concerning St. Romanus, "has brought in these sophists to deny the worship of the gods? How doth this chief sorcerer mock us, skilled by his Thessalian charm (*carmine*) to laugh at punishment."[30]

Hence we gather the meaning of the word "*carmine*" as used by Pliny; when he speaks of the Christians "saying with one another a *carmen* to Christ as to a god," he meant pretty much what Suetonius expressed by the "*malefica superstitio.*"[31] And the words of the last-mentioned writer and Tacitus are still more exactly, and I may say, singularly illustrated by clauses which occur in the {226} Theodosian code; which seems to show that these historians were using formal terms and phrases to express their notion of Christianity. For instance, Tacitus says, "*Quos per flagitia invisos, vulgus Christianos appellabat*;" and the Law against the Malefici and Mathematici in the Code speaks of those, "*quos ob facinorum magnitudinem vulgus maleficos appellat.*"[32] Again, Tacitus charges Christians with the "*odium humani generis:*" this is the very characteristic of a practiser in magic; the Laws call the Malefici, "*humani generis hostes,*" "*humani generis inimici,*" "*naturae peregrini,*" "*communis salutis hostes.*"[33]

Here we see the meaning of words which have created so much surprise to certain moderns;—that a grave well-informed historian like Tacitus should apply to Christians what sounds like abuse. Yet what is the difficulty, supposing that Christians were considered mathematici and magi, and these were the secret intriguers against established government, the resort of desperate politicians, the enemies of the established religion, the disseminators of lying rumours, the perpetrators of poisonings and other crimes? "Read this," says Paley, after quoting some of the most beautiful and subduing passages of St. Paul, "read this, and then think of *exitiabilis superstitio*;" and he goes on to express a wish "in contending with heathen authorities, to produce our books against theirs,"[34] as if it were {227} a matter of books. Public men care very little for books; fine sentiments, the most luminous philosophy, the deepest theology, inspiration itself, moves them but little; they look at facts, and care only for facts. The question was, What was the worth, what the tendency of the Christian body in the state? what Christians said, what they thought, was to little purpose. They might exhort to peaceableness and passive obedience as strongly as words could speak; but what did they *do*, what was their political position? This is what statesmen thought of then, as they do now. It is little to refer men of the world to abstract truths or first principles; a statesman measures parties, and sects, and writers by their bearing upon *him*; and he has a practised eye in this sort of judgment, and is not likely to be mistaken. "What is Truth?" said jesting Pilate. Apologies, however eloquent or true, availed nothing with the Roman magistrate against the sure instinct which taught him to dread Christianity. It was a dangerous enemy to any power not built upon itself; he felt it, and the event justified his apprehension.

We must not forget the well-known character of the Roman state in its dealings with its subjects. It had had from the first an extreme jealousy of secret societies; it was prepared to grant a large toleration and a broad comprehension, but, as is the case with modern governments, it wished to have jurisdiction and the ultimate authority in every movement of the body politic and its members; and its institutions were based, or essentially depended, on its religion. Accordingly, every innovation upon the established paganism, except it was allowed by the law, was rigidly repressed. Hence the professors of low superstitions, of mysteries, of magic, of astrology, were the outlaws of society, and were in a condition analogous, if the comparison may be allowed, to smugglers or {228} poachers among ourselves, or perhaps to burglars and highwaymen. The modern robber is sometimes made to ask in novels or essays, why the majority of a people should bind the minority, and why he is amenable to laws which he does not enact; but the magistrate, relying on the power of the sword, wishes all men to gain a living indeed, and to prosper, but only in his own legally sanctioned ways, and he hangs or transports dissenters from his authority. The Romans applied this rule to religion. Lardner protests against Pliny's application of the words "contumacy and inflexible obstinacy" to the Christians of Pontus. "Indeed, these are hard words," he says, "very improperly applied to men who were open to conviction, and willing to satisfy others, if they might have leave to speak."[35] And he says, "It seems to me that Pliny acted very arbitrarily and unrighteously, in his treatment of the Christians in his province. What right had Pliny to act in this manner? by what law or laws did he punish [them] with death?"—but the Romans had ever burnt the sorcerer, and banished his consulters for life.[36] It was an ancient custom. And at mysteries they looked with especial suspicion, because, since the established religion did not include them in its provisions, they really did supply what may be called a demand of the age. The Greeks of an earlier day had naturalized among themselves the Eleusinian and other mysteries, which had come from Egypt and Syria, and had little fear from a fresh invasion from the same quarter; yet even in Greece, as Plutarch tells us, the *"carmina"* of the itinerants of Cybele and Serapis threw the Pythian verses out of fashion, and henceforth the responses from the temple were given in prose. Soon the oracles altogether ceased. What would cause still greater jealousy in the Roman mind was the general infidelity which {229} prevailed among all classes about the mythological fables of Charon, Cerberus, and the realms of punishment.[37]

We know what opposition had been made in Rome even to the philosophy of Greece; much greater would be the aversion of constitutional statesmen and lawyers to the ritual of barbarians. Religion was the Roman point of honour. "Spaniards might rival them in numbers," says Cicero, "Gauls in bodily strength, Carthaginians in address, Greeks in the arts, Italians and Latins in sense, but the Romans surpassed all nations in piety and devotion."[38] It was one of their laws, "Let no one have gods by himself, nor worship in private new gods nor adventitious, unless added on public authority."[39] Lutatius,[40] at the end of the first Punic war, was forbidden by the senate to consult the Sortes Praenestinae as being *"auspicia alienigena."* Some years afterwards the Consul took axe in hand, and commenced the destruction of the temples of Isis and Serapis. In the second Punic war, the senate had commanded the surrender of the *libri vaticini* or *precationes*, and any written art of sacrificing. When a secret confraternity was discovered, at a later date, the Consul spoke of the rule of their ancestors which forbade the forum, circus, and city to Sacrificuli and prophets, and burnt their books. In the next age banishment was inflicted on individuals who were introducing the worship of the Syrian Sabazius; and in the next the Iseion and Serapeion were destroyed a second time. Maecenas in Dio advises Augustus to honour the gods according to the national custom, because the contempt of the country's deities leads to civil insubordination, reception of foreign {230} laws, conspiracies, and secret meetings.[41] "Suffer no one," he adds, "to deny the gods or to practise sorcery." The civilian Julius Paulus lays it down as one of the leading principles of Roman Law, that those who introduce new or untried religions should be degraded, and if in the lower orders put to death.[42] In like manner, it is enacted in one of Constantine's Laws that the Haruspices should not exercise their art in private; and there is a law of Valentinian's against nocturnal sacrifices or magic. It is more immediately to our purpose that Trajan had been so earnest in his resistance to *Hetaeriae* or secret societies, that, when a fire had laid waste Nicomedia, and Pliny proposed to him to incorporate a body of a hundred and fifty firemen in consequence,[43] he was afraid of the precedent and forbade it.

What has been said will suggest another point of view in which the Oriental rites were obnoxious to the government, viz., as being vagrant and proselytizing religions. If it tolerated foreign superstitions, this would be on the ground that districts or countries within its jurisdiction held them; to proselytize to a rite hitherto unknown, to form a new party, and to propagate it through the Empire,—a religion not local but Catholic,—was an offence against both order and reason. The state desired peace everywhere, and no change; "considering," according to Lactantius, "that they were rightly and deservedly punished who execrated the public religion handed down to them by their ancestors."[44]

It is impossible surely to deny that, in assembling for religious purposes, the Christians were breaking a solemn law, a vital principle of the Roman constitution; and this is the light in which their conduct {231} was regarded by historians and philosophers of the Empire. This was a very strong act on the part of the disciples of the great Apostle, who had enjoined obedience to the powers that be. Time after time they resisted the authority of the magistrate; and this is a phenomenon inexplicable on the theory of what is now called the Voluntary Principle. The justification of such disobedience lies simply in the necessity of obeying the higher authority of some divine law; but if Christianity were in its essence only private and personal, as so many now think, there was no necessity of their meeting together at all. If, on the other hand, in assembling for worship and holy communion, they were fulfilling an indispensable observance, Christianity has imposed a social law on the world, and formally enters the field of politics. Gibbon says that, in consequence of Pliny's edict, "the prudence of the Christians suspended their Agape; but it was *impossible* for them to omit the exercise of public worship."[45] We can draw no other conclusion.

At the end of three hundred years, a more remarkable violation of law seems to have been admitted by the Christians. It shall be given in the words of Dr. Burton; he has been speaking of Maximin's edict, which provided for the restitution of any of their lands or buildings which had been alienated from them. "It is plain," he says, "from the terms of this edict, that the Christians had for some time been in possession of property. It speaks of houses and lands which did not belong to individuals, but to the whole body. Their possession of such property could hardly have escaped the notice of the government; but it seems to have been held in direct violation of a law of Diocletian, which prohibited corporate bodies, or associations {232} which were not legally recognised, from acquiring property. The Christians were certainly not a body recognised by law at the beginning of the reign of Diocletian, and it might almost be thought that this enactment was specially directed against them. But, like other laws which are founded upon tyranny, and are at variance with the first principles of justice, it is probable that this law about corporate property was evaded. We must suppose that Christians had purchased lands and houses before the law was passed; and their disregard of the prohibition may be taken as another proof that their religion had now taken so firm a footing that the executors of the laws were obliged to connive at their being broken by so numerous a body."[46]

No wonder that the magistrate who presided at the martyr-dom of St. Romanus calls them in Prudentius "a rebel people;"[47] that Galerius speaks of them as "a nefarious conspiracy;" the heathen in Minucius, as "men of a desperate faction;" that others make them guilty of sacrilege and treason, and call them by those other titles which, more closely resembling the language of Tacitus, have been noticed above. Hence the violent accusations against them as the destruction of the Empire, the authors of physical evils, and the cause of the anger of the gods.

"Men cry out," says Tertullian, "that the state is beset, that the Christians are in their fields, in their forts, in their islands. They mourn as for a loss that every sex, condition, and now even rank, is going over to this sect. And yet they do not by this very means advance their minds to the idea of some good therein hidden; they allow not themselves to conjecture more rightly, they choose not to examine more closely. The generality run upon a hatred of this name, with eyes so closed that in {233} bearing favourable testimony to any one they mingle with it the reproach of the name. "A good man Caius Seius, only he is a Christian." So another, "I marvel that that wise man Lucius Titius hath suddenly become a Christian." No one reflecteth whether Caius be not therefore good and Lucius wise because a Christian, or therefore a Christian because wise and good. They praise that which they know, they revile that which they know not. Virtue is not in such account as hatred of the Christians. Now, then, if the hatred be of the name, what guilt is there in names? What charge against words? Unless it be that any word which is a name have either a barbarous or ill-omened, or a scurrilous or an immodest sound. If the Tiber cometh up to the walls, if the Nile cometh not up to the fields, if the heaven hath stood still, if the earth hath not moved, if there be any famine, if any pestilence, 'The Christians to the lions' is forthwith the word."

"Men of a desperate, lawless, reckless faction," says the heathen Caecilius, in the passage above referred to, "who collect together out of the lowest rabble the thoughtless portion, and credulous women seduced by the weakness of their sex, and form a mob of impure conspirators, of whom nocturnal assemblies, and solemn fastings, and unnatural food, no sacred rite but pollution, is the bond. A tribe lurking and light-hating, dumb for the public, talkative in corners; they despise our temples as if graves, spit at our gods, deride our religious forms; pitiable themselves, they pity, forsooth, our priests; half-naked themselves, they despise our honours and purple; monstrous folly and incredible impudence!. . . Day after day, their abandoned morals wind their serpentine course; over the whole world are those most hideous rites of an impious association growing into shape: . . . they recognise each other by marks and signs, and love each other almost before they {234} recognise; promiscuous lust is their religion. Thus does their vain and mad superstition glory in crimes. . . The writer who tells the story of a criminal capitally punished, and of the gibbet (*ligna feralia*) of the cross being their observance (*ceremonias*), assigns to them thereby an altar in keeping with the abandoned and wicked, that they may worship (*colant*) what they merit. . . . Why their mighty effort to hide and shroud whatever it is they worship (*colunt*), since things honest ever like the open day, and crimes are secret? Why have they no altars, no temples, no images known to us, never speak abroad, never assemble freely, were it not that what they worship and suppress is subject either of punishment or of shame?. . . What monstrous, what portentous notions do they fabricate! that that God of theirs, whom they can neither show nor see, should be inquiring diligently into the characters, the acts, nay the words and secret thoughts of all men; running to and fro, forsooth, and present everywhere, troublesome, restless, nay impudently curious they would have him; that is, if he is close at every deed, interferes in all places, while he can neither attend to each as being distracted through the whole, nor suffice for the whole as being engaged about each. Think too of their threatening fire, meditating destruction to the whole earth, nay the world itself with its stars! . . . Nor content with this mad opinion, they add and append their old wives' tales about a new birth after death, ashes and cinders, and by some strange confidence believe each other's lies. Poor creatures! consider what hangs over you after death, while you are still alive. Lo, the greater part of you, the better, as you say, are in want, cold, toil, hunger, and your God suffers it; but I omit common trials. Lo, threats are offered to you, punishments, torments; crosses to be undergone now, not worshipped (*adorandae*; fires too which ye predict and fear; where is that God who can {235} recover, but cannot preserve your life? The answer of Socrates, when he was asked about heavenly matters, is well known, "What is above us does not concern us." My opinion also is, that points which are doubtful, as are the points in question, must be left; nor, when so many and such great men are in controversy on the subject, must judgment be rashly and audaciously given on either side, lest the consequence be either anile superstition or the overthrow of all religion."

Such was Christianity in the eyes of those who witnessed its rise and propagation;—one of a number of wild and barbarous rites which were pouring in upon the empire from the ancient realms of superstition, and the mother of a progeny of sects which were faithful to the original they had derived from Egypt or Syria; a religion unworthy an educated person, as appealing, not to the intellect, but to the fears and weaknesses of human nature, and consisting, not in the rational and cheerful enjoyment, but in a morose rejection of the gifts of Providence; a horrible religion, as inflicting or enjoining cruel sufferings, and monstrous and loathsome in its very indulgence of the passions; a religion leading by re-action to infidelity; a religion of magic, and of the vulgar arts, real and pretended, with which magic was accompanied; a secret religion which dared not face the day; an itinerant, busy, proselytizing religion, forming an extended confederacy against the state, resisting its authority and breaking its laws. There may be some exceptions to this general impression, such as Pliny's discovery of the innocent and virtuous rule of life adopted by the Christians of Pontus; but this only proves that Christianity was not the infamous religion which the heathen thought it; it did not reverse their general belief to the contrary.

Now it must be granted that, in some respects, this view of Christianity depended on the times, and {236} would alter with their alteration. When there was no persecution, Martyrs could not be obstinate; and when the Church was raised aloft in high places, it was no longer in caves. Still, I believe, it continued substantially the same in the judgment of the world external to it, while there was an external world to judge of it. "They thought it enough," says Julian in the fourth century, of our Lord and His Apostles, "to deceive women, servants, and slaves, and by their means wives and husbands." "A human fabrication," says he elsewhere, "put together by wickedness, having nothing divine in it, but making a perverted use of the fable-loving, childish, irrational part of the soul, and offering a set of wonders to create belief." "Miserable men," he says elsewhere, "you refuse to worship the ancile, yet you worship the wood of the cross, and sign it on your foreheads, and fix it on your doors. Shall one for this hate the intelligent among you, or pity the less understanding, who in following you have gone to such an excess of perdition as to leave the everlasting gods and go over to a dead Jew?" He speaks of their adding other dead men to Him who died so long ago. "You have filled all places with sepulchres and monuments, though it is nowhere told you in your religion to haunt the tombs and to attend upon them." Elsewhere he speaks of their "leaving the gods for corpses and relics." On the other hand, he attributes the growth of Christianity to its humanity towards strangers, care in burying the dead, and pretended religiousness of life. In another place he speaks of their care of the poor.[48]

Libanius, Julian's preceptor in rhetoric, delivers the same testimony, as far as it goes. He addressed his Oration for the Temples to a Christian Emperor, and would in consequence be guarded in his language; however it runs in one direction. He speaks {237} of "those black-habited men," meaning the monks, "who eat more than elephants, and by the number of their potations trouble those who send them drink in their chantings, and conceal this by paleness artificially acquired." They "are in good condition out of the misfortunes of others, while they pretend to serve God by hunger." Those whom they attack "are like bees, they like drones." I do not quote this passage to prove that there were monks in Libanius's days, which no one doubts, but to show his impression of Christianity, as far as his works betray it.

Numantian, in the same century, describes in verse his voyage from Rome to Gaul: one book of the poem is extant; he falls in with Christianity on two of the islands which lie in his course. He thus describes them on one of them: "The island is in a squalid state, being full of light-haters. They call themselves monks, because they wish to live alone without witness. They dread the gifts, from fearing the reverses, of fortune. Thus Homer says that melancholy was the cause of Bellerophon's anxiety; for it is said that after the wounds of grief mankind displeased the offended youth." He meets on the other island a Christian, whom he had known, of good family and fortune, and happy in his marriage, who "impelled by the Furies had left men and gods, and, credulous exile, was living in base concealment. Is not this herd," he continues, "worse than Circean poison; then bodies were changed, now minds."

In the Philopatris, which is the work of an Author of the fourth century,[49] Critias is introduced pale and wild. His friend asks him if he has seen Cerberus or Hecate; and he answers that he has heard a rigmarole from certain "thrice-cursed sophists;" which he thinks would drive him mad, if he heard it again, and was nearly sending him headlong over some cliff as it was. He retires for relief with his inquirer to {238} a pleasant place, shadowed by planes, where swallows and nightingales are singing, and a quiet brook is purling. Triephon, his friend, expresses a fear lest he has heard some incantation, and is led by the course of the dialogue, before his friend tells his tale, to give some account of Christianity, being himself a Christian. After speaking of the creation, as described by Moses, he falls at once upon that doctrine of a particular providence which is so distasteful to Plutarch, Velleius in Cicero, and Caecilius, and generally to unbelievers. "He is in heaven," he says, "looking at just and unjust, and causing actions to be entered in books; and he will recompense all on a day which He has appointed." Critias objects that he cannot make this consistent with the received doctrine about the Fates, "even though he has perhaps been carried aloft with his master, and initiated in unspeakable mysteries." He also asks if the deeds of the "Scythians are written in heaven; for if so, there must be many scribes there. After some more words, in course of which, as in the earlier part of the dialogue, the doctrine of the Trinity is introduced, Critias gives an account of what befel him. He says, he fell in with a crowd in the streets; and while asking a friend the cause of it, others joined them (Christians or monks), and a conversation ensues, part of it corrupt or obscure, on the subject, as Gesner supposes, of Julian's oppression of the Christians, especially of the clergy. One of these interlocutors is a wretched old man, whose "phlegm is paler than death;" another has "a rotten cloke on, and no covering on head or feet," who says he has been told by some ill-clad person from the mountains with a shorn crown, that in the theatre was a name hieroglyphically written of one who would flood the highway with gold. On his laughing at his story, his friend Crato, whom he had joined, bids him be silent, using a Pythagorean word; for he has "most excellent matters {239} to initiate him into, and that the prediction is no dream but true," and will be fulfilled in August, using the Egyptian name of the month. He attempts to leave them in disgust, but Crato pulls him back "at the instigation of that old demon." He is in consequence persuaded to go "to those conjurers," *eis goetas anthropous*, who, says Crato, would "initiate in all mysteries." He finds, in a building which is described in the language used by Homer of the Palace of Menelaus, "not Helen, no, but men pale and downcast," who ask whether there was any bad news; "for they seemed," he says, "wishing the worst; and rejoicing in misfortune, as the Furies in the theatres." On their asking him how the city and the world went on, and his answering that things went on smoothly and seemed likely to do so still, they frown, and say that "the city is in travail with a bad birth." "You who dwell aloft," he answers, "and see everything from on high, doubtless have a keen perception in this matter; but tell me how is the sky? will the Sun be eclipsed?" will Mars be in quadrature with

Jupiter? &c.;" and he goes on to jest upon their celibacy. On their persisting in prophesying evil to the state, he says, "This evil will fall on your own head, since you are so hard upon your country; for not as high-flyers have ye heard this, nor are ye adepts in the restless astrological art, but if divinations and conjurings have seduced you, double is your stupidity; for they are the discoveries of old women and things to laugh at." The interview then draws to an end; but more than enough has been quoted already to show the author's notion of Christianity.

Such was the language of paganism after Christianity had for fifty years been exposed to the public gaze; after it had been before the world for fifty more, St. Augustine had still to defend it against the charge of being the cause of the calamities of the Empire. And for the charge of magic, when {240} the Arian bishops were in formal disputations with the Catholic, before Gungebald, Burgundian King of France, at the end of the fifth century, we find that they charged them with being "*proestigia-tores*," and worshipping a number of gods; and when the Catholics proposed that the king should repair to the shrine of St. Justus, where both parties might ask him concerning their respective faiths, the Arians cried out that "they would not seek enchantments like Saul, for Scripture was enough for them, which was more powerful than all bewitchments."[50] This was said, not against strangers of whom they knew nothing, as Ethelbert might be suspicious of St. Augustine and his brother missionaries, but against a body of men who lived among them.

I do not think it can be doubted then that, had Tacitus, Suetonius, and Pliny, Celsus, Porphyry, and the other opponents of Christianity, lived in the fourth century, their evidence concerning Christianity would be very much the same as it has come down to us from the centuries before it. In either case, a man of the world and a philosopher would have been disgusted at the gloom and sadness of its profession, its mysteriousness, its claim of miracles, the want of good sense evident in its rule of life, and the unsettlement and discord it was introducing into the social and political world.

On the whole I conclude as follows:—if there is a form of Christianity, now in the world which is accused of gross superstition, of borrowing its rites and customs from the heathen, and of ascribing to forms and ceremonies an occult virtue;—a religion which is considered to burden and enslave the mind by its requisitions, to address itself to the weak-minded and ignorant, to be supported by sophistry and imposture, and to contradict reason and exalt {241} mere irrational faith;—a religion which impresses on the serious mind very distressing views of the guilt and consequences of sin, sets upon the minute acts of the day, one by one, their definite value for praise or blame, and thus casts a grave shadow over the future;—a religion which holds up to admiration the surrender of wealth, and disables serious persons from enjoying it if they would;—a religion, the doctrines of which, be they good or bad, are to the generality of men unknown; which is considered to bear on its very surface sighs of folly and falsehood so distinct that a glance suffices to judge of it, and careful examination is preposterous; which is felt to be so simply bad, that it may be calumniated at hazard and at pleasure, it being nothing but absurdity to stand upon the accurate distribution of its guilt among its particular sects, or painfully to determine how far this or that story is literally true, what must be allowed in candour, or what is improbable, or what cuts two ways, or what is not proved, or what may be plausibly defended;—a religion such, that men look at a convert to it with a feeling which no other sect raises except Judaism, Socialism, or Mormonism, with curiosity, suspicion, fear, disgust, as the case may be, as if something strange had befallen him, as if he had had an initiation into a mystery, and had come into communion with dreadful influences, as if he were now one of a confederacy which claimed him, absorbed him, stripped him of his personality, reduced him to a mere organ or instrument of a whole;—a religion which men hate as proselytizing, anti-social, revolutionary, as dividing families, separating chief friends, corrupting the maxims of government, making a mock at law, dissolving the empire, the enemy of human nature, and a "conspirator against its rights and privileges;"[51]—a religion which they consider the champion and instrument {242} of darkness, and a pollution calling down upon the land the anger of heaven;—a religion which they associate with intrigue and conspiracy, which they speak about in whispers, which they detect by an anticipation in whatever goes wrong, and to which they impute whatever is unaccountable;—a religion, the very name of which they cast out as evil, and use simply as a bad epithet, and which from the impulse of self-preservation they would persecute if they could;—if there be such a religion now in the world, it is not unlike Christianity as that same world viewed it, when first it came forth from its Divine Author.

SECTION II.

THE CHURCH OF THE FOURTH CENTURY.

Till the Imperial Government had become Christian, and heresies were put down by the arm of power, the face of Christendom presented much the same appearance all along as on the first propagation of the religion. What Gnosticism, Montanism, Judaism and, I may add, the Oriental mysteries were to the nascent Church as described in the foregoing Section, such were the Manichean, Donatist, Apollinarian and contemporary sects afterwards. The Church in each place looked at first sight as but one out of a number of religious communions, with little of a very distinctive character except to the careful inquirer. Still there were external indications of essential differences within; and, as we have already compared it in the first centuries, we may no contrast it in the fourth, with the rival religious bodies with which it was encompassed.

How was the man to guide his course who {243} wished to join himself to the doctrine and fellowship of the Apostles in the times of St. Athanasius, St. Basil, and St. Augustine? Few indeed were the districts in the *orbis terrarum*, which did not then, as in the Ante-nicene era, present a number of creeds and communions for his choice. Gaul is said at that era to have been perfectly free from heresies; at least none are mentioned as belonging to that country in the Theodosian Code. But in Egypt, in the earlier part of the fourth century, the Meletian schism numbered one-third as many bishops as were contained in the whole Patriarchate. In Africa, towards the end of it, while the Catholic Bishops amounted in all to 466, the Donatists almost rivalled them with 400. In Spain Priscillianism was spread from the Pyrenees to the Ocean. It seems to have been the religion of the population in the province of Gallicia, while its author, Priscillian, whose death had been contrived by the Ithacians, was honoured as a Martyr. The detestable sect of the Manichees, hiding itself under a variety of names in different localities, was not in the least flourishing condition at Rome. Rome and Italy were the seat of the Marcionites. The Origenists, too, are mentioned by St. Jerome as "bringing a cargo of blasphemies into the port of Rome." And Rome was the seat of a Novatian, a Donatist, and a Luciferian bishop, in addition to the legitimate occupant of the See of St. Peter. The Luciferians, as was natural under the circumstances of their schism, were sprinkled over Christendom from Spain to Palestine, and from Treves to Lybia; while in its parent country Sardinia, as a centre of that extended range, Lucifer seems to

have received the honours of a Saint. When St. Gregory Nazianzen began to preach at Constantinople, the Arians were in
possession of its hundred churches; they had the populace in their
favour, and, after their legal dislodgement, edict after edict was
{244} ineffectually issued against them. The Novatians too
abounded there; and the Sabbatians, who had separated from
them, had a church, where they prayed at the tomb of their
founder. Moreover, Apollinarians, Eunomians, and Semi-arians,
mustered in great numbers at Constantinople. The Semi-arian
bishops were as popular in the neighbouring provinces, as the
Arian doctrine in the capital. They had possession of the coast of
the Hellespont and Bithynia; and were found in Phrygia, Isauria,
and the neighbouring parts of Asia Minor. Phrygia was the head-
quarters of the Montanists, and was overrun by the Messalians,
who had advanced thus far from Mesopotamia, spreading through
Syria, Lycaonia, Pamphylia, and Cappadocia in their way. In the
lesser Armenia, the same heretics had penetrated into the
monasteries. Phrygia, too, and Paphlagonia were the seat of the
Novatians, who besides were in force at Nicaea and Nicomedia,
were found in Alexandria, Africa, and Spain, and had a bishop
even in Scythia. The whole tract of country from the Hellespont
to Cilicia had nearly lapsed into Eunomianism, and the tract from
Cilicia as far as Phoenicia to Apollinarianism. The disorders of
the Church of Antioch are well known: an Arian succession, two
orthodox claimants, and a bishop of the Apollinarians. Palestine
abounded in Origenists, if at that time they may properly be
called a sect; Palestine, Egypt, and Arabia were overrun with
Marcionites; Osrhoëne was occupied by the followers of Bardesanes and Harmonius, whose hymns so nearly took the place of
national tunes that St. Ephrem found no better way of resisting
heresy than setting them to fresh words. Theodoret in Comagene
speaks in the next century of reclaiming eight villages of
Marcionites, one of Eunomians, and one of Arians.

These sects were of various character. Learning, eloquence, and talent were the characteristics {245} of the Apollinarians, Manichees, and Pelagians; Tichonius the Donatist was distinguished in biblical interpretation; the Semi-arian and Apollinarian leaders were men of grave and correct behaviour; the Novatians had sided with the Orthodox during the Arian persecution; the Montanists and Messalians addressed themselves to an almost heathen population; the atrocious fanaticism of the Priscillianists, the fury of the Arian women of Alexandria and Constantinople, and the savage cruelty of the Circumcellions can hardly be exaggerated. They had their orders of clergy, bishops, priests and deacons; their readers and ministers; their celebrants and altars, their hymns and litanies. They preached to the crowds in public and their meeting-houses bore the semblance of churches. They had their sacristies and cemeteries; their farms; their professors and doctors; their schools. Miracles were ascribed to the Arian Theophilus, to the Luciferian Gregory of Elvira, to a Macedonian in Cyzicus, and to the Donatists in Africa.

How was an individual inquirer to find, or a private Christian to keep the Truth, amid so many rival teachers? The misfortunes or perils of holy men and saints show us the difficulty; St. Augustine was nine years a Manichee; St. Basil for a time was in admiration of the Semi-arians; St. Sulpicius gave a momentary countenance to the Pelagians; St. Paula listened, and Melania assented, to the Origenists. Yet the rule was simple, which would direct every one right; and in that age, at least, no one could be wrong for any long time without his own fault. The Church is everywhere, but it is one; sects are everywhere, but they are many, independent, and discordant. Catholicity is the attribute of the Church, independency of sectaries. It is true that some sects might seem almost Catholic in their diffusion; Novatians or Marcionites were in all quarters of the empire; yet it is hardly more than {246} the name, or the general doctrine of philosophy, that was universal: the different portions which professed it seem to have been bound together by no strict or definite tie. The Church might be evanescent or lost for a while in particular countries, or it might be levelled and buried among sects, when the eye was confined to one spot, or it might be confronted by the one and same heresy in various places; but, on looking round the *orbis terrarum*, there was no mistaking that body which, and which alone, had possession of it. The Church is a kingdom: and as a family continually divides and sends out branches, founding new houses, and propagating itself in colonies, each of them as independent as its original head, so was it with heresy. Simon Magus, the first heretic, had been Patriarch of Menandrians, Basilidians, Valentinians, and the whole family of Gnostics; Tatian of Encratites, Severians, Aquarians, Apotactites, and Saccophori. The Montanists had been propagated into Tascodrugites, Pepuzians, Artotyrites, and quartodecimans. Eutyches, in a later time, gave birth to the Dioscorians, Gaianites, Theodosians, Agnoetae, Theopaschites, Acephali, Semidalitae, Nagranitae, Jacobites, and others. This is the uniform history of heresy. The patronage of the civil power might for a time counteract the law of its nature, but it showed it as soon as the obstacle was removed. Scarcely was Arianism deprived of the churches of Constantinople, and left to itself, than it split in that very city into the Dorotheans, the Psathyrians, and the Curtians; and the Eunomians into the Theophronians and Eutychians. One fourth part of the Donatists speedily became Maximinianists; and besides these were the Rogatians, the Primianists, the Urbanists, and the Claudianists. If such was the fecundity of the heretical principle in one place, it is not to be supposed that Novatians or Marcionites {247} in Africa or the East would feel themselves bound to think or to act with their fellow-sectaries of Rome or Constantinople; and the great varieties or inconsistencies of statement, which have come down to us concerning the tenets of heresies, may thus be explained. This had been the case with the pagan rites, whether indigenous or itinerant, to which heresy succeeded. The established priesthoods were local properties, as independent theologically as they were geographically of each other; the fanatical companies which spread over the Empire dissolved and formed again as the circumstances of the moment occasioned. So was it with heresy: it was, by its very nature, its own master, free to change, self-sufficient; and, having thrown off the yoke of the Church, it was little likely to submit to any usurped and spurious authority. Montanism and Manicheeism might perhaps in some sort furnish an exception to this remark.

In one point alone the heresies seem universally to have agreed,—in hatred to the Church. This might at that time be considered one of her surest and most obvious signs. She was that body of which all sects, however divided among themselves, spoke ill; according to the prophecy, "If they have called the Master of the house Beelzebub, how much more them of His household." They disliked and they feared her; they did their utmost to overcome their mutual differences, in order to unite against her. Their utmost indeed was little, for independency was the law of their being; they could not exert themselves without fresh quarrels, both in the bosom of each, and one with another. *"Bellum hoereticorum pax est ecclesiae,"* had become a proverb; but they felt the great desirableness of union against the only body which was the natural antagonist of all, and various are the instances which occur in ecclesiastical history of attempted coalitions. The Meletians of Africa united with the Arians against {248} St. Athanasius; the Semi-arians of the Council of Sardica correspond with the Donatists of Africa; Nestorius received and protected the Pelagians; Aspar, the Arian minister of Leo the Emperor, favoured the Monophysites of Egypt; the Jacobites of Egypt sided with the Moslem, who are charged with holding a Nestorian doctrine. It had been so from the beginning: "They huddle up a peace with all everywhere," says Tertullian, "for it maketh no matter to them, although they hold different doctrines, so long as they conspire together in their siege against the one thing, Truth."[52] And though active co-operation was impracticable, at least hard words cost nothing, and could express that common hatred at all seasons. Accordingly, by Montanists, Catholics were called "carnal;" by Novatians, "the apostates;" by Valentinians, "the worldly;" by Manichees, "the simple;" by Aërians, "the ephemeral;"[53] by Apollinarians, "the man-worshippers;" by Origenists, "the flesh-lovers;" and "the slimy;" by the Nestorians, "Egyptians;" by Monophysites, "the Chalcedonians;" by Donatists, "the traitors," and "the sinners," and "servants of Antichrist;" and St. Peter's chair, "the seat of pestilence;" and by the Luciferians, the Church was called "a brothel;" "the devil's harlot;" and "synagogue of Satan:" so that it was almost a note of the Church, for the use of the most busy and the most ignorant, that she was on one side and yet all other bodies on the other.

Yet, strange as it may appear, there was one title of the Church of a very different character from those which have been enumerated, a title of honour, in which all heretics agreed, which furnished a still more simple direction for the busy and ignorant where she lay, and was used by the Fathers for that purpose. It was one which the sects could not claim for themselves, and which they could not help giving to its rightful owner, though it seemed to {249} surrender the whole controversy between the parties. Balaam could not keep from blessing the ancient people of God; and the whole world, heresies inclusive, were irresistibly constrained to call God's second election by its prophetical title of the "Catholic" Church. St. Paul tells us that the heretic is "condemned by himself;" and no clearer witness against the sects of the earlier centuries was needed by the Church, than their own testimony to the fact of her actual position and their own. Sects, say the Fathers, are called after the name of their founders, or from their locality, or from their doctrine. So was it from the beginning: "I am of Paul, and I of Apollos, and I of Cephas;" but it was promised to the Church that she should have no master upon earth, and that she should "gather together in one the children of God that were scattered abroad." Her every-day name, which was understood in the market-place and which state-edicts recognised, was the "Catholic" Church. This was that very *description* of Christianity in those times which we are all along engaged in determining. And it had been recognised as such from the first; the name or the fact is put forth by St. Ignatius, St. Justin, St. Clement; the Church of Smyrna, St. Irenaeus, Rhodon or another, Tertullian, Origen, St. Cyprian, St. Cornelius; the Martyrs, Pionius, Sabina, and Asclepiades; Lactantius, Eusebius, Adimantius, St. Athanasius, St. Pacian, St. Optatus, St. Epiphanius, St. Cyril, St. Basil, St. Ambrose, St. Chrysostom, St. Jerome, St. Augustine, and Facundus. St. Clement uses it as an argument against the Gnostics, St. Augustine against the Donatists and Manichees, St. Jerome against the Luciferians, and St. Pacian against the Novatians.

It was an argument for educated and simple. When St. Ambrose would convert the cultivated Augustine, he bade him study the book of Isaiah, {250} who is the prophet, as of the Messiah, so of the calling of the Gentiles and of the Imperial power of the Church. And when St. Cyril would give a rule to his crowd of Catechumens, "If ever thou art sojourning in any city," he says, "inquire not simply where the Lord's house is (for the sects of the profane also make an attempt to call their own dens houses of the Lord,) nor merely where the Church is, but where is the Catholic Church. For this is the peculiar name of this Holy Body, the Mother of us all, which is the Spouse of our Lord Jesus Christ."[54] "In the Catholic Church," says St. Augustine to the Manichees, "not to speak of that most pure wisdom, to the knowledge of which few spiritual men attain in this life so

as to know it even in its least measure,—as men, indeed, yet
without any doubt,—(for the multitude of Christians are safest,
not in understanding with quickness, but in believing with
simplicity,) not to speak of this wisdom, which ye do not believe
to be in the Catholic Church, there are many other considerations
which most sufficiently hold me in her bosom. I am held by the
consent of people and nations; by that authority which began in
miracles, was nourished in hope, was increased by charity, and
made steadfast by age; by that succession of priests from the
chair of the Apostle Peter, to whose feeding the Lord after His
resurrection commended His Sheep, even to the present episcopate; lastly, by the very title of Catholic, which, not without
cause, hath this Church alone, amid so many heresies, obtained
in such sort, that, whereas all heretics wish to be called Catholics,
nevertheless to any stranger, who asked how to find the "Catholic" Church, no one would dare to point to his own basilica or
house. These dearest bonds, then, of the Christian Name, so
many and such, rightly hold a man in belief in the Catholic
Church, even though, by reason {251} of the slowness of our
understanding or our deserts, truth hath not yet shown herself in
her clearest tokens. But among you, who have none of these
reasons to invite and detain me, I hear but the sound of the
promise of the truth; which truth, verily, if it be so manifestly
displayed that there can be no mistake about it, is to be preferred
to all those things by which I am held in the Catholic Church;
but if it is promised alone, and not produced, no one shall move
me from that faith which by so many and great ties binds my
mind to the Christian religion."[55] When Adimantius asked his
Marcionite opponent, how he was a Christian who did not eve
bear that name, but was called from Marcion, he retorts, "And
you are called from the Catholic Church, and therefore you are
not Christians either;" Adimantius answers, "Did we profess
man's name, you would have spoken to the point; but if we are

called from being all over the world, what is there bad in this?"[56]

"Whereas there is one God and one Lord," says St. Clement, "therefore also that which is at the summit of veneration is praised as being sole, being after the pattern of the One Principle. In the nature then of the One, the Church, which is one, hath its portion, which they would forcibly cut up into many heresies. In substance then, and in idea, and in principle, and in pre-eminence, we call the ancient Catholic Church sole; in order to the unity of one faith, the faith according to her own covenants, or rather that one covenant in different times, which, by the will of one God and through one Lord, is gathering together those who are already ordained, whom God hath predestined, having known that they would be just from the foundation of the world. . . . But of heresies, some are called from a name, as Valentine's heresy, Marcion's, and Basilides' (though they profess to bring the opinion of Matthias, for all {252} the Apostles had, as one teaching, so one tradition); and others from place, as the Peratici; and others from nation, as that of the Phrygians; and others from their actions, as that of their Encratites; and others from their peculiar doctrines, as the Docetae and Hematites; and others from their hypotheses, and what they have honoured, as Cainists and the Ophites; and others from their wicked purposes and enormities, as those Simonians who are called Eutychites."[57] "There are and there have been," says St. Justin, "many who have taught atheistic and blasphemous words and deeds, coming in the name of Jesus; and they are called by us from the appellation of the man whence each doctrine and opinion began. Some are called Marcians, others Valentinians, others Basilidians, others Saturnilians."[58] "When men are called Phrygians, or Novatians, or Valentinians, or Marcionites, or Anthropians," says Lactantius, "or by any other name, they cease to be Christians; for they have lost Christ's Name and clothe themselves in human and foreign titles. It is the Catholic Church alone which retains the true worship."[59] "We never heard of Petrines, or Paulines, or Bartholomeans, or Thaddeans," says St. Epiphanius; "but from the first there was one preaching of all the Apostles, not preaching themselves, but Christ Jesus the Lord. Wherefore also they gave one name to the Church, not their own, but that of their Lord Jesus Christ, since they began to be called Christians first at Antioch; which is the Sole Catholic Church, having nought else but Christ's, being a Church of Christians; not of Christs, but of Christians, He being One, they from that One being called Christians. None, but this Church and her preachers, are of this character, as they show by their own epithets, Manicheans, and Simonians, and Valentinians, {253} and Ebionites."[60] "If you ever hear those who are called Christians," says St. Jerome, "named, not from the Lord Jesus Christ, but from some other, say Marcionites, Valentinians, Mountaineers, Campestrians, know that it is not Christ's Church, but the Synagogue of Antichrist."[61]

St. Pacian's letters to the Novatian Bishop Sympronian require a more extended notice. The latter had required the Catholic faith to be proved to him, without distinctly stating from what portion of it he dissented; and he boasted that he had never found any one to convince him of its truth. St. Pacian observes that there is one point which Sympronian cannot dispute, and which settles the question, the very name Catholic. He then supposes Sympronian to object that, "under the Apostles no one was called Catholic." He answers, "Be it thus;[62] it shall have been so; allow even that. When, after the Apostles, heresies had burst forth, and were striving under various names to tear piecemeal and divine "the Dove" and "the Queen" of God, did not the Apostolic people require a name of their own, whereby to mark the unity of the people that was uncorrupted, lest the error of some should rend limb by limb "the undefiled virgin" of God? Was it not seemly that the chief head should be distinguished by its own peculiar appellation: Suppose this very day I entered a populous city. When I had found Marcionites, Apollinarians, Cataphrygians, Novatians, and others of the kind, who call themselves Christians, by what name should I recognize the congregation of my own people, unless it were named Catholic?. . . . Whence was it delivered to me? Certainly that which has stood through so many ages was not borrowed from man. This name 'Catholic' sounds not of Marcion, nor {254} of Apelles, nor of Montanus, nor does it take heretics for its authors."

In his second letter, he continues, "Certainly that was no accessory name which endured through so many ages. And, indeed, I am glad for thee, that, although thou mayest have preferred others, that thou agreeest that the name attaches to us. What should you deny? nature would cry out. But, and if you still have doubts, let us hold our peace. We will both be that which we shall be named." After alluding to Sympronian's remark that, though Cyprian was holy, "his people bear the name of Apostaticum, Capitolinum, or Synedrium," which were some of the Novatian titles of the Church, St. Pacian replies, "Ask a century, brother, and all its years in succession, whether this name has adhered to us; whether the people of Cyprian have been called other than Catholic? No one of these names have I ever heard." It followed that such appellations were "taunts, not names," and therefore unmannerly. On the other hand, it seems that Sympronian did not like to be called a Novatian, though he could not call himself a Catholic. "Tell me yourselves," says St. Pacian, "what ye are called. Do ye deny that the Novatians are called from Novatian? Impose on them whatever name ye like; that will ever adhere to them. Search, if you please, whole annals, and trust so many ages. You will answer, 'Christian.' But if I inquire the genus of the sect, you will not deny that it is Novatian. . . . Confess it without deceit; there is no wickedness in the name. Why, when so often inquired for, do you hide yourself?

Why ashamed of the origin of your name? When you first wrote, I thought you a Cataphrygian. . . . Dost thou grudge me my name, and yet shun thine own? Think what there is of shame in a cause which shrinks from its own name."

In a third letter: "The Church is the Body of {255} Christ." Truly, the body, not a member; the body composed of many parts, and members knit in one, as saith the Apostle, "For the Body is no one member, but many." Therefore, the Church is the full body, compacted, and diffused now throughout the whole world; like a city, I mean, all whose parts are united, not as ye are, O Novatians, some small and insolent portion, and a mere swelling that has gathered and separated from the rest of the body. . . Great is the progeny of the Virgin, and without number her offspring, wherewith the whole world is filled, wherewith the populous swarms ever through the circumfluous hive." And he founds this characteristic of the Church upon the prophecies: "At length, brother Sympronian, be not ashamed to be with the many; at length consent to despise these festering spots of the Novatians, and these parings of yours; at length to look upon the flocks of the Catholics, and the people of the Church extending so far and wide . . . Hear what David saith, 'I will sing unto Thy name in the great congregation;' and again, 'I will praise Thee among much people;' and 'the Lord, even the most mighty God, hath spoken, and called the world from the rising up of the sun unto the going down thereof.' What! shall the seed of Abraham, which is as the stars and the sand on the seashore for number, be contented with your poverty?. . . Recognise now, brother, the Church of God extending her tabernacles and fixing the stakes of her curtains on the right and on the left; understand that "the Lord's name is praised from the rising up of the sun unto the going down thereof."

In citing these passages, I am not proving what was the *doctrine* of the Fathers concerning the Church in those early times, or what were the *promises* made to it in Scripture; but simply ascertaining what, in matter of fact, was its *then* condition relatively to the various Christian bodies among which it was {256} found. That the Fathers were able to put forward a certain doctrine, that they were able to appeal to the prophecies, proves the matter of fact; for unless the Church, and the Church alone, had been one body everywhere, they could not have argued on the supposition that it was so. And so as to the word "Catholic;" it is enough that the Church was so called; that title was a confirmatory proof and symbol of what is otherwise so plain, that she, as St. Pacian explains the word, was everywhere one, while the sects of the day were nowhere one, but everywhere divided. They might, indeed, be everywhere, but they were in no two places the same; every spot had its own independent communion, or at least to this result they were inevitably and continually tending.

St. Pacian writes in Spain: the same contrast between the Church and sectarianism is presented to us in Africa in the instance of the Donatists; and St. Optatus is a witness both to the fact, and to its notoriety, and to the deep impression which it made on all parties. Whether or not the Donatists identified themselves with the true Church, and cut off the rest of Christendom from it, is not the question here, nor alters the fact which I wish distinctly brought out and recognised, that in those ancient times the Church was that Body which was spread over the *orbis terrarum*, and sects were those bodies which were local or transitory.

"What is that one Church," says St. Optatus, "which Christ calls 'Dove' and 'Spouse?' It cannot be in the multitude of heretics and schismatics. Does it follow that it is in one place? Yet thou, brother Parmenian, hast said that it is with you alone; unless, perhaps, you aim at claiming for yourselves a special sanctity from your pride, so that where you will, there the Church may be, and may not be, where you will not. Must it then be in a small portion of Africa, in the corner of a {257} small realm, among you, but not among us in another part of Africa? And not in Spain, in Gaul, in Italy, where you are not? And, if you will have it only among you, not in the three Pannonian provinces, in Dacia, Maesia, Thrace, Achaia, Macedonia, and in all Greece, where you are not? And that you may keep it among yourselves, not in Pontus, Galatia, Cappadocia, Pamphylia, Phrygia, Cilicia, in the three Syrias, in the two Armenias, in all Egypt, and in Mesopotamia, where you are not? Not among such innumerable islands and other provinces, scarcely numerable, where you are not? What will become then of the meaning of the word Catholic, which is given to the Church, as being according to reason[63] and diffused everywhere? For if thus at your pleasure you narrow the church, if you withdraw from her all the nations, where will be the earnings of the Son of God? where will be that which the Father hath so amply accorded to Him, saying in the second Psalm, "I will give Thee the heathen for Thine inheritance and the uttermost parts of the earth for Thy possession," &c.? . . The whole earth is given Him with the nations; its whole circuit (*orbis*) is Christ's one possession."[64]

An African writer contemporary with St. Augustine, if not St. Augustine himself, enumerates the small portions of the Donatist Sect, in and out of Africa, and asks if they can be imagined to be the fulfilment of the Scripture promise to the Church. "If the holy Scriptures have assigned the Church to Africa alone, or to the scanty· Cutzupitans or Mountaineers of Rome, or to the house or patrimony of one Spanish woman, however the argument may stand from other writings, let none but the Donatists have possession of the Church. If holy Scripture determines it to the few Moors of {258} the Caesarian province we must go over to the Rogatists; if to the few Tripolitans or Byzacenes and Provincials, the Maximianists have attained to it;

if in the Orientals only, it is to be sought for among Arians, Eunomians, Macedonians, and others that may be there; for who can enumerate every heresy of every nation? But if Christ's Church, by the divine and most certain testimonies of Canonical Scriptures, is assigned to all nations, whatever may be adduced, and from whatever quarter cited, by those who say, 'Lo, here is Christ and lo there,' let us rather hear, if we be His sheep, the voice of our Shepherd saying unto us, 'Do not believe.' For they are not each found in the many nations where she is; but she, who is everywhere, is found where they are."[65]

Lastly, let us hear St. Augustine himself in the same controversy: "They do not communicate with us, as you say," he observes to Cresconius, "Novatians, Arians, Patripassians, Valentinians, Patricians, Apellites, Marcionites, Ophites, and the rest of those sacrilegious names, as you call them, of nefarious pests rather than sects. Yet, wheresoever they are, there is the Catholic Church; as in Africa it is where you are. On the other hand, neither you, nor any one of those heresies whatever, is to be found wherever is the Catholic Church. Whence it appears, which is that tree whose boughs extend over all the earth by the richness of its fruitfulness, and which be those broken branches which have not the life of the root but lie each in its own place, drying up."[66]

It may be possibly suggested that this universality which the Fathers ascribe to the Catholic Church lay in its Apostolical descent, or again in its Episcopacy; and that it was one, not as being one kingdom or *civitas* "at unity with itself," with {259} one and the same intelligence in every part, one sympathy, one ruling principle, one organization, one communion, but because, though consisting of a number of independent communities, at variance (if so be) with each other even to a breach of communion, nevertheless all these were possessed of a legitimate succession of clergy, or all governed by Bishops, Priests, and Deacons. But who will in seriousness maintain that relationship, or that resemblance, makes two bodies one? England and Prussia are both monarchies; are they therefore one kingdom? England and the United States are from one stock; can they therefore be called one state? England and Ireland are peopled by different races; yet are they not one kingdom still? If unity lies in the Apostolical succession, an act of schism is from the nature of the case impossible; for as no one can reverse his parentage, so no Church can undo the fact that its clergy have come by lineal descent from the Apostles. Either there is no such sin as schism, or unity does not lie in the Episcopal form or in Episcopal ordination. And this is felt by the controversialists alluded to; who in consequence are obliged to invent a sin, and to consider not division of Church from Church, but the interference of Church with Church to be the sin of schism, as if local dioceses and bishops with restraint were more than ecclesiastical arrangements, and by-laws of the Church, however sacred, while schism is a sin against her essence. Thus they strain out a gnat, and swallow a camel. Division is the schism, if schism there be, not interference. If interference is a sin, division which is the cause of it is a greater; but where division is a duty, there can be no sin of interference.

Far different from such a theory is the picture which the ancient Church presents to us; true, it was governed by Bishops, and those Bishops came {260} from the Apostles, but it was a kingdom besides; and as a kingdom admits of the possibility of rebels, so does such a Church admit of sectaries and schismatics, but not of independent portions. Let us hear Gibbon's description of it, an external witness suited to our present purpose, whose facts we may accept, while we reject his imputations: "The Catholic Church,"[67] he says, "was administered by the spiritual and legal jurisdiction of 1800 bishops; of whom one thousand were seated in the Greek, and eight hundred in the Latin provinces of the Empire. . . Episcopal Churches were closely planted along the banks of the Nile, on the seacoast of Africa, in the proconsular Asia, and through the Southern provinces of Italy. The bishops of Gaul and Spain, of Thrace and Pontus, reigned over an ample territory, and delegated their rural suffragans to execute the subordinate duties of the pastoral office. A Christian diocese might be spread over a province, or reduced to a village; but all the bishops possessed an equal and indelible character; they all derived the same powers and privileges from the Apostles, from the people, and from the laws. . .

"The whole body of the Catholic clergy, more numerous perhaps than the legions, was exempted by the Emperors from all service, private or public, all municipal offices, and all personal taxes and contributions, which pressed on their fellow-citizens with intolerable weight; and the duties of their holy profession were accepted as a full discharge of their obligations to the republic. Each bishop acquired an absolute and indefeasible right to the perpetual obedience of the clerk whom he ordained; the clergy of each Episcopal Church, with its dependent parishes, formed a regular and permanent society, and the Cathedrals of Constantinople and Carthage maintained their peculiar establishment of five hundred ecclesiastical ministers. Their ranks and numbers were insensibly multiplied by {261} the superstition of the times, which introduced into the Church the splendid ceremonies of a Jewish or Pagan temple; and a long train of priests, deacons, sub-deacons, acolytes, exorcists, readers, singers, and doorkeepers, contributed in their respective stations to swell the pomp and harmony of religious worship. The clerical name and privilege were extended to many pious fraternities, who devoutly supported the ecclesiastical throne. Six hundred *parabolani*, or adventurers, visited the sick at Alexandria; eleven hundred *copiatœ*, or grave-diggers, buried the dead of Constantinople; and the swarms of monks, who arose from the Nile, overspread and darkened the face of the Christian world. . .

"Under a despotic government, the bishops alone enjoyed and asserted the inestimable privilege of being tried only by their peers; and, even in a capital accusation, a synod of their brethren were the sole judges of their guilt or innocence. . . The domestic jurisdiction of the bishops was at once a privilege and restraint of the ecclesiastical order, whose civil causes were decently withdrawn from the cognizance of a secular judge. . . The arbitration of the bishops was ratified by a positive law; and the judges were instructed to execute, without appeal or delay, the Episcopal decrees, whose validity had hitherto depended on the consent of the parties. The conversion of the magistrates themselves, and of the whole empire, might gradually remove the fears and scruples of the Christians; but they still resorted to the tribunals of the bishops, whose abilities and integrity they esteemed; and the venerable Austin enjoyed the satisfaction of complaining that his spiritual functions were perpetually interrupted by the invidious labour of deciding the claim or the possession of silver and gold, of lands and cattle. The ancient privilege of sanctuary was transferred to the Christian temples, {262} and the lives or fortunes of the most eminent subjects might be protected by the mediation of the Bishop.

"The Bishop was the perpetual censor of the morals of his people. The discipline of penance was digested into a system of canonical jurisprudence, which accurately defined the duty of private or public confession, the rules of evidence, the degrees of guilt, and the measure of punishment. . . . St. Athanasius excommunicated one of the ministers of Egypt; and the interdict which he pronounced, of fire and water, was solemnly transmitted to the Churches of Cappadocia . . . [Synesius of Ptolemais] vanquished the monster of Libya, the president Andronicus, who abused the authority of a venal office, invented new modes of rapine and torture, and aggravated the guilt of oppression by that of sacrilege. After a fruitless attempt to reclaim the haughty magistrate by mild and religious admonition, Synesius proceeds to inflict the last sentence of ecclesiastical justice, which devotes Andronicus, with his associates and their families, to the abhorrence of earth and heaven. . . . The Church of Ptolemais, obscure and contemptible as she may appear, addresses this declaration to all her sister Churches of the world; and the profane who reject her decrees will be involved in the guilt and punishment of Andronicus and his impious followers. . . .

"Every popular government has experienced the effects of rude or artificial eloquence. . . . The Bishop or some distinguished presbyter, to whom he cautiously delegated the powers of preaching, harangued, without the danger of interruption or reply, a submissive multitude, whose minds had been prepared or subdued by the awful ceremonies of religion. Such was the strict subordination of the Catholic Church, that the same concerted sounds might issue at once from a hundred pulpits of Italy {263} or Egypt, if they were tuned by the masterhand of the Roman or Alexandrian primate. . . . The representatives of the Christian republic were regularly assembled in the spring and autumn of each year; and these synods diffused the spirit of ecclesiastical discipline and legislation through the hundred and twenty provinces of the Roman world. . . . At an early period, when Constantine was the protector rather than the proselyte of Christianity, he referred the African controversy to the Council of Arles, in which the Bishops of York, of Treves, of Milan, and of Carthage met as friends and brethren, to debate in their native tongue on the common interest of the Latin or Western Church. Eleven years afterwards, a more numerous and celebrated assembly was convened at Nice in Bithynia, to extinguish, by their final sentence, the subtle disputes which had arisen in Egypt on the subject of the Trinity. Three hundred and eighteen Bishops obeyed the summons of their indulgent master; the ecclesiastics, of every rank, and sect,[68] and denomination, have been computed at 2048 persons; the Greeks appeared in person; and the consent of the Latins was expressed by the Legates of the Roman Pontiff."

Here is assuredly abundant evidence of the nature of the unity, by which the Church of those ages was distinguished from the sects among which it lay. It was a vast organized association, co-extensive with the Roman Empire, or rather overflowing it. Its Bishops were not mere local officers, but possessed a power essentially ecumenical, extending wherever a Christian was to be found. "No Christian," says Bingham, "would pretend to {264} travel without taking letters of credence with him from his own bishop, if he meant to communicate with the Christian Church in a foreign country. Such was the admirable unity of the Church Catholic in those days, and the blessed harmony and consent of her bishop among another one."[69] St. Gregory Nazianzen calls St. Cyprian an universal Bishop, "presiding," as the same author presently quotes him, "not only over the Church of Carthage and Africa, but over all the regions of the West, and over the East, and the South, and Northern parts of the world also." This is evidence of a unity throughout Christendom, not of mere origin or of Apostolical succession, but of government. He continues "[Gregory] says the same of Athanasius; that, in being made Bishop of Alexandria, he was made Bishop of the whole world. Chrysostom, in like manner, styles Timothy, Bishop of the universe. . . . The great Athanasius, as he returned from his exile, made no scruple to ordain in several cities as he went along, though they were not in his own diocese. And the famous Eusebius of Samosata did the like, in the times of the Arian persecution under Valens . . . Epiphanius made us of the same power and privilege in a like case, ordaining Paulinianus, St. Jerome's brother, first deacon, and then presbyter, in a monastery out of his own diocese in Palestine."[70] And so in respect of teaching, before Councils met on any large scale, St. Ignatius of Antioch had addressed letters to the Churches along the coast of Asia Minor, when on his way to martyrdom at Rome. St. Irenaeus, when a disciple of the Church of Smyrna, betakes himself to Gaul, and answers in Lyons the heresies of Syria. The see of St. Hippolytus, as if he belonged to all parts of the *orbis terrarum*, cannot be located, and is variously placed in the neighbourhood of Rome and in Arabia. Hosius, a Spanish Bishop, {265} arbitrates in an Alexandrian controversy. St. Athanasius, driven from his Church, makes all Christendom his home, from Treves to Ethiopia, and introduces into the West the discipline of the Egyptian Antony. St. Jerome is born in Dalmatia, studies at Constantinople and Alexandria, is secretary to St. Damasus at Rome, and settles and dies in Palestine. Above all, the See of Rome itself is the centre of teaching as well as of action, is visited by Fathers and heretics as tribunal in controversy, and by ancient custom sends her alms to the poor Christians of all Churches, to Achaia and Syria, Palestine, Arabia, Egypt, and Cappadocia.

Moreover, this universal Church was not only one; it was exclusive also. The vehemence with which Christians of the Ante-nicene period had denounced the idolatries and sin of paganism, and proclaimed the judgments which would be their consequence, in great measure accounts for their being reputed in the heathen world as "enemies of mankind." "Worthily doth God exert the lash of His stripes and scourges," says St. Cyprian to a heathen magistrate; "and since they avail so little, and convert not men to God by all this dreadfulness of havoc, there abides beyond the prison eternal and the ceaseless flame of the everlasting penalty. . . . Why humble yourself, and bend to false gods? Why bow your captive body before helpless images and moulded earth? Why grovel in the prostration of death, like the serpent whom ye worship? Why rush into the downfal of the devil, his fall the cause of yours, and he your companion?. . . Believe and live; you have been our persecutors in time; in eternity, be companions of our joy."[71] "These rigid sentiments," says Gibbon, "which had been unknown to the ancient world, appear to have infused a spirit of bitterness into a system of love and harmony."[72] Such, however, was the judgment {266} passed by the first Christians upon all who did not join their own society; and such was the judgment of their successors on those who lived and died in the sects and heresies which had issued from it. That very father, whose denunciation of the heathen has just been quoted, had declared it in the third century. "He who leaves the Church of Christ," he says, "attains not to Christ's reward. He is an alien, an outcast, an enemy. He can no longer have God for a Father, who has not the Church for a Mother. If any man was able to escape who remained without the Ark of Noah, then will that man escape who is out of doors beyond the church. What sacrifice do they believe they celebrate who are rivals of the Priests? If such men were even killed for confession of the Christian name, not even by their blood is this stain washed out. Inexplicable and heavy is the sin of discord, and is purged by no suffering. They cannot dwell with God who have refused to be of one mind in God's Church; a man of such sort may indeed be killed, crowned he cannot be."[73] And so St. Chrysostom, in the following century, with an allusion to St. Cyprian's sentiment: "Though we have achieved ten thousand glorious acts, yet shall we, if we cut to pieces the fulness of the Church, suffer punishment no less sore than they who mangled His body."[74] In like manner St. Augustine seems to consider a conversion from idolatry to a schismatical communion is no gain. "Those whom Donatists baptize, they heal of the wound of idolatry or infidelity, but inflict a more grievous stroke in the wound of schism; for idolaters among God's people the sword destroyed, but schismatics the gaping earth devoured."[75] Else-where, he speaks of the "sacrilege of schism, which surpasses all wickedness."[76] St. Optatus, {267} too, marvels at the Donatist Parmenian's inconsistency in maintaining, what is true doctrine, that "Schismatics are cut off as branches from the vine, are destined for punishments, and reserved, as dry wood, for hell-fire."[77] "Let us hate them who are worthy of hatred," says St. Cyril, "withdraw we from them whom God withdraws from; let us also say unto God with all boldness concerning all heretics, 'Do not I hate them, O Lord, that hate thee?'"[78] "Most firmly hold, and doubt in no wise," says St. Fulgentius, "that every heretic and schismatic soever, baptized in the name of Father, Son, and Holy Ghost, unless brought into the Catholic Church, how great soever have been his alms, though for Christ's Name he has even shed his blood, can in no wise be saved."[79] The Fathers ground this doctrine on St. Paul's words that, though we have knowledge, and give our goods to the poor, and our body to be burned, we are nothing without love.

One more remark shall be made: that the Catholic teachers, far from recognizing any ecclesiastical relation as existing between the Sectarian Bishops and Priests, and their flocks, address the latter immediately, as if those Bishops did not exist, and call on them to come over to the Church individually without respect to any one besides; and that because it is a matter of life and death. To take the instance of the Donatists: it was nothing to the purpose that their Churches in Africa nearly equalled those of the Catholics, or that they had a case to produce in their controversy with the Catholic Church; the very fact that they were separated from the *orbis terrarum* was a public, a manifest, a simple, a sufficient argument against them. "The question is not about your gold and silver," says St. Augustine to Glorius and others, "not your lands, or farms, nor even your bodily health {268} is in peril, but we address your souls about obtaining eternal

life and fleeing eternal death. Rouse yourselves therefore. . . .
You see it all, and know it, and groan over it; yet God sees that
there is nothing to detain you in so pestiferous and sacrilegious a
separation, if you will not overcome your carnal affection, for
the obtaining the spiritual kingdom, and shake off the fear of
wounding friendships, which will avail nothing in God's judgment, in order to escape eternal punishment. Go, think over the
matter, consider what can be said in answer. . . No one blots out
from heaven the Ordinance of God, no one blots out from earth
the Church of God: He hath promised, she hath filled the whole
world." "Some carnal intimacies," he says to his kinsman Severi-
nus, "hold you where you are. . . . What avails temporal health or
relationship, if with it we neglect Christ's eternal heritage, and
our perpetual health?" "I ask," he says to Celer, a person of
influence, "that you would more earnestly urge upon your men
Catholic Unity in the region of Hippo." "Why," he says, in the
person of the Church, to the whole Donatist population, "Why
open your ears to the words of men, who say what they never
have been able to prove and close them to the word of God,
saying, 'Ask of Me, and I will give Thee the heathen for Thine
inheritance?' At another time he says to them, "Some of the
presbyters of your party have sent to us to say, 'Retire from our
flocks, unless you would have us kill you.' How much more
justly do we say to them, 'Nay, do you not, retire from, but come
in peace to, not our flocks, but the flocks of Him whose we are
all; or, if you will not, and are far from peace, then do you rather
retire from flocks, for which Christ shed His Blood.'" "I call on
you for Christ's sake," he says to a late pro-consul, "to write me
an answer, and to urge gently and kindly all your people in the
district of Sinis or Hippo into {269} the communion of the
Catholic Church." He publishes an address to the Donatists at
another time to inform them of the defeat of their Bishops in a
conference: "Whoso," he says, "is separated from the Catholic

Church, however laudably he thinks he is living, by this crime alone, that he is separated from Christ's Unity, he shall not have life, but the wrath of God abideth in him." "Let them ascribe to the Catholic Church," he writes to some converts about their friends who are still in schism, "that is, to the Church diffused over the whole world, rather what the Scriptures say than what human tongues utter in calumny." The idea of acting upon the Donatists only as a body, and through their bishops, does not appear to have occurred to St. Augustine at all.[80]

On the whole, then, we have reason to say, that if there be a form of Christianity at this day distinguished for its careful organization, and its consequent power; if it is spread over the world; if it is conspicuous for zealous maintenance of its own creed; if it is intolerant towards what it considers error; if it is engaged in ceaseless war with all other bodies called Christian; if it, and it alone, is called "Catholic" by the world, nay, by those very bodies, and if it makes much of the title; if it names them heretics, and warns them of coming woe, and calls on them one by one to come over to itself, overlooking every other tie; and if they, on the other hand, call it seducer, harlot, apostate, Anti-Christ, devil; if, however they differ one with another, they consider it their common enemy; if they strive to unite together against it, and cannot; if they are but local; if they continually subdivide, and it remains one; if they fall one after another, and make way for new sects, and it remains the same; such a form of religion is not unlike the Christianity of the Nicene Era.

---

[1] Vid. Muller de Hierarch. et Ascetic. <P. E. Müller, *De hierarchia et studio vitae asceticae in sacris et mysteriis Graecorum Romanorumque latentibus quam . . . accedit auctarum eodem autore De disciplina arcana eleusiniorum* (Havniae: J. F. Schultz, 1803)>. Warburton Div. Leg. ii. 4. <W. Warburton, *A Letter to the Author of the Divine Legislation of Moses, demonstrated . . .* (1765)>, Selden de Diis Syr. <J. Selden (1584-1654), *De diis Syris syntagmata*

II adversaria nempe de numinibus commentitiis in veteri instrumento memoratis,
(rev. ed. Leipzig: L. S. Corneri, 1668).> Acad. des Inscript. t. 3, hist. p. 296, t.
5, mem. p. 63, t. 16, mem. p. 267. Lucian. Pseudomant. Cod. Theod. ix. 16.
2 Acad. t. 16, mem. p. 274.
3 Apol. 25. Vid. also Prudent. in hon. Romani. circ. fin. and Lucian de Deo
Syr. 50.
4 Vid. also the scene in Jul. Firm. p. 449.
5 Tac. Ann. ij. 85; Sueton. Tiber. 36.
6 August. 93.
7 De Superst. 3.
8 de Art. Am. i. init.
9 Sat. iij. vj.
10 Tertul. Ap. 5.
11 Vit. Hel. 3.
12 Vid. Tillemont, Mem. <Louis Sébastien Le Nain de Tillemont (1637-98),
Mémoires pour servir à l'histoire ecclésiastique des six premiers siècles (Paris,
1693-1712) in 12 vols.> and Lardner's Hist. Heretics. <Nathaniel Lardner
(1684-1768), *A History of the Heretics of the Two First Centuries containing
the Account of their Time, Opinions and Testimonies to the Books of the New
Testament,* with long additions by J. Hogg (London, 1780.>
13 Bampton Lect. 2. <Edward Burton (1794-1836), *An Inquiry into the
Heresies of the Apostolic Age* (Bampton Lectures, 1829; Oxford, printed by
Samuel Collingwood, 1829).>
14 Burton, Bampton Lect. note 61.
15 Burton, Bampton Lect. note 44.
16 Montfaucon, Antiq. t. ii. part 2, p. 353. <Bernard de Montfaucon (1655-
1741), *L'Antiquité expliquée et représentée en figures* (Paris, 1719) in 10 vols.>
17 Haer. i. 20.
18 De Praeser. 43.
19 Vid. Kortholt, in Plin. et Traj. Epp. p. 152 <Christian Kortholt (1633-
1694), Lutheran theologian, *In Plinii et Trajani de christianis primaevis
epistulas commentarius* (Kiel, 1674).; Comment. in Minuc. F. &c.
20 Itaque imposuistis in cervicibus nostris sempiternum dominum, quem
dies et noctes timeremus; quis enim non timeat omnia providentem et
cogitantem et animadvertentem et omnia ad se pertinere putantem, curiosum, et
plenum negotii Deum?—*Cic. de Nat. Deor. i. 20.*
21 Min. c. ll, Lact. v. 1, 2, vid. Arnob. ij. 8, &c.
22 Origen contr. Cels. i. 9, iii. 44, 50, vi. 44.
23 Prudent. in hon. Fruct. 37.
24 Evan. Dem. iii. 3, 4.
25 Mort. Peregr. 13.
26 c. 108.
27 Philos. 16.

[28] De Mort. Pereg. ibid.

[29] Ruin. Mart. pp. 100, 594, &c. <Thierry Ruinart (1657-1709), *Acta primorum martyrum sincera* (Paris, 1689)>

[30] Prud. in hon. Rom. vv. 404, 868.

[31] We have specimens of *carmina* ascribed to Christians in the Philopatris. <Newman still ascribes this 10th-century satire to Lucian of Samosata of the second century).>

[32] Goth. in Cod. Th. t. 5, p. 120, ed. 1665. <*Codex Theodosianus cum perpetuis commentariis Iacobi Gothofredi . . . opus posthumum . . .* opera et studio A. Maurillii (1665) six vols. (Mantua, 1750-60)>. Again, "Qui malefici vulgi consuetudine nuncupantur." Leg. 6. So Lactantius, "Magi et ii quos verè maleficos vulgus appellat." Inst. ij. 17. "Quos vulgus mathematicos vocat." Hieron. in Dan. c. ij. Vid. Gothof. in loc. Other laws speak of those who were "maleficiorum labe polluti," and of the "maleficiorum scabies."

[33] Tertullian too mentions the charge of "hostes principum Romanorum, populi, generis humani, Deorum, Imperatorum, legum, morum, naturae totius inimici." Apol. 2, 35, 38, ad Scap. 4, ad. Nat. i. 17.

[34] Evid. part. ij. ch. 4.

[35] Heathen Test. 9. <See note 4 to ch. 3>

[36] Gothof. in Cod. Th. t. 5, p. 121. <see note 32 above>

[37] Cic. pro. Cluent. 61. Gieseler transl. vol. i. p. 21, note 5. Acad. Inscr. t. 34. hist. p. 110.

[38] De Harus. Resp. 9.

[39] De Leg. ii. 8.

[40] Acad. Inscr. ibid.

[41] Neander, Eccl. Hist. tr. vol. i. p. 81. <August Neander (1789-1850), *History of the Christian Religion and Church during the First Three Centuries*, tr. H. J. Rose (Philadelphia 1831).>

[42] Muller, p. 21, 22, 30 <see note 1 above>; Tertull. Ox. tr. p. 12, note *p*.

[43] Gibbon, Hist. ch. 16, note 14.

[44] Epit. Instit. 55.

[45] Gibbon, ibid. Origen admits and defends the violation of the laws: οὐκ ἄλογον συνθήκας παρὰ τὰ νενομισμένα ποιεῖν, τὰς ὑπὲρ ἀληθείας. c. Cels. i. 1.

[46] Hist. p. 418.

[47] In hon. Rom. 62, In Act. S. Cypr. 4, Tert. Apol. 10, &c.

[48] Julian, ap. Cyril, pp. 39, 194, 206, 335. Epp. pp. 305, 429, 438, ed. Spauh.

[49] Niebuhr ascribes it to the beginning of the tenth.

[50] Sirm. Opp. ii. p. 225, ed. Ven. <Jacques Sirmond (1553-1651), *Opera Sancti Aviti . . .* (Paris: apud Sebastianum Cramoisy, 1643).>

[51] Proph. Office, p. 132.

[52] De Praeser. Haer. 41, Oxf. tr.

53 Grk!
54 Cat. xviij. 26.
55 Contr. Ep. Man. 5.
56 Origen, Opp. t. i. p. 809.
57 Strom. vii. 17.
58 Tryph. 35.
59 Instit. 4, 20.
60 Haer. 42, p. 366
61 In Lucif. fin.
62 The Oxford translation is used.
63 *Rationabilis*; apparently an allusion to the civil officer called *Catholicus* or *Rationalis*, receiver-general.
64 Ad Parm. ii. init.
65 De Unit. Eccles. 6.
66 Contr. Cresc. iv. 75; also iii. 77.
67 Hist. ch. xx.
68 This is an apparent allusion to the Emperor's having called the Novatian Bishop Acesius to the Council. Gibbon argues also that the number 2048 *must* have included sectaries. As far as this fact or opinion is a deduction from the force of his general description, *valeat quantum*.
69 Antiq. ii. 4, § 5. <see note 22 to ch. 3.>
70 Ibid. 5, § 3.
71 Ad Demetr. 4, &c. Oxf. tr.
72 Hist. ch. xv.
73 De. Unit. 5, 12.
74 Chrys. in Eph. iv.
75 De Baptism. 20.
76 c. Ep. Parm. i. 7.
77 De Schism. Donat. i. 10.
78 Cat. xvi. 10.
79 De Fid. ad. Petr. 39.
80 Epp. 43, 52, 57, 76, 105, 112, 141, 144.

CHAPTER V.

ILLUSTRATIONS CONTINUED.

APPLICATION OF THE FIRST TEST CONTINUED.

THE CHURCH OF THE FIFTH AND SIXTH CENTURIES.

THE patronage extended by the first Christian Emperors to Arianism, its adoption by the barbarians who succeeded to their power, the subsequent expulsion of all heresy beyond the limits of the Empire, and then again the Monophysite tendencies of Egypt and part of Syria, changed in some measure the aspect of the Church, and claim our further attention. It was still a body in possession, or approximating to the possession, of the *orbis terrarum*; but it did not altogether lie among the sects, as we have been surveying it in the earlier periods, rather it lay between or over against schisms. That same vast Association, which, and which only, had existed from the first, which had been identified by all parties with Christianity, which had been ever called Catholic by people and by laws, took a different shape; collected itself in far greater strength on some points of her extended territory than on others; possessed whole kingdoms with scarcely as rival; lost others partially or wholly, temporarily or for good; was stemmed in its course here or there by external obstacles; and was confronted by heresy, in a substantive shape and in mass, from {271} foreign lands, and with the support of the temporal power. Thus, not to mention the Arianism of the Eastern Empire in the

256

fourth century, the whole of the West was possessed by the same heresy in the fifth; and nearly the whole of Asia, east of the Euphrates, as far as it was Christian, by the Nestorians, in the centuries which followed; while the Monophysites had almost the possession of Egypt, and at times of the whole Eastern Church. I think it no assumption to call Arianism, Nestorianism, and Eutychianism heresies, or to identify the contemporary Catholic Church with Christianity. Now, then, let us consider the mutual relation of Christianity and heresy under these circumstances.

SECTION I.

THE ARIANS OF THE GOTHIC RACE.

No heresy has started with greater violence or more sudden success than the Arian; and it presents a still more remarkable exhibition of these characteristics among the barbarians than in the civilized world. Even among the Greeks it had shown a missionary spirit. Theophilus in the reign of Constantine had introduced the popular heresy, not without some promising results, to the Sabeans of the Arabian peninsula; but, under Valens, Ulphilas became the apostle of a whole race. He taught the Arian doctrine, which he had unhappily learned in the Imperial Court, first to the pastoral Maesogoths; who, unlike the other branches of their family, multiplied under the Maesian mountains with neither military nor religious triumphs. The Visigoths were next corrupted; by whom does not appear. It is one of the singular traits in the history of this vast family of heathens that they so {272} instinctively caught, and so impetuously communicated, and so fiercely maintained, a heresy, which had excited in the Empire, except at Constantinople, little interest in the body of the people. The Visigoths are said to have been converted by the influence of Valens; but Valens reigned for only

fourteen years, and the barbarian population which had been
admitted to the Empire amounted to nearly a million persons. It
is as difficult to trace how the heresy was conveyed from them to
the other barbarian tribes. Gibbon seems to suppose that the
Visigoths acted the part of missionaries in their career of
predatory warfare from Thrace to the Pyrenees. But such is the
fact, however it was brought about, that the success in arms and
the conversion to Arianism, of Ostrogoths, Alani, Suevi, Vandals,
and Burgundians stand as concurrent events in the history of the
times; and by the end of the fifth century the heresy had been
established by the Visigoths in France and Spain, in Portugal by
the Suevi, in Africa by the Vandals, and by the Ostrogoths in
Italy. For a while the title of Catholic as applied to the Church
seemed a misnomer; for not only was she buried beneath these
populations of heresy, but that heresy was one, and maintained
the same distinctive tenet, whether at Carthage, Seville, Toulouse,
or Ravenna.

It cannot be supposed that these northern warriors had
attained to any high degree of mental cultivation; but they
understood their own religion enough to hate the Catholics, and
their bishops were learned enough to hold disputations for its
propagation. They professed to stand upon the faith of Ariminum,
administering Baptism under an altered form of words, and re-
baptizing Catholics whom they gained over to their sect. It must
be added that, whatever was their cruelty or tyranny, both Goths
and Vandals were a moral people, and put to shame the Catholics
whom they dispossessed.

{273} "What can the prerogative of a religious name profit
us," says Salvian, "that we call ourselves Catholic, boast of being
the faithful, taunt Goths and Vandals with the reproach of an
heretical appellation, while we live in heretical wickedness?"[1]
The barbarians were chaste, temperate, just, and devout; the
Visigoth Theodoric repaired every morning with his domestic

officers to his chapel, where service was performed by the Arian priests; and one singular instance is on record of the defeat of a Visigoth force by the Imperial troops on a Sunday, when instead of preparing for battle they were engaged in the religious services of the day.[2] Many of their princes were men of great ability, as the two Theodorics, Euric and Leovigild.

Successful warriors, animated by a fanatical spirit of religion, were not likely to be content with a mere profession of their own creed; they proceeded to place their own priests in the religious establishments which they found, and to direct a bitter persecution against the vanquished Catholics. The savage cruelties of the Vandal Hunneric in Africa have often been enlarged upon; Spain was the scene of repeated persecutions; Sicily, too, had its Martyrs. Compared with these enormities, it was but a little thing to rob the Catholics of their {274} churches and the shrines of their treasures. Lands, immunities, and jurisdiction, which had been given by the Emperors to the African Church, were made over to the clergy of its conquerors; and by the time of Belisarius, the Catholic Bishops had been reduced to less than a third of their original number. In Spain, as in Africa, bishops were driven from their sees, churches were destroyed, cemeteries profaned, martyries rifled. When it was possible, the Catholics concealed the relics in caves, keeping up a perpetual memory of their provisional hiding places.[3] Repeated spoliations were exercised upon the property of the Church. Leovigild applied[4] its treasures partly to increase the splendour of his throne, partly to national works. At other times, the Arian clergy themselves must have been the gainers from the plunder: for when Childebert the Frank had been brought into Spain by the cruelties exercised against the Catholic queen of the Goths, who was his sister, he carried away with him from the Arian churches, as St. Gregory of Tours informs us, sixty chalices, fifteen patens, twenty cases in which the gospels were kept, all of pure gold and ornamented with jewels.[5]

In France, and especially in Italy, the rule of the heretical power was much less oppressive; Theodoric, the Ostrogoth, reigned from the Alps to Sicily, and till the close of a long reign he gave an ample toleration to his Catholic subjects. He respected their property, suffered their churches and sacred places to remain in their hands, and had about his court some of their eminent Bishops, since known as Saints, St. Caesarius of Arles, and St. Epiphanius of Pavia. Still he brought into the country a new population, devoted to Arianism, or, as we now speak, a new Church. His "march," says Gibbon,[6] "must be considered as the emigration {275} of an entire people; the wives and children of the Goths, their aged parents, and most precious effects, were carefully transported; and some idea may be formed of the heavy luggage that now followed the camp by the loss of two thousand waggons, which had been sustained in a single action in the war of Epirus." To his soldiers he assigned a third of the soil of Italy, and the barbarian families settled down with their slaves and cattle. The original number of the Vandal conquerors of Africa had only been fifty thousand men, but the military colonists of Italy soon amounted to the number of two hundred thousand; which, according to the calculation adopted by the same author elsewhere, involves a population of a million. The least that could be expected was, that an Arian ascendency established through the extent of Italy would provide for the sufficient celebration of the Arian worship, and we hear of the Arians having a Church even in Rome.[7] The rule of the Lombards in the north of Italy succeeded to that of the Goths—Arians, like their predecessors, without their toleration. The clergy they brought with them seem to have claimed their share in the possession of the Catholic churches;[8] and though the court was converted at the end of thirty years, many cities in Italy were for some time afterwards disputed by the heretical bishops.[9] The rule of Arianism in France lasted for eighty years; in Spain for a hundred and eighty; in Africa for a hundred; for about a hundred in Italy. These periods were not contemporaneous; but extend altogether from the beginning of the fifth to the end of the sixth century.

It will be anticipated that the duration of this ascendency of error had not the faintest tendency to deprive the ancient Church of the West of the title of Catholic; and it is needless to produce evidence {276} of a fact which is on the very face of the history. The Arians seem never to have claimed the Catholic name. It is more remarkable that the Catholics during this period were denoted by the additional title of "Romans." Of this there are many proofs in the histories of St. Gregory of Tours, Victor of Vite, and the Spanish Councils. Thus St. Gregory speaks of Theodegisid, a king of Portugal, expressing his incredulity at a miracle, by saying, "It is the temper of the Romans, for," interposes the author, "they call men of our religion Romans,) and not the power of God."[10] "Heresy is everywhere an enemy to Catholics," says the same St. Gregory in a subsequent place, and he proceeds to illustrate it by the story of a "Catholic woman," who had a heretic husband, to whom, he says, came "a presbyter of our religion very Catholic;" and whom the husband matched at table with his own Arian presbyter, "that there might be the priests of each religion" in their house at once. When they were eating, the husband said to the Arian, "Let us have some sport with this presbyter of the Romans."[11] The Arian Count Gomachar seized on the lands of the Church of Adge <Agde> in France, and was attacked with a fever; on his recovery, at the prayers of the Bishop, he repented of having asked them, observing, "What will these Romans say now? that my fever came of taking their land."[12] When the Vandal Theodoric would have killed the Catholic Armogastes, after torturing him to recant in vain, his presbyter dissuaded him, "lest the Romans should begin to call him a Martyr."[13]

This appellation had two meanings; one, which will readily suggest itself, is its use in contrast to the word "barbarian," as denoting the faith of the Empire, as "Greek" occurs in St. Paul's Epistles. {277} In this sense it would more naturally be used by the Romans themselves than by others. Thus Salvian says, that "nearly all the Romans are greater sinners than the barbarians;"[14] and he speaks of "Roman heretics, of which there is an innumerable multitude,"[15] meaning heretics of the Empire. And so St. Gregory the Great complains, that he "had become Bishop of the Lombards rather than of the Romans."[16] And Evagrius, speaking even of the East, contrasts "Romans and Barbarians"[17] in his account of St. Simeon; and at a later date, and even to this day, Thrace and part of Asia Minor derive their name from Rome. In like manner, we find Syrian writers sometimes speaking of the religion of the Romans, sometimes of the Greeks,[18] as synonymes.

But the word certainly contains also an allusion to the faith and communion of the Roman See. In this sense the Emperor Theodosius, in his letter to Acacius of Berrhoea, contrasts it with Nestorianism, which was within the Empire as well as Catholicism; during the controversy raised by that heresy, he exhorts him and others to show themselves "approved priests of the Roman religion."[19] Again, when the Ligurian nobles were persuading the Arian Ricimer to come to terms with Athemius, the orthodox representative of the Greek Emperor,[20] they propose to him to send St. Epiphanius as ambassador, a man "whose life is venerable to every Catholic and Roman, and at least amiable in the eyes of a Greek (Graeculus) if he deserves the sight of him."[21] It must be recollected, too, that the Spanish and African Churches actually were in the closest communion with the See of Rome at that time, and that that communion was the visible ecclesiastical {278} distinction between them and their Arian rivals. The chief ground of the Vandal Hunneric's persecution of the African Catholics seems to have been their connexion with their brethren beyond the sea,[22] which he looked at with jealousy, as introducing a foreign power into his territory. Prior to this he had published an edict calling on the "Homoüsian" Bishops (for on this occasion he did not call them Catholic, to meet his own bishops and treat concerning the faith, that "their meetings to the seduction of Christian souls might not be held in the territory of the Vandals."[23] Upon this invitation, Eugenius of Carthage replied that all the transmarine Bishops of the orthodox communion ought to be summoned, "in particular because it is a matter for the whole world, not special to the African provinces," that "they could not undertake a point of faith *sine universitatis assensu*." Hunneric answered that if Eugenius would make him sovereign of the *orbis terrarum*, he would comply with his request. This led Eugenius to say that the orthodox faith was "the only true faith;" that the king ought to write to his allies abroad, if he wished to know it, and that he himself would write to his brethren for foreign bishops, "who," he says, "may assist us in setting before you the true faith, common to them and to us, and especially the Roman Church, which is the head of all Churches." Moreover, the African Bishops in their banishment in Sardinia, to the number of sixty, with St. Fulgentius at their head, quote with approbation the words of Pope Hormisdas, to the effect that they hold, "on the point of freewill and divine grace, what the Roman, that is, the Catholic, Church follows and preserves."[24] Again, the Spanish Church was under the superintendence of the Pope's Vicar[25] during the persecutions, whose duty it was to hinder all encroachments {279} upon "the Apostolical decrees, or the limits of the Holy Fathers," through the whole of the country.

Nor was the association of Catholicism with the See of Rome an introduction of that age. The Emperor Gratian, in the fourth century, had ordered that the Churches which the Arians had usurped should be restored, not to those who held "the Catholic faith," or "the Nicene Creed," or were "in communion with the *orbis terrarum*" but "who chose the communion of Damasus,"[26] the then Pope. It was St. Jerome's rule, also, in some well-known passages:—Writing against Ruffinus, who had spoken of "our faith," he says, "What does he mean by 'his faith?' that which is the strength of the Roman Church? or that which is contained in the volumes of Origen? If he answer, 'The Roman,' then we are Catholics who have borrowed nothing of Origen's error; but if Origen's blasphemy be his faith, then, while he is charging me with inconsistency, he proves himself to be an heretic."[27] The other passage, already quoted, is still more exactly to the point, because it was written on occasion of a schism. The divisions at Antioch had thrown the Catholic Church into a remarkable position; there were two Bishops in the See, one in connexion with the East, the other with Egypt and the West,—with which then was "Catholic Communion?" St. Jerome has no doubt on the subject:—Writing to St. Damasus, he says, "Since the East tears into pieces the Lord's coat . . . therefore by me is the chair of Peter to be consulted, and that faith which is praised by the Apostle's mouth. . . . Though your greatness terrifies me, yet your kindness invites me. From the Priest the sacrifice claims salvation, from the Shepherd the sheep claims protection. Let us speak without offence; I court not the Roman height: I speak with the successor of the Fisherman and the disciple of the {280} Cross. I, who follow none as my chief but Christ, am associated in communion with thy blessedness, that is, with the See of Peter. On that rock the Church is built, I know. Whoso shall eat the Lamb outside that House is profane. . . . I know not Vitalis" (the Apollinarian), "Meletius I reject, I am ignorant of Paulinus. Whoso gathereth not with thee, scattereth; that is, he who is not of Christ is of Antichrist."[28] Again, "The ancient authority of the monks, dwelling round about, rises against me; I meanwhile cry out, If any be joined to Peter's chair, he is mine."[29]

Here was what may be considered a *dignus vindice nodus*, the Church being divided and an arbiter wanted. Such a case has also occurred in Africa in the controversy with the Donatists. Four hundred bishops, though but in one region, were a fifth part of the whole Episcopate of Christendom, and might seem too many for a Schism, and in themselves too large a body to be cut off from God's inheritance by a mere majority, even had it been overwhelming. St. Augustine, then, who so often appeals to the *orbis terrarum*, sometimes adopts a more prompt criterion. He tells certain Donatists to whom he writes, that the Catholic Bishop of Carthage "was able to make light of the thronging multitude of his enemies, when he found himself by letters of credence joined both to the Roman Church, in which ever had flourished the principality of the Apostolical See, and to the other lands whence the gospel came to Africa itself."[30]

There are good reasons then for explaining the Gothic and Arian use of the word "Roman," when applied to the Catholic Church and faith, of something beyond its mere connexion with the Empire, which the barbarians were assaulting; nor would "Roman" surely be the most obvious word to denote the orthodox faith in the mouths of a people {281} who had learned their heresy from a Roman Emperor and Court, and who professed to direct their belief by the great Latin Council of Ariminum.

As then the fourth century presented to us in its external aspect the Catholic Church lying in the midst of a multitude of sects, all enemies to it, so in the fifth and sixth we see the same Church in the West lying under the oppression of a huge, far-spreading and schismatical communion. Heresy is no longer a domestic enemy intermingled with the Church, but it occupies its own ground and is extended over against her, even though on the same territory, and is more or less organized, and cannot be so promptly refuted by the simple test of Catholicity.

SECTION II.

THE NESTORIANS.

The Churches of Syria and Asia Minor were the most intellectual portion of early Christendom. Alexandria was but one metropolis in a large region, and contained the philosophy of the whole Patriarchate; but Syria abounded in wealthy and luxurious cities, the creation of the Seleucidae, where the arts and the schools of Greece had full opportunities of cultivation. For a time too, for the first two hundred years, as some think, Alexandria was the only See as well as the only school of Egypt; while Syria was divided into smaller Dioceses, each of which had at first an authority of its own, and which, even after the growth of the Patriarchal power, received their respective bishops, not from the See of Antioch, but from their own metropolitan. In Syria too the schools were private, a circumstance which would tend both to diversity in religious opinion, and incaution in the expression of it; but the {282} sole catechetical school of Egypt was the organ of the Church, and its Bishop could banish Origen for speculations which developed and ripened with impunity in Syria.

But the immediate source of that fertility in heresy, which is the unhappy characteristic of the Syrian Church, was its celebrated Exegetical School. The causes of the connexion of that school with doctrinal error need not here be discussed, and will be alluded to again in a subsequent place; here only the fact need be stated, on the one hand that it devoted itself to the literal and critical interpretation of Scriptures, and on the other that it gave rise first to the Arian and then to the Nestorian heresy. If additional evidence be wanted of the connexion of heterodoxy and biblical criticism in that age, it is found in the fact that, not long after their contemporaneous appearance in Syria, they are found combined in the person of Theodore of Heraclea, so called from the place both of his birth and his bishoprick, an able commentator and an active enemy of St. Athanasius, but a Thracian unconnected except by sympathy with the Patriarchate of Antioch.

This school appears to have risen in the middle of the third century; but there is no evidence to determine whether it was a local institution, or, as is more probable, a discipline or method characteristic of the Syrian Church. Dorotheus is one of its earliest teachers; he is known as a Hebrew scholar, as well as a commentator on the sacred text, and he was the master of Eusebius of Caesarea. Lucian, the friend of the notorious Paul of Samosata, and for three successive Episcopates after him a seceder from the Church, though afterwards a martyr in it, was the editor of a new edition of the Septuagint, and master of the chief original teachers of {283} Arianism. Eusebius of Caesarea, Asterius called the Sophist, and Eusebius of Emesa, Arians of the Nicene period, and Diodorus, a zealous opponent of Arianism, but the master of Theodore of Mopsuestia, have all a place in the Exegetical School. St. Chrysostom and Theodoret, both Syrians, and the former pupil of Diodorus, adopted the literal interpretation, though preserved from its abuse. But the principal doctor of the School was that Theodore, the master of Nestorius, who has just been mentioned, and who with his writings, and with the writings of Theodoret against St. Cyril, and the letter written by Ibas of Edessa to Maris, was condemned by the fifth Ecumenical Council. Ibas was the translator into Syriac, and Maris into Persian, of the books of Theodore and Diodorus;[31] and in so doing they became the immediate instruments of the formation of the great Nestorian school and Church in farther Asia.

As many as ten thousand tracts of Theodore are said in this way to have been introduced to the knowledge of the Christians of Mesopotamia, Adiabene, Babylonia, and the neighbouring countries. He was called by those Churches absolutely "the Interpreter," and it eventually became the very profession of the Nestorian communion to follow him as such. "The doctrine of all our Eastern Churches," says the Council under the patriarch Marabas, "is founded on the Creed of Nicaea; but in the exposition of the Scriptures we follow St. Theodore." "We must by all means remain firm to the commentaries of the great Commentator," says the Council under Sabarjesus; "whoso shall in any manner oppose them, or think otherwise, be he anathema."[32] No one since the beginning of Christianity, except Origen and St. Augustine, has had such great influence on his brethren as Theodore.[33]

The original Syrian school had possessed very marked characteristics, which it did not lose when it passed into a new country and into strange {284} tongues. Its comments on Scripture seem to have been clear, natural, methodical, apposite, and logically exact. "In all Western Aramaea," says Lengerke, that is, in Syria, "there was but one mode of treating whether exegetics or doctrine, the practical."[34] Thus Eusebius of Caesarea, whether as a disputant or a commentator, is commonly a writer of sense and judgment; and he is to be referred to the Syrian school, though he does not enter so far into its temper as to exclude the mystical interpretation or to deny the verbal inspiration of Scripture. Again, we see in St. Chrysostom a direct, straightforward treatment of the sacred text, and a pointed application of it to things and persons; and Theodoret abounds in modes of thinking and reasoning which without any great impropriety may be called English. Again, St. Cyril of Jerusalem, though he does not abstain from allegory, shows the character of his school by the great stress he lays upon the study of Scripture, and, I may add, by the peculiar characteristics of his style, which will be appreciated by a modern reader.

It would have been well, had the genius of the Syrian theology been ever in the safe keeping of men such as St. Cyril, St. Chrysostom, and Theodoret; but in Theodore of Mopsuestia, nay in Diodorus before him, it developed into those errors, of which Paul of Samosata had been the omen on its rise. As its attention was chiefly directed to the examination of the Scriptures, in its interpretation of the Scriptures was its heretical temper discovered; and though allegory can be made an instrument of evading Scripture doctrine, criticism may more readily be turned to the destruction of doctrine and Scripture together. Bent on ascertaining the literal sense, Theodore was naturally led to the Hebrew text instead of the Septuagint, and thence to Jewish commentators. Jewish Commentators naturally suggested events and objects {285} short of evangelical as the fulfilment of the prophetical announcements, and when it was possible, an ethical sense instead of a prophetical. The eighth chapter of Proverbs ceased to bear a Christian meaning, because, as Theodore maintained, a writer of the book had received the gift, not of prophecy, but of wisdom. The Canticles must be interpreted literally; and then it was but an easy, or rather a necessary step, to exclude the book from the Canon. The book of Job too professed to be historical; yet what was it really but a Gentile drama? He also gave up the books of Chronicles and Ezra, and, strange to say, the Epistle of St. James, though it was contained in the Peschito Version of his Church. He denied Psalms xxii. and lxix. applied to our Lord; rather he limited the Messianic passages of the whole book to four; of which the eighth Psalm was one, and the forty-fifth another. The rest he explained of Hezekiah and Zerubbabel, without denying that they might be accommodated to an evangelical sense.[35] He explained St. Thomas's words, "My Lord and my God," as a joyful exclamation; and our Lord's "Receive ye the Holy Ghost," as an anticipation of the day of Pentecost. As may be expected, he denied the verbal inspiration of Scripture. Also, he held that the deluge did not cover the earth; and, as others before him, he was heterodox on the doctrine of original sin, and denied the eternity of punishment.

Maintaining that the real sense of Scripture was, not the scope of a Divine Intelligence, but the intention of the mere human organ of inspiration, Theodore was led to hold, not only that that sense was one in each text, but that it was continuous and single in a context; that what was the subject of the composition in one verse, must be the subject in the next, and that if a Psalm was historical or prophetical in its commencement, it was the one or the other to its termination. Even that fulness of {286} meaning, refinement of thought, subtle versatility of feeling, and delicate reserve or reverent suggestiveness, which poets exemplify, seem to have been excluded from his idea of a sacred composition. Accordingly, if a Psalm contained passages which could not be applied to our Lord, it followed that that Psalm did not properly apply to Him at all, except by accommodation. Such at least is the doctrine of Cosmas, a writer of Theodore's school, who on this ground passes over the twenty-second, sixty-ninth, and other Psalms, and limits the Messiasnic to the second, the eighth, the forty-fifth, and the hundred and tenth. "David," he says, "did not make common to the servants what belongs to the Lord[36] Christ, but what was proper to the servants, of servants."[37] Accordingly the twenty-second could not properly belong to Christ, because in the beginning it spoke of the "*verba delictorum meorum.*" A remarkable consequence would follow from this doctrine, that as Christ was divided from his Saints, so the Saints were divided from Christ; and an opening was made for a denial of the doctrine of their *cultus*, though this denial in the event has not been developed among Nestorians. But a more serious consequence is latently contained in it, and nothing else than the Nestorian heresy, viz. that our Lord's manhood is not so intimately included in His Divine Personality that His brethren according to the flesh may be associated with the Image of the One Christ. Here St. Chrysostom pointedly contradicts the doctrine of Theodore, though his fellow-pupil and friend;[38] as does St. Ephrem, though a Syrian also;[39] and St. Basil.[40]

{287} One other characteristic of the Syrian school, viewed as independent of Nestorius, should be added:—As it tended to the separation of the Divine Person of Christ from His manhood, so did it tend to explain away His Divine Presence in the Sacramental elements. Ernesti seems to consider the school, in modern language, Sacramentarian: and certainly some of the most cogent passages brought by moderns against the Catholic doctrine of the Eucharist are taken from writers who are connected with that school; as the author, said to be St. Chrysostom, of the Epistle to Caesarius, Theodoret in his Eranistes, and Facundus. Some countenance too is given to the same view of the Eucharist, at least in some parts of his works, by Origen, whose language concerning the Incarnation also leans to what was afterwards Nestorianism. To these may be added Eusebius,[41] who, far removed as he was from that heresy, was a disciple of the Syrian school. The language of the later Nestorian writers seems to have been of the same character.[42] Such then on the whole is the character of that theology of Theodore which passed from Cilicia and Antioch to Edessa first, and then to Nisibis.

Edessa, the metropolis of Mesopotamia, had remained an oriental city till the third century, when it was made a Roman colony by Caracalla.[43] Its position on the confines of two empires gave it great ecclesiastical importance, as the channel by which the theology of Rome and Greece was conveyed to a family of Christians, dwelling in contempt and persecution amid a still heathen world. It was the seat of various schools; apparently of a Greek school, where the classics were studied as well as theology, where Eusebius of Emesa[44] had originally been trained, and where perhaps Protogenes {288} taught.[45] There were Syrian schools asttended by heathen and Christian youths in common. The cultivation of the native language had been an especial object of its masters since the time of Vespasian, so that the pure and refined dialect went by the name of the Edessene.[46] At Edessa too St. Ephrem formed his own Syrian school, which lasted long after him; and there too was the celebrated Persian Christian school, over which Maris presided, who has been already mentioned as the translator of Theodore into Persian.[47] Even in the time of the predecessor of Ibas in the See (before A.D. 435) the Nestorianism of this Persian School was so notorious that Rabbula the Bishop had expelled its masters and scholars;[48] and they, taking refuge in the country with which they were connected, had introduced the heresy to the Churches subject to the Persian King.

Something ought to be said of these Churches; though little is known except what is revealed by the fact, in itself of no slight value, that they had sustained two persecutions at the hands of the heathen government in the fourth and fifth centuries. One testimony is extant as early as the end of the second century, to the effect that in Parthia, Media, Persia, and Bactria there were Christians who "were not overcome by evil laws and customs."[49] In the early part of the fourth century, a bishop of Persia attended the Nicene Council, and about the same time Christianity is said to have pervaded nearly the whole of Assyria.[50] Monachism had been introduced there before the middle of the fourth century, and shortly after commenced that fearful persecution in which sixteen thousand Christians are said to have suffered. It lasted thirty years, {289} and is said to have recommenced at the end of the Century. The second persecution lasted for at least another thirty years of the next, at the very time when the Nestorian troubles were in progress in the Empire. Trials such as these show the populousness as well as the faith of the Churches in those parts; and the number of the Sees, for the names of twenty-seven Bishops are preserved who suffered in the former persecution. One of them was apprehended together with sixteen priests, nine deacons, besides monks and nuns of the diocese; another with twenty-eight companions, ecclesiastics or regulars; another with one hundred ecclesiastics of different orders; another with one hundred and twenty-eight; another with his chorepiscopus and two hundred and fifty of his clergy. Such was the Church, consecrated by the blood of so many martyrs, which immediately after its glorious confession fell a prey to the theology of Theodore; and which through a succession of ages discovered the energy, when it had lost the purity of Saints.

The members of the Persian school, who had been driven out of Edessa by Rabbula, found a wide field open for their exertions under the pagan government with which they had taken refuge. The Persian monarchs, who had often prohibited by edict[51] the intercommunion of the Church under their sway, with the countries towards the west, readily extended their protection to exiles, who professed the means of destroying its Catholicity. Barsumas, the most energetic of them, was placed in the metropolitan See of Nisibis, where also the fugitive school was settled under the presidency of another of their party; while Maris was promoted to the See of Ardaschir. The primacy of the Church had from an early period belonged to the See of Seleucia in Babylonia. Catholicus was the title appropriated to its occupant, as well as to the Persian Primate, as {290} being deputies of the Patriarch of Antioch, and was derived apparently from the Imperial dignity so called, denoting their function as Procurators-general, or officers in chief for the regions in which they were placed. Acacius, another of the Edessene party, was put into this principal See, and suffered, if he did not further, the innovations of Barsumas. The mode by which the latter effected these measures has been left on record by an enemy. "Barsumas accused Babuaeus, the Catholicus, before King Pherozes, whispering, "These men hold the faith of the Romans, and are their spies. Give me power against them to arrest them."[52] It is said that in this way he obtained the death of Babuaeus, whom Acacius succeeded. When a minority resisted[53] the process of schism, a persecution followed. The death of seven thousand seven hundred Catholics is said by Monophysite authorities to have been the price of the severance of the Chaldaic Churches from Christendom.[54] Their loss was compensated in the eyes of the government by the multitude of Nestorian fugitives, who flocked into Persia from the Empire, numbers of them industrious artizans, who sought a country where their own religion was in the ascendant.

The foundation of that religion lay, as we have already seen, in the literal interpretation of Scripture, of which Theodore was the principal teacher. The doctrine, in which it formally consisted, is known by the name of Nestorius: it lay in the ascription of a human as well as a Divine Personality to our Lord; and it showed itself in denying the title of "Mother of God," or θεοτόκος. to St. Mary. As to our Lord's Personality, it is to be observed that the question of language casme in, which always serves to perplex a subject and make a controversy seem a matter of words. The native Syrians made a distinction between the word "Person," and "Prosopon," which stands for it in Greek; they allowed that there was one Prosopon or Parsopa, as they called it, and they held that there were two Persons. If it asked what they meant by *parsopa*, the answer seems to be, that they took the word merely in the sense of *character*, or *aspect*, a sense familiar to the Greek *prosopon*, {291} and quite irrelevant as a guarantee of their orthodoxy. It follows moreover that, since the *aspect* of a thing is its impression upon the beholder, the personality to which they ascribed unity must have lain in our Lord's manhood, and not in His Divine Nature. But it is hardly worth while pursuing the heresy to its limits. Next, as to the phrase "Mother of God," they rejected it as unscriptural; they maintained that St. Mary was Mother of the humanity of Christ, not of the Word, and they fortified themselves by the Nicene Creed, in which no such title is ascribed to her.

Whatever might be the obscurity or the plausibility of their original dogma, there is nothing obscure or attractive in the developments, whether of doctrine or of practice, in which it issued. The first act of the exiles of Edessa, on their obtaining power in the Chaldean community, was to abolish the celibacy of the clergy, or in Gibbon's forcible words, to allow "the public and reiterated nuptials of the priests, the bishops, and even the patriarch himself." Barsumas, the great instrument of the change of religion, was the first to set an example of the new usage, and is even said by a Nestorian writer to have married a nun.[55] He passed a Canon at Councils, held at Seleucia and elsewhere, that Bishops and priests might marry, and might renew their wives as often as they lost them. The Catholicus who followed Acacius went so far as to extend the benefit of the Canon to Monks, that is, to destroy the Monastic order; and his two successors availed {292} themselves of this liberty, and are recorded to have been fathers. A restriction, however, was afterwards placed upon the Catholicus, and upon the Episcopal order.

Such were the circumstances, and such the principles, under which the See of Seleucia became the Rome of the East. In the course of time the Catholicus took on himself the loftier and independent title of Patriarch of Babylon; and though Seleucia was changed for Ctesiphon and for Bagdad,[56] still the name of Babylon was preserved from first to last as a formal or ideal Metropolis. In the time of the Caliphs, it was at the head of as many as twenty-five Archbishops; its Communion extended from China to Jerusalem; and its numbers, with those of the Monophysites, are said to have surpassed those of the Greek and Latin

Churches together. The Nestorians seem to have been unwilling, like the Novatians, to be called by the name of their founder,[57] though they confessed it had adhered to them; one instance may be specified of their assuming the name of Catholic,[58] but there is nothing to show it was given them by others.

"From the conquest of Persia," says Gibbon, "they carried their spiritual arms to the North, the East, and the South; and the simplicity of the Gospel was fashioned and painted with the colours of the Syriac theology. In the sixth century, according to the report of a Nestorian traveller, Christianity was successfully preached to the Bactrians, the Huns, the Persians, the Indians, the Persarmenians, the Medes, and the Elamites: the Barbaric Churches from the Gulf of Persia to the Caspian Sea were almost infinite; and their recent faith was conspicuous in the number and sanctity of their monks and martyrs. The pepper coast of Malabar and the isles of the ocean, Socotora and Ceylon, were peopled with an increasing multitude of Christians, {293} and the bishops and clergy of those sequestered regions derived their ordination from the Catholicus of Babylon. In a subsequent age, the zeal of the Nestorians overleaped the limits which had confined the ambition and curiosity both of the Greeks and Persians. The missionaries of Balch and Samarcand pursued without fear the footsteps of the roving Tartar, and insinuated themselves into the camps of the valleys of Imaus and the banks of the Selinga."[59]

SECTION III.

THE MONOPHYSITES.

Eutyches was Archimandrite, or Abbot, of a Monastery in the suburbs of Constantinople; he was a man of unexceptionable character, and was of the age of seventy years, and had been Abbot for thirty, at the date of his unhappy introduction into ecclesiastical history. He had been the friend and assistant of St. Cyril of Alexandria, and had lately taken part against Ibas, Bishop of Edessa, whose name has occurred in the foregoing Section. For some time he had been engaged in teaching a doctrine concerning the Incarnation, which he maintained indeed to be none other than that of St. Cyril's in his controversy with Nestorius, but which others denounced as an heresy in the opposite extreme, and substantially a re-assertion of Apollinarianism. The subject was brought before a Council of Constantinople, under the presidency of Flavian, the Patriarch, in the year 448; and Eutyches was condemned by the assembled Bishops of holding the doctrine of One, instead of Two Natures in Christ.

It is but indirectly to our present purpose to ascertain accurately what he held, and there has been a great deal of controversy on the subject; {294} partly from confusion between him and his successors, partly from the indecision or the ambiguity which commonly attaches to the professions of heretics. If a statement must be made of the doctrine of Eutyches himself, in whom the controversy began, let it be said to consist in these two tenets:—in maintaining, first, that "before the Incarnation there were two natures, after their union one," or that our Lord was of or from two natures, but not in two;—and, secondly, that His flesh was not of one substance with ours, that is, not of the substance of St. Mary. Of these two points, he seemed willing to abandon the second, but was firm in his maintenance of the first. But let us return to the Council of Constantinople.

On examination Eutyches allowed that the Holy Virgin was consubstantial with us, and that "our God was incarnate of her;" but he would not allow that He was therefore, as man, consubstantial with us, his notion apparently being that union with the Divinity had changed what otherwise would have been human nature. However, when pressed, he said that, though up to that day he had not permitted himself to discuss the nature of Christ, or to affirm that "God's body is man's body though it was human," yet he would allow, if commanded, our Lord's consubstantiality with us. Upon this Flavian observed that "the Council was introducing no innovation, but declaring the faith of the Fathers." To his other position, however, that our Lord had but one nature after the Incarnation, he adhered: when the Catholic doctrine was put before him, he answered, "Let St. Athanasius be read; you will find nothing of the kind there."

His condemnation followed: it was signed by twenty-two Bishops and twenty-three Abbots;[60] among the former were Flavian of Constantinople, Basil metropolitan of Seleucia in Isauria, the metropolitans {295} of Amasea in Pontus and Marcianopolis in Maesia, and the Bishop of Cos, the Pope's minister at Constantinople.

Eutyches appealed to the Pope of the day, St. Leo, who at first hearing took his part. He wrote to Flavian that, "judging by the statement of Eutyches, he did not see with what justice he had been separated from the communion of the Church." "Send therefore," he continued, "some suitable person to give us a full account of what has occurred, and let us know what the new error is." St. Flavian, who had behaved with great forbearance throughout the proceedings, had not much difficulty in setting the controversy before the Pope in its true light.

Eutyches was supported by the Imperial Court, and by Dioscorus the Patriarch of Constantinople; the proceedings therefore at Constantinopole were not allowed to settle the question. A general Council was summoned for the ensuing summer at Ephesus, where the Third Ecumenical Council had been held twenty years before against Nestorius. It was attended by sixty metropolitans, ten from each of the great divisions of the East; the whole number of bishops assembled amounted to one hundred and thirty-five.[61] Dioscorus was appointed President by the Emperor, and the object of the assembly was said to be the settlement of a question of faith which had arisen between Flavian and Eutyches. St. Leo, dissatisfied with the measure altogether, nevertheless sent his legates, but with the object, as their commission stated, and a letter he addressed to the Council, of "condemning the heresy, and reinstating Eutyches if he retracted." His legates took precedence after Dioscorus and before the other Patriarchs. He also published at this time his celebrated Tome on the Incarnation, in a letter addressed to Flavian.

{296} The proceedings which followed were of so violent a character, that the Council has gone down to posterity under the name of the Latrocinium or "Gang of Robbers." Eutyches was honourably acquitted, and his doctrine received; but the assembled fathers showed some backwardness to depose St. Flavian. Dioscorus had been attended by a multitude of monks, furious zealots for the Monophysite doctrine from Syria and Egypt, and by an armed force. These broke into the Church at his call; Flavian was thrown down and trampled on, and received injuries of which he died the third day after. The Pope's legates escaped as they could; and the Bishops were compelled to sign a blank paper, which was afterwards filled with the condemnation of Flavian. These outrages, however, were subsequent to the Synodical acceptance of the Creed of Eutyches, which seems to have been the spontaneous act of the assembled Fathers. The proceedings ended by Dioscorus excommunicating the Pope, and the emperor issuing an edict in approval of the decision of the Council.

Before continuing the narrative, let us pause awhile to consider what it has already brought before us. An aged and blameless man, the friend of a Saint, and him the great champion of the faith against the heresy of the day, is found in the belief and maintenance of a doctrine which he declares to be the very doctrine which that Saint taught in opposition to that heresy. To prove it, he and his friends refer to the very words of St. Cyril;

Eustathius of Berytus quoting from him at Ephesus as follows: "We must not then conceive two natures, but one nature of the Word incarnate."[62] Moreover, it seems that St. Cyril had been called to account for this very phrase, and had appealed more than once to a passage, which is extant as he quoted it, of a work by St. Athanasius.[63] Whether the passage {297} in question is genuine is very doubtful, but that is not to the purpose; for the phrase which it contains is also attributed by St. Cyril to other Fathers, and was admitted by Catholics generally, as by St. Flavian, who deposed Eutyches, nay was indirectly adopted by the Council of Chalcedon itself.

But Eutyches did not merely insist upon a phrase; he appealed for his doctrine to the Fathers generally, "I have read the blessed Cyril, and the holy Fathers, and the holy Athanasius;" he says at Constantinople, "that they said, "Of two natures before the union," but that "after the union" they said "but one."[64] In his letter to St. Leo, he appeals in particular to St. Julius, Pope Felix, St. Gregory Thaumaturgus, St. Gregory Nazianzen, St. Basil, Atticus, and St. Proclus. He did not appeal to them unreservedly certainly, as shall be presently noticed; he allowed that they might err, and perhaps had erred, in their expressions: but it is plain, even from what has been said, that there could be no *consensus* against him, as the word is now commonly understood. It is also undeniable that, though the word "nature" is applied to our Lord's manhood by St. Ambrose, St. Gregory Nazianzen, and others, yet on the whole it is for whatever reason avoided by the previous Fathers; certainly by St. Athanasius, who uses the words "manhood," "flesh," "the man," "economy," where a later writer would have used "nature:" and the same is true of St. Hilary.[65] In like manner, the Athanasian Creed, written as it is supposed, some twenty years before the date of Eutyches, does not contain the word "nature." Much might be said on the plausibility of the defence, which Eutyches might have made for his doctrine from the history and documents of the Church before his time.

{298} Further, Eutychus professed to subscribe heartily the decrees of the Council of Nicaea and Ephesus, and his friends appealed to the latter of these Councils and to the previous Fathers, that nothing was to be added to the Creed of the Church. "I," he says to St. Leo, "even from my elders have so understood, and from my childhood have so been instructed, as the holy and Ecumenical Council at Nicaea of the three hundred and eighteen most blessed Bishops settled the faith, and which the Holy Council held at Ephesus maintained and defined anew as the only faith; and I have never understood otherwise than as the right or only true orthodox faith hath enjoined." He says at the Latrocinium, "When I declared that my faith was conformable to the decision of Nicaea, confirmed at Ephesus, they demanded that I should add some words to it; and I, fearing to act contrary to the decrees of the First Council of Ephesus and of the Council of Nicaea, desired that your holy Council might be made acquainted with it, since I was ready to submit to whatever you should approve."[66] Dioscorus states the matter more strongly: "We have heard," he says, "what this Council" of Ephesus "decreed, that if any one affirm or opine anything, or raise any question, beyond the Creed aforesaid" of Nicaea, "he is to be condemned."[67] It is remarkable that the Council of Ephesus, which laid down this rule, had itself {299} sanctioned the δεοτόκος, an addition, greater perhaps than any before or since, to the letter of the primitive faith.

Further, Eutyches appealed to Scriptures, and denied that a human nature was there given to our Lord; and this appeal obliged him in consequence to refuse an unconditional assent to the Councils and Fathers, though he so confidently spoke about them at other times. It was urged against him that the Nicene Council itself had introduced into the Creed extra-scriptural terms. "'I have never found in Scripture,' he said, reports one of the Priests who were sent to him, "'that there are two natures.' I replied, 'Neither is the Consubstantiality,'" the Homoüsion of Nicaea, "'to be found in the Scriptures, but in the Holy Fathers, who well understood them and faithfully expounded them.'"[68] Accordingly, on another occasion, a report was made of him, that "he professed himself ready to assent to the Exposition of Faith made by the Holy Fathers of the Nicene and Ephesine Councils, and he engaged to subscribe their interpretations. However, if there were any accidental fault or error in any expressions which they made, this he would neither blame nor accept; but only search the Scriptures, as being surer than the expositions of the Fathers; that since the time of the Incarnation of God the Word . . . . he worshipped one Nature: that the doctrine that our Lord Jesus Christ came of Two Natures personally united, this it was that he had not learned from the expositions of the Holy Fathers; nor did he accept, if aught was read to him from any author to that effect, because the Holy Scriptures, as he said, were better than the teaching of the Fathers."[69] This appeal to the Scriptures will remind us of what has lately been said of the school of Theodore in the history of Nestorianism, and of the challenge of the Arians to St. Avitus before the Gothic King.[70] It {300} had also been the characteristic of heresy in the antecedent period. St. Hilary brings together a number of instances in point, from the history of Marcellus, Photinus, Sabellius, Montanus, and Manes; then he adds, "They all speak Scripture without the sense of Scripture, and profess a faith without faith."[71]

Once more, the Council of Latrocinium, though tyrannized over by Dioscorus in the matter of St. Flavian, certainly did acquit Eutyches and accept his doctrine canonically, and, as it would appear, cordially; though their change at Chalcedon, and the subsequent variations of the East, make it a matter of little moment how they decided. The Acts of Constantinople were read to the Fathers of the Latrocinium; when they came to the part where Eusebius of Dorylaeum, the accuser of Eutyches, asked him whether he confessed Two Natures after the Incarnation, and the Consubstantiality according to the flesh, the Fathers broke in upon the reading:—"Away with Eusebius; burn him; burn him alive; cut him in two; as he divided, so let him be divided."[72] The Council seems to have been unanimous, with the exception of the Pope's Legates, in the restoration of Eutyches; a more complete decision can hardly be imagined. It is true the whole number of signatures now extant, one hundred and eight, may seem small out of a thousand, the number of Sees in the East; but the attendance of Councils always bore a representative character. The whole number of East and West was about eighteen hundred, yet the Second Ecumenical Council was attended by only one hundred and fifty, which is but a twelfth part of the whole number; the Third Council by about two hundred, or a ninth; the Council of Nicaea itself numbered only three hundred and eighteen Bishops. Moreover, when we look through the names subscribed to the Synodal decision, we {301} find that the misbelief, or misapprehension, or weakness, to which this great offence must be attributed, was no local phenomenon, but the unanimous sin of every patriarchate and every school of the East. Three out of the four Patriarchs were in favour of the heresiarch, the fourth being on his trial. Of these, Domnus of Antioch and Juvenal of Jerusalem acquitted him, on the ground of his confessing the faith of Nicaea and Ephesus; and Domnus was a man of the fairest and purest character, and originally a disciple of St. Euthemius, however inconsistent on this occasion, and ill-advised in former steps of his career. Dioscorus, violent and bad man as he showed himself, had been Archdeacon to St. Cyril, whom he attended at the Council of Ephesus; and was on this occasion supported by those Churches which had so nobly stood by their Patriarch Athanasius in the great Arian conflict. These three Patriarchs were supported by the Exarchs of Ephesus and

Caesarea in Cappadocia; and both of them, as well as Domnus and Juvenal, were supported in turn by their subordinate Metropolitans. Even the Sees under the influence of Constantinople, which was the remaining sixth division of the East, took part with Eutyches. Thus among the signatures to his acquittal are the Bishops of Dyrrachium, of Heraclea in Macedonia, of Messene in the Peloponnese, of Sebaste in Armenia, of Tarsus, of Damascus, of Berytus, of Bostra in Arabia, of Amida in Mesopotamia, of Himeria in Osrhoëne, of Babylon, of Arsinoe in Egypt, and of Cyrene. The Bishops of Palestine, of Macedonia, and of Achaia, where the keen eye of St. Athanasius had detected the doctrine in its germ, while Apollinarianism was but growing into form, were his actual partizans. Barsumas, a Syrian Abbot, ignorant of Greek, attended the Latrocinium, as the representative of the monks of his nation, whom he formed into a force, material or moral, of a thousand strong, and {302} whom at that infamous assembly he cheered on to the murder of St. Flavian.

Such was the state of Eastern Christendom in the year 449; a heresy, appealing to the Fathers, to the Creed, and above all to Scripture, was by a general Council, professing to be Ecumenical, received as true in the person of its promulgator. If the East could determine a matter of faith independently of the West, certainly the Monophysite heresy was established as Apostolic truth in all its provinces from Macedonia to Egypt.

There had been a time in the history of Christianity when it had been Athanasius against the world, and the world against Athanasius. The need and straitness of the Church had been great, and one man was raised up for her deliverance. In this second necessity, who was the destined champion of her who cannot fail? whence did he come, and what was his name? He came with an augury of victory upon him, which even Athanasius could not show; it was Leo, Bishop of Rome.

Leo's augury of success, which even Athanasius had not, was this, that he was seated in the chair of St. Peter and the heir of his prerogatives. In the very beginning of the controversy, St. Peter Chrysologus had urged this grave consideration upon Eutyches himself, in words which have already been cited: "I exhort you, my venerable brother," he had said, "to submit yourself in every thing to what has been written by the blessed Pope of Rome; for St. Peter, who lives and presides in his own See, gives the true faith to those who seek it."[73] This voice had come from Ravenna, and now after the Latrocinium it was echoed back from the depths of Syria by the learned Theodoret. "That all-holy See," he says in a letter to one of the Pope's Legates, "has the office of heading (ἡγεμονίαν) the whole world's Churches for many reasons; and above all others, {303} because it has remained free of the communion of heretical taint, and no one of heterodox sentiments hath sat in it, but it hath preserved the Apostolic grace unsullied."[74] And a third testimony in encouragement of the faithful at the same dark moment issued from the Imperial Court of the West. "We are bound," says Valentinian to the Emperor of the East, "to preserve inviolate in our times the prerogative of particular reverence to the blessed Apostle Peter; that the most blessed Bishop of Rome, to whom Antiquity assigned the priesthood over all (κατὰ π ντ ων) may have place and opportunity of judging concerning the faith and the priests."[75] Nor had Leo himself been wanting at the same time in "the confidence" he had "obtained from the most blessed Peter and head of the Apostles, that he had authority to defend the truth for the peace of the Church."[76] Such are the words with which we are introduced to the Council of Chalcedon.

The Council met on the 8th of October, 451, and was attended by the largest number of Bishops of any Council before or since; some say by as many as six hundred and thirty. Of these, only four came from the West, two Roman Legates and two Africans.[77]

Its proceedings were opened by the Pope's Legates, who said that they had it in charge from the Bishop of Rome, "which is the head of all the Churches," to demand that Dioscorus should not sit, on the ground that "he had presumed to hold as Council without the authority of the Apostolic See, which had never been done nor was lawful to do."[78] This was immediately allowed them.

The next act of the Council was to give admission to Theodoret, who had been deposed at the Latrocinium. The Imperial officers present urged his {304} admission on the ground that "the most holy Archbishop Leo that restored him to the Episcopal office, and the most pious Emperor has ordered that he should assist at the holy Council."[79]

Presently, a charge was brought forward against Dioscorus, that though the Legates had presented a letter from the Pope to the Council, it had not been read. Dioscorus admitted not only the fact, but its relevancy; but alleged in excuse that he had twice ordered it to be read in vain.

In the course of the reading of the Acts of the Latrocinium and Constantinople, a number of Bishops moved from the side of Dioscorus and placed themselves with the opposite party. When Peter, Bishop of Corinth, crossed over, the Orientals whom he joined shouted, "Peter thinks as does Peter; orthodox Bishop welcome."

In the second Session the duty of the Fathers was to draw up a confession of faith condemnatory of the heresy. A committee was formed for the purpose, and the Creed of Nicaea and Constantinople was read; then some of the Epistles of St. Cyril; lastly, St. Leo's Tome, which had been passed over in silence at the Latrocinium. Some discussion followed upon the last of these documents, but at length the Bishops cried out, "This is the faith of the Fathers; this is the faith of the Apostles: we all believe thus; the orthodox believe thus; anathema to him who does not believe thus. Peter has thus spoken through Leo; the Apostles taught thus." Readings from the Fathers followed; and then some days were allowed for private discussion, before drawing up the confession of faith.

During the interval, Dioscorus was tried and condemned; the sentence was pronounced against him by the Pope's Legates, and ran this: "The most holy Archbishop of Rome, Leo, through us and this present Council, with the Apostle St. Peter, who is {305} the rock and foundation of the Catholic Church and of the orthodox faith, deprives him of the Episcopal dignity and every sacerdotal ministry."

In the fourth Session the question of the definition of faith came on again, and the Council got no further than this, that it received the definition of the three previous Ecumenical Councils, but would not add to them. One hundred and sixty Bishops however subscribed the Tome of St. Leo.

In the fifth Session the question came on once more; a definition of faith was the result of the labours of the committee, and was accepted by the great majority of the Council. The Bishops cried out, "We are all satisfied with the definition; it is the faith of the Fathers; anathema to him who thinks otherwise: drive out the Nestorians." Objectors appeared, but Anatolius, the new Patriarch of Constantinople, asked "Did not every one yesterday consent to the definition of faith?" The Bishops answered, "Everyone consented; we do not believe otherwise; it is the Faith of the Fathers; be it set down that Holy Mary is the Mother of God: let this be added to the Creed; put out the Nestorians."[80] The objectors were the Pope's Legates, who were supported by some Orientals: those clear-sighted, firm-minded Latins understood full well what and what alone was the true expression of orthodox doctrine under the emergency of the existing heresy. They had been instructed to induce the Council to pass a declaration to the effect, that Christ was not only "of" but "in" two natures. However, they did not enter upon disputation on the point, but they used a more intelligible argument: "If the Fathers did not consent to the letter of the blessed Bishop Leo," they would leave the Council and go home. The Imperial officers took the part of the Legates. The Council however persisted: "Every one approved the definition; let {306} it be subscribed: he who refuses to subscribe it is a heretic." They even proceeded to refer it to Divine inspiration. The officers asked if they received St. Leo's Tome; they answered that they had subscribed it, but that they would not introduce its contents into their definition of faith. "We are for no other definition," they said; "nothing is wanting in this."

Notwithstanding, the Pope's Legates gained their point through the support of the Emperor Marcian, who had succeeded Theodosius. A fresh committee was obtained under the threat that, if they resisted, the Council should be transferred to the West. Some voices were raised against this measure; the cries were repeated against the Roman part, "They are Nestorians; let them go to Rome." The Imperial officers remonstrated, "Dioscorus said, 'Of two natures;' Leo says, 'Two natures:' which will you follow, Leo or Dioscorus?" On their answering "Leo," they continued, "Well then, add to the definition according to the judgment of our most holy Leo." Nothing more was to be said. The committee immediately proceeded to their work, and in a short time returned to the assembly with such a definition as the Pope required. After reciting the Creed of Nicaea and Constantinople, it observes, "This Creed were sufficient for the perfect knowledge of religion, but the enemies of the truth have invented novel expressions;" and therefore it proceeds to state the faith more explicitly. When this was read through, the Bishops all exclaimed, "This is the faith of the Fathers; we all follow it." And thus ended the controversy once for all.

The Council, after its termination, addressed a letter to St. Leo; in it the Fathers acknowledge him as "constituted interpreter of the voice of Blessed Peter,"[81] {307} with an allusion to St. Peter's Confession in Matthew xvi., and speak of him as "the very one commissioned with the guardianship of the Vine by the Saviour."

Such is the external aspect of those proceedings by which the Catholic faith has been established in Christendom against the Monophysites. That the definition passed at Chalcedon is the Apostolic Truth once delivered to the Saints is most firmly to be received, from faith in that overruling Providence which is by special promise extended over the acts of the Church; moreover, that it is in simple accordance with the faith of St. Athanasius, St. Gregory Nazianzen, and all the other Fathers, will be evident to the theological student in proportion as he becomes familiar with their works; but the historical account of the Council is this, that a doctrine which the Creed did not declare, which the Fathers did not unanimously witness, and which some eminent Saints had almost in set terms opposed, which the whole East refused as a symbol, not once, but twice, patriarch by patriarch, metropolitan by metropolitan, first by the mouth of above a hundred, then by the mouth of above six hundred of its Bishops, and refused upon the grounds of its being an addition to the Creed, was forced upon the Council, not indeed as a Creed, yet, on the other hand, not for subscription merely, but for its acceptance as a definition of faith under the sanction of an anathema, forced on the Council by the resolution of the Pope of the day, acting through his Legates and supported by the civil power.

It cannot be supposed that such a transaction would approve itself to the Churches of Egypt, and the event showed it: they disowned the authority of the Council, and called its adherents Chalcedonians,[82] and Synodites.[83] Here was the West tyranniz-ing {308} over the East, forcing it into agreement with itself, resolved to have one and one only form of words, rejecting the definition of faith which the East had drawn up in Council, bidding it and making it frame another, dealing peremptorily and sternly with the assembled Bishops, and casting contempt on the most sacred traditions of Egypt. What was Eutyches to them? He might be guilty or innocent; they gave him up: Dioscorus had given him up at Chalcedon;[84] they did not agree with him:[85] he was an extreme man; they would not call themselves by human titles; they were not Eutychians; Eutyches was not their master, but Athanasius and Cyril were their doctors.[86] The two great lights of their Church, the two greatest and most successful polemical Fathers that Christianity had seen, had both pronounced "One Nature Incarnate," though allowing Two before the Incarnation, and though Leo and his Council had not gone so far as to deny the phrase, they had proceeded to say what was contrary to it, to explain away, to overlay the truth, by defining that the Incarnate Saviour was "in Two Natures." At Ephesus it had been declared that the Creed should not be touched; the Chalcedonian Fathers had, not literally, but virtually added to it: by subscribing Leo's Tome, and promulgating their definition of faith, they had added what might be called, "The Creed of Pope Leo."

It is remarkable, as has been just stated, that Dioscorus, wicked man as he was in act, was of the moderate or middle school in doctrine, as the violent and able Severus after him; and from the first the great body of the protesting party disowned Eutyches, whose form of the heresy took refuge in Armenia, where it remains to this day. The Armenians alone were pure Eutychians, and {309} so zealously such that they innovated on the ancient and recognised custom of mixing water with the wine in the Holy Eucharist, and consecrated the wine by itself in token of the one nature, as they considered, of the Christ. Elsewhere both name and doctrine of Eutyches were abjured; the heretical bodies in Egypt and Syria took a title from their tenet, and formed the Monophysite communion. Their theology was at once simple and specious. They based it upon the illustration which is familiar to us in the Athanasian Creed, and which had been used by St. Gregory Nazianzen, St. Cyril, St. Augustine, Vincent of Lerins, not to say St. Leo himself. They argued that as body and soul made up one man, so God and man made up but one, though one compound Nature, in Christ. It might have been charitably hoped that their difference from the Catholics had been a simple matter of words, as it is allowed by Vigilius of Thapsa really to have been in many cases; but their refusal to obey the voice of the Church was an omen of error in their faith, and its secret heterodoxy is proved by their connexion, in spite of themselves, with the extreme or ultra party whom they so vehemently disowned. It is very observable that, ingenious as is their theory and sometimes perplexing to a disputant, the Monophysites never could shake themselves free of the Eutychians; and though they could draw intelligible lines on paper between the two doctrines, yet in fact by a hidden fatality their partizans were ever running into or forming alliance with the anathematized extreme. Thus Peter the Fuller, the Theopaschite (Eutychian), is at one time in alliance with Peter the Stammerer, who advocated the Henoticon (Monophysite). The Acephali, though separating from the latter Peter for that advocacy, and accused by Leontius of being Gaianites[87] (Eutychians), are considered {310} by Facundus as Monophysites.[88] Timothy the Cat, who is said to have agreed with Dioscorus and Peter the Stammerer, who signed the Henoticon, that is, with two Monophysite Patriarchs, is said nevertheless, according to Anastasius, to have maintained the extreme tenet that "the Divinity is the sole nature in Christ."[89] Severus, according to Anastasius, symbolized with the Phantasiasts (Eutychians), yet he is more truly, according to Leontius, the chief doctor and leader of the Monophysites. And at one time there was a union, though temporary, between the Theodosians (Mono-physites) and the Gaianites.

Such a division of an heretical party, into the maintainers of a moderate and an extreme view, perspicuous and plausible on paper, yet in fact unreal, impracticable, and hopeless, was no new phenomenon in the history of the Church. As Eutyches put forward an extravagant tenet, which was first corrected into the Monophysite, and then relapsed recklessly into the doctrine of the Phantasiasts and the Theopaschites, so had Arius been superseded by the Eusebians, and had revived in Eunomius; and as the moderate Eusebians had formed the great body of the dissentients to the Nicene Council, so did the Monophysites include the mass of those who protested against Chalcedon; and as the Eusebians had been moderate in creed, yet unscrupulous in act, so were the Monophysites. And as the Eusebians were ever running individu-ally into pure Arianism, so did the Monophysites run into pure Eutychianism. And as the Monophysites set themselves against Pope Leo, so had the Eusebians, with even less provocation, withstood and complained of Pope Julius. In like manner, the Apollinarians had divided into two sects; one, with Timotheus, going the whole length of the inferences which the tenet of their master involved, and the more cautious {311} or timid party making an unintelligible stand with Valentinus. Again, in the history of Nestorianism, though it admitted less opportunity for division of opinion, the See of Rome was with St. Cyril in one extreme, Nestorius in the other, and between them the great Eastern party, headed by John of Antioch and Theodoret, not heretical, but for a time dissatisfied with the Council of Ephesus.

The Nestorian heresy, I have said, gave less opportunity for doctrinal varieties than the heresy of Eutyches. Its spirit was rationalizing, and had the qualities which go with rationalism. When cast out of the Roman Empire, it addressed itself, as we have seen, to a new and rich field of exertion, got possession of an Established Church, co-operated with the civil government, adopted secular fashions, and, by whatever means, pushed itself out into an Empire. Apparently, though it requires a very intimate knowledge of its history to speak, except conjecturally, it was a political power rather than a dogma, and despised the science of theology. Eutychianism, on the other hand, was mystical, severe, enthusiastic; with the exception of Severus, and one or two more, it was supported by little polemical skill; it had little hold upon the intellectual Greeks of Syria and Asia Minor, but flourished in Egypt, which was far behind the East in civilization, and among the native Syrians. Nestorianism, like Arianism before it, was a cold religion, and more fitted for the schools than for the many;[90] but the Monophysites carried the people with them. Like modern Jansenism, and unlike Nestorianism, the Monophysites were famous for their austerities. They have, or had, five Lents in the year, during which laity as well as clergy abstain not only from flesh and eggs, but from wine, oil, and fish.[91]

{312} Monachism was a characteristic part of their ecclesiastical system: their Bishops, and Maphrian or Patriarch, were always taken from the Monks, who are even said to have worn an iron shirt or breastplate as a part of their monastic habit.[92]

Severus, Patriarch of Antioch at the end of the fifth century, has already been mentioned as an exception to the general character of the Monophysites, and, by his learning and ability, may be accounted the founder of its theology. Their cause, however, had been undertaken by the Emperors themselves before him. For the first thirty years after the Council of Chalcedon, the protesting Church of Egypt had been the scene of continued tumult and bloodshed. Dioscorus had been popular with the people for his munificence, in spite of the extreme laxity of his morals, and for a while the Imperial Government did not succeed in obtaining the election of a successor. At length Proterius, a man of fair character, and the Vicar-general of

Dioscorus on his absence at Chalcedon, was chosen, consecrated, and enthroned; but the people rose against the civil authorities, and the military, coming to their defence, were attacked with stones, and pursued into a church, where they were burned alive by the mob. Next, the popular leaders prepared to intercept the supplies of grain which were destined for Constantinople; and a defensive retaliation taking place, Alexandria was starved. Then a force of two thousand men were sent for the restoration of order, and permitted themselves in scandalous excesses towards the women of Alexandria. Proterius's life was attempted, and he was obliged to be attended by a guard. The Bishops of Egypt would not submit to him; two of his own clergy, who afterwards succeeded him, Timothy and Peter, seceded, and were joined by four or five of the Bishops and by the mass of the population[93] and the Catholic {313} Patriarch was left without a communion in Alexandria. He held a council, and condemned the schismatics; and the Emperor, seconding his efforts, sent them out of the country, and enforced the laws against the Eutychians. An external quiet succeeded; then Marcian died; and then forthwith Timothy the Cat made his appearance again, first in Egypt, then in Alexandria. The people rose in his favour, and carried in triumph their persecuted champion to the great Caesarean Church, where he was consecrated Patriarch by two deprived Bishops, who had been put out of their sees, whether by a Council of Egypt or of Palestine.[94] Timothy, now raised to the Episcopal rank, began to create a new succession; he ordained Bishops for the Churches of Egypt, and drove into exile those who were in possession. The Imperial troops, who had been stationed in Upper Egypt, returned to Alexandria; the mob rose again, broke into the Church, where St. Proterius was in prayer, and murdered him. A general ejectment of the Catholic clergy throughout Egypt followed. On their betaking themselves to Constantinople to the new Emperor, Timothy and his party addressed him also. They quoted the Fathers, and demanded the abrogation of the Council of Chalcedon. Next, they demanded a conference; the Catholics said that what was once done could not be undone; they agreed, and urged it, as their very argument against Chalcedon, that it had added to the faith, and reversed former decisions.[95] After a rule of three years, Timothy was driven out and Catholicism restored; but then in turn the Monophysites rallied, and this state of warfare and alternate success continued for thirty years.

At length the Imperial Government, wearied out with a dispute which was interminable, came to {314} the conclusion that the only way of restoring peace to the Church was to abandon the Council of Chalcedon. In the year 482 was published the famous *Henoticon* or Pacification of Zeno, in which the Emperor took upon himself to determine a matter of faith. The Henoticon declared that no symbol of faith but that of the Nicene Creed, commonly so called, should be received in the Churches; it anathematized the opposite heresies of Nestorius and Eutyches, and it was silent on the question of the "One" or "Two Natures" after the Incarnation. This middle measure had the various effects which might be anticipated. It united the great body of the Eastern Bishops, who readily relapsed into the vague profession of doctrine from which they had been roused by the authority of St. Leo. All the Eastern Bishops signed this Imperial formulary. But this unanimity of the East was purchased by a breach with the West; the Popes cut off the communication between the two divisions of Christendom for thirty-five years. On the other hand, the more zealous Monophysites, disgusted at their leaders for accepting what they considered an unjustifiable compromise, split off from the heretical Churches, and formed a sect themselves, which remained without Bishops (*acephali*) for three hundred years, when at length they were received back into the communion of the Catholic Church.

Dreary and waste was the condition of the Church, and forlorn her prospects, at the period which we have been reviewing. After the brief triumph which attended the conversion of Constantine, trouble and trial had returned upon her. Her imperial protectors were failing in power or in faith. Strange forms of evil were rising in the distance and were thronging for the conflict. There was but one spot in the whole of Christendom, one voice in the whole {315} Episcopate, to which the faithful turned in hope that miserable day. In the year 493, in the Pontificate of Gelasius, the whole of the East was in the hands of traitors to Chalcedon, and the whole of the West under the tyranny of the open enemies of Nicaea. Italy was the prey of robbers; mercenary bands had overrun its territory, and barbarians were seizing on its farms and settling in its villas. The peasants were thinned by famine and pestilence; Tuscany might be even said, as Gelasius words it, to contain scarcely a single inhabitant.[96] Odoacer was sinking before Theodoric, and the Pope was changing one Arian master for another. And as if one heresy were not enough, Pelagianism was spreading with the connivance of the Bishops in the territory of Picenum. In the North of the dismembered Empire, the Britons had first been infected by Pelagianism, and now were dispossessed by the heathen Saxons. The Armoricans still preserved a witness of Catholicism in the West of Gaul; but Picardy, Champagne, and the neighbouring provinces, where some remnant of its supremacy had been found, had lately submitted to the yet heathen Clovis. The Arian kingdom of Burgundy in France, and of the Visigoths in Aquitaine and Spain, oppressed a zealous and Catholic clergy. Africa was in still more deplorable condition under the cruel sway of the Vandal Gundamond: the people indeed uncorrupted by the heresy,[97] but their clergy in exile and their worship suspended. While such was the state of the Latins, what had happened in the East? Acacius, the Patriarch of Constantinople, had secretly taken part against the Council of

Chalcedon and was under Papal excommunication. Nearly all the whole East had sided with Acacius, and a schism had begun between East and West, which lasted for thirty-five years. The Henoticon was in force, and {316} at the Imperial command had been signed by all the Patriarchs and Bishops throughout the Eastern Empire.[98] In Armenia the Churches were ripening for the pure Eutychianism which they adopted in the following Century; and in Egypt the Acephali had already broken off from the Monophysite Patriarch, were extending in the east and west of the country, and preferred the loss of the Episcopal Succession to the reception of the Council of Chalcedon. And while Monophysites or their favourers occupied the Churches of the Eastern Empire, Nestorianism was making progress in the territories beyond it. Barsumas had filled the See of Nisibis, Theodore was read in the schools of Persia, and the successive Catholici of Seleucia had abolished Monachism and were secularizing the clergy.

If then there is now a form of Christianity such that it extends throughout the world, though with varying measures of prominence or prosperity in separate places;—that it lies under the power of sovereigns and magistrates, in different ways alien to its faith;—that flourishing nations and great empires, professing or tolerating the Christian name, lie over against it as antagonists;—that schools of philosophy and learning are supporting theories, and following out conclusions hostile to it, and establishing an exegetical system subversive of its Scriptures;—that it has lost whole Churches by schism, and is now opposed by powerful communions once part of itself;—that it has been altogether or almost driven from some countries;—that in others its line of teachers is overlaid, its flocks oppressed, its Churches occupied, its property held by what may be called a duplicate succession;—that in others its members are degenerate and corrupt, and surpassed in conscientiousness and in virtue, as in gifts of intellect, by the very heretics whom it condemns;—that heresies are rife {317} and bishops negligent within its own pale;—and that amid its disorders and fears there is but one Voice for whose decisions its people wait with trust, one Name and one See to which they look with hope, and that name Peter, and that see Rome;—such a religion is not unlike the Christianity of the fifth and sixth Centuries.

---

[1] De Gubern. Dei. vii. p. 142. Elsewhere, "Apud Aquitanicos quae civitas, in locupletissimâ ac nobilissimâ sui parte non quasi lupanar fuit? Quis potentum ac divitum non in luto libidinis vixit? Haud multum matrona abest à vilitate servarum, ubi paterfamilias ancillarum maritus est? Quis autem Aquitanorum divitum non hoc fuit?" (pp. 134, 135.) "Offenduntur barbari ipsi impuritatibus nostris. Esse inter Gothos non licet scortatorem Gothum; soli inter eos praejudicio nationis ac nominis permittuntur impuri esse Romani." (p. 137.) "Quid? Hispanias nonne vel eadem vel majora forsitan vitia perdiderunt?. . . Accessit hoc ad manifestandam illic impudicitiae damnationem, ut Wandalis potissimum, id est, pudicis barbaris traderentur." (p. 137.) Of Africa and Carthage, "In urbe Christianâ, in urbe ecclesiasticâ, . . viri in semetipsis feminas profitebantur," &c. (p. 152.) <See *The Writings of Salvian, the Presbyter*, tr. J. F. O'Sullivan (New York: CIMA, 1947), pp. 190-91, 193-94, 211-12.>

[2] Dunham, Hist. Spain. vol. i. p. 112. <see note 20 to ch. 3.>

[3] Aguirr. Concil. t. 2, p. 191. <See note 20 to ch. 3.>

[4] Dunham, p. 125.

[5] Hist. Franc. iii. 10.

[6] Ch. 39.

[7] Greg. Dial. iii. 30.

[8] Ibid. 29.

[9] Gibbon, Hist. Ch. 37.

[10] De Glor. Mart. i. 25.

[11] Ibid. 80.

[12] Ibid. 79.

[13] Vict. Vit. i. 14. <Victor, bishop of Vite, fl. 480, *Historia persecutionis in Africae Provinciae*, PL 58:179-276.>

[14] De Gub. D. iv. p. 73.

[15] Ibid. v. p. 88.

[16] Epp. i. 31.

[17] Hist. vi. 23.

[18] Cf. Assem. t. i. p. 351, not. 4, t. 3, p. 393. <Joseph Assemani (1710-1782), *Codex liturgicus ecclesiae universae in XV libros distributae* (Rome, 1749-66).>

[19] Baron. Ann. 432, 47. <Cesare Baronius (1538-1607), *Annales ecclesiastici*, (1588-1607), in 12 vols.>

[20] Gibbon, Hist. Ch. 36.

[21] Baron. Ann. 471, 18.

[22] Vict. Vit. iv. 4.

[23] Vict. Vit. ii. 13-15.

[24] Aguirr. Conc. t. 2, p. 262. <See note 20 to ch. 3>

[25] Aguirr. ibid. p. 232.

[26] Theod. Hist. v. 2.

[27] c. Ruff. i. 4.

[28] Ep. 15.

[29] Ep. 16.

[30] Aug. Epp. 43, 7.

[31] Assem. iij. p. 68.

[32] Ibid. t. 3, p. 84, note 3.

[33] Wegnern, Proleg. in Theod. Opp. p. ix. <August F. V. von Wegnern, *Theodori Antiocheni. . . quae supersunt opera* (Leipzig, 1831).>

[34] De Ephrem Syr. p. 61. <see note below.>

[35] Lengerke, de Ephrem Syr. pp. 73-75. <Cäsar von Lengerke (1803-55), *De Ephraemi Syri arte hermeneutica liber* (Königsberg: J.H. Bon, 1831).>

[36] δεςπότου, vid La Croze, Thesaur. Ep. t. 3. § 145. <Mathurier Veyssière de la Croze (1661-1739), *Theasuri epistolici Lacroziani tomi 1-3*, ed. J. L. Uhlius (Leipzig, 1742-46).>

[37] Montf. Coll. Nov. t. 2, p. 227.

[38] Rosenmuller, Hist. Interpr. t. 3, p. 278. <Io. Georgii Rosenmülleri (1736-1815), *Historia interpretationis librorum sacrorum in ecclesia christiana, inde ab apostolurum aetate usque ad Origenem* (Hildburg: Jo. G. Hanisch, 1795-1814), in 5 vols.>

[39] Lengerke, de Ephr. Syr. pp. 165-167. <See note 34 above.>

[40] Ernest. de Proph. Mess. p. 462. <J. A. Ernesti, *Narratio critica de interpretatione prophetarum messianarum in ecclesia christiana* in *Opuscula theologica* (Leipzig, 1773).>

[41] Eccl. Theol. iij. 12.

[42] Professor Lee's Serm. Oct. 1838, p. 144-152. <Either James Prince Lee (1804-69), Master at Rugby at that time and subsequently Bishop of Manchester, or Samuel Lee (1783-1852), canon of Bristol.>

[43] Noris. Opp. t. 2, p. 112. <Enrico Cardinal Noris (1631-1704), *Opera varia* (Lyon: Posuil, 1707) including his *Historia pelagiana* and *Vindiciae augustinianae*.

[44] Augusti. Euseb. Em. Opp. <Johann C. W. Augusti (1771-1841), critical editor of *Eusebii Emesini quae supersunt opsucula* . . . (Elberfeld, 1829).

[45] Asseman. p. cmxxv.

[46] Hoffman, Gram. Syr. Proleg. § 4. <A. G. Hoffmann (1796-1864, Grammaticae syriacae libri III (Halae: Impensis Orphanotrophei, 1827).>

[47] The educated Persians were also acquainted with Syriac. Assem. t. i. p. 351, note.

[48] Asseman. p. lxx.

[49] Euseb. Praep. vi. 10.

[50] Tillemont, Mem. t. 7. p. 77.

[51] Gibbon, ch. 47.

[52] Asseman, p. lxxviii.

[53] Gibbon, ibid.

[54] Asseman, t. 2, p. 403, t. 3, p. 393.

[55] Asseman. t. 3, p. 67.

[56] Gibbon, ibid.

[57] Assem. p. lxxvi.

[58] Ibid. 3, p. 441.

[59] Ch. 47.

[60] Fleur. Hist. xxvii. 29. <See note 22 to ch. 3.>

[61] Gibbon, ch. 47.

[62] Concil. Hard. t. 2. p. 127. <Jean Hardouin (1646-1729), *Conciliorum collectio regia maxima*. . . (Paris, 1714-15), 12 vols.>

[63] Petav. de Incarn. iv. 6, § 4. <in D. Petavius, *De theologicis dogmatibus* (1643-1650).>

[64] Concil. Hard. t. 2. p. 167.

[65] Vid. Athan. Ar. Oxf. trans. p. 345, note *g*, p. 480, note *d*.

[66] Fleury, Oxf. tr. xxvii. 39. <See note 22 to ch. 3.>

[67] Ibid. 41. In like manner, St. Athanasius in the foregoing age had said, "The faith confessed at Nicaea by the Fathers, according to the Scriptures, is sufficient for the overthrow of all misbelief." ad Epict. init. Elsewhere, however, he explains his statement, "The decrees of Nicaea are right, and sufficient for the overthrow of all heresy, *especially* the Arian." ad Max. fin. St. Gregory Nazianzen, in like manner, appeals to Nicaea; but he "adds an explanation on the doctrine of the Holy Spirit which was left deficient by the Fathers, because the question had not been raised." Ep. 102, init. This exclusive maintenance, and yet extension of the Creed, according to the exigences of the times, is instanced in other Fathers. Vid. Athan. Oxf. tr. p. 49, note *p*.

[68] Fleury, ibid. 27. <See note 22 to ch. 3.>

[69] Concil. Hard. t. 2, p. 142.

[70] supr. p. 240.

[71] Ad Const. ii. 9. Vid. Athan. Ar. Oxf. tr. p. 386, note.

[72] Concil. Hard. t. 2, p. 162.

[73] Fleury, Hist. Oxf. tr. xxvii. 37. <See note 22 to ch. 3.>

[74] Ep. 116.

[75] Conc. Hard. t. 2, p. 36.

[76] Ep. 43.

[77] Fleury, Hist. Oxf. tr. xxviii. 17, note *l.*

[78] Concil. Hard. t. 2, p. 68.

[79] Fleury, Oxf. tr. xxviii. 2, 3.

[80] Ibid. 20.

[81] Conc. Hard. t. 2, p. 656.

[82] I cannot find my reference for this fact; the sketch is formed from notes made some years since, though I have now verified them.

[83] Leont. de Sect. v. p. 512.

[84] Concil. Hard. t. 2, p. 99, vid. also p. 418.

[85] Renaud. Patr. Alex. p. 115. <See note 21 to ch. 3).>

[86] Assem. B. O. t. 2, pp. 133-137. <*Bibliotheca orientalis Clementino vaticana.* ed., G. Assemani (Roma: typis Sacrae Congregationis de Propaganda fidei, 1719-28).>

[87] Leont. de. Sect. vii. pp. 521, 2. <see note to ch. >

[88] Fac. i. 5, circ. init.

[89] Hodeg. 20, p. 319. <The *Hodegos* was a work written by Anastasius the Sinaite against the Monophysites (PG 89:274).>

[90] i.e. in Greece: "Sanctiores aures plebis quam corda sunt sacerdotum" S. Hil. cóntr. Auxent. 6. It requires some research to account for its hold on the barbarians.. Vid. Supr. pp. 271, 2.

[91] Gibbon, ch. 47.

[92] Assem. B. O. t. 2, de Monoph. circ. fin. <see note 84 above.>

[93] Leont. Sect. v. init.

[94] Tillemont, t. 15, p. 784.

[95] Tillemont, Mem. t. 15, pp. 790-811.

[96] Gibbon, Hist. ch. 36, fin.

[97] Ibid.

[98] Gibbon, Hist. ch. 47.

CHAPTER VI.

ILLUSTRATIONS CONTINUED.

SECTION I.

APPLICATION OF THE SECOND TEST OF FIDELITY IN DEVELOPMENT.

IT appears then that there has been a certain general type of Christianity in every age, by which it is known at first sight, as any physical production, animal or vegetable, is named at once by those to whom such forms of nature are familiar; or as some work of literature or art is at once assigned to its right author by the critic, difficult as may be the analysis of that specific impression by which he is enabled to do so. And it appears that this type has remained entire from first to last, in spite of that process of development which seems to be attributed by all parties, for good or bad, to the doctrines, rites, and usages in which Christianity consists; or, in other words, that the changes which have taken place in Christianity have not been such as to destroy that type,—that is, that they are not corruptions, because they are consistent with that type. Here then, in the *preservation of type*, we have a first proof of the fidelity of the existing developments of Christianity. Now we proceed to a second.

When the Christian developments are spoken of, it is sometimes supposed that they are deductions {319} and divertions made at random, according to accident or the caprice of individuals; whereas, if they really deserve the name, they must be conducted all along on definite and continuous principles, which determine their course. Thus Judaism did but develop, while it bore in mind its imperfection, and its subordination to a coming Messiah; and it became corrupt as soon, and in proportion, as it fancied itself self-sufficient and rejected the Gospel. What then are the principles of Christian development? Have they been the same from the first to the present age? For *continuity of principle* will become a second evidence that the so-called Catholic doctrines are true developments, and not corruptions. Principles of development, thus continuous, may I think be assigned; and I proceed to mention two or three by way of specimen.

§ 1.

Scripture and its Mystical Interpretation.

Several passages have occurred in the course of the Chapters last preceding, to suggest the rule of development on which a few words are first to be said. Theodore's exclusive adoption of the literal, and repudiation of the mystical interpretation of Scripture, suggests to us the consideration of the latter, as one of the characteristic conditions or principles on which the development of doctrine has proceeded. Again, Christianity developed, as we have incidentally seen, in the form, first, of a Catholic, then of a Papal Church. Now Scripture was made the rule on which this development proceeded in each case, and Scripture moreover interpreted in a mystical sense; and, whereas at first certain texts were inconsistently confined to the letter, and a Millenium was in consequence expected, the very course of events, as time went on, interpreted the prophesies {320} about the Church more truly, and that first in respect of her prerogative as occupying the *orbis terrarum*, next in support of the claims of the See of St. Peter.[1]

This is but one specimen of a certain law of Christian development, which is this, —a reference to Scripture throughout, and
especially in its mystical sense.

1. This is a characteristic which will become more and more
evident to us, the more we look for it. The divines of the Church
are in every age engaged in regulating themselves by Scripture,
appealing to Scripture in proof of their conclusions, and exhort-
ing and teaching in the thoughts and language of Scripture.
Scripture may be said to be the medium in which the mind of the
Church has energized and developed.[2] When St. Methodius
would enforce the doctrine of vows of celibacy, he refers to the
book of Numbers; and if St. Irenaeus proclaims the dignity of St.
Mary, it is from a comparison of St. Luke's Gospel with Genesis.
And thus St. Cyprian, in his Testimonies, rests the prerogatives
of martyrdom, as indeed the whole circle of Christian doctrine,
on the declaration of certain texts; and when in his letter to
Antonian he seems to allude to Purgatory, he refers to our Lord's
words about "the prison" and "paying the last farthing." And if
St. Ignatius exhorts to unity, {321} it is from St. Paul; and he
quotes St. Luke against the Phantasiasts of his day. We have a
first instance of this law in the Epistle of St. Polycarp, and a last
in the practical works of St. Alphonso Liguori. St. Cyprian, or St.
Ambrose, or St. Bede, or St. Bernard, or St. Carlo, or such
popular books as Horstius's *Paradisus Animae*, are specimens of
a rule which is too obvious to need formal proof. It is exemplified in the theological decisions of St. Athanasius in the fourth
century, and of St. Thomas in the thirteenth; in the structure of
the Canon Law, and in the Bulls and Letters of Popes. It is
instanced in the notion so long prevalent in the Church, which
philosophers of this day do not allow us to forget, that all truth,
all science, must be derived from the inspired volume. And it is
recognised as well as exemplified; recognised as distinctly by

writers of the Society of Jesus, as it is copiously exemplified by the Ante-nicene Fathers.

"Scriptures are called canonical," says Salmeron, "as having been received and set apart by the Church into the Canon of sacred books, and because they are to us a rule of right belief and good living; also because they ought to rule and moderate all other doctrines, laws, writings, whether ecclesiastical, apocryphal, or human. For as these agree with them, or at least do not disagree, so far are they admitted; but they are repudiated and reprobated so far as they differ from them even in the least matter."[3] Again: "The main subject of Scripture is nothing else than to treat of the God-Man, or the Man-God, Christ Jesus, not only in the New Testament, which is open, but in the Old . . . . . . For whereas Scripture contains nothing but the precepts of belief and conduct, or faith and works, the end and the means towards it, the Creator and the Creature, love of God, and of our neighbour, creation and redemption, {322} and whereas all these are found in Christ, it follows that Christ is the proper subject of Canonical Scripture. For all matters of faith, whether concerning Creator or creatures, are recapitulated in Jesus, whom every heresy denies, according to that text, "Every spirit that denies (*solvit*) Jesus is not of God;" for He as man is united to the Godhead, and as God to the manhood, to the Father from whom He is born, to the Holy Ghost who proceeds at once from Christ and the Father, to Mary His most Holy Mother, to the Church, to Scriptures, Sacraments, Saints, Angels, the Blessed, to Divine Grace, to the authority and ministers of the Church, so that it is rightly said that every heresy denies Jesus."[4] And again: "Holy Scripture is so fashioned and composed by the Holy Ghost as to be accommodated to all plans, times, persons, difficulties, dangers, diseases, the expulsion of evil, the obtaining of good, the stifling of errors, the establishment of doctrines, the ingrafting of virtues, the averting of vices. Hence it is deservedly compared by St. Basil to a dispensary which supplies various medicines against every complaint. From it did the Church in the age of Martyrs draw her firmness and fortitude; in the age of Doctors, her wisdom and light of knowledge; in the time of heretics, the overthrow of error; in time of prosperity, humility and moderation; fervour and diligence, in a lukewarm time; and in times of depravity and growing abuse, reformation from corrupt living and return to the first estate."[5]

"Holy Scripture," says Cornelius à Lapide, "contains the beginnings of all theology: for theology is nothing but the science of conclusions which are drawn from principles certain to faith, and therefore is of all sciences most august as well as certain; but the principles of faith and faith itself doth Scripture contain; whence it evidently {323} follows that Holy Scripture lays down those principles of theology by which the theologian begets of the mind's reasoning his demonstrations. He, then, who thinks he can tear away Scholastic Science from the work of commenting on Holy Scripture is hoping for offspring without a mother."[6] Again: "What is the subject-matter of Scripture? Must I say it in a word? Its aim is *de omni scibili;* it embraces in its bosom all studies, all that can be known: and thus it is a certain university of sciences containing all sciences either "formally" or "eminently.""[7]

Nor am I aware that Post-tridentine writers deny that the whole Catholic faith may be proved from Scripture, though they would certainly maintain that it is not to be found on the surface of it, nor in such sense that it may be gained from Scripture without the aid of Tradition.

2. And this has been the doctrine of all ages of the Church, as is shown by the disinclination of her teachers to confine themselves to the mere literal interpretation of Scripture. Her most subtle and powerful method of proof, whether in ancient or modern times, is the mystical sense, which is so frequently used in doctrinal controversy as on many occasions to supersede any

other. Thus the Council of Trent appeals to the peace-offering spoken of in Malachi i. in proof of the Eucharistic Sacrifice; to the water and blood issuing from our Lord's side, and to the mention of "waters" in the Apocalypse, in admonishing on the subject of the mixture of water with the wine in the Oblation. Thus Bellarmine defends Monastic celibacy by our Lord's words in Matthew xix., and refers to "We went through fire and water," &c. in the Psalm, as an argument for Purgatory; and these, as is plain, are but specimens of a rule. Now, on turning to primitive controversy, we find this method of interpretation to be the {324} very basis of the proof of the Catholic doctrine of the Holy Trinity. Whether we betake ourselves to the Ante-nicene writers or the Nicene, certain texts will meet us, which do not obviously refer to that doctrine, yet are put forward as palmary proofs of it. Such are, in respect of our Lord's divinity, "My heart is inditing of a good matter," or "has burst with a good Word;" "The Lord made" or "possessed Me in the beginning of His ways;" "I was with Him, in whom He delighted;" "In thy Light shall we see Light;" "Who shall declare His generation?" "She is the Breath of the Power of God;" and "His Eternal Power and Godhead." On the other hand, the School of Antioch, which adopted the literal interpretation, was the very metropolis of heresy. Not to speak of Lucian, whose history is but imperfectly known,—one of the first masters of this school, and also teacher of Arius and his principal supporters,—Diodorus and Theodore of Mopsuestia, who were the most eminent masters of literalism in the succeeding generation, were, as we have seen, the forerunners of Nestorianism. The case had been the same in a stil earlier age;—the Jews clung to the literal sense of the Old Testament and rejected the Gospel; the Christian Apologists proved its divinity by means of the allegorical. The formal connexion of this mode of interpretation with Christian theology is noticed by Porphyry, who speaks of Origen and others as borrowing it from heathen philosophy, both in explanation of the Old Testament and in defence of their own doctrine. It may be almost laid down as an historical fact, that the mystical interpretation and orthodoxy will stand or fall together. This is clearly seen, as regards the primitive theology, by a recent writer, in the course of a Dissertation upon St. Ephrem. After observing that Theodore of Heraclea, Eusebius, and Diodorus gave a systematic opposition to the mystical interpretation, {325} which had a sort of sanction from Antiquity and the orthodox Church, he proceeds; "Ephrem is not as sober in his interpretations, *nor could he be, since* he was a zealous disciple of the orthodox faith. For all those who are most eminent in such sobriety were as far as possible removed from the faith of the Councils. . . . On the other hand, all who retained the faith of the Church never entirely dispensed with the spiritual sense of the Scriptures. For the Councils watched over the orthodox faith; nor was it safe in those ages, as we learn especially from the instance of Theodore of Mopsuestia, to desert the spiritual for an exclusive cultivation of the literal method. Moreover, the allegorical interpretation, even when the literal sense was not injured, was also preserved; because in those times, when both heretics and Jews in controversy were stubborn in their objections to Christian doctrine, maintaining that the Messiah was yet to come, or denying the abrogation of the Sabbath and ceremonial law, or ridiculing the Christian doctrine of the Trinity, and especially that of Christ's Divine Nature, under such circumstances ecclesiastical writers found it to their purpose, in answer to such exceptions, violently to refer every part of Scripture by allegory to Christ and His Church."[8]

With this passage from a learned German, illustrating the bearing of the allegorical method upon the Judaic and Athanasian controversies, it will be well to compare the following passage from the latitudinarian Hales's "Golden Remains," as directed against the theology of Rome. "The literal, plain, and uncontroversable meaning of Scripture," he says, "without any addition or supply by way of interpretation, is that alone which for ground of faith we are necessarily bound to accept; except it be there, where the Holy Ghost Himself treads us out another way. I take not this to be any particular conceit of {326} mine but that unto which our Church stands necessarily bound. When we receded from the Church of Rome, one motive was, because she added unto Scripture her glosses as Canonical, to supply what the plain text of Scripture could not yield. If, in place of hers, we set up our own glosses, thus to do were nothing else but to pull down Baal, and set up an Ephod, to run round and meet the Church of Rome again in the same point in which at first we left her. This doctrine of the literal sense was never grievous or prejudicial to any, but only to those who were inwardly conscious that their positions were not sufficiently grounded. When Cardinal Cajetan, in the days of our grandfathers, had forsaken that vein of postilling and allegorising on Scripture, which for a long time had prevailed in the Church, and betaken himself unto the literal sense, it was a thing so distasteful unto the Church of Rome that he was forced to find out many shifts and make many apologies for himself. The truth is, (as it will appear to him that reads his writings,) this sticking close to the literal sense was that alone which made him to shake off many of those tenets upon which the Church of Rome and the reformed Churches differ. But when the importunity of the reformers, and the great credit of Calvin's writings in that kind, had forced the divines of Rome to level their interpretations by the same line; when they saw that no pains, no subtlety of wit was strong enough to defeat the literal evidence of Scripture, it drove them on those desperate shoals, on which at this day they stick, to call in question, as far as they durst, the credit of the Hebrew text, and countenance against it a corrupt translation; to add traditions unto Scripture, and to make the Church's interpretation, so pretended, to be above exception."[9]

He presently adds concerning the allegorical sense: "If we absolutely condemn these interpretations, {327} then must we condemn a great part of Antiquity, who are very much conversant in this kind of interpreting. For the most partial for Antiquity cannot choose but see and confess thus much, that for the literal sense, the interpreters of our own times, because of their skill in the original languages, their care of pressing the circumstances and coherence of the text, of comparing like places of Scripture with like, have generally surpassed the best of the ancients."[10]

The use of Scripture then, especially its spiritual or second sense, as a medium of thought and deduction, is a characteristic principle of the developments of doctrine in the Church.

§ 2.

Supremacy of Faith.

Though, in the two preceding Chapters, our sole business was to take an external view of Christianity, as it would appear to a bystander, yet some of the principles on which it has developed came, as it were, to the surface, and were incidentally mentioned. Such was the rejection of the mere literal interpretation of Scripture on which I have been speaking; and such again was its special preference of Faith to Reason, which was so great a jest to Celsus and Julian.

The latter principle, when brought out into words, is as follows: that belief is in itself better than unbelief; that it is safer to believe; that we must begin with believing, and that conviction will follow; that as for the reasons of believing, they are for the most part implicit, and but slightly recognised by the mind that is under their influence; that they consist moreover rather of presumptions and guesses, ventures after the truth than of accurate proofs; and that probable arguments are sufficient {328} for conclusions which we even embrace as most certain, and turn to the most important uses. On the other hand, it has ever been the heretical principle to prefer Reason to Faith, and to hold that things must be considered true only so far as they are proved. This shall be shown in the words of Locke, and will illustrate the ecclesiastical principle of Faith by the contrast:—

He says, "Whatever God hath revealed is certainly true; no doubt can be made of it. This is the proper object of Faith; but whether it be a divine revelation or no, reason must judge."[11] Now, if he merely means that proofs can be given for Revelation, and that Reason comes in logical order before Faith, such a doctrine is in no sense uncatholic; but he certainly holds that for individuals to act on Faith without Reason, or to make Faith a primary principle of conduct for themselves, without waiting till they have got their reasons accurately drawn out and serviceable for controversy, is enthusiastic and absurd. "How a man may know whether he be [a lover of truth for truth's sake] is worth inquiry; and I think there is this one unerring mark of it, viz., the not entertaining any proposition with greater assurance, than the proofs it is built upon, will warrant. Whoever goes beyond this measure of assent, it is plain, receives not truth in the love of it; loves not truth for truth's sake, but for some other by-end. For the evidence that any proposition is true, except such as are self-evident, lying only in the proofs a man has of it, whatsoever degrees of assent he affords it, beyond the degrees of that evidence, it is plain all that surplusage of assurance is owing to some other affection, and not to the love of truth; it being as impossible that the love of truth should carry my assent above the evidence there is to me that it is true, as that the love of truth should make me assent to any proposition {329} for the sake of that evidence which it has not, that it is true; which is in effect to love it as a truth, because it is possible or probable that it may not be true.[12] . . . What I see,[13] I know to be so by the evidence of the thing itself: what I believe, I take to be so upon the testimony of another; but this testimony I must know to be given, or else what ground have I of believing? . . . Enthusiasm fails of the evidence it pretends to; for men, thus possessed, boast of a light whereby, they say, they are enlightened, and brought into the knowledge of this or that truth. But if they know it to be a truth, they must know it to be so, either by its own self-evidence to natural reason, or by the rational proofs that make it out to be so." Here this author lays down, that a lover of truth is he who loves a valid argument, and that such faith as is not credulity or enthusiasm is always traceable to a process of reason, and varies with its cogency.

I will but observe on such philosophy as this, that, were it received, no great work ever would have been done for God's glory and the welfare of man. Enthusiasm may do much harm, and act at times absurdly; but calculation never made a hero. But it is not to our present purpose to examine this theory, and I have done so elsewhere. Here I have but to show that both ancient and modern Catholics reject it. For instance, it is the very objection urged by Celsus, that Christians were but parallel to the credulous victims of jugglers or of devotees, who itinerated through the pagan population. He says "that some do not even wish to give or to receive a reason for their faith, but say, 'Do not inquire but believe,' and 'Thy faith will save thee;' and 'A bad thing is the world's wisdom, and foolishness is a good.'" How does Origen answer the charge? by denying the fact, and speaking of Reason as proving the Scriptures to be divine, and Faith {330} after that conclusion receiving the contents, as it is now popular to maintain? Far from it; he grantŝ the fact alleged against the Church and defends it. He observes that considering the engagements and the necessary ignorance of the multitude of men, it is a very happy circumstance that a substitute is provided for those philosophical exercises, which Christianity allows and encourages, but does not impose on the individual. "Which," he asks, "is the better for them to believe without reason, and thus to reform any how and gain a benefit, from their belief in the punishment of sinners and the reward of well-doers, or to refuse their conversion on mere belief, except they devote themselves to an intellectual inquiry?"[14] Such a provision then is a mark of divine wisdom and mercy. In like manner, St. Irenaeus, after observing that the Jews had the evidence of prophecy, which the Gentiles had not, and that to the latter it was a foreign teaching and a new doctrine to be told that the gods of the Gentiles were not only not gods, but were idols of devils, and that in consequence St. Paul laboured more upon them, as needing it more, adds, "On the other hand, the faith of the Gentiles is thereby shown to be more generous, who followed the word of God without the assistance of Scriptures." To believe on less evidence was generous faith, not enthusiasm. And so again, Eusebius, while he contends of course that Christians are influenced by "no irrational faith," that is, by a faith which is capable of a logical basis, fully allows that, in the individual believing, it is not necessary or ordinarily based upon Reason, and maintains that it is connected with that very "hope," and inclusively with that desire of the things beloved, which Locke in the above extract considers incompatible with the love of truth. "What do we find," he says, "but that the whole life of man is suspended on {331} these two, hope and faith?"[15] and Clement calls faith a "presumption." The natural tendency of the heretical doctrine concerning Faith is to make men over-confident, in cases where they do not become sceptical and unbelieving. Thus the same Father says that the Valentinians attribute to themselves Knowledge and to Catholics Faith." Tertullian too observes of heretics generally: "All are puffed up, all promise knowledge, their catechumens are perfected before they are taught."[16]

I do not mean to imply that the Fathers were opposed to inquiries into the intellectual basis of Christianity, but that they held that men were not obliged to wait for proof before believing; on the contrary, that the majority were to believe first and prove afterwards.

St. Augustine, who had tried both ways, strikingly contrasts them in his *De Utilitate credendi*, though his direct object in that work is to decide, not between Reason and Faith, but between Reason and Authority. He addresses in it a very dear friend, who, like himself, had become a Manichee, but who, with less happiness than his own, was still retained in heresy. "The Manichees," he observes, "inveigh against those who, following the authority of the Catholic faith, fortify themselves in the first instance with believing, and, before they are able to set eyes upon the truth, which is discerned by the pure soul, prepare themselves for a God who shall illuminate. You, Honoratus, know that nothing else was the cause of my falling into their hands, than their professing to put away Authority which was so terrible, and by absolute and simple Reason to lead their hearers to God's presence, and to rid them of all {332} error. For what was there that forced me, for nearly nine years, to slight the religion which was sown in me when a child by my parents, and to follow them and diligently attend their lectures, but their assertion that I was terrified by superstition, and was bidden to have Faith before I had Reason, whereas they pressed no one to believe before the truth had been discussed and unravelled? Who would not be seduced by these promises, and especially a youth, such as they found me then, desirous of truth, nay conceited and forward, by reason of the disputations of certain men of school learning, with a contempt of old-wives' tales, and a desire of possessing and drinking that clear and unmixed truth which they promised me?"[17] Presently he goes on to describe how he was reclaimed. He found the Manichees more successful in pulling down than in building up; he was disappointed in Faustus, whom we found eloquent and nothing besides. Upon this, he did not know what to hold, and was tempted to a general scepticism. At length he found he must be guided by Authority; then came the question, Which authority among so many teachers? He cried earnestly to God for help, and at last was led to the Catholic Church. He then returns to the question urged against that Church, that "she bids those who come to her believe," whereas heretics "boast that they do not impose a yoke of believing, but open a fountain of teaching." On which he observes, "True religion cannot in any manner be rightly embraced, without a belief in those things which each individual afterwards attains and perceives, if he behave himself well and shall deserve it, nor altogether without some weighty and imperative Authority."[18]

These are specimens of the teaching of the Ancient Church on the subject of Faith and Reason; if, on the other hand, we know what has been taught on {333} the subject in those modern schools, in and through which the subsequent developments of Catholic doctrines have proceeded, we may turn to the extracts made from their writings by Huet, in his "Essay on the Human Understanding;" and in so doing, we need not perplex ourselves with the particular theory, true or not, for the sake of which he has collected them. Speaking of the weakness of the Understanding, Huet says:—

"God, by His goodness, repairs this defect of human nature, by granting us the inestimable gift of Faith, which confirms our staggering Reason, and corrects that perplexity of doubts which we must bring to the knowledge of things. For example: my reason not being able to inform me with absolute evidence, and perfect certainty, whether there are bodies, what was the origin of the world, and many other like things; after I have received the Faith, all those doubts vanish, as darkness at the rising of the sun. This made St. Thomas Aquinas say: 'It is necesssary for man to receive as articles of Faith, not only the things which are above Reason, but even those that for their certainty may be known by Reason. For human Reason is very deficient in things divine; a sign of which we have from philosophers, who, in the search of human things by natural methods, have been deceived, and opposed each other on many heads. To the end then that men may have a certain undoubted cognizance of God, it was necessary things divine should be taught them by way of Faith, as being revealed of God Himself, who cannot lie.'[19] . . .

"Then St. Thomas adds afterwards: 'No search by natural Reason is sufficient to make man know things divine, nor even those which we can prove by Reason.' And in another place he speaks thus: 'Things which may be proved demonstratively, as the Being of God, the Unity of the Godhead, and other points are placed among articles we are to believe, {334} because previous to other things thast are of Faith; and these must be presupposed, at least by such as have no demonstration of them.'

"What St. Thomas says of the cognizance of divine things extends also to the knowledge of human, according to the doctrine of Suarez. 'We often correct,' he says, 'the light of Nature by the light of Faith, even in things which seem to be first principles, as appears in this: those things that are the same to a third, are the same between themselves; which, if we have respect to the Trinity, ought to be restrained to finite things. And in other mysteries, especially in those of the Incarnation and the Eucharist, we use many other limitations, that nothing may be repugnant to the Faith. This is then an indication that the light of Faith is most certain, because founded on the first truth, which is God, to whom it's more impossible to deceive or be deceived than for the natural science of man to be mistaken and erroneous.'[20] . . .

"If we hearken not to Reason, say you, you overthrow that great foundation of Religion which Reason has established in our understanding, viz. God is. To answer this objection, you must be told that men know God in two manners. By Reason, with entire human certainty; and by Faith, with absolute and divine certainty. Although by Reason we cannot acquire any knowledge more certain than that of the Being of God; insomuch that all the arguments, which the impious oppose to this knowledge are of no more validity and easily refuted; nevertheless this certainty is not absolutely perfect.[21] . . .

"Now, although to prove the existence of the Deity, we can bring arguments which, accumulated and connected together, are not of less power to convince men than geometrical principles, and theorems deduced from them, and which are of entire human certainty; notwithstanding, because learned philosophers {335} have openly opposed even these principles, 'tis clear we cannot, neither is the natural knowledge we have of God, which is acquired by Reason, nor in science founded on geometrical principles and theorems, find absolute and consummate certainty, but only that human certainty I have spoken of, to which nevertheless every wise man ought to submit his understanding. This being not repugnant to the testimony of the Book of Wisdom and the Epistle to the Romans, which declares that men who do not from the make of the world acknowledge the power and divinity of the Maker are senseless and inexcusable.

"For to use the terms of Vasquez: 'By these words the Holy Scripture means only that there has ever been a sufficient testimony of the Being of a God in the fabrick of the world, and in His other works, to make Him known unto men: but the Scripture is not under any concern whether this knowledge be evident or of greatest probability; for these terms are seen and understood, in their common and usual acceptance, to signify all the knowledge of the mind with a determined assent.' He adds after: 'For if any one should at this time deny Christ, that which would render him inexcusable would not be because he might have had an evident knowledge and reason for believing in Him, but because he might have believed it by Faith and a prudential knowledge.'

" 'Tis with reason then that Suarez teaches that 'the natural evidence of this principle, God is the first truth, who cannot be deceived, is not necessary, nor sufficient enough to make us believe by infused Faith, what God reveals.' He proves, by the testimony of experience, that it is not necessary; for ignorant and illiterate Christians, though they know nothing clearly and certainly of God, do {336} believe nevertheless that God is. Even Christians of parts and learning, as St. Thomas has observed, believe that God is, before they know it by Reason. Suarez shows afterwards that the natural evidence of this principle is not sufficient, because divine Faith, which is infused into our understanding, cannot be bottomed upon human faith alone, how clear and firm soever it is, as upon a formal object, because an assent most firm, and of an order most noble and exalted, cannot derive its certainty from a more infirm assent.[22]

"As touching the motives of credibility, which, preparing the mind to receive Faith, ought according to you to be not only certain by supreme and human certainty, but by supreme and absolute certainty. I will oppose Gabriel Biel to you, who pronounces that to receive Faith 'tis sufficient that the motives of credibility be proposed as probable. Do you believe that children, illiterate, gross, ignorant people, who have scarcely the use of Reason, and notwithstanding have received the gift of Faith, do most clearly, and most steadfastly conceive those forementioned motives of credibility? No, without doubt; but the grace of God comes into their assistance, and sustains the imbecility of Nature and Reason.

"This is the common opinion of divines. Reason has need of divine grace, not only in gross, illiterate persons, but even in those of parts and learning; for how clear-sighted soever that may be, yet it cannot make us have Faith, if celestial light does not illuminate us within, because, as I have said already, divine Faith being of a superior order cannot derive its efficacy from human faith.[23]

"This is likewise the doctrine of St. Thomas Aquinas: 'The light of Faith makes things seen that are believed.' He says moreover, 'Believers have knowledge of the things of Faith, not in a demonstrative way, but so as by the light of Faith, it appears to them that they ought to be believed.'"[24]

{337} It is very evident, what a special influence a view such as this must have on the controversial method of those who hold it. Arguments will come to be considered rather as representatives and persuasives than as logical proofs; and developments as the spontaneous, gradual and ethical growth, not as intentional and arbitrary deductions, of existing opinions.

SECTION II.

APPLICATION OF THE SECOND AND THIRD TESTS.

THE DOGMATIC AND SACRAMENTAL PRINCIPLES, AND THE FORMATION OF A THEOLOGY BY MEANS OF THEM.

Since religious systems, true and false, have one and the same great and comprehensive subject-matter, they necessarily interfere with one another as rivals, both in those points in which they agree together, and in those in which they differ. That Christianity on its rise was in these circumstances of competition and controversy, is sufficiently evident even from a foregoing Chapter: it was surrounded by rites, sects, and philosophies, which contemplated the same questions, sometimes advocated the same truths, and in no slight degree wore the same external appearance. It could not stand still, it could not take its own way, and let them take theirs; they came across its path, and a conflict was inevitable. The very nature of a true philosophy relatively to other systems is to be polemical, eclectic, unitive: Christianity was polemical; it could not but be eclectic; but was it also unitive? Had it the power, keeping its own identity, of absorbing its antagonists, as Aaron's rod, according to St. Jerome's illustration, devoured the rods of the sorcerers of Egypt? Did it incorporate them into {338} itself, or was it dissolved into them? Did it assimilate them into its own substance, or, keeping its name, was it simply infected by them? In a word, were its developments faithful or corrupt? Nor is this a question merely of the early centuries. When we consider the deep interest of the controversies which Christianity raises, the various minds it has swayed, the range of subjects which it embraces, the many countries it has entered, the deep philosophies it has encountered, the vicissitudes it has undergone, and the length of time through which it has lasted, it requires some assignable explanation, why we should not consider it modified and changed, that is, corrupted, from the first by the numberless influences to which it has been exposed.

Now there was this cardinal distinction between Christianity and the religions and philosophies by which it was surrounded, nay even the Judaism of the day, that it referred all truth and revelation to one source, and that the Supreme and Only God. Pagan rites which honoured one out of ten thousand deities; philosophies which scarcely taught any source of revelation at all; Gnostic heresies which were based on Dualism, adored angels, or ascribed the two Testaments to distinct authors, could not regard truth as one, unalterable, consistent, imperative, and saving. But Christianity started with the principle that there was but "one God and one Mediator," and that He "who at sundry times and in divers manners spake in time past unto the fathers by the Prophets, had in these last days spoken unto us by His Son."

Hence Christianity and it alone, revered and protected the Divine word which it had received, as both sacred and as sanctifying. It was grace, and it was truth.

In other words, Christianity has from first to last kept fixed principles in view in the course of its developments, and thereby has been able to incorporate doctrine which was external to it without {339} losing its own. Such continuity of principle, and such assimilating power, are each of them incompatible with the idea of a corruption, as was laid down in an early part of the Volume. The two special principles which the foregoing paragraph introduces, may be called the Dogmatic and the Sacramental, and their assimilating power shall now be illustrated.

1. That opinions in religion are not matters of indifference, but have a definite bearing on the position of their holders in the Divine Sight, is a principle on which the Evangelical Faith has from the first developed, and on which that Faith has been the first to develope. I suppose, it hardly had any exercise under the Law; the zeal and obedience of the ancient people being employed in the maintenance of divine worship and the overthrow of idolatry, not in the assertion of opinion. Faith is in this, as in other respects, a characteristic of the Gospel, except so far as it was anticipated, as its time drew near. Elijah and the Prophets down to Ezra resisted Baal or restored the Temple Service; the Three Children refused to bow down before the golden image; Daniel would turn his face towards Jerusalem; the Maccabees spurned the Grecian paganism. On the other hand, the Greek Philosophers were authoritative indeed in their teaching, used the "*Ipse dixit*," and demanded the faith of their disciples; but they did not commonly attach sanctity or reality to opinions, or view them in a religious light. Our Saviour was the first to "bear witness to the Truth," and to die for it, when "before Pontius Pilate he witnessed a good confession." St. John and St. Paul,

following his example, both pronounce anathema on those who denied "the Truth" or "brought in another Gospel." Tradition tells us that the Apostle of love seconded his word with his deed, and on one occasion hastily quitted a bath {340} because an heresiarch of the day had entered it. St. Ignatius, his contemporary, compares false teachers to raging dogs; and St. Polycarp, his disciple, exercised the same severity upon Marcion which St. John had shown towards Cerinthus.

St. Irenaeus exemplifies the same doctrine after St. Polycarp: "I saw thee," he says to the heretic Florinus, "when I was yet a boy, in lower Asia, with Polycarp, when thou was living splendidly in the Imperial Court, and trying to recommend thyself to him. I remember indeed what then happened better than more recent occurrences, for the lessons of boyhood grow with the mind and become one with it. Thus I can name the place where blessed Polycarp sat and conversed, and his goings out and comings in, and the fashion of his life, and the appearance of his person, and his discourses to the people, and his familiarity with John, which he used to tell of, and with the rest who had seen the Lord, and how he used to repeat their words, and what it was that he had learned about the Lord from them. . . . And in the sight of God, I can protest, that, if that blessed and apostolical Elder had heard aught of this doctrine, he had cried out and stopped his ears, saying after his wont, 'O Good God, for what times hast thou reserved me that I should endure this?' and he had fled the place where he was sitting or standing when he heard it." It seems to have been the duty of every individual Christian from the first to witness in his place what he had received in his baptismal catechizing, and to shun the society of those who maintained them. "So religious," says Irenaeus after giving his account of St. Polycarp, "were the Apostles and their disciples, in not even conversing with those who counterfeited the truth."[25]

Such a principle, however, would but have broken up the Church the sooner, resolving it into the individuals {341} of which it was composed, unless the Truth, to which they were to bear witness, had been a something definite, and formal, and independent of themselves. Christians were bound to defend and to transmit the faith which they had received, and they received it from the rulers of the Church; and, on the other hand, it was the duty of those rulers to watch over and define this traditionary faith. It is unnecessary to go over ground which has been traversed so often of late years. St. Irenaeus brings the subject before us in his description of St. Polycarp, part of which has already been quoted; and to it we may limit ourselves. "Polycarp," he says when writing against the Gnostics, "whom we have seen in our first youth, ever taught those lessons which he learned from the Apostles, which the Church also transmits, which alone are true. All the Churches of Asia bear witness to them; and the successors of Polycarp down to this day, who is a much more trustworthy and sure witness of truth than Valentinus, Marcion, or their perverse companions. The same was in Rome in the time of Anicetus, and converted many of the aforenamed heretics to the Church of God, preaching that he had received from the Apostles this one and only truth, which had been transmitted by the Church."[26]

{342} Nor was this the doctrine and practice of one school only, which might be ignorant of philosophy; the cultivated minds of the Alexandrian Fathers, who are said to owe so much to Pagan science, certainly showed no gratitude or reverence towards their alleged instructress, but maintained the supremacy of Catholic Tradition. Clement[27] speaks of heretical teachers as perverting Scripture, and essaying the gate of heaven with a false key, not raising the veil, as he and his, by means of tradition from Christ, but digging through the Church's wall, and becoming mystagogues of misbelief; "for," he continues, "few words are enough to prove they have formed their human assemblies later than {343} the Catholic Church," and "from that previously existing and most true Church it is very clear that these later heresies, and others which have been since, are counterfeit and novel inventions."[28] "When the Marcionites, Valentinians, and the like," says Origen, "appeal to apocryphal works, they are saying, 'Christ is in the desert;' when to canonical Scripture, 'Lo, He is in the chambers;' but we must not depart from that first and ecclesiastical tradition, nor believe otherwise than as the Churches of God by succession have transmitted to us." And it is recorded of him in his youth, that he never could be brought to attend the prayers of a heretic who was in the house of his patroness, from abomination of his doctrine, "observing," adds Eusebius, "the rule of the Church." Eusebius too himself, unsatisfactory as is his own theology, cannot break from this fundamental rule; he ever speaks of the Gnostic teachers, the chief heretics of his period, (at least before the rise of Arianism,) in terms most expressive of abhorrence and disgust.

The African, Syrian, and Asian schools are additional witnesses; Tertullian at Carthage was strenuous for the dogmatic principle even after he had given up the traditional. The Fathers of Asia Minor, who excommunicated Noëtus, rehearse the Creed, and add, "We declare as we have learned;" the Fathers of Antioch, who depose Paul of Samosata set down in writing the Creed from Scripture, "which," they say, "we received from the beginning, and have, by tradition and in custody, in the Catholic and Holy Church, until this day, by succession, as preached by the blessed Apostles, who were eye-witnesses and ministers of the Word."[29]

{344} And it is as plain, or even plainer, that what the Christians of the first ages anathematized, included deductions from the Articles of Faith, that is, developments, as well as those Articles of Faith themselves. For, since the reason they commonly gave for using the anathema was that the doctrine in question was strange and startling, it follows that the truth, which was its contradictory, had also been unknown to them hitherto; which is also shown by their temporary perplexity, and their difficulty of meeting heresy, in particular cases. "Who ever heard the like hitherto?" says St. Athanasius of Apollinarianism; "who was the teacher of it, who the hearer? 'From Sion shall go forth the Law of God, and the Word of the Lord from Jerusalem;' but from whence hath this gone forth? What hell hath burst out with it?"[30] The Fathers at Nicaea stopped their ears; St. Irenaeus, as above quoted, says that St. Polycarp, had he heard the Gnostic blasphemies, would have stopped his ears, and deplored the times for which he was reserved. They anathematized the doctrine, not because it was old, but because it was new: the anathema would have altogether slept, if it could not have been extended to propositions not anathematized in the beginning; for the very characteristic of heresy is this novelty and originality of manifestation.

2. That there is a truth then; that there is one truth; that religious error is in itself of an immoral nature; that its maintainers, unless involuntarily such, are guilty in maintaining it; that it is to be dreaded; that the search for truth is not the gratification of curiosity; that its attainment has nothing of the excitement of a discovery; that the mind is below truth, not above it, and is bound, not to descant upon it, but to venerate it; that truth and falsehood are set before us for the trial {345} of our hearts; that our choice is an awful giving forth of lots on which salvation or rejection is inscribed; that "before all things it is necessary to hold the Catholic faith;" that "he that would be saved must thus think," and not otherwise; that "if thou criest after knowledge, and liftest up thy voice for understanding, if thou seekest her as silver, and searchest for her as for hid treasure, then shalt thou understand the fear of the Lord, and find the knowledge of God,"—this is the dogmatical principle, which has strength.

That truth and falsehood in religion are but matter of opinion; that one doctrine is as good as another; that the Governor of the world does not intend that we should gain the truth; that there is no truth; that we are not more acceptable to God by believing this than by believing that; that no one is answerable for his opinions; that they are a matter of necessity or accident; that it is enough if we sincerely hold what we profess; that our merit lies in seeking, not in possessing; that it is a duty to follow what seems to us true, without a fear lest it should not be true; that it may be a gain to succeed, and can be no harm to fail; that we may take up and lay down opinions at pleasure; that belief belongs to the mere intellect, not to the heart; that we may safely trust ourselves in matters of Faith, and need no other guide,—this is the principle of philosophies and heresies, which is very weakness.

Two opinions encounter; each may be abstractedly true; or again, each may be a subtle, comprehensive doctrine, vigorous, elastic, expansive, various; one is held as a matter of indifference, the other as a matter of life and death; one is held by the intellect, the other by the heart: it is plain which of the two must succumb to the other. Such was the conflict of Christianity with the old established Paganism, which was almost dead before Christianity appeared; with the Oriental Mysteries, flitting {346} wildly to and fro like spectres; with the Gnostics, who made Knowledge all in all, despised the many, and called Catholics mere children in the Truth; with the Neo-platonists, men of literature, pedants, visionaries, or courtiers; with the Manichees, who professed to seek Truth by Reason, not by Faith; with the fluctuating teachers of the school of Antioch, the time-serving Eusebians, and the reckless variable Arians; with the fanatic Montanists and harsh Novatians, who hated the Catholic doctrine, without loving their own. These sects had no stay or consistence, yet they contained elements of truth amid their error, and had

Christianity been as they, it might have resolved into them; but it had that hold of the truth which gave its teaching a gravity, a directness, a consistency, a sternness, and a force, to which they were strangers. It could not call evil good, or good evil, because it discerned the difference between them; it could not make light of what was solemn, or fall from what was so solid. Hence, in the collision, it broke in pieces its antagonists, and divided the spoils.

This was but another form of the spirit that made martyrs. Dogmatism was in teaching, what confession was in act. Each was the same strong principle of life in a different aspect, distinguishing the faith which was displayed in it from the world's philosophies on the one side, and the world's religions on the other. The heathen sects and the heresies of Christian history were dissolved by the breath of opinion which made them; paganism shuddered and died at the very sight of the sword of persecution, which it had itself unsheathed. Intellect and force were applied as tests both upon the Divine and upon the human work; they prevailed with the human, they did but become instruments of the Divine. "No one," says St. Justin, "has so believed Socrates as to die for the doctrine which he taught." "No one was ever {347} found undergoing death for faith in the sun."[31] Thus Christianity grew in its proportions, gaining aliment and medicine from all that it came near, yet preserving its original type, from its perception and its love of what had been revealed once for all and was no private imagination.

There are writers who refer to the first centuries of the Church as a time when opinion was free, and the conscience exempt from the obligation or temptation to take on trust what it had not proved; and that, apparently on the mere ground that the series of great theological decisions did not commence till the fourth. This seems to be M. Guizot's meaning when he says that Christianity "in the early ages was a belief, a sentiment, an individual conviction;"[32] that "the Christian society appears as a pure association of men, animated by the same sentiments and professing the same creed. The first Christians," he continues, "assembled to enjoy together the same emotions, the same religious convictions. We do not find any doctrinal system established, any form of discipline or of laws, or any body of magistrates."[33] What can be meant by saying that Christianity had no magistrates in the earliest ages?—but, any how, in statements such as these the distinction is not properly recognised between a principle and its developments, even if the fact were as is represented. The principle indeed of Dogmatism develops into Councils in the course of time; but it is active, nay sovereign from the first, in every part of Christendom. A conviction that truth was one; that it was a gift from without, a sacred trust, an inestimable blessing; that it was to be reverenced, guarded, defended, transmitted; that its absence was a grievous want, that its loss an unutterable calamity;—all this is quite consistent with perplexity or mistake as to what was truth in particular cases, {348} in what way doubtful questions were to be decided, or what were the limits of the Revelation. Councils and Popes are the guardians and instruments of the dogmatic principle: they are not that principle themselves; they presuppose the principle; they are summoned into action at the call of the principle, and the principle might act even before they had their legitimate place, and exercised as recognised power, in the movements of the Christian body.

The instance of Conscience, which has already served us in illustration, may assist us here. What Conscience is in the history of an individual mind, such was the dogmatic principle in the history of Christianity. Both in the one case and the other, there is the gradual formation of a directing power out of a principle. The natural voice of Conscience is far more imperative in testifying and enforcing as rule of duty, than successful in determining that duty in particular cases. It acts as a messenger from above, and says that there is a right and a wrong, and that the right must be followed; but it is variously, and therefore erroneously, trained in the instance of various persons. It mistakes error for truth; and yet we believe that on the whole, and even in those cases where it is ill-instructed, if its voice be diligently obeyed, it will gradually be cleared, simplified, and perfected, so that minds, starting differently, will, if honest, in course of time converge to one and the same truth. I would not imply that there is indistinctness so great as this in the knowledge of the first centuries; but so far is plain, that the early Church and Fathers exercised far more a ruler's than a doctor's office: it was the age of Martyrs, of acting not of thinking. Doctors succeeded Martyrs, as light and peace of conscience follow upon obedience to it; yet, even before the Church had grown into the full measure of its doctrines, it was rooted in its principles.

{349} So far, however, may be granted to M. Guizot, that even principles were not so well understood and so carefully handled at first, as they were afterwards. In the early period, we see traces of a conflict, as well as of a variety, in theological elements, which were in course of combination, but which required adjustment and management before they could be used with precision as one. In a thousand instances of a minor character, the statements of the early Fathers are but tokens of the multiplicity of openings which the mind of the Church was making into the treasure-house of Truth; real openings, but incomplete or irregular. Nay, the doctrines even of the heretical bodies are indices and anticipations of the mind of the Church. As the first step in settling a point of doctrine is to raise and debate it, so heresies in every age may be taken as the measure of the existing state of thought in the Church, and of the movement of her theology; they determine in what way the current is setting, and the rate at which it flows.

Thus, St. Clement may be called the representative of the ecclectic element, and Tertullian of the dogmatic; and Clement perhaps went too far in his accommodation to philosophy, and Tertullian asserted with exaggeration the immutability of the Creed. Nay, the two antagonist principles of dogmatism and development are found in Tertullian alone, though with some deficiency of amalgamation, and with a greater leaning towards the dogmatic. Though the Montanists professed to pass over the subject of doctrine, it is chiefly in Tertullian's Montanistic works that his strong statements occur of the unalterableness of the Creed; and extravagance on the subject is not only in keeping with the stern and vehement temper of that Father, but with the general severity and harshness of his sect. On the other hand the very foundation of Montanism is development, though not of doctrine, yet of discipline {350} and conduct. It is said that its founder professed himself the promised Comforter, through whom the Church was to be perfected; he provided prophets as organs of the new revelation, and called Catholics Psychici or carnal. Tertullian distinctly recognises even the process of development in one of his Montanistic works. After speaking of an innovation upon usage, which his newly revealed truth required, he proceeds, "Therefore hath the Lord sent the Paraclete, that, since human infirmity could not take all things in at once, discipline might be gradually directed, regulated and brought to perfection by the Lord's Vicar, the Holy Ghost. 'I have yet many things to say you,' he saith, 'but ye, &c.' What is this dispensation of the Paraclete but this, that discipline is directed, Scriptures revealed, intellect informed, improvements effected? Nothing can take place without age, and all things wait their time. In short, the Preacher says 'There is a time for all things.' Behold the creature itself gradually advancing to fruit. At first there is a seed, and a stalk springs out of the seed, and from the stalk bursts out a shrub, and then its branches and foliage grow vigorous, and all that we mean by a tree is unfolded; then there is the swelling of the bud, and the bud is resolved into a blossom, and the blossom is opened into a fruit, and it for a while rudimental and unformed, till, by degrees tempering its own age, it is matured into mildness of flavour. So too righteousness, for there is the same God both of righteousness and of the creature, was at first, in its rudiments, a nature fearing God; thence, by means of Law and Prophets, it advanced into infancy; thence, by the gospel, it burst forth into its youth; and now by the Paraclete, it is fashioned into maturity.[34]

Not in one principle or doctrine only, but in its whole system, Montanism is a remarkable anticipation {351} or presage of developments which soon began to show themselves in the Church, though they were not perfected for centuries after. Its rigid maintenance of the original Creed, yet its admission of a development, at least in the ritual, has just been instanced in the person of Tertullian. Equally Catholic in their principle, whether in fact or anticipation, were most of the other peculiarities of Montanism: its rigorous fasts, its visions, its commendation of celibacy, and martyrdom, its contempt of temporal goods, its penitential discipline, and its centre of unity. The doctrinal determinations and the ecclesiastical usages of the middle ages are the true fulfilment of its self-willed and abortive attempts at precipitating the growth of the Church. The favour shown to it for a while by Pope Victor is an evidence of its external resemblance to orthodoxy; and the celebrated Martyrs and Saints in Africa, in the beginning of the third century, Perpetua and Felicitas, or at least their Acts, betoken that same peculiar temper of religion, which, when cut off from the Church a few years afterwards, quickly degenerated into a heresy. A parallel instance occurs in the case of the Donatists. They held a doctrine on the subject of Baptism similar to that of St. Cyprian: "Vincentius Lirinensis," says Gibbon, referring to Tillemont's remarks on that resemblance, "has explained why the Donatists are eternally burning with the devil, while St. Cyprian reigns in heaven with Jesus Christ."[35] And his reason is intelligible: it is, says Tillemont, as Augustine often says, because the Donatists had broken the bond of peace and charity with the other Churches which St. Cyprian had preserved so carefully.[36]

These are specimens of the raw material, as it may be called, which whether as found in individual Fathers within the pale of the Church, or in heretics {352} external to it, she had the power, by means of the continuity and firmness of her principles, to convert to her own uses. She alone has succeeded in thus rejecting evil without sacrificing the good, and in holding together in one things which in all other schools are incompatible. Gnostic or Platonic words are found in the inspired theology of St. John. Unitarian writers trace the doctrine of our Lord's divinity to the Platonists; Gibbon the idea of the Incarnation to the Gnostics. The Gnostics too seem first to have systematically directed the intellect upon matters of faith; and the very term "Gnostic" has been taken by Clement to express his perfect Christian. And, though ascetics existed from the beginning, the notion of a religion higher than the Christianity of the many, was first prominently brought forward by the Gnostics, Montanists, Novatians, and Manachees. And while the prophets of the Montanists prefigure the Church's Doctors, and their inspiration her infallibility, and their revelations her developments, and the heresiarch himself is the unsightly anticipation of St. Francis, in Novatian again we discern the aspiration of nature after such creations of grace as St. Benedict or St. Bruno. And so the effort of Sabellius to complete the mystery of the Ever-blessed Trinity failed: it became a heresy; grace would not be constrained; the course of thought could not be forced;—at length it was realized in the true Unitarianism of St. Augustine.

Doctrine too is percolated, as it were, through different minds, beginning with writers of inferior authority in the Church, and issuing at length in the enunciation of her Doctors. Origen, Tertullian, nay Eusebius and the Antiochenes, supply the materials from which the Fathers have wrought out comments, or treatises. St. Gregory Nazianzen and St. Basil digested into form the theological principles of Origen; St. Hilary and St. Ambrose are both indebted {353} to the same great writer in their interpretations of Scripture; St. Ambrose again has taken his comment on St. Luke from Eusebius, and certain of his Tracts from Philo; St. Cyprian called Tertullian his Master; and traces of Tertullian, in his almost heretical treatises, may be detected in the most finished sentences of St. Leo. The school of Antioch, in spite of its heretical taint, formed the genius of St. Chrysostom. And the Apocryphal gospels have contributed many things for the devotion and edification of Catholic believers.[37]

The deep meditation which seems to have been exercised by the Fathers on points of doctrine, the debate and turbulence yet lucid determination of Councils, the indecision of Popes, are all in different ways, at least when viewed together, portions and indications of the same process. The theology of the Church is no random combination of various opinions, but a diligent, patient working out of one doctrine out of many materials. The conduct of Popes, Councils, Fathers, betokens the slow, painful, anxious taking up of new elements into an existing body of belief. St. Athanasius, St. Augustine, St. Leo are conspicuous for the repetition *in terminis* of their own theological statements; on the contrary it has been observed of Tertullian, that his works "indicate no ordinary fertility of mind in that he so little repeats himself or recurs to favorite thoughts, as is frequently the case even with the great St. Augustine."[38]

Here we see the difference between originality of mind and the gift and calling of a Doctor in the Church; the holy Fathers just mentioned were intently fixing their minds on what they taught, grasping it more and more closely, viewing it on various sides, trying its consistency, weighing their own separate expressions. And thus if in some {354} cases they were even left in ignorance, the next generation of teachers completed their work, for the same unwearied anxious process of thought went on. St. Gregory Nyssen finishes the investigations of St. Athanasius; St. Leo guards the polemical statements of St. Cyril. Clement may hold a purgatory, yet tend to consider all punishment purgatorial; St. Cyprian may hold the unsanctified state of heretics, but include in his doctrine a denial of their baptism; St. Hippolytus may believe in the personal existence of the Word from eternity, yet speak confusedly on the eternity of His Sonship; the Council of Antioch might put aside the Homoüsion, and the Council of Nicaea impose it; St. Hilary may believe in a purgatory, yet confine it to the day of judgment; St. Athanasius and other Fathers may treat with almost supernatural exactness the doctrine of our Lord's incarnation, yet imply, as far as words go, that He was ignorant in His human nature; the Athanasian Creed may admit the illustration of soul and body, and later Fathers discountenance it; St. Augustine might first be opposed to the employment of force in religion, and then acquiesce in it. Prayers for the faithful departed may be found in the early liturgies, yet with an indistinctness which included St. Mary and the Martyrs in the same rank with the imperfect Christian whose sins were as yet unexpiated; and succeeding times might keep what was exact, and supply what was deficient. Aristotle might be reprobated by certain early Fathers, yet furnish the phraseology for theological definitions afterwards. And in a different subject-matter, St. Isidore and others might be suspicious of the decoration of churches; St. Paulinus and St. Helena advance it.

3. There is in truth a certain virtue or grace in the Gospel which changes the quality of doctrines, opinions, usages, actions, and personal characters which become incorporated with it, and makes them right and acceptable to its Divine Author, {355}

when before they were either contrary to truth, or at best but shadows of it. This is the second principle, above spoken of, which I have called the Sacramental. "We know that we are of God, and the whole world lieth in wickedness," is an enunciation of the principle;—or, the declaration of the Apostle of the Gentiles, "If any man be in Christ, he is a new creature; old things are passed away, behold all things are become new." Thus outward rites, which are but worthless in themselves, lose their own character and become Sacraments under the gospel; circumcision, as St. Paul says, is carnal and has come to an end, yet Baptism is a perpetual ordinance, as being grafted upon a system which is grace and truth. Elsewhere, he parallels, while he contrasts, "the cup of the Lord" and "the cup of devils," in this respect, that to partake of either is to hold communion with the source from which it comes; and he adds presently, that "we have been all made to drink into one Spirit." So again he says, no one is justified by the works of the Law; while both St. Paul implies, and St. James declares, that Christians are justified by works of the Spirit. Again he contrasts the exercises of the intellect as exhibited by heathen and Christian. "Howbeit," he says, after condemning heathen wisdom, "we speak wisdom among them that are perfect, yet not the wisdom of this world;" and it is plain that no where need we look for more glowing eloquence, more distinct profession of reasoning, more careful assertion of principles, than are to be found in the Apostle's writings.

In like manner when the Jewish exorcists attempted to "call over them which had evil spirits the Name of the Lord Jesus," the evil spirit professed not to know them, and inflicted on them a bodily injury; on the other hand, the occasion of this attempt of theirs was a stupendous instance or type, in the person of St. Paul, of the very principle I am illustrating. "God wrought special miracles {356} by the hands of Paul, so that from his body were brought unto the sick handkerchiefs and aprons, and the diseases departed from them, and the evil spirits went out of them." The grace given him was communicable, diffusive; an influence, as enthusiasm may be, or moral habits and principles, or tastes, or knowledge.

Parallel instances occur of the operation of this principle in the history of the Church as soon as the Apostles were taken from it. St. Paul denounces distinctions in meat and drink, the observance of Sabbaths and holydays, and of ordinances, and the worship of Angels; yet Christians, from the first, were rigid in their stated fastings, venerated, as St. Justin tells us, the Angelic intelligences,[39] and established the observance of the Lord's day as soon as persecution ceased.

In like manner Celsus objects that Christians did not "endure the sight of temples, altars, and statues;" Porphyry, that "they blame the rites of worship, victims, and frankincense;" the heathen disputant in Minucius asks, "Why have Christians no altars, no temples, no conspicuous images?" and "no sacrifices;" and yet it is plain from Tertullian that Christians had altars of their own, and sacrifices and priests. And that they had churches is again and again proved by Eusebius who had seen "the houses of prayer levelled" in the Dioclesian persecution; from the history too of St. Gregory Thaumaturgus, nay from Clement.[40] Again, St. Justin and Minucius speak of the form of the Cross in terms of reverence, quite inconsistent with the doctrine that external emblems of religion may not be venerated. Tertullian speaks of Christians signing themselves with it whatever they set about, whether they walk, eat, or lie down to sleep. In Eusebius's {357} life of Constantine, the figure of the Cross holds a most conspicuous place; the Emperor sees it in the sky and is converted; he places it upon his standards; he places it in his own hand when he puts up his statue; wherever the Cross is displayed in his battles, he conquers; he appoints fifty men to carry it; he engraves it on his soldiers' arms; and Licinius dreads its power.

Shortly after, Julian plainly accuses Christians of worshipping the wood of the Cross, though they refused to worship the ancile. In a later age the worship of images was introduced.[41]

The principle of the distinction, on which these observances were pious in Christianity and superstitious in paganism, is implied in such passages of Tertullian, Lactantius, and others, as speak of evil spirits lurking under the pagan statues. It is intimated also by Origen, who, after saying that Scripture so strongly "forbids temples, altars, and images," that Christians are "ready to go to death, if necessary, rather than pollute their notion of the God of all by any such transgression," assigns as a reason "that, as far as possible, they might not fall into the notion that images were gods." St. Augustine, in replying to Porphyry, is more express; "Those," he says," who are acquainted with Old and New Testament do not blame in the pagan religion the erection of temples or institution of priesthoods, but that these are done to idols and devils . . . True religion blames in their superstitions, not so much their sacrificing, for the ancient saints sacrificed to the True God, as their sacrificing to false gods."[42] To Faustus the Manichee he answers, "We have some things in common with the gentiles, but our purpose is different."[43] And St. Jerome asks Vigilantius, who made objections to lights and oil, "Because we once worshipped idols, is that a reason why we should not worship God, for fear of seeming {358} to address him with an honour like that which was paid to idols and then was detestable, whereas this is paid to Martyrs and therefore to be received?"[44]

Confiding then in the power of Christianity to resist the infection of evil, and to transmute the very instruments and appendages of demon-worship to an evangelical use, and feeling also that these usages had originally come from primitive revelations and from the instinct of nature, though they had been corrupted; and that they must invent what they needed, if they did not use what they found; and that they had moreover with them the very archetypes, of which paganism attempted the shadows; the rulers of the Church from early times were prepared, should the occasion arise, to adopt, or imitate, or sanction the existing rites and customs of the populace, as well as the philosophy of the educated class. St. Gregory Thaumaturgus supplies the first instance on record of this economy. He was the Apostle of Pontus, which since Pliny's time seems to have fallen back into heathenism, and one of his methods for governing an untoward population is thus related by St. Gregory of Nyssa. "Returning," he says, "from the city, and revisiting its environs, he increased the devotion of the people everywhere by instituting festive meetings in honour of those who had fought for the faith. The bodies of the Martyrs were distributed in different places, and the people assembled and made merry, as the year came round, holding festival in their honour. This indeed was a proof of his great wisdom . . . for, perceiving that the childish and untrained populace were retained in their idolatrous error by sensual indulgences, in order that what was of first importance should at any rate be secured to them, viz. that they should look to God in place of their vain rites, he allowed them to be merry and solace {359} themselves at the monuments of the holy Martyrs, as if their behaviour would in time undergo a spontaneous change into greater seriousness and strictness, and faith would lead them to it; which has actually been the happy issue in that population, all sensual gratification having turned into a spiritual form of rejoicing."[45] There is no reason to suppose that the license here spoken of passed the limits of harmless though rude festivity; for it is observable that the same reason, the need of holydays for the multitude, is assigned by Origen, St. Gregory's master, to explain the establishment of the Lord's Day also, and the Paschal and the Pentecostal festivals, which have never been viewed as unlawful compliances; and, moreover, the people were eventually reclaimed from their gross habits by his indulgent policy, a successful issue which could not have followed an accommodation to what was sinful.

The example set by St. Gregory in an age of persecution was impetuously followed when a time of peace succeeded. In the course of the fourth century two movements or developments spread over the face of Christendom, with a rapidity characteristic of the Church; the one ascetic, the other ritual or ceremonial. We are told in various ways by Eusebius,[46] that Constantine, in order to recommend the new religion to the heathen, transferred into it the outward ornaments to which they had been accustomed in their own. It is not necessary to go into a subject which the diligence of Protestant writers has made familiar to most of us. The use of temples, and these dedicated to particular saints, and ornamented on occasions with branches of trees; incense, lamps, and candles; votive offerings on recovery from illness; holy water; asylums; holydays and seasons, use of calendars, processions, blessings on the fields; sacerdotal vestments, {360} the tonsure, the ring in marriage, turning to the East, images at a later date, perhaps the ecclesiastical chant, and the Kyrie Eleison,[47] are all of pagan origin, and sanctified by their adoption into the Church.

The eighth book of Theodoret's work, *Adversus Gentiles*, which is "On the Martyrs," treats so largely on the subject, that we must content ourselves with but a specimen of the illustrations which it affords, to the principle acted on by St. Gregory Thaumaturgus. "Time, which makes all things decay," he says, speaking of the Martyrs, "has preserved their glory incorruptible. For as the noble souls of those conquerors traverse the heavens, and take part in the spiritual choirs, so their bodies are not consigned to separate tombs, but cities and towns have distributed them; and they call them saviours of souls and bodies, and physicians, and honour them as the protectors and guards of cities, and, using their intervention with the Lord of all, through them they obtain divine gifts. And though the body be divided, the grace remains indivisible; and that small and tiny particle is equal in power with the Martyr that hath never been dispersed about. For the grace which thrives distributes the gifts, measuring the bounty according to the faith of comers.

"Yet not even this persuades you to celebrate their God, but ye laugh and mock at the honour which is paid them by all, and consider it as pollution to approach their tombs. But though all men made a jest of them, yet at least the Greeks could not decently complain, to whom belonged libations and expiations, and heroes and demi-gods and deified men. To Hercules, though a man, and compelled to serve Eurystheus, they built temples, and constructed altars, and offered sacrifices in honour, and allotted feasts; and that, not Spartans {361} only and Athenians, but the whole of Greece and the greater part of Europe."

Then, after going through the history of many heathen deities, and referring to the doctrine of the philosophers about great men, and to the monuments of kings and emperors, all of which at once are witnesses and are inferior, to the greatness of the Martyrs, he continues: "To their temples we come, not once or twice a year or five times, but often do we hold celebrations; often, nay daily, do we present hymns to their Lord. And the sound in health ask for its preservation, and those who struggle with any disease for a release from their sufferings; the childless for children, the barren to become mothers, and those who enjoy the blessing for its safe-keeping. Those too who are setting out for a foreign land beg that they may be their fellow-travellers and guides of the journey; those who have come safe back acknowl-edge the grace, not coming to them as to gods, but beseeching them as divine men, and asking their intercession. And that they obtain what they ask in faith, their dedications openly witness, in token of their care. For some bring likenesses of eyes, others of feet; others of hands; some of gold, others of silver; and their Lord accepts even the small and cheap, measuring the gift by the offerer's ability. . . . Philosophers and Orators are consigned to oblivion, and kings and captains are not known even by name to the many; but the names of the Martyrs are better known to all than the names of those dearest to them. And they make a point of giving them to their children, with a view of gaining for them thereby safety and protection. . . . Nay, of the so-called gods, so utterly have the sacred places been destroyed, that not even their outline remains, nor the shape of their altars is known to me of this generation, while their materials have been devoted to the shrines of the Martyrs. For the Lord has introduced His own dead in {362} the place of your gods, of the one He hath made a riddance, on the other He hath conferred their honours. For the Pandian festival, the Diasia, and the Dionysia, and your other feasts, we have the celebrations of Peter, of Paul, of Thomas, of Sergius, of Marcellus, of Leontius, of Panteleëmon, of Antony, of Maurice, and of the other Martyrs; and for that ancient procession, and the indecency of work and word, are held modest festivities, without intemperance, or revel, or laughter, but with divine hymns, and attendance on holy discourses and prayers, adorned with laudable tears." This was the view of the "Evidences of Christianity" which a Bishop of the fifth century offered for the conversion of unbelievers.

The introduction of Images was still later, and met with more opposition in the West than in the East. It is grounded on the same principle which I am illustrating; and as I have given extracts from Theodoret for the developments of the fourth and fifth centuries, so will I now cite St. John Damascene in defense of the further developments in the eighth.[48]

"As to the passages you adduce," he says to his opponents, "they abominate not the worship paid to our Images, but that of the Greeks, who made them gods. It needs not therefore, because of the absurd use of the Greeks, to abolish our use which is so pious. Enchanters and wizards adjure, so does the Church its Catechumens; but they invoke devils, and she invokes God against devils. Greeks dedicate images to devils, and call them gods; but we to True God Incarnate, and to God's servants and friends, who drive away the troop of devils." Again, "As the holy Fathers overthrew the temples and shrines of the devils, and raised in their places shrines in the names of Saints and we worship them, so also they overthrew the images of the devils, and {363} in their stead raised images of Christ, and God's Mother, and the Saints. And under the Old Covenant, Israel neither raised temples in the name of men, nor was memory of man made a festival; for, as yet, man's nature was under a curse, and death was condemnation, and therefore was lamented, and a corpse was reckoned unclean and he who touched it; but now that the Godhead has been combined with our nature, as some life-giving and saving medicine, our nature has been glorified and is transelemented into incorruption. Wherefore the death of Saints is made a feast, and temples are raised to them, and Images are painted. . . . For the Image is a triumph, and a manifestation, and a monument in memory of the victory of those who have done nobly and excelled, and of the shame of the devils defeated and overthrown."[49] Once more, "If because of the Law thou dost forbid Images, you will soon have to sabbatise and be circumcised, for these ordinances the Law commands as indispensable; nay, to observe the whole law, and not to keep the festival of the Lord's Pascha out of Jerusalem: but know that if you keep the Law, Christ hath profited you nothing. . . . But away with this, for whoever of you are justified in the Law have fallen from grace."

It is quite consistent with the tenor of these remarks to observe, or to allow, that real superstitions have sometimes obtained in parts of the Church from its intercourse with the heathen; or have even been admitted, or all but admitted, though commonly strenuously resisted, by its authorities, in consequence of the resemblance which exists between the heathen rites and certain portions of its ritual. As philosophy has at times corrupted its divines, so has paganism corrupted its worshippers; and as the more intellectual have been involved in heresy, so have the ignorant been corrupted by superstition. {364} Thus St. Chrysostom is vehement against the superstitious usages which Jews and Gentiles were introducing among Christians at Antioch and Constantinople. "What shall we say," he asks in one place, "about the amulets and bells which are hung upon the hands, and the scarlet woof, and other things full of such extreme folly; when they ought to invest the child with nothing else save the protection of the Cross? But now that is despised which hath converted the whole world, and given the sore wound to the devil, and overthrown all his power; while the thread, and the woof, and the other amulets of that kind, are entrusted with the child's safety." After mentioning further superstitions, he proceeds, "Now that among Greeks such things should be done, is no wonder; but among the worshippers of the Cross, and partakers in unspeakable mysteries, and professors of such morality, that such unseemliness should prevail, this is especially to be deplored again and again."[50] And in like manner St. Augustine suppressed the feasts called Agapae, which had been allowed the African Christians on their first conversion. "It is time," he says, "for men who dare not deny that they are Christians, to begin to live according to the will of Christ, and, now being Christians, to reject what was only allowed that they might become Christians." The people objected the example of the Vatican Church at Rome, where such feasts were observed every day; St. Augustine answered, "I have heard that it has often been prohibited, but the place is far off from the Bishop's abode (the Lateran), and in so large a city there is a multitude of carnal persons, especially of strangers who resort daily thither."[51] And in like manner it certainly is possible that the consciousness of the sanctifying power in Christianity may have acted as a temptation to sins, {365} whether of deceit or of violence; as if the habit or state of grace destroyed the sinfulness of certain acts, or as if the end justified the means.

It is but enunciating in other words the principle we are tracing, to say that the Church has been entrusted with the dispensation of grace. For if she can convert heathen appointments into spiritual rites and usages, what is this but to be in possession of a treasure, and to exercise discretionary power in its application? Hence there has been from the first much variety and change, in the Sacramental issues and instruments which the Church has used. While the Eastern and African Churches baptized heretics on their reconciliation, the Church of Rome, as the Catholic Church since, maintained that imposition of hands was sufficient, if their prior baptism had been formally correct. The ceremony of imposition of hands was used on various occasions with a distinct meaning; at the rite of Catechumens, on admitting heretics, in Confirmation, in Ordination, in Benediction. The Eastern Church seemed to consider the consecration of the elements in Baptism and the Eucharist to lie in the invocatory prayer; the Latin placed it in the recitation of the words of institution. Baptism was sometimes administered by immersion, sometimes by infusion. Infant Baptism was not enforced as afterwards. Children or even infants were admitted to the Eucharist in the African Church and the rest of the West, as now in the Greek. The Bread or the Wine was sometimes administered without the corresponding element. Oil had various uses, as for healing the sick, or as in the rite of Extreme Unction. Confession and Penance were at first public, afterwards private, as in the Church of Rome at this day. Indulgences of works or of periods of penance, had a different meaning, according to circumstances. In like {366} manner the Sign of the Cross was one of the earliest means of grace; then holy seasons, and holy places, and pilgrimage to them; holy water; prescribed prayers, or other observances; garments, as the scapular, or coronation robes; the rosary; the crucifix. And for some wise purpose doubtless, such as that of showing the power of the Church in the dispensation of divine grace, as well as the perfection and spirituality of the Eucharistic Presence, the Cup is witheld from all but the celebrant in the Holy Eucharist.

In the foregoing sketch I have been tracing the gradual consolidation of doctrine and ritual in the Christian Church, and describing the principles on which the process was conducted.

1. The Dogmatic and Sacramental principles have in consequence been enlarged upon here, while others were specified in a former Section; such as the mystical interpretation of Scripture, and the substitution of Faith for Reason as a principle of conduct.

2. The continuity of these various principles down to this day, and the vigour of their operation, are two distinct guarantees that the theological conclusions to which they are subservient are, in accordance with the Divine Promise, true developments, and not corruptions of the Revelation.

3. Moreover, if it be true that the principles of the later Church are the same as those of the earlier, then, whatever are the variations of belief between the two periods, the earlier in reality agrees more than it differs with the later, for principles are responsible for doctrine. Hence they who assert that the modern Roman system is the corruption of primitive theology are forced to discover some difference of principle between the one and the other; for instance, that the right of private judgment was secured to the early Church and has been lost to the later, or, again, that the later Church rationalizes and the earlier went by faith.

{367} 4. On this point I will but remark as follows. It cannot be doubted that the horror of heresy, the law of implicit obedience to ecclesiastical authority, and the doctrine of the mystical virtue of unity, were as strong and active in the Church of St. Ignatius and St. Cyprian as in that of St. Carlo and St. Pius the Fifth, whatever be thought of the theology respectively taught in the one and in the other. Now we have before our eyes the effect of these principles in the instance of the later Church; they have entirely succeeded in preventing innovation upon the doctrine of Trent for three hundred years. Have we any reason for doubting, that from the strictness the same fidelity would follow, in the first three, or any three, centuries of the Ante-tridentine period? Where then was the opportunity of corruption in the three hundred years between St. Ignatius and St. Augustine? or between St. Augustine and St. Bede? or between St. Bede and St. Peter Damiani? or again, between St. Irenaeus and St. Leo, St. Cyprian and St. Gregory the Great, St. Athanasius and St. John Damascene? Thus the tradition of eighteen centuries becomes a chain of indefinitely many links, one crossing the other; and each year, as it comes, is guaranteed with various degrees of cogency by every year which has gone before it.

5. Moreover, the various heresies which have from time to time arisen, have all in one respect or other violated those principles with which the Church rose into existence, and which she still retains. Thus Arian and Nestorian schools denied the allegorical rule of Scripture interpretation; the Gnostics and Eunomians for Faith professed to substitute Knowledge; and the Manichees also, as St. Augustine so touchingly declares in the beginning of his work, *De Utilitate Credendi*. The Dogmatic Rule, at least so far as regards it traditional {368} character was thrown aside by all those sects which, as Tertullian tells us, claimed to judge for themselves from Scripture; and the Sacramental principle was violated, *ipso facto*, by all who separated

from the Church was denied too by Faustus the Manichee when he argued against the Catholic ceremonial, by Vigilantius in his opposition to relics, and by the Iconoclasts. In like manner the contempt of mystery, of reverence, of devoutness, of sanctity, are other notes of the heretical spirit. It is plain in how many ways Protestantism has reversed the principles of Catholic theology.

6. Further, these principles of Catholic development admit of development themselves, and have in fact developed, as was above suggested, though not to the prejudice of their manifest identity throughout. For instance, the principle of Dogmatism involves the philosophy, as it may be called, of the intellectual exhibition of mysteries, and the principle of infallibility. Again, it is plain that such writers as St. Thomas and Suarez speak more definitely on the subject of Faith and Reason than Origen or Eusebius. And, in like manner, for the assertion of the Sacramental principle we shall have recourse, not to St. Gregory Thaumaturgus, who acted upon it, but to St. Augustine or St. John Damascene.

7. And, lastly, it might be expected that the Catholic principles would be later in development than the Catholic doctrines, as lying deeper in the mind, and as being its assumptions rather than its objective professions. This has been the case. The Protestant controversy has mainly turned, or is turning, on one or other of the principles of Catholicity; and to this day the rule of Scripture Interpretation, the doctrine of Inspiration, the revelation of Faith to Reason, moral responsibility, private judgment, inherent grace, the seat of infallibility, remain, I suppose, more or less undeveloped, or at least, undefined, by the Church.

[1] Vid. Proph. Off. pp. 226-230.

[2] A late writer goes farther, and maintains that it is not determined by the Council of Trent, whether the whole of the Revelation is in Scripture or not. Though this position be untenable, at least it is a remarkable testimony on the part of opponents to the Church's reverence for the written word. "The Synod declares that the Christian "truth and discipline are contained in written books and unwritten traditions." They were well aware that the controversy then was, whether the Christian doctrine was only *in part* contained in Scripture. But they did not dare to frame their decree openly in accordance with the modern Romish view; they did not venture to affirm, as they might easily have done, that the Christian verity "was contained *partly* in written books, and *partly* in unwritten traditions."—*Palmer on the Church*, vol. 2, p. 15. <William Palmer (1803-1885), *Treatise on the Church of Christ, Designed Chiefly for the Use of Students in Theology* (London: Rivingtom, 1839).>

[3] Opp. t. 1, p. 4. <Alfonso Salmeron, *Commentarii in evangelicam historiam* (Madrid, 1597-1601), 11 vols.>

[4] Opp. t. i. pp. 4, 5. The six dots, twice the usual number, occur also in the second edition, which Newman pruned of typos. By those six dots Newman may have emphasized, however elliptically, the blindness of the Old Testament. He would have surely opposed those who on recent decades wanted to remove from the wall of the Cathedral of Strasbourg blindfolded female figure that represents the Synagogue.

[5] Ibid. p. 9.

[6] Proem. 5. <Cornelius a Lapide (van den Steen, 1567-1637), *Opera*, (Antwerp, 1681).>

[7] p. 4.

[8] Lengerke, de Ephr. S. pp. 78-80. <see note 34 to ch. 5.>

[9] pp. 24-26. <John Hales (1584-1656), *Golden Remains.* . . (London: R. Pawlet, 1673). On account of his eirenicism, Hales, whose best known work was *Schism and Schismaticks* (1636), had difficulties with Archbishop Laud.>

[10] p. 27.

[11] Of Hum. Underst. iv. 18, 19.

[12] p. 334.

[13] p. 336.

[14] c. Cels. i. 9.

[15] Haer. iv. 24. Euseb. Praep. Ev. i. 5. vid. also Clem. Strom. ii. 2. Arnob. ii. 8. Cyril, Cat. v. 3. Greg. Naz. Orat. 32, 26. Pseudo-Basil in Ps 115, init. Theod. Graec. Aff. i. p. 717, &c.

[16] Clement. Strom. ii. 6. (Vid. the word *praesumptio* in Tertullian, Oxf. tr. p. 136, note *t* Kortholt (<see note 19 to ch. 4>. Calumn. 10, p. 83.) Ibid. 3. Tertull. de Praeser. Haer. 41.

[17] Init.

[18] De Util. Cred. init.

¹⁹ pp. 142, 143, Combe's tr. <Pierre-Daniel Huet (1630-1721), bp. of Avranche, *Traité philosophique de la faiblesse de l'esprit humaine* (Amsterdam, 1728), tr. *An Essay concerning the Weakness of Human Understanding* (London, 1732).>
²⁰ pp. 144, 145.
²¹ p. 219.
²² pp. 221, 223.
²³ pp. 229, 230.
²⁴ pp. 230, 231.
²⁵ Euseb. Hist. iv. 14, v. 20.
²⁶ Contr. Haer. iii. 3, § 4. This whole passage, by the way, supplies an answer to a statement which has sometimes been made that in the Fathers "Evangelical" Tradition and "Apostolical" Tradition properly stand, not for what is now meant by Tradition, but for the Gospels and Epistles respectively. On the contrary, St. Irenaeus, who is here plainly speaking of Tradition commonly so called, expressed it thus, "Traditio quae est ab Apostolis;" "Neque Scripturis neque Traditioni consentire;" "Traditio Apostolorum;" τὸ κήρυγμα τῶν ἀποστόλων καὶ τὴν παράδοσιν ἥν ἀπὸ τῶν ἀποστόλων παράδοσιν εἰλήφει· "Apostolicam Ecclesiae Traditionem;" "Veterem Apostolorum Traditionem." Again, Theodoret says that the word θεοτόκος was used, κατὰ τὴν ἀποστολικὴν παράδοσιν. Haer. iv. 12. And St. Basil contrasts τὰ ἐκ τῆς ἐγγράφου διδασκαλίας, and τὰ ἐκ τῆς τῶν ἀποστόλων παραδόσεως. de Sp. S. § 66. Presently he speaks of οὔτε τῆς θεοπνεύστου γραφῆς, οὔτε τῶν ἀποστολικῶν παραδόσεων. § 77. Origen speaks of a dogma, οὔτε παραδιδόμενον ὑπὸ τῶν ἀποστόλων, οὔτε ἐμφαινόμενόν που τῶν γραφῶν. Tom. in Matth. xii. 1. Vid. also t. 4, p. 696, and de Princ. praef. 2, and Euseb. Hist. v. 23. So in Athanasius (de Synod. 21, fin.) we read of "the Apostolical Tradition and teaching which is acknowledged by all." And soon after of a believing conformably, τῇ εὐαγγελικῇ καὶ ἀποστολικῇ ταραδόσει." 23, init, where παράδοσις means *doctrine*, not *books*, for the Greek would run τῇ εὐαγγ· καὶ τῇ ἀποστ· were the Gospels and Epistles intended. (Thus St. Leo, "secundum evangelicam apostolicamque *doctrinam*," Ep. 124, 1.) And he makes ἡ εὐαγγελικὴ παράδοσις, and ἡ ἐκκλησιαστικὴ παρ· synonymous. Cf. contr. Apoll. i. 22., with ad Adelph. 2, init. In like manner, Neander <see note   to ch.   > speaks of two kinds of so called Apostolical traditions, doctrinal and ecclesiastical, Eccl. Hist. t. 2, p. 333, transl. And <Etienne> Le Moyne <d. 1789> considers the Apostolical Tradition of St. Hippolytus to be what St. Irenaeus means by it, doctrine as distinct from Scripture. Var. Sacr. p. 1062. <Varia sacra seu Sylloge . . . (Leiden, 1785)>; Vid. also Pearson, Vindic. Ignat. i. 4, circ. fin. <John Pearson, bishop of Chester, *S. Ignatii epistulae genuinae* (1709).>. In like manner, St. Augustine contrasts Apostolical Tradition, and writings. De Bapt. contr. Don. ii. 7, v. 23.

And calls Infant Baptism an Apostolical Tradition. De Peccat. Mer. i, 26. And St. Cyprian speaks of, not only wine, but the mixed Cup in the Holy Eucharist, as an "Evangelical truth and tradition of the Lord." Epist. 63. Sometimes the phrase, on the other hand, is almost synonymous with Scripture, *E.g.* "The Apostolical Tradition teaches, blessed Peter saying, &c. and Paul writing, &c." Athan. ad Adelph. 6. Suicer <Johannes Caspar Suicerus, *Theasurus ecclesiasticus e patribus graecis* (Amsterdam, 1682), 2 vols.> refers to Greg. Nys. de Virg. xi. Cyril in Is. lxvi. 5, Balsamon, ad Can. vi. Nic. 2, Cyprian, Ep. 74, &c. A recent controversalist has also adduced these same passages and one or two others, in illustration of a sentence in Athan. cont. Apoll. i. 22, which the writer of these pages had understood of tradition; his tone is not such as claims a more distinct notice here.

27 ed. Potter, p. 897. <John Potter, Oxford, 1715, 2 vols.)>

28 ed. Potter, p. 899.

29 Clem. Strom. vii. 17. Origen. in Matth. Comm. Ser. 46. Euseb. Hist. vi. 2, fin. Epiph. Haer. 57, p. 480. Routh <see note 18 to ch. 7>, t. 2, p. 465.

30 Ad Epict. 2.

31 Justin, Apol. ii. 10, Tryph. 121.

32 Europ. Civ. p. 56. tr. <see note 7 to ch. 1>

33 p. 58.

34 De Virg. Vel. 1.

35 Hist. t. 3, p. 312.

36 Mem. Eccl. t. 6, p. 83. <See note 12 to ch. 4.>

37 Galland. t. 3, p. 673, note 3. <A. Galland (1709-1780), *Bibliotheca veterum patrum antiquorumque scriptorum ecclesiasticorum graeco-latina* (Venice, 1765-81), 14 vols.>

38 Vid. Preface to Oxford Transl. of Tertullian, where the character of his mind is admirably drawn out.

39 Infra. p. 377, &c.

40 Orig. c. Cels. vii. 63, viii. 17, (vid. not. Bened. in loc.) August. Ep. 102, 16; Minuc. F. 10, and 32; Tertull. de Orat. fin. ad Uxor. i. fin. Euseb. Hist. viii. 2; Clem. Strom. vii. 6, p. 846.

41 Tertull. de Cor. 3; Just. Apol. i. 55; Minuc. F. 29; Julian ap. Cyr. vi. p. 194, Spanh. <Ezechiel Spanheim (1629-1710), whose introduction is taken over by Migne PG 76:490-504).>

42 Epp. 102, 18.

43 Contr. Faust, 20, 23.

44 Lact. ii. 15, 16; Tertull. Sput. 12; Origen, c. Cels. vii. 64-66; August. Ep. 102, 18; Contr. Faust. xx. 23; Hirom. <Hieronymus> c. Vigil. 8.

45 Vit. Thaum. c. 27.

46 V. Const. iii. 1, iv. 23, &c.

47 According to Dr. E. D. Clarke, Travels, vol. i. p. 352. <Edward Daniel

Clarke (1769-1827), *Travels in Various Countries of Europe, Asia and Africa* (London: Cadell and Davies, 1811-12).>

[48] De Imag. 1. 24.

[49] ii. 11.

[50] Hom. xii. in Cor. 1, Oxf. Tr.

[51] Fleury, Hist. xx. 11, Oxf. Tr.

CHAPTER VII.

ILLUSTRATIONS CONTINUED.

APPLICATION OF THE FOURTH TEST OF
FIDELITY IN DEVELOPMENT.

IT has been set down above as a fourth argument in favour of the fidelity of developments, ethical or political, if the doctrine from which they have proceeded, in any early stage of its history, gave indications of those opinions and practices in which it has ended. Supposing then the so-called Catholic doctrines and practices are true and legitimate developments, and not corruptions, we may expect to find traces of them in the first centuries. And this I conceive to be the case: the records indeed of those times are scanty, and we have little means of determining what daily Christian life then was: we know little of the thoughts, and the prayers, and the meditations, and the discourses of the early disciples of Christ, at a time when these professed developments were not recognised and duly located in the theological system; yet it appears, even from what remains, that the atmosphere of the Church was, as it were, charged with them from the first, and delivered itself of them from time to time, in this way or that, in various places and persons, as occasion elicited them, testifying the presence of a vast body of thought within it, which one day would take shape and position.

§ 1.

Resurrection and Relics.

As a chief specimen of what I would say, I will direct attention to a characteristic principle {370} of Christianity, which may almost be considered as a modification or instance of the great Sacramental Principle on which I have lately insisted; I mean the view which Christianity takes of Matter as susceptible of grace, or as capable of a union with a Divine Presence and influence. This principle, as we shall see, was in the first age both strongly manifested and variously developed; and that chiefly in consequence of the diametrically opposite doctrine of the schools and the religions of the day. And thus its exhibition in that primitive time becomes also an instance of a statement often made in controversy, that the profession and the developments of a doctrine are according to the emergency of the time, and that silence at a certain period implies, not that it was not then held, but that it was not questioned.

Christianity began by considering Matter as a creature of God, and in itself "very good." It taught that Matter, as well as Spirit, had become corrupt, in the instance of Adam; and it contemplated its recovery. It taught that the Highest had taken a portion of that corrupt mass upon Himself, in order to its sanctification. It taught that, as a firstfruits of His purpose, He had purified from all sin that very portion of it which He took into His Eternal Person, and thereunto had taken it from a Virgin Womb, which He had filled with the abundance of His Spirit. Moreover, it taught that during His earthly sojourn He had been subject to all the natural infirmities of man, and had suffered all those ills to which flesh is heir. It taught that the Highest had in that flesh died on the Cross, and that His blood had an expiatory power; moreover, that He had risen again in that flesh, and had carried that flesh with Him into heaven, and that from that flesh, glorified and deified in Him, He never would be divided. As a first consequence of these awful doctrines comes that of the resurrection of {371} the bodies of His Saints, and their future glorification with Him; next, that of the sanctity of relics; further, that of the Real Presence in the Eucharist; further, that of the merit of Virginity; and lastly, that of the prerogatives of Mary, Mother of God. All these doctrines are more or less developed in the Ante-nicene period though in various degrees, from the nature of the case.

And they were all objects of offence or of scorn to philosophers, priests, or populace of the day. With varieties of opinions which need not be mentioned, it was a fundamental doctrine in the schools, whether Greek or Oriental, that Matter was essential-ly evil. It had not been created by the Supreme God; it was in eternal enmity with Him; it was the source of all pollution; and it was irreclaimable. Such was the doctrine of Platonist, Gnostic, and Manichee:—whereas then St. John had laid it down that "Every spirit that confesseth not that Jesus Christ is come in the flesh is the spirit of Antichrist," the Gnostics obstinately denied the Incarnation, and held that Christ was but a phantom, or had come on the man Jesus at his baptism, and left him at his passion. The one great topic of preaching with Apostles and Evangelists was the Resurrection of Christ and of all mankind after Him; but when the philosophers of Athens heard St. Paul, "some mocked," and others contemptuously put aside the doctrine. The birth from a Virgin implied, not only that the body was intrinsically evil, but that one state of it was holier than another, and St. Paul explained that, while marriage was good, celibacy was better; but the Gnostics, holding the utter malignity of Matter, one and all condemned marriage as sinful, and, whether they observed continence or not, or abstained from eating flesh or not, maintained that all functions of our animal nature were evil and abominable.

"Perish the thought," says Manes, "that our {372} Lord Jesus Christ should have descended through the womb of a woman." "He descended," said Marcion, "but without touching her or taking aught from her." "Through her, not of her," said another. "It is absurd to assert," says a disciple of Bardesanes, "that this flesh in which we are imprisoned shall rise again, for it is well called a burden, a tomb, and a chain." "They execrate the funeral pile," says Caecilius of Christians, "as if bodies, though withdrawn from the flames, did not all resolve into dust by years, whether beasts tear, or sea swallows, or earth covers, or flame wastes." According to the old Paganism, both the educated and the vulgar held corpses and sepulchres in aversion. They quickly rid themselves of the remains even of their friends, thinking of their presence a pollution, and felt the same terror even of burying-places which assails the ignorant and superstitious now. It is recorded of Hannibal that, on his return to the African coast from Italy, he changed his landing-place to avoid a ruined sepulchre. "For that falsehood," says Apuleius in his *Apology*, "may the god who passes between heaven and hell present to thy eyes, O Emilian, all that haunts the night, all that alarms in burying-places, all that terrifies in tombs." George of Cappadocia could not direct a more bitter taunt against the Alexandrian Pagans than to call the temple of Serapis a sepulchre. The case had been the same even among the Jews; the Rabbins taught, that even the corpses of holy men "did but serve to diffuse infection and defilement." "When deaths were Judaical," says the writer who goes under the name of St. Basil, "corpses were an abomination; when death is for Christ, the relics of Saints are precious. It was anciently said to the Priests and the Nazarites, 'If any one shall touch a corpse, he shall be unclean till evening, and he shall wash his garment;' now, on the contrary, if any one shall touch a Martyr's bones, by reason of the {373} grace dwelling in the body, he receives some participation in his sanctity."[1] Nay, Christianity taught a reverence for the bodies even of heathen. The care of the dead is one of the praises which, as we have seen above, is extorted in their favour from the Emperor Julian; and it was exemplified during the mortality which spread through the Roman world in the time of St. Cyprian. "They did good," says Pontius of the Christians of Carthage, "in the profusion of exuberant works to all, and not only to the household of faith. They did somewhat more than is recorded of the incomparable benevolence of Tobias. The slain of the king and the outcasts, whom Tobias gathered together, were of his own kin only."[2]

It was far more of course than such general reverence which they showed to the bodies of the Saints. They ascribed virtues to their martyred tabernacles, and treasured, as something supernatural, their blood, their ashes, and their bones. When St. Cyprian was beheaded, his brethren brought napkins to soak up his blood. "Only the harder portion of the holy relics remained," say the Acts of St. Ignatius, who was exposed to the beasts in the amphitheatre, "which were conveyed to Antioch, and deposited in linen, bequeathed by the grace that was in the Martyr to that holy Church as a priceless treasure." The Jews attempted to deprive the brethren of St. Polycarp's body, "lest leaving the Crucified, they begin to worship him," says his Acts; "ignorant," they continue, "that we can never leave Christ;" and they add, "We, having taken up his bones which were more costly than precious stones, and refined more {374} than gold, deposited them where was fitting; and there when we meet together as we can, the Lord will grant us to celebrate with joy and gladness the birthday of his martyrdom." On one occasion in Palestine, the Imperial authorities disinterred the bodies and cast them into the sea, "lest, as their opinion went," says Eusebius, "there should be those who in their sepulchres and monuments might think them gods, and treat them with divine worship." Julian, who had been a Christian, and knew the Christian history more intimately than a mere infidel would know it, traces the superstition, as he considers it, to the very life-time of St. John, that is, as early as there were Martyrs to honour; makes their observance contemporaneous with the worship paid to our Lord, and equally distinct and formal; and, moreover, declares that first it was secret, which for various reasons it was likely to have been. "Neither Paul," he says, "nor Matthew, nor Luke, nor Mark, dared to call Jesus God; but honest John, having perceived that a great multitude had been caught by this disease in many of the Greek and Italian cities, and hearing, I suppose, that the monuments of Peter and Paul were, secretly indeed, but still hearing that they were honoured, first dared to say it." "Who can feel worthy abomination?" he says elsewhere; "you have filled all places with tombs and monuments though it has been no where told you to tumble down at tombs or to honour them. . . . If Jesus said that they were full of uncleanness, why do ye invoke God at them?" The tone of Faustus the Manichaean is the same. "Ye have turned," he says to St. Augustine, "the idols" of the heathen "into your Martyrs whom ye observe (*colitis*) with similar prayers (*votis*)."[3]

It is remarkable that both Christians and their opponents proceeded from the subject of the relics of the Martyrs to that of their persons. Basilides at least, {375} who was founder of one of the most impious Gnostic sects, spoke of them with disrespect; he considered that their sufferings were the penalty of secret sins or evil desires, or transgressions committed in another body, and a sign of divine favour only because they were allowed to connect them with the cause of Christ.[4] On the other hand, it was the doctrine of the Church that Martyrdom was meritorious, that it had a certain supernatural efficacy in it, and that the blood of the Saints received from the grace of the One Redeemer a certain expiatory power. Martyrdom stood in the place of

Baptism, where the Sacrament had not been administered. It exempted the soul from all preparatory waiting, and gained its immediate admittance into glory. "All crimes are pardoned for the sake of this work," says Tertullian. And in proportion to the Martyrs' near approach to their Almighty Judge, such was their high dignity and power. St. Dionysius speaks of their reigning with Christ; Origen even conjectures that "as we are redeemed by the precious blood of Jesus, so some are redeemed by the precious blood of the Martyrs." St. Cyprian seems to explain his meaning when he says, "We believe that the merits of Martyrs and works of the just avail much with the Judge," that is, for those who were lapsed, "when, after the end of this age and the world, Christ's people shall stand before His Judgment-seat." Accordingly they were considered to intercede for the Church below in their state of glory, and for individuals whom they had known. St. Potamiaena of Alexandria, in the first years of the third century, when taken out for execution, promised to obtain after her departure the salvation of the officer who led her out; and did appear to him, according to Eusebius, on the third day, and prophesied his own speedy martyrdom. And St. Theodosia in {376} Palestine came to certain confessors who were in bonds, "to request them," as Eusebius tells us, "to remember her when they came to the Lord's Presence." Tertullian, when a Montanist, betrays the existence of the doctrine in the Church by protesting against it.[5]

§ 2.

Cultus of Saints and Angels.

Little as is known of the early Spanish Church, it furnishes one point of detail about itself, which seems to be a further development of the doctrine of the Intercession of Saints. The

Canons are extant of a Council of Illiberis, held shortly before the Council of Nicaea, and representative of course of the doctrine of the third century. Among these occurs the following: "It is decreed, that pictures ought not to be in the Church, lest what is worshipped or adored be painted on the walls."[6] Now these words are commonly taken to be decisive against the use of pictures in the Spanish Church at that era. Let us grant it; let us grant that the use of all pictures is forbidden, pictures not only of our Lord, and sacred emblems, as of the Lamb and Dove, but pictures of Angels and Saints also. It is not fair to restrict the words, nor are controversialists found desirous of doing so; they take them to include the images of the Saints. "For keeping of pictures out of the Church, the Canon of the Eliberine or Illiberitine Council, held in Spain, about the time of Constantine the Great, is most plain,"[7] says Usher: he is speaking of "the representations of God and of Christ, and of Angels and of Saints."[8] "The Council of Eliberis is very {377} ancient and of great fame," says Taylor, "in which it is expressly forbidden that what is worshipped should be depicted on the walls, and that therefore pictures ought not to be in churches."[9] He too is speaking of the Saints. Let us grant this freely. This inference seems to follow, that the Spanish Church considered the Saints to be in the number of objects either of "worship or adoration'"; for it is of such objects that the representations are forbidden. The very drift of the prohibition is this—*lest* what is in itself an object of worship (*quod colitur*) should be worshipped *in painting*; unless then Saints and Angels were objects of worship, their pictures would have been allowed.[10]

The glorious reign of Saints and Martyrs with Christ leads to a subject which incidentally came before us in the Introduction to this Essay, the association of His Angels with Him; though to speak of incorporeal beings will be a digression from the line of inquiry which we are pursuing.

St. Justin, after "answering the charge of Atheism," as Dr. Burton says, "which was brought against Christians of his day, and observing that they were punished for not worshipping evil demons which were not really gods," continues, "But Him, (God,) and the Son who came from Him, and taught us these things, and the host of the other good Angels which attend upon and resemble them, and the prophetic Spirit, we worship and adore, paying them a reasonable and true honour, and not refusing to deliver to any one else, who wishes to be taught, what we ourselves have learned."[11]

{378} A more express testimony to the *cultus angelorum* cannot be required; nor is it unnatural in the connexion in which it occurs, considering St. Justin has been speaking of the heathen worship of demons, and therefore would be led without effort to mention, not only the incommunicable adoration paid to the One God, who "will not give His glory to another," but such inferior honour as may be paid to creatures without sin, on the side of giver or receiver. Nor is the construction of the original Greek harsher than is found in other authors; nor need it surprise us in one whose style is not accurate, that two words should be used to express worship, and that one should include Angels, and that the other should not.

The following is Dr. Burton's account of the passage:

"Scultetus, a Protestant divine of Heidelberg, in his *Medulla Theologiae Patrum*, which appeared in 1605, gave a totally different meaning to the passage; and instead of connecting "the host" with "*we worship*," connected it with "*taught us*." The words would then be rendered thus: "But Him, and the Son who came from Him, who also gave us instructions concerning these things, and concerning the host of the other good angels we worship," &c. This interpretation is adopted and defended at some length by Bishop Bull, and by Stephen Le Moyne; and even the Benedictine Le Nourry supposed Justin to mean that

Christ had taught us not to worship the bad angels, as well as the existence of good angels. Grabe, in his edition of "Justin's Apology," which was printed in 1703, adopted another interpretation, which had {379} been before proposed by Le Moyne and by Cave. This also connects "*the host*" with "*taught these things.*" Both of them certainly are ingenious, and are not perhaps opposed to the literal construction of the Greek words; but I cannot say that they are satisfactory, or that I am surprised at Roman Catholic writers describing them as forced and violent attempts to evade a difficulty. If the words enclosed in brackets were removed, the whole passage would certinly contain a strong argument in favour of the Trinity; but as they now stand, Roman Catholic writers will naturally quote them as supporting the worship of Angels. There is, however, this difficulty in such a construction of the passage: it proves too much. By coupling the Angels with the three persons of the Trinity, as objects of religious adoration, it seems to go beyond even what Roman Catholics themselves would maintain concerning the worship of Angels. Their well-known distinction between *latria* and *dulia* would be entirely confounded; and the difficulty felt by the Benedictine editor appears to have been as great, as his attempt to explain it is unsuccessful when he wrote as follows: "Our adversaries in vain object the twofold expression, *we worship and adore*. For the former is applied to Angels themselves, regard being had to the distinction between the creature and the Creator; the latter by no means necessarily includes the Angels." This sentence requires concessions, which no opponent could be expected to make; and if one of the two terms, *we worship* and *adore* may be applied to Angels, it is unreasonable {380} to contend that the other must not also. Perhaps, however, the passage may be explained so as to admit a distinction of this kind. The interpretations of Scultetus and Grabe have not found many advocates; and upon the whole I should be inclined to conclude, that the clause, which relates to the Angels, is connected particularly with the words, 'paying them a reasonable and true honour.'"12

Two violent alterations of the text have been proposed: one to transfer the clause which creates the difficulty, after the words *paying them honour*; the other to substitute στρατηγὸν (*commander*) for στρατὸν (*host*).

Presently Dr. Burton continues:—"Justin, as I observed, is defending the Christians from the charge of Atheism; and after saying that the gods, whom they refused to worship, were no gods, but evil demons, he points out what were the Beings who were worshipped by the Christians. He names the true God, who is the source of all virtue; the Son, who proceeded from Him; the good and ministering spirits; and the Holy Ghost. To these Beings, he says, we pay all the worship, adoration, and honour, which is due to each of them; *i. e.* worship where worship is due, honour where honour is due. The Christians were accused of worshipping no gods, that is, of acknowledging no superior beings at all. Justin shows that so far was this from being true, that they acknowledged more than one order of spiritual Beings; they offered divine worship to the true God, and they also believed in the existence of good spirits, which were entitled to honour and respect. If the reader will view the passage as a whole, he will perhaps see that there is nothing violent in thus restricting the words *worship and adore*, and *honouring*, to certain parts of it respectively. It may seem strange that Justin {381} should mention the ministering spirit before the Holy Ghost; but this is a difficulty which presses upon the Roman Catholics as much as upon ourselves; and we may perhaps adopt the explanation of the Bishop of Lincoln, who says, 'I have sometimes thought that in this passage, '*and the host*' is equivalent to '*with the host*,' and that Justin had in his mind the glorified state of Christ, when He should come to judge the world, surrounded by the host of heaven." The bishop then brings several passages from Justin, where the Son of God is spoken of as attended by a company of Angels; and if this idea was then in Justin's mind, it might account for naming the ministering spirits immediately after the Son of God, rather than after the Holy Ghost, which would have been the natural and proper order."[13]

This passage is the more remarkable, because it cannot be denied that there was a worship of the Angels at that day, of which St. Paul speaks, which was Jewish and Gnostic, and utterly reprobated by the Church.

§ 3.

The merit of Virginity.

Next to the prerogatives of bodily suffering or Martyrdom came, in the estimation of the early Church, the prerogatives of bodily purity or Virginity; another form of the general principle which I am here illustrating. "The first reward," says St. Cyprian to the Virgins, "is for the Martyrs an hundred fold; the second sixty fold is for yourselves."[14] Their state and its merit is recognised by a *consensus* of the Ante-nicene writers; of whom Athenagoras distinctly connects Virginity with the privilege of divine communion: "You will find many of our people," he says to the Emperor Marcus, "both {382} men and women, grown old in their single state, in hope thereby of a closer union with God."[15]

Among the numerous authorities which might be cited, I will confine myself to a work, elaborate in itself, and important from its author. St. Methodius was a Bishop and Martyr of the latter years of the Ante-nicene period, and is celebrated as the most variously endowed divine of his day. His learning, elegance in composition, and eloquence, are all commemorated.[16] The work in question, the *Convivium Virginum*, is a conference in which ten Virgins successively take part, in praise of the state of life to which they have themselves been specially called. I do not wish to deny that there are portions of it which strangely grate upon the feelings of an age, which is formed on principles of which marriage is the centre. But here we are concerned with its doctrine. Of the speakers in this Colloquy, three at least are real persons prior to St. Methodius' time; of these Thecla, whom tradition associates with St. Paul, is one, and Marcella, who in the Roman Breviary is considered to be St. Martha's servant, and who is said to have been the woman who exclaimed, "Blessed is the womb that bare Thee," &c., is described as a still older servant of Christ. The latter opens the discourse, and her subject is the gradual development of the doctrine of Virginity in the Divine Dispensations; Theophila, who follows, enlarges on the sanctity of Matrimony, with which the special glory of the higher state does not interfere; Thalia discourses on the mystical union which exists between Christ and His Church, and on the Seventh chapter of the first Epistle to the Corinthians; Theopatra on the merit of Virginity; Thallusa exhorts to a watchful guardianship of the gift; Agatha shows the necessity of other virtues and good works, in order to the real praise of their peculiar profession; Procilla extols Virginity {383} as the special instrument of becoming a spouse of Christ; Thecla treats of it as the great combatant in the warfare between heaven and hell, good and evil; and Domnina allegorizes Jothan's parable in Judges ix. Virtue, who has been introduced as the principal personage in the representation from the first, closes the discussion with an exhortation to inward purity, and they answer her by an hymn to our Lord as the Spouse of His Saints.

It is observable that St. Methodius plainly speaks of the profession of Virginity as a vow. "I will explain," says one of his speakers, "how we are dedicated to the Lord. What is enacted in the Book of Numbers," to vow a vow mightily," shows what I am insisting on at great length, that Chastity is a mighty vow

beyond all vows."[17] This language is not peculiar to St. Methodius among the Ante-nicene Fathers. "Let such as promise
Virginity and break their profession be ranked among digamists,"
says the Council of Ancyra in the beginning of the fourth
century. Tertullian speaks of being "married to Christ," and
marriage implies a vow; he proceeds, "to Him thou has pledged
(*sponsasti*) thy ripeness of age;" and before he had expressly
spoken of the *continentiae votum*, Origen speaks of "devoting
one's body to God" in chastity; and St. Cyprian "of Christ's
Virgin, dedicated to Him and destined for His sanctity," and
elsewhere of "members dedicated to Christ, and for ever devoted
to virtuous chastity to the praise of continence;" and Eusebius of
those "who had consecrated themselves body and soul to a pure
and all-holy life."[18]

{384}   §. 4.

Office of St. Mary.

The special prerogatives of St. Mary, the *Virgo Virginum*,
are intimately involved in the doctrine of the Incarnation itself,
with which these remarks began. As is well known, they were
not fully recognised in the Catholic ritual till a late date, but they
were not a new thing in the Church, or strange to her earlier
teachers. St. Justin, St. Irenaeus, and others, had distinctly laid it
down, that she not only had an office, but bore a part, and was
a voluntary agent, in the actual process of redemption, as Eve
had been instrumental and responsible in Adam's fall. They
taught that, as the first woman might have foiled the Tempter and
did not, so had Mary been disobedient or unbelieving on
Gabriel's message, the Divine Economy would have been
frustrated. And certainly the parallel between "the Mother of all
living" and the Mother of the Redeemer may be gathered from a

comparison of the first chapters of Scripture with the last. It was noticed in a former place, that the only passage where the serpent is directly identified with the evil spirit occurs in the twelfth chapter of Revelations; now it is observable that the recognition, when made, is found in the course of a vision of a "woman clothed with the sun and the moon under her feet:" thus two women are brought into contrast with each other. Moreover, as it is said in the Apocalypse, "The dragon was wroth with the woman, and went about to make war with the remnant of her seed," so it is prophesied in Genesis, "I will put enmity between thee and the woman, and between thy seed and her Seed. He shall bruise thy head, and thou shalt bruise His heel." Also the enmity was to exist, not only between the Serpent and the Seed of the woman, but between the serpent and the woman herself; and here too there {385} is a correspondence in the Apocalyptic vision. If then there is a reason for thinking that this mystery at the close of Revelation answers to the mystery in the beginning of it and that "the Woman" mentioned in both passages is one and the same, then she can be none other than St. Mary, thus introduced prophetically to our notice immediately on the transgression of Eve.

Here, however, we are not so much concerned to interpret Scripture as to examine the Fathers. Thus St. Justin says, "Eve, being a virgin and incorrupt, having conceived the word from the Serpent, bore disobedience and death; but Mary the Virgin, receiving faith and joy, when Gabriel the Angel evangelized her, answered, "Be it unto me according to thy word."[19] And Tertullian says that, whereas Eve believed the Serpent, and Mary believed Gabriel, "what Eve failed in believing, Mary by believing hath blotted out."[20] St. Irenaeus speaks more explicitly: "As Eve," he says, "was seduced by the Angel's speech so as to flee God, having transgressed his word, so also Mary by an Angel's speech was evangelized as to contain God, being obedient to his Word. And as the one was seduced to flee God, having transgressed His word, so also Mary by an Angel's speech was evangelized so as to contain God, being obedient to His Word. And as the one was seduced to flee God, so the other was persuaded to obey God, that the Virgin Mary might become the Advocate (Paraclete) of the Virgin Eve, that as mankind has been bound to death through a Virgin, through a Virgin it may be saved,—virginal disobedience by virginal obedience, the balance being made equal." And elsewhere, "As Eve, becoming disobedi-ent, became the cause of death to herself and to all mankind, so Mary too, having the predestined Man, and yet a Virgin, being obedient, became cause of salvation both to herself and to all mankind. . . . The knot formed by Eve's disobedience was untied through the obedience of Mary; for what the Virgin Eve tied through unbelief, that {386} the Virgin Mary unties through faith."[21] This becomes the received doctrine in the Post-nicene Church.

One well-known instance occurs in the history of the third century of St. Mary's interposition, and it is remarkable from the names of the two persons, who were, one the subject, the other the historian of it. St. Gregory of Nyssen, a native of Cappadocia in the fourth century, relates that his name-sake Bishop of Neo-caesarea, surnamed Thaumaturgus, in the preceding century, shortly before he was called to the priesthood, received in a vision a Creed, which is still extant, from St. Mary at the hands of St. John. The account runs thus: He was deeply pondering theological doctrine, which the heretics of the day depraved. "In such thoughts," says his name-sake of Nyssa, "he was passing the night, when one appeared, as if in human form, aged in appear-ance, saintly in the fashion of his garments, and very venerable both in grace of countenance and general mien. Amazed at the sight, he started from his bed, and asked who it was, and why he came; but on the other calming the perturbation of his mind with his gentle voice, and saying he had appeared to him by divine command on account of his doubts, in order that the truth of the orthodox faith might be revealed to him, he took courage at the word, and regarded him with a mixture of joy and fright. Then on his stretching his hand forward, and pointing with his fingers at something on one side, he followed with his eyes the extended hand, and saw another appearance opposite to the former, in shape of a woman, but more than human. . . . When his eyes could not bear the apparition, he heard them conversing together on the subject of his doubts; and thereby not only gained a true knowledge of the faith, but learned their names, as they addressed each other by their respective appellations. And thus he is said to have heard the person in woman's {387} shape bid "John the Evangelist" disclose to the young man the mystery of godliness; and he answered that he was ready to comply in this matter with the wish of "the Mother of the Lord," and enunciated a formulary, well-turned and complete, and so vanished. He, on the other hand, immediately committed to writing that divine teaching of his mystagogue, and henceforth preached in the Church according to that form, and bequeathed to posterity, as an inheritance, that heavenly teaching, by means of which his people are instructed down to this day, being preserved from all heretical evil." He proceeds to rehearse the Creed thus given, "There is one God, Father of a Living Word," &c.[22] Bull, after quoting it in his work upon the Nicene Faith, alludes to this history of its origin, and adds, "No one should think it incredible that such a providence should befall a man whose whole life was conspicuous for revelations and miracles, as all ecclesiastical writers who have mentioned him (and who has not?) witness with one voice.[23]

It is remarkable that St. Gregory Nazianzen relates an instance, even more pointed, of St. Mary's intercession, contemporaneous with this appearance to Thaumaturgus; but it is attended with mistake in the narrative, which weakens its cogency as an evidence of the belief, not indeed of the fourth century, in which St. Gregory lived, but of the third. He speaks of a Christian woman having recourse to the protection of St. Mary, and obtaining the conversion of a heathen who had attempted to practise on her by magical arts. They were both martyred.

In both these instances the Blessed Virgin appears especially in that character of Patroness or Paraclete, which St. Irenaeus and other Fathers describe, and which the Medieval Church exhibits,—a loving Mother with clients.

{388}   § 5.

Specimens of Theological Science.

It will be observed that in nothing that has hitherto been adduced from the Ante-nicene Church, is there any evidence of a theology, that is, of a conscious deduction of proposition from proposition, and the formation of a doctrinal system. Though the series of divine truths proceeded from the Incarnation and the Resurrection to the merit of Martyrdom, the sanctity of Relics, the intercession of Saints, the excellence of Virginity, and the prerogatives of St. Mary, yet there was no very clear evidence that the preachers of these doctrines understood their connexion with each other. Thus I am not aware of any passage in which the religious observance of Relics is clearly connected with the doctrine of the Resurrection, from which it undoubtedly proceeds. This may afford matter for an objection. It may be said that we are connecting together for a particular purpose certain opinions or practices, which are found among others in primitive times, and which are really unconnected and accidental. It may be urged moreover, that there are many things in the documents or the history of the period which have a contrary bearing; that the Fathers also speak against idols, and invocation of Angels; that some of them have been betrayed into statements which savour of heresy or pagan philosophy; and that by putting all these together we might form as imposing a *catena* against the Catholic doctrines as can be formed in their favour.

But this is to misunderstand the drift of this argument, which is merely to determine whether certain developments, which did afterwards and do exist, have not such sufficient countenance in early times, that we may pronounce them to be true developments and not corruptions. If existing developments can be produced of an opposite kind, {389} and the question arises whether these also are really such or corruptions, then will be the time, and then will it be fair, to make mention of such antagonist instances as shall be forthcoming. Nay, if there be but an hypothesis which has never been realized, with which they fall in, which interprets more consistently than the Catholic creed the whole mass of Ante-nicene testimony, this will have its weight, though it rest on no historical foundation. But this is not the case. Stray heterodox expressions, Sabellian or Unitarian, or what was afterwards Arian, Platonisms, *argumenta ad hominem*, assertions in controversy, omissions in practice, silence in public teaching, and the like, such as alone can be adduced, can be made up into no system. They are "a rope of sand," to use the familiar phrase, not a *catena*; each stands by itself, with an independence, or an irrelevancy, which precludes the chance of assimilation or coalition. On the other hand, the Catholic anticipations which have been instanced, are parts of a whole, and have innate attractions towards each other, and have been proved to have them by the event; and therefore, it is no paradox to say, that even were they much fewer than those of a contrary character, they would be the rule, and the majority would be the exception: for they have a principle of consistency, and tend to be something; whereas the others must be mere accidents and errors, because they have no meaning, and come to nothing.

However in fact there is very clear evidence of the formation of a theology in Christianity from the first, and that founded on the very views of the relation of Matter to the Evangelical Dispensation, which has been above selected for illustration; though that theology in the primitive age does not extend to all the developments, which have been already instanced in their popular and devotional aspects. In order to make this plain, I shall make use {390} of an article which appeared in a Review some years ago,[24] on the subject of St. Ignatius' Epistles.

"Men fancy," it was observed, "that though they have never seen Clement or Ignatius, or any other Father before, they are quite as well qualified to interpret the words λειτουργία or προφορά as if they knew them and their brethren well. How different is their judgment in other matters! Who will not grant, except in the case of theology, that an experienced eye is an important qualification for understanding the distinction of things or detecting their force and tendency? In politics, the sagacious statesman puts his finger on some apparently small or not confessedly great event, promptly declares it to be 'no little matter,' and is believed. Why? because he is conceived to have scholarship in the language of political history, and to be well read in the world's events. In the same way the comparative anatomist falls in with a little bone, and confidently declares, from it, the make, habits, and age of the animal to which it belonged. What should we say to the unscientific hearer who disputed his accuracy and attempted to argue against him? Yet, is this not just the case of sciolists, or less than sciolists in theology, who, when persons who have given time to the Fathers recognise in some phrase or word in Clement or Ignatius a Catholic doctrine, object that the connexion between the phrase and the doctrine is not clear *to them*, and allow nothing to the judgment of the experienced, over that of ordinary men? Or again, surely it needs to be formally proved that sympathy and congeniality of mind are concerned in enabling us to enter into another's meaning. His single words or tones are nothing to one man, they tell a story to another: the one man passes them over; the other is arrested by them, and {391} never forgets them. Such is the difference between reading the Apostolical Father with or without a knowledge of theological language."

After quoting various passages from St. Ignatius, the writer continued,

"In these extracts there are a number of remarkable expressions, which the student in Catholic theology alone will recognize, and he at once, as belonging to that theology, and having a special reference to the heretical perversions of it. He will enter into, and another might pass over such words and phrases as γεννητὸς καὶ αγέννητος,—ἐν σαρκὶ γενό-μενος θεὸς—ἐκ Μαρίας καὶ ἐκ θεοῦ,—παθητὸς καὶ ἀπαθὴς,—ἄχρονος—ἀόρατος, δι'ἡμᾶς ὁρατός,—τέλειος ἄνδρωπος γενόμενος,—σαρκόφορος,—πάθος τοῦ θεοῦ. He will perceive such expressions to be dogmatic, and will be at home in them.

"For instance, take the words τέλειος ἄνθρωπος, 'perfect man.' A heresy existed in the beginning of the fourth century, which was in fact a revival of the error of the Docetae, in St. John's times, viz. that our Lord was not really a man as other men are, that he had no intellectual soul, and, as they went on to say, not even a real body. Such was the tenet of Apollinarianism, and the Catholics protested against it by maintaining that Christ was "perfect man" (τέλειος). This was their special symbol against the heresy, as we find it in the Athanasian Creed, "perfect man, subsisting of a reasonable soul and human flesh." The Apollinarians joined issue on this point; they contended that it was impossible for one and the same person to contain in him δύο τέλεια, and that since our Lord was perfect God, he could not be perfect man. In consequence, this became a turning point of the controversy, and is treated as such, among other authors, by Athanasius, Nazianzen, Epiphanius, Leontius, and Maximus.

"The importance of the word is most readily {392} shown by its occurrence in Creeds. The Athanasian has already been mentioned; in like manner a confession ascribed by Theodoret to St. Ambrose speaks of our Lord Jesus Christ, 'who in the last days became incarnate, and took on Him a *perfect* manhood of rational soul and body;' so that 'of two *perfect* natures an union has been made ineffably,' &c. In a Creed of Pelagius, who was orthodox on this point, we are told that 'they who own in the Son an imperfect God and *imperfect* man, are to be accounted not to hold truly either God or man.' And John of Antioch, in his explanation to St. Cyril, confesses that our Lord is 'perfect God and *perfect* man, of a reasonable soul and body.'

"The expression, then, 'perfect man,' was a portion of the dogmatic Catholic view existing in the fourth and fifth centuries. Now, as we have above quoted, it belongs also to Ignatius: 'I endure all,' he says, 'as He who became *perfect* man, enables me.' Here, then, on the one hand, we find a word in Ignatius, which is scarcely taken from Scripture, which is uncongenial to modern sentiments, which is uncalled for by the context, which has the air of a dogmatic expression, which was well adapted to oppose existing errors, and which is found in a work which does oppose heresies of various sorts. On the other hand, we find this word undeniably and prominently a dogmatic term in the fourth century; can we doubt that it is dogmatic in Ignatius? or, in other words, that Ignatius's tone of writing is inconsistent with the modern theory, whether of feelings or of good lives being the whole of religion, and formal creeds being superfluous or burdens?

"Take another instance: he speaks of those who 'blaspheme' Christ, 'not confessing that He bore flesh' (σαρκοφόρον). This word is of a dogmatic character on the very face of the passage; and it is notoriously such in after-controversy. It is so {393} used by Clement of Alexandria, Athanasius and in the Confessions of the Emperors Valentinian, Valens, and Gratian. It was used both in the Apollinarian and Nestorian controversies; by the Catholics against Nestorius, who asserted that our Lord was not θεὸς σαρκοφόρος, but ἄνθρωπος θεοφόρος and by the Apollinarians with a view of imputing to the Catholics what was really the Nestorian tenet.

"Again: Nestorius considering, after the Cerinthians and other early Gnostics, that the Son of God was distinct from Christ, a man, as if Christ had a separate existence or personality, the Catholics met the heresy, among other strong statements, by the phrases that 'God was born and suffered on the cross,' and that the Blessed Virgin was θεοτόκος, 'the Mother of God.' On the other hand, such phrases, it is scarcely necessary to say, are considered in the judgment of this day's religion at once incorrect and unbecoming. This is not the place to go into the history of the controversy, and to show their propriety and necessity. The latter of the two is found in Origen, who, moreover, engaged in an inquiry into its real meaning, which is remarkable as showing that it was at that time a received word; for we do not investigate what we have invented. It is used by Alexander, Nazianzen, and Athanasius, and as many think, by Dionysius. As to the former phrase, Irenaeus speaks of our Lord's 'descensio in Mariam;' Tertullian of His descending 'in vulvam de vulvâ carnem participaturus;' or of 'Dei passiones', 'Dei interemptores;' and Athanasius of the 'σῶμα θεοῦ,' and of the consequent duty of worshipping it. Athanasius, indeed, as is well known, objected to the phrase that 'God suffered,' as used by Apollinaris, who by θεὸς meant θεότης, but that it was a usual and received phrase in the Church Catholic cannot be disputed. Now turning to Ignatius, we find it in a passage above quoted from his Epistles; as he speaks {394} of being 'a follower of the πάθος τοῦ θεοῦ. In like manner, he says that 'our God, Jesus the Christ, was born in the womb, ἐκυοφορηθη, by

Mary.' Is this the language of the modern school and not rather of the Catholic Church?"

And then after adding other instances: "To draw out fully the case for Catholic doctrine, which this apostolical Father supplies, would lead us beyond both the literal and moral bounds of a review. It would be a great service if some divine would publish the text of these Epistles, with a running comment from the Fathers after them. It is hardly too much to say that almost the whole system of Catholic doctrine may be discovered in them, at least in outline, not to say filled up in parts. There are indeed one or two remarkable omissions, as if on purpose to prove to us their genuineness; for in a later age these certainly would have been supplied; the chief of which is the scanty notices they contain of the Catholic doctrine of the Trinity, and of baptismal regeneration, which in Ignatius's time were not subjects of controversy. But after all the deductions from the completeness of his theological system, let us see what we have in the course of these seven short compositions. We have, first, the principle of dogmatic faith; next the doctrine of the Incarnation, almost as theologically laid down as it is in the fourth and fifth centuries; then that of the dissemination of a new and divine nature in the fallen stock of Adam, and that by means of the Eucharist. Further, we read in them of the divine origin and duty of the Episcopal regimen; the divine authority of the Bishop, as the representative of our unseen Maker and Redeemer; the doctrine of the three orders; the doctrine of unity; the doctrine of the Church's Catholicity; the diocesan system; the sin of going by individual judgments in matters of faith; what may be called the sacramental character of unity; the consecrating {395} power and authority of Bishops over all Ecclesiastical appointments, and the importance of united prayer. To these might be added his implied praise of virginity, and his implied countenance of resolves for that purpose; apparently too his recognition of what has since been called the *Disciplina Arcani*, of what has been called the *Limbus Patrum*, of the Lord's day, of the acceptableness of good works, of grace as inherent, not external, of Ecclesiastial Councils, of departed Saints remembering, or at least benefitting us, and of communion with them in life and death; and, not least important as throwing a light on all that has been said by the contrast, his hatred and condemnation of Judaism."

The writer continues, "Are these Epistles genuine? Are they but genuine on the whole? Are they genuine all but certain corruptions which cannot now be detected? Let it be granted only as far as this, that the substance of them is what Ignatius wrote, —and those who deny this may wrestle, as best they can, with the greater difficulties in which they will find themselves,— and is any further witness wanting to prove that the Catholic system, not in an inchoate state, not in doubtful dawnings, not in tendencies, or in implicit teaching, or in temper, or in surmises, but in a definite, complete, and dogmatic form, was the religion of St. Ignatius; and if so, where in the world did he come by it? How came he to lose, to blot out from his mind, the true Gospel, if this was not it? How came he to possess this, except it be apostolic? One does not know which of the two most to be struck with his precise unhesitating tone, or the compass of doctrine he goes through; the latter, however, has this particular force, which the former has not, that it quite cuts off the suspicion, if any lingers on the mind, that the conciseness with which his sentiments are conveyed has given opportunity for their being practised on by theologians, and tortured into {396} Church meanings which they really have not. Granting that, by a mere coincidence, some one form of words in his Epistles might have been misinterpreted into an apparent countenance of some later doctrine, or that some one word like θυσιαστήριον or εὐχαριστία might be laden with a sense which came in later, it is quite impossible surely that so great a number of coincidences should have occurred, that so many distinct doctrines afterwards existing in the Church should accidently find a place, find form of words capable of denoting them, and used afterwards to denote them, in so short a document. Either the Epistles of St. Ignatius have been the document from which the Church system has been historically developed, which no one maintains, or the Church system is the basis on which St. Ignatius wrote his Epistles."

It is only necessary to add, on a sentence near the commencement of this last extract, that though certain Catholic doctrines are found in St. Ignatius, "not in an inchoate state, not in doubtful dawnings, not in tendencies, or in implicit teaching, or in temper, or in surmises, but in a definite, complete, and dogmatic form," yet certain other doctrines are found in his Epistles, at most only in their rudiments; as, for instance, the doctrine of the Holy Trinity, of Original Sin, or of Baptismal Regeneration, as indeed is expressly stated in one of the above passages.

The capabilities, so to speak, of the text of St. Ignatius for the process of subsequent development, which are most striking in the writings of other Fathers also, as in St. Athanasius and St. Augustine, might have been mentioned under the next Test; but it seems more natural to refer to them here. So much then in proof of the existence from the first, whether in individual minds or popular belief, of those doctrinal developments which afterwards became recognised portions of the Church's Creed.

---

[1] Act. Arch. p. 85. <*Acta Archelai et Manetis disputationis*, PG 73-74>. Athan. c. Apoll. ii. 3.—Adam. Dial. iii. init. <Adamantius, Dialogus de recta in Deum fide>. Minuc. Dial. ll. Apul. Apol. p. 535. Kortholt. Cal. <see note 19 to ch. 3> p. 63. Calmet, Dict. t. 2, p. 736. <A. Calmet (1672-1757), *Dictionnaire critique, historique, chronologique, géographique et littéral de la Bible* (Paris: 1720)>. Basil in Ps. 115, 4.

[2] Vit. S. Cypr. 10.

[3] Act. Procons. 5. Ruinart, Act. Mart. pp. 22, 44. Euseb. Hist. viii. 6. Julian. ap. Cyr. pp. 327, 335. August. c. Faust. xx. 4.

[4] Clem. Strom. iv. 12.

[5] Tertull. Apol. fin. Euseb. Hist. vi. 42. Orig. ad Martyr. 50. Ruinart, Act. Mart. pp. 122, 323.

[6] Placuit picturas in ecclesiâ esse no debere, ne, quod colitur aut adoratur, in parietibus depingatur. Can. 36.

[7] Answ. to a Jes. 10, p. 437. <James Usher (1581-1656), *An Answer to a Challenge made by a Jesuit* [i.e. W. B.] *in Ireland, wherein the Judgment of Antiquity in the Points questioned is truly delivered, and the novelties of the New Romish Doctrine plainly discovered* (Dublin, 1624), a work reprinted in Cambridge in 1835 with the subtitle, *with other Tracts on Popery*.>

[8] p. 430. The "colitur *aut* adoratur" marks a difference of worship.

[9] Dissuasive, i. 1, 8. <Jeremy Taylor (1613-1667), *A Dissuasive from Popery to the People of Ireland*, 3d ed. corrected by the author, London, 1664>

[10] The canon runs "ne quod colitur . . . depingatur; if it merely meant "lest what *may become* an object of worship," &c. it would have been "ne quod colatur."

[11] Εκεῖνον τε, καὶ τὸν παρ᾽ αὐτοῦ υἱὸν ἐλθόντα καὶ διδάξαντα ἡμᾶς ταῦτα, [καὶ τὸν τῶν ἀλλων ἑπομένων καὶ ἐξομοιουμένων ἀγαθῶν ἀγγέλων στρατὸν,] πνεῦμα τε τὸ προφητικὸν σεβόμεθα καὶ προσκυνοῦμεν, λόγῳ καὶ ἀληθέια τίμῶντες, καὶ παντὶ βουλομένῳ μαθεῖν, ὡς ἐδιδάχθημεν, ἀφθόνως παραδιδόντες. *Apol.* i. 6. The passage is parallel to the Prayer in the Breviary: "Sacrosanctae et individuae Trinitati, Crucufixi Domini nostri Jesu Christi humanitati, beatissimae et gloriosissimae semperque Virginis Mariae faecundae integritati, et omnium Sanctorum universitati, sit sempiterna laus, honor, virtus, et gloria ab omni creaturâ," &c.

[12] Test. Trin. pp. 16, 17, 18. <See note 15 to Introduction.>

[13] p. 19-21.

[14] De Hab. Virg. 12.

[15] Athenag. Leg. 33.

[16] Lumper, Hist. t. 13, p. 439. <R. Gottfried Lumper, *Historia theologico-critica de viat scriptis atque doctrina Sanctorum Patrum Ecclesiasticorum trium priorum saeculorum* (Augsburg, 1783-99).>

[17] Galland. t. 3, p. 700. <see note 37 to ch. 6.>

[18] Routh, Reliqu. t. 3, p. 414. <M. J. Routh, *Reliquiae sacrae, sive auctorum fere iam perditorum, secundi tertiique saeculi, quae supersunt* (Oxford,1814-18), 4 vols.> Tertull. de Virg. Vel. 16 and 11. Orig. in Num. Hom. 24, 2. Cyprian. Ep. 4, p. 8, ed. Fell. Ep. 62, p. 147. Euseb. v. Const. iv. 26.

[19] Tryph. 100.

[20] Resurr. Carn. 17.

[21] Haer. iii. 22, § 4, v. 19.

[22] Nyss. Opp. t. ii. p. 977.

[23] Def. F. N. ii. 12. <see note 8 to Introduction.>

[24] British Critic, January, 1839, pp. 57-74. <Part of a review of an edition by W. Jacobson (Oxford, 1838), of the Letter of S. Clement, and of the letters of S. Ignatius of Antioch and the writings of other early Fathers.>

CHAPTER VIII.

ILLUSTRATIONS CONCLUDED.

SECTION I.

APPLICATION OF THE FIFTH TEST OF FIDELITY IN DEVELOPMENT.

LOGICAL sequence was set down in the first Chapter of this Essay as a fifth test of fidelity in development, and shall now be briefly illustrated in the history of Christian doctrine. That is, I mean to give instances of one doctrine leading to another; so that, if the former be admitted, the latter can hardly be denied, and the latter can hardly be called a corruption without reflecting on the former. And I use "logical sequence," in contrast to that process of incorporation and assimilation which has lately been under review, to denote an internal growth of doctrine and usage in the way of reasoning. Accordingly it will include any progress of the mind from one judgment to another, as, for instance, by way of moral fitness, which may not admit of analysis into premiss and conclusion. Thus St. Peter argued in the case of Cornelius and his friends, "Can any man forbid water that these should not be baptized, which have received the Holy Ghost as well as we?"

§ 1.

Developments growing out of the Question of our Lord's Divinity.

No one who has looked ever so little into the theological works of the ancient Church, but is {398} aware that the language of the Ante-nicene Fathers, on the subject of our Lord's Divinity, may be far more easily accomodated to the Arian hypothesis than the language of the Post-nicene. Thus St. Justin speaks of the Son as subservient to the Father in the creation of the world, as seen by Abraham, as speaking to Moses from the bush, as appearing to Joshua before the fall of Jericho,[1] as Minister and Angel, and as numerically distinct from the Father. Clement, again, speaks of the Word[2] as the "Instrument of God," "close to the Sole Almighty;" "ministering to the Omnipotent Father's will;"[3] an energy, so to say, or operation of the Father,"[4] and "constituted as the causer of all good by the Almighty Father's will." The Council of Antioch, which condemned Paul of Samosata, says that He "appears to the Patriarchs and converses with them, being testified sometimes to be an Angel, at other times Lord, at others God;" that, while "it is impious to think that the God of all is called an Angel, the Son is the Angel of the Father."[5] Formal proof, however, is unnecessary; had not the fact been as I have stated it, neither Sandius would have attacked the Post-nicene Fathers, nor would Bull have had to defend the Ante-nicene.

One principal change which took place, as time went on, was the following: the Ante-nicene Fathers, as in some of the foregoing extracts, speak of the Angelic visions in the Old Testament as if they were appearances of the Son; but St. Augustine introduced the explicit doctrine, which has been received since his date, that they were simply Angels, through whom the Omnipresent Son manifested Himself. This indeed is the only interpretation which could be put on the Ante-nicene statements, as soon as reason began to examine what they meant. They could not mean that the Eternal {399} God could really be seen by bodily eyes; if anything was seen, that must have been some created glory or other symbol, by which it pleased the Almighty to signify His Presence. What was heard was a sound, as external to His Essence, and as distinct from His Nature, as the thunder, or the voice of the trumpet, which pealed along Mount Sinai; what it was had not come under discussion till St. Augustine; both questions and answers were alike undeveloped. The earlier Fathers spoke as if there were no medium interposed between the Creator and the creature, and so they seemed to make the Eternal Son the medium; what it really was, they had not determined. St. Augustine ruled, and his ruling has been accepted in later times, that it was not a mere atmospheric phenomenon, or an impression on the senses, but the material form proper to an Angelic presence, or the presence of an Angel in that material garb in which blessed Spirits do ordinarily appear to men. Henceforth the Angel in the bush, the voice which spoke with Abraham, and the man who wrestled with Jacob, were not regarded as the Son of God, but as Angelic ministers, whom He employed, and through whom He signified His presence and His will. Thus the tendency of the controversy with the Arians was to raise our view of our Lord's Mediatorial acts, to impress them on us in their divine rather than their human aspect, and to associate them more intimately with the ineffable glories which surround the Throne of God. The Mediatorship was no longer regarded in itself in that prominently subordinate place which it had once occupied in the thoughts of Christians, but as an office assumed by One, who, though having become man in order to bear it, was still God. Works and attributes, which had hitherto been assigned to the Economy or to Sonship, were now simply assigned to the Manhood. A tendency was also elicited, as the

{400} controversy proceeded, to contemplate our Lord more distinctly in His absolute perfections, than in His relation to the First Person of the Blessed Trinity. Thus, whereas the Nicene Creed speaks of the "Father Almighty," and "His Only-begotten Son, our Lord, God from God, Light from Light, Very God from Very God," and of the Holy Ghost, "the Lord and Giver of Life," we are told in the Athanasian of "the Father Eternal, the Son Eternal, and the Holy Ghost Eternal," and that "none is afore or after other, none is greater or less than another."

The Apollinarian and Monophysite controversy, which followed in the course of the next century, tended towards a development in the same direction. Since the heresies, which were in question, maintained, at least virtually, that our Lord was not man, it was obvious to insist on the passages of Scripture which describe His created and subservient nature, and this had the immediate effect of interpreting of His manhood texts which had hitherto been understood more commonly of His Divine Sonship. Thus for instance, "My Father is greater than I," which had been understood even by St. Athanasius of our Lord as God, is applied by later writers more commonly to His humanity; and in this way the doctrine of His subordination to the Eternal Father, which formed so prominent a feature in the Ante-nicence theology, comparatively fell into the shade.

And coincident with these changes, a most remarkable result is discovered. The treatment of the Arian and Monophysite errors, being of this character, became the natural introduction of the *cultus Sanctorum*; for in proportion as words descriptive of created mediation ceased to be applied to our Lord, so was a room opened for created mediators. Nay, as regards the instance of Angelic appearances itself, as St. Augustine explained them, if those appearances were creatures, certainly creatures were worshipped by the Patriarchs, not indeed {401} in themselves, but as the token of a Presence greater than themselves. When "Moses hid his face, for he was afraid to look upon God," he hid his face before a creature; when Jacob said, "I have seen God face to face, and my life is preserved," the Son of God was there, but what he saw, what he wrestled with, was an Angel. When "Joshua fell on his face to the earth and did worship before the captain of the Lord's host, and said unto him, What saith my Lord unto his servant?" what was seen and heard was a glorified creature, if St. Augustine is to be followed; and the Son of God was in him.

And there were plain precedents in the Old Testament for the religiousness of such adoration. When "the people saw the cloudy pillar stand at the tabernacle door," "all the people rose up and worshipped, every man in his tent-door."[6] When Daniel too saw "a certain man clothed in linen" "there remained no strength" in him, for his "comeliness was turned" in him "into corruption." He fell down on his face, and next remained on his knees and hands, and at length "stood trembling," and said, "O my Lord, by the vision my sorrows are turned upon me, and I have retained no strength. For how can the servant of this my Lord talk with this my Lord?"[7] It might be objected perhaps to this argument, that a worship which was allowable in an elementary system might be unlawful when "grace and truth" had come "through Jesus Christ;" but then it might be retorted surely, that the elementary system had been emphatically opposed to all idolatry, and had been minutely jealous of everything which might approach to favouring it. Nay, the very prominence given in the Pentateuch to the doctrine of a Creator, and the comparative silence concerning the {402} Angelic creation, and the prominence given to the Angelic creation in the later Prophets, taken together, were a token both of that jealousy, and of its cessation in course of time. Nor can anything be concluded from St. Paul's censure of Angel worship, since the sin which he is denouncing was that of "not holding the Head," and of worshipping creatures *instead* of the Creator as the source of good. The same explanation avails for passages like those in St. Athanasius and Theodoret, in which the worship of Angels is discountenanced.

The Arian controversy had led to another development, which confirmed by anticipation the *cultus* to which St. Augustine's doctrine pointed. In answer to the objection urged against our Lord's supreme Divinity from texts which speak of His exaltation, St. Athanasius is led to insist largely on the benefits which have accrued to man through it. He says that, in truth, not Christ, but that human nature which He had assumed, was raised and glorified in Him. The more plausible was the heretical argument from those texts against his Divinity, the more emphatic is St. Athanasius' exaltation of our regenerate nature by way of explaining them. But intimate indeed must be the connexion between Christ and His brethren, and high their glory, if the language which seemed to belong to the Incarnate word really belonged to them. Thus the pressure of the controversy elicited and developed a truth, which till then was held indeed by Christians, but less perfectly realized and not publicly recognized. The sanctification, or rather the deification of the nature of man, is one main subject of St. Athanasius' theology. Christ, in rising, raises His Saints with Him to the right hand of power. They become instinct with His Life, of one body with His flesh, sons, kings, gods. He is in them, because He is in human nature; and He comunicates to them that nature deified by becoming His, that it may deify them. He is in them by the {403} Presence of His Spirit, and in them is He seen. They have those titles of honour by participation, which are properly His. Without misgiving we may apply to them the most sacred language of Psalmists and Prophets. "Thou art a Priest for ever" may be said of St. Polycarp or St. Martin as well as of their Lord. "He hath dispersed abroad, he hath given to the poor," was fulfilled in St. Laurence. "I have found David My servant" was first said of the King of Israel, belongs really to Christ, is transferred again by grace to His Vice-gerents upon earth. "I have given thee the nations for thine inheritance" is the prerogative of Popes. "Thou hast given him his heart's desire," the record of a Martyr; "thou has loved righteousness and hated iniquity," the praise of Virgins.

"As Christ," says St. Athanasius, "died, and was exalted as man, so, as man, is He said to take what, as God, He ever had, that even this so high a grant of grace might reach to us. For the Word was not impaired in receiving a body, that He should seek to receive a grace, but rather He deified that which He put on, nay, gave it graciously to the race of man. For it is the Father's glory, that man made and then lost should be found again; and, when the prey of death, that he should be made alive, and should become God's temple. For whereas the powers in heaven, both Angels and Archangels, were ever worshipping the Lord, as they are now worshipping Him in the Name of Jesus, this is our grace and high exaltation, that, even when He became man, the Son of God is worshipped, and the heavenly powers are not startled at seeing all of us, who are of one body with Him, introduced into their realms."[8] In this passasge it is almost said that the glorified Saints will partake in the homage paid by Angels to Christ, the True Object of all worship; and at least as reason is suggested by it {404} for the Angel's shrinking in the Apocalypse from the homage of St. John, the Theologian and Prophet of the Church. But St. Athanasius proceeds still more explicitly, "In that the Lord, even when come in human body and called Jesus, was worshipped and believed to be God's Son, and that through Him the Father is known, it is plain, as has been said, that *not the Word*, considered as the Word, received this so great grace, *but we*. For, because of our relationshiop to His Body, we too have become God's temple, and in consequence are made God's sons, so that *even in us the Lord is now worshipped*, and beholders report, as the Apostle says, that "God is there of a truth."[9] It would appear to be distinctly stated in this passage, that those who are known to be God's adopted sons in Christ are fit objects of worship on account of Him who is in them; a doctrine which both interprets and accounts for the invocation of Saints, the observance of relics, and the religious veneration in which the living have sometimes been held, who, being saintly, were distinguished by miraculous gifts.[10] Worship then is the necessary correlative of glory; and in the same sense in which created natures can share in the Creator's incomunicable glory, do they also share in that worship which is His property alone.

There was one other subject on which the Arian controversy had a more intimate, though not an immediate influence. Its tendency to give a new interpretation to the texts which speak of our Lord's subordination, has already been noticed; such as admitted of it were henceforth explained more prominently of His manhood than of His Economy or His Sonship. But there were other texts which did not admit of this interpretation, but which, without ceasing to belong to Him, might seem more directly applicable to a creature than to a Creator. He indeed was really the "Wisdom in whom the Father eternally delighted," yet it would be but natural, if, under the circumstances of Arian misbelief, theologians looked out for other than the Eternal Son to be immediate object of such descriptions. And thus the controversy opened a question which it {405} did not settle. It discovered a new sphere, if we may so speak, in the realms of light, to which the Church had not yet assigned its inhabitant. Arianism had admitted that our Lord was both the God of the Evangelical covenant, and the actual Creator of the Universe; but even this was not enough, because it did not confess Him to be the One, Everlasting, Infinite, Supreme Being, but to be made by Him. It was not enough with that heresy to proclaim Him to be begotten ineffably before all worlds; not enough to place Him high above all creatures as the type of all the works of God's

Hands; not enough to make Him the Lord of His Saints, the Mediator between God and man, the Object of worship, the Image of the Father; not enough, because it was not all, and between all, and anything short of all, there was an infinite interval. The highest of creatures is levelled with the lowest in comparison of the One Creator Himself. That is, the Nicene Council recognised the eventful principle, that, while we believe and profess any being to be a creature, such a being is really no God to us, though honoured by us with whatever high titles and with whatever homage. Arius or Asterius did all but confess that Christ was the Almighty; they said much more than St. Bernard or St. Alphonso have since said of St. Mary; yet they left Him a creature and were found wanting. Thus there was "a wonder in heaven:" a throne was seen, far above all created powers, mediatorial, intercessory; a title archetypal; a crown bright as {406} the morning star; a glory issuing from the Eternal Throne; robes pure as the heavens; and a sceptre over all; and who was the predestined heir of that Majesty? Who was that Wisdom, and what was her name, "the Mother of fair love, and fear, and holy hope," "exalted like a palm-tree in Engaddi, and a rose-plant in Jericho," "created from the beginning of the world" in God's counsels, and "in Jerusalem was her power?" The vision is found in the Apocalypse, a Woman clothed with the sun, and the moon under her feet, and upon her head a crown of twelve stars. The votaries of Mary do not exceed the true faith, unless the blasphemers of her Son came up to it. The Church of Rome is not idolatrous, unless Arianism is orthodoxy.

I am not stating conclusions which were drawn out in the controversy, but of premises which were laid, broad and deep. It was then shown, it was then determined, that to exalt a creature was no recognition of its divinity. Nor am I speaking of the Semi-arians, who, holding our Lord's derivation from the Substance of the Father, yet denying His Consubstantiality, really did lie open to the charge of maintaining two Gods, and present no parallel to the defenders of the prerogatives of St. Mary. But I speak of the Arians who taught that our Lord's Substance was created; and concerning them it is true that St. Athanasius' condemnation of their theology is a vindication of the Medieval. Yet it is not wonderful, considering how Socinians, Sabellians, Nestorians, and the like, abound in these days, without their even knowing it themselves, if those who never rise higher in their notions of our Lord's Divinity than to consider Him a man singularly inhabited by a Divine Presence, that is, a Catholic Saint,—if such men should recognise, in the honour paid by the Church to St. Mary, the very honour which, and which alone, they offer to her Eternal Son.

{407} I have said that there was in the first ages no public and ecclesiastical recognition of the place which St. Mary holds in the Economy of grace; this was reserved for the fifth century, as the definition of our Lord's proper Divinity had been the work of the fourth. There was a controversy contemporary with those already mentioned, I mean the Nestorian, which brought out the complement of the development, to which they had been subservient; and which, if I may so speak, supplied the subject of that august proposition of which Arianism had provided the predicate. In order to do honour to Christ, in order to defend the true doctrine of the Incarnation, in order to secure a right faith in the manhood of the Eternal Son, the Council of Ephesus determined the Blessed Virgin to be the Mother of God. Thus all heresies of that day, though opposite to each other, tended in a most wonderful way to her exaltation; and the School of Antioch, the fountain of primitive rationalism, led the Church to lay down first the conceivable greatness of a creature, and then the incommunicable dignity of St. Mary.

But the spontaneous or traditional feeling of Christians, as we saw in the foregoing Chapter, had in great measure anticipated the formal ecclesiastical decision. Thus the title *Theotocos*, or Mother of God, was familiar to Christians from primitive times, and is used, among other writers, by Origen, Eusebius, St. Alexander, St. Athanasius, St. Ambrose, St. Gregory Nazianzen, St. Gregory Nysse, and St. Nilus. She had been called Ever-Virgin by St. Epiphanius, Didymus, and others. By others, "The Mother of all living," as being the anti-type of Eve; for, as St. Epiphanius observes, "in truth," not in shadow, "from Mary was Life itself brought into the world, that Mary might bear things living, and might become Mother of living things."[11] St. Augustine says that all have sinned "except {408} the Holy Virgin Mary, concerning whom, for the honour of the Lord, I wish no question to be raised at all, when we are treating of sins." "She was alone and wrought the world's salvation," says St. Ambrose, alluding to her conception of the Redeemer. She is signified by the Pillar of the cloud which guided the Israelites, according to the same Father; and she had "so great grace, as not only to have virginity herself, but to impart it to those to whom she came;"—the Rod out of the stem of Jesse," says St. Jerome, and "the Eastern gate through which the High Priest alone goes in and out, yet is ever shut;"—the wise woman, says St. Nilus, who "hath clad all believers, from the fleece of the Lamb born from her, with the clothing of incorruption, and delivered them from their invisible nakedness;"—"the Mother of Life, beauty, of majesty, the Morning Star," according to Antiochus;—"the mystical new heavens," "the heavens carrying the Divinity," "the fruitful vine by whom we are translated from death unto life," according to St. Ephraim; "the manna which is delicate, bright, sweet, and virgin, which, as though coming from heaven, has poured down on all the people of the Churches a food pleasanter than honey," according to St. Maximus.

St. Proclus calls her "the unsullied shell which contains the pearl of price," "the sacred shrine of sinlessness," "the golden altar of holocaust," "the holy oil of anointing," "the costly alabaster box of spikenard," "the ark gilt within and without," "the heifer whose ashes, that is, the Lord's Body taken from her, cleanses those who are defiled by the pollution of sin," "the fair bride of the Canticles," "the stay (στήριγμα) of believers," "the Church's diadem," "the expression of orthodoxy." These are oratorical expressions; but we use oratory on great subjects, not small. Elsewhere he calls her "God's only bridge to man;" and elsewhere {409} he breaks forth, "Run through all creation in your thoughts, and see if there be equal to, or greater than the Holy Virgin Mother of God."

Theodotus too, one of the Fathers of Ephesus, or whoever it is whose Homilies are given to St. Amphilochius: "As debtors and God's well-affected servants, let us make confession to God the Word and to His Mother, of the gift of words, as far as we are able . . . Hail, Mother, clad in light, of the light which sets not; hail all-undefiled mother of holiness; hail most pellucid fountain of the life-giving stream!" After speaking of the Incarnation, he continues, "Such paradoxes doth the Divine Virgin Mother ever bring to us in her holy irradiations, for with her is the Fount of Life, and breasts of the spiritual and guileless milk; from which to suck the sweetness, we have even now earnestly run to her, not as in forgetfulness of what has gone before, but in desire of what is to come."

St. Fulgentius of the same date says, "Mary became the window of heaven, for through her God poured the True light upon the world; the heavenly ladder, for through her did God descend upon earth. . . . Come, Virgin, to a Virgin, come ye who conceive to one who did conceive, ye who bear to one who bore, mothers to a Mother, ye who give suck to one who suckled, young women to the Young." Lastly, "Thou has found grace," says St. Peter Chrysologus, "how much? he had said above, Full.

And full indeed, which with full shower might pour upon and into the whole creation."[12]

{410} Such was the state of sentiment on the subject of St. Mary, which the Arian, Nestorian, and Monophysite heresies found in the Church; and on which the doctrinal decisions consequent upon them impressed as form and consistency which has been handed on in the Church to this day.

§ 2.

Developments following the Doctrine of Baptism.

1. It is not necessary here to enlarge on the benefits which the primitive Church considered to be conveyed to the soul by means of the Sacrament of Baptism. Its distinguishing gift, which is in point to mention, was the plenary forgiveness of sins past. It was also believed that the Sacrament could not be repeated. The question immediately followed, how was the guilt of such sin to be removed as was incurrred after its administration.

This question was felt to be so intimately and acutely personal by the early Christians, that they delayed the rite, as Christians now delay attendance on the Holy Eucharist. Of course it is difficult for us at this day to enter into the assemblage of notions which led to the postponement; other reasons besides a sense of the benefit of the baptismal privilege would concur, such as reluctance to be committed to a rule of life, and fear of the responsibilities which the baptized incur. But so it was, that Infant Baptism, which is happily a fundamental rule of Christian duty with us, was less clearly appreciated in the {411} early Church. Even in the fourth century St. Gregory Nazianzen, St. Basil, and St. Augustine, with Christian mothers, were not baptized till they were adults. St. Gregory's mother dedicated him to God immediately on his birth; and again when he had come to years of discretion, with the rite to taking the sacred books into his hands by way of consecration. He was religiously-minded from his youth, and had devoted himself to a single life. Yet his baptism did not take place till after he had attended the schools of Caesarea, Palestine, and Alexandria, and was on his voyage to Athens. He had embarked during the November gales, and for twenty days his life was in danger. He presented himself for baptism as soon as he got to land. St. Basil was the son of Christian confessors on both father's and mother's side. His grandmother Macrina, who brought him up, had for seven years lived with her husband in the woods of Pontus during the Decian persecution. His father was said to have wrought miracles; his mother, an orphan of great personal beauty, was forced from her unprotected state to abandon the hope of a single life, and was conspicuous in matrimony for her care of strangers and the poor, and for her offerings to the Churches. How religiously she brought up her children is shown by the singular blessing, that four of ten have since been canonized as Saints. St. Basil was one of these; yet the child of such parents was not baptized till he had come to man's estate,—till, according to the Benedictine Editor, his twenty-first, and perhaps his twenty-ninth year. St. Augustine's mother, who is herself a Saint, was a Christian when he was born, though his father was not. Immediately on his birth, he was made a catechumen; in his childhood he fell ill, and asked for baptism. His mother was alarmed, and was taking measures for his reception into the Church, when he suddenly got better, and it was deferred. He did not receive {412} baptism till the age of thirty-three, after he had for nine years been a victim of Manichaean error.

Evidently then the position of Baptism in the received system was not the same in the first ages as in later times; and still less was it clearly ascertained in the first three centuries. The problem which required an answer was this, as I have already stated it. Since there was but one Baptism, what could be done for those who had received the one remission of sins, and had sinned since? The primitive Fathers appear to have conceived that the Church was empowered to grant one, and one only, reconciliation after grievous offences; at least this was the practice of the times. Three sins however, at least in the West, seem to have been irremissible, idolatry, murder, and adultery. Such a system of Church discipline, suited as it was to a small community, and even expedient in a time of persecution, could not exist in Christianity, as it spread into the *orbis terrarum*, and gathered like a net of every kind. A more indulgent rule gradually gained ground; yet the Spanish Church adhered to it even in the fourth century, and a portion of the African in the third, and in the remaining portion there was a relaxation only as regards the crime of incontinence. Meanwhile a protest was made against the growing innovation: at the beginning of the third century Montanus, who was a zealot for the more primitive rule, shrank from the laxity, as he considered it, of the Asian Churches;[13] as in a different subject-matter, Jovinian and Vigilantius were offended at the developments in divine worship in the century which followed. The Montanists had recourse to the See of Rome, and at first with some prospect of success. Again, in Africa, where there had been in the first instance a schism headed by Felicissimus in favour of Antiquity, headed by Novatus, who originally had {413} been of the party of Felicissimus. This was taken up at Rome by Novatian, who professed to adhere to the original, or at least the primitive rule of the Church, viz. that those who had once fallen from the faith could in no case be received again.[14] The controversy seems to have found the following issue,—whether the Church had the *means* of pardoning sins committed after Baptism, which the Novatians, at least practically, denied. "It is fitting," says the Novatian Acesius, "to exhort those who have sinned after Baptism to repentance, but to expect hope of remission, not from the priests, but from God, who hath power to forgive sins."[15] The schism spread into the East, and led to the appointment of a penitentiary priest in the Catholic Churches. By the end of the third century as many as four degrees of penance were appointed, through which offenders had to pass in order to a reconciliation.

The length and severity of the penance varied with times and places. Sometimes, as we have seen, it lasted, in the case of grave offences, through life, and on to death, without any reconciliation; at other times it ended only in the *viaticum*; and if, after reconciliation they recovered, their ordinary penance was still binding on them either for life or for a certain time. In other cases it lasted ten, fifteen, or twenty years. But in all cases, from the first, the Bishop had the power of shortening it, and of altering the nature and quality of the punishment. Thus in the instance of the Emperor Theodosius, whom St. Ambrose shut out from communion for the massacre at Thessalonica, "according to the mildest rules of ecclesiastical discipline, which were established in the fourth century," says Gibbon, "the crime of homicide was expiated by the penitence of twenty years; and as it was impossible in the period of human life, to purge the accumulated guilt of the massacre . . . the murderer should have been excluded from the holy communion {414} till the hour of his death." He goes on to say that the public edification which resulted from the humiliation of so illustrious a penitent was a reason for abridging the punishment. "It was sufficient that the Emperor of the Romans, stripped of the ensigns of royalty, should appear in a mournful and suppliant posture, and that, in the midst of the Church of Milan, he should humbly solicit with signs and tears the pardon of his sins." His penance was shortened to an interval of about eight months. Hence arose the phrase of a "*poenitentia legitima, plena, et justa;*" which signifies a penitence sufficient, perhaps in length of time, perhaps in intensity of punishment.

2. Here a serious question presented itself to the minds of Christians, which was now to be wrought out:—Were these punishments merely signs of contrition, or in any sense satisfactions for sin? If the former, they might be absolutely remitted at the discretion of the Church, as soon as true repentance was discovered; the end had then been attained, and nothing more was necessary. Thus St. Chrysostom says in one of his Homilies,[16] "I require not continuance of time, but the correction of the soul. Show your contrition, show your reformation, and all is done." Yet, though there might be a reason of the moment for shortening the penance imposed by the Church, this does not at all decide the question whether that ecclesiastical penance be not part of an expiation made to the Almighty Judge for the sin; and supposing this really to be the case, the question follows, How is the complement of that satisfaction to be wrought out, which on just grounds of present expedience has been suspended by the Church now?

As to this question it cannot be doubted that the Fathers considered penance as not a mere {415} expression of contrition, but as an act done directly towards God and a means of averting His anger. "If the sinner spare not himself, he will be spared by God," says the writer who goes under the name of St. Ambrose. "Let him lie in sackcloth, and by the austerity of his life make amends for the offence of his past pleasures," says St. Jerome. "As we have sinned greatly," says St. Cyprian, "let us weep greatly; for a deep wound diligent and long tending must not be wanting, the repentance must not fall short of the offence." "Take heed to thyself," says St. Basil, "that, in proportion to the fault, thou admit also the restoration from the remedy."[17] If so, the question follows which was above contemplated,—if in consequence of death, or the exercise of the Church's discretion, the "*plena poenitentia*" is not accomplished in its ecclesiastical shape, how and when will the residue be exacted?

Clement of Alexandria answers this particular question very distinctly, according to Bishop Kaye, though not in some other points expressing himself conformably to the doctrine afterwards received. "Clement," says that Author, "distinguishes between sins committed before and after baptism: the former are remitted at baptism; the latter are purged by discipline. . . . The necessity of this purifying discipline is such, that if it does not take place in this life, it must after death, and is then to be effected by fire, not by a destructive, but a discriminating fire, pervading the soul which passes through it."[18]

There is a celebrated passage in St. Cyprian, on the subject of the punishment of lapsed Christians, which certainly seems to express the same doctrine. "St. Cyprian is arguing in favour of re-admitting the lapsed, when penitent; and his argument seems to be that it does not follow that we absolve them simply because we simply restore {416} them to the Church. He writes this to Antonian: 'It is one thing to stand for pardon, another to arrive at glory; one to be sent to prison (*missum in carcerem*) and not to go out till the last farthing is paid, another to receive at once the reward of faith and virtue; one thing to be tormented for sin in long pain, and so to be cleansed, and to be purged a long while in the fire (*purgari diu igne*), another to be washed from all sin in suffering; one thing, in short, to wait for the Lord's sentence in the Day of Judgment, another at once to be crowned by Him.' Some understand this passage to refer to the penitential discipline of the Church which was imposed on the penitent; and, as far as the context goes, certainly no sense could be more apposite. Yet . . . the words in themselves seem to go beyond any mere ecclesiastical, though virtually divine censure; especially '*missum in carcerem*' and '*purgari diu igne*'."[19]

The Acts of the Martyrs St. Perpetua and St. Felicitas, which are prior to St. Cyprian, confirm this interpretation. In the course of the narrative, St. Perpetua prays for her brother Dinocrates, who had died at the age of seven; and has a vision of a dark place, and next of a pool of water, which he was not tall enough to reach. She goes on praying; and in a second vision the water descended to him, and he was able to drink, and went to play as children use. "Then I knew," she says, "that he was translated from his place of punishment."[20]

The prayers in the Eucharistic Service for the faithful departed inculcate, at least according to the belief of the fourth century, the same doctrine, that the sins of accepted and elect souls, which were not expiated here, would receive punishment hereafter. Certainly such was St. Cyril's belief: "I know that many say," he observes, "what is a soul profited, {417} which departs from this world either with sins or without sins, if it be commemorated in the [Eucharistic] Prayer? Now, surely, if when a king had banished certain who had given him offence, their connexions should weave a crown and offer it to him on behalf of those under his vengeance, would he not grant a respite to their punishments? In the same way we, when we offer Him our supplications for those who have fallen asleep, though they be sinners, weave no crown, but offer up Christ, sacrificed for our sins, propitiating our merciful God, both for them and for ourselves."[21]

Thus we see how, as time went on, the doctrine of Purgatory was opened upon the comprehension of the Church, as a portion or form of Penance due for sins committed after Baptism. And thus the belief in this doctrine and the practice of Infant Baptism would grow into general reception together.

The process of thought, of which it is the result, is drawn out in the following passage, which may be suitably introduced in this place, though I wish to express my dissent from it in various incidental points. One point of difference is important, though it does not interfere with its serviceableness here; the writer considers the growth of the doctrine as an instance of the action of private judgment, whereas I should now call it an instance of the mind of the Church working out dogmatic truths from implicit feelings under secret supernatural guidance. The passage runs thus: "How Almighty God will deal with the mass of Christians, who are neither very bad nor very good, is a problem with which we are not concerned, and which it is our wisdom, and may be our duty, to put from our thoughts. But when it has once forced itself upon the mind, we are led in self-defence, with a view of keeping ourselves from dwelling unhealthily on particular cases, which come under our experience and perplex us, {418} to imagine modes, not by which God *does* (for that would be presumptuous to conjecture), but by which He may solve the difficulty. Most men, to our apprehensions, are too unformed in religious habits either for heaven or for hell, yet there is no middle state when Christ comes in judgment. In consequence it is obvious to have recourses to the interval before His coming, as a time during which this incompleteness might be remedied; as a season, not of changing the spiritual bent and character of the soul departed, whatever that be, for probation ends with mortal life, but of developing it in a more determinate form, whether of good or of evil. Again, when the mind once allows itself to speculate, it will discern in such a provision a means, whereby those, who, not without true faith at bottom, yet have committed great crimes, or those who have been carried off in youth while still undecided, or who die after a barren though not an immoral or scandalous life, may receive such chastisements as may prepare them for heaven, and render it consistent with God's justice to admit them thither. Again the inequality of the sufferings of Christians in this life, compared one with another, leads the unguarded mind to the same speculations; the intense suffering, for instance, which some men undergo on their death-bed, seeming as if but an anticipation in their case of what comes after death upon others, who, without greater claim on God's forbearance, live without chastisement, and die easily. I say, the mind will inevitably dwell upon such thoughts, unless it has been taught to subdue them by education or by the experience of their dangerousness.

"Various suppositions have, accordingly, been made, as pure suppositions, as mere specimens of the capabilities (if one may so speak) of the Divine Dispensation, as efforts of the mind reaching forward and venturing beyond its depth into the abyss of the Divine Counsels. If one supposition could be {419} produced, sufficient to solve the problem, ten thousand others are conceivable, unless indeed the resources of God's Providence are exactly commensurate with man's discernment of them. Religious men, amid these searchings of heart, have naturally gone to Scripture for relief; to see if the inspired word anywhere gave them any clue for their inquiries. And from what was there found, and from the speculations of reason upon it, various notions have been hazarded at different times; for instance, that there is a certain momentary ordeal to be undergone by all men after this life, more or less severe according to their spiritual state; or that certain gross sins in good men will be thus visited, or their lighter failings and habitual imperfections; or that the very sight of Divine Perfection in the invisible world will be in itself a pain, while it constitutes the purification of the imperfect but believing soul; or that, happiness admitting of various degrees of intensity, penitents late in life may sink for ever into a state, blissful as far as it goes, but more or less approaching to unconsciousness; and infants dying after baptism may be as gems paving the courts of heaven, or as the living wheels of the Prophet's vision; while matured Saints may excel in capacity of bliss, as well as in dignity, the highest archangels.

Such speculations are dangerous when indulged; the event proves it; from some of them, in fact, seems to have resulted the doctrine of Purgatory.

"Now the texts to which the minds of the early Christians seem to have been principally drawn, and from which they ventured to argue in behalf of these vague notions, were these two: 'The fire shall try every man's work,' &c., and 'He shall baptize you with the Holy Ghost and with fire.' These texts, with which many more were found to accord, directed their thoughts one way, as making mention of 'fire,' whatever was meant by the word, as the instrument of trial and {420} purification; and that, at some time between the present time and the Judgment, or at the Judgment. And accordingly, without perhaps having any definite or consistent meaning in what they said, or being able to say whether they spoke literally or figuratively, and with an indefinite reference to this life, as well as to the Intermediate State, they sometimes named fire as the instrument of recovering those who had sinned after their baptism. That this is the origin of the notion of a Purgatorial fire, I gather from these circumstances: first, that they do frequently insist on the texts in question; next, that they do not agree in the particular sense they put upon them. That they quote them shows that they rest upon them; that they vary in explaining them; that they had no Catholic sense to guide them. Nothing can be clearer, if these facts be so, than that the doctrine of the Purgatorial fire in all its senses, as far as it was more than a surmise, and was rested on argument, was the result of private judgment exerted, in defect of tradition, upon the text of Scripture. . . .

"As to the doctrine, thus suggested by certain striking texts, grew in popularity and definiteness, and verged towards its present Roman form, it seemed a key to many others. Great portions of the books of Psalms, Job, and the Lamentations, which express the feelings of religious men under suffering, would powerfully recommend it by the forcible and most affecting and awful meaning which they received from it. When this was once suggested, all other meanings would seem tame and inadequate.

"To these may be added various passages from the Prophets, as that in the beginning of the third chapter of Malachi, which speaks of fire as the instrument of judgment and purification, when Christ comes to visit His Church.

"Moreover, there were other texts of obscure and {421} indeterminate bearing, which seemed on this hypothesis to receive a profitable meaning; such as our Lord's words in the Sermon on the Mount, 'Verily, I say unto thee, thou shalt by no means come out thence till thou has paid the uttermost farthing;' and St. John's expression in the Apocalypse, that 'no man in heaven, nor in earth, neither under the earth, was able to open the book.'

"Further, the very circumstance that no second instrument of a plenary and entire cleansing from sin was given after Baptism, such as Baptism, led Christians to expect that that unknown means, when accorded, would be of a more painful nature than that which they had received so freely and instantaneously in infancy; and confirmed, not only the text already cited, 'He shall baptize you with the Holy Ghost and with fire,' but also St. Paul's announcement of the 'judgment and fiery indignation' which await those who sin after having been once 'enlightened,' and by Christ's warning to the impotent man to sin no more, lest a worse thing come unto him.

"Lastly, the universal and apparently Apostolical custom of praying for the dead in Christ, called for some explanation, the reason for it not having come down to posterity with it. Various reasons may be supposed quite clear of this distressing doctrine; but it supplied an adequate and a most constraining motive for its

observance, to those who were not content to practise it in ignorance."[22]

The doctrine of post-baptismal sin, especially when realized
in the doctrine of Purgatory, leads the recipient to fresh developments beyond itself. Its effect is to convert a Scripture statement,
which might seem only of temporary application, into a universal
and perpetual truth. When St. Paul and St. Barnabas would
"confirm the souls of the disciples," they taught them "that we
must through much tribulation enter into the kingdom of God." It
is {422} obvious what very practical results would follow on such
an announcement in the instance of those who simply accepted
the Apostolic decision; and in like manner a conviction that sin
must have its punishment, here or hereafter, and that we all must
suffer, how overpowering will be its effect, what a new light
does it cast on the history of the soul, what a change does it
make in our judgment of the external world, what a reversal of
our natural wishes and aims for the future! Is a doctrine conceivable which would so elevate the mind above this present state
and teach it so successfully to dare difficult things, and to be
reckless of danger and pain? Infidels, nay writers of our own,
have enlarged upon the influence which will attend upon it; and
though they express it in terms of their own philosophy, we may
make much of their testimony. "The Ascetics," says Gibbon,
"who obeyed and abused the rigid precepts of the gospel, were
inspired by the savage enthusiasm which represents man as a
criminal and God as a tyrant. They seriously renounced the
business and the pleasures of the age, abjured the use of wine, of
flesh, and of marriage, chastised their body, mortified their
affections, and embraced a life of misery as the price of eternal
happiness. In the reign of Constantine, the Ascetics fled from a
profane and degenerate world to perpetual solitude or religious
society. The monks might contend with Stoics in the contempt of
fortune, of pain, and of death; the Pythagorean silence and

submission were revived in their servile discipline; and they disdained, as firmly as the Cynics themselves, all the forms and decencies of civil society."[23] What is this but to say, that he who believes that suffer he must, and that delayed punishment may be the greater, will be above the world, will admire nothing, fear nothing, desire nothing? He has within his breast a source of greatness, self-denial, heroism. This is the secret spring of {423} strenuous efforts and persevering toil, of the sacrifice of fortune, friends, ease, reputation, happiness. There is, it is true, a higher class of motives which will be felt by the Saint; who will do from love what all Christians, who act acceptably, do from faith. And, moreover, the ordinary measures of charity which Christians possess, suffice for securing such respectable attention to religious duties as the routine necessities of the Church require. But if we would raise an army of devoted men to resist the world, to oppose sin and error, to relieve misery, or to propagate the truth, we must be provided with motives which keenly affect the many. Christian love is too rare a gift, philanthropy is too weak a material, for the occasion. Nor is an influence to be found to suit our purpose, besides this solemn conviction, which arises out of the very rudiments of Christian theology, and is taught by its most primitive masters,—this sense of the awfulness of post-baptismal sin. It is in vain to look out for missionaries in China, or Africa, or evangelists for our great towns, or Christian attendants on the sick, or teachers of the ignorant, on such a scale of numbers as the need requires, without the doctrine of Purgatory. For thus the sins of youth are turned to account by the profitable penance of manhood; and terrors, which the philosopher scorns in the individual, become the benefactors and earn the gratitude of nations.

3. But there is one form of Penance which has been more prevalent and uniform than any other, out of which the forms just

noticed have grown, or on which they have been engrafted, the Monastic Rule. In the first ages, the doctrine of the punishments of sin, whether in this world or in the next, was little called for. The rigid discipline of the infant Church was the preventative of greater offences and its persecutions the penance of their {424} commission; but when the Canons were relaxed and confessorship ceased, then some substitute was needed, and such was Monachism, being at once a sort of continuation of primeval innocence, and a school of self-chastisement. And, as it is a great principle in economical and political science that everything should be turned to account, and there should be no waste, so, in the instance of Christianity, the penitential observances of individuals, which were necessarily on a large scale as its professors increased, took the form of works, whether for the defence of the Church, or the spiritual and temporal good of mankind. In no aspect of the Divine system do we see more striking developments than in the successive fortunes of Monachism.

Little did the youth Antony foresee, when he set off to fight the evil one in the wilderness, what a sublime and various history he was opening, a history which had its first developments even in his own lifetime. He was himself a hermit in the desert; but when others followed his example, he was obliged to give them guidance, and thus he found himself, by degrees, at the head of a large family of solitaries, five thousand of whom were scattered in the distric of Nitria alone. He lived to see a second stage in the development; the huts in which they lived were brought together, sometimes round a church, and a sort of subordinate community, or college, formed among certain individuals of their number. St. Pachomius was the first who imposed a general rule of discipline upon the brethren, gave them a common dress, and set before them the objects to which the religious life was dedicated. Manual labour, study, devotion, bodily mortification, were now their peculiarities; and the institution, thus defined, spread and established through Eastern and Western Christendom.

The penitential character of Monachism is not {425} prominent in St. Antony, though it is distinctly noticed by Pliny in his description of the Essenes of the Dead Sea, who anticipated the monastic life at the rise of Christianity. In St. Basil, however, it becomes a distinguishing feature;—so much so that the monastic profession was made a disqualification for the pastoral office,[24] and in theory involved an absolute separation from mankind; though in St. Basil's, as well as St. Antony's disciples, it performed the office of resisting heresy.

Next, the monasteries, which in their ecclesiastical capacity had been at first separate churches under a Presbyter or Abbot, became schools for the education of the clergy.[25]

Centuries past, and after many extravagant shapes of the institution, and much wildness and insubordination in its members, a new development took place under St. Benedict. Revising and digesting the provisions of St. Antony, St. Pachomius, and St. Basil, he bound together his monks by a perpetual vow, brought them into the cloister, united the separate convents into one Order,[26] and added objects of an ecclesiastical and political nature to that of personal edification. Of these objects, agriculture seemed to St. Benedict himself of first importance; but in a very short time it was superseded by study and education, and the monasteries of the following centuries became the schools and libraries, and the monks the chroniclers and copyists, of a dark period. Centuries later, the Benedictine Order was divided into separate Congregations, and propagated in separate monastic societies. The Congregation of Cluni was the most celebrated of the former; and of the latter, the hermit order of the Camaldoli and the agricultural Cistercians.

{426} Both a unity and an originality are observable in the successive phases under which Monachism has shown itself;

while its developments bring it more and more into the ecclesiastical system, and subordinate it to the governing power, they are
true to their first idea, and spring fresh and fresh from the parent
stock, which from time immemorial had thriven in Syria and
Egypt. The sheepskin and desert of St. Antony did but revive
"the mantle"[27] and the mountain of the first Carmelite, and St.
Basil's penitential exercises had already been practised by the
Therapeutae. In like manner the Congregational principle, which
is ascribed to St. Benedict, had been anticipted by St. Antony and
St. Pachomius; and after centuries of disorder, another function
of early Monachism, for which there had been little call for
centuries, the defence of Catholic truth, was exercised with
singular success by the rival orders of Dominicans and
Franciscans.

St. Benedict had come as if to preserve a principle of
civilization, and a refuge for learning, at a time when the old
framework of society was falling, and new political creations
were taking place. And when the young intellect within them
began to stir, and a change of another kind discovered itself,
then appeared St. Francis and St. Dominic to teach and
chastise it; and in proportion as Monachism assumed this
public office, so did the principle of penance, which had been
the chief characteristic of earlier forms, hold a less prominent
place. The Tertiaries indeed, or members of the third order of
St. Francis and St. Dominic, were penitents; but the friar
himself, instead of a penitent, was made a priest, and was
allowed to quit cloister. Nay, they assumed the character of
what may be called an Ecumenical Order, as {427} being
supported by begging, not by endowments, and being under
the jurisdiction, not of the local Bishop, but of the Holy See.
The Dominicans too came forward especially as a learned
body, and as entrusted with the office of preaching, at a time
when the mind of Europe seemed to be developing into

infidelity. They filled the chairs at the Universities, while the strength of the Franciscans lay among the lower orders.

At length, in the last era of ecclesiastical revolution, another principle of early Monachism, which had been but partially developed, was brought out into singular prominence in the history of the Jesuits. "Obedience," said an ancient abbot, "is a monk's service, with which he shall be heard in prayer, and shall stand with confidence by the Crucified, for so the Lord came to the cross, being made obedient even unto death;"[28] but it was reserved for modern times to furnish the perfect illustration of this virtue, and to receive the full blessing which follows it. The great Society, which bears no earthly name, still more secular in its organization, and still more simply dependent on the See of St. Peter, has been still more distinguished than any Order before it for the rule of obedience, while it has compensated the danger of its free intercourse with the world by its scientific treatment of devotional exercises. The hermitage, the cloister, the inquisitor, and the friar were suited to other states of society; with the Jesuits, as well as with the religious Communities, which are their juniors, usefulness, secular and religious, literature, education, the confessional, preaching, the oversight of the poor, missions, the care of the sick, have been chief objects of attention; great cities have been the scene of operation: bodily austerities and the ceremonial of devotion have been made of but secondary importance. Yet it may fairly be questioned, whether, in an intellectual age, when freedom {428} both of thought and of action is so dearly prized, a greater penance can be devised for the soldier of Christ than the absolute surrender of judgment and will to the command of another.

SECTION II.

APPLICATION OF THE SIXTH TEST OF FIDELITY IN DEVELOPMENT.

It is the general pretext of heretics that they are but serving and protecting Christianity by their innovations; and it is their charge against what by this time may surely be called the Catholic Church, that her successive definitions of doctrine have but overlaid and obscured it. That is, they assume what we have no wish to deny, that a true development is that which is conservative of its original, and a corruption is that which tends to its destruction. This has already been set down as a Sixth Test, discriminative of a development from a corruption, and must now be applied to the Catholic doctrines; though this Essay has so far exceeded its proposed limits, that both reader and writer may well be weary, and may content themselves with a brief consideration of the portions of the subject which remain.

It has been observed already[29] that a strict correspondence between the various members of a development, and those of the doctrine from which it is derived, is more than we have any right to expect. The bodily structure of a grown man is not merely that of a magnified boy; he differs from what he was in his make and proportions; still manhood is the perfection of boyhood, adding something of its own, yet keeping what it finds. *"Nihil novum,"* says Vincentius, *"proferatur in senibus, quod non in pueris jam antea latitaverit."* This character of {429} *addition,*—that is, of a change which is in one sense real and perceptible, yet without loss or reversal of what was before, but, on the contrary, protective and confirmative of it,—in many respects and in a special way belongs to Christians.

1. If we take the simplest and most general view of its history, as existing in an individual mind, or in the Church at

large, we shall see in it an instance of this peculiarity. It is the birth of something virtually new, because latent in what was before. We know that no temper of mind is acceptable, in the Divine Presence but love; it is love which makes Christian fear differ from servile dread; yet in the beginning of the religious life, fear is the prominent evangelical grace, and love is but latent in fear, and has in course of time to be developed out of what seems its contradictory. Then, when it is developed, it takes that prominent place which fear held before, yet protecting not superseding it. Love is added, not fear removed, and the mind is but perfected in grace by what seems a revolution. "They that sow in tears, reap in joy;" yet afterwards still they are "sorrowful," though "always rejoicing."

And so was it with the Church at large. She started with suffering, which turned to victory; but when she was set free from the house of her prison, she did not quit it so much as turn it into a cell. Meekness inherited the earth; strength came forth from weakness; the poor made many rich; yet meekness and poverty remained. The rulers of the world were Monks, when they could not be Martyrs.

2. Immediately on the overthrow of the heathen power, two movements simultaneously ran through the world from East to West, as quickly as the lightning in the prophecy, a development of worship and of asceticism. Hence, while the world's first reproach in heathen times had been that {430} Christianity was a dark malevolent magic, its second has been that it is a joyous carnal paganism;—according to that saying, "We have piped unto you, and ye have not danced; we have mourned unto you, and ye have not lamented. For John came neither eating nor drinking, and they say, He hath a devil. The son of man came eating and drinking, and they say, Behold a man gluttonous and a winebibber, a friend of publicans and sinners." Yet our Lord too was "a man of sorrows" all the while, but softened his austerity by His gracious gentleness.

3. The like characteristic attends also on the mystery of His Incarnation. He was first God and He became man; but Eutyches and heretics of his school refused to admit that He was man, lest they should deny that He was God. In consequence the Catholic Fathers are frequent and unanimous in their asseverations, that "the Word" had become flesh, not to His loss, but by an addition. Each Nature is distinct, but the created Nature lives in and by the Eternal. *"Non amittendo quod erat, sed sumendo quod non erat,"* is the Church's principle. And hence, though the course of development, as was observed in a former Chapter, has been to bring into prominence that divine aspect of our Lord's mediation, this has been attended by even a more open manifestation of the doctrine of His atoning sufferings. The passion of our Lord is one of the most imperative and engrossing subjects of Catholic teaching. It is the great topic of meditations and prayers; it is brought into continual remembrance by the sign of the Cross; it is preached to the world in the Crucifix; it is variously honored by the many houses of prayer, and associations of religious men, and pious institutions and undertakings, which in some way or other are placed under the name and the shadow of Jesus, or the Saviour, or the Redeemer, or His Cross, or His Passion, or His sacred Heart.

{431} 4. Here a singular development may be mentioned of the doctrine of the Cross, which some have thought so contrary to its original meaning,[30] as to be manifest corruption; I mean the introduction of the Sign of the meek Jesus into the armies of men, and the use of an emblem of peace as a protection in battle. If light has no communion with darkness, or Christ with Belial, what has He to do with Moloch, who would not call down fire on His enemies, and came not to destroy but to save? Yet this seeming anomaly is but one instance of a great law which is seen in developments generally, that changes which appear at first sight to contradict that out of which they grew, are really its protection or illustration. Our Lord Himself is represented in the Prophets as a combatant inflicting wounds while He received them, as coming from Bozrah with dyed garments, sprinkled and red in His apparel with the blood of His enemies; and whereas no war is lawful but what is just, it surely beseems that they who are engaged in so dreadful a commission as that of taking away life at the price of their own, should at least have the support of His Presence, and fight under the mystical influence of His Name, who redeemed His elect as a combatant by the Blood of Atonement, with the slaughter of His foes, the sudden overthrow of the Jews, and the slow and awful fall of the Pagan Empire. And if the wars of Christian nations have often been unjust, this is a reason against much more than the use of religious symbols by the parties who engage in them, though the pretence of religion may increase the sin.

5. The same rule of development has been observed in respect of the doctrine of the Blessed Trinity. It is the objection of the School of Socinus, that belief in the Trinity is destructive of any true maintenance of the Divine Unity, however {432} strongly the latter may be professed; but Petavius, as we have seen,[31] sets it down as one especial recommendation of the Catholic doctrine, that it subserves that original truth which at first sight it does but obscure and compromise.

6. M. Guizot has contrasted the consistency of the Church of Rome with the inconsistency of its heretical opponents in the points which came into controversy between them. "The Reformers are told," he says, "'You provoke licentiousness, you produce it; but yet when you discover it, you wish to constrain and repress it. And how do you repress it? By the most hard and violent means,—you persecute heresy too, by virtue of an illegitimate authority.' These reproaches much embarrassed the Reformers. When the multitude of different sects was charged against them, instead of acknowledging the legitimacy of their

free development, they sought to anathematize dissenters, were annoyed by their existence, and sought some apology for it. And when the dominant party amongst the Reformers were reproached with persecution, not by their enemies, but by the children of the Reformation; when the sects which they anathematized ex- claimed, 'We only do what you did; we separate ourselves from you, as you separated yourselves from Rome,' they were still more embarrassed, and too frequently their only reply was an increase in severity. The reason of their inconsistency is, that the religious revolution of the sixteenth century had never ascended to the first cause, it had never descended to the ultimate conse- quences of its work. The rights and claims of tradition have not been reconciled with those of liberty; and the cause of this must undoubtedly be sought in the fact that the Reformation did not fully comprehend and accept either its own principles or effects."

With this inconsistency he contrasts the {433} harmonious completeness and the decision of the Roman Catholic theology. "The adversaries of the Reformation," he says, "knew very well what they were about, and what they required; they could point to their first principles, and boldly admit all the consequences that might result from them. No government was ever more consistent and systematic than that of the Romish Church. In fact, the Court of Rome was much more accomodating, yielded much more than the Reformers; but in principle it much more com- pletely adopted its own system, and maintained a much more consistent conduct. There is an immense power in this full confidence of what is done; this perfect knowledge of what is required; this complete and rational adaptation of a system and a creed." Then he goes on to the history of the Society of Jesus in illustration. "Everything," he says, "was unfavourable to the Jesuits, both fortune and appearances; neither practical sense which requires success, nor the imagination which looks for splendour, were gratified by their destiny. Still it is certain that they possessed the elements of greatness; a grand idea is attached to their name, to their influence, and to their history. Why? because they worked from fixed principles, which they fully and clearly understood, and the tendency of which they entirely comprehended. In the Reformation, on the contrary, when the event surpassed its conception, something incomplete, inconsequent, and narrow has remained, which has placed the conquerors themselves in a state of rational and philosophical inferiority, the influence of which has occasionally been felt in events. The conflict of the new spiritual order of things against the old, is, I think, the weak side of the Reformation."[32]

7. This representation of the consistency of the Catholic system will be found to be true, even in respect of those peculiarities of it, which have been {434} considered by Protestants most open to the charge of corruption and innovation. It is maintained, for instance, that the veneration paid to Images in the Catholic Church directly contradicts the command of Scripture, and the usage of the primitive ages. As to primitive usage, that part of the subject was incidentally observed upon in a foregoing Chapter; here I will make one remark on the argument from Scripture.

It may be reasonably questioned, then, whether the Commandment which stands second in our Decalogue, on which the prohibition of Images is principally grounded, was intended for more than temporary observance in the letter. So far is certain, that none could surpass the Jews in its literal observance; yet this did not save them from the punishments attached to the violation of it. If this be so, the literal observance is not its true and evangelical import.

"When the generation to come of your children shall rise up after you," says their inspired law-giver, "and the stranger that shall come from a far land shall say, when they see the plagues of that land, and its sicknesses which the Lord hath laid upon it;

and that the whole land thereof is brimstone, and salt, and burning, that it is not sown, nor beareth, nor any grass groweth therein, . . even all nations shall say, Wherefore hath the Lord done this unto the land? What meaneth the heat of this great anger? Then men shall say, Because they have forsaken the covenants of the Lord God of their fathers, which He made with them when He brought them forth out of the land of Egypt; for they went and served other gods, and worshipped them, gods whom they knew not, and whom He had not given them." Now the Jews of our Lord's day did not keep this covenant, for they incurred the penalty; yet they kept the letter of the Command-ment rigidly, and were {435} known among the heathen far and wide for their devotion to the "Lord God of their fathers who brought them out of the land of Egypt," and for their abhorrence of the "gods whom He had not given them." If then adherence to the letter was no protection to the Jews, departure from the letter may be no guilt in Christians.

It should be observed, moreover, that there certainly is a difference between the two covenants in their respective view of symbols of the Almighty. In the Old, it was blasphemy to represent Him under "the similitude of a calf that eateth hay;" in the New, the Third Person of the Holy Trinity has signified His Presence by the appearance of a Dove, and the Second Person has presented His sacred Humanity for worship under the name of the Lamb.

It follows that, if the letter of the Decalogue is but partially binding on Christians, it is as justifiable, in setting it before persons under instruction, to omit such parts as do not apply to them, as, when we quote passages from the Pentateuch in Sermons or Lectures generally, to pass over verses which refer simply to the temporal promises or the ceremonial law, which we are accustomed to do without any intention or appearance of dealing irreverently with the sacred text.

8. It has been anxiously asked, whether the honours paid to St. Mary, which have grown out of devotion to her Almighty Lord and Son, do not, in fact, tend to weaken that devotion; and whether, from the nature of the case, it is possible so to exalt a creature without withdrawing the heart from the Creator.

In addition to what has been said on this subject in this Chapter and the foregoing, I observe that the question is one of fact, not of presumption or conjecture. The abstract lawfulness of the honours paid to St. Mary, and their distinction in {436} theory from the incommunicable worship paid to God, have already been insisted on; but here the question turns upon their practicability or expedience, which must be determined by the fact whether they are practicable, and whether they have been found to be expedient.

Here I observe, first, that to those who admit the authority of the Council of Ephesus, the question is in no slight degree answered by its sanction of the δεοτόκος, or "Mother of God," as a title of St. Mary, and that in order to protect the doctrine of the Incarnation, and to preserve the faith of Catholics from a specious Humanitarianism. And if we take a survey of Europe at least, we shall find that those religious communions which are characterized by the observance of St. Mary, are not the Churches which have ceased to adore her Eternal Son, but such as have renounced that observance. The regard for His glory, which was professed in that keen jealousy of her exaltation, has not been supported by the event. They who were accused of worshipping a creature in His stead, still worship Him; their accusers, who hoped to worship Him so purely, where obstacles to the development of their principles have been removed, have ceased to worship Him altogether.

Next, it must be observed, that the tone of the devotion paid to St. Mary is altogether distinct from that which is paid to Her Eternal Son, and to the Holy Trinity, as we shall certainly allow on inspection of the Catholic services. The supreme and true worship paid to the Almighty is severe, profound, awful. Christ is addressed as true God, while He is true Man; as our Creator and Judge, while He is most loving, tender, and gracious. On the other hand, towards St. Mary the language employed is affectionate and ardent, as towards a mere child of Adam; though subdued, as coming from her sinful kindred. How different, for instance, {437} is the tone of the *Dies Irae* from that of the *Stabat Mater*. In the "Tristis et afflicta Mater Unigeniti," in the "Mater fons amoris," the "Sancta Mater," the "Virgo virginum praeclara Mihi jam non sis amara, Poenas mecum divide,"the "Fac me verè tecum flere," we have an expression of the feelings with which we regard one who is a creature and a mere human being; but in the "Rex tremendae majestatis qui salvandos salvas gratis, salva me Fons pietatis," the "Ne me perdas illâ die," the "Juste judex ultionis, donum fac remissionis," the "Oro supplex et aclinis, cor contritum quasi cinis," the "Pie Jesu Domine, dona eis requiem," we hear the voice of the creature raised in hope and love, yet in deep awe to his Creator, Infinite Benefactor, and Judge. Or again, how distinct is the language of the Breviary Services on the Festival of Pentecost, or of the Holy Trinity, from the language of the Services for the Assumption! How indescribably majestic, solemn, and soothing is the "Veni Creator Spiritus," the "Altissimi donum Dei, Fons vivus, ignis, charitas," or the "Vera et una Trinitas, una et summa Deitas, sancta et una Deitas," the "Spes nostra, salus nostra, honor noster, O beata Trinitas," the "Charitas Pater, gratia Filius, communicatio Spiritus Sanctus, O beata Trinitas;" "Libera nos, salva nos vivifica nos, O beata Trinitas;" How gentle, on the contrary, how full of sympathy and affection, how stirring and animating, in the Office for the Assumption, is the "Virgo prudentissima, quo progrederis, quasi aurora valde rutilans? filia Sion, tota formosa et suavis es, pulcra ut luna, electa ut sol;" the "Sicut dies verni circumdabant eam flores rosarum, et lilia convallium;" the "Maria Virgo assumpta est ad aethereum thalamum in quo Rex regum stellato sedet solio;" and the "Gaudent Angeli, laudantes benedicunt Dominum." Or again the Antiphon, the "Ad te clamamus exules filii Hevae, ad te suspiramus gementes et {438} flentes in hac lacrymarum valle," and "Eia ergo, advocata nostra, illos tuos misericordes oculos ad nos converte," and "O clemens, O pia, O dulcis Virgo Maria." Or the Hymn, "Ave Maris stella, Dei Mater alma," and "Virgo singularis, inter omnes mitis, nos culpis solutos, mites fac et castos."

Nor does it avail to object that, in this contrast of devotional exercises, the human will supplant the Divine, from the infirmity of our nature; for, I repeat, the question is one of fact, whether it has done so. And next it must be asked, whether the character of Protestant devotion towards our Lord has been that of worship at all; and not rather such as we pay to an excellent human being, that is, no higher devotion than that which Catholics pay to St. Mary, differing from it, however, in being familiar, rude, and earthly. Carnal minds will ever create a carnal worship for themselves; and to forbid them the service of the Saints will have no tendency to teach them the worship of God.

Moreover, it must be observed, what is very important, that great and constant devotion which the Catholic pays to St. Mary, it has a special province, and has far more connexion with the public services and the festive aspect of Christianity, and with certain extraordinary offices which she holds, than with what is strictly personal and primary in religion. Two instances will serve in illustration, and they are but samples of many others.[33]

(1.) For example, St. Ignatius' Spiritual Exercises are among the most approved methods of devotion in the modern Catholic Church; they proceed from one of the most celebrated of her Saints, and have the praises of Popes, and of the most {439} eminent masters of the spiritual life. A Bull of Paul the Third's "approves, praises, and sanctions all and everything contained in them;" indulgences are granted to the performance of them by the same Pope, by Alexander the Seventh, and by Benedict the Fourteenth. St. Carlo Borromeo declared that he learned more from them than from all other books together; St. Francis de Sales calls it "a holy method of reformation," and they are the model on which all the extraordinary devotions of religious men or bodies, and the course of missions, are conducted. If there is a document which is the authoritative exponent of the inward communion of the members of the modern Catholic Church with their God and Saviour, it is this work.

The Exercises are directed to the removal of obstacles in the way of the soul's receiving and profiting by the gifts of God. They undertake to effect this in three ways; by removing all objects of this world, and, as it were, bringing the soul "into the solitude where God may speak to its heart;" next, by setting before it the ultimate end of man, and its own deviations from it, the beauty of holiness, and the pattern of Christ; and lastly, by giving rules for its correction. They consist of course of prayers, meditations, self-examinations, and the like, which in its complete extent lasts thirty days; and these are divided into three stages, —the *Via Purgativa*, in which sin is the main subject of consideration; the *Via Illuminativa*, which is devoted to the contemplation of our Lord's passion, involving the process of the determination of our calling; and the *Via Unitiva*, in which we proceed to the contemplation of our Lord's resurrection and ascension.

No more need be added in order to introduce the remark for which I have referred to these Exercises; viz., that in a work so highly sanctioned, so widely received, so intimately bearing upon the most {440} sacred points of personal religion, very slight mention occurs of devotion to the Blessed Virgin, Mother of God. There is one mention of her in the rule given for the first

Prelude or preparation, in which the person meditating is directed to consider before him a church, or other place with Christ in it, St. Mary, and whatever else is suitable to the subject of meditation. Another in the third Exercise, in which one of the three addresses is made to our Lady, Christ's Mother, requesting earnestly "her intercession with her Son;" to which is to be added the Ave Mary. In the beginning of the Second Week there is a form of offering ourselves to God in the presence of "His infinite goodness," and with the witness of His "glorious Virgin Mother Mary, and the whole host of heaven." At the end of the Meditation upon the Angel Gabriel's mission to St. Mary, an address to each Divine Person, "the Word Incarnate, and His Mother." In the Meditation upon the Two Standards, there is an address prescribed to St. Mary to implore grace from her Son through her, with an Ave Mary after it. In the beginning of the Third Week one address is prescribed to Christ; or three, if devotion incites, to Mother, Son, and Father. In the description given of three different modes of prayer we are told, if we would imitate St. Mary, we must recommend ourselves to her, as having power with her Son, and presently the Ave Mary, *Salve Regina*, and other forms are prescribed, as is usual after all prayers. And this is about the whole of the devotion, if it may so be called, which is recommended towards St. Mary in the course of so many apparently as a hundred and fifty Meditations, and those chiefly on the events of our Lord's earthly history as recorded in Scripture. It would seem then that whatever be the influence of the doctrines connected with St. Mary and the Saints in the Catholic Church, at least they do not impede or obscure the freeest exercise {441} and the fullest manifestation of the devotional feelings towards God and Christ.

(2.) The other instance which I give in illustration is of a different kind, but is suitable to mention. About forty little books have come into my possession which are in circulation among the laity at Rome, and answer to the smaller publications of the Christian Knowledge Society among ourselves. They have been taken almost at hazard from a number of such works, and are of various lengths; some running to as many as two or three hundred pages, others consisting of scarce a dozen. They may be divided into four classes:—a third part consists of books on practical subjects; another third is upon the Incarnation and Passion; and of the rest, the greater part are on St. Mary, and the remainder upon the Sacraments, especially the Holy Eucharist. There are two or three besides for the use of Missions.

As to the first class, they are on such subjects as the following: "La Consolazione degl'Infermi;" "Pensieri di una donna sul vestire moderno;" "L'Inferno Aperto;" "Il Purgatorio Aperto;" St. Alphnso Liguori's "Massime eterne;" other Maxims by St. Francis de Sales for every day in the year; "Pratica per ben confessasrsi e communicarsi;" and the like. The titles of the second class are such as "Gesu dalla Croce al cuore del peccatore;" "Novena de Ss. Natale di G. C.; "Associazone pel culto perpetuo del divin cuore;" "Compendio della Passione." In the third are "Il Mese Eucaristico," and a few others.

These books are, as even the titles of some of them show, in great measure made up of Meditations; such are the "Breve e pie Meditazioni" of P. Crasset; the "Meditazioni per ciascun giorno del mese sulla Passione;" the "Meditazioni per l'ora Eucaristica." Now of these it may be said generally, that in the body of the Meditation St. Mary {442} is hardly mentioned at all. For instance, the Meditations on the Passion, a book used for distribution, through two hundred and seventy-seven pages St. Mary is not once named. In the Prayers for Mass which are added, she is introduced at the Confiteor, thus, "I pray the Virgin, the Angels, the Apostles, and all the Saints of heaven to intercede," &c.; and in the Preparation for Penance, she is once addressed, after our Lord, as the Refuge of sinners, with the

Saints and Guardian Angel; and at the end of the Exercise there is a similar prayer of four lines for the intercession of St. Mary, Angels and Saints, of heaven. In the Exercise for Communion, in a prayer to our Lord, "my only and infinite good, my treasure, my life, my paradise, my all," the merits of the Saints are mentioned, "especially of St. Mary." She is also mentioned with Angels and Saints at the termination.

In a collection of "Spiritual Lauds" for Missions, of thirty-six Hymns, we find as many as eleven addressed to St. Mary, or relating to her, among which are translations of the *Ave Maris Stella*, and the *Stabat Mater*, and the *Salve Regina*; and one is on "the sinner's reliance on Mary." Five, however, which are upon Repentance, are entirely engaged upon the subjects of our Lord and sin, with the exception of an address to St. Mary at the end of two of them. Seven others, upon sin, the Crucifixion, and the Four Last Things, do not mention St. Mary's name.

To the Manual for the Perpetual Adoration of the Divine Heart of Jesus there is appended one chapter on the Immaculate Conception.

The most important of the first class is the French *Pensez y bien*, which seems a favourite book, since there are two transla-tions of it, one of them being the fifteenth edition; and it is used for distribution to Missions. In these Reflections there is scarcely a word of St. Mary. At the end there is a Method of {443} reciting the Crown of the Seven Dolours of the Virgin Mary, which contains seven prayers to her, and the *Stabat Mater*.

One of the longest books in the whole collection is one consisting principally of Meditations on the Holy Communion; under the title of the "Eucharistic Month," as already mentioned. In these "Preparations," "Aspirations," &c., St. Mary is but once mentioned, and that in a prayer addressed to our Lord. "O my sweetest Brother," it says with an allusion to the Canticles, "who, being made Man for my salvation, hast sucked the milk from the virginal breast of her, who is my Mother by grace," &c. In a small "Instruction" given to children on their first Communion, there are the following questions and answers: "Is our Lady in the Host? No. Are the Angels and the Saints? No. Why not? Because they have no place there."

Of the fourth class, which relate to St. Mary, such as "Esercizio ad Onore dell' addolorato cuore di Maria," "Novena di Preparazione alla festa dell' Assunzione," "Li Quindici Misteri del Santo Rosario," the principal is a remarkable book by Father Segneri, called "Il divoto di Maria," which requires a distinct notice. It is far from the intention of these remarks to deny the high place which the Holy Virgin holds in the devotion of Catholics; I am but bringing evidence of its not interfering with that incommunicable and awful relation which exists between the creature and the Creator; and, as the following instances show, as far as they go, that relation is preserved inviolate by such honours as are paid to St. Mary, so will this treatise throw light upon the rationale by which the distinction is preserved between the worship of God and the honour of an exalted creature, and that in singular accordance with the remarks made in the foregoing Section.

This work of Segneri is written against persons {444} who continue in sins under pretence of their devotion to St. Mary, and in consequence it is led to draw out the idea which good Catholics have of her. This idea is this, that she is absolutely the first of created beings. Thus the treatise says, that "God might have easily made a more beautiful firmament, and a greener earth, but it was not possible to make a higher Mother than the Virgin Mary; and in her formation there has been conferred on mere creatures all the glory of which they are capable, remaining mere creatures," p. 34. And as containing all created perfection, she has all those attributes, which, as was noticed above, the Arians and other heretics applied to our Lord, and which the

Church denied of Him as infinitely below His Supreme Majesty. Thus she is "the created Idea in the making of the world," p. 20; "which, as being a more exact copy of the Incarnate Idea than was elsewhere to be found, was used as the original of the rest of the creation," p. 21. To her are applied the words, "Ego primogenita prodivi ex ore Altissimi," because she was predestinated in the Eternal Mind coevally with the Incarnation of her Divine Son. But to Him alone the title of Wisdom Incarnate is reserved, p. 25. Again, Christ is the First-born by nature; the Virgin in a less sublime order, viz. that of adoption. Again, if omnipotence is ascribed to her, it is a participated omnipotence (as she and all Saints have a participated sonship, divinity, glory, holiness, and worship), and is explained by the words "Quod Deus imperio, tu prece, Virgo potes."

Again, a special office is assigned to St. Mary, that is, special as compared with all other Saints; but it is marked off with the utmost precision from that assigned to our Lord. Thus she is said to have been made "the arbitress of every *effect* coming from God's mercy." Because she is the Mother of God, the salvation of mankind is said to be given to {445} her prayers, "*de congruo*, but *de condigno* it is due only to the blood of the Redeemeer," p. 113. "Merit is ascribed to Christ, and prayer to St. Mary," p. 162. In a word, the whole may be expressed in the words, "*Unica* spes mea Jesus, et post Jesum Virgo Maria. Amen."

Again, a distinct *cultus* is assigned to St. Mary, but the reason of it is said to be the transcendant dignity of her Son. "A particular *cultus* is due to the Virgin beyond comparison greater than that given to any other Saint because her dignity belongs to another order, namely to one which in some sense belongs to the order of the Hypostatic Union itself, and is necessarily connected with it," p. 41. And "Her being the Mother of God is the source of all the extraordinary honours due to Mary," p. 35.

It is remarkable that the "Monstra te esse Matrem" is explained, p. 158, as "Show thyself to be *our* Mother;" an interpretation which I think I have found elsewhere in these Tracts, and also in a book commonly used in religious houses, called the "Journal of Meditations," and elsewhere.

We have reason then to wait for clearer proof before we say that the *cultus* of St. Mary obscures the divine glory of her Son. And so much may suffice on the Sixth Test of fidelity in the development of an idea, as applied to the Catholic system.

SECTION III.

APPLICATION OF THE SEVENTH TEST OF FIDELITY IN DEVELOPMENT.

We have arrived at length at the seventh and last test, which was laid down in the beginning of this Essay, for distinguishing true development {446} of an idea from its corruptions and perversions. A corruption is of brief duration, runs itself out quickly, and ends in death. This general law gives us additional assistance in determining the character of the developments of Christianity commonly called Catholic.

When we consider the succession of ages during which the Catholic system has endured, the severity of the trials it has undergone, the sudden and wonderful changes without and within which have befallen it, the incessant mental activity and the intellectual gifts of its maintainers, the enthusiasm which it has kindled, the fury of the controversies which have been carried on among its professors, the impetuosity of the assaults made upon it, the ever-increasing responsibilities to which it has been committed by the continuous development of its dogmas, it is quite inconceivable that it should not have been broken up and lost, were it a corruption of Christianity. Yet it is still living, if there be a living religion or philosophy in the world; vigorous, energetic, persuasive, progressive; *vires acquirit eundo*; it grows and is not overgrown; it spreads out, yet is not enfeebled; it is ever germinating, yet ever consistent with itself. Corruptions indeed are to be found which sleep and are suspended; and these are usually called "decays;" such is not the case with Catholicity; it does not sleep, it is not stationary even now; and that its long series of developments should be corruptions would be an instance of sustained error, so novel, so unaccountable, so preternatural, as to be little short of a miracle, and to rival those manifestations of Divine Power which constitute the evidence of Christianity. We sometimes view with surprise and awe the degree of pain and disarrangement which the human frame can undergo without succumbing; yet at length it comes to an end. Fevers have their crisis, fatal or favourable; but this corruption of {447} a thousand years, if corruption it be, has ever been growing nearer death, yet never reaching it, and has been strengthened, not debilitated, by its excesses.

For instance: when the Empire was converted, multitudes, as is very plain, came into the Church on but partially religious motives, and with habits and opinions infected with the false worship which they had professedly abandoned. History shows us what anxiety and effort it cost her rulers to keep Paganism out of her pale. To this tendency must be added the hazard which attended on the development of the Catholic ritual, such as the honours publicly assigned to Saints and Martyrs, the formal veneration of their relics, and the usages and observances which followed. What was to hinder the rise of a sort of refined Pantheism, and the overthrow of dogmatism *pari passu* with the multiplication of heavenly intercessors and patrons? If what is called in reproach "Saint-worship" resembled the polytheism which it supplanted, or was a corruption, how did Dogmatism survive? Dogmatism is a religion's profession of its own reality as contrasted with other systems; but polytheists are liberals, and hold that one religion is as good as another. Yet the theological system was developing and strengthening, as well as the monastic rule, all the while the ritual was assimilating itself, as Protestants say, to the Paganism of former ages.

Nor was the development of dogmatic theology, which was then taking place, a silent and spontaneous process. It was wrought out and carried through under the fiercest controversies, and amid the most fearful risks. The Catholic faith was placed in a succession of perils, and rocked to and fro like a vessel at sea. Large portions of Christendom were, one after another, in heresy or in schism; the leading Churches and the most authoritative schools fell from time to time into serious error; {448} three Popes, Liberius, Vigilius, Honorius, have left to posterity the burden of their defence: but these disorders were no interruption to the sustained and steady march of the sacred science from implicit belief to formal statement. The series of ecclesiastical decisions, in which its progress was ever and anon signified, alternate between the one and the other side of the theological dogma especially in question, as if fashioning it into shape by opposite strokes. The controversy began in Apollinaris, who confused or denied the Two Natures in Christ, and was condemned by Pope Damasus. A reaction followed, and Theodore of Mopsuestia ventured to teach the doctrine of Two Persons. After Nestorius had brought that heresy into public view, and had incurred in consequence the anathema of the Third Ecumenical Council, the current controversy again shifted its direction; for Eutyches appeared, maintained the One Nature, and was condemned at Chalcedon. Something however was still wanting to the overthrow of the Nestorian doctrine of Two Persons, and the Fifth Council was formally directed against the writings of

Theodore and his party. Then followed the Monothelite heresy, which was a revival of the Euthycian or Monophysite, and was condemned in the Sixth. Lastly, Nestorianism once showed itself in the Adoptionists of Spain, and gave occasion to the great Council of Frankfort. Any one false step would have thrown the whole theory of the doctrine into irretrievable confusion; but it was as if some one individual and perspicacious intellect, to speak humanly, ruled the theological discussion from first to last. That in the long course of centuries, and in spite of the failure, in points of detail, of the most gifted Fathers and Saints, the Church thus wrought out the one and only consistent theory which can be taken on the great doctrine in dispute, proves how {449} clear, simple, and exact her vision of that doctrine was. But it proves more than this. Is it not utterly incredible, that with this thorough comprehension of so great a mystery, as far as the human mind can know it, she should be at that very time in the commission of the grossest errors in religious worship, and should be hiding the God and Mediator, whose Incarnation she contemplated with so clear an intellect, behind a crowd of idols?

The integrity of the Catholic developments is still more evident when they are viewed in contrast with the history of other doctrinal systems. Philosophies and religions of the world have each its day, and are parts of a succession. They supplant and are in turn supplanted. But the Catholic religion alone has had no limits; it alone has ever been greater than the emergence, and can do what others cannot do. If it were a falsehood, or a corruption, like the systems of men, it would be weak as they are; whereas it is able even to impart to them a strength which they have not, and it uses them for its own purposes, and locates them in its own territory. The Church can extract good from evil, or at least gets no harm from it. She inherits the promise made to the disciples, that they should take up serpents, and, if they drank any deadly thing, it should not hurt them. When evil has clung to her, and the barbarian people have looked on with curiosity or in malice, till she should have swollen or fallen down suddenly, she has shaken the venomous beast into the fire, and felt no harm.

Eusebius has sent before us this tribute of Catholicism in a passage in his history. "These attempts," he says, speaking of the acts of the enemy, "did not long avail him, Truth ever consolidating itself, and as time goes on, shining into broader day. For while the devices of adversaries were extinguished at once, undone by their very impetuousity,—one heresy after another presenting {450} its own novelty, the former specimens ever dissolving and wasting variously in manifold and multiform shapes,—the brightness of the Catholic and only true Church went forward increasing and enlarging, yet ever in the same things, and in the same way, beaming on the whole race of Greeks and barbarians with the awfulness, and simplicity, and nobleness, and sobriety, and purity of its divine polity and philosophy. Thus the calumny against our whole creed died with its day, and there continued alone our Discipline, sovereign among all, and acknowledged to be pre-eminent in awfulness, sobriety, and divine and philosophical doctrines; so that no one of this day dares to cast any base reproach upon our faith, nor any such calumny, such as it was once usual for our enemies to use."[34]

The Psalmist says, "We went through fire and water;" nor is it possible to imagine trials fiercer or more various than those from which Catholicism has come forth uninjured, as out of the Egyptian sea or the Babylonian furnace. First of all were the bitter persecutions of the Pagan Empire in the early centuries; then its sudden conversion, the liberty of Christian worship, the development of the *cultus sanctorum*, and the reception of Monachism into the ecclesiastical system. Then came the irruption of the barbarians; and then occupation of the *orbis terrarum*, first from the North, then by the Saracens from the South. Meanwhile the anxious and protracted controversy concerning the Incarnation hung like some terrible disease upon the faith of the Church. Then came the time of thick darkness; and afterwards two great struggles, one with material power, the other with the intellect, of the world, terminating in the ecclesiastical monarchy, and in the theology of the schools. And lastly came the great changes consequent upon the controversies of the sixteenth century. Is it conceivable {451} that any one of those heresies, with which ecclesiastical history abounds, should have gone through a hundredth part of these trials, yet have come out of them so nearly what it was before, as Catholicism has done? Could such a theology as Arianism have lasted through the scholastic contest? Or Montanism have borne the possession of the world, without coming to a crisis, and failing? or could the imbecility of the Manichean system, as a religion, have escaped exposure, had it been brought into conflict with the barbarians of the Empire, or the feudal system?

A similar contrast discovers itself in the effects and fortunes of certain influential principles or usages, which have been introduced into the Catholic system, and are seen in operation elsewhere. When a system really is corrupt, powerful agents, when applied to it, do but develop that corruption, and bring it the more speedily to an end. They stimulate it preternaturally; it puts forth its strength, and dies in some memorable act. Very different has been the history of Catholicism, when it has committed itself to such formidable influences. It has borne, and can bear, principles or doctrines, which in other systems of religion quickly degenerate into fanaticism or infidelity. This might be shown at great length in the history of the Aristotelic philosophy within and without the Church; or in the history of Monachism, or of Mysticism;—not that there has not been at first a conflict between these powerful and unruly elements and the Divine System into which they were entering, but that it ended in the victory of Catholicism. The theology of St. Thomas, nay of the Church of his period, is built on that very Aristotelism, which the early Fathers denounce as the source of all misbelief, and in particular of the Arian and Monophysite heresies. The exercises of asceticism, which are so graceful in St. Antony, so touching in St. Basil, and so awful in St. Germanus, do but become {452} a melancholy and gloomy superstition even in the most pious persons who are cut off from Catholic communion. And while the highest devotion in the Church is the mystical, and contemplation has been the token of the most singularly favoured Saints, we need not look deeply into the history of modern sects, for evidence of the excesses in conduct, or the errors in doctrine, to which mystics have been led, who have boasted of their possession of reformed truth, and have rejected what they called the corruptions of Catholicism.

It is true, there have been seasons when, from the operation of external or internal causes, the Church has been thrown into what was almost a state of *deliquium*; but her wonderful revivals, while the world was triumphing over her, is a further evidence of the absence of corruption, in the system of doctrine and worship into which she has developed. If corruption be an incipient disorganization, surely an abrupt and absolute recurrence to such a state, after an interval during which it has ceased to be, is even less conceivable than its sustained existence. Now this is the case with the revivals I speak of. After violent exertion men are exhausted and fall asleep; they awake the same as before, refreshed by the temporary cessation of their activity; and such has been the slumber and such the restoration of the Church. She pauses in her course, and almost suspends her functions; she rises again, and she is herself once more; all things are in their place and ready for action. Doctrine is where it was, and usage, and precedence, and principle, and policy; there may be changes, but they are consolidations or adaptations; all is unequivocal and determinate, with an identity which there is no disputing. Indeed it is one of the most popular charges against the Catholic Church at this very time, that she is "incorrigible;"—change she cannot, if we listen to St. Athanasius or St. Leo; change {453} she never will, if we believe the controversialist or alarmist of the present day.

Such were the thoughts concerning the "Blessed Vision of Peace," of one whose long-continued petition had been that the Most Merciful would not despise the work of His own Hands, nor leave him to himself;—while yet his eyes were dim, and his breast laden, and he could but employ Reason in the things of Faith. And now, dear Reader, time is short, eternity is long. Put not from you what you have here found; regard it not as mere matter of present controversy; set not out resolved to refute it, and looking about for the best way of doing so; seduce not yourself with the imagination that it comes of disappointment, or disgust, or restlessness, or wounded feeling, or undue sensibility, or other weakness. Wrap not yourself round in the associations of years past; nor determine that to be truth which you wish to be so, nor make an idol of cherished anticipations. Time is short, eternity is long.

NUNC DIMITTIS SERVUM TUUM, DOMINE,

SECUNDUM VERBUM TUUM IN PACE:

QUIA VIDERUNT OCULI MEI SALUTARE TUUM.

THE END.

---

[1] Kaye's Justin, p. 59, &c. <John Kay (1783-1853), *Some Account of the Writings and Opinions of Justin Martyr* (London: F. J. Rivington, 1843).>

[2] Kaye's Clement, p. 335. <*Some Account of the Writings and Opinions of Clement of Alexandria* (London: J. G. and F. Rivington, 1835).>

[3] p. 341.

[4] Ib. 342.

[5] Reliqu. Sacr. t. ii. p. 469, 470. <see note 18 to ch. 7.>

[6] Ex. xxxiii. 10.

[7] Dan. x. 5-17.

[8] Athan. Orat. i. 42, Oxf. tr.

[9] Athan. ibid.

[10] And so Eusebius, in his Life of Constantine: "The all-holy choir of God's perpetual virgins, he was used almost to worship (σέβων), believing that that God, to whom they had consecrated themselves, was an inhabitant in the souls of such." Vit. Const. iv. 28.

[11] Haer. 78, 18.

[12] Aug. de Nat. et Grat. 42. Ambros. Ep. 1. 49, § 2, in Psalm 118; v. 3. de Instit. Virg. 50. Hier. in Is. xi. 1, contr. Pelag. ii. 4. Nil. Ep. i. p. 267. Antioch. ap. Cyr. de Rect. Fid. p. 49. Ephr. Opp. Syr. t. 3, p. 607. Max. Hom. 45. Procl. Orat. vi. pp. 225-228, p. 60, p. 179, 180, ed. 1630. Theodot. ap. Amphiloch. pp. 39, &c. Fulgent. Serm. 3, p. 125. Chrysol. Serm. 142. A striking passage from another Sermon of the last-mentioned author, on the words "She cast in her mind what manner of salutation," &c., may be added: "Quantus sit Deus satis ignorat ille, qui hujus Virginis mentem non stupet, animam non miratur. Pavet coelum, tremunt Angeli, creatura non sustinet, natura non sufficit; et una puella sic Deum in sui pectoris capit, recipit, oblectat hospitio, ut pacem terris, coelis gloriam, salutem perditis, vitam mortuis, terrenis cum coelestibus parentelam, ipsius Dei cum carne commercium, pro ipsâ domûs exigat pensione, pro ipsius uteri mercede conquirat." &c. Serm. 140. St. Basil, St. Chrysostom, and St. Cyril of Alexandria sometimes speak, it is true, in a different tone; but this is irrelevant to the argument, as will be seen by pp. 388, 389.

[13] Gieseler, Text-book, vol. i. p. 108. <See note 19 to ch. 1).>

[14] Gieseler, ibid. p. 164.

[15] Socr. Hist. i. 10.

[16] Hom. 14, in 2 Cor. fin.

[17] Vid. Tertull. Oxf. tr. pp. 374, 5.

[18] Clem. ch. 12.

[19] Tracts for the Times, No. 79, p. 38. <"On Purgatory," par. 3, "History of the rise of the Doctrine of Purgatory, and opinions in the early Church concerning it," A Tract written by Newman himself.>

[20] Ruinart. Mart. p. 96. <See note 29 to ch. 4.>

[21] Mystagog. 5.

[22] Proph. Office, pp. 213-220.

[23] Hist. ch. 37. init.

[24] Gieseler, vol. ii. p. 288.

[25] Ibid. p. 279.

[26] Or rather his successors, as St. Benedict of Aniene, were the founders of the Order; but minute accuracy on these points is unnecessary in a mere sketch of the history.

[27] μηλωτής, 2 Kings ii. Sept. vid. also, "They wandered about in sheepskins and goatskins." Heb. xi. 37.

[28] Rosweyde. V<itae>. P<atrum>. p. 618. <De vita et moribus seniorum, historiam eremeticam complectentes . . . opera et studio Heriberti Rosweydi (1615), also in Migne PL, vols. 73 and 74.>

[29] p. 63.

[30] Supr. p. 65.

[31] Supr. p. 60.

[32] Hist. Eur. Civil. pp. 394-398. <See note 7 to ch. 1.>

[33] E. g. the "De Imitatione," the "Introduction à la Vie Dévote," the "Spiritual Combat," the "Anima Divota," the "Paradisus Animae," the "Regula Cleri," the "Garden of the Soul," the "Journal of Meditations," &c. &c.

[34] Euseb. Hist. iv. 7, ap. Church of the Fathers, p. 285.

Books by the editor

Les tendances nouvelles de l'ecclésiologie

The Relevance of Physics

Brain, Mind and Computers
(Lecomte du Nouy Prize, 1970)

The Paradox of Olbers' Paradox

The Milky Way: An Elusive Road for Science

*Science and Creation: From Eternal Cycles
to an Oscillating Universe*

*Planets and Planetarians: A History of Theories
of the Origin of Planetary Systems*

The Road of Science and the Ways to God
(Gifford Lectures: University of Edinburgh, 1975 and 1976)

The Origin of Science and the Science of its Origin
(Fremantle Lectures, Oxford, 1977)

*And on This Rock: The Witness of One Land
and Two Covenants*

Cosmos and Creator

Angels, Apes and Men

Uneasy Genius: The Life and Work of Pierre Duhem

Chesterton: A Seer of Science

The Keys of the Kingdom: A Tool's Witness to Truth

Lord Gifford and His Lectures: A Centenary Retrospect

Chance or Reality and Other Essays

The Physicist as Artist: The Landscapes of Pierre Duhem

The Absolute beneath the Relative and Other Essays

The Savior of Science
(Wethersfield Institute Lectures, 1987)

Miracles and Physics

[434]

(continued from p. [434])

Books by the editor

God and the Cosmologists
(Farmington Institute Lectures, Oxford, 1988)

The Only Chaos and Other Essays

The Purpose of It All
(Farmington Institute Lectures, Oxford, 1989)

Catholic Essays

Cosmos in Transition: Studies in the History of Cosmology

Olbers Studies

Scientist and Catholic: Pierre Duhem

Reluctant Heroine: The Life and Work of Hélène Duhem

Universe and Creed

Genesis 1 through the Ages

Is There a Universe?

Patterns or Principles and Other Essays

Bible and Science

Theology of Priestly Celibacy

Means to Message: A Treatise on Truth

God and the Sun at Fatima

The Limits of a Limitless Science and Other Essays

A Mind's Matter: An Intellectual Autobiography

Why the Question: Is There a God?

Why the Question: Is There a Soul?

Advent and Science

Why Believe in the Church?

Why Believe in Jesus?

Fifteen Mysteries

(continued from p. [435])

Books by the editor

The Litany of Saint Joseph

Why the Mass?

Twenty Mysteries

Original Sin?

Numbers Decide and Other Essays

* * *

Translations with introduction and notes:

The Ash Wednesday Supper (Giordano Bruno)

Cosmological Letters on the Arrangement of the World Edifice (J.-H. Lambert)

Universal Natural History and Theory of the Heavens (I. Kant)

Note on the Editor

Stanley L. Jaki, a Hungarian-born Catholic priest of the Benedictine Order, is Distinguished University Professor at Seton Hall University, South Orange, New Jersey. With doctorates in theology and physics, he has for the past forty years specialized in the history and philosophy of science. The author of almost forty books and over a hundred articles, he served as Gifford Lecturer at the University of Edinburgh and as Fremantle Lecturer at Balliol College, Oxford. He has lectured at major universities in the United States, Europe, and Australia. He is honorary member of the Pontifical Academy of Sciences, *membre correspondant* of the Académie Nationale des Sciences, Belles-Lettres et Arts of Bordeaux, and the recipient of the Lecomte du Nouy Prize for 1970 and of the Templeton Prize for 1987.

www.sljaki.com